DARWIN

A NORTON CRITICAL EDITION

-))) (((-

DARWIN

A NORTON CRITICAL EDITION

SECOND EDITION

-))) (((-

Edited by

PHILIP APPLEMAN

INDIANA UNIVERSITY

"It was characteristic of Darwin on his journeys
that when he saw a mountain he always tried to
climb it."   —Sir Gavin de Beer

W · W · NORTON & COMPANY

New York · London

THIS BOOK IS DEDICATED TO

William Madden
Michael Wolff
Donald Gray
George Levine

COMRADES

W. W. Norton & Company, Inc., 500 Fifth Avenue, New York, N.Y. 10110
W. W. Norton & Company Ltd., 10 Coptic Street, London, WC1A 1PU

Copyright © 1979, 1970 by W. W. Norton & Company, Inc.

Printed in the United States of America. All Rights Reserved

Library of Congress Cataloging in Publication Data
Appleman, Philip, 1926–   comp.
    Darwin.

    (A Norton critical edition)
    Bibliography: p.
    Includes index.
    1. Evolution—History. 2. Darwin, Charles Robert,
1809–1882. 3. Naturalists—Great Britain—Biography.
QH365.Z9A7   1979   575'.0092'4   79–13599
ISBN 0-393-01192-5
ISBN 0-393-95009-3 pbk.
                    5 6 7 8 9 0

ACKNOWLEDGEMENTS

Sir Gavin de Beer: "Biology Before the Beagle" from *Charles Darwin: A Scientific Biography*. Reprinted by permission of Thomas Nelson & Sons Limited.

Arthur Caplan: "Ethics, Evolution and the Milk of Human Kindness," *The Hastings Center Report*, April 1976. Reprinted by permission of the Hastings Center Report. Copyright © Institute of Society, Ethics, and the Life Sciences, 360 Broadway, Hastings-on-Hudson, New York 10706.

Pierre Teilhard de Chardin: Abridgement of the Preface and "The Convergence of the Person and the Omega Point" from *The Phenomenon of Man* by Pierre Teilhard de Chardin, translated by Bernard Wall. Copyright 1955 by Editions du Seuil. Copyright © 1959 in the English translation by William Collins Sons & Co., Ltd., London and Harper and Row, Publishers, New York.

Noam Chomsky: "The Fallacy of Richard Herrnstein's 'I.Q.,'" *Cognition* I (1973). Reprinted by permission of Elsevier Sequoia S.A., Switzerland.

Preston Cloud: "'Scientific Creationism'—A New Inquisition Brewing?" *The Humanist,* January/February 1977. Reprinted by permission of the publisher.

John Dewey: "The Influence of Darwinism on Philosophy" from *Tne Influence of Darwin on Philosophy* by John Dewey. Copyright © 1910 by Holt, Rinehart and Winston, Inc. Copyright 1938 by John Dewey. Reprinted by permission of Holt, Rinehart and Winston, Inc.

Theodosius Dobzhansky: From *Heredity and the Nature of Man*, © 1964 by Theodosius Dobzhansky. Reprinted by permission of Harcourt Brace Jovanovich, Inc. and Allen & Unwin, Ltd.

Jane van Lawick-Goodall: From *In the Shadow of Man*. Copyright © 1971 by Hugo and Jane van Lawick-Goodall. Reprinted by permission of Houghton Mifflin Company and William Collins Sons & Co., Ltd.

Stephen Jay Gould: Adapted from "This View of Life: Biological Potential vs. Biological Determinism" and reprinted with permission from *Natural History* Magazine, May 1976. Copyright © The American Museum of Natural History, 1976.

Richard J. Herrnstein: From *I. Q. in the Meritocracy*. Copyright © 1971, 1973 by Richard J. Herrnstein. Originally published in *Atlantic Monthly*. Reprinted by permission of Little, Brown and Co. in association with Atlantic Monthly Press and Penguin Books Ltd.

Richard Hofstadter: From *Social Darwinism in American Thought*. Copyright © 1944, 1955, by the American Historical Association. Reprinted by permission of Beacon Press.

Julian Huxley and Thomas Henry Huxley: From the Introduction to *Evolution: The Modern Synthesis*, Second Edition, 1964, by Julian Huxley. Reprinted by permission of John Wiley & Sons, Inc. From pp. 13–28 in *Evolution: The Modern Synthesis* by Julian Huxley. Copyright 1942 by Julian Huxley. Reprinted by permission of Harper & Row, Publishers, Inc. and A. D. Peters & Co. "Evolution and Ethics" by Thomas Henry Huxley and "Evolutionary Ethics" by Julian Huxley from *Touchstone for Ethics* by Thomas Henry Huxley and Julian Huxley. Copyright 1947 by Julian Huxley. Reprinted by permission of Harper & Row, Publishers, Inc.

Joseph Wood Krutch: Excerpted from *The Modern Temper*. Copyright © 1929, by Harcourt Brace Jovanovich, Inc.; renewed, 1957, by Joseph Wood Krutch. Reprinted by permission of the publishers.

Richard E. Leakey and Roger Lewin: From *Origins*. Copyright 1977 by Richard E. Leakey and Roger Lewin. Reprinted by permission of the publishers, E. P. Dutton.

John C. Loehlin, Gardner Lindzey, and J. N. Spuhler: Excerpted with permission from *Race Differences in Intelligence* published by W. H. Freeman and Company. Copyright © 1975.

Bert James Loewenberg: "The Mosaic of Darwinian Thought" *Victorian Studies*, III (1959). Reprinted by permission of *Victorian Studies* and the author.

Contents

Part III: Darwin and Science

Part IV: Darwin, Philosophy, and Theology

Part V: Darwin and Society

Preface

The purpose of this anthology is to demonstrate some of the ways in which Darwin's work exercised an influence on our intellectual history, and our day-to-day lives. To fulfill such a task at really satisfying length would of course require many volumes as large as this. Nevertheless, I hope that by excerpting primary materials and carefully selecting scholarly commentary, I have succeeded in drawing into one book the main outlines of this vast subject. Those who wish to explore further will find suggestions in the contents themselves and in the Selected Readings.

I want to thank those scholars who have advised me in various ways in planning this collection: Walter F. Cannon, Frederick B. Churchill, Sir Gavin de Beer, P. J. Gautrey, Donald Gray, George Levine, Bert James Loewenberg, William Madden, Herbert J. Muller, Morse Peckham, George Gaylord Simpson, and Michael Wolff. I should add that any faults in the book are mine alone.

I cannot release to the world so Victorian a product without an extra word of nostalgic gratitude to those extraordinarily fine gentlemen, my colleagues for years at *Victorian Studies*, to whom this work is dedicated. Nor is it by force of habit that I publicly thank yet again that able critic whose intelligence, and whose presence at breakfast, have alike been indispensable to me.

P.A.
Bloomington, Indiana
December 1969

Preface to the Second Edition

After nine years and twelve printings in its first edition, this book has been revised in order to include the important recent work in paleontology, sociobiology, ethology, DNA research, primate research, and other fields, little of which was available when *Darwin* first went to press, and all of which (as is pointed out in the Postscript, pp. 551-571) is explicitly based upon Darwinian postulates and principles. Most of these new materials are, in one way or another, controversial, which makes them especially useful in a textbook dealing with the history of ideas.

In addition to reiterating my gratitude to the generous people named in the original Preface (to several of whom I am again indebted), I should like to thank the following for invaluable services to the present edition. Needless to say, not all of them agree with everything included here; but they have all been helpful to me: Charles Blinderman, John Broderick, Harold Burstyn, Bette Chambers, Erwin Chargaff, Preston Cloud, Philip Daghlian, Kay Dinsmoor, Stephen Jay Gould, Loren Graham, Richard Levine, James L. Mairs, Peter Medawar, Craig Nelson, Francine Simring, Robert Sinsheimer, George Stade, and John Woodcock.

Once again I register my gratitude to my wife, Marjorie, whose critical and appreciative presence is my own natural selection.

P.A.
Bloomington, Indiana
January 1979

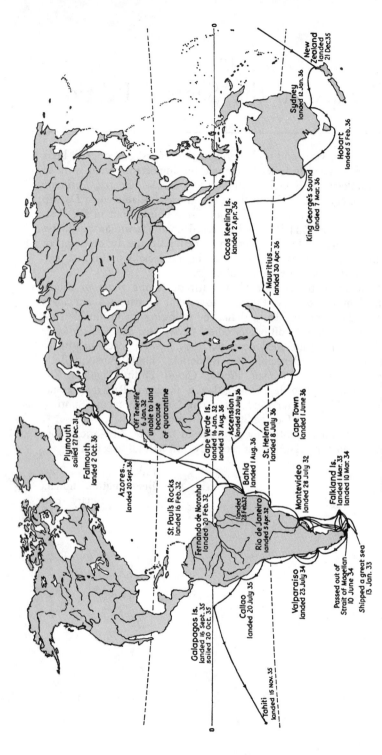

The Voyage of the *Beagle* 1831–1836

(The dates of Darwin's landings are not always those of the ship's arrival.)

Plymouth
sailed 27 Dec. 31

Falmouth
landed 2 Oct. 36

Azores—
landed 20 Sept. 36

Off Tenerife
6 Jan. 32
unable to land
because
of quarantine

Cape Verde Is.
landed 16 Jan. 32

Ascension I.
landed 20 July 36

St. Paul's Rocks
landed 16 Feb. 32

St. Helena
landed 8 July 36

Fernando de Noronha
landed 20 Feb. 32

Cape Town
landed 1 June 36

landed
28 Feb. 32

Bahia
landed 1 Aug. 32

Rio de Janeiro
landed 5 Apr. 32

Montevideo
landed 28 July 32

Falkland Is.
landed 1 Mar. 33
landed 10 Mar. 34

Valparaiso
landed 23 July 34

Passed out of
Strait of Magellan
10 June 34

Shipped a great sea
13 Jan. 33

Galapagos Is.
landed 16 Sept. 35
sailed 20 Oct. 35

Callao
landed 20 July 35

Tahiti
landed 15 Nov. 35

Cocos Keeling Is.
landed 2 Apr. 36

Mauritius
landed 30 Apr. 36

King George's Sound
landed 7 Mar. 36

Sydney
landed 12 Jan. 36

Hobart
landed 5 Feb. 36

New
Zealand
landed
21 Dec. 35

Introduction

Charles Darwin's youth was unmarked by signs of genius. Born in 1809 into the well-to-do Darwin and Wedgwood clans (his mother was a Wedgwood, and Darwin himself was to marry another), he led a secure and carefree childhood, happy with his family, indifferent to books, responsive to nature. The son and grandson of impressively successful physicians, he eventually tried medical training himself, but found the studies dull and surgery (before anesthesia) too ghastly even to watch. So, for want of anything better, he followed the advice of his awesome father (6'2," 336 pounds, domineering in temperament) and studied for the ministry, taking his B.A. at Christ's College, Cambridge, in 1831.

Then a remarkable turn of events saved Darwin from a country parsonage. His science teacher at Cambridge, John Stevens Henslow, arranged for Darwin the invitation to join H.M.S. *Beagle* during a long voyage of exploration. Despite his father's initial reluctance, Darwin got the position, and at the end of 1831 left England for a five-year voyage around the globe that turned out to be not only a crucial experience for Darwin himself, but a passage of consequence for the whole world.

The voyage of the *Beagle* made a scientist of Darwin—an industrious collector, a keen observer, a canny theorist—and it set him a momentous problem that he was to spend the next twenty years struggling with: the problem of the origin of species. By 1858, when another young naturalist, Alfred Russel Wallace, was pondering the same problem, Darwin had collected enormous masses of detail relating to species and supporting his theory of natural selection. Faced, after decades of work, with the threat of being anticipated by Wallace's independent discoveries, Darwin quickly finished and published his great work, *The Origin of Species*, in 1859.

The effects of that publication were many and profound; hardly any kind of thought—scientific, philosophical, social, literary, historical—remained long unchanged by the implications of the *Origin*. That is what this anthology is about, and what is reviewed in the Epilogue.

Except for the voyage of the *Beagle*, however, Darwin's adventures were mostly intellectual, his life deliberately domestic. A chronic sufferer from a mysterious ailment, he had neither the strength nor the temperament for an active and public career; he remained secluded at his country house at Down, shunning the furious post-*Origin* controversies and leaving the defense of "Darwinism" to his more pugnacious friends. But always he worked. Good Victorian that he was, he worked as much every day as his strength permitted, and his industrious life was studded with solid contributions to science in articles, reviews, and books: *The Descent of Man* . . . (1871), *The Expression of the Emotions* . . . (1872), *The Formation of Vegetable Mould* . . . (1881), and so on, and on.*

There was something paradoxical but eminently admirable about both Darwin's character and his devotion to his task. Intellectually he was a revolutionary, but the gentlest of revolutionaries. Spiritually he became an agnostic, but never a simple materialist; like many another Victorian agnostic, he exemplified in his life and work a high-minded benevolence not only toward his fellow men but for all creatures, and he continued always to write of the "grandeur" of "beautiful" and "wonderful" forms of life, and of men's high "destiny" in the future.

When he died in 1882, the man whose sacrilegious ideas had once been publicly assailed, from pulpit and periodical, by a multitude of critics, was buried, with the cordial acquiescence of the Dean, in Westminster Abbey—a few feet from the grave of the other immortal among British scientists, Sir Isaac Newton.

* See the Selected Readings at the end of this volume.

PART I

Scientific Opinion in the Early Nineteenth Century

As a record of a former state of things, I have retained in the foregoing paragraphs, and elsewhere, several sentences which imply that naturalists believe in the separate creation of each species; and I have been much censured for having thus expressed myself. But undoubtedly this was the general belief when the first edition of the present work appeared. I formerly spoke to very many naturalists on the subject of evolution, and never once met with any sympathetic agreement. It is probable that some did then believe in evolution, but they were either silent, or expressed themselves so ambiguously that it was not easy to understand their meaning. Now things are wholly changed, and almost every naturalist admits the great principle of evolution.

—Charles Darwin, 1872

He succeeded in putting the *whole* of past life into *every* aspect of *every* form of present life. In this respect Darwin has no precursor.

—Bert James Loewenberg, 1965

SIR GAVIN DE BEER

Biology Before the *Beagle* (1964) †

* * * The subject of mutability of species had been taken up in speculative manner by a group of French philosophers including Montesquieu, Maupertuis, and Diderot. Basing themselves on certain facts such as the gradations that can be imagined between different species arranged in series, the appearance of new varieties of cultivated plants and domestic animals and of hereditary sports such as six-fingered men, the significance of monstrous births and imperfections of development, and the changes undergone by animals during their own life-histories, these thinkers concluded by deduction that species must have been mutable. Diderot even suggested that there was a prototype from which all living beings were descended and that the agent responsible for change was the age-old folk-belief that characters impressed on an organism during its life were transmitted by inheritance to the offspring. This, in his view, would account for the supposed perpetuation of the effects of use and disuse of organs, while the principle that if an animal experienced a need this need would provoke the formation of an organ that satisfied the need, accounted for the origin of such an organ.

In substantial agreement with these speculations was Erasmus Darwin, physician-philosopher-poet, whose work *Zoönomia or the Laws of Organic Life* was published in 1794. Like his French predecessors, Erasmus Darwin believed in the mutability of species because of the changes undergone by animals during embryonic development, particularly the metamorphoses of the caterpillar into the moth and the tadpole into the frog, because of the changes brought about by domestication and resulting from hybridization, because of the significance of monstrous births, and the similarity in plan of structure of vertebrate animals. He believed that the modification of species was brought about by the satisfaction of wants due to "lust, hunger, and danger," and as a result of "their own exertions in consequence of their desires and aversions, of their pleasures and pains, or of irritations, or of associations; and many of these acquired forms or propensities are transmitted to their posterity." He recognized the importance of adaptation of organisms to their environments in the struggle for existence, of protective coloration; of artificial selection and sexual selection in bringing about change; of cross-fertilization in maintaining vigor; of the

† From Chapter 1 of *Charles Darwin: A Scientific Biography* (New York, 1964). Sir Gavin de Beer (1899–1972) was formerly director of the Natural History Department of the British Museum and professor of embryology at the University of London.

significance of vestigial organs that were without function in their possessors but presupposed a former function; of monstrous births as disproof of the notion that the embryo is preformed in the germ; and of sports or mutations such as six-toed cats and rumpless fowls. But when it came to explaining how adaptations were produced in an organism, Erasmus Darwin had nothing to offer but "the power of acquiring new parts, attended with new propensities, directed by irritations, sensations, volitions, and associations; and thus possessing the faculties of continuing to improve by its own inherent activity, and of delivering down those improvements to its posterity, world without end."

Independently, although heir to the same speculative background, Jean-Baptiste de Lamarck came to conclusions very similar to those of Erasmus Darwin. A soldier of outstanding gallantry in the Seven Years War who had subsequently become fascinated by the luxuriance of plants in his garrison stations in the south of France, Lamarck abandoned the army as a profession and took up the study of natural history. In his book *Hydrogéologie* published in 1802 he opposed the "catastrophic" theories of geological causes then in vogue which required fantastic catastrophes to explain the state of the earth and, like James Hutton, advocated the uninterrupted continuity of past and present causes and effects. Lamarck recognized the unlimited amount of time required to account for the history of the earth, deduced the organic origin of sedimentary rocks, and pointed out the importance of fossils for the estimation of past changes of climate, valuable services to science, largely ignored even today.

It is for his *Philosophie zoologique* published in 1809 that Lamarck is remembered in the history of science. Confronted with the task of classifying the collections in the Paris Museum of Natural History, he experienced such difficulty in distinguishing between species and varieties of species that he concluded that there was no basic difference between them. He argued that if enough closely related species were studied together, differences between them could no longer be made out and they merged into one another. In fact this is not the case, because the barrier between species is always discernible even if very difficult to detect, but the appearance that species graded into one another led Lamarck to put forward a full theory of "transformism" or evolution, which he was the first to do, invoking descent of species during long periods of time from other species, so that the Animal Kingdom could be represented by a genealogy of branching lines, the last branch being that of man. Fossil organisms he thought had not become extinct but had been transmuted into their living descendants.

Lamarck accounted for evolution by means of the action of two factors. The first was a supposed tendency to perfection and to increased complexity, which he held responsible for the existence of the scale of beings from the simplest organisms at the bottom to man at the top. He regarded this concept as so self-evident as not to require proof, of which in fact it is incapable, being inaccessible to scientific investigation. It led him to suppose that as simple lowly organisms exist today without having been perfected or made complex, they must have arisen recently by spontaneous generation. Lamarck's second factor was introduced because the scale of beings is not a perfect series graded from the lowest to the highest but shows anomalies, deviations, and branchings from what it might and in his view would have been if the environment had not interfered. Like Diderot and Erasmus Darwin, Lamarck supposed that as a result of new needs experienced by the animal in its environment, its "inner feeling," comparable to Erasmus Darwin's "internal impulse" or "living force," set in motion bodily movements and instituted habits that produced new organs satisfying those needs, in other words, adapting the animal to its environment. These organs, and the effects of their use and disuse, he thought were then transmitted by heredity. As this explanation could not be applied to plants or to the lowest animals, Lamarck concluded that their evolution was conditioned by the direct effects of the environment. He was therefore unable to provide a unitary theory of evolution.

These views led contemporary scientists to reject them, and with them the theory of transmutation. Even Étienne Geoffroy-Saint-Hilaire, who accepted the transmutation of species, regretted that by his speculations Lamarck had compromised it. Scientists like Baron Georges Cuvier who rejected transmutation were even more opposed to Lamarck. It is, however, only fair to say that Lamarck has been treated with less than justice by history, for his name is associated with a hypothetic cause of evolution that he did not invent and that is unacceptable, whereas it was his genius in proposing a scheme of evolution that deserves commemoration in the term Lamarckism.

As a result of his extensive researches in comparative anatomy and paleontology published in 1812, Cuvier was struck by the fact that in the rocks of the Paris basin some strata contained fossils of marine animals, others fossils of fresh-water animals, and others again no fossils at all. From the apparently sudden appearance and equally sudden disappearance of these remains of bygone life, Cuvier concluded that catastrophes similar to the Biblical Flood had repeatedly destroyed life, and that after each catastrophe it had blossomed out afresh through successive creations and immigrations of such organisms as had escaped destruction because they had previously lived elsewhere on earth, out of reach of that particular catastrophe. There had therefore been extensive extinction of species, which was a new concept involving the abandonment of some objects of creation to their melancholy fate by the Supreme Being.

It was not many years since John Wesley, in 1770, had written, "Death . . . is never permitted to destroy the most inconsiderable species," and Thomas Jefferson, referring to fossil bones of the American mastodon, which he refused to regard as extinct, wrote, "Such is the economy of nature, that no instance can be produced, of her having permitted any one race of her animals to become extinct; of her having formed any link in her great work, so weak as to be broken."

It was also obvious to Cuvier that after each "catastrophe" there was an advance in the complexity of life, so that each new wave of living beings showed a superiority of organization over their extinct predecessors. The younger the strata, the more fossils they contained belonging to animals similar to those living. A transcendental principle of progressionism had therefore to be invoked to account for this, since two reasons prevented him from accepting transmutation: the absence of any known intermediate forms, and the fact that organisms found in the oldest tombs of Egypt were identical with those still living and had therefore undergone no transmutation during the intervening period of time. Finally, Cuvier showed that the anatomical diversity exhibited by different groups of animals could not be accommodated on any single plan of structure undergoing progression from the simplest to the most complex. He therefore introduced the concept of four major groups or *embranchements* into which the Animal Kingdom was divided: Radiata (jellyfish, starfish), Articulata (worms, insects), Mollusca (snails, octopus), and Vertebrata. In other words, for the single scale of beings Cuvier substituted four plans of structure, which introduced the concept of divergence.

Another concept introduced by Cuvier was that of correlation of parts. His mastery of comparative anatomy enabled him to claim that "the smallest fragment of bone, even the most apparently insignificant apophysis, possesses a fixed and determinate character, relative to the class, order, genus and species of the animal to which it belonged; insomuch, that when we find merely the extremity of a well-preserved bone, we are able by careful examination, assisted by analogy and exact comparison, to determine the species to which it once belonged, as certainly as if we had the entire animal before us." * * *

Cuvier's principle of correlation was, in fact, based on his recognition of the fact and importance of adaptation; organs serve functions that adapt the organisms to their environments or conditions of existence, and in his view, as in that of many of his contemporaries, this fact of adaptation was evidence of purpose or of final causes: organisms had been created with their organs as they are in order that they might exploit their several ways of life and enjoy their environments. Teleology had been introduced into the details of anatomy and physiology.

To the geologist Charles Lyell, Cuvier's theories of catastrophism and progressionism were unacceptable, first because Lyell's observations and researches had convinced him that the geological agents that were to be seen operating in the present could, given sufficient time, have caused everything that had happened in the past history of the earth. This was the principle of uniformitarianism, first introduced by James Hutton in 1785 and developed independently by Lyell in his *Principles of Geology* (1830) to a point where it could not fail to prevail over the speculations of catastrophism. Lyell's objection to progressionism was due partly to its association with catastrophism and partly to his opinion that the paleontological evidence obtainable from the fossil record as known in his day was insufficient to support progressionism. Dicotyledonous plants, the highest types of the vegetable kingdom, had been found in coal measures of the Carboniferous period, and mammals in Secondary strata. Lyell therefore rejected progressionism and, with it, Lamarck's theory of transmutation, all the more because "if we look for some of those essential changes which would be required to lend even the semblance of a foundation for the theory of Lamarck, respecting the growth of new organs and the gradual obliteration of others, we find nothing of the kind." In his view, the theory lacked evidence, no intermediate forms were known, he thought it extravagant to claim that organisms could vary sufficiently to account for the differences between species, and the notion that when organs were needed they arose, removed the problem out of the realm of science into that of fanciful speculation. It must be added that Lamarck's inclusion of man in his scheme of evolution could not fail to disturb Lyell, for he was not yet prepared to contemplate unorthodox opinion where man was concerned, notwithstanding his scientific approach and rejection of scriptural interpretation in problems of geology. The result was that Lyell accepted the fact that species could become extinct, as a result of failure in the struggle for existence, and he knew that extinct species had been replaced by other species, but as to how this occurred and by what process fresh species originated, he had nothing to offer.

The problem of the origination of fresh species had, however, to be answered somehow, and the inability of the uniformitarian view to provide an answer drove its critics to adopt the only alternative known to them, namely miraculous interposition by the Creator. * * * The theory of evolution was tinged with political overtones that still persist. Then, they resulted in the writing of two books that had profound though unexpected effects on the future of natural history. On the sociological plane, a valiant attempt to stem the tide of the French ungodly was made by Thomas Robert Malthus with his *Essay on Population*, while on the theological side William Paley set out in his *Natural Theology* to prove that the study of natural history inevitably led to belief in a divine Creator.

* * * [Malthus] generalized the principle that "Population, when unchecked, increases in a geometrical ratio. Subsistence increases only in an arithmetical ratio. . . . I can see no way by which man can escape from the weight of this law which pervades all animate nature." Unwittingly, no doubt, Malthus here placed man on the same plane as the rest of the animal kingdom. Among plants and animals the growth of population was kept down by mortality due to "want of room and nourishment" and falling a prey to predators. In man, if in spite of famines and epidemics and the preventive checks imposed by reason, population nevertheless increased too fast, those of its members who could least afford the necessities of life were doomed to misery and death. On the other hand, if the checks to the increase in numbers of a population through delayed marriage and abstinence were artificial and too effective, there would be no competition or compulsion to work exerted on those whose livelihood depended on it, and the results would equally be misery from the effects of immorality, idleness, and sloth.

It followed, as H. N. Brailsford has pointed out, that all attempts to preserve life were contrary to the correct application of principle, charity was an economic sin, altruism "unscientific," and presumably the medical profession pursued an anti-social aim. Since the possibilities of variation, shown by cultivated plants and domestic animals, were in Malthus' view strictly limited, progress was impossible; attempts to achieve it as in the French Revolution were doomed to failure; and mankind could neither improve nor be perfected. Malthus' book was reprinted several times and the main lines of evidence on which his argument rested were on his own admission more and more undermined, but he nevertheless stuck to the sloganlike antithesis between geometrical and arithmetical rates of increase for growth of population and of subsistence. In this, Malthus performed a service to science, because most of those of his contemporaries who were aware of the struggle for existence in nature ran away from the horrors of tooth and claw and tried to veil it, minimize it, or moralize on the greater resulting happiness for the survivors. As will be seen, this aspect of Malthus' work had far-reaching effects.

Among Malthus' adherents was William Paley, who based his *Natural Theology* (1802) on the argument that a contrivance implies a contriver, just as a design implies a designer, and illustrated this analogy by means of a watch. Passing from horology to natural history he pointed out that the lens of the eye in fishes is more spherical than that of the eye of land vertebrates, which showed that each eye is *adapted* to the refractive index of the medium, water or air, in which the animal lives. "What plainer manifestation of design can there be than this instance?" he asked. The function of the iris diaphragm, accommodation for distance, the fact that the blind spots of the two eyes of an individual are not at conjugate points on the retina, that the eyebrow and eyelid protect the eye, all pointed to intelligent construction: "it is only by the display of contrivance, that the existence, the agency, the wisdom, of the Deity *could* be testified to his rational creatures." The same argument applied to the ear and to the function of all organs and tissues: down-feathers for warmth, flight-feathers for flight, webbed feet for progression in water, poison-fangs for defense in snakes, pouches for containing the young in marsupials, the long tongue of the woodpecker for catching grubs, the complicated life history of mistletoe. Some adaptations are even anticipatory, such as migration in birds, a contrivance to avoid and survive a cold season that has not yet arrived, or the foramen ovale and ductus arteriosus of the mammalian embryo, which enable it to switch instantly at birth from the intra-uterine to the aerial type of respiration and blood-circulation. All these were adaptations and Paley summed them up with the words: "The marks of *design* are too strong to be gotten over. Design must have had a designer. That designer must have been a person. That person is God." * * *

It is in the treatment of the problem of suffering that Paley had the greatest difficulty in making his case. "Pain, no doubt, and privations exist . . . Evil, no doubt, exists; but it is never, that we can perceive, the *object* of contrivance. Teeth are contrived to eat, not to ache." The "aches" caused in what teeth kill and eat are ignored, although the undeniable carnage of nature forces Paley to admit that "We cannot avoid the difficulty by saying that the effect was not intended. The only question open to us is whether it be ultimately evil. From the confessed and felt imperfection of our knowledge, we ought to presume that there may be consequences of this economy which are hidden from us," a form of argument that will be met again in very different circumstances. In an attempt to minimize the horror of the war of nature, he continues, "I believe the cases of bites which produce death in large animals (of stings I think there are none) to be very few."

Again, "Pain also itself is not without its *alleviations*. It may be violent and frequent; but it is seldom violent and long-continued; and its pauses and intermissions become positive pleasures. Of *mortal* diseases the great use is to reconcile us to death." In any case, by Malthus' principle, death is necessary to prevent over-population, and therefore beneficial. In compensation, "The Deity has super-added *pleasure* to animal sensations, beyond what was necessary for any purpose . . . it is a happy world after all." Then, as a parting shot, "The appearance of chance will always bear a proportion to the ignorance of the observer," with which Paley was confident that he had defended his religion and confounded the infidel. * * *

What Paley had, in fact, done was to provide a catalogue of adaptations that was shortly to come in very useful, and this is why it has been necessary to allot to Paley, as to Malthus, more space than would be justified by the intrinsic merits of their special pleading, masquerading as science. Furthermore, Paley's works, which were prescribed reading in British universities for many years, represent the prevailing points of view and attitudes of mind that had to be overcome by hard scientific evidence before the theory of evolution could be established, and, by an astonishing irony of history, his and Malthus' works unwittingly contributed more than any other publications to the establishment of that theory.

Such were the tides, currents, and backwaters of thought when on December 27, 1831 H.M.S. *Beagle* set sail from Plymouth.

SIR CHARLES LYELL

Principles of Geology (1830–1833) †

* * *

Whether species have a real existence in nature

Before we can advance a step in our proposed inquiry, we must be able to define precisely the meaning which we attach to the term species. This is even more necessary in geology than in the ordinary studies of the naturalist; for they who deny that such a thing as a species exists, concede nevertheless that a botanist or zoologist may reason as if the specific character were constant, because they confine their observations to a brief period of time. Just as the geographer, in constructing his maps from century to century, may proceed as if the apparent places of the fixed stars remained absolutely the same, and as if no alteration were brought about by the

† Sir Charles Lyell (1797–1875) was a Fellow of the Royal Society and president of the British Association. His three-volume *Principles of Geology*, which went through eleven editions in his lifetime, illustrates by its continual accretions the progress of geology over half a century. The following passage, critical of Lamarck's theory of transformation, is from Volume II of the *Principles*, which Darwin received, while aboard the *Beagle* in 1832.

Lyell's relationship with Darwin was a complex one. His "Uniformitarian" principle (the view that past changes in the earth's surface are to be accounted for by processes still in operation) was part of the underlying rationale for Darwin's work, and was an unorthodox geological opinion in the 1830's. Yet Lyell, though a friend of (and constant devil's advocate for) Darwin, could not bring himself to accept Darwin's theory until some years after the publication of the *Origin*.

The present text is from Volume II, Book III, Chapter 24, of the ninth edition of the *Principles* (1853), the last edition before the appearance of Darwin's book.

precession of the equinoxes; so, it is said, in the organic world, the stability of a species may be taken as absolute, if we do not extend our views beyond the narrow period of human history; but let a sufficient number of centuries elapse, to allow of important revolutions in climate, physical geography, and other circumstances, and the characters, say they, of the descendants of common parents may deviate indefinitely from their original type. * * *

Lamarck's arguments in favour of the transmutation of species

The name of species, observes Lamarck, has been usually applied to "every collection of similar individuals produced by other individuals like themselves." [1] This definition, he admits, is correct; because every living individual bears a very close resemblance to those from which it springs. But this is not all which is usually implied by the term species; for the majority of naturalists agree with Linnæus in supposing that all the individuals propagated from one stock have certain distinguishing characters in common, which will never vary, and which have remained the same since the creation of each species.

In order to shake this opinion, Lamarck enters upon the following line of argument:—The more we advance in the knowledge of the different organized bodies which cover the surface of the globe, the more our embarrassment increases, to determine what ought to be regarded as a species, and still more how to limit and distinguish genera. In proportion as our collections are enriched, we see almost every void filled up, and all our lines of separation effaced! we are reduced to arbitrary determinations, and are sometimes fain to seize upon the slight differences of mere varieties, in order to form characters for what we choose to call a species; and sometimes we are induced to pronounce individuals but slightly differing, and which others regard as true species, to be varieties.

The greater the abundance of natural objects assembled together, the more do we discover proofs that every thing passes by insensible shades into something else; that even the more remarkable differences are evanescent, and that nature has, for the most part, left us nothing at our disposal for establishing distinctions, save trifling, and, in some respects, puerile particularities. * * *

Every considerable alteration in the local circumstances in which each race of animals exists causes a change in their wants, and these new wants excite them to new actions and habits. These actions require the more frequent employer of some parts before but slightly exercised, and then greater development follows as a consequence of their more frequent use. Other organs no longer in use are impoverished and diminished in size, nay, are sometimes en-

1. Lamarck, *Philosophie Zoologique*, I, 54.

tirely annihilated, while in their place new parts are insensibly produced for the discharge of new functions.[2]

I must here interrupt the author's argument, by observing, that no positive fact is cited to exemplify the substitution of some *entirely new* sense, faculty, or organ, in the room of some other suppressed as useless. All the instances adduced go only to prove that the dimensions and strength of members and the perfection of certain attributes may, in a long succession of generations, be lessened and enfeebled by disuse; or, on the contrary, be matured and augmented by active exertion; just as we know that the power of scent is feeble in the greyhound, while its swiftness of pace and its acuteness of sight are remarkable—that the harrier and stag-hound, on the contrary, are comparatively slow in their movements, but excel in the sense of smelling.

It was necessary to point out to the reader this important chasm in the chain of evidence, because he might otherwise imagine that I had merely omitted the illustrations for the sake of brevity; but the plain truth is, that there were no examples to be found; and when Lamarck talks "of the efforts of internal sentiment," "the influence of subtle fluids," and "acts of organization," as causes whereby animals and plants may acquire *new organs,* he substitutes names for things; and, with a disregard to the strict rules of induction, resorts to fictions, as ideal as the "plastic virtue," and other phantoms of the geologists of the middle ages.

It is evident that, if some well-authenticated facts could have been adduced to establish one complete step in the process of transformation, such as the appearance, in individuals descending from a common stock, of a sense or organ entirely new, and a complete disappearance of some other enjoyed by their progenitors, time alone might then be supposed sufficient to bring about any amount of metamorphosis. The gratuitous assumption, therefore, of a point so vital to the theory of transmutation, was unpardonable on the part of its advocate.

But to proceed with the system: it being assumed as an undoubted fact, that a change of external circumstances may cause one organ to become entirely obsolete, and a new one to be developed, such as never before belonged to the species, the following proposition is announced, which, however staggering and absurd it may seem, is logically deduced from the assumed premises. It is not the organs, or, in other words, the nature and form of the parts of the body of an animal, which have given rise to its habits, and its particular faculties; but, on the contrary, its habits, its manner of living, and those of its progenitors, have in the course of time determined the form of its body, the number and condition of its organs—in short, the faculties which it enjoys. Thus otters, beavers,

2. *Ibid.,* I, 234.

waterfowl, turtles, and frogs, were not made web-footed in order that they might swim; but their wants having attracted them to the water in search of prey, they stretched out the toes of their feet to strike the water and move rapidly along its surface. By the repeated stretching of their toes, the skin which united them at the base acquired a habit of extension, until, in the course of time, the broad membranes which now connect their extremities were formed.

In like manner, the antelope and the gazelle were not endowed with light agile forms, in order that they might escape by flight from carnivorous animals; but, having been exposed to the danger of being devoured by lions, tigers, and other beasts of prey, they were compelled to exert themselves in running with great celerity; a habit which, in the course of many generations, gave rise to the peculiar slenderness of their legs, and the agility and elegance of their forms. * * *

Lamarck's theory of the transformation of the orang-outang into the human species

Such is the machinery of the Lamarckian system; but the reader will hardly, perhaps, be able to form a perfect conception of so complicated a piece of mechanism, unless it is exhibited in motion, so that we may see in what manner it can work out, under the author's guidance, all the extraordinary effects which we behold in the present state of the animate creation. I have only space for exhibiting a small part of the entire process by which a complete metamorphosis is achieved, and shall therefore omit the mode by which, after a countless succession of generations, a small gelatinous body is transformed into an oak or an ape; passing on at once to the last grand step in the progressive scheme, by which the orang-outang, having been already evolved out of a monad, is made slowly to attain the attributes and dignity of man.

One of the races of quadrumanous animals which had reached the highest state of perfection, lost, by constraint of circumstances (concerning the exact nature of which tradition is unfortunately silent), the habit of climbing trees, and of hanging on by grasping the boughs with their feet as with hands. The individuals of this race being obliged, for a long series of generations, to use their feet exclusively for walking, and ceasing to employ their hands as feet, were transformed into bimanous animals, and what before were thumbs became mere toes, no separation being required when their feet were used solely for walking. Having acquired a habit of holding themselves upright, their legs and feet assumed, insensibly, a conformation fitted to support them in an erect attitude, till at last these animals could no longer go on all-fours without much inconvenience. * * *

Among other ideas which the natural *tendency to perfection* engendered, the desire of ruling suggested itself, and this race succeeded at length in getting the better of the other animals, and made themselves masters of all those spots on the surface of the globe which best suited them. They drove out the animals which approached nearest them in organization and intelligence, and which were in a condition to dispute with them the good things of this world, forcing them to take refuge in deserts, woods, and wildernesses, where their multiplication was checked, and the progressive development of their faculties retarded; while, in the meantime, the dominant race spread itself in every direction, and lived in large companies, where new wants were successively created, exciting them to industry, and gradually perfecting their means and faculties.

In the supremacy and increased intelligence acquired by the ruling race, we see an illustration of the natural tendency of the organic world to grow more perfect; and, in their influence in repressing the advance of others, an example of one of those disturbing causes before enumerated, that *force of external circumstances* which causes such wide chasms in the regular series of animated being.

When the individuals of the dominant race became very numerous, their ideas greatly increased in number, and they felt the necessity of communicating them to each other, and of augmenting and varying the signs proper for the communication of ideas. Meanwhile the inferior quadrumanous animals, although most of them were gregarious, acquired no new ideas, being persecuted and restless in the deserts, and obliged to fly and conceal themselves, so that they conceived no new wants. Such ideas as they already had remained unaltered, and they could dispense with the communication of the greater part of these. To make themselves, therefore, understood by their fellows, required merely a few movements of the body or limbs—whistling, and the uttering of certain cries varied by the inflexions of the voice.

On the contrary, the individuals of the ascendant race, animated with a desire of interchanging their ideas, which became more and more numerous, were prompted to multiply the means of communication, and were no longer satisfied with mere pantomimic signs, nor even with all the possible inflexions of the voice, but made continual efforts to acquire the power of uttering articulate sounds, employing a few at first, but afterwards varying and perfecting them according to the increase of their wants. The habitual exercise of their throat, tongue, and lips, insensibly modified the conformation of these organs, until they became fitted for the faculty of speech.[3]

3. *Ibid.,* I, 356.

In effecting this mighty change, "the exigencies of the individuals were the sole agents; they gave rise to efforts, and the organs proper for articulating sounds were developed by their habitual employment." Hence, in this peculiar race, the origin of the admirable faculty of speech; hence also the diversity of languages, since the distance of places where the individuals composing the race established themselves soon favored the corruption of conventional signs.[4]

In conclusion, it may be proper to observe that the above sketch of the Lamarckian theory is no exaggerated picture, and those passages which have probably excited the greatest surprise in the mind of the reader are literal translations from the original.

SIR JOSEPH DALTON HOOKER

Flora Nova-Zelandiae (1853) †

* * * The arguments in favour of the permanence of specific characters in plants are:—

1. The fact that the amount of change produced by external causes does not warrant our assuming the contrary as a general law. Though there are many notorious cases in which cultivation and other causes produce changes of greater apparent value than specific characters generally possess, this happens in comparatively very few families, and only in such as are easily cultivated. In the whole range of the vegetable kingdom it is difficult to produce a change of specific value, however much we may alter conditions; it is much more difficult to prevent an induced variety from reverting to its original state, though we persevere in supplying the original conditions; and it is most difficult of all to reproduce a variety with similar materials and processes.[1]

4. *Ibid.*, I, 357.
† Sir Joseph Dalton Hooker (1817–1911), Fellow (and for five years president) of the Royal Society, shared with Darwin, Huxley, Wallace, and other Victorian naturalists the valuable experience of a long voyage of exploration. The fruits of his travels are three volumes under the general title, *The Botany of the Antarctic Voyage of H.M. Discovery Ships Erebus and Terror, in the Years 1839–1843*, of which the present text is from Chapter 2 of the Introductory Essay to Volume II. Hooker was an old friend and correspondent of Darwin's, but as this 1853 essay shows, he too was skeptical of Darwin's ideas.
1. I am quite aware that this argument will be met by many instances of change produced in our garden plants: but, after all, the skill of the gardener is successfully exerted in but few cases upon the whole: out of more than twenty thousand species cultivated at one time or another in the Royal Gardens of Kew, how few there are which do not come up, not only true to their species, but even to the race or variety from which they spring; yet it would be difficult to suggest a more complete change than that from the Alps or Polar regions to Surrey, or from the free air of the tropics to the thoroughly artificial conditions of our hothouses. Plants do not accommodate themselves to these changes: either they have passive powers of resisting their effects to a greater or less degree, or they succumb to them.

2. In tracing widely dispersed species, the permanence with which they retain their characters strikes the most ordinary observer; and this, whether we take such plants as have been dispersed without the aid of man (as *Sonchus oleraceus, Callitriche*, and *Montia*) through all latitudes from England to New Zealand; or such as have within modern times followed the migrations of man (as *Poa annua, Phalaris Canariensis*, Dock, Clover, *Alsine media, Capsella bursa-pastoris*, and a host of others); or such as man transports with him, whether such temperate climate plants as the cerealia, fruits, and flowers of the garden or field, or such tropical forms as *Convolvulus Batatas* and yams, which were introduced into New Zealand by its earliest inhabitants;—all these, in whatever climate to which we may follow them, retain the impress of their kind, unchanged save in a trifling degree.

3. With comparatively few exceptions, plants are confined within well-marked limits, which, though often very wide, are sometimes as much the reverse; while the instances are rare of sporadic species, as such are called which are found in small numbers in widely sundered localities. These facts seem incompatible on the one hand with the theory of species spreading from many centres, and on the other with their varying indefinitely; for were it otherwise, sporadic distribution would be the rule, insular floras would not necessarily be peculiar, and similar climates would have similar, if not identical species, which is not the case.

4. A multitude of allied species of plants grow close together without any interchange of specific character; and there are instances of exceedingly closely allied plants keeping company under many modifications of climate, soil, and elevation, yet never losing their distinctive marks.

5. The individuals that inhabit the circumference of the area occupied by a species, are not found passing into other species, but ceasing more or less abruptly; their limits may meet or overlap those of one or more very similar species, when the individuals associate, but do not amalgamate.

6. One negative argument in favour of distribution from one centre only, is, that taking the broadest view of the dispersion of species, we find that the more extensive families [2] are more or less widely distributed, very much in proportion to the facilities they present for dispersion. Thus the most minute-spored Cryptograms [3]

2. This rule does not extend to the Natural Orders themselves. The *Compositæ*, whose facilities for dispersion are proverbial, are amongst the most local; and the same may be said of *Leguminosæ* and *Solaneæ*, whose seeds retain their vitality in a remarkable degree: a few of their species are remarkably cosmopolite, but the greater number have generally narrow ranges.
3. The fact (first communicated to me by the Rev. M. J. Berkeley) of the spores of Fungi having been found by Professor Ehrenberg mingled with the atmospheric dust that has fallen on ships far out at sea, is one of the most decisive proofs of this.

are the most widely dispersed of all organized nature; plants that resist the influence of climate best, range furthest; water-plants are more cosmopolite than land-plants, and inhabitants of salt, more than those of fresh water: the more equable and uniform is the climate of a tract of land, the more uniformly and widely will its plants be distributed.

7. The species of the lowest Orders are not only the most widely diffused, but their specific characters are not modified by the greatest changes of climate, however much their stature and luxuriance may vary. Fungi offer a remarkable instance of this: their microscopic spores are wafted in myriads through the air; the life of the individuals is often of very short duration, and many of them being as sensitive as insects to temperature and humidity, they are ephemeral in all senses; sometimes appearing only once in the same spot, and remaining but a few days, never to reappear within the observer's experience. The specific characters of many reside in the diameter, form, colour, and arrangement of their most minute organs, whose analysis demands a refinement of microscopic skill; yet the most accomplished and profound botanist in this Natural Order (who has favoured me with the descriptions of the New Zealand Fungi) fails to find the most trifling character by which to separate many New Zealand species from European.

8. The fact, now universally conceded by all intelligent horticulturists, that no plant has been acclimated in England within the experience of man, is a very suggestive one, though not conclusive; for it may be answered, that plants which cannot survive a sudden change, might a slow and progressive one. On the other hand, plants have powers of enduring change when self-propagated that they have not in our gardens; thus I find a great difference in the hardiness of individual species of several Himalayan plants,[4] depending upon the altitude at which they were gathered. In these cases the species is the same, and the parent individuals were not even varieties of one another, except so far as regards hardiness, in other words, the specific character remains unaltered in spite of the change of constitution, just as the climate of one part of the globe disagrees with the human race of another, and is even fatal to it.

Such are a few of the leading phenomena or facts that appear to me to give the greatest weight to the opinion that individuals of a species are all derived from one parent: for such arguments as the New Zealand Flora furnishes, I must refer my readers to the following chapter. I would again remind the student that the hasty adop-

---

4. Thus some of the seedling Pines whose parents grew at 12,000 feet appear hardy, whilst those of the same species from 10,000 are tender. The common scarlet *Rhododendron* of Nepal and the North-west Himalaya is tender, but seedlings of the same species from Sikkim, whose parents grew at a greater elevation, have proved perfectly hardy.

tion of any of these theories is not advisable: plants should be largely collected, and studied both in the living and dried states, and the result of their dissection noted, without reference to any speculations, which are too apt to lead the inquirer away from the rigorous investigation of details, from which alone truth can be elicited. When however the opportunity or necessity arises for combining results, and presenting them in that systematic form which can alone render them available for the purposes of science, it becomes necessary for the generalizer to proceed upon some determinate principle; and I cannot conclude this part of the subject better than by adopting the words of the most able of Transatlantic botanists, who is no less sound as a generalizer than profound in his knowledge of details:—"All classification and system in Natural History rests upon the fundamental idea of the original creation of certain forms, which have naturally been perpetuated unchanged, or with such changes only as we may conceive or prove to have arisen from varying physical influences, accidental circumstances, or from cultivation." [5] * * *

In the above speculative review of some of the causes which appear to affect the life and range of species in the vegetable kingdom, I have not touched upon one point, namely, that which concerns the original introduction of existing species of plants upon the earth. I have assumed that they have existed for ages in the forms they now retain, that assumption agreeing, in my opinion, with the facts elicited by a survey of all the phenomena they present, and, according to the most eminent zoologists, with those laws that govern animal life also; but there is nothing in what is assumed above, in favour of the antiquity of species and their wide distribution, that is inconsistent with any theory of their origin that the speculator may adopt. My object has not so much been to ascertain what may, or may not, have been the original condition of species, as to show that, granting more scope for variation than is generally allowed, still there are no unassailable grounds for concluding that they now vary so as to obliterate specific character; in other words, I have endeavoured to show that they are, for all practical purposes of progress in botanical science, to be regarded as permanently distinct creations, which have survived great geological changes, and which will either die out, or be destroyed, with their distinctive marks unchanged. * * *

5. Botanical Text-book, p. 303, by Professor Asa Gray, of Cambridge University, U.S. (Hooker means, of course, Harvard University.—Ed.)

CHARLES DARWIN

An Historical Sketch of the Progress of Opinion on the Origin of Species, previously to the Publication of This Work (1861) †

I will here give a brief sketch of the progress of opinion on the Origin of Species. Until recently the great majority of naturalists believed that species were immutable productions, and had been separately created. This view has been ably maintained by many authors. Some few naturalists, on the other hand, have believed that species undergo modification and that the existing forms of life are the descendants by true generation of pre-existing forms. Passing over allusions to the subject in the classical writers,[1] the first author who in modern times has treated it in a scientific spirit was Buffon. But as his opinions fluctuated greatly at different periods, and as he does not enter on the causes or means of the transformation of species, I need not here enter on details.

Lamarck was the first man whose conclusions on the subject excited much attention. This justly celebrated naturalist first published his views in 1801; he much enlarged them in 1809 in his 'Philosophie Zoologique,' and subsequently, in 1815, in the Introduction to his 'Hist. Nat. des Animaux sans Vertèbres.' In these works he upholds the doctrine that all species, including man, are descended from other species. He first did the eminent service of arousing attention to the probability of all changes in the organic, as well as in the inorganic world, being the result of law, and not of

† This sketch was first added to the *Origin of Species* in the third edition (1861) and was supplemented in later editions. Darwin had been criticized from various quarters for giving insufficient credit to his "predecessors."

The present text is from the sixth edition of the *Origin*, the last in Darwin's lifetime.

1. Aristotle, in his 'Physicae Auscultationes' (lib. 2, cap. 8, s. 2), after remarking that rain does not fall in order to make the corn grow, any more than it falls to spoil the farmer's corn when threshed out of doors, applies the same argument to organisation; and adds (as translated by Mr. Clair Grece, who first pointed out the passage to me), "So what hinders the different parts [of the body] from having this merely accidental relation in nature? as the teeth, for example, grow by necessity, the front ones sharp, adapted for dividing, and the grinders flat, and serviceable for masticating the food; since they were not made for the sake of this, but it was the result of accident. And in like manner as to the other parts in which there appears to exist an adaptation to an end. Wheresoever, therefore, all things together (that is all the parts of one whole) happened like as if they were made for the sake of something, these were preserved, having been appropriately constituted by an internal spontaneity; and whatsoever things were not thus constituted, perished, and still perish." We here see the principle of natural selection shadowed forth, but how little Aristotle fully comprehended the principle, is shown by his remarks on the formation of the teeth.

miraculous interposition. Lamarck seems to have been chiefly led to his conclusion on the gradual change of species, by the difficulty of distinguishing species and varieties, by the almost perfect gradation of forms in certain groups, and by the analogy of domestic productions. With respect to the means of modification, he attributed something to the direct action of the physical conditions of life, something to the crossing of already existing forms, and much to use and disuse, that is, to the effects of habit. To this latter agency he seems to attribute all the beautiful adaptations in nature;—such as the long neck of the giraffe for browsing on the branches of trees. But he likewise believed in a law of progressive development; and as all the forms of life thus tend to progress, in order to account for the existence at the present day of simple productions, he maintains that such forms are now spontaneously generated.[2]

Geoffroy Saint-Hilaire, as is stated in his 'Life,' written by his son, suspected, as early as 1795, that what we call species are various degenerations of the same type. It was not until 1828 that he published his conviction that the same forms have not been perpetuated since the origin of all things. Geoffroy seems to have relied chiefly on the conditions of life, or the *'monde ambiant'* as the cause of change. He was cautious in drawing conclusions, and did not believe that existing species are now undergoing modification; and, as his son adds, "C'est donc un problème à réserver entièrement à l'avenir, supposé même que l'avenir doive avoir prise sur lui."

In 1813, Dr. W. C. Wells read before the Royal Society 'An Account of a White female, part of whose skin resembles that of a Negro'; but his paper was not published until his famous 'Two Essays upon Dew and Single Vision' appeared in 1818. In this paper he distinctly recognises the principle of natural selection, and this is the first recognition which has been indicated; but he applies it only to the races of man, and to certain characters alone. After remarking that Negroes and mulattoes enjoy an immunity from certain tropical diseases, he observes, firstly, that all animals tend to vary in some degree, and, secondly, that agriculturists improve their

---

2. I have taken the date of the first publication of Lamarck from Isid. Geoffroy Saint-Hilaire's ('Hist. Nat. Générale,' tom. ii. p. 405, 1859) excellent history of opinion on this subject. In this work a full account is given of Buffon's conclusions on the same subject. It is curious how largely my grandfather, Dr. Erasmus Darwin, anticipated the views and erroneous grounds of opinion of Lamarck in his 'Zoonomia' (vol. i. pp. 500–510), published in 1794. According to Isid. Geoffroy there is no doubt that Goethe was an extreme partisan of similar views, as shown in the Introduction to a work written in 1794 and 1795, but not published till long afterwards: he has pointedly remarked ('Goethe als Naturforscher,' von Dr. Karl Meding, s. 34) that the future question for naturalists will be how, for instance, cattle got their horns, and not for what they are used. It is rather a singular instance of the manner in which similar views arise at about the same time, that Goethe in Germany, Dr. Darwin in England, and Geoffroy Saint-Hilaire (as we shall immediately see) in France, came to the same conclusion on the origin of species, in the years 1794–5.

domesticated animals by selection; and then, he adds, but what is done in this latter case "by art, seems to be done with equal efficacy, though more slowly, by nature, in the formation of varieties of mankind, fitted for the country which they inhabit. Of the accidental varieties of man, which would occur among the first few and scattered inhabitants of the middle regions of Africa, some one would be better fitted than the others to bear the diseases of the country. This race would consequently multiply, while the others would decrease; not only from their inability to sustain the attacks of disease, but from their incapacity of contending with their more vigorous neighbours. The colour of this vigorous race I take for granted, from what has been already said, would be dark. But the same disposition to form varieties still existing, a darker and a darker race would in the course of time occur: and as the darkest would be the best fitted for the climate, this would at length become the most prevalent, if not the only race, in the particular country in which it had originated." He then extends these same views to the white inhabitants of colder climates. I am indebted to Mr. Rowley, of the United States, for having called my attention, through Mr. Brace, to the above passage in Dr. Wells' work.

The Hon. and Rev. W. Herbert, afterwards Dean of Manchester, in the fourth volume of the 'Horticultural Transactions,' 1822, and in his work on the 'Amaryllidaceæ' (1837, pp. 19, 339), declares that "horticultural experiments have established, beyond the possibility of refutation, that botanical species are only a higher and more permanent class of varieties." He extends the same view to animals. The Dean believes that single species of each genus were created in an originally highly plastic condition, and that these have produced, chiefly by intercrossing, but likewise by variation, all our existing species.

In 1826 Professor Grant, in the concluding paragraph in his well-known paper ('Edinburgh Philosophical Journal,' vol. xiv. p. 283) on the Spongilla, clearly declares his belief that species are descended from other species, and that they become improved in the course of modification. This same view was given in his 55th Lecture, published in the 'Lancet' in 1834.

In 1831 Mr. Patrick Matthew published his work on 'Naval Timber and Arboriculture,' in which he gives precisely the same view on the origin of species as that (presently to be alluded to) propounded by Mr. Wallace and myself in the 'Linnean Journal,' and as that enlarged in the present volume. Unfortunately the view was given by Mr. Matthew very briefly in scattered passages in an Appendix to a work on a different subject, so that it remained unnoticed until Mr. Matthew himself drew attention to it in the 'Gardener's Chronicle,' on April 7th, 1860. The differences of

Mr. Matthew's view from mine are not of much importance: he seems to consider that the world was nearly depopulated at successive periods, and then re-stocked; and he gives as an alternative, that new forms may be generated "without the presence of any mould or germ of former aggregates." I am not sure that I understand some passages; but it seems that he attributes much influence to the direct action of the conditions of life. He clearly saw, however, the full force of the principle of natural selection.

The celebrated geologist and naturalist, Von Buch, in his excellent 'Description Physique des Isles Canaries' (1836, p. 147), clearly expresses his belief that varieties slowly become changed into permanent species, which are no longer capable of intercrossing.

Rafinesque, in his 'New Flora of North America,' published in 1836, wrote (p. 6) as follows:—"All species might have been varieties once, and many varieties are gradually becoming species by assuming constant and peculiar characters"; but farther on (p. 18) he adds, "except the original types or ancestors of the genus."

In 1843–44 Professor Haldeman ('Boston Journal of Nat. Hist. U. States,' vol. iv. p. 468) has ably given the arguments for and against the hypothesis of the development and modification of species: he seems to lean towards the side of change.

The 'Vestiges of Creation' appeared in 1844. In the tenth and much improved edition (1853) the anonymous author says (p. 155):—"The proposition determined on after much consideration is, that the several series of animated beings, from the simplest and oldest up to the highest and most recent, are, under the providence of God, the results, *first*, of an impulse which has been imparted to the forms of life, advancing them, in definite times, by generation, through grades of organisation terminating in the highest dicotyledons and vertebrata, these grades being few in number, and generally marked by intervals of organic character, which we find to be a practical difficulty in ascertaining affinities; *second*, of another impulse connected with the vital forces, tending, in the course of generations, to modify organic structures in accordance with external circumstances, as food, the nature of the habitat, and the meteoric agencies, these being the 'adaptations' of the natural theologian." The author apparently believes that organisation progresses by sudden leaps, but that the effects produced by the conditions of life are gradual. He argues with much force on general grounds that species are not immutable productions. But I cannot see how the two supposed "impulses" account in a scientific sense for the numerous and beautiful coadaptations which we see throughout nature; I cannot see that we thus gain any insight how, for instance, a woodpecker has become adapted to its peculiar habits of life. The work, from its powerful and brilliant style, though displaying in the earlier editions little accurate knowledge and a great want of scientific caution, immediately had a very wide circulation. In my opinion it has done excellent service in this country in calling attention to the subject, in removing prejudice, and in thus preparing the ground for the reception of analogous views.

In 1846 the veteran geologist M. J. d'Omalius d'Halloy published in an excellent though short paper ('Bulletins de l'Acad. Roy. Bruxelles,' tom. xiii. p. 581) his opinion that it is more probable that new species have been produced by descent with modification than that they have been separately created: the author first promulgated this opinion in 1831.

Profesor Owen, in 1849 ('Nature of Limbs,' p. 86), wrote as follows:—"The archetypal idea was manifested in the flesh under diverse such modifications, upon this planet, long prior to the existence of those animal species that actually exemplify it. To what natural laws or secondary causes the orderly succession and progression of such organic phenomena may have been committed, we, as yet, are ignorant." In his Address to the British Association, in 1858, he speaks (p. li.) of "the axiom of the continuous operation of creative power, or of the ordained becoming of living things." Farther on (p. xc.), after referring to geographical distribution, he adds, "These phenomena shake our confidence in the conclusion that the Apteryx of New Zealand and the Red Grouse of England were distinct creations in and for those islands respectively. Always, also, it may be well to bear in mind that by the word 'creation' the zoologist means 'a process he knows not what.' " He amplifies this idea by adding that when such cases as that of the Red Grouse are "enumerated by the zoologist as evidence of distinct creation of the bird in and for such islands, he chiefly expresses that he knows not how the Red Grouse came to be there, and there exclusively; signifying also, by this mode of expressing such ignorance, his belief that both the bird and the islands owed their origin to a great first Creative Cause." If we interpret these sentences given in the same Address, one by the other, it appears that this eminent philosopher felt in 1858 his confidence shaken that the Apteryx and the Red Grouse first appeared in their respective homes, "he knew not how," or by some process "he knew not what."

This Address was delivered after the papers by Mr. Wallace and myself on the Origin of Species, presently to be referred to, had been read before the Linnean Society. When the first edition of this work was published, I was so completely deceived, as were many others, by such expressions as "the continuous operation of creative power," that I included Professor Owen with other palæontologists as being firmly convinced of the immutability of species; but it appears ('Anat. of Vertebrates,' vol. iii. p. 796) that this was on my part a preposterous error. In the last edition of this work I inferred, and the inference still seems to me perfectly just, from a passage beginning with the words "no doubt the type-form," &c. (Ibid. vol. i. p. xxxv.), that Professor Owen admitted that natural selection may have done something in the formation of a new species; but this it appears (Ibid. vol. iii. p. 798) is inaccurate and without evidence. I also gave some extracts from a correspondence between Professor Owen and the Editor of the 'London Review,' from which it appeared manifest to the Editor as well as myself, that Professor Owen claimed to have promulgated the theory of natural selection before I had done so; and I expressed my surprise and satisfaction at this announcement; but as far as it is possible to understand certain recently published passages (Ibid vol. iii. p. 798) I have either partially or wholly again fallen into error. It is consolatory to me that others find Professor Owen's controversial writings as difficult to understand and to reconcile with each other, as I do. As far as the mere enunciation of the principle of natural selection is concerned, it is quite immaterial whether or not Professor Owen preceded me, for both of us, as shown in this historical sketch, were long ago preceded by Dr. Wells and Mr. Matthew.

M. Isidore Geoffroy Saint-Hilaire, in his lectures delivered in 1850 (of which a Résumé appeared in the 'Revue et Mag. de Zoolog.,' Jan. 1851), briefly gives his reason for believing that specific characters "sont fixés, pour chaque espèce, tant qu'elle se perpétue au milieu des mêmes circonstances: ils se modifient, si les circonstances ambiantes viennent à changer." "En-résumé, *l'observation* des animaux sauvages démontre déjà la variabilité *limitée* des espèces. Les *expériences* sur les animaux sauvages, devenus domestiques, et sur les animaux domestiques redevenus sauvages, la démontrent plus clairement encore. Ces mêmes expériences prouvent, de plus, que les différences produites peuvent être de *valeur générique.*" In his 'Hist. Nat. Générale' (tom. ii. p. 430, 1859) he amplifies analogous conclusions.

From a circular lately issued it appears that Dr. Freke, in 1851 ('Dublin Medical Press,' p. 322), propounded the doctrine that all organic beings have descended from one primordial form. His grounds of belief and treatment of the subject are wholly different from mine; but as Dr. Freke has now (1861) published his Essay on the 'Origin of Species by means of Organic Affinity,' the difficult attempt to give any idea of his views would be superfluous on my part.

Mr. Herbert Spencer, in an Essay (originally published in the 'Leader,' March, 1852, and republished in his 'Essays,' in 1858), has contrasted the theories of the Creation and the Development of organic beings with remarkable skill and force. He argues from the analogy of domestic productions, from the changes which the embryos of many species undergo, from the difficulty of distinguishing species and varieties, and from the principle of general gradation, that species have been modified; and he attributes the modification to the change of circumstances. The author (1855) has also treated Psychology on the principle of the necessary acquirement of each mental power and capacity by gradation.

In 1852 M. Naudin, a distinguished botanist, expressly stated, in an admirable paper on the Origin of Species ('Revue Horticole,' p. 102; since partly republished in the 'Nouvelles Archives du Muséum,' tom. i. p. 171), his belief that species are formed in an analogous manner as varieties are under cultivation; and the latter process he attributes to man's power of selection. But he does not show how selection acts under nature. He believes, like Dean Herbert, that species, when nascent, were more plastic than at present. He lays weight on what he calls the principle of finality, "puissance mystérieuse, indéterminée; fatalité pour les uns; pour les autres, volonté providentielle, dont l'action incessante sur les êtres vivants détermine, à toutes les époques de l'existence du monde, la forme, le volume, et la durée de chacun d'eux, en raison de sa destinée dans l'ordre de choses dont il fait partie. C'est cette puissance qui harmonise chaque membre à l'ensemble, en l'appropriant à la fonction qu'il doit remplir dans l'organisme général de la nature, fonction qui est pour lui sa raison d'être." [3]

In 1853 a celebrated geologist, Count Keyserling ('Bulletin de la Soc. Géolog.,' 2nd Ser., tom x. p. 357), suggested that as new diseases, supposed to have been caused by some miasma, have arisen and spread over the world, so at certain periods the germs of existing species may have been chemically affected by circumambient molecules of a particular nature, and thus have given rise to new forms.

In this same year, 1853, Dr. Schaaffhausen published an excellent pamphlet ('Verhand. des Naturhist. Vereins der Preuss. Rheinlands,' &c.), in which he maintains the development of organic forms on the earth. He infers that many species have kept true for

---

3. From references in Bronn's 'Untersuchungen über die Entwickelungs-Gesetze,' it appears that the celebrated botanist and palaeontologist Unger published, in 1852, his belief that species undergo development and modification. Dalton, likewise, in Pander and Dalton's work on Fossil Sloths, expressed, in 1821, a similar belief. Similar views have, as is well known, been maintained by Oken in his mystical 'Natur-Philosophie.' From other references in Godron's work 'Sur l'Espèce,' it seems that Bory St. Vincent, Burdach, Poiret, and Fries, have all admitted that new species are continually being produced.

I may add, that of the thirty-four authors named in this Historical Sketch, who believe in the modification of species, or at least disbelieve in separate acts of creation, twenty-seven have written on special branches of natural history or geology.

long periods, whereas a few have become modified. The distinction of species he explains by the destruction of intermediate graduated forms. "Thus living plants and animals are not separated from the extinct by new creations, but are to be regarded as their descendants through continued reproduction."

A well-known French botanist, M. Lecoq, writes in 1854 (Etudes sur Géograph. Bot.,' tom. i. p. 250), "On voit que nos recherches sur la fixité ou la variation de l'espèce, nous conduisent directement aux idées émises, par deux hommes justement célèbres, Geoffroy Saint-Hilaire et Goethe." Some other passages scattered through M. Lecoq's large work, make it a little doubtful how far he extends his views on the modification of species.

The 'Philosophy of Creation' has been treated in a masterly manner by the Rev. Baden Powell, in his 'Essays on the Unity of Worlds,' 1855. Nothing can be more striking than the manner in which he shows that the introduction of new species is "a regular, not a casual phenomenon," or, as Sir John Herschel expresses it, "a natural in contradistinction to a miraculous process."

The third volume of the 'Journal of the Linnean Society' contains papers, read July 1st, 1858, by Mr. Wallace and myself, in which, as stated in the introductory remarks to this volume, the theory of Natural Selection is promulgated by Mr. Wallace with admirable force and clearness.

Von Baer, towards whom all zoologists feel so profound a respect, expressed about the year 1859 (see Prof. Rudolph Wagner, 'Zoologisch-Anthropologische Untersuchungen,' 1861, s. 51) his conviction, chiefly grounded on the laws of geographical distribution, that forms now perfectly distinct have descended from a single parent-form.

In June, 1859, Professor Huxley gave a lecture before the Royal Institution on the 'Persistent Types of Animal Life.' Referring to such cases, he remarks, "It is difficult to comprehend the meaning of such facts as these, if we suppose that each species of animal and plant, or each great type of organisation, was formed and placed upon the surface of the globe at long intervals by a distinct act of creative power; and it is well to recollect that such an assumption is as unsupported by tradition or revelation as it is opposed to the general analogy of nature. If, on the other hand, we view 'Persistent Types' in relation to that hypothesis which supposes the species living at any time to be the result of the gradual modification of preexisting species, a hypothesis which, though unproven, and sadly damaged by some of its supporters, is yet the only one to which physiology lends any countenance; their existence would seem to show that the amount of modification which living beings have undergone during geological time is but very small in relation to the whole series of changes which they have suffered."

In December, 1859, Dr. Hooker published his 'Introduction to the Australian Flora.' In the first part of this great work he admits the truth of the descent and modification of species, and supports this doctrine by many original observations.

The first edition of this work was published on November 24th, 1859, and the second edition on January 7th, 1860.

MILTON MILLHAUSER

"In the Air" (1959) †

* * *

Evolution, then, was "in the air" in the years immediately preceding the publication of V*estiges* [Robert Chambers, V*estiges of* * * * *Creation*, 1844], in a number of specific senses. First, a fair number of scientists, from Buffon and Maupertius to Lamarck and Saint-Hilaire and Meckel, had given it the cachet of their approval; and while most of these were obscure enough, a few were of some importance in their fields or had taken pains to be noticed. Second, the idea had also attracted several nonscientific writers, ranging in influence and quality from Kant to Erasmus Darwin and Monboddo. Third, there had been of late a considerable accumulation of technical findings leading in the same direction, most strikingly in geology, embryology, and comparative anatomy. Fourth, a good many of the neutral and half-convinced were recording the hypothesis honestly enough, sometimes even in popular treatises, as at least a possibility. Fifth, these influences had rendered the idea sufficiently conspicuous that even hostile writers, when addressing an informed audience, were forced to deal seriously with it, thereby giving it a sort of disagreeable publicity of their own. (Herbert Spencer was first seriously interested in evolution by Lyell's refutation of it in the *Principles*.)

And, finally, there was a sixth, contributory influence, the weight of which cannot be estimated but can hardly have been negligible. The idea of development had entered the world and was touching other fields than biology; thinking in terms of growth and change was becoming a familiar habit of the age.

History, for instance, was never in much danger of neglecting change; but since the eighteenth century it had turned noticeably from an earlier habit of chronicle to tracing the development and

† From Chapter 3 of *Just before Darwin* (Middletown, Conn., 1959). Milton Millhauser (b. 1910) is professor of English at the University of Bridgeport.

transformation of institutions, or to emphasizing the uniqueness and organic unity of the societies out of which had sprung our own. (The Victorians tended sometimes to think of it as synonymous with "progress.") John Henry Newman, then still a Protestant, had introduced roughly comparable ideas into English theology (and, by one reviewer of V*estiges*, was sharply criticized for so doing). A similar line was being followed by the German "higher critics," who regarded the sacred documents of theology as the products of tradition and subject to the processes of history. The historical novel, which tells us that our fathers' world was unlike our own, was an eighteenth-century invention and a nineteenth-century speciality; it was a typical outgrowth of the romantic spirit, which looks back, and traces continuity through change. Romantic psychology, under the influence of Rousseau, drove back the concept of growth and change into our own mental life; emphasizing the kinship of the youth's intellectual processes with those of the savage, it introduced a kind of "recapitulation" of its own. German philosophy had centered, from Lessing to Hegel, on the idea of "becoming"; Comtism, with its "three stages," might also be considered in a crude and elementary way a developmental system. Economics was still in 1844 the domain of absolute principles; but, if this is any comfort to the generalizing mind, it was not long to remain so. In 1848 two solemn theorizers, one British and empirical, one metaphysical and German, were to found a new type of forward-looking economic science, in which the socialism of the future —whether Mill's or Marx's—was to work itself into being out of the structure and process of contemporary society.

The sciences were also moving in this direction. Geology and embryology, those vigorous nineteenth-century growths, were both (aside from their connection with evolution) sciences of "becoming," which taught the mind to look on development as not magnification but change. Chemistry was investigating elements whose properties changed unpredictably when they were combined; it had also synthesized an organic substance, urea. G. J. Mulder, a Dutch physicist of the time, was merely the latest of a long line of "gradationists" who believed that the organic world shaded off into the inorganic, and that the nature of vital activity might be found in a study of the biochemical processes. (The great Schleiden himself had said that the growth of the cell was of the same order of phenomena with the growth of the crystal.) Even more mystifying was electricity, which also had been shown to have its obscure relations with life. From Mesmer and Galvani, this exciting notion had filtered down to reach a literary public; so generally metaphysical a thinker as S. T. Coleridge (not to speak of the "Vestigitarian") thought it worth his while to attempt to trace out, or at least to point to, a connection. Biology was still—in those far days—divided over the question whether life proceeded from a specifically "vital" or merely physical "principle"; any circumstance that favored the latter answer, any observation that extended the bounds and subtlety of the realm of matter, naturally encouraged that intellectual materialism which was the soil in which evolution flourished.

Of all the sciences that contributed incidentally or analogically to this effect, none was more potent over men's imaginations than astronomy. To the young man of the 1830's, the single most impressive contribution to astronomy since Newton was the nebular hypothesis. Suggested independently by Kant and Emanuel Swedenborg, elaborated by Laplace, buttressed by Comte's mathematics, and supported inferentially by the observations of the elder Herschel, it enjoyed throughout the first part of the century a tremendous vogue; it seemed to explain and fulfil the universe of simple laws and ordered forces that previous centuries had spread across the sky. Theoretical objections were early raised against it; but in the 1840's, though it had already been abandoned by most astronomers, it still exercised a powerful sway over the popular mind. The great Baron von Humboldt, who did not accept it, nevertheless afforded it a certain prominence, and his English reviewers treated it with respect.[1] The effect of this theory was much the same as that of uniformitarian geology: it set back infinitely far the date of any possible Creation, adding the aeons of the nebula to the aeons of the earth; and it disposed men's minds to think of their universe as *generated*, developed through successive stages and in accordance with mechanical laws, rather than created miraculously in virtually its present form. Even the observations that had recently shaken faith in the nebular hypothesis, "resolving" what had appeared to be diffuse masses of primitive matter into swarms of distant stars, were not calculated to buttress the old ways of thinking. The awe-inspiring reaches of interstellar space, the compounded infinitudes of galaxies and systems that the modern telescope was thus opening to men's gaze, militated with a terrible force against the notion that mankind, masters of certain circumscribed areas on the accidental satellite of a half-burnt-out star, could possibly have any special value—let alone a central and decisive position—in the whole stupendous scheme of things.

Here was a whole concatenation of influences, ranging from the direct and explicit to the vaguely suggestive and remote, some diffused through the entire intellectual atmosphere, others inaccessible

---

1. The *Quarterly Review*, in 1845, obviously believes that Humboldt was on this account a follower of Erasmus Darwin, and that he was willing to ascribe the power of "indefinite development" to matter.

except to the specialist, but all finally inclining the mind in the same general direction. Nevertheless, the force of these influences, as compared to that of clerical conservatism and the hostility of many eminent scientists to the very idea of evolution, was limited and slight. The mere habit of thinking developmentally (which had not yet filtered down effectively to the popular level) would be of trifling effect without the science; and among popular writers, it was precisely the technical studies that were least read and therefore least reflected. Science reached the public—the large public of which we are now speaking—through the Scriptural Geologist and the reconciling divine; through skilled expositors like Lyell and Whewell, both conservative on the issue of evolution; and through popular treatises, which tended, by and large, to assume a safe, conventional position. Biology was a difficult subject to follow, especially in its microscopic phases (geology, by contrast, was spread out across a vast specimen case that any healthy pedestrian Englishman could inspect at leisure); its more specialized findings and more questionable theories were not particularly well advertised. The sense of an impending crisis, which was beginning to be felt by men like Lyell and Whewell and the Scriptural Geologists—and by a few of their most discerning readers—was not generally shared. Buffon was read as a descriptive naturalist, Erasmus Darwin as a literary curiosity, and Lamarck not at all. There was a widespread interest in "natural history," and some in paleontology, which were both serviceable as far as they went; but theoretical biology, for all its recent strides, was virtually unknown.[2]

Thus the actual effect of the influences we have traced out was not to spread the idea broadcast, in however attenuated a form, but rather to trouble the minds of an informed few; and, beyond that, to prepare an atmosphere or temper of mind that—when at long last it did come irresistibly—might fit the theory of evolution into its place among the opinions of the age. Even the scientist, bound by his own prejudices or dubious of a rather sketchy demonstration, might require this sort of prodding and encouragement; how long it took for Lyell to come round! As for the general reader, even the rather studious and thoughtful one, he was being readied by forces he did not recognize for a revelation of which he did not dream. Meanwhile it was inevitable that the idea should occur at intervals to scattered thinkers, each of whom formed a little focus whence it radiated for a space; or that, to those who first encountered it in some slighting reference, it should have seemed less strange, less wholly unexpected, than it might have been without the work of preparation. We must draw a twofold distinction, which is also

2. That is, by popular writers on general subjects. Naturally, the physicians and other specialists were acquainted with it.

something—but not too much—of an oversimplification: between a specially informed small public and an only generally informed large one; between widespread but inconclusive influences such as geology and comparative anatomy, and narrowly restricted but powerfully suggestive ones such as biochemistry and embryology. Only then can we comprehend the paradox that evolution, when it came, struck an unprepared British audience as a profound moral shock; and that it still seemed in retrospect, to the Victorians themselves, to have been for a generation before 1859 "in the air." * * *

PART II

Selections from Darwin's Work

Darwin's *essential* achievement was the demonstration that the almost incredible variety of life, with all its complex and puzzling relations to its environment, was explicable in scientific terms.
—Julian Huxley, 1958

This second supposed cause of evolution was known as "the inheritance of acquired characters," a doctrine that had been accepted generally for well over two thousand years. Not until late in the nineteenth century was its validity questioned seriously. Then the critical experiments, designed to test its validity, gave negative results * * * and now the belief has been abandoned by all honest and critical biologists.
—Conway Zirkle, 1958

CHARLES DARWIN

The Origin of Species (1859) †

Introduction

When on board H.M.S. 'Beagle,' as naturalist, I was much struck with certain facts in the distribution of the organic beings inhabiting South America, and in the geological relations of the present to the past inhabitants of that continent. These facts, as will be seen in the latter chapters of this volume, seemed to throw some light on the origin of species—that mystery of mysteries, as it has been called by one of our greatest philosophers. On my return home, it occurred to me, in 1837, that something might perhaps be made out on this question by patiently accumulating and reflecting on all sorts of facts which could possibly have any bearing on it. After five years' work I allowed myself to speculate on the subject, and drew up some short notes; these I enlarged in 1844 into a sketch of the conclusions, which then seemed to me probable: from that period to the present day I have steadily pursued the same object. I hope that I may be excused for entering on these personal details, as I give them to show that I have not been hasty in coming to a decision.

My work is now (1859) nearly finished; but as it will take me many more years to complete it, and as my health is far from strong, I have been urged to publish this Abstract. I have more especially been induced to do this, as Mr. Wallace, who is now studying the natural history of the Malay archipelago, has arrived at almost exactly the same general conclusions that I have on the origin of species. In 1858 he sent me a memoir on this subject, with a request that I would forward it to Sir Charles Lyell, who sent it to the Linnean Society, and it is published in the third volume of the Journal of that society. Sir C. Lyell and Dr. Hooker, who both knew of my work—the latter having read my sketch of 1844—honoured me by thinking it advisable to publish, with Mr. Wallace's excellent memoir, some brief extracts from my manuscripts.

This Abstract, which I now publish, must necessarily be imperfect. I cannot here give references and authorities for my several statements; and I must trust to the reader reposing some confidence in my accuracy. No doubt errors will have crept in, though I hope I

† The present text is excerpted from the sixth edition of the *Origin* (1872), the last edition during Darwin's lifetime.

have always been cautious in trusting to good authorities alone. I can here give only the general conclusions at which I have arrived, with a few facts in illustration, but which, I hope, in most cases will suffice. No one can feel more sensible than I do of the necessity of hereafter publishing in detail all the facts, with references, on which my conclusions have been grounded; and I hope in a future work to do this. For I am well aware that scarcely a single point is discussed in this volume on which facts cannot be adduced, often apparently leading to conclusions directly opposite to those at which I have arrived. A fair result can be obtained only by fully stating and balancing the facts and arguments on both sides of each question; and this is here impossible. * * *

In considering the Origin of Species, it is quite conceivable that a naturalist, reflecting on the mutual affinities of organic beings, on their embryological relations, their geographical distribution, geological succession, and other such facts, might come to the conclusion that species had not been independently created, but had descended, like varieties, from other species. Nevertheless, such a conclusion, even if well founded, would be unsatisfactory, until it could be shown how the innumerable species inhabiting this world have been modified, so as to acquire that perfection of structure and coadaptation which justly excites our admiration. Naturalists continually refer to external conditions, such as climate, food, &c., as the only possible source of variation. In one limited sense, as we shall hereafter see, this may be true; but it is preposterous to attribute to mere external conditions, the structure, for instance, of the woodpecker, with its feet, tail, beak, and tongue, so admirably adapted to catch insects under the bark of trees. In the case of the mistletoe, which draws its nourishment from certain trees, which has seeds that must be transported by certain birds, and which has flowers with separate sexes absolutely requiring the agency of certain insects to bring pollen from one flower to the other, it is equally preposterous to account for the structure of this parasite, with its relations to several distinct organic beings, by the effects of external conditions, or of habit, or of the volition of the plant itself.

It is, therefore, of the highest importance to gain a clear insight into the means of modification and coadaptation. At the commencement of my observations it seemed to me probable that a careful study of domesticated animals and of cultivated plants would offer the best chance of making out this obscure problem. Nor have I been disappointed; in this and in all other perplexing cases I have invariably found that our knowledge, imperfect though it be, of variation under domestication, afforded the best and safest clue. * * *

From these considerations, I shall devote the first chapter of this Abstract to Variation under Domestication. We shall thus see that a large amount of hereditary modification is at least possible; and, what is equally or more important, we shall see how great is the power of man in accumulating by his Selection successive slight variations. I will then pass on to the variability of species in a state of nature; but I shall, unfortunately, be compelled to treat this subject far too briefly, as it can be treated properly only by giving long catalogues of facts. We shall, however, be enabled to discuss what circumstances are most favourable to variation. In the next chapter the Struggle for Existence amongst all organic beings throughout the world, which inevitably follows from the high geometrical ratio of their increase, will be considered. This is the doctrine of Malthus, applied to the whole animal and vegetable kingdoms. As many more individuals of each species are born than can possibly survive; and as, consequently, there is a frequently recurring struggle for existence, it follows that any being, if it vary however slightly in any manner profitable to itself, under the complex and sometimes varying conditions of life, will have a better chance of surviving, and thus be *naturally selected*. From the strong principle of inheritance, any selected variety will tend to propagate its new and modified form.

This fundamental subject of Natural Selection will be treated at some length in the fourth chapter; and we shall then see how Natural Selection almost inevitably causes much Extinction of the less improved forms of life, and leads to what I have called Divergence of Character. In the next chapter I shall discuss the complex and little known laws of variation. In the five succeeding chapters, the most apparent and gravest difficulties in accepting the theory will be given: namely, first, the difficulties of transitions, or how a simple being or a simple organ can be changed and perfected into a highly developed being or into an elaborately constructed organ; secondly, the subject of Instinct, or the mental powers of animals; thirdly, Hybridism, or the infertility of species and the fertility of varieties when intercrossed; and fourthly, the imperfection of the Geological Record. In the next chapter I shall consider the geological succession of organic beings throughout time; in the twelfth and thirteenth, their geographical distribution throughout space; in the fourteenth, their classification or mutual affinities, both when mature and in an embryonic condition. In the last chapter I shall give a brief recapitulation of the whole work, and a few concluding remarks.

No one ought to feel surprise at much remaining as yet unexplained in regard to the origin of species and varieties, if he make due allowance for our profound ignorance in regard to the mutual relations of the many beings which live around us. Who can explain why one species ranges widely and is very numerous, and why another allied species has a narrow range and is rare? Yet these relations are of the highest importance, for they determine the present welfare and, as I believe, the future success and modification of every inhabitant of this world. Still less do we know of the mutual relations of the innumerable inhabitants of the world during the many past geological epochs in its history. Although much remains obscure, and will long remain obscure, I can entertain no doubt, after the most deliberate study and dispassionate judgment of which I am capable, that the view which most naturalists until recently entertained, and which I formerly entertained—namely, that each species has been independently created—is erroneous. I am fully convinced that species are not immutable; but that those belonging to what are called the same genera are lineal descendants of some other and generally extinct species, in the same manner as the acknowledged varieties of any one species are the descendants of that species. Furthermore, I am convinced that Natural Selection has been the most important, but not the exclusive, means of modification.

Chapter I

VARIATION UNDER DOMESTICATION

Causes of variability —Effects of habit and the use or disuse of parts—Correlated variation—Inheritance—Character of domestic varieties—Difficulty of distinguishing between varieties and species —Origin of domestic varieties from one or more species—Domestic pigeons, their differences and origin—Principles of selection, anciently followed, their effects—Methodical and unconscious selection—Unknown origin of our domestic productions—Circumstances favourable to man's power of selection.

CAUSES OF VARIABILITY

When we compare the individuals of the same variety or sub-variety of our older cultivated plants and animals, one of the first points which strikes us is, that they generally differ more from each other than do the individuals of any one species or variety in a state of nature. And if we reflect on the vast diversity of the plants and animals which have been cultivated, and which have varied during all ages under the most different climates and treatment, we are driven to conclude that this great variability is due to our domestic productions having been raised under conditions of life not so uniform as, and somewhat different from, those to which the parent species had been exposed under nature. There is, also, some probability in the view propounded by Andrew Knight, that this variability may be partly connected with excess of food. It seems

clear that organic beings must be exposed during several generations to new conditions to cause any great amount of variation;
and that, when the organisation has once begun to vary, it generally continues varying for many generations. No case is on record
of a variable organism ceasing to vary under cultivation. Our oldest
cultivated plants, such as wheat, still yield new varieties: our oldest
domesticated animals are still capable of rapid improvement or
modification.

As far as I am able to judge, after long attending to the subject,
the conditions of life appear to act in two ways,—directly on the
whole organisation or on certain parts alone, and indirectly by
affecting the reproductive system. With respect to the direct action,
we must bear in mind that in every case, as Professor Weismann
has lately insisted, and as I have incidentally shown in my work on
'Variation under Domestication,' there are two factors: namely,
the nature of the organism, and the nature of the conditions. The
former seems to be much the more important; for nearly similar
variations sometimes arise under, as far as we can judge, dissimilar
conditions; and, on the other hand, dissimilar variations arise under
conditions which appear to be nearly uniform. The effects on the
offspring are either definite or indefinite. They may be considered
as definite when all or nearly all the offspring of individuals exposed
to certain conditions during several generations are modified in the
same manner. It is extremely difficult to come to any conclusion in
regard to the extent of the changes which have been thus definitely
induced. There can, however, be little doubt about many slight
changes,—such as size from the amount of food, colour from the
nature of the food, thickness of the skin and hair from climate, &c.
Each of the endless variations which we see in the plumage of our
fowls must have had some efficient cause; and if the same cause were
to act uniformly during a long series of generations on many individuals, all probably would be modified in the same manner. * * *

EFFECTS OF HABIT AND OF THE USE OR DISUSE OF PARTS; CORRELATED
VARIATION; INHERITANCE

* * * The laws governing inheritance are for the most part unknown. No one can say why the same peculiarity in different
individuals of the same species, or in different species, is sometimes
inherited and sometimes not so; why the child often reverts in
certain characters to its grandfather or grandmother or more remote
ancestor; why a peculiarity is often transmitted from one sex to
both sexes, or to one sex alone, more commonly but not exclusively
to the like sex. It is a fact of some importance to us, that peculiarities appearing in the males of our domestic breeds are often transmitted, either exclusively or in a much greater degree, to the males

alone. A much more important rule, which I think may be trusted, is that, at whatever period of life a peculiarity first appears, it tends to reappear in the offspring at a corresponding age, though sometimes earlier. In many cases this could not be otherwise; thus the inherited peculiarities in the horns of cattle could appear only in the offspring when nearly mature; peculiarities in the silkworm are known to appear at the corresponding caterpillar or cocoon stage. But hereditary diseases and some other facts make me believe that the rule has a wider extension, and that, when there is no apparent reason why a peculiarity should appear at any particular age, yet that it does tend to appear in the offspring at the same period at which it first appeared in the parent. I believe this rule to be of the highest importance in explaining the laws of embryology. * * *

CHARACTER OF DOMESTIC VARIETIES; DIFFICULTY OF DISTINGUISHING BETWEEN VARIETIES AND SPECIES; ORIGIN OF DOMESTIC VARIETIES FROM ONE OR MORE SPECIES

When we look to the hereditary varieties or races of our domestic animals and plants, and compare them with closely allied species, we generally perceive in each domestic race, as already remarked, less uniformity of character than in true species. Domestic races often have a somewhat monstrous character; by which I mean, that, although differing from each other, and from other species of the same genus, in several trifling respects, they often differ in an extreme degree in some one part, both when compared one with another, and more especially when compared with the species under nature to which they are nearest allied. With these exceptions (and with that of the perfect fertility of varieties when crossed,—a subject hereafter to be discussed), domestic races of the same species differ from each other in the same manner as do the closely-allied species of the same genus in a state of nature, but the differences in most cases are less in degree. This must be admitted as true, for the domestic races of many animals and plants have been ranked by some competent judges as the descendants of aboriginally distinct species, and by other competent judges as mere varieties. If any well marked distinction existed between a domestic race and a species, this source of doubt would not so perpetually recur. It has often been stated that domestic races do not differ from each other in character of generic value. It can be shown that this statement is not correct; but naturalists differ much in determining what characters are of generic value; all such valuations being at present empirical. When it is explained how genera originate under nature, it will be seen that we have no right to expect often to find a generic amount of difference in our domesticated races.

In attempting to estimate the amount of structural difference between allied domestic races, we are soon involved in doubt, from not knowing whether they are descended from one or several parent species. This point, if it could be cleared up, would be interesting; if, for instance, it could be shown that the greyhound, bloodhound, terrier, spaniel, and bull-dog, which we all know propagate their kind truly, were the offspring of any single species, then such facts would have great weight in making us doubt about the immutability of the many closely allied natural species—for instance, of the many foxes—inhabiting different quarters of the world. I do not believe, as we shall presently see, that the whole amount of difference between the several breeds of the dog has been produced under domestication, I believe that a small part of the difference is due to their being descended from distinct species. In the case of strongly marked races of some other domesticated species, there is presumptive or even strong evidence, that all are descended from a single wild stock. * * *

BREEDS OF THE DOMESTIC PIGEON, THEIR DIFFERENCES AND ORIGIN

Believing that it is always best to study some special group, I have, after deliberation, taken up domestic pigeons. I have kept every breed which I could purchase or obtain, and have been most kindly favoured with skins from several quarters of the world, more especially by the Hon. W. Elliot from India, and by the Hon. C. Murray from Persia. Many treatises in different languages have been published on pigeons, and some of them are very important, as being of considerable antiquity. I have associated with several eminent fanciers, and have been permitted to join two of the London Pigeon Clubs. The diversity of the breeds is something astonishing. Compare the English carrier and the short-faced tumbler, and see the wonderful difference in their beaks, entailing corresponding differences in their skulls. The carrier, more especially the male bird, is also remarkable from the wonderful development of the carunculated skin about the head; and this is accompanied by greatly elongated eyelids, very large external orifices to the nostrils, and a wide gape of mouth. The short-faced tumbler has a beak in outline almost like that of a finch; and the common tumbler has the singular inherited habit of flying at a great height in a compact flock, and tumbling in the air head over heels. The runt is a bird of great size, with long massive beak and large feet; some of the sub-breeds of runts have very long necks, others very long wings and tails, others singularly short tails. The barb is allied to the carrier, but, instead of a long beak has a very short and broad one. The pouter has a much elongated body, wings, and legs; and its enormously developed crop, which it glories in inflating, may well excite astonishment and even laughter. The turbit has a short and conical beak, with a line of reversed feathers down the breast; and it has the habit of continually expanding slightly, the upper part of the œsophagus. The Jacobin has the feathers so much reversed along the back of the neck that they form a hood; and it has, proportionately to its size, elongated wing and tail feathers. The trumpeter and laugher, as their names express, utter a very different coo from the other breeds. The fantail has thirty or even forty tail-feathers, instead of twelve or fourteen—the normal number in all the members of the great pigeon family: these feathers are kept expanded, and are carried so erect, that in good birds the head and tail touch: the oil-gland is quite aborted. Several other less distinct breeds might be specified.

In the skeletons of the several breeds, the development of the bones of the face in length and breadth and curvature differs enormously. The shape, as well as the breadth and length of the ramus of the lower jaw, varies in a highly remarkable manner. The caudal and sacral vertebræ vary in number; as does the number of the ribs, together with their relative breadth and the presence of processes. The size and shape of the apertures in the sternum are highly variable; so is the degree of divergence and relative size of the two arms of the furcula. The proportional width of the gape of mouth, the proportional length of the eyelids, of the orifice of the nostrils, of the tongue (not always in strict correlation with the length of beak), the size of the crop and of the upper part of the œsophagus; the development and abortion of the oil-gland; the number of the primary wing and caudal feathers; the relative length of the wing and tail to each other and to the body; the relative length of the leg and foot; the number of scutellæ on the toes, the development of skin between the toes, are all points of structure which are variable. The period at which the perfect plumage is acquired varies, as does the state of the down with which the nestling birds are clothed when hatched. The shape and size of the eggs vary. The manner of flight, and in some breeds the voice and disposition, differ remarkably. Lastly, in certain breeds, the males and females have come to differ in a slight degree from each other.

Altogether at least a score of pigeons might be chosen, which, if shown to an ornithologist, and he were told that they were wild birds, would certainly be ranked by him as well-defined species. Moreover, I do not believe that any ornithologist would in this case place the English carrier, the short-faced tumbler, the runt, the barb, pouter, and fantail in the same genus; more especially as in each of these breeds several truly-inherited sub-breeds, or species, as he would call them, could be shown him.

Great as are the differences between the breeds of the pigeon, I am fully convinced that the common opinion of naturalists is correct, namely, that all are descended from the rock-pigeon (Columba livia), including under this term several geographic races or sub-species, which differ from each other in the most trifling respects. * * *

From these several reasons, namely,—the improbability of man having formerly made seven or eight supposed species of pigeons to breed freely under domestication;—these supposed species being quite unknown in a wild state, and their not having become anywhere feral;—these species presenting certain very abnormal characters, as compared with all other Columbidæ, though so like the rock-pigeon in most respects;—the occasional re-appearance of the blue colour and various black marks in all the breeds, both when kept pure and when crossed;—and lastly, the mongrel offspring being perfectly fertile;—from these several reasons taken together, we may safely conclude that all our domestic breeds are descended from the rock-pigeon or Columba livia with its geographical sub-species.

In favour of this view, I may add, firstly, that the wild C. livia has been found capable of domestication in Europe and in India; and that it agrees in habits and in a great number of points of structure with all the domestic breeds. Secondly, that, although an English carrier or a short-faced tumbler differs immensely in certain characters from the rock-pigeon, yet that, by comparing the several sub-breeds of these two races, more especially those brought from distant countries, we can make, between them and the rock-pigeon, an almost perfect series; so we can in some other cases, but not with all the breeds. Thirdly, those characters which are mainly distinctive of each breed are in each eminently variable, for instance the wattle and length of beak of the carrier, the shortness of that of the tumbler, and the number of tail-feathers in the fantail; and the explanation of this fact will be obvious when we treat of Selection. Fourthly, pigeons have been watched and tended with the utmost care, and loved by many people. They have been domesticated for thousands of years in several quarters of the world * * * The paramount importance of these considerations in explaining the immense amount of variation which pigeons have undergone, will likewise be obvious when we treat of Selection. We shall then, also, see how it is that the several breeds so often have a somewhat monstrous character. It is also a most favourable circumstance for the production of distinct breeds, that male and female pigeons can be easily mated for life; and thus different breeds can be kept together in the same aviary.

I have discussed the probable origin of domestic pigeons at some, yet quite insufficient, length; because when I first kept pigeons and watched the several kinds, well knowing how truly they breed, I felt fully as much difficulty in believing that since they had been domesticated they had all proceeded from a common parent, as any naturalist could in coming to a similar conclusion in regard to the many species of finches, or other groups of birds, in nature. One circumstance has struck me much; namely, that nearly all the breeders of the various domestic animals and the cultivators of plants, with whom I have conversed, or whose treatises I have read, are firmly convinced that the several breeds to which each has attended, are descended from so many aboriginally distinct species. Ask, as I have asked, a celebrated raiser of Hereford cattle, whether his cattle might not have descended from Long-horns, or both from a common parent-stock, and he will laugh you to scorn. I have never met a pigeon, or poultry, or duck, or rabbit fancier, who was not fully convinced that each main breed was descended from a distinct species. Van Mons, in his treatise on pears and apples, shows how utterly he disbelieves that the several sorts, for instance a Ribston-pippin or Codlin-apple, could ever have proceeded from the seeds of the same tree. Innumerable other examples could be given. The explanation, I think, is simple: from long-continued study they are strongly impressed with the differences between the several races; and though they well know that each race varies slightly, for they win their prizes by selecting such slight differences, yet they ignore all general arguments, and refuse to sum up in their minds slight differences accumulated during many successive generations. May not those naturalists who, knowing far less of the laws of inheritance than does the breeder, and knowing no more than he does of the intermediate links in the long lines of descent, yet admit that many of our domestic races are descended from the same parents—may they not learn a lesson of caution, when they deride the idea of species in a state of nature being lineal descendants of other species?

PRINCIPLES OF SELECTION ANCIENTLY FOLLOWED, AND THEIR
EFFECTS

Let us now briefly consider the steps by which domestic races have been produced, either from one or from several allied species. Some effect may be attributed to the direct and definite action of the external conditions of life, and some to habit; but he would be a bold man who would account by such agencies for the differences between a dray- and race-horse, a greyhound and bloodhound, a carrier and tumbler pigeon. One of the most remarkable features in our domesticated races is that we see in them adaptation, not indeed to the animal's or plant's own good, but to man's use or fancy. Some variations useful to him have probably arisen suddenly, or by one step; many botanists, for instance, believe that the fuller's teasel, with its hooks, which cannot be rivalled by any mechanical contrivance, is only a variety of the wild Dipsacus; and this amount of change may have suddenly arisen in a seedling. So it has probably been with the turnspit dog; and this is known to have been the case with the ancon sheep. But when we compare the dray-horse and race-horse, the dromedary and camel, the various breeds of sheep fitted either for cultivated land or mountain pasture, with the wool of one breed good for one purpose, and that of another breed for another purpose; when we compare the many breeds of dogs, each good for man in different ways; when we compare the game-cock, so pertinacious in battle, with other breeds so little quarrelsome, with "everlasting layers" which never desire to sit, and with the bantam so small and elegant; when we compare the host of agricultural, culinary, orchard, and flower-garden races of plants, most useful to man at different seasons and for different purposes, or so beautiful in his eyes, we must, I think, look further than to mere variability. We cannot suppose that all the breeds were suddenly produced as perfect and as useful as we now see them; indeed, in many cases, we know that this has not been their history. The key is man's power of accumulative selection: nature gives successive variations; man adds them up in certain directions useful to him. In this sense he may be said to have made for himself useful breeds. * * *

At the present time, eminent breeders try by methodical selection, with a distinct object in view, to make a new strain or sub-breed, superior to anything of the kind in the country. But, for our purpose, a form of Selection, which may be called Unconscious, and which results from every one trying to possess and breed from the best individual animals, is more important. Thus, a man who intends keeping pointers naturally tries to get as good dogs as he can, and afterwards breeds from his own best dogs, but he has no wish or expectation of permanently altering the breed. Nevertheless we may infer that this process, continued during centuries, would improve and modify any breed, in the same way as Bakewell, Collins, &c., by this very same process, only carried on more methodically, did greatly modify, even during their lifetimes, the forms and qualities of their cattle. Slow and insensible changes of this kind can never be recognised unless actual measurements or careful drawings of the breeds in question have been made long ago, which may serve for comparison. In some cases, however, unchanged, or but little changed individuals of the same breed exist in less civilised districts, where the breed has been less improved. There is reason to believe that King Charles's spaniel has been unconsciously modified to a large extent since the time of that monarch. Some highly competent authorities are convinced that the setter is directly derived from the spaniel, and has probably been slowly altered from it. It is known that the English pointer has been greatly changed within the last century, and in this case the change has, it is believed, been chiefly effected by crosses with the fox-hound; but what concerns us is, that the change has been effected unconsciously and gradually, and yet so effectually, that, though the old Spanish pointer certainly came from Spain, Mr. Borrow has not seen, as I am informed by him, any native dog in Spain like our pointer.

By a similar process of selection, and by careful training, English racehorses have come to surpass in fleetness and size the parent Arabs, so that the latter, by the regulations for the Goodwood Races, are favoured in the weights which they carry. Lord Spencer and others have shown how the cattle of England have increased in weight and in early maturity, compared with the stock formerly kept in this country. By comparing the accounts given in various old treatises of the former and present state of carrier and tumbler pigeons in Britain, India, and Persia, we can trace the stages through which they have insensibly passed, and come to differ so greatly from the rock-pigeon. * * *

CIRCUMSTANCES FAVOURABLE TO MAN'S POWER OF SELECTION

* * * To sum up on the origin of our domestic races of animals and plants, Changed conditions of life are of the highest importance in causing variability, both by acting directly on the organisation, and indirectly by affecting the reproductive system. It is not probable that variability is in inherent and necessary contingent, under all circumstances. The greater or less force of inheritance and reversion, determine whether variations shall endure. Variability is governed by many unknown laws, of which correlated growth is probably the most important. Something, but how much we do not know, may be attributed to the definite action of the conditions of life. Some, perhaps a great, effect may be attributed to the increased use or disuse of parts. The final result is thus rendered infinitely complex. In some cases the intercrossing of aboriginally distinct species appears to have played an important part in the origin of our breeds. When several breeds have once been formed in any country, their occasional intercrossing, with the aid of selection, has, no doubt, largely aided in the formation of new sub-breeds; but the importance of crossing has been much exaggerated, both in regard to animals and to those plants which are propagated by seed. With plants which are temporarily propagated by cuttings, buds, &c., the importance of crossing is immense; for the cultivator may here disregard the extreme variability both of hybrids and of mongrels, and the sterility of hybrids; but plants not propagated by seed are of little importance to us, for their endurance is only temporary. Over all these causes of Change, the accumulative action of Selection, whether applied methodically and quickly, or unconsciously and slowly but more efficiently seems to have been the predominant Power.

Chapter II

VARIATION UNDER NATURE

Variability — Individual differences — Doubtful species — Wide-ranging, much diffused, and common species vary most—Species of the larger genera in each country vary more frequently than the species of the smaller genera—Many of the species of the larger genera resemble varieties in being very closely, but unequally, related to each other, and in having restricted ranges.

Before applying the principles arrived at in the last chapter to organic beings in a state of nature, we must briefly discuss whether these latter are subject to any variation. To treat this subject properly, a long catalogue of dry facts ought to be given; but these I shall reserve for a future work. Nor shall I here discuss the various definitions which have been given of the term species. No one definition has satisfied all naturalists; yet every naturalist knows vaguely what he means when he speaks of a species. Generally the term includes the unknown element of a distant act of creation. The term "variety" is almost equally difficult to define; but here community of descent is almost universally implied, though it can rarely be proved. * * *

WIDE-RANGING, MUCH DIFFUSED, AND COMMON
SPECIES VARY MOST

* * * Alphonse de Candolle and others have shown that plants which have very wide ranges generally present varieties; and this might have been expected, as they are exposed to diverse physical conditions, and as they come into competition (which, as we shall hereafter see, is an equally or more important circumstance) with different sets of organic beings. But my tables further show that, in any limited country, the species which are the most common, that is abound most in individuals, and the species which are most widely diffused within their own country (and this is a different consideration from wide range, and to a certain extent from commonness), oftenest give rise to varieties sufficiently well marked to have been recorded in botanical works. Hence it is the most flourishing, or, as they may be called, the dominant species,—those which range widely, are the most diffused in their own country, and are the most numerous in individuals,—which oftenest produce well-marked varieties, or, as I consider them, incipient species. And this, perhaps, might have been anticipated; for, as varieties, in order to become in any degree permanent, necessarily have to struggle with the other inhabitants of the country, the species

which are already dominant will be the most likely to yield off-spring, which, though in some slight degree modified, still inherit those advantages that enabled their parents to become dominant over their compatriots. * * *

SUMMARY

Finally, varieties cannot be distinguished from species,—except, first, by the discovery of intermediate linking forms; and, secondly, by a certain indefinite amount of difference between them; for two forms, if differing very little, are generally ranked as varieties, notwithstanding that they cannot be closely connected; but the amount of difference considered necessary to give to any two forms the rank of species cannot be defined. In genera having more than the average number of species in any country, the species of these genera have more than the average number of varieties. In large genera the species are apt to be closely, but unequally, allied together, forming little clusters round other species. Species very closely allied to other species apparently have restricted ranges. In all these respects the species of large genera present a strong analogy with varieties. And we can clearly understand these analogies, if species once existed as varieties, and thus originated; whereas, these analogies are utterly inexplicable if species are independent creations.

We have, also, seen that it is the most flourishing or dominant species of the larger genera within each class which on an average yield the greatest number of varieties; and varieties, as we shall hereafter see, tend to become converted into new and distinct species. Thus the larger genera tend to become larger; and throughout nature the forms of life which are now dominant tend to become still more dominant by leaving many modified and dominant descendants. But by steps hereafter to be explained, the larger genera also tend to break up into smaller genera. And thus, the forms of life throughout the universe become divided into groups subordinate to groups.

Chapter III

STRUGGLE FOR EXISTENCE

Its bearing on natural selection—The term used in a wide sense— Geometrical ratio of increase—Rapid increase of naturalised animals and plants—Nature of the checks in increase—Competition universal—Effects of climate—Protection from the number of individuals—Complex relations of all animals and plants throughout nature—Struggle for life most severe between individuals and varieties of the same species: often severe between species of the same genus—The relation of organism to organism the most important of all relations.

Before entering on the subject of this chapter, I must make a few preliminary remarks, to show how the struggle for existence bears on Natural Selection. It has been seen in the last chapter that amongst organic beings in a state of nature there is some individual variability: indeed I am not aware that this has ever been disputed. It is immaterial for us whether a multitude of doubtful forms be called species or sub-species or varieties; what rank, for instance, the two or three hundred doubtful forms of British plants are entitled to hold, if the existence of any well-marked varieties be admitted. But the mere existence of individual variability and of some few well-marked varieties, though necessary as the foundation for the work, helps us but little in understanding how species arise in nature. How have all those exquisite adaptations of one part of the organisation to another part, and to the conditions of life, and of one organic being to another being, been perfected? We see these beautiful co-adaptations most plainly in the woodpecker and the mistletoe; and only a little less plainly in the humblest parasite which clings to the hairs of a quadruped or feathers of a bird; in the structure of the beetle which dives through the water; in the plumed seed which is wafted by the gentlest breeze; in short, we see beautiful adaptations everywhere and in every part of the organic world.

Again, it may be asked, how is it that varieties, which I have called incipient species, become ultimately converted into good and distinct species which in most cases obviously differ from each other far more than do the varieties of the same species? How do those groups of species, which constitute what are called distinct genera, and which differ from each other more than do the species of the same genus, arise? All these results, as we shall more fully see in the next chapter, follow from the struggle for life. Owing to this struggle, variations, however slight and from whatever cause proceeding, if they be in any degree profitable to the individuals of a species, in their infinitely complex relations to other organic beings and to their physical conditions of life, will tend to the preservation of such individuals, and will generally be inherited by the offspring. The offspring, also, will thus have a better chance of surviving, for, of the many individuals of any species which are periodically born, but a small number can survive. I have called this principle, by which each slight variation, if useful, is preserved, by the term Natural Selection, in order to mark its relation to man's power of selection. But the expression often used by Mr. Herbert Spencer of the Survival of the Fittest is more accurate, and is sometimes equally convenient. We have seen that man by selection can certainly produce great results, and can adapt organic beings to his own uses, through the accumulation of slight but useful variations, given to him by the hand of Nature. But Natural Selection, as we shall hereafter see, is a power incessantly ready for action, and is as immeasurably superior to man's feeble efforts, as the works of Nature are to those of Art.

We will now discuss in a little more detail the struggle for existence. In my future work this subject will be treated, as it well deserves, at greater length. The elder De Candolle and Lyell have largely and philosophically shown that all organic beings are exposed to severe competition. In regard to plants, no one has treated this subject with more spirit and ability than W. Herbert, Dean of Manchester, evidently the result of his great horticultural knowledge. Nothing is easier than to admit in words the truth of the universal struggle for life, or more difficult—at least I have found it so—than constantly to bear this conclusion in mind. Yet unless it be thoroughly engrained in the mind, the whole economy of nature, with every fact on distribution, rarity, abundance, extinction, and variation, will be dimly seen or quite misunderstood. We behold the face of nature bright with gladness, we often see superabundance of food; we do not see or we forget, that the birds which are idly singing round us mostly live on insects or seeds, and are thus constantly destroying life; or we forget how largely these songsters, or their eggs, or their nestlings, are destroyed by birds and beasts of prey; we do not always bear in mind, that, though food may be now superabundant, it is not so at all seasons of each recurring year.

THE TERM, STRUGGLE FOR EXISTENCE, USED IN A LARGE SENSE

I should premise that I use this term in a large and metaphorical sense including dependence of one being on another, and including (which is more important) not only the life of the individual, but success in leaving progeny. Two canine animals, in a time of dearth, may be truly said to struggle with each other which shall get food and live. But a plant on the edge of a desert is said to struggle for life against the drought, though more properly it should be said to be dependent on the moisture. A plant which annually produces a thousand seeds, of which only one of an average comes to maturity, may be more truly said to struggle with the plants of the same and other kinds which already clothe the ground. The mistletoe is dependent on the apple and a few other trees, but can only in a far-fetched sense be said to struggle with these trees, for, if too many of these parasites grow on the same tree, it languishes and dies. But several seedling mistletoes, growing close together on the same branch, may more truly be said to struggle with each other. As the mistletoe is disseminated by birds, its existence depends on them; and it may methodically be said to struggle with other fruit-bearing plants, in tempting the birds to devour and thus disseminate its seeds. In these several senses, which pass into each other, I use for convenience' sake the general term of Struggle for Existence.

GEOMETRICAL RATIO OF INCREASE

A struggle for existence inevitably follows from the high rate at which all organic beings tend to increase. Every being, which during its natural lifetime produces several eggs or seeds, must suffer destruction during some period of its life, and during some season or occasional year, otherwise, on the principle of geometrical increase, its numbers would quickly become so inordinately great that no country could support the product. Hence, as more individuals are produced than can possibly survive, there must in every case be a struggle for existence, either one individual with another of the same species, or with the individuals of distinct species, or with the physical conditions of life. It is the doctrine of Malthus applied with manifold force to the whole animal and vegetable kingdoms; for in this case there can be no artificial increase of food, and no prudential restraint from marriage. Although some species may be now increasing, more or less rapidly, in numbers, all cannot do so, for the world would not hold them.

There is no exception to the rule that every organic being naturally increases at so high a rate, that, if not destroyed, the earth would soon be covered by the progeny of a single pair. Even slow-breeding man has doubled in twenty-five years, and at this rate, in less than a thousand years, there would literally not be standing-room for his progeny. Linnæus has calculated that if an annual plant produced only two seeds—and there is no plant so unproductive as this—and their seedlings next year produced two, and so on, then in twenty years there should be a million plants. The elephant is reckoned the slowest breeder of all known animals, and I have taken some pains to estimate its probable minimum rate of natural increase; it will be safest to assume that it begins breeding when thirty years old, and goes on breeding till ninety years old, bringing forth six young in the interval, and surviving till one hundred years old; if this be so, after a period of from 740 to 750 years there would be nearly nineteen million elephants alive, descended from the first pair.

But we have better evidence on this subject than mere theoretical calculations, namely, the numerous recorded cases of the astonishingly rapid increase of various animals in a state of nature, when circumstances have been favourable to them during two or three following seasons. Still more striking is the evidence from our domestic animals of many kinds which have run wild in several parts of the world; if the statements of the rate of increase of slow-breeding cattle and horses in South America, and latterly in Australia, had not been well authenticated, they would have been incredible. So it is with plants; cases could be given of introduced plants which have become common throughout whole islands in a period of less than ten years. Several of the plants, such as the cardoon and a tall thistle, which are now the commonest over the whole plains of La Plata, clothing square leagues of surface almost to the exclusion of every other plant, have been introduced from Europe; and there are plants which now range in India, as I hear from Dr. Falconer, from Cape Comorin to the Himalaya, which have been imported from America since its discovery. In such cases, and endless others could be given, no one supposes, that the fertility of the animals or plants has been suddenly and temporarily increased in any sensible degree. The obvious explanation is that the conditions of life have been highly favourable, and that there has consequently been less destruction of the old and young, and that nearly all the young have been enabled to breed. Their geometrical ratio of increase, the result of which never fails to be surprising, simply explains their extraordinarily rapid increase and wide diffusion in their new homes.

In a state of nature almost every full-grown plant annually produces seed, and amongst animals there are very few which do not annually pair. Hence we may confidently assert, that all plants and animals are tending to increase at a geometrical ratio,—that all would rapidly stock every station in which they could anyhow exist, —and that this geometrical tendency to increase must be checked by destruction at some period of life. Our familiarity with the larger domestic animals tends, I think, to mislead us: we see no great destruction falling on them, but we do not keep in mind that thousands are annually slaughtered for food, and that in a state of nature an equal number would have somehow to be disposed of.

The only difference between organisms which annually produce eggs or seeds by the thousand, and those which produce extremely few, is, that the slow-breeders would require a few more years to people, under favourable conditions, a whole district, let it be ever so large. The condor lays a couple of eggs and the ostrich a score, and yet in the same country the condor may be the more numerous of the two; the Fulmar petrel lays but one egg, yet it is believed to be the most numerous bird in the world. One fly deposits hundreds of eggs, and another, like the hippobosca, a single one; but this difference does not determine how many individuals of the two species can be supported in a district. A large number of eggs is of some importance to those species which depend on a fluctuating amount of food, for it allows them rapidly to increase in number. But the real importance of a large number of eggs or seeds is to make up for much destruction at some period of life; and this period in the great majority of cases is an early one. If an animal can in any way protect its own eggs or young, a small number may be produced, and yet the average stock be fully kept up; but if many eggs or young are destroyed, many must be produced, or the species will become extinct. It would suffice to keep up the full number of a tree, which lived on an average for a thousand years, if a single seed were produced once in a thousand years, supposing that this seed were never destroyed, and could be ensured to germinate in a fitting place. So that, in all cases, the average number of any animal or plant depends only indirectly on the number of its eggs or seeds.

In looking at Nature, it is most necessary to keep the foregoing considerations always in mind—never to forget that every single organic being may be said to be striving to the utmost to increase in numbers; that each lives by a struggle at some period of its life; that heavy destruction inevitably falls either on the young or old, during each generation or at recurrent intervals. Lighten any check, mitigate the destruction ever so little, and the number of the species will almost instantaneously increase to any amount. * * *

Chapter IV

NATURAL SELECTION; OR THE SURVIVAL OF THE FITTEST

Natural Selection—its power compared with man's selection—its power on characters of trifling importance—its power at all ages and on both sexes—Sexual selection—On the generality of intercrosses between individuals of the same species—Circumstances favourable and unfavourable to the results of natural selection, namely, intercrossing, isolation, number of individuals—Slow action—Extinction caused by natural selection—Divergence of character, related to the diversity of inhabitants of any small area, and to naturalisation—Action of natural selection, through divergence of character and extinction, on the descendants from a common parent—Explains the grouping of all organic beings—Advance in organisation—Low forms preserved—Convergence of character—Indefinite multiplication of species—Summary.

How will the struggle for existence, briefly discussed in the last chapter, act in regard to variation? Can the principle of selection, which we have seen is so potent in the hands of man, apply under nature? I think we shall see that it can act most efficiently. Let the endless number of slight variations and individual differences occurring in our domestic productions, and, in a lesser degree, in those under nature, be borne in mind; as well as the strength of the hereditary tendency. Under domestication, it may be truly said that the whole organisation becomes in some degree plastic. But the variability, which we almost universally meet with in our domestic productions, is not directly produced, as Hooker and Asa Gray have well remarked, by man; he can neither originate varieties, nor prevent their occurrence; he can preserve and accumulate such as do occur. Unintentionally he exposes organic beings to new and changing conditions of life, and variability ensues; but similar changes of conditions might and do occur under nature. Let it also be borne in mind how infinitely complex and close-fitting are the mutual relations of all organic beings to each other and to their physical conditions of life; and consequently what infinitely varied diversities of structure might be of use to each being under changing conditions of life. Can it, then, be thought improbable, seeing that variations useful to man have undoubtedly occurred, that other variations useful in some way to each being in the great and complex battle of life, should occur in the course of many successive generations. If such do occur, can we doubt (remembering that many more individuals are born than can possibly survive) that individuals having any advantage, however slight, over others, would have the best chance of surviving and of procreating their kind? On the other hand, we may feel sure that any variation in the least degree injurious would be rigidly destroyed. This preservation of favourable individual differences and variations, and the destruction of those which are injurious, I have called Natural Selection, or the Survival of the Fittest. Variations neither useful nor injurious would not be affected by natural selection, and would be left either a fluctuating element, as perhaps we see in certain polymorphic species, or would ultimately become fixed, owing to the nature of the organism and the nature of the conditions.

Several writers have misapprehended or objected to the term Natural Selection. Some have even imagined that natural selection induces variability, whereas it implies only the preservation of such variations as arise and are beneficial to the being under its conditions of life. No one objects to agriculturists speaking of the potent effects of man's selection; and in this case the individual differences given by nature, which man for some object selects, must of necessity first occur. Others have objected that the term selection implies conscious choice in the animals which become modified; and it had even been urged that, as plants have no volition, natural selection is not applicable to them! In the literal sense of the word, no doubt, natural selection is a false term; but who ever objected to chemists speaking of the elective affinities of the various elements?—and yet an acid cannot strictly be said to elect the base with which it in preference combines. It has been said that I speak of natural selection as an active power or Deity; but who objects to an author speaking of the attraction of gravity as ruling the movements of the planets? Every one knows what is meant and is implied by such metaphorical expressions; and they are almost necessary for brevity. So again it is difficult to avoid personifying the word Nature; but I mean by Nature, only the aggregate action and product of many natural laws, and by laws the sequence of events as ascertained by us. With a little familiarity such superficial objections will be forgotten.

We shall best understand the probable course of natural selection by taking the case of a country undergoing some slight physical change, for instance, of climate. The proportional numbers of its inhabitants will almost immediately undergo a change, and some species will probably become extinct. We may conclude, from what we have seen of the intimate and complex manner in which the inhabitants of each country are bound together, that any change in the numerical proportions of the inhabitants, independently of the change of climate itself, would seriously affect the others. If the country were open on its borders, new forms would certainly immigrate, and this would likewise seriously disturb the relations of some of the former inhabitants. Let it be remembered how powerful the influence of a single introduced tree or mammal has been shown to be. But in the case of an island, or of a country partly surrounded by barriers, into which new and better adapted forms could not freely enter, we should then have places in the economy of nature which would assuredly be better filled up, if some of the original inhabitants were in some manner modified; for, had the area been open to immigration, these same places would have been seized on by intruders. In such cases, slight modifications, which in any way favoured the individuals of any species, by better adapting them to their altered conditions, would tend to be preserved; and natural selection would have free scope for the work of improvement.

We have good reason to believe, as shown in the first chapter, that changes in the conditions of life give a tendency to increased variability; and in the foregoing cases the conditions have changed, and this would manifestly be favourable to natural selection, by affording a better chance of the occurrence of profitable variations. Unless such occur, natural selection can do nothing. Under the term of "variations," it must never be forgotten that mere individual differences are included. As man can produce a great result with his domestic animals and plants by adding up in any given direction individual differences, so could natural selection, but far more easily from having incomparably longer time for action. Nor do I believe that any great physical change, as of climate, or any unusual degree of isolation to check immigration, is necessary in order that new and unoccupied places should be left, for natural selection to fill up by improving some of the varying inhabitants. For as all the inhabitants of each country are struggling together with nicely balanced forces, extremely slight modifications in the structure or habits of one species would often give it an advantage over others; and still further modifications of the same kind would often still further increase the advantage, as long as the species continued under the same conditions of life and profited by similar means of subsistence and defence. No country can be named in which all the native inhabitants are now so perfectly adapted to each other and to the physical conditions under which they live, that none of them could be still better adapted or improved; for in all countries, the natives have been so far conquered by naturalised productions, that they have allowed some foreigners to take firm possession of the land. And as foreigners have thus in every country beaten some of the natives, we may safely conclude that the natives might have been modified with advantage, so as to have better resisted the intruders.

As man can produce, and certainly has produced, a great result by his methodical and unconscious means of selection, what may not natural selection effect? Man can act only on external and visible characters: Nature, if I may be allowed to personify the natural preservation or survival of the fittest, cares nothing for appearances, except in so far as they are useful to any being. She can act on every internal organ, on every shade of constitutional difference, on the whole machinery of life. Man selects only for his own good: Nature only for that of the being which she tends. Every selected character is fully exercised by her, as is implied by the fact of their selection. Man keeps the natives of many climates in the same country; he seldom exercises each selected character in some peculiar and fitting manner; he feeds a long and a short beaked pigeon on the same food; he does not exercise a long-backed or long-legged quadruped in any peculiar manner; he exposes sheep with long and short wool to the same climate. He does not allow the most vigorous males to struggle for the females. He does not rigidly destroy all inferior animals, but protects during each varying season, as far as lies in his power, all his productions. He often begins his selection by some half-monstrous form; or at least by some modification prominent enough to catch the eye or to be plainly useful to him. Under Nature, the slightest differences of structure or constitution may well turn the nicely balanced scale in the struggle for life, and so be preserved. How fleeting are the wishes and efforts of man! how short his time! and consequently how poor will be his results, compared with those accumulated by Nature during whole geological periods! Can we wonder, then, that Nature's productions should be far "truer" in character than man's productions that they should be infinitely better adapted to the most complex conditions of life and should plainly bear the stamp of far higher workmanship?

It may metaphorically be said that natural selection is daily and hourly scrutinising, throughout the world, the slightest variations; rejecting those that are bad, preserving and adding up all that are good; silently and insensibly working, *whenever and wherever opportunity offers*, at the improvement of each organic being in relation to its organic and inorganic conditions of life. We see nothing of these slow changes in progress, until the hand of time has marked the lapse of ages, and then so imperfect is our view into long-past geological ages, that we see only that the forms of life are now different from what they formerly were.

In order that any great amount of modification should be effected in a species, a variety when once formed must again, perhaps after a long interval of time, vary or present individual differences of the same favourable nature as before; and these must be again preserved, and so onwards step by step. Seeing that individual differences of the same kind perpetually recur, this can hardly be considered as an unwarrantable assumption. But whether it is true, we can judge only by seeing how far the hypothesis accords with and explains the general phenomena of nature. On the other hand, the ordinary belief that the amount of possible variation is a strictly limited quantity is likewise a simple assumption.

Although natural selection can act only through and for the good of each being, yet characters and structures, which we are apt to consider as of very trifling importance, may thus be acted on. When we see leaf-eating insects green, and bark-feeders mottled-grey; the alpine ptarmigan white in winter, the red-grouse the colour of heather, we must believe that these tints are of service to these birds and insects in preserving them from danger. Grouse, if not destroyed at some period of their lives would increase in countless numbers; they are known to suffer largely from birds of prey; and hawks are guided by eyesight to their prey—so much so, that on parts of the Continent persons are warned not to keep white pigeons, as being the most liable to destruction. Hence natural selection might be effective in giving the proper colour to each kind of grouse, and in keeping that colour, when once acquired, true and constant. Nor ought we to think that the occasional destruction of an animal of any particular colour would produce little effect: we should remember how essential it is in a flock of white sheep to destroy a lamb with the faintest trace of black. We have seen how the colour of the hogs, which feed on the "paint-root" in Virginia, determines whether they shall live or die. In plants, the down on the fruit and the colour of the flesh are considered by botanists as characters of the most trifling importance: yet we hear from an excellent horticulturist, Downing, that in the United States, smooth-skinned fruits suffer far more from a beetle, a Curculio, than those with down; that purple plums suffer far more from a certain disease than yellow plums; whereas another disease attacks yellow-fleshed peaches far more than those with other coloured flesh. If, with all the aids of art, these slight differences make a great difference in cultivating the several varieties, assuredly, in a state of nature, where the trees would have to struggle with other trees, and with a host of enemies, such differences would effectually settle which variety, whether a smooth or downy, a yellow or purple fleshed fruit, should succeed.

In looking at many small points of difference between species, which, as far as our ignorance permits us to judge, seem quite unimportant, we must not forget that climate, food, &c., have no doubt produced some direct effect. It is also necessary to bear in mind that, owing to the law of correlation, when one part varies, and the variations are accumulated through natural selection, other modifications, often of the most unexpected nature, will ensue.

As we see that those variations which, under domestication, appear at any particular period of life, tend to reappear in the offspring at the same period;—for instance, in the shape, size, and flavour of the seeds of the many varieties of our culinary and agricultural plants; in the caterpillar and cocoon stages of the varieties of the silk-worm; in the eggs of poultry, and in the colour of the down of their chickens; in the horns of our sheep and cattle when nearly adult;—so in a state of nature natural selection will be enabled to act on and modify organic beings at any age, by the accumulation of variations profitable at that age, and by their inheritance at a corresponding age. If it profit a plant to have its seeds more and more widely disseminated by the wind, I can see no greater difficulty in this being effected through natural selection, than in the cotton-planter increasing and improving by selection the down in the pods on his cotton-trees. Natural selection may modify and adapt the larva of an insect to a score of contingencies, wholly different from those which concern the mature insect; and these modifications may effect, through correlation, the structure of the adult. So, conversely, modifications in the adult may affect the structure of the larva; but in all cases natural selection will ensure that they shall not be injurious: for if they were so, the species would become extinct.

Natural selection will modify the structure of the young in relation to the parent, and of the parent in relation to the young. In social animals it will adapt the structure of each individual for the benefit of the whole community; if the community profits by the selected change. What natural selection cannot do, is to modify the structure of one species, without giving it any advantage, for the good of another species; and though statements to this effect may be found in works of natural history, I cannot find one case which will bear investigation. A structure used only once in an animal's life, if of high importance to it, might be modified to any extent by natural selection; for instance, the great jaws possessed by certain insects, used exclusively for opening the cocoon—or the hard tip to the beak of unhatched birds, used for breaking the egg. It has been asserted, that of the best short-beaked tumbler-pigeons a greater number perish in the egg than are able to get out of it; so that fanciers assist in the act of hatching. Now if nature had to make the beak of a full-grown pigeon very short for the bird's own advantage, the process of modification would be very slow, and there would be simultaneously the most rigorous selection of all the young birds within the egg, which had the most powerful and hardest beaks, for all with weak beaks would inevitably perish; or, more delicate and more easily broken shells might be selected, the thickness of the shell being known to vary like every other structure.

It may be well here to remark that with all beings there must be much fortuitous destruction, which can have little or no influence on the course of natural selection. For instance a vast number of eggs or seeds are annually devoured, and these could be modified through natural selection only if they varied in some manner which protected them from their enemies. Yet many of these eggs or seeds would perhaps, if not destroyed, have yielded individuals better adapted to their conditions of life than any of those which happened to survive. So again a vast number of mature animals and plants, whether or not they be the best adapted to their conditions, must be annually destroyed by accidental causes, which would not be in the least degree mitigated by certain changes of structure or constitution which would in other ways be beneficial to the species. But let the destruction of the adults be ever so heavy, if the number which can exist in any district be not wholly kept down by such causes,—or again let the destruction of eggs or seeds be so great that only a hundredth or a thousandth part are developed,—yet of those which do survive, the best adapted individuals, supposing that there is any variability in a favourable direction, will tend to propagate their kind in larger numbers than the less well adapted. If the numbers be wholly kept down by the causes just indicated, as will often have been the case, natural selection will be powerless in certain beneficial directions; but this is no valid objection to its efficiency at other times and in other ways; for we are far from having any reason to suppose that many species ever undergo modification and improvement at the same time in the same area.

SEXUAL SELECTION

Inasmuch as peculiarities often appear under domestication in one sex and become hereditarily attached to that sex, so no doubt it will be under nature. Thus it is rendered possible for the two sexes to be modified through natural selection in relation to different habits of life, as is sometimes the case; or for one sex to be modified in relation to the other sex, as commonly occurs. This leads me to say a few words on what I have called Sexual Selection. This form of selection depends, not on a struggle for existence in relation to other organic beings or to external conditions, but on a struggle between the individuals of one sex, generally the males, for the possession of the other sex. The result is not death to the unsuccessful competitor, but few or no offspring. Sexual selection is, therefore, less rigorous than natural selection. Generally, the most vigorous males, those which are best fitted for their places in nature, will leave most progeny. But in many cases, victory depends not so much on general vigor, as on having special weapons, confined to the male sex. A hornless stag or spurless cock would have poor chance of leaving numerous offspring. Sexual selection, by always allowing the victor to breed, might surely give indomitable courage, length to the spur, and strength to the wing to strike in the spurred leg, in nearly the same manner as does the brutal cock-fighter by the careful selection of his best cocks. How low in the scale of nature the law of battle descends, I know not; male alligators have been described as fighting, bellowing, and whirling round, like Indians in a war-dance, for the possession of the females; male salmons have been observed fighting all day long; male stag-beetles sometimes bear wounds from the huge mandibles of other males; the males of certain hymenopterous insects have been frequently seen by that inimitable observer M. Fabre, fighting for a particular female who sits by, an apparently unconcerned beholder of the struggle, and then retires with the conqueror. The war is, perhaps, severest between the males of polygamous animals, and these seem oftenest provided with special weapons. The males of carnivorous animals are already well armed; though to them and to others, special means of defence may be given through means of sexual selection, as the mane of the lion, and the hooked jaw to the male salmon; for the shield may be as important for victory, as the sword or spear.

Amongst birds, the contest is often of a more peaceful character. All those who have attended to the subject, believe that there is the severest rivalry between the males of many species to attract, by singing, the females. The rock-thrush of Guiana, birds of paradise, and some others, congregate; and successive males display with the most elaborate care, and show off in the best manner, their gorgeous plumage; they likewise perform strange antics before the females, which, standing by as spectators, at last choose the most attractive partner. Those who have closely attended to birds in confinement well know that they often take individual preferences and dislikes: thus Sir R. Heron has described how a pied peacock was eminently attractive to all his hen birds. I cannot here enter on the necessary details; but if man can in a short time give beauty and an elegant carriage to his bantams, according to the standard of beauty, I can see no good reason to doubt that female birds, by selecting, during thousands of generations, the most melodious or beautiful males according to their standard of beauty, might produce a marked effect. Some well-known laws, with respect to the plumage of male and female birds, in comparison with the plumage of the young, can partly be explained through the action of sexual selection on variations occurring at different ages, and transmitted to the males alone or to both sexes at corresponding ages; but I have not space here to enter on this subject.

Thus it is, as I believe, that when the males and females of any animal have the same general habits of life, but differ in structure, colour, or ornament, such differences have been mainly caused by sexual selection: that is, by individual males having had, in successive generations, some slight advantage over other males, in their weapons, means of defence, or charms, which they have transmitted to their male offspring alone. Yet, I would not wish to attribute all sexual differences to this agency: for we see in our domestic animals peculiarities arising and becoming attached to the male sex, which apparently have not been augmented through selection by man. The tuft of hair on the breast of the wild turkey-cock cannot be of any use, and it is doubtful whether it can be ornamental in the eyes of the female bird;—indeed, had the tuft appeared under domestication, it would have been called a monstrosity.

ILLUSTRATIONS OF THE ACTION OF NATURAL SELECTION, OR THE SURVIVAL OF THE FITTEST

In order to make it clear how, as I believe, natural selection acts, I must beg permission to give one or two imaginary illustrations. Let us take the case of a wolf, which preys on various animals, securing some by craft, some by strength and some by fleetness; and let us suppose that the fleetest prey, a deer for instance, had from any change in the country increased in numbers or that other prey had decreased in numbers, during that season of the year when the wolf was hardest pressed for food. Under such circumstances the swiftest and slimmest wolves would have the best chance of surviving and so be preserved or selected,—provided always that they retained strength to master their prey at this or some other period of the year, when they were compelled to prey on other animals. I can see no more reason to doubt that this would be the result, than that man should be able to improve the fleetness of his greyhounds by careful and methodical selection, or by that kind of unconscious selection which follows from each man trying to keep the best dogs without any thought of modifying the breed. I may add, that, according to Mr. Pierce, there are two varieties of the wolf inhabiting the Catskill Mountains, in the United States, one with a light greyhound-like form, which pursues deer, and the other more bulky, with shorter legs, which more frequently attacks the shepherd's flocks.

It should be observed that, in the above illustration, I speak of the slimmest individual wolves, and not of any single strongly-marked variation having been preserved. In former editions of this work I sometimes spoke as if this latter alternative had frequently occurred. I saw the great importance of individual differences, and this led me fully to discuss the results of unconscious selection by man, which depends on the preservation of all the more or less valuable individuals, and on the destruction of the worst. I saw, also, that the preservation in a state of nature of any occasional deviation of structure, such as a monstrosity, would be a rare event; and that, if at first preserved, it would generally be lost by subsequent intercrossing with ordinary individuals. Nevertheless, until reading an able and valuable article in the 'North British Review' (1867), I did not appreciate how rarely single variations, whether slight or strongly marked, could be perpetuated. The author takes the case of a pair of animals, producing during their lifetime two hundred offspring, of which, from various causes of destruction, only two on an average survive to procreate their kind. This is rather an extreme estimate for most of the higher animals, but by no means so for many of the lower organisms. He then shows that if a single individual were born, which varied in some manner, giving it twice as good a chance of life as that of the other individuals, yet the chances would be strongly against its survival. Supposing it to survive and to breed, and that half its young inherited the favourable variation; still, as the Reviewer goes on to show, the young would have only a slightly better chance of surviving and breeding; and this chance would go on decreasing in the succeeding generations. The justice of these remarks cannot, I think, be disputed. If, for instance, a bird of some kind could procure its food more easily by having its beak curved, and if one were born with its beak strongly curved, and which consequently flourished, nevertheless there would be a very poor chance of this one individual perpetuating its kind to the exclusion of the common form; but there can hardly be a doubt, judging by what we see taking place under domestication, that this result would follow from the preservation during many generations of a large number of individuals with more or less strongly curved beaks, and from the destruction of a still larger number with the straightest beaks.

It should not, however, be overlooked that certain rather strongly marked variations, which no one would rank as mere individual differences, frequently recur owing to a similar organisation being similarly acted on—of which fact numerous instances could be given with our domestic productions. In such cases, if the varying individual did not actually transmit to its offspring its newly-acquired character, it would undoubtedly transmit to them, as long as the existing conditions remained the same, a still stronger tendency to vary in the same manner. There can also be little doubt that the tendency to vary in the same manner has often been so strong that all the individuals of the same species have been similarly modified without the aid of any form of selection. Or only a third, fifth, or tenth part of the individuals may have been thus affected, of which fact several instances could be given. Thus Graba estimates that about one-fifth of the guillemots in the Faroe Islands consist of a variety so well marked, that it was formerly ranked as a distinct species under the name of Uria lacrymans. In cases of this kind, if the variation were of a beneficial nature, the original form would soon be supplanted by the modified form, through the survival of the fittest.

To the effects of intercrossing in eliminating variations of all kinds, I shall have to recur; but it may be here remarked that most animals and plants keep to their proper homes, and do not needlessly wander about; we see this even with migratory birds, which almost always return to the same spot. Consequently each newly-formed variety would generally be at first local, as seems to be the common rule with varieties in a state of nature; so that similarly modified individuals would soon exist in a small body together, and would often breed together. If the new variety were successful in its battle for life, it would slowly spread from a central district, competing with and conquering the unchanged individuals on the margins of an ever-increasing circle.

It may be worth while to give another and more complex illustration of the action of natural selection. Certain plants excrete sweet juice, apparently for the sake of eliminating something injurious from the sap: this is effected, for instance, by glands at the base of the stipules in some Leguminosæ, and at the backs of the leaves of the common laurel. This juice, though small in quantity, is greedily sought by insects; but their visits do not in any way benefit the plant. Now, let us suppose that the juice or nectar was excreted from the inside of the flowers of a certain number of plants of any species. Insects in seeking the nectar would get dusted with pollen, and would often transport it from one flower to another. The flowers of two distinct individuals of the same species would thus get crossed; and the act of crossing, as can be fully proved, gives rise to vigorous seedlings which consequently would have the best chance of flourishing and surviving. The plants which produced flowers with the largest glands or nectaries, excreting most nectar, would oftenest be visited by insects, and would oftenest be crossed;

and so in the long-run would gain the upper hand and form a local variety. The flowers, also, which had their stamens and pistils placed, in relation to the size and habits of the particular insects which visited them, so as to favour in any degree the transportal of the pollen, would likewise be favoured. We might have taken the case of insects visiting flowers for the sake of collecting pollen instead of nectar; and as pollen is formed for the sole purpose of fertilisation, its destruction appears to be a simple loss to the plant; yet if a little pollen were carried, at first occasionally and then habitually, by the pollen-devouring insects from flower to flower, and a cross thus effected, although nine-tenths of the pollen were destroyed it might still be a great gain to the plant to be thus robbed; and the individuals which produced more and more pollen, and had larger anthers, would be selected.

When our plant, by the above process long continued, had been rendered highly attractive to insects, they would, unintentionally on their part, regularly carry pollen from flower to flower; and that they do this effectually, I could easily show by many striking facts. I will give only one, as likewise illustrating one step in the separation of the sexes of plants. Some holly-trees bear only male flowers, which have four stamens producing a rather small quantity of pollen, and a rudimentary pistil: other holly-trees bear only female flowers; these have a full-sized pistil, and four stamens with shrivelled anthers, in which not a grain of pollen can be detected. Having found a female tree exactly sixty yards from a male tree, I put the stigmas of twenty flowers, taken from different branches, under the microscope, and on all, without exception, there were a few pollen-grains, and on some a profusion. As the wind had set for several days from the female to the male tree, the pollen could not thus have been carried. The weather had been cold and boisterous, and therefore not favourable to bees, nevertheless every female flower which I examined had been effectually fertilised by the bees, which had flown from tree to tree in search of nectar. But to return to our imaginary case: as soon as the plant had been rendered so highly attractive to insects that pollen was regularly carried from flower to flower, another process might commence. No naturalist doubts the advantage of what has been called the "physiological division of labour"; hence we may believe that it would be advantageous to a plant to produce stamens alone in one flower or on one whole plant, and pistils alone in another flower or on another plant. In plants under culture and placed under new conditions of life, sometimes the male organs and sometimes the female organs become more or less impotent; now if we suppose this to occur in ever so slight a degree under nature, then, as pollen is already carried regularly from flower to flower, and as a more complete separation of the sexes of our plant would be advantageous on the principle of the division of labour, individuals with this tendency more and more increased would be continually favoured or selected, until at last a complete separation of the sexes might be effected. It would take up too much space to show the various steps, through dimorphism and other means, by which the separation of the sexes in plants of various kinds is apparently now in progress; but I may add that some of the species of holly in North America, are, according to Asa Gray, in an exactly intermediate condition, or, as he expresses it, are more or less diœciously polygamous.

Let us now turn to the nectar-feeding insects; we may suppose the plant, of which we have been slowly increasing the nectar by continued selection, to be a common plant; and that certain insects depended in main part on its nectar for food. I could give many facts showing how anxious bees are to save time: for instance, their habit of cutting holes and sucking the nectar at the bases of certain flowers, which, with a very little more trouble, they can enter by the mouth. Bearing such facts in mind, it may be believed that under certain circumstances individual differences in the curvature or length of the proboscis, &c., too slight to be appreciated by us, might profit a bee or other insect, so that certain individuals would be able to obtain their food more quickly than others; and thus the communities to which they belonged would flourish and throw off many swarms inheriting the same peculiarities. The tubes of the corolla of the common red and incarnate clovers (Trifolium pratense and incarnatum) do not on a hasty glance appear to differ in length; yet the hive-bee can easily suck the nectar out of the incarnate clover, but not out of the common red clover, which is visited by humble-bees alone; so that whole fields of red clover offer in vain an abundant supply of precious nectar to the hive-bee. That this nectar is much liked by the hive-bee is certain; for I have repeatedly seen, but only in the autumn, many hive-bees sucking the flowers through holes bitten in the base of the tube by bumble-bees. The difference in the length of the corolla in the two kinds of clover, which determines the visits of the hive-bee, must be very trifling; for I have been assured that when red clover has been mown, the flowers of the second crop are somewhat smaller, and that these are visited by many hive-bees. I do not know whether this statement is accurate; nor whether another published statement can be trusted, namely, that the Ligurian bee which is generally considered a mere variety of the common hive-bee, and which freely crosses with it, is able to reach and suck the nectar of the red clover. Thus, in a country where this kind of clover abounded, it might be a great advantage to the hive-bee to have a slightly longer or differently constructed proboscis. On the other hand, as the fertility of this clover absolutely depends on bees visiting the flowers, if humble-bees were to become rare in any country, it might be a great advantage to the plant to have a shorter or more deeply divided corolla, so that the hive-bees should be enabled to suck its flowers. Thus I can understand how a flower and a bee might slowly become, either simultaneously or one after the other, modified and adapted to each other in the most perfect manner, by the continued preservation of all the individuals which presented slight deviations of structure mutually favourable to each other.

I am well aware that this doctrine of natural selection, exemplified in the above imaginary instances, is open to the same objections which were first urged against Sir Charles Lyell's noble views on "the modern changes of the earth, as illustrative of geology"; but we now seldom hear the agencies which we see still at work, spoken of as trifling or insignificant, when used in explaining the excavation of the deepest valleys of the formation of long lines of inland cliffs. Natural selection acts only by the preservation and accumulation of small inherited modifications, each profitable to the preserved being; and as modern geology has almost banished such views as the excavation of a great valley by a single diluvial wave, so will natural selection banish the belief of the continued creation of new organic beings, or of any great and sudden modification in their structure. * * *

CIRCUMSTANCES FAVOURABLE FOR THE PRODUCTION OF NEW FORMS THROUGH NATURAL SELECTION

This is an extremely intricate subject. A great amount of variability, under which term individual differences are always included, will evidently be favourable. A large number of individuals, by giving a better chance within any given period for the appearance of profitable variations, will compensate for a lesser amount of variability in each individual, and is, I believe, a highly important element of success. Though Nature grants long periods of time for the work of natural selection, she does not grant an indefinite period; for as all organic beings are striving to seize on each place in the economy of nature, if any one species does not become modified and improved in a corresponding degree with its competitors, it will be exterminated. Unless favourable variations be inherited by some at least of the offspring, nothing can be effected by natural selection. The tendency to reversion may often check or prevent the work; but as this tendency has not prevented man from forming by selection numerous domestic races, why should it prevail against natural selection?

In the case of methodical selection, a breeder selects for some definite object, and if the individuals be allowed freely to intercross, his work will completely fail. But when many men, without intending to alter the breed, have a nearly common standard of perfection, and all try to procure and breed from the best animals, improvement surely but slowly follows from this unconscious process of selection, notwithstanding that there is no separation of selected individuals. Thus it will be under nature; for within a confined area, with some place in the natural polity not perfectly occupied, all the individuals varying in the right direction, though in different degrees, will tend to be preserved. But if the area be large, its several districts will almost certainly present different conditions of life; and then, if the same species undergoes modification in different districts, the newly-formed varieties will intercross on the confines of each. But we shall see in the sixth chapter that intermediate varieties, inhabiting intermediate districts, will in the long run generally be supplanted by one of the adjoining varieties. Intercrossing will chiefly affect those animals which unite for each birth and wander much, and which do not breed at a very quick rate. Hence with animals of this nature, for instance, birds, varieties will generally be confined to separated countries; and this I find to be the case. With hermaphrodite organisms which cross only occasionally, and likewise with animals which unite for each birth, but which wander little and can increase at a rapid rate, a new and improved variety might be quickly formed on any one spot, and might there maintain itself in a body and afterwards spread, so that the individuals of the new variety would chiefly cross together. On this principle, nurserymen always prefer saving seed from a large body of plants, as the chance of intercrossing is thus lessened.

Even with animals which unite for each birth, and which do not propagate rapidly, we must not assume that free intercrossing would always eliminate the effects of natural selection; for I can bring forward a considerable body of facts showing that within the same area, two varieties of the same animal may long remain distinct, from haunting different stations, from breeding at slightly different seasons, or from the individuals of each variety preferring to pair together.

Intercrossing plays a very important part in nature by keeping the individuals of the same species, or of the same variety, true and uniform in character. It will obviously thus act far more efficiently with those animals which unite for each birth; but, as already stated, we have reason to believe that occasional intercrosses take place with all animals and plants. Even if these take place only at long intervals of time, the young thus produced will gain so much in vigour and fertility over the offspring from long-continued self-fertilisation, that they will have a better chance of surviving and propagating their kind; and thus in the long run the influence of crosses, even at rare intervals, will be great. With respect to organic beings extremely low in the scale, which do not propagate sexually, nor conjugate, and which cannot possibly intercross, uniformity of character can be retained by them under the same conditions of life, only through the principle of inheritance, and through natural selection which will destroy any individuals departing from the proper type. If the conditions of life change and the form undergoes modification, uniformity of character can be given to the modified offspring, solely by natural selection preserving similar favourable variations.

Isolation, also, is an important element in the modification of species through natural selection. In a confined or isolated area, if not very large, the organic and inorganic conditions of life will generally be almost uniform; so that natural selection will tend to modify all the varying individuals of the same species in the same manner. Intercrossing with the inhabitants of the surrounding districts will, also, be thus prevented. Moritz Wagner has published an interesting essay on this subject, and has shown that the service rendered by isolation in preventing crosses between newly-formed varieties is probably greater even than I supposed. But from reasons already assigned I can by no means agree with this naturalist, that migration and isolation are necessary elements for the formation of new species. The importance of isolation is likewise great in preventing, after any physical change in the conditions, such as of climate, elevation of the land, &c., the immigration of better adapted organisms; and thus new places in the natural economy of the district will be left open to be filled up by the modification of the old inhabitants. Lastly, isolation will give time for a new variety to be improved at a slow rate; and this may sometimes be of much importance. If, however, an isolated area be very small, either from being surrounded by barriers, or from having very peculiar physical conditions, the total number of the inhabitants will be small; and this will retard the production of new species, through natural selection by decreasing the chances of favourable variations arising.

The mere lapse of time by itself does nothing, either for or against natural selection. I state this because it has been erroneously asserted that the element of time has been assumed by me to play an all-important part in modifying species, as if all the forms of life were necessarily undergoing change through some innate law. Lapse of time is only so far important, and its importance in this respect is great, that it gives a better chance of beneficial variations arising and of their being selected, accumulated, and fixed. It likewise tends to increase the direct action of the physical conditions of life, in relation to the constitution of each organism.

If we turn to nature to test the truth of these remarks, and look at any small isolated area, such as an oceanic island, although the number of species inhabiting it is small, as we shall see in our chapter on Geographical Distribution; yet of these species a very large proportion are endemic,—that is, have been produced there and nowhere else in the world. Hence an oceanic island at first sight seems to have been highly favourable for the production of new species. But we may thus deceive ourselves, for to ascertain whether a small isolated area, or a large open area like a continent, has been most favourable for the production of new organic forms, we ought to make the comparison within equal times; and this we are incapable of doing.

Although isolation is of great importance in the production of new species, on the whole I am inclined to believe that largeness of area is still more important, especially for the production of species which shall prove capable of enduring for a long period, and of spreading widely. Throughout a great and open area, not only will there be a better chance of favourable variations, arising from the large number of individuals of the same species there supported, but the conditions of life are much more complex from the large number of already existing species; and if some of these many species become modified and improved, others will have to be improved in a corresponding degree, or they will be exterminated. Each new form, also, as soon as it has been much improved, will be able to spread over the open and continuous area, and will thus come into competition with many other forms. Moreover, great areas, though now continuous, will often, owing to former oscillations of level, have existed in a broken condition; so that the good effects of isolation will generally, to a certain extent, have concurred. Finally, I conclude that, although small isolated areas have been in some respects highly favourable for the production of new species, yet that the course of modification will generally have been more rapid on large areas; and what is more important, that the new forms produced on large areas, which already have been victorious over many competitors, will be those that will spread most widely, and will give rise to the greatest number of new varieties and species. They will thus play a more important part in the changing history of the organic world.

In accordance with this view, we can, perhaps, understand some facts which will be again alluded to in our chapter on Geographical Distribution; for instance, the fact of the productions of the smaller continent of Australia now yielding before those of the larger Europæo-Asiatic area. Thus, also, it is that continental productions have everywhere become so largely naturalised on islands. On a small island, the race for life will have been less severe, and there will have been less modification and less extermination. Hence, we can understand how it is that the flora of Madeira, according to Oswald Heer, resembles to a certain extent the extinct tertiary flora of Europe. All fresh-water basins, taken together, make a small area compared with that of the sea or of the land. Consequently, the competition between fresh-water productions will have been less severe than elsewhere; new forms will have been then more slowly produced, and old forms more slowly exterminated.

And it is in fresh-water basins that we find seven genera of Ganoid fishes, remnants of a once preponderant order: and in fresh water we find some of the most anomalous forms now known in the world as the Ornithorhynchus and Lepidosiren which, like fossils, connect to a certain extent orders at present widely sundered in the natural scale. These anomalous forms may be called living fossils; they have endured to the present day, from having inhabited a confined area, and from having been exposed to less varied, and therefore less severe, competition.

To sum up, as far as the extreme intricacy of the subject permits, the circumstances favourable and unfavourable for the production of new species through natural selection. I conclude that for terrestrial productions a large continental area, which has undergone many oscillations of level, will have been the most favourable for the production of many new forms of life, fitted to endure for a long time and to spread widely. Whilst the area existed as a continent, the inhabitants will have been numerous in individuals and kinds, and will have been subjected to severe competition. When converted by subsidence into large separate islands, there will still have existed many individuals of the same species on each island: intercrossing on the confines of the range of each new species will have been checked: after physical changes of any kind, immigration will have been prevented, so that new places in the polity of each island will have had to be filled up by the modification of the old inhabitants; and time will have been allowed for the varieties in each to become well modified and perfected. When, by renewed elevation, the islands were reconverted into a continental area, there will again have been very severe competition: the most favoured or improved varieties will have been enabled to spread: there will have been much extinction of the less improved forms, and the relative proportional numbers of the various inhabitants of the reunited continent will again have been changed; and again there will have been a fair field for natural selection to improve still further the inhabitants, and thus to produce new species.

That natural selection generally acts with extreme slowness I fully admit. It can act only when there are places in the natural polity of a district which can be better occupied by the modification of some of its existing inhabitants. The occurrence of such places will often depend on physical changes, which generally take place very slowly, and on the immigration of better adapted forms being prevented. As some few of the old inhabitants become modified, the mutual relations of others will often be disturbed; and this will create new places, ready to be filled up by better adapted forms, but all this will take place very slowly. Although all the individuals of the same species differ in some slight degree from each other, it would often be long before differences of the right nature in various parts of the organisation might occur. The result would often be greatly retarded by free intercrossing. Many will exclaim that these several causes are amply sufficient to neutralise the power of natural selection. I do not believe so. But I do believe that natural selection will generally act very slowly, only at long intervals of time, and only on a few of the inhabitants of the same region. I further believe that these slow, intermittent results accord well with what geology tells us of the rate and manner at which the inhabitants of the world have changed.

Slow though the process of selection may be, if feeble man can do much by artificial selection, I can see no limit to the amount of change, to the beauty and complexity of the coadaptations between all organic beings, one with another and with their physical conditions of life, which may have been effected in the long course of time through nature's power of selection, that is by the survival of the fittest. * * *

DIVERGENCE OF CHARACTER

The principle, which I have designated by this term, is of high importance, and explains, as I believe, several important facts. In the first place, varieties, even strongly-marked ones, though having somewhat of the character of species—as is shown by the hopeless doubts in many cases how to rank them—yet certainly differ far less from each other than do good and distinct species. Nevertheless, according to my view, varieties are species in the process of formation, or are, as I have called them, incipient species. How, then, does the lesser difference between varieties become augmented into the greater difference between species? That this does habitually happen, we must infer from most of the innumerable species throughout nature presenting well-marked differences; whereas varieties, the supposed prototypes and parents of future well-marked species, present slight and ill-defined differences. Mere chance, as we may call it, might cause one variety to differ in some character from its parents, and the offspring of this variety again to differ from its parent in the very same character and in a greater degree; but this alone would never account for so habitual and large a degree of difference as that between the species of the same genus.

As has always been my practice, I have sought light on this head from our domestic productions. We shall here find something analogous. It will be admitted that the production of races so different as short-horn and Hereford cattle, race and cart horses, the several breeds of pigeons, &c., could never have been effected by the mere chance accumulation of similar variations during many successive generations. In practice, a fancier is, for instance, struck by a pigeon having a slightly shorter beak; another fancier is struck by a pigeon having a rather longer beak; and on the acknowledged principle that "fanciers do not and will not admire a medium standard, but like extremes," they both go on (as has actually occurred with the sub-breeds of the tumbler-pigeon) choosing and breeding from birds with longer and longer beaks, or with shorter and shorter beaks. Again, we may suppose that at an early period of history, the men of one nation or district required swifter horses, whilst those of another required stronger and bulkier horses. The early differences would be very slight; but, in the course of time, from the continued selection of swifter horses in the one case, and of stronger ones in the other, the differences would become greater, and would be noted as forming two sub-breeds. Ultimately, after the lapse of centuries, these sub-breeds would become converted into two well-established and distinct breeds. As the differences became greater, the inferior animals with intermediate characters, being neither swift nor very strong, would not have been used for breeding, and will thus have tended to disappear. Here, then, we see in man's productions the action of what may be called the principle of divergence, causing differences, at first barely appreciable, steadily to increase, and the breeds to diverge in character, both from each other and from their common parent.

But how, it may be asked, can any analogous principle apply in nature? I believe it can and does apply most efficiently (though it was a long time before I saw how), from the simple circumstance that the more diversified the descendants from any one species become in structure, constitution, and habits, by so much will they be better enabled to seize on many and widely diversified places in the polity of nature, and so be enabled to increase in numbers.

We can clearly discern this in the case of animals with simple habits. Take the case of a carnivorous quadruped, of which the number that can be supported in any country has long ago arrived at its full average. If its natural power of increase be allowed to act, it can succeed in increasing (the country not undergoing any change in conditions) only by its varying descendants seizing on places at present occupied by other animals: some of them, for instance, being enabled to feed on new kinds of prey, either dead or alive; some inhabiting new stations, climbing trees, frequenting water, and some perhaps becoming less carnivorous. The more diversified in habits and structure the descendants of our carnivorous animals become, the more places they will be enabled to occupy. What applies to one animal will apply throughout all time to all animals—that is, if they vary—for otherwise natural selection can effect nothing. So it will be with plants. It has been experimentally proved, that if a plot of ground be sown with one species of grass, and a similar plot be sown with several distinct genera of grasses, a greater number of plants and a greater weight of dry herbage can be raised in the latter than in the former case. The same has been found to hold good when one variety and several mixed varieties of wheat have been sown on equal spaces of ground. Hence, if any one species of grass were to go on varying, and the varieties were continually selected which differed from each other in the same manner, though in a very slight degree, as do the distinct species and genera of grasses, a greater number of individual plants of this species, including its modified descendants, would succeed in living on the same piece of ground. And we know that each species and each variety of grass is annually sowing almost countless seeds; and is thus striving, as it may be said, to the utmost to increase in number. Consequently, in the course of many thousand generations, the most distinct varieties of any one species of grass would have the best chance of succeeding and of increasing in numbers, and thus of supplanting the less distinct varieties; and varieties, when rendered very distinct from each other, take the rank of species.

The truth of the principle that the greatest amount of life can be supported by great diversification of structure, is seen under many natural circumstances. In an extremely small area, especially if freely open to immigration, and where the contest between individual and individual must be very severe, we always find great diversity in its inhabitants. For instance, I found that a piece of turf, three feet by four in size, which had been exposed for many years to exactly the same conditions, supported twenty species of plants, and these belonged to eighteen genera and to eight orders, which shows how much these plants differed from each other. So it is with the plants and insects on small and uniform islets: also in small ponds of fresh water. Farmers find that they can raise most food by a rotation of plants belonging to the most different orders: nature follows what may be called a simultaneous rotation. Most of the animals and plants which live close round any small piece of ground, could live on it (supposing its nature not to be in any way peculiar), and may be said to be striving to the utmost to live there; but, it is seen, that where they come into the closest competition, the advantages of diversification of structure, with the accompanying differences of habit and constitution, determine that the inhabitants, which thus jostle each other most closely, shall, as a general rule, belong to what we call different genera and orders.

The same principle is seen in the naturalisation of plants through man's agency in foreign lands. It might have been expected that the plants which would succeed in becoming naturalised in any land would generally have been closely allied to the indigenes; for these are commonly looked at as specially created and adapted for their own country. It might also, perhaps, have been expected that naturalised plants would have belonged to a few groups more especially adapted to certain stations in their new homes. But the case is very different; and Alph. de Candolle has well remarked, in his great and admirable work, that floras gain by naturalisation, proportionally with the number of the native genera and species far more in new genera than in new species. To give a single instance: in the last edition of Dr. Asa Gray's 'Manual of the Flora of the Northern United States,' 260 naturalised plants are enumerated, and these belong to 162 genera. We thus see that these naturalised plants are of a highly diversified nature. They differ, moreover, to a large extent, from the indigenes, for out of the 162 naturalised genera, no less than 100 genera are not there indigenous, and thus a large proportional addition is made to the genera now living in the United States.

By considering the nature of the plants or animals which have in any country struggled successfully with the indigenes and have there become naturalised, we may gain some crude idea in what manner some of the natives would have to be modified, in order to gain an advantage over their compatriots; and we may at least infer that diversification of structure, amounting to new generic differences, would be profitable to them.

The advantage of diversification of structure in the inhabitants of the same region is, in fact, the same as that of the physiological division of labour in the organs of the same individual body—a subject so well elucidated by Milne Edwards. No physiologist doubts that a stomach adapted to digest vegetable matter alone, or flesh alone, draws most nutriment from these substances. So in the general economy of any land, the more widely and perfectly the animals and plants are diversified for different habits of life, so will a greater number of individuals be capable of there supporting themselves. A set of animals, with their organisation but little diversified, could hardly compete with a set more perfectly diversified in structure. It may be doubted, for instance, whether the Australian marsupials, which are divided into groups differing but little from each other, and feebly representing, as Mr. Waterhouse and others have remarked, our carnivorous, ruminant, and rodent mammals, could successfully compete with these well-developed orders. In the Australian mammals, we see the process of diversification in an early and incomplete stage of development.

THE PROBABLE EFFECTS OF THE ACTION OF NATURAL SELECTION THROUGH DIVERGENCE OF CHARACTER AND EXTINCTION, ON THE DESCENDANTS OF A COMMON ANCESTOR

After the foregoing discussion, which has been much compressed, we may assume that the modified descendants of any one species will succeed so much the better as they become more diversified in structure, and are thus enabled to encroach on places occupied by other beings. Now let us see how this principle of benefit being de-

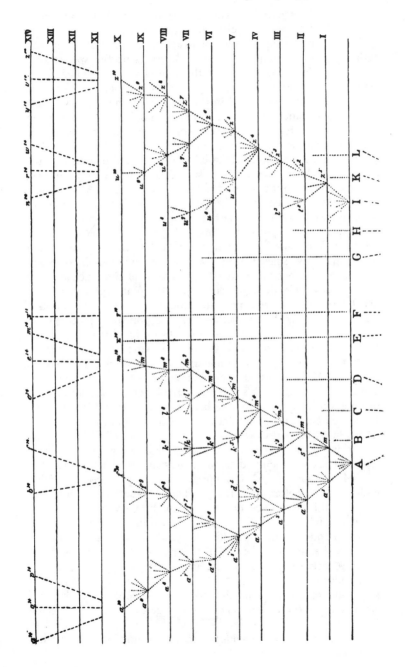

rived from divergence of character, combined with the principles of natural selection and of extinction, tends to act.

The accompanying diagram will aid us in understanding this rather perplexing subject. Let A to L represent the species of a genus large in its own country; these species are supposed to resemble each other in unequal degrees, as is so generally the case in nature, and as is represented in the diagram by the letters standing at unequal distances. I have said a large genus, because as we saw in the second chapter, on an average more species vary in large genera than in small genera; and the varying species of the large genera present a greater number of varieties. We have, also, seen that the species, which are the commonest and the most widely diffused, vary more than do the rare and restricted species. Let (A) be a common, widely-diffused, and varying species, belonging to a genus large in its own country. The branching and diverging dotted lines of unequal lengths proceeding from (A), may represent its varying offspring. The variations are supposed to be extremely slight, but of the most diversified nature; they are not supposed all to appear simultaneously, but often after long intervals of time; nor are they all supposed to endure for equal periods. Only those variations which are in some way profitable will be preserved or naturally selected. And here the importance of the principle of benefit derived from divergence of character comes in; for this will generally lead to the most different or divergent variations (represented by the outer dotted lines) being preserved and accumulated by natural selection. When a dotted line reaches one of the horizontal lines, and is there marked by a small numbered letter, a sufficient amount of variation is supposed to have been accumulated to form it into a fairly well-marked variety, such as would be thought worthy of record in a systematic work.

The intervals between the horizontal lines in the diagram, may represent each a thousand or more generations. After a thousand generations, species (A) is supposed to have produced two fairly well-marked varieties, namely a^1 and m^1. These two varieties will generally still be exposed to the same conditions which made their parents variable, and the tendency to variability is in itself hereditary; consequently they will likewise tend to vary, and commonly in nearly the same manner as did their parents. Moreover, these two varieties, being only slightly modified forms, will tend to inherit those advantages which made their parent (A) more numerous than most of the other inhabitants of the same country; they will also partake of those more general advantages which made the genus to which the parent-species belonged, a large genus in its own country. And all these circumstances are favourable to the production of new varieties.

If, then, these two varieties be variable, the most divergent of their variations will generally be preserved during the next thousand generations. And after this interval, variety a^1 is supposed in the diagram to have produced variety a^2, which will, owing to the principle of divergence, differ more from (A) than did variety a^1. Variety m^1 is supposed to have produced two varieties, namely m^2 and s^2, differing from each other, and more considerably from their common parent (A). We may continue the process by similar steps for any length of time; some of the varieties, after each thousand generations, producing only a single variety, but in a more and more modified condition, some producing two or three varieties, and some failing to produce any. Thus the varieties or modified descendants of the common parent (A), will generally go on increasing in number and diverging in character. In the diagram the process is represented up to the ten-thousandth generation, and under a condensed and simplified form up to the fourteen-thousandth generation.

But I must here remark that I do not suppose that the process ever goes on so regularly as is represented in the diagram, though in itself made somewhat irregular, nor that it goes on continuously; it is far more probable that each form remains for long periods unaltered, and then again undergoes modification. Nor do I suppose that the most divergent varieties are invariably preserved: a medium form may often long endure, and may or may not produce more than one modified descendant; for natural selection will always act according to the nature of the places which are either unoccupied or not perfectly occupied by other beings; and this will depend on infinitely complex relations. But as a general rule, the more diversified in structure the descendants from any one species can be rendered, the more places they will be enabled to seize on, and the more their modified progeny will increase. In our diagram the line of succession is broken at regular intervals by small numbered letters marking the successive forms which have become sufficiently distinct to be recorded as varieties. But these breaks are imaginary, and might have been inserted anywhere, after intervals long enough to allow the accumulation of a considerable amount of divergent variation.

As all the modified descendants from a common and widely-diffused species, belonging to a large genus, will tend to partake of the same advantages which made their parent successful in life, they will generally go on multiplying in number as well as diverging in character: this is represented in the diagram by the several divergent branches proceeding from (A). The modified offspring from the later and more highly improved branches in the lines of descent, will, it is probable, often take the place of, and so de-

stroy, the earlier and less improved branches: this is represented in
the diagram by some of the lower branches not reaching to the
upper horizontal lines. In some cases no doubt the process of modification will be confined to a single line of descent and the number
of modified descendants will not be increased; although the amount
of divergent modification may have been augmented. This case
would be represented in the diagram, if all the lines proceeding
from (A) were removed, excepting that from a^1 to a^{10}. In the
same way the English racehorse and English pointer have apparently
both gone on slowly diverging in character from their original
stocks, without either having given off any fresh branches or races.

After ten thousand generations, species (A) is supposed to have
produced three forms, a^{10}, f^{10}, and m^{10}, which, from having
diverged in character during the successive generations, will have
come to differ largely, but perhaps unequally, from each other and
from their common parent. If we suppose the amount of change
between each horizontal line in our diagram to be excessively
small, these three forms may still be only well-marked varieties;
but we have only to suppose the steps in the process of modification
to be more numerous or greater in amount, to convert these three
forms into doubtful or at least into well-defined species. Thus the
diagram illustrates the steps by which the small differences distinguishing varieties are increased into the larger differences distinguishing species. By continuing the same process for a greater
number of generations (as shown in the diagram in a condensed
and simplified manner), we get eight species, marked by the letters
between a^{14} and m^{14}, all descended from (A). Thus, as I believe,
species are multiplied and genera are formed.

In a large genus it is probable that more than one species would
vary. In the diagram I have assumed that a second species (I) has
produced, by analogous steps, after ten thousand generations, either
two well-marked varieties (w^{10} and z^{10}) or two species, according
to the amount of change supposed to be represented between the
horizontal lines. After fourteen thousand generations, six new species marked by the letters n^{14} to z^{14}, are supposed to have been
produced. In any genus, the species which are already very different
in character from each other, will generally tend to produce the
greatest number of modified descendants; for these will have the
best chance of seizing on new and widely different places in the
polity of nature: hence in the diagram I have chosen the extreme
species (A), and the nearly extreme species (I), as those which have
largely varied, and have given rise to new varieties and species. The
other nine species (marked by capital letters) of our original genus,
may for long but unequal periods continue to transmit unaltered
descendants; and this is shown in the diagram by the dotted lines
unequally prolonged upwards.

But during the process of modification, represented in the diagram, another of our principles, namely that of extinction, will have played an important part. As in each fully stocked country natural selection necessarily acts by the selected form having some advantage in the struggle for life over other forms, there will be a constant tendency in the improved descendants of any one species to supplant and exterminate in each stage of descent their predecessors and their original progenitor. For it should be remembered that the competition will generally be most severe between those forms which are most nearly related to each other in habits, constitution, and structure. Hence all the intermediate forms between the earlier and later states, that is between the less and more improved states of the same species, as well as the original parent-species itself, will generally tend to become extinct. So it probably will be with many whole collateral lines of descent, which will be conquered by later and improved lines. If, however, the modified offspring of a species get into some distinct country, or become quickly adapted to some quite new station, in which offspring and progenitor do not come into competition, both may continue to exist.

If, then, our diagram be assumed to represent a considerable amount of modification, species (A) and all the earlier varieties will have become extinct, being replaced by eight new species (a^{14} to m^{14}); and species (I) will be replaced by six (n^{14} to z^{14}) new species.

But we may go further than this. The original species of our genus were supposed to resemble each other in unequal degrees, as is so generally the case in nature; species (A) being more nearly related to B. C, and D, than to the other species; and species (I) more to G, H, K, L, than to the others. These two species (A) and (I) were also supposed to be very common and widely diffused species, so that they must originally have had some advantage over most of the other species of the genus. Their modified descendants, fourteen in number at the fourteen-thousandth generation, will probably have inherited some of the same advantages: they have also been modified and improved in a diversified manner at each stage of descent, so as to have become adapted to many related places in the natural economy of their country. It seems, therefore, extremely probable that they will have taken the places of, and thus exterminated not only their parents (A) and (I), but likewise some of the original species which were most nearly related to their parents. Hence very few of the original species will have transmitted offspring to the fourteen-thousandth generation. We may suppose that only one, (F), of the two species (E and F) which were least closely related to the other nine original species, has transmitted descendants to this late stage of descent.

The new species in our diagram descended from the original eleven species, will now be fifteen in number. Owing to the divergent tendency of natural selection, the extreme amount of difference in character between species a^{14} and z^{14} will be much greater than that between the most distinct of the original eleven species. The new species, moreover, will be allied to each other in a widely different manner. Of the eight descendants from (A) the three marked a^{14}, q^{14}, p^{14}, will be nearly related from having recently branched off from a^{10}, b^{14}, and f^{14}, from having diverged at an earlier period from a^5, will be in some degree distinct from the three first-named species; and lastly, o^{14}, e^{14}, and m^{14}, will be nearly related one to the other, but, from having diverged at the first commencement of the process of modification, will be widely different from the other five species, and may constitute a sub-genus or a distinct genus.

The six descendants from (I) will form two sub-genera or genera. But as the original species (I) differed largely from (A), standing nearly at the extreme end of the original genus, the six descendants from (I) will, owing to inheritance alone, differ considerably from the eight descendants from (A); the two groups, moreover, are supposed to have gone on diverging in different directions. The intermediate species, also (and this is a very important consideration), which connected the original species (A) and (I), have become, excepting (F), extinct, and have left no descendants. Hence the six new species descended from (I), and the eight descendants from (A), will have to be ranked as very distinct genera, or even as distinct sub-families.

Thus it is, as I believe, that two or more genera are produced by descent with modification, from two or more species of the same genus. And the two or more parent-species are supposed to be descended from some one species of an earlier genus. In our diagram, this is indicated by the broken lines, beneath the capital letters, converging in sub-branches downwards towards a single point; this point represents a species, the supposed progenitor of our several new sub-genera and genera.

It is worth while to reflect for a moment on the character of the new species F^{14}, which is supposed not to have diverged much in character, but to have retained the form of (F), either unaltered or altered only in a slight degree. In this case, its affinities to the other fourteen new species will be of a curious and circuitous nature. Being descended from a form which stood between the parent-species (A) and (I), now supposed to be extinct and unknown, it will be in some degree intermediate in character between the two groups descended from these two species. But as these two groups have gone on diverging in character from the type of their parents, the new species (F^{14}) will not be directly intermediate between them, but rather between types of the two groups; and every naturalist will be able to call such cases before his mind.

In the diagram, each horizontal line has hitherto been supposed to represent a thousand generations, but each may represent a million or more generations; it may also represent a section of the successive strata of the earth's crust including extinct remains. We shall, when we come to our chapter on Geology, have to refer again to this subject, and I think we shall then see that the diagram throws light on the affinities of extinct beings, which, though generally belonging to the same orders, families, or genera, with those now living, yet are often, in some degree, intermediate in character between existing groups; and we can understand this fact, for the extinct species lived at various remote epochs when the branching lines of descent had diverged less.

I see no reason to limit the process of modification, as now explained, to the formation of genera alone. If, in the diagram, we suppose the amount of change, represented by each successive group of diverging dotted lines to be great, the forms marked a^{14} to p^{14}, those marked b^{14} and f^{14}, and those marked o^{14} to m^{14}, will form three very distinct genera. We shall also have two very distinct genera descended from(I), differing widely from the descendants of (A). These two groups of genera will thus form two distinct families, or orders, according to the amount of divergent modification supposed to be represented in the diagram. And the two new families, or orders, are descended from two species of the original genus, and these are supposed to be descended from some still more ancient and unknown form.

We have seen that in each country it is the species belonging to the larger genera which oftenest present varieties or incipient species. This, indeed, might have been expected; for, as natural selection acts through one form having some advantage over other forms in the struggle for existence, it will chiefly act on those which already have some advantage; and the largeness of any group shows that its species have inherited from a common ancestor some advantage in common. Hence, the struggle for the production of new and modified descendants will mainly lie between the larger groups which are all trying to increase in number. One large group will slowly conquer another large group, reduce its numbers, and thus lessen its chance of further variation and improvement. Within the same large group, the later and more highly perfected sub-groups, from branching out and seizing on many new places in the polity of Nature, will constantly tend to supplant and destroy the earlier and less improved sub-groups. Small and broken groups and sub-groups will finally disappear. Looking to the future, we can predict that the groups of organic beings which are now large and triumphant, and which are least broken up, that is, which have as yet suffered least extinction, will, for a long period, continue to increase. But which groups will ultimately prevail, no man can predict; for we know that many groups formerly most extensively developed, have now become extinct. Looking still more remotely to the future, we may predict that, owing to the continued and steady increase of the larger groups, a multitude of smaller groups will become utterly extinct, and leave no modified descendants; and consequently that, of the species living at any one period, extremely few will transmit descendants to a remote futurity. I shall have to return to this subject in the chapter on Classification, but I may add that as, according to this view, extremely few of the more ancient species have transmitted descendants to the present day, and, as all the descendants of the same species form a class, we can understand how it is that there exist so few classes in each main division of the animal and vegetable kingdoms. Although few of the most ancient species have left modified descendants, yet, at remote geological periods, the earth may have been almost as well peopled with species of many genera, families, orders, and classes, as at the present time.

ON THE DEGREE TO WHICH ORGANISATION TENDS TO ADVANCE

Natural Selection acts exclusively by the preservation and accumulation of variations, which are beneficial under the organic and inorganic conditions to which each creature is exposed at all periods of life. The ultimate result is that each creature tends to become more and more improved in relation to its conditions. This improvement inevitably leads to the gradual advancement of the organisation of the greater number of living beings throughout the world. But here we enter on a very intricate subject, for naturalists have not defined to each other's satisfaction what is meant by an advance in organisation. Amongst the vertebrata the degree of intellect and an approach in structure to man clearly come into play. It might be thought that the amount of change which the various parts and organs pass through in their development from the embryo to maturity would suffice as a standard of comparison; but there are cases, as with certain parasitic crustaceans, in which several parts of the structure become less perfect, so that the mature animal cannot be called higher than its larva. Von Baer's standard seems the most widely applicable and the best, namely, the amount of differentiation of the parts of the same organic being, in the adult state as I should be inclined to add, and their specialisation for different functions; or, as Milne Edwards would express it, the completeness of the division is physiological labour. But we shall see how obscure this subject is if we look, for instance, to fishes, amongst which some naturalists rank those as highest which, like the sharks, approach nearest to amphibians; whilst other naturalists rank the common bony or teleostean fishes as the highest, inasmuch as they are most strictly fish-like and differ most from the other vertebrate classes. We see still more plainly the obscurity of the subject by turning to plants, amongst which the standard of intellect is of course quite excluded; and here some botanists rank those plants as highest which have every organ, as sepals, petals, stamens, and pistils, fully developed in each flower; whereas other botanists, probably with more truth, look at the plants which have their several organs much modified and reduced in number as the highest.

If we take as the standard of high organisation, the amount of differentiation and specialisation of the several organs in each being when adult (and this will include the advancement of the brain for intellectual purposes), natural selection clearly leads towards this standard: for all physiologists admit that the specialisation of organs, inasmuch as in this state they perform their functions better, is an advantage to each being; and hence the accumulation of variations tending towards specialisation is within the scope of natural selection. On the other hand, we can see, bearing in mind that all organic beings are striving to increase at a high ratio and to seize on every unoccupied or less well occupied place in the economy of nature, that it is quite possible for natural selection gradually to fit a being to a situation in which several organs would be superfluous or useless: in such cases there would be retrogression in the scale of organisation. Whether organisation on the whole has actually advanced from the remotest geological periods to the present day will be more conveniently discussed in our chapter on Geological Succession.

But it may be objected that if all organic beings thus tend to rise in the scale, how is it that throughout the world a multitude of the lowest forms still exist; and how is it that in each great class some forms are far more highly developed than others? Why have not the more highly developed forms everywhere supplanted and exterminated the lower? Lamarck, who believed in an innate and inevitable tendency towards perfection in all organic beings, seems to have felt this difficulty so strongly, that he was led to suppose that new and simple forms are continually being produced by spontaneous generation. Science has not as yet proved the truth of this belief, whatever the future may reveal. On our theory the continued existence of lowly organisms offers no difficulty; for natural selection, or the survival of the fittest, does not necessarily include progressive development—it only takes advantage of such variations as arise and are beneficial to each creature under its complex relations of life. And it may be asked what advantage, as far as we can see, would it be to an infusorian animalcule—to an intestinal worm—or even to an earthworm, to be highly organised. If it were no advantage, these forms would be left, by natural selection, un-improved or but little improved, and might remain for indefinite ages in their present lowly condition. And geology tells us that some of the lowest forms, as the infusoria and rhizopods, have remained for an enormous period in nearly their present state. But to suppose that most of the many now existing low forms have not in the least advanced since the first dawn of life would be extremely rash; for every naturalist who has dissected some of the beings now ranked as very low in the scale, must have been struck with their really wondrous and beautiful organisation.

Nearly the same remarks are applicable if we look to the different grades of organisation within the same great group; for instance, in the vertebrata, to the co-existence of mammals and fish —amongst mammalia, to the co-existence of man and the ornitho-rhynchus—amongst fishes, to the co-existence of the shark and the lancelet (Amphioxus), which latter fish in the extreme simplicity of its structure approaches the invertebrate classes. But mammals and fish hardly come into competition with each other; the advancement of the whole class of mammals, or of certain members in this class, to the highest grade would not lead to their taking the place of fishes. Physiologists believe that the brain must be bathed by warm blood to be highly active, and this requires aërial respiration; so that warm-blooded mammals when inhabiting the water lie under a disadvantage in having to come continually to the surface to breathe. With fishes, members of the shark family would not tend to supplant the lancelet; for the lancelet, as I hear from Fritz Müller, has as sole companion and competitor on the barren sandy shore of South Brazil, an anomalous annelid. The three lowest orders of mammals, namely, marsupials, edentata, and rodents, co-exist in South America in the same region with numerous monkeys, and probably interfere little with each other. Although organisation, on the whole, may have advanced and be still advancing throughout the world, yet the scale will always present many degrees of perfection; for the high advancement of certain whole classes, or of certain members of each class, does not at all necessarily lead to the extinction of those groups with which they do not enter into close competition. In some cases, as we shall hereafter see, lowly organised forms appear to have been preserved to the present day, from inhabiting confined or peculiar stations, where they have been subjected to less severe competition, and where their scanty numbers have retarded the chance of favourable variations arising.

Finally, I believe that many lowly organised forms now exist throughout the world, from various causes. In some cases variations or individual differences of a favourable nature may never have arisen for natural selection to act on and accumulate. In no case, probably, has time sufficed for the utmost possible amount of development. In some few cases there has been what we must call retrogression of organisation. But the main cause lies in the fact that under very simple conditions of life a high organisation would be of no service,—possibly would be of actual disservice, as being of a more delicate nature, and more liable to be put out of order and injured.

Looking to the first dawn of life, when all organic beings, as we may believe, presented the simplest structure, how, it has been asked, could the first steps in the advancement or differentiation of parts have arisen? Mr. Herbert Spencer would probably answer that, as soon as simple unicellular organism came by growth or division to be compounded of several cells, or became attached to any supporting surface, his law "that homologous units of any order become differentiated in proportion as their relations to incident forces become different" would come into action. But as we have no facts to guide us, speculation on the subject is almost useless. It is, however, an error to suppose that there would be no struggle for existence, and, consequently, no natural selection, until many forms had been produced: variations in a single species inhabiting an isolated station might be beneficial, and thus the whole mass of individuals might be modified, or two distinct forms might arise. But, as I remarked towards the close of the Introduction, no one ought to feel surprise at much remaining as yet unexplained on the origin of species, if we make due allowance for our profound ignorance on the mutual relations of the inhabitants of the world at the present time, and still more so during past ages. * * *

SUMMARY OF CHAPTER

If under changing conditions of life organic beings present individual differences in almost every part of their structure, and this cannot be disputed; if there be, owing to their geometrical rate of increase, a severe struggle for life at some age, season, or year, and this certainly cannot be disputed; then, considering the infinite complexity of the relations of all organic beings to each other and to their conditions of life, causing an infinite diversity in structure, constitution, and habits, to be advantageous to them, it would be a most extraordinary fact if no variations had ever occurred useful to each being's own welfare, in the same manner as so many variations have occurred useful to man. But if variations useful to any organic being ever do occur, assuredly individuals thus characterised will have the best chance of being preserved in the struggle for life; and from the strong principle of inheritance, these will tend to produce offspring similarly characterised. This principle of preservation, or the survival of the fittest, I have called Natural Selection. It leads to the improvement of each creature in relation to its organic and inorganic conditions of life; and consequently, in most cases, to what must be regarded as an advance in organisation. Nevertheless, low and simple forms will long endure if well fitted for their simple conditions of life.

Natural selection, on the principle of qualities being inherited at corresponding ages, can modify the egg, seed, or young, as easily as the adult. Amongst many animals, sexual selection will have given its aid to ordinary selection, by assuring to the most vigorous and best adapted males the greatest number of offspring. Sexual selection will also give characters useful to the males alone, in their struggles or rivalry with other males; and these characters will be transmitted to one sex or to both sexes, according to the form of inheritance which prevails.

Whether natural selection has really thus acted in adapting the various forms of life to their several conditions and stations, must be judged by the general tenor and balance of evidence given in the following chapters. But we have already seen how it entails extinction; and how largely extinction has acted in the world's history, geology plainly declares. Natural selection, also leads to divergence of character; for the more organic beings diverge in structure, habits, and constitution, by so much the more can a large number be supported on the area,—of which we see proof by looking to the inhabitants of any small spot, and to the productions naturalised in foreign lands. Therefore, during the modification of the descendants of any one species, and during the incessant struggle of all species to increase in numbers, the more diversified the descendants become, the better will be their chance of success in the battle for life. Thus the small differences distinguishing varieties of the same species, steadily tend to increase, till they equal the greater differences between species of the same genus, or even of distinct genera.

We have seen that it is the common, the widely-diffused and widely-ranging species, belonging to the larger genera within each class, which vary most; and these tend to transmit to their modified offspring that superiority which now makes them dominant in their own countries. Natural selection, as has just been remarked, leads to divergence of character and to much extinction of the less improved and intermediate forms of life. On these principles, the nature of the affinities, and the generally well-defined distinctions between the innumerable organic beings in each class throughout the world, may be explained. It is a truly wonderful fact—the wonder of which we are apt to overlook from familiarity—that all animals and all plants throughout all time and space should be related to each other in groups, subordinate to groups, in the manner which we everywhere behold—namely, varieties of the same species most closely related, species of the same genus less closely and unequally related, forming sections and sub-genera, species of distinct genera much less closely related, and genera related in different degrees, forming sub-families, families, orders, sub-classes and classes. The several subordinate groups in any class cannot be ranked in a single file, but seem clustered round points, and these round other points, and so on in almost endless cycles. If species had been independently created, no explanation would have been possible of this kind of classification; but it is explained through inheritance and the complex action of natural selection, entailing extinction and divergence of character, as we have seen illustrated in the diagram.

The affinities of all the beings of the same class have sometimes been represented by a great tree. I believe this simile largely speaks the truth. The green and budding twigs may represent existing species; and those produced during former years may represent the long succession of extinct species. At each period of growth all the growing twigs have tried to branch out on all sides, and to overtop and kill the surrounding twigs and branches, in the same manner as species and groups of species have at all times overmastered other species in the great battle for life. The limbs divided into great branches, and these into lesser and lesser branches, were themselves once, when the tree was young, budding twigs, and this connection of the former and present buds by ramifying branches may well represent the classification of all extinct and living species in groups subordinate to groups. Of the many twigs which flourished when the tree was a mere bush, only two or three, now grown into great branches, yet survive and bear the other branches; so with the species which lived during long-past geological periods, very few have left living and modified descendants. From the first growth of the tree, many a limb and branch has decayed and dropped off; and these fallen branches of various sizes may represent those whole orders, families, and genera which have now no living representatives, and which are known to us only in a fossil state. As we here and there see a thin straggling branch springing from a fork low down in a tree, and which by some chance has been favoured and is still alive on its summit, so we occasionally see an animal like the Ornithorhynchus or Lepidosiren, which in some small degree connects by its affinities two large branches of life, and which has apparently been saved from fatal competition by having inhabited a protected station. As buds give rise by growth to fresh buds, and these, if vigorous, branch out and overtop on all sides many a feebler branch, so by generation I believe it has been with the great Tree of Life, which fills with its dead and broken branches the crust of the earth, and covers the surface with its ever-branching and beautiful ramifications.

Chapter VI

DIFFICULTIES OF THE THEORY

Difficulties of the theory of descent with modification—Absence or rarity of transitional varieties—Transitions in habits of life—Diversified habits in the same species—Species with habits widely different from those of their allies—Organs of extreme perfection—Modes of transition—Cases of difficulty—Natura non facit saltum—Organs of small importance—Organs not in all cases absolutely perfect—The law of unity of type and of the conditions of existence embraced by the theory of natural selection.

Long before the reader has arrived at this part of my work, a crowd of difficulties will have occurred to him. Some of them are so serious that to this day I can hardly reflect on them without being in some degree staggered; but, to the best of my judgment, the greater number are only apparent, and those that are real are not, I think, fatal to the theory.

These difficulties and objections may be classed under the following heads:—First, why, if species have descended from other species by fine gradations, do we not everywhere see innumerable transitional forms? Why is not all nature in confusion instead of the species being, as we see them, well defined?

Secondly, is it possible that an animal having, for instance, the structure and habits of a bat, could have been formed by the modification of some other animal with widely different habits and structure? Can we believe that natural selection could produce, on the one hand, an organ of trifling importance, such as the tail of a giraffe, which serves as a fly-flapper, and, on the other hand, an organ so wonderful as the eye?

Thirdly, can instincts be acquired and modified through natural selection? What shall we say to the instinct which leads the bee to make cells, and which has practically anticipated the discoveries of profound mathematicians?

Fourthly, how can we account for species, when crossed, being sterile and producing sterile offspring, whereas, when varieties are crossed, their fertility is unimpaired?

The two first heads will here be discussed; some miscellaneous objections in the following chapter; Instinct and Hybridism in the two succeeding chapters.

ON THE ABSENCE OR RARITY OF TRANSITIONAL VARIETIES

As natural selection acts solely by the preservation of profitable modifications, each new form will tend in a fully-stocked country to take the place of, and finally to exterminate, its own less improved parent-form and other less favoured forms with which it comes into competition. Thus extinction and natural selection go hand in hand. Hence, if we look at each species as descended from some unknown form, both the parent and all the transitional varieties will generally have been exterminated by the very process of the formation and perfection of the new form.

But, as by this theory innumerable transitional forms must have existed, why do we not find them embedded in countless numbers in the crust of the earth? It will be more convenient to discuss this question in the chapter on the Imperfection of the Geological Record; and I will here only state that I believe the answer mainly lies in the record being incomparably less perfect than is generally supposed. The crust of the earth is a vast museum; but the natural collections have been imperfectly made, and only at long intervals of time.

But it may be urged that when several closely-allied species inhabit the same territory, we surely ought to find at the present time many transitional forms. Let us take a simple case: in travelling from north to south over a continent, we generally meet at successive intervals with closely allied or representative species, evidently filling nearly the same place in the natural economy of the land. These representative species often meet and interlock; and as the one becomes rarer and rarer, the other becomes more and more frequent, till the one replaces the other. But if we compare these species where they intermingle, they are generally as absolutely distinct from each other in every detail of structure as are specimens taken from the metropolis inhabited by each. By my theory these allied species are descended from a common parent; and during the process of modification, each has become adapted to the conditions of life of its own region, and has supplanted and exterminated its original parent-form and all the transitional varieties between its past and present states. Hence we ought not to expect at the present time to meet with numerous transitional varieties in each region, though they must have existed there, and may be embedded there in a fossil condition. But in the intermediate region, having intermediate conditions of life, why do we not now find closely-linking intermediate varieties? This difficulty for a long time quite confounded me. But I think it can be in large part explained.

In the first place we should be extremely cautious in inferring, because an area is now continuous, that it has been continuous during a long period. Geology would lead us to believe that most continents have been broken up into islands even during the later tertiary periods; and in such islands distinct species might have been separately formed without the possibility of intermediate varieties existing in the intermediate zones. By changes in the form of the land and of climate, marine areas now continuous must often have existed within recent times in a far less continuous and uniform condition than at present. But I will pass over this way of escaping from the difficulty; for I believe that many perfectly defined species have been formed on strictly continuous areas; though I do not doubt that the formerly broken condition of areas now continuous, has played an important part in the formation of new species, more especially with freely-crossing and wandering animals.

In looking at species as they are now distributed over a wide area, we generally find them tolerably numerous over a large territory, then becoming somewhat abruptly rarer and rarer on the confines, and finally disappearing. Hence the neutral territory, between two representative species is generally narrow in comparison with the territory proper to each. We see the same fact in ascending mountains, and sometimes it is quite remarkable how abruptly, as Alph. de Candolle has observed, a common alpine species disappears. The same fact has been noticed by E. Forbes in sounding the depths of the sea with the dredge. To those who look at climate and the physical conditions of life as the all-important elements of distribution, these facts ought to cause surprise, as climate and height or depth graduate away insensibly. But when we bear in mind that almost every species, even in its metropolis, would increase immensely in numbers, were it not for other competing species; that nearly all either prey on or serve as prey for others; in short, that each organic being is either directly or indirectly related in the most important manner to other organic beings,—we see that the range of the inhabitants of any country by no means exclusively depends on insensibly changing physical conditions, but in a large part on the presence of other species, on which it lives, or by which it is destroyed, or with which it comes into competition; and as these species are already defined objects, not blending one into another by insensible gradations, the range of any one species, depending as it does on the range of others, will tend to be sharply defined. Moreover, each species on the confines of its range, where it exists in lessened numbers, will, during fluctuations in the number of its enemies or of its prey, or in the nature of the seasons, be extremely liable to utter extermination; and thus its geographical range will come to be still more sharply defined.

As allied or representative species, when inhabiting a continuous area, are generally distributed in such a manner that each has a wide range, with a comparatively narrow neutral territory between them, in which they become rather suddenly rarer and rarer; then, as varieties do not essentially differ from species, the same rule will probably apply to both; and if we take a varying species inhabiting a very large area, we shall have to adapt two varieties to two large areas, and a third variety to a narrow intermediate zone. The intermediate variety, consequently, will exist in lesser numbers from inhabiting a narrow and lesser area; and practically, as far as I can make out, this rule holds good with varieties in a state of nature. I have met with striking instances of the rule in the case of varieties intermediate between well-marked varieties in the genus Balanus. And it would appear from information given me by Mr. Watson, Dr. Asa Gray, and Mr. Wollaston, that generally, when varieties intermediate between two other forms occur, they are much rarer numerically than the forms which they connect. Now, if we may trust these facts and inferences, and conclude that varieties linking two other varieties together generally have existed in lesser numbers than the forms which they connect, then we can understand why intermediate varieties should not endure for very long periods: —why, as a general rule, they should be exterminated and disappear, sooner than the forms which they originally linked together.

For any form existing in lesser numbers would, as already remarked, run a greater chance of being exterminated than one existing in large numbers; and in this particular case the intermediate form would be eminently liable to the inroads of closely-allied forms existing on both sides of it. But it is a far more important consideration, that during the process of further modification, by which two varieties are supposed to be converted and perfected into two distinct species, the two which exist in larger numbers, from inhabiting larger areas, will have a great advantage over the intermediate variety, which exists in smaller numbers in a narrow and intermediate zone. For forms existing in larger numbers will have a better chance, within any given period, of presenting further favourable variations for natural selection to seize on, than will the rarer forms which exist in lesser numbers. Hence, the more common forms, in the race for life, will tend to beat and supplant the less common forms, for these will be more slowly modified and improved. It is the same principle which, as I believe, accounts for the common species in each country, as shown in the second chapter, presenting on an average a greater number of well-marked varieties than do the rarer species. I may illustrate what I mean by supposing three varieties of sheep to be kept, one adapted to an extensive mountainous region; a second to a comparatively narrow, hilly tract; and a third to the wide plains at the base; and that the inhabitants are all trying with equal steadiness and skill to improve their stocks by selection; the chances in this case will be strongly in favour of the great holders on the mountains or on the plains, improving their breeds more quickly than the small holders on the intermediate narrow, hilly tract; and consequently the improved mountain or plain breed will soon take the place of the less improved hill breed; and thus the two breeds, which originally existed in greater numbers, will come into close contact with each other, without the interposition of the supplanted, intermediate hill variety.

To sum up, I believe that species come to be tolerably well-defined objects, and do not at any one period present an inextricable chaos of varying and intermediate links; first, because new varieties are very slowly formed, for variation is a slow process, and natural selection can do nothing until favourable individual differences or variations occur, and until a place in the natural polity of the country can be better filled by some modification of some one or more of its inhabitants. And such new places will depend on slow changes of climate, or on the occasional immigration of new inhabitants, and, probably, in a still more important degree, on some of the old inhabitants becoming slowly modified, with the new forms thus produced, and the old ones acting and reacting on each other. So that, in any one region and at any one time, we ought to see only a few species presenting slight modifications of structure in some degree permanent; and this assuredly we do see.

Secondly, areas now continuous must often have existed within the recent period as isolated portions, in which many forms, more especially amongst the classes which unite for each birth and wander much, may have separately been rendered sufficiently distinct to rank as representative species. In this case, intermediate varieties between the several representative species and their common parent, must formerly have existed within each isolated portion of the land, but these links during the process of natural selection will have been supplanted and exterminated, so that they will no longer be found in a living state.

Thirdly, when two or more varieties have been formed in different portions of a strictly continuous area, intermediate varieties will, it is probable, at first have been formed in the intermediate zones, but they will generally have had a short duration. For these intermediate varieties will, from reasons already assigned (namely from what we know of the actual distribution of closely allied or representative species, and likewise of acknowledged varieties), exist in the intermediate zones in lesser numbers than the varieties which they tend to connect. From this cause alone the intermediate varieties will be liable to accidental extermination; and during the process of further modification through natural selection, they will almost certainly be beaten and supplanted by the forms which they connect; for these from existing in greater numbers will, in the aggregate, present more varieties, and thus be further improved through natural selection and gain further advantages.

Lastly, looking not to any one time, but to all time, if my theory be true, numberless intermediate varieties, linking closely together all the species of the same group, must assuredly have existed; but the very process of natural selection constantly tends, as has been so often remarked, to exterminate the parent-forms and the intermediate links. Consequently evidence of their former existence could be found only amongst fossil remains, which are preserved, as we shall attempt to show in a future chapter, in an extremely imperfect and intermittent record.

ON THE ORIGIN AND TRANSITIONS OF ORGANIC BEINGS WITH PECULIAR HABITS AND STRUCTURE

It has been asked by the opponents of such views as I hold, how, for instance, could a land carnivorous animal have been converted into one with aquatic habits; for how could the animal in its transitional state have subsisted? It would be easy to show that there now exist carnivorous animals presenting close intermediate grades from strictly terrestrial to aquatic habits; and as each exists by a struggle for life, it is clear that each must be well adapted to its place in nature. Look at the Mustela vison of North America, which has webbed feet, and which resembles an otter in its fur, short legs, and form of tail. During the summer this animal dives for and preys on fish, but during the long winter it leaves the frozen waters, and preys, like other pole-cats, on mice and land animals. If a different case had been taken, and it had been asked how an insectivorous quadruped could possibly have been converted into a flying bat, the question would have been far more difficult to answer. Yet I think such difficulties have little weight.

Here, as on other occasions, I lie under a heavy disadvantage, for, out of the many striking cases which I have collected, I can only give one or two instances of transitional habits and structures in allied species; and of diversified habits, either constant or occasional, in the same species. And it seems to me that nothing less than a long list of such cases is sufficient to lessen the difficulty in any particular case like that of the bat.

Look at the family of squirrels; here we have the finest gradation from animals with their tails only slightly flattened, and from others, as Sir J. Richardson has remarked, with the posterior part of their bodies rather wide and with the skin on their flanks rather full, to the so-called flying squirrels; and flying squirrels have their limbs and even the base of the tail united by a broad expanse of skin, which serves as a parachute and allows them to glide through the air to an astonishing distance from tree to tree. We cannot doubt that each structure is of use to each kind of squirrel in its own country, by enabling it to escape birds or beasts of prey, to collect food more quickly, or, as there is reason to believe, to lessen the danger from occasional falls. But it does not follow from this fact that the structure of each squirrel is the best that it is possible to conceive under all possible conditions. Let the climate and vegetation change, let other competing rodents or new beasts of prey immigrate, or old ones become modified, and all analogy would lead us to believe that some at least of the squirrels would decrease in numbers or become exterminated, unless they also become modified and improved in structure in a corresponding manner. Therefore, I can see no difficulty, more especially under changing conditions of life, in the continued preservation of individuals with fuller and fuller flank-membranes, each modification being useful, each being propagated, until by the accumulated effects of this process of natural selection, a perfect so-called flying squirrel was produced.

Now look at the Galeopithecus or so-called flying lemur, which formerly was ranked amongst bats, but is now believed to belong to the Insectivora. An extremely wide flank-membrane stretches from the corners of the jaw to the tail, and includes the limbs with the elongated fingers. This flank-membrane is furnished with an extensor muscle. Although no graduated links of structure, fitted for gliding through the air, now connect the Galeopithecus with the other Insectivora, yet there is no difficulty in supposing that such links formerly existed, and that each was developed in the same manner as with the less perfectly gliding squirrels; each grade of structure having been useful to its possessor. Nor can I see any insuperable difficulty in further believing that the membrane connected fingers and fore-arm of the Galeopithecus might have been greatly lengthened by natural selection; and this, as far as the organs of flight are concerned, would have converted the animal into a bat. In certain bats in which the wing-membrane extends from the top of the shoulder to the tail and includes the hind-legs, we perhaps see traces of an apparatus originally fitted for gliding through the air rather than for flight.

If about a dozen genera of birds were to become extinct, who would have ventured to surmise that birds might have existed which used their wings solely as flappers, like the logger-headed duck (Micropterus of Eyton); as fins in the water and as front-legs on the land, like the penguin; as sails, like the ostrich; and functionally for no purpose, like the Apteryx? Yet the structure of each of these birds is good for it, under the conditions of life to which it is exposed, for each has to live by a struggle; but it is not necessarily the best possible under all possible conditions. It must not be inferred from these remarks that any of the grades of wing-structure here alluded to, which perhaps may all be the result of disuse, indicate the steps by which birds actually acquired their perfect power of flight; but they serve to show what diversified means of transition are at least possible.

Seeing that a few members of such water-breathing classes as the Crustacea and Mollusca are adapted to live on the land; and seeing that we have flying birds and mammals, flying insects of the most diversified types, and formerly had flying reptiles, it is conceivable that flying-fish, which now glide far through the air, slightly rising and turning by the aid of their fluttering fins, might have been modified into perfectly winged animals. If this had been effected, who would have ever imagined that in an early transitional state they had been the inhabitants of the open ocean, and had used their incipient organs of flight exclusively, as far as we know, to escape being devoured by other fish?

When we see any structure highly perfected for any particular habit, as the wings of a bird for flight, we should bear in mind that animals displaying early transitional grades of the structure will seldom have survived to the present day, for they will have been supplanted by their successors, which were gradually rendered more perfect through natural selection. Furthermore, we may conclude that transitional states between structures fitted for very different habits of life will rarely have been developed at an early period in great numbers and under many subordinate forms. Thus, to return to our imaginary illustration of the flying-fish, it does not seem probable that fishes capable of true flight would have been developed under many subordinate forms, for taking prey of many kinds in many ways, on the land and in the water, until their organs of flight had come to a high stage of perfection, so as to have given them a decided advantage over other animals in the battle for life. Hence the chance of discovering species with transitional grades of structure in a fossil condition will always be less, from their having existed in lesser numbers, than in the case of species with fully developed structures.

I will now give two or three instances both of diversified and of changed habits in the individuals of the same species. In either case it would be easy for natural selection to adapt the structure of the animal to its changed habits, or exclusively to one of its several habits. It is, however, difficult to decide, and immaterial for us, whether habits generally change first and structure afterwards; or whether slight modifications of structure lead to changed habits; both probably often occurring almost simultaneously. Of cases of changed habits it will suffice merely to allude to that of the many British insects which now feed on exotic plants, or exclusively on artificial substances. Of diversified habits innumerable instances could be given: I have often watched a tyrant flycatcher (Saurophagus sulphuratus) in South America, hovering over one spot and then proceeding to another, like a kestrel, and at other times standing stationary on the margin of water, and then dashing into it like a king-fisher at a fish. In our own country the larger titmouse (Parus major) may be seen climbing branches, almost like a creeper; it sometimes, like a shrike, kills small birds by blows on the head; and I have many times seen and heard it hammering the seeds of the yew on a branch, and thus breaking them like a nuthatch. In North America the black bear was seen by Hearne swimming for hours with widely open mouth, thus catching, almost like a whale, insects in the water.

As we sometimes see individuals following habits different from those proper to their species and to the other species of the same genus, we might expect that such individuals would occasionally give rise to new species, having anomalous habits, and with their structure either slightly or considerably modified from that of their type. And such instances occur in nature. Can a more striking instance of adaptation be given than that of a woodpecker for climbing trees and seizing insects in the chinks of the bark? Yet in North America there are woodpeckers which feed largely on fruit, and others with elongated wings which chase insects on the wing. On the plains of La Plata, where hardly a tree grows, there is a woodpecker (Colaptes campestris) which has two toes before and two behind, a long pointed tongue, pointed tail-feathers, sufficiently stiff to support the bird in a vertical position on a post, but not so stiff as in the typical woodpeckers, and a straight strong beak. The beak, however, is not so straight or so strong as in the typical woodpeckers, but it is strong enough to bore into wood. Hence this Colaptes in all the essential parts of its structure is a woodpecker. Even in such trifling characters as the colouring, the harsh tone of the voice, and undulatory flight, its close blood-relationship to our common woodpecker is plainly declared; yet, as I can assert, not only from my own observation, but from those of the accurate Azara, in certain large districts it does not climb trees, and it makes its nest in holes in banks! In certain other districts, however, this same woodpecker, as Mr. Hudson states, frequents trees, and bores holes in the trunk for its nest. I may mention as another illustration of the varied habits of this genus, that a Mexican Colaptes has been described by De Saussure as boring holes into hard wood in order to lay up a store of acorns.

Petrels are the most aërial and oceanic of birds, but in the quiet sounds of Tierra del Fuego, the Puffinuria berardi, in its general habits, in its astonishing power of diving, in its manner of swimming and of flying when made to take flight, would be mistaken by any one for an auk or a grebe; nevertheless it is essentially a petrel, but with many parts of its organisation profoundly modified in relation to its new habits of life; whereas the woodpecker of La Plata has had its structure only slightly modified. In the case of the water-ouzel, the acutest observer by examining its dead body would never have suspected its sub-aquatic habits; yet this bird, which is allied to the thrush family, subsists by diving—using its wings under water, and grasping stones with its feet. All the members of the great order of Hymenopterous insects are terrestrial, excepting the genus Proctotrupes, which Sir John Lubbock has discovered to be aquatic in its habits; it often enters the water and dives about by the use not of its legs but of its wings, and remains as long as four hours beneath the surface; yet it exhibits no modification in structure in accordance with its abnormal habits.

He who believes that each being has been created as we now see it, must occasionally have felt surprise when he has met with an animal having habits and structure not in agreement. What can be plainer than that the webbed feet of ducks and geese are formed for swimming? Yet there are upland geese with webbed feet which rarely go near the water; and no one except Audubon has seen the frigate-bird, which has all its four toes webbed, alight on the surface of the ocean. On the other hand, grebes and coots are eminently aquatic, although their toes are only bordered by membrane. What seems plainer than that the long toes, not furnished with membrane of the Grallatores are formed for walking over swamps and floating plants?—the waterhen and landrail are members of this order, yet the first is nearly as aquatic as the coot, and the second nearly as terrestrial as the quail or partridge. In such cases, and many others could be given, habits have changed without a corresponding change of structure. The webbed feet of the upland goose may be said to have become almost rudimentary in function, though not in structure. In the frigate-bird, the deeply scooped membrane between the toes shows that structure has begun to change.

He who believes in separate and innumerable acts of creation may say, that in these cases it has pleased the Creator to cause a being of one type to take the place of one belonging to another type; but this seems to me only re-stating the fact in dignified language. He who believes in the struggle for existence and in the principle of natural selection, will acknowledge that every organic being is constantly endeavouring to increase in numbers; and that if any one being varies ever so little, either in habits or structure, and thus gains an advantage over some other inhabitant of the same country, it will seize on the place of that inhabitant, however different that may be from its own place. Hence it will cause him no surprise that there should be geese and frigate-birds with webbed feet, living on the dry land and rarely alighting on the water, that there should be long-toed corncrakes, living in meadows instead of in swamps; that there should be woodpeckers where hardly a tree grows; that there should be diving thrushes and diving Hymenoptera, and petrels with the habits of auks.

ORGANS OF EXTREME PERFECTION AND COMPLICATION

To suppose that the eye with all its inimitable contrivances for adjusting the focus to different distances, for admitting different amounts of light, and for the correction of spherical and chromatic aberration, could have been formed by natural selection, seems, I freely confess, absurd in the highest degree. When it was first said that the sun stood still and the world turned round, the common sense of mankind declared the doctrine false; but the old saying of Vox *populi*, *vox Dei*, as every philosopher knows, cannot be trusted in science. Reason tells me, that if numerous gradations from a simple and imperfect eye to one complex and perfect can be shown to exist, each grade being useful to its possessor, as is certainly the case; if further, the eye ever varies and the variations be inherited, as is likewise certainly the case; and if such variations should be useful to any animal under changing conditions of life, then the difficulty of believing that a perfect and complex eye could be formed by natural selection, though insuperable by our imagination, should not be considered as subversive of the theory. How a nerve comes to be sensitive to light, hardly concerns us more than how life itself originated; but I may remark that, as some of the lowest organisms, in which nerves cannot be detected, are capable of perceiving light, it does not seem impossible that certain elements in their sarcode should become aggregated and developed into nerves, endowed with this special sensibility.

In searching for the gradations through which an organ in any species has been perfected, we ought to look exclusively to its lineal progenitors; but this is scarcely ever possible, and we are forced to look to other species and genera of the same group, that is to the collateral descendants from the same parent-form, in order to see what gradations are possible, and for the chance of some gradations having been transmitted in an unaltered or little altered condition. But the state of the same organ in distinct classes may incidentally throw light on the steps by which it has been perfected.

The simplest organ which can be called an eye consists of an optic nerve, surrounded by pigment-cells and covered by translucent skin, but without any lens or other refractive body. We may, however, according to M. Jourdain, descend even a step lower and find aggregates of pigment-cells, apparently serving as organs of vision, without any nerves, and resting merely on sarcodic tissue. Eyes of the above simple nature are not capable of distinct vision, and serve only to distinguish light from darkness. In certain starfishes, small depressions in the layer of pigment which surrounds the nerve are filled, as described by the author just quoted, with transparent gelatinous matter, projecting with a convex surface, like the cornea in the higher animals. He suggests that this serves not to form an image, but only to concentrate the luminous rays and render their perception more easy. In this concentration of the rays we gain the first and by far the most important step towards the formation of a true, picture-forming eye; for we have only to place the naked extremity of the optic nerve, which in some of the lower animals lies deeply buried in the body, and in some near the surface, at the right distance from the concentrating apparatus, and an image will be formed on it.

In the great class of the Articulata, we may start from an optic nerve simply coated with pigment, the latter sometimes forming a sort of pupil, but destitute of a lens or other optical contrivance. With insects it is now known that the numerous facets on the cornea of their great compound eyes form true lenses, and that the cones include curiously modified nervous filaments. But these organs in the Articulata are so much diversified that Müller formerly made three main classes with seven subdivisions, besides a fourth main class of aggregated simple eyes.

When we reflect on these facts, here given much too briefly, with respect to the wide, diversified, and graduated range of structure in the eyes of the lower animals; and when we bear in mind how small the number of all living forms must be in comparison with those which have become extinct, the difficulty ceases to be very great in believing that natural selection may have converted the simple apparatus of an optic nerve, coated with pigment and invested by transparent membrane, into an optical instrument as perfect as is possessed by any member of the Articulate Class.

He who will go thus far, ought not to hesitate to go one step further, if he finds on finishing this volume that large bodies of facts, otherwise inexplicable, can be explained by the theory of modification through natural selection; he ought to admit that with a structure even as perfect as an eagle's eye might thus be formed, although in this case he does not know the transitional states. It has been objected that in order to modify the eye and still preserve it as a perfect instrument, many changes would have to be effected simultaneously, which, it is assumed, could not be done through natural selection; but as I have attempted to show in my work on the variation of domestic animals, it is not necessary to suppose that the modifications were all simultaneous, if they were extremely slight and gradual. Different kinds of modification would, also, serve for the same general purpose: as Mr. Wallace has remarked, "if a lens has too short or too long a focus, it may be amended either by an alteration of curvature, or an alteration of density; if the curvature be irregular, and the rays do not converge to a point, then any increased regularity of curvature will be an improvement. So the contraction of the iris and the muscular movements of the eye are neither of them essential to vision, but only improvements which might have been added and perfected at any stage of the construction of the instrument." Within the highest division of the animal kingdom, namely, the Vertebrata, we can start from an eye so simple, that it consists, as in the lancelet, of a little sack of transparent skin, furnished with a nerve and lined with pigment, but destitute of any other apparatus. In fishes and reptiles, as Owen has remarked, "the range of gradations of dioptric structures is very great." It is a significant fact that even in man, according to the high authority of Virchow, the beautiful crystalline lens is formed in the embryo by an accumulation of epidermic cells, lying in a sack-like fold of the skin; and the vitreous body is formed from embryonic subcutaneous tissue. To arrive, however, at a just conclusion regarding the formation of the eye, with all its marvellous yet not absolutely perfect characters, it is indispensable that the reason should conquer the imagination; but I have felt the difficulty far too keenly to be surprised at others hesitating to extend the principle of natural selection to so startling a length.

It is scarcely possible to avoid comparing the eye with a telescope. We know that this instrument has been perfected by the long-continued efforts of the highest human intellects; and we naturally infer that the eye has been formed by a somewhat analogous process. But may not this inference be presumptuous? Have we any right to assume that the Creator works by intellectual powers like those of man? If we must compare the eye to an optical instrument, we ought in imagination to take a thick layer of transparent tissue, with spaces filled with fluid, and with a nerve sensitive to light beneath, and then suppose every part of this layer to be continually changing slowly in density, so as to separate into layers of different densities and thicknesses, placed at different distances from each other, and with the surfaces of each layer slowly changing in form. Further we must suppose that there is a power, represented by natural selection or the survival of the fittest, always intently watching each slight alteration in the transparent layers; and carefully preserving each which, under varied circumstances, in any way or in any degree, tends to produce a distincter image. We must suppose each new state of the instrument to be multiplied by the million; each to be preserved until a better one is produced, and then the old ones to be all destroyed. In living bodies, variation will cause the slight alterations, generation will multiply them almost infinitely, and natural selection will pick out with unerring skill each improvement. Let this process go on for millions of years; and during each year on millions of individuals of many kinds; and may we not believe that a living optical instrument might thus be formed as superior to one of glass, as the works of the Creator are to those of man? * * *

SUMMARY: THE LAW OF UNITY OF TYPE AND OF THE CONDITIONS OF
    EXISTENCE EMBRACED BY THE THEORY OF NATURAL SELECTION

We have in this chapter discussed some of the difficulties and objections which may be urged against the theory. Many of them are serious; but I think that in the discussion light has been thrown on several facts, which on the belief of independent acts of creation are utterly obscure. We have seen that species at any one period are not indefinitely variable, and are not linked together by a multitude of intermediate gradations, partly because the process of natural selection is always very slow, and at any one time acts only on a few forms; and partly because the very process of natural selection implies the continual supplanting and extinction of preceding and intermediate gradations. Closely allied species, now living on a continuous area, must often have been formed when the area was not continuous, and when the conditions of life did not insensibly graduate away from one part to another. When two varieties are formed in two districts of a continuous area, an intermediate variety will often be formed, fitted for an intermediate zone; but from reasons assigned, the intermediate variety will usually exist in lesser numbers than the two forms which it connects; consequently the two latter, during the course of further modification, from existing in greater numbers, will have a great advantage over the less numerous intermediate variety, and will thus generally succeed in supplanting and exterminating it.

We have seen in this chapter how cautious we should be in concluding that the most different habits of life could not graduate into each other; that a bat, for instance, could not have been formed by natural selection from an animal which at first only glided through the air.

We have seen that a species under new conditions of life may change its habits; or it may have diversified habits, with some very unlike those of its nearest congeners. Hence we can understand, bearing in mind that each organic being is trying to live wherever it can live, how it has arisen that there are upland geese with webbed feet, ground woodpeckers, diving thrushes, and petrels with the habits of auks.

Although the belief that an organ so perfect as the eye could have been formed by natural selection, is enough to stagger any one; yet in the case of any organ, if we know of a long series of gradations in complexity, each good for its possessor, then, under changing conditions of life, there is no logical impossibility in th

acquirement of any conceivable degree of perfection through natural selection. In the cases in which we know of no intermediate or transitional states, we should be extremely cautious in
concluding that none can have existed, for the metamorphoses of
many organs show what wonderful changes in function are at least
possible. For instance, a swimbladder has apparently been converted into an air-breathing lung. The same organ having performed simultaneously very different functions, and then having
been in part or in whole specialised for one function; and two distinct organs having performed at the same time the same function, the one having been perfected whilst aided by the other, must
often have largely facilitated transitions.

We have seen that in two beings widely remote from each other
in the natural scale, organs serving for the same purpose and in
external appearance closely similar may have been separately and
independently formed; but when such organs are closely examined,
essential differences in their structure can almost always be detected; and this naturally follows from the principle of natural
selection. On the other hand, the common rule throughout nature
is infinite diversity of structure for gaining the same end; and this
again naturally follows from the same great principle.

In many cases we are far too ignorant to be enabled to assert that
a part or organ is so unimportant for the welfare of a species, that
modifications in its structure could not have been slowly accumulated by means of natural selection. In many other cases, modifications are probably the direct result of the laws of variation or of
growth, independently of any good having been thus gained. But
even such structures have often, as we may feel assured, been subsequently taken advantage of, and still further modified, for the
good of species under new conditions of life. We may, also, believe
that a part formerly of high importance has frequently been
retained (as the tail of an aquatic animal by its terrestrial descendants), though it has become of such small importance that it
could not, in its present state, have been acquired by means of
natural selection.

Natural selection can produce nothing in one species for the
exclusive good or injury of another; though it may well produce
parts, organs, and excretions highly useful or even indispensable,
or again highly injurious to another species, but in all cases at the
same time useful to the possessor. In each well-stocked country
natural selection acts through the competition of the inhabitants,
and consequently leads to success in the battle for life, only in
accordance with the standard of that particular country. Hence the
inhabitants of one country, generally the smaller one, often yield
to the inhabitants of another and generally the larger country. For
in the larger country there will have existed more individuals and

more diversified forms, and the competition will have been severer, and thus the standard of perfection will have been rendered higher. Natural selection will not necessarily lead to absolute perfection; nor, as far as we can judge by our limited faculties, can absolute perfection be everywhere predicated.

On the theory of natural selection we can clearly understand the full meaning of that old canon in natural history, "Natura non facit saltum." This canon, if we look to the present inhabitants alone of the world, is not strictly correct; but if we include all those of past times, whether known or unknown, it must on this theory be strictly true.

It is generally acknowledged that all organic beings have been formed on two great laws—Unity of Type, and the Conditions of Existence. By unity of type is meant that fundamental agreement in structure which we see in organic beings of the same class, and which is quite independent of their habits of life. On my theory, unity of type is explained by unity of descent. The expression of conditions is fully embraced by the principle of natural selection. For natural selection acts by either now adapting the varying parts of each being to its organic and inorganic conditions of life; or by having adapted them during past periods of time: the adaptations being aided in many cases by the increased use or disuse of parts, being affected by the direct action of the external conditions of life, and subjected in all cases to the several laws of growth and variation. Hence, in fact, the law of the Conditions of Existence is the higher law; as it includes, through the inheritance of former variations and adaptations, that of Unity of Type.

Chapter X

ON THE IMPERFECTION OF THE GEOLOGICAL RECORD

On the absence of intermediate varieties at the present day—On the nature of extinct intermediate varieties; on their number—On the lapse of time, as inferred from the rate of denudation and of deposition—On the lapse of time as estimated by years—On the poorness of our palæontological collections—On the intermittence of geological formations—On the denudation of granitic areas—On the absence of intermediate varieties in any one formation—On the sudden appearance of groups of species—On their sudden appearance in the lowest known fossiliferous strata—Antiquity of the habitable earth.

In the sixth chapter I enumerated the chief objections which might be justly urged against the views maintained in this volume.

Most of them have now been discussed. One, namely the distinctness of specific forms, and their not being blended together by innumerable transitional links, is a very obvious difficulty. I assigned reasons why such links do not commonly occur at the present day under the circumstances apparently most favourable for their presence, namely, on an extensive and continuous area with graduated physical conditions. I endeavoured to show, that the life of each species depends in a more important manner on the presence of other already defined organic forms, than on climate, and, therefore, that the really governing conditions of life do not graduate away quite insensibly like heat or moisture. I endeavoured, also, to show that intermediate varieties, from existing in lesser numbers than the forms which they connect, will generally be beaten out and exterminated during the course of further modification and improvement. The main cause, however, of innumerable intermediate links not now occurring everywhere throughout nature, depends on the very process of natural selection, through which new varieties continually take the places of and supplant their parent-forms. But just in proportion as this process of extermination has acted on an enormous scale, so must the number of intermediate varieties, which have formerly existed, be truly enormous. Why then is not every geological formation and every stratum full of such intermediate links? Geology assuredly does not reveal any such finely-graduated organic chain; and this, perhaps, is the most obvious and serious objection which can be urged against the theory. The explanation lies, as I believe, in the extreme imperfection of the geological record.

In the first place, it should always be borne in mind what sort of intermediate forms must, on the theory, have formerly existed. I have found it difficult, when looking at any two species, to avoid picturing to myself forms *directly* intermediate between them. But this is a wholly false view; we should always look for forms intermediate between each species and a common but unknown progenitor; and the progenitor will generally have differed in some respects from all its modified descendants. To give a simple illustration: the fantail and pouter pigeons are both descended from the rock-pigeon; if we possessed all the intermediate varieties which have ever existed, we should have an extremely close series between both and the rock-pigeon; but we should have no varieties directly intermediate between the fantail and pouter; none, for instance, combining a tail somewhat expanded with a crop somewhat enlarged, the characteristic features of these two breeds. These two breeds, moreover, have become so much modified, that, if we had no historical or indirect evidence regarding their origin, it would not have been possible to have determined, from a mere comparison of their structure with that of the rock-pigeon, C. livia, whether they had descended from this species or from some allied form, such as C. œnas.

So, with natural species, if we look to forms very distinct, for instance to the horse and tapir, we have no reason to suppose that links directly intermediate between them ever existed, but between each and an unknown common parent. The common parent will have had in its whole organisation much general resemblance to the tapir and to the horse; but in some points of structure may have differed considerably from both, even perhaps more than they differ from each other. Hence, in all such cases, we should be unable to recognise the parent-form of any two or more species, even if we closely compared the structure of the parent with that of its modified descendants, unless at the same time we had a nearly perfect chain of the intermediate links.

It is just possible by the theory, that one of two living forms might have descended from the other; for instance, a horse from a tapir; and in this case *direct* intermediate links will have existed between them. But such a case would imply that one form had remained for a very long period unaltered, whilst its descendants had undergone a vast amount of change; and the principle of competition between organism and organism, between child and parent, will render this a very rare event; for in all cases the new and improved forms of life tend to supplant the old and unimproved forms.

By the theory of natural selection all living species have been connected with the parent-species of each genus, by differences not greater than we see between the natural and domestic varieties of the same species at the present day; and these parent-species, now generally extinct, have in their turn been similarly connected with more ancient forms; and so on backwards, always converging to the common anestor of each great class. So that the number of intermediate and transitional links, between all living and extinct species, must have been inconceivably great. But assuredly, if this theory be true, such have lived upon the earth.

ON THE LAPSE OF TIME, AS INFERRED FROM THE RATE OF DEPOSITION AND EXTENT OF DENUDATION

Independently of our not finding fossil remains of such infinitely numerous connecting links, it may be objected that time cannot have sufficed for so great an amount of organic change, all changes having been effected slowly. It is hardly possible for me to recall to the reader who is not a practical geologist, the facts leading the mind feebly to comprehend the lapse of time. He who can read Sir Charles Lyell's grand work on the Principles of Geology, which the future historian will recognise as having produced a revolution in natural science, and yet does not admit how vast have been the past periods of time, may at once close this volume. Not that it suffices to study the Principles of Geology, or to read special treatises by different observers on separate formations, and to mark how each author attempts to give an inadequate idea of the duration of each formation, or even of each stratum. We can best gain some idea of past time by knowing the agencies at work, and learning how deeply the surface of the land has been denuded, and how much sediment has been deposited. As Lyell has well remarked, the extent and thickness of our sedimentary formations are the result and the measure of the denudation which the earth's crust has elsewhere undergone. Therefore a man should examine for himself the great piles of superimposed strata, and watch the rivulets bringing down mud, and the waves wearing away the sea-cliffs, in order to comprehend something about the duration of past time, the monuments of which we see all around us. * * *

ON THE POORNESS OF PALAEONTOLOGICAL COLLECTIONS

Now let us turn to our richest geological museums, and what a paltry display we behold! That our collections are imperfect is admitted by every one. The remark of that admirable palæontologist, Edward Forbes, should never be forgotten, namely, that very many fossil species are known and named from single and often broken specimens, or from a few specimens collected on some one spot. Only a small portion of the surface of the earth has been geologically explored, and no part with sufficient care, as the important discoveries made every year in Europe prove. No organism wholly soft can be preserved. Shells and bones decay and disappear when left on the bottom of the sea, where sediment is not accumulating. We probably take a quite erroneous view, when we assume that sediment is being deposited over nearly the whole bed of the sea, at a rate sufficiently quick to embed and preserve fossil remains. Throughout an enormously large proportion of the ocean, the bright blue tint of the water bespeaks its purity. The many cases on record of a formation conformably covered, after an immense interval of time, by another and later formation, without the underlying bed having suffered in the interval any wear and tear, seem explicable only on the view of the bottom of the sea not rarely lying for ages in an unaltered condition. The remains which do become embedded, if in sand or gravel, will, when the beds are upraised generally be dissolved by the percolation of rain-water charged with carbonic acid. Some of the many kinds of animals which live on the beach between high and low water mark seem to be rarely preserved. For instance, the several species of the Chthamalinæ (a subfamily of sessile cirripedes) coat the rocks all over the world in infinite numbers: they are all strictly littoral, with the exception of a single Mediterranean species, which inhabits deep water, and this has been found fossil in Sicily, whereas not one other species has hitherto been found in any tertiary formation: yet it is known that the genus Chthamalus existed during the Chalk period. Lastly, many great deposits requiring a vast length of time for their accumulation, are entirely destitute of organic remains, without our being able to assign any reason: one of the most striking instances is that of the Flysch formation, which consists of shale and sandstone, several thousand, occasionally even six thousand feet in thickness, and extending for at least 300 miles from Vienna to Switzerland; and although this great mass has been most carefully searched, no fossils, except a few vegetable remains, have been found.

With respect to the terrestrial productions which lived during the Secondary and Palæozoic periods, it is superfluous to state that our evidence is fragmentary in an extreme degree. For instance, until recently not a land-shell was known belonging to either of these vast periods, with the exception of one species discovered by Sir C. Lyell and Dr. Dawson in the carboniferous strata of North America; but now land-shells have been found in the lias. In regard to mammiferous remains, a glance at the historical table published in Lyell's Manual will bring home the truth, how accidental and rare is their preservation, far better than pages of detail. Nor is their rarity surprising, when we remember how large a proportion of the bones of tertiary mammals have been discovered either in caves or in lacustrine deposits; and that not a cave or true lacustrine bed is known belonging to the age of our secondary or palæozoic formations.

But the imperfection in the geological record largely results from another and more important cause than any of the foregoing; namely, from the several formations being separated from each other by wide intervals of time. This doctrine has been emphatically admitted by many geologists and palæontologists, who, like E. Forbes, entirely disbelieve in the change of species. When we see the formations tabulated in written works, or when we follow them in nature, it is difficult to avoid believing that they are closely consecutive. But we know, for instance, from Sir R. Murchison's great work on Russia, what wide gaps there are in that country between the superimposed formations; so it is in North America, and in many other parts of the world. The most skilful geologist, if his attention had been confined exclusively to these large territories, would never have suspected that, during the periods which were blank and barren in his own country, great piles of sediment, charged with new and peculiar forms of life, had elsewhere been accumulated. And if, in each separate territory, hardly any idea can be formed of the length of time which has elapsed between the consecutive formations, we may infer that this could nowhere be ascertained. The frequent and great changes in the mineralogical composition of consecutive formations, generally implying great changes in the geography of the surrounding lands, whence the sediment was derived, accord with the belief of vast intervals of time having elapsed between each formation. * * *

* * * Those who believe that the geological record is in any degree perfect, will undoubtedly at once reject the theory. For my part, following out Lyell's metaphor, I look at the geological record as a history of the world imperfectly kept, and written in a changing dialect; of this history we possess the last volume alone, relating only to two or three countries. Of this volume, only here and there a short chapter has been preserved; and of each page, only here and there a few lines. Each word of the slowly-changing language, more or less different in the successive chapters, may represent the forms of life, which are entombed in our consecutive formations, and which falsely appear to have been abruptly introduced. On this view, the difficulties above discussed are greatly diminished, or even disappear.

Chapter XV

RECAPITULATION AND CONCLUSION

Recapitulation of the objections to the theory of natural selection —Recapitulation of the general and special circumstances in its favour—Causes of the general belief in the immutability of species —How far the theory of natural selection may be extended—Effects of its adoption on the study of natural history—Concluding remarks.

As this whole volume is one long argument, it may be convenient to the reader to have the leading facts and inferences briefly recapitulated.

That many and serious objections may be advanced against the theory of descent with modification through variation and natural selection, I do not deny. I have endeavored to give to them their full force. Nothing at first can appear more difficult to believe than that the more complex organs and instincts have been perfected, not by means superior to, though analogous with, human reason, but by the accumulation of innumerable slight variations, each good for the individual possessor. Nevertheless, this difficulty, though appearing to our imagination insuperably great, cannot be considered real if we admit the following propositions, namely, that all parts of the organisation and instincts offer, at least, individual differences—that there is a struggle for existence leading to the preservation of profitable deviations of structure or instinct—and, lastly, that gradations in the state of perfection of each organ may have existed, each good of its kind. The truth of these propositions cannot, I think, be disputed.

It is, no doubt, extremely difficult even to conjecture by what gradations many structures have been perfected, more especially amongst broken and failing groups of organic beings, which have suffered much extinction, but we see so many strange gradations in nature, that we ought to be extremely cautious in saying that any organ or instinct, or any whole structure, could not have arrived at its present state by many graduated steps. There are, it must be admitted, cases of special difficulty opposed to the theory of natural selection; and one of the most curious of these is the existence in the same community of two or three defined castes of workers or sterile female ants; but I have attempted to show how these difficulties can be mastered.

With respect to the almost universal sterility of species when first crossed, which forms so remarkable a contrast with the almost universal fertility of varieties when crossed, I must refer the reader to the recapitulation of the facts given at the end of the ninth chapter, which seem to me conclusively to show that this sterility is no more a special endowment than is the incapacity of two distinct kinds of trees to be grafted together; but that it is incidental on differences confined to the reproductive systems of the intercrossed species. We see the truth of this conclusion in the vast difference in the results of crossing the same two species reciprocally,—that is, when one species is first used as the father and then as the mother. Analogy from the consideration of dimorphic and trimorphic plants clearly leads to the same conclusion, for when the forms are illegitimately united, they yield few or no seed, and their offspring are more or less sterile; and these forms belong to the same undoubted species, and differ from each other in no respect except in their reproductive organs and functions.

Although the fertility of varieties when intercrossed and of their mongrel offspring has been asserted by so many authors to be universal, this cannot be considered as quite correct after the facts given on the high authority of Gärtner and Kölreuter. Most of the varieties which have been experimented on have been produced under domestication; and as domestication (I do not mean mere confinement) almost certainly tends to eliminate that sterility which, judging from analogy, would have affected the parent-species if intercrossed, we ought not to expect that domestication would likewise induce sterility in their modified descendants when crossed. This elimination of sterility apparently follows from the same cause which allows our domestic animals to breed freely under diversified circumstances; and this again apparently follows from their having been gradually accustomed to frequent changes in their conditions of life.

A double and parallel series of facts seems to throw much light on the sterility of species, when first crossed, and of their hybrid offspring. On the one side, there is good reason to believe that slight changes in the conditions of life give vigour and fertility to all organic beings. We know also that a cross between the distinct individuals of the same variety, and between distinct varieties, increases the number of their offspring, and certainly gives to them increased size and vigour. This is chiefly owing to the forms which are crossed having been exposed to somewhat different conditions of life; for I have ascertained by a laborious series of experiments that if all the individuals of the same variety be subjected during several generations to the same conditions, the good derived from crossing is often much diminished or wholly disappears. This is one side of the case. On the other side, we know that species which have long been exposed to nearly uniform conditions, when they are subjected under confinement to new and greatly changed conditions, either perish, or if they survive, are rendered sterile, though retaining perfect health. This does not occur, or only in a very slight degree, with our domesticated productions, which have long been exposed to fluctuating conditions. Hence when we find that hybrids produced by a cross between two distinct species are few in number, owing to their perishing soon after conception or at a very early age, or if surviving that they are rendered more or less sterile, it seems highly probable that this result is due to their having been in fact subjected to a great change in their conditions of life, from being compounded of two distinct organisations. He who will explain in a definite manner why, for instance, an elephant or a fox will not breed under confinement in its native country, whilst the domestic pig or dog will breed freely under the most diversified conditions, will at the same time be able to give a definite answer to the question why two distinct species, when crossed, as well as their hybrid offspring, are generally rendered more or less sterile, whilst two domesticated varieties when crossed and their mongrel offspring are perfectly fertile.

Turning to geographical distribution, the difficulties encountered on the theory of descent with modification are serious enough. All the individuals of the same species, and all the species of the same genus, or even higher group, are descended from common parents; and therefore, in however distant and isolated parts of the world they may now be found, they must in the course of successive generations have travelled from some one point to all the others. We are often wholly unable even to conjecture how this could have been effected. Yet, as we have reason to believe that some species have retained the same specific form for very long periods of time, immensely long as measured by years, too much stress ought not to be laid on the occasional wide diffusion of the same species; for during very long periods there will always have been a good chance for wide migration by many means. A broken or interrupted range may often be accounted for by the extinction of the species in the intermediate regions. It cannot be denied that we are as yet very ignorant as to the full extent of the various climatal and geographical changes which have affected the earth during modern periods; and such changes will often have facilitated migration. As an example, I have attempted to show how potent has been the influence of the Glacial period on the distribution of the same and of allied species throughout the world. We are as yet profoundly ignorant of the many occasional means of transport. With respect to distinct species of the same genus inhabiting distant and isolated regions, as the process of modification has necessarily been slow, all the means of migration will have been possible during a very long period; and consequently the difficulty of the wide diffusion of the species of the same genus is in some degree lessened.

As according to the theory of natural selection an interminable number of intermediate forms must have existed, linking together all the species in each group by gradations as fine are our existing varieties, it may be asked: Why do we not see these linking forms all around us? Why are not all organic beings blended together in an inextricable chaos? With respect to existing forms, we should remember that we have no right to expect (excepting in rare cases) to discover *directly* connecting links between them, but only between each and some extinct and supplanted form. Even on a wide area, which has during a long period remained continuous, and of which the climatic and other conditions of life change insensibly in proceeding from a district occupied by one species into another district occupied by a closely allied species, we have no just right to expect often to find intermediate varieties in the intermediate zones. For we have reason to believe that only a few species of a genus ever undergo change; the other species becoming utterly extinct and leaving no modified progeny. Of the species which do change, only a few within the same country change at the same time; and all modifications are slowly effected. I have also shown that the intermediate varieties which probably at first existed in the intermediate zones, would be liable to be supplanted by the allied forms on either hand; for the latter, from existing in greater numbers, would generally be modified and improved at a quicker rate than the intermediate varieties, which existed in lesser numbers; so that the intermediate varieties would, in the long run, be supplanted and exterminated.

On this doctrine of the extermination of an infinitude of connecting links, between the living and extinct inhabitants of the world, and at each successive period between the extinct and still older species, why is not every geological formation charged with such links? Why does not every collection of fossil remains afford plain evidence of the gradation and mutation of the forms of life? Although geological research has undoubtedly revealed the former existence of many links, bringing numerous forms of life much closer together, it does not yield the infinitely many fine gradations between past and present species required on the theory; and this is the most obvious of the many objections which may be urged against it. Why, again, do whole groups of allied species appear, though this appearance is often false, to have come in suddenly on the successive geological stages? Although we now know that organic beings appeared on this globe, at a period incalculably remote, long before the lowest bed of the Cambrian system was deposited, why do we not find beneath this system great piles of strata stored with the remains of the progenitors of the Cambrian fossils? For on the theory, such strata must somewhere have been deposited at these ancient and utterly unknown epochs of the world's history.

I can answer these questions and objections only on the supposition that the geological record is far more imperfect than most geologists believe. The number of specimens in all our museums is absolutely as nothing compared with the countless generations of countless species which have certainly existed. The parent-form of any two or more species would not be in all its characters directly intermediate between its modified offspring, any more than the rock-pigeon is directly intermediate in crop and tail between its descendants, the pouter and fantail pigeons. We should not be able to recognise a species as the parent of another and modified species, if we were to examine the two ever so closely, unless we possessed most of the intermediate links; and owing to the imperfection of the geological record, we have no just right to expect to find so many links. If two or three, or even more linking forms were discovered, they would simply be ranked by many naturalists as so many new species, more especially if found in different geological sub-stages, let their differences be ever so slight. Numerous existing doubtful forms could be named which are probably varieties; but who will pretend that in future ages so many fossil links will be discovered, that naturalists will be able to decide whether or not these doubtful forms ought to be called varieties? Only a small portion of the world has been geologically explored. Only organic beings of certain classes can be preserved in a fossil condition, at least in any great number. Many species when once formed never undergo any further change but become extinct without leaving modified descendants; and the periods, during which species have undergone modification, though long as measured by years, have probably been short in comparison with the periods during which they retain the same form. It is the dominant and widely ranging species which vary most frequently and vary most, and varieties are often at first local—both causes rendering the discovery of inter-mediate links in any one formation less likely. Local varieties will not spread into other and distant regions until they are consider-ably modified and improved; and when they have spread, and are discovered in a geological formation, they appear as if suddenly created there, and will be simply classed as new species. Most formations have been intermittent in their accumulation; and their duration has probably been shorter than the average duration of specific forms. Successive formations are in most cases separated from each other by blank intervals of time of great length; for fossiliferous formations thick enough to resist future degradations can as a general rule be accumulated only where much sediment is deposited on the subsiding bed of the sea. During the alternate periods of elevation and of stationary level the record will generally be blank. During these latter periods there will probably be more variability in the forms of life; during periods of subsidence, more extinction.

With respect to the absence of strata rich in fossils beneath the Cambrian formation, I can recur only to the hypothesis given in the tenth chapter; namely, that though our continents and oceans have endured for an enormous period in nearly their present rela-tive positions, we have no reason to assume that this has always been the case; consequently formations much older than any now known may lie buried beneath the great oceans. With respect to the lapse of time not having been sufficient since our planet was consolidated for the assumed amount of organic change, and this objection, as urged by Sir William Thompson, is probably one of the gravest as yet advanced, I can only say, firstly, that we do not know at what rate species change as measured by years, and sec-ondly, that many philosophers are not as yet willing to admit that we know enough of the constitution of the universe and of the in-terior of our globe to speculate with safety on its past duration.

That the geological record is imperfect all will admit; but that it is imperfect to the degree required by our theory, few will be in-clined to admit. If we look to long enough intervals of time, geology plainly declares that species have all changed; and they have changed in the manner required by the theory, for they have changed slowly and in a graduated manner. We clearly see this in the fossil remains from consecutive formations invariably being much more closely related to each other, than are the fossils from widely separated formations.

Such is the sum of the several chief objections and difficulties which may be justly urged against the theory; and I have now briefly recapitulated the answers and explanations which, as far as I can see, may be given. I have felt these difficulties far too heavily during many years to doubt their weight. But it deserves especial notice that the more important objections relate to questions on which we are confessedly ignorant; nor do we know how ignorant we are. We do not know all the possible transitional gradations between the simplest and the most perfect organs; it cannot be pretended that we know all the varied means of distribution during the long lapse of years, or that we know how imperfect is the Geological Record. Serious as these several objections are, in my judgment they are by no means sufficient to overthrow the theory of descent with subsequent modification.

Now let us turn to the other side of the argument. Under domestication we see much variability, caused, or at least excited, by changed conditions of life; but often in so obscure a manner, that we are tempted to consider the variations as spontaneous. Variability is governed by many complex laws,—by correlated growth, compensation, the increased use and disuse of parts, and the definite action of the surrounding conditions. There is much difficulty in ascertaining how largely our domestic productions have been modified; but we may safely infer that the amount has been large, and that modifications can be inherited for long periods. As long as the conditions of life remain the same, we have reason to believe that a modification, which has already been inherited for many generations, may continue to be inherited for an almost infinite number of generations. On the other hand, we have evidence that variability when it has once come into play, does not cease under domestication for a very long period; nor do we know that it ever ceases, for new varieties are still occasionally produced by our oldest domesticated productions.

Variability is not actually caused by man; he only unintentionally exposes organic beings to new conditions of life, and then nature acts on the organisation and causes it to vary. But man can and does select the variations given to him by nature, and thus accumulates them in any desired manner. He thus adapts animals and plants for his own benefit or pleasure. He may do this methodically, or he may do it unconsciously by preserving the individuals most useful or pleasing to him without any intention of altering the breed. It is certain that he can largely influence the character of a breed by selecting, in each successive generation, individual differences so slight as to be inappreciable except by an educated eye. This unconscious process of selection has been the great agency in the formation of the most distinct and useful domestic breeds. That many breeds produced by man have to a large extent the character of natural species, is shown by the inextricable doubts whether many of them are varieties or aboriginally distinct species.

There is no reason why the principles which have acted so efficiently under domestication should not have acted under nature. In the survival of favoured individuals and races, during the constantly-recurrent Struggle for Existence, we see a powerful and ever-acting form of Selection. The struggle for existence inevitably follows from the high geometrical ratio of increase which is common to all organic beings. This high rate of increase is proved by calculation,—by the rapid increase of many animals and plants during a succession of peculiar seasons, and when naturalised in new countries. More individuals are born than can possibly survive. A grain in the balance may determine which individuals shall live and which shall die,—which variety or species shall increase in number, and which shall decrease, or finally become extinct. As the individuals of the same species come in all respects into the closest competition with each other, the struggle will generally be most severe between them; it will be almost equally severe between the varieties of the same species, and next in severity between the species of the same genus. On the other hand the struggle will often be severe between beings remote in the scale of nature. The slightest advantage in certain individuals, at any age or during any season, over those with which they come into competition, or better adaptation in however slight a degree to the surrounding physical conditions, will, in the long run, turn the balance.

With animals having separated sexes, there will be in most cases a struggle between the males for the possession of the females. The most vigorous males, or those which have most successfully struggled with their conditions of life, will generally leave most progeny. But success will often depend on the males having special weapons, or means of defense, or charms; and a slight advantage will lead to victory.

As geology plainly proclaims that each land has undergone great physical changes, we might have expected to find that organic beings have varied under nature, in the same way as they have varied under domestication. And if there has been any variability under nature, it would be an unaccountable fact if natural selection had not come into play. It has often been asserted, but the assertion is incapable of proof, that the amount of variation under nature is a strictly limited quantity. Man, though acting on external characters alone and often capriciously, can produce within a short period a great result by adding up mere individual differences in his domestic productions; and every one admits that species present individual differences. But, besides such differences, all naturalists admit that natural varieties exist, which are considered sufficiently distinct to be worthy of record in systematic works. No one has drawn any clear distinction between individual differences and slight varieties; or between more plainly marked varieties and sub-species, and species. On separate continents, and on different parts of the same continent when divided by barriers of any kind, and on outlying islands, what a multitude of forms exist, which some experienced naturalists rank as varieties, others as geographical races or sub-species, and others as distinct, though closely allied species!

If then, animals and plants do vary, let it be ever so slightly or slowly, why should not variations or individual differences, which are in any way beneficial, be preserved and accumulated through natural selection, or the survival of the fittest? If man can by patience select variations useful to him, why, under changing and complex conditions of life, should not variations useful to nature's living products often arise, and be preserved or selected? What limit can be put to this power, acting during long ages and rigidly scrutinising the whole constitution, structure, and habits of each creature,—favouring the good and rejecting the bad? I can see no limit to this power, in slowly and beautifully adapting each form to the most complex relations of life. The theory of natural selection, even if we look no farther than this, seems to be in the highest degree probable. I have already recapitulated, as fairly as I could, the opposed difficulties and objections: now let us turn to the special facts and arguments in favour of the theory.

On the view that species are only strongly marked and permanent varieties, and that each species first existed as a variety, we can see why it is that no line of demarcation can be drawn between species, commonly supposed to have been produced by special acts of creation, and varities which are acknowledged to have been produced by secondary laws. On this same view we can understand how it is that in a region where many species of a genus have been produced, and where they now flourish, these same species should present many varieties; for where the manufactory of species has been active, we might expect, as a general rule, to find it still in action; and this is the case if varieties be incipient species. Moreover, the species of the larger genera, which afford the greater number of varieties or incipient species, retain to a certain degree the character of varieties; for they differ from each other by a less amount of difference than do the species of smaller genera. The closely allied species also of the larger genera apparently have restricted ranges, and in their affinities they are clustered in little groups round other species—in both respects resembling varieties. These are strange relations on the view that each species was independently created, but are intelligible if each existed first as a variety.

As each species tends by its geometrical rate of reproduction to increase inordinately in number; and as the modified descendants of each species will be enabled to increase by as much as they become more diversified in habits and structure, so as to be able to seize on many and widely different places in the economy of nature, there will be a constant tendency in natural selection to preserve the most divergent offspring of any one species. Hence, during a long-continued course of modification, the slight differences characteristic of varieties of the same species, tend to be augmented into the greater differences characteristic of the species of the same genus. New and improved varieties will inevitably supplant and exterminate the older, less improved, and intermediate varieties; and thus species are rendered to a large extent defined and distinct objects. Dominant species belonging to the larger groups within each class tend to give birth to new and dominant forms; so that each large group tends to become still larger, and at the same time more divergent in character. But as all groups cannot thus go on increasing in size, for the world would not hold them, the more dominant groups beat the less dominant. This tendency in the large groups to go on increasing in size and diverging in character, together with the inevitable contingency of much extinction, explains the arrangement of all the forms of life in groups subordinate to groups, all within a few great classes, which has prevailed throughout all time. This grand fact of the grouping of all organic beings under what is called the Natural System, is utterly inexplicable on the theory of creation.

As natural selection acts solely by accumulating slight, successive, favourable variations, it can produce no great or sudden modifications; it can act only by short and slow steps. Hence, the canon of "Natura non facit saltum," which every fresh addition to our knowledge tends to confirm, is on this theory intelligible. We can see why throughout nature the same general end is gained by an almost infinite diversity of means, for every peculiarity when once acquired is long inherited, and structures already modified in many different ways have to be adapted for the same general purpose. We can, in short, see why nature is prodigal in variety, though niggard in innovation. But why this should be a law of nature if each species has been independently created no man can explain.

Many other facts are, as it seems to me, explicable on this theory. How strange it is that a bird, under the form of a woodpecker, should prey on insects on the ground; that upland geese which rarely or never swim, should possess webbed feet; that a thrush-like bird should dive and feed on sub-aquatic insects; and that a petrel should have the habits and structure fitting it for the life of an auk! and so in endless other cases. But on the view of each species constantly trying to increase in number, with natural selection always ready to adapt the slowly varying descendants of each to any unoccupied or ill-occupied place in nature, these facts cease to be strange, or might even have been anticipated.

We can to a certain extent understand how it is that there is so much beauty throughout nature; for this may be largely attributed to the agency of selection. That beauty, according to our sense of it, is not universal, must be admitted by every one who will look at some venomous snakes, at some fishes, and at certain hideous bats with a distorted resemblance to the human face. Sexual selection has given the most brilliant colours, elegant patterns, and other ornaments to the males, and sometimes to both sexes of many birds, butterflies, and other animals. With birds it has often rendered the voice of the male musical to the female, as well as to our ears. Flowers and fruit have been rendered conspicuous by brilliant colours in contrast with the green foliage, in order that the flowers may be readily seen, visited and fertilised by insects, and the seeds disseminated by birds. How it comes that certain colours, sounds, and forms should give pleasure to man and the lower animals,—that is, how the sense of beauty in its simplest form was first acquired,—we do not know any more than how certain odours and flavours were first rendered agreeable.

As natural selection acts by competition, it adapts and improves the inhabitants of each country only in relation to their co-inhabitants; so that we need feel no surprise at the species of any one country, although on the ordinary view supposed to have been created and specially adapted for that country, being beaten and supplanted by the naturalised productions from another land. Nor ought we to marvel if all the contrivances in nature be not, as far as we can judge, absolutely perfect, as in the case even of the human eye; or if some of them be abhorrent to our ideas of fitness. We need not marvel at the sting of the bee, when used against an enemy, causing the bee's own death; at drones being produced in such great numbers for one single act, and being then slaughtered by their sterile sisters; at the astonishing waste of pollen by our fir-trees; at the instinctive hatred of the queenbee for her own fertile daughters; at the ichneumonidæ feeding within the living bodies of caterpillars; or at other such cases. The wonder indeed is, on the theory of natural selection, that more cases of the want of absolute perfection have not been detected.

The complex and little known laws governing the production of varieties are the same, as far as we can judge, with the laws which have governed the production of distinct species. In both cases physical conditions seem to have produced some direct and definite effect, but how much we cannot say. Thus, when varieties enter any new station, they occasionally assume some of the characters proper to the species of that station. With both varieties and species, use and disuse seem to have produced a considerable effect;

for it is impossible to resist this conclusion when we look, for instance, at the logger-headed duck, which has wings incapable of flight, in nearly the same condition as in the domestic duck; or when we look at the burrowing tucu-tucu, which is occasionally blind, and then at certain moles, which are habitually blind and have their eyes covered with skin; or when we look at the blind animals inhabiting the dark caves of America and Europe. With varieties and species, correlated variation seems to have played an important part, so that when one part has been modified other parts have been necessarily modified. With both varieties and species, reversions to long-lost characters occasionally occur. How inexplicable on the theory of creation is the occasional appearance of stripes on the shoulders and legs of the several species of the horse-genus and of their hybrids! How simply is this fact explained if we believe that these species are all descended from a striped progenitor, in the same manner as the several domestic breeds of the pigeon are descended from the blue and barred rock-pigeon!

On the ordinary view of each species having been independently created, why should specific characters, or those by which the species of the same genus differ from each other, be more variable than generic characters in which they all agree? Why, for instance, should the colour of a flower be more likely to vary in any one species of a genus, if the other species possess differently coloured flowers, than if all possessed the same coloured flowers? If species are only well-marked varieties, of which the characters have become in a high degree permanent, we can understand this fact; for they have already varied since they branched off from a common progenitor in certain characters, by which they have come to be specifically distinct from each other; therefore these same characters would be more likely again to vary than the generic characters which have been inherited without change for an immense period. It is inexplicable on the theory of creation why a part developed in a very unusual manner in one species alone of a genus, and therefore, as we may naturally infer, of great importance to that species, should be eminently liable to variation; but, on our view, this part has undergone, since the several species branched off from a common progenitor, an unusual amount of variability and modification, and therefore we might expect the part generally to be still variable. But a part may be developed in the most unusual manner, like the wing of a bat, and yet not be more variable than any other structure, if the part be common to many subordinate forms, that is, if it has been inherited for a very long period; for in this case, it will have been rendered constant by long-continued natural selection.

Glancing at instincts, marvellous as some are, they offer no greater difficulty than do corporeal structures on the theory of the natural selection of successive slight, but profitable modifications. We can thus understand why nature moves by graduated steps in endowing different animals of the same class with their several instincts. I have attempted to show how much light the principle of gradation throws on the admirable architectural powers of the hive-bee. Habit no doubt often comes into play in modifying instincts; but it certainly is not indispensable, as we see in the case of neuter insects, which leave no progeny to inherit the effects of long-continued habit. On the view of all the species of the same genus having descended from a common parent, and having inherited much in common, we can understand how it is that allied species, when placed under widely different conditions of life, yet follow nearly the same instincts; why the thrushes of tropical and temperate South America, for instance, line their nests with mud like our British species. On the view of instincts having been slowly acquired through natural selection, we need not marvel at some instincts being not perfect and liable to mistakes, and at many instincts causing other animals to suffer.

If species be only well-marked and permanent varieties, we can at once see why their crossed offspring should follow the same complex laws in their degrees and kinds of resemblance to their parents,—in being absorbed into each other by successive crosses, and in other such points,—as do the crossed offspring of acknowledged varieties. This similarity would be a strange fact, if species had been independently created and varieties had been produced through secondary laws.

If we admit that the geological record is imperfect to an extreme degree, then the facts, which the record does give, strongly support the theory of descent with modifications. New species have come on the stage slowly and at successive intervals; and the amount of change, after equal intervals of time, is widely different in different groups. The extinction of species and of whole groups of species which has played so conspicuous a part in the history of the organic world, almost inevitably follows from the principle of natural selection; for old forms are supplanted by new and improved forms. Neither single species nor groups of species reappear when the chain of ordinary generation is once broken. The gradual diffusion of dominant forms, with the slow modification of their descendants, causes the forms of life, after long intervals of time, to appear as if they had changed simultaneously throughout the world. The fact of the fossil remains of each formation being in some degree intermediate in character between the fossils in the formations above and below, is simply explained by their intermediate position in the chain of descent. The grand fact that all extinct beings can be classed with all recent beings, naturally follows from the living and the extinct being the offspring of common parents. As species have generally diverged in character during their long course of descent and modification, we can understand why it is that the more ancient forms, or early progenitors of each group, so often occupy a position in some degree intermediate between existing groups. Recent forms are generally looked upon as being, on the whole, higher in the scale of organisation than ancient forms; and they must be higher, in so far as the later and more improved forms have conquered the older and less improved forms in the struggle for life; they have also generally had their organs more specialised for different functions. This fact is perfectly compatible with numerous beings still retaining simple and but little improved structures, fitted for simple conditions of life; it is likewise compatible with some forms having retrograded in organisation, by having become at each stage of descent better fitted for new and degraded habits of life. Lastly, the wonderful law of the long endurance of allied forms on the same continent,—of marsupials in Australia, of edentata in America, and other such cases,—is intelligible, for within the same country the existing and the extinct will be closely allied by descent.

Looking to geographical distribution, if we admit that there has been during the long course of ages much migration from one part of the world to another, owing to former climatal and geographical changes and to the many occasional and unknown means of dispersal, then we can understand, on the theory of descent with modification, most of the great leading facts in Distribution. We can see why there should be so striking a parallelism in the distribution of organic beings throughout space, and in their geological succession throughout time; for in both cases the beings have been connected by the bond of ordinary generation, and the means of modification have been the same. We see the full meaning of the wonderful fact, which has struck every traveller, namely, that on the same continent, under the most diverse conditions, under heat and cold, on mountain and lowland, on deserts and marshes, most of the inhabitants within each great class are plainly related; for they are the descendants of the same progenitors and early colonists. On this same principle of former migration, combined in most cases with modification, we can understand, by the aid of the Glacial period, the identity of some few plants, and the close alliance of many others, on the most distant mountains, and in the northern and southern temperate zones; and likewise the close alliance of some of the inhabitants of the sea in the northern and southern temperate latitudes, though separated by the whole intertropical ocean. Although two countries may present physical conditions as closely similar as the same species ever require, we need feel no surprise at their inhabitants being widely different, if they have been for a long period completely sundered from each other; for as the relation of organism to organism is the most important of all relations, and as the two countries will have received colonists at various periods and in different proportions, from some other country or from each other, the course of modification in the two areas will inevitably have been different.

On this view of migration, with subsequent modification, we see why oceanic islands are inhabited by only few species, but of these, why many are peculiar or endemic forms. We clearly see why species belonging to those groups of animals which cannot cross wide spaces of the ocean, as frogs and terrestrial mammals, do not inhabit oceanic islands; and why, on the other hand, new and peculiar species of bats, animals which can traverse the ocean, are found on islands far distant from any continent. Such cases as the presence of peculiar species of bats on oceanic islands and the absence of all other terrestrial mammals, are facts utterly inexplicable on the theory of independent acts of creation.

The existence of closely allied or representative species in any two areas, implies, on the theory of descent with modification, that the same parent-forms formerly inhabited both areas; and we almost invariably find that wherever many closely allied species inhabit two areas, some identical species are still common to both. Wherever many closely allied yet distinct species occur, doubtful forms and varieties belonging to the same groups likewise occur. It is a rule of high generality that the inhabitants of each area are related to the inhabitants of the nearest source whence immigrants might have been derived. We see this in the striking relation of nearly all plants and animals of the Galapagos archipelago, of Juan Fernandez, and of the other American islands, to the plants and animals of the neighbouring American mainland; and of those of the Cape de Verde Archipelago, and of the other African islands to the African mainland. It must be admitted that these facts receive no explanation on the theory of creation.

The fact, as we have seen, that all past and present organic beings can be arranged within a few great classes, in groups subordinate to groups, and with the extinct groups often falling in between the recent groups, is intelligible on the theory of natural selection with its contingencies of extinction and divergence of character. On these same principles we see how it is, that the mutual affinities of the forms within each class are so complex and circuitous. We see why certain characters are far more serviceable than others for classification;—why adaptive characters, though of paramount importance to the beings, are of hardly any importance in classification; why characters derived from rudimentary parts, though of no service to the beings, are often of high classificatory value; and why embryological characters are often the most valuable of all. The real affinities of all organic beings, in contradistinction to their adaptive resemblances, are due to inheritance or community of descent. The Natural System is a genealogical arrangement, with the acquired grades of difference, marked by the terms, varieties, species, genera, families, &c.; and we have to discover the lines of descent by the most permanent characters whatever they may be and of however slight vital importance.

The similar framework of bones in the hand of a man, wing of a bat, fin of the porpoise, and leg of the horse,—the same number of vertebræ forming the neck of the giraffe and of the elephant,—and innumerable other such facts, at once explain themselves on the theory of descent with slow and slight successive modifications. The similarity of pattern in the wing and in the leg of a bat, though used for such different purpose,—in the jaws and legs of a crab,—in the petals, stamens, and pistils of a flower, is likewise, to a large extent, intelligible on the view of the gradual modification of parts or organs, which were aboriginally alike in an early progenitor in each of these classes. On the principle of successive variations not always supervening at an early age, and being inherited at a corresponding not early period of life, we clearly see why the embryos of mammals, birds, reptiles, and fishes should be so closely similar, and so unlike the adult forms. We may cease marvelling at the embryo of an airbreathing mammal or bird having branchial slits and arteries running in loops, like those of a fish which has to breathe the air dissolved in water by the aid of well-developed branchiæ.

Disuse, aided sometimes by natural selection, will often have reduced organs when rendered useless under changed habits or conditions of life; and we can understand on this view the meaning of rudimentary organs. But disuse and selection will generally act on each creature, when it has come to maturity and has to play its full part in the struggle for existence, and will thus have little power on an organ during early life; hence the organ will not be reduced or rendered rudimentary at this early age. The calf, for instance, has inherited teeth, which never cut through the gums of the upper jaw, from an early progenitor having well-developed teeth; and we may believe, that the teeth in the mature animal were formerly reduced by disuse, owing to the tongue and palate, or lips, having become excellently fitted through natural selection to browse without their aid; whereas in the calf, the teeth have been left unaffected, and on the principle of inheritance at corresponding ages have been inherited from a remote period to the present day. On the view of each organism with all its separate parts having been specially created, how utterly inexplicable is it that organs bearing the plain stamp of inutility, such as the teeth in the embryonic calf or the shrivelled wings under the soldered wing-covers of many beetles, should so frequently occur. Nature may be said to have taken pains to reveal her scheme of modification, by means of rudimentary organs, of embryological and homologous structures, but we are too blind to understand her meaning.

I have now recapitulated the facts and considerations which have thoroughly convinced me that species have been modified, during a long course of descent. This has been effected chiefly through the natural selection of numerous successive, slight, favourable variations; aided in an important manner by the inherited effects of the use and disuse of parts; and in an unimportant manner, that is in relation to adaptive structures, whether past or present, by the direct action of external conditions, and by variations which seem to us in our ignorance to arise spontaneously. It appears that I formerly underrated the frequency and value of these latter forms of variation, as leading to permanent modifications of structure independently of natural selection. But as my conclusions have lately been much misrepresented, and it has been stated that I attribute the modification of species exclusively to natural selection, I may be permitted to remark that in the first edition of this work, and subsequently, I placed in a most conspicuous position—namely, at the close of the Introduction—the following words: "I am convinced that natural selection has been the main but not the exclusive means of modification." This has been of no avail. Great is the power of steady misrepresentation; but the history of science shows that fortunately this power does not long endure.

It can hardly be supposed that a false theory would explain, in so satisfactory a manner as does the theory of natural selection, the several large classes of facts above specified. It has recently been objected that this is an unsafe method of arguing; but it is a method used in judging of the common events of life, and has often been used by the greatest natural philosophers. The undulatory theory of light has thus been arrived at; and the belief in the revolution of the earth on its own axis was until lately supported by hardly any direct evidence. It is no valid objection that science as yet throws no light on the far higher problem of the essence or origin of life. Who can explain what is the essence of the attraction of gravity? No one now objects to following out the results consequent on this unknown element of attraction; notwithstanding that Leibnitz formerly accused Newton of introducing "occult qualities and miracles into philosophy."

I see no good reason why the views given in this volume should shock the religious feelings of any one. It is satisfactory, as showing how transient such impressions are, to remember that the greatest discovery ever made by man, namely, the law of the attraction of gravity, was also attacked by Leibnitz, "as subversive of natural, and inferentially of revealed, religion." A celebrated author and divine has written to me that "he has gradually learnt to see that it is just as noble a conception of the Deity to believe that He created a few original forms capable of self-development into other and needful forms, as to believe that He required a fresh act of creation to supply the voids caused by the action of His laws."

Why, it may be asked, until recently did nearly all the most eminent living naturalists and geologists disbelieve in the mutability of species? It cannot be asserted that organic beings in a state of nature are subject to no variation; it cannot be proved that the amount of variation in the course of long ages is a limited quality; no clear distinction has been, or can be, drawn between species and well-marked varieties. It cannot be maintained that species when intercrossed are invariably sterile, and varieties invariably fertile; or that sterility is a special endowment and sign of creation. The belief that species were immutable productions was almost unavoidable as long as the history of the world was thought to be of short duration; and now that we have acquired some idea of the lapse of time, we are too apt to assume, without proof, that the geological record is so perfect that it would have afforded us plain evidence of the mutation of species, if they had undergone mutation.

But the chief cause of our natural unwillingness to admit that one species has given birth to clear and distinct species, is that we are always slow in admitting great changes of which we do not see the steps. The difficulty is the same as that felt by so many geologists, when Lyell first insisted that long lines of inland cliffs had been formed, the great valleys excavated, by the agencies which we see still at work. The mind cannot possibly grasp the full meaning of the term of even a million years; it cannot add up and perceive the full effects of many slight variations, accumulated during an almost infinite number of generations.

Although I am fully convinced of the truth of the views given in this volume under the form of an abstract, I by no means expect to convince experienced naturalists whose minds are stocked with a multitude of facts all viewed, during a long course of years, from a point of view directly opposite to mine. It is so easy to hide our ignorance under such expressions as the "plan of creation," "unity of design," &c., and to think that we give an explanation when we only re-state a fact. Any one whose disposition leads him to attach more weight to unexplained difficulties than to the explanation of a certain number of facts will certainly reject the theory. A few naturalists, endowed with much flexibility of mind, and who have already begun to doubt the immutability of species, may be influenced by this volume; but I look with confidence to the future,— to young and rising naturalists, who will be able to view both sides of the question with impartiality. Whoever is led to believe that species are mutable will do good service by conscientiously expressing his conviction; for thus only can the load of prejudice by which this subject is overwhelmed be removed.

Several eminent naturalists have of late published their belief that a multitude of reputed species in each genus are not real species; but that other species are real, that is, have been independently created. This seems to me a strange conclusion to arrive at. They admit that a multitude of forms, which till lately they themselves thought were special creations, and which are still thus looked at by the majority of naturalists, and which consequently have all the external characteristic features of true species,—they admit that these have been produced by variation, but they refuse to extend the same view to other and slightly different forms. Nevertheless they do not pretend that they can define, or even conjecture, which are the created forms of life, and which are those produced by secondary laws. They admit variation as a *vera causa* in one case, they arbitrarily reject it in another, without assigning any distinction in the two cases. The day will come when this will be given as a curious illustration of the blindness of preconceived opinion. These authors seem no more startled at a miraculous act of creation than at an ordinary birth. But do they really believe that at innumerable periods in the earth's history certain elemental atoms have been commanded suddenly to flash into living tissues? Do they believe that at each supposed act of creation one individual or many were produced? Were all the infinitely numerous kinds of animals and plants created as eggs or seed, or as full grown? and in the case of mammals, were they created bearing the false marks of nourishment from the mother's womb? Undoubtedly some of these same questions cannot be answered by those who believe in the appearance or creation of only a few forms of life, or of some one form alone. It has been maintained by several authors that it is as easy to believe in the creation of a million beings as of one; but Maupertuis' philosophical axiom "of least action" leads the mind more willingly to admit the smaller number; and certainly we ought not to believe that innumerable beings within each great class have been created with plain, but deceptive, marks of descent from a single parent.

As a record of a former state of things, I have retained in the foregoing paragraphs, and elsewhere, several sentences which imply that naturalists believe in the separate creation of each species; and I have been much censured for having thus expressed myself. But undoubtedly this was the general belief when the first edition of the present work appeared. I formerly spoke to very many naturalists on the subject of evolution, and never once met with any sympathetic agreement. It is probable that some did then believe in evolution, but they were either silent, or expressed themselves so ambiguously that it was not easy to understand their meaning. Now things are wholly changed, and almost every naturalist admits the great principle of evolution. There are, however, some who still think that species have suddenly given birth, through quite unexplained means, to new and totally different forms: but, as I have attempted to show, weighty evidence can be opposed to the admission of great and abrupt modifications. Under a scientific point of view, and as leading to further investigation, but little advantage is gained by believing that new forms are suddenly developed in an inexplicable manner from old and widely different forms, over the old belief in the creation of species from the dust of the earth.

It may be asked how far I extend the doctrine of the modification of species. The question is difficult to answer, because the more distinct the forms are which we consider, by so much the arguments in favour of community of descent become fewer in number and less in force. But some arguments of the greatest weight extend very far. All the members of whole classes are connected together by a chain of affinities, and all can be classed on the same principle, in groups subordinate to groups. Fossil remains sometimes tend to fill up very wide intervals between existing orders.

Organs in a rudimentary condition plainly show that an early progenitor had the organ in a fully developed condition; and this in some cases implies an enormous amount of modification in the descendants. Throughout whole classes various structures are formed on the same pattern, and at a very early age the embryos closely resemble each other. Therefore I cannot doubt that the theory of descent with modification embraces all the members of the same great class or kingdom. I believe that animals are descended from at most only four or five progenitors, and plants from an equal or lesser number.

Analogy would lead me one step farther, namely, to the belief that all animals and plants are descended from some one prototype. But analogy may be a deceitful guide. Nevertheless all living things have much in common, in their chemical composition, their cellular structure, their laws of growth, and their liability to injurious influences. We see this even in so trifling a fact as that the same poison often similarly affects plants and animals; or that the poison secreted by the gall-fly produces monstrous growths on the wild rose or oak-tree. With all organic beings excepting perhaps some of the very lowest, sexual production seems to be essentially similar. With all, as far as is at present known the germinal vesicle is the same; so that all organisms start from a common origin. If we look even to the two main divisions—namely, to the animal and vegetable kingdoms—certain low forms are so far intermediate in character that naturalists have disputed to which kingdom they should be referred. As Professor Asa Gray has remarked, "the spores and other reproductive bodies of many of the lower algæ may claim to have first a characteristically animal, and then an unequivocally vegetable existence." Therefore, on the principle of natural selection with divergence of character, it does not seem incredible that, from such low and intermediate form, both animals and plants may have been developed; and, if we admit this, we must likewise admit that all the organic beings which have ever lived on this earth may be descended from some one primordial form. But this inference is chiefly grounded on analogy and it is immaterial whether or not it be accepted. No doubt it is possible, as Mr. G. H. Lewes has urged, that at the first commencement of life many different forms were evolved; but if so we may conclude that only a very few have left modified descendants. For, as I have recently remarked in regard to the members of each great kingdom, such as the Vertebrata, Articulata &c., we have distinct evidence in their embryological homologous and rudimentary structures that within each kingdom all the members are descended from a single progenitor.

When the views advanced by me in this volume, and by Mr. Wallace, or when analogous views on the origin of species are generally admitted, we can dimly foresee that there will be a considerable revolution in natural history. Systematists will be able to pursue their labours as at present; but they will not be incessantly haunted by the shadowy doubt whether this or that form be a true species. This, I feel sure and I speak after experience, will be no slight relief. The endless disputes whether or not some fifty species of British brambles are good species will cease. Systematists will have only to decide (not that this will be easy) whether any form be sufficiently constant and distinct from other forms, to be capable of definition; and if definable, whether the differences be sufficiently important to deserve a specific name. This latter point will become a far more essential consideration than it is at present; for differences, however slight, between any two forms if not blended by intermediate gradations, are looked at by most naturalists as sufficient to raise both forms to the rank of species.

Hereafter we shall be compelled to acknowledge that the only distinction between species and well-marked varieties is, that the latter are known, or believed, to be connected at the present day by intermediate gradations, whereas species were formerly thus connected. Hence, without rejecting the consideration of the present existence of intermediate gradations between any two forms we shall be led to weigh more carefully and to value higher the actual amount of difference between them. It is quite possible that forms now generally acknowledged to be merely varieties may hereafter be thought worthy of specific names; and in this case scientific and common language will come into accordance. In short, we shall have to treat species in the same manner as those naturalists treat genera, who admit that genera are merely artificial combinations made for convenience. This may not be a cheering prospect; but we shall at least be free from the vain search for the undiscovered and undiscoverable essence of the term species.

The other and more general departments of natural history will rise greatly in interest. The terms used by naturalists, of affinity, relationship, community of type, paternity, morphology, adaptive characters, rudimentary and aborted organs, &c., will cease to be metaphorical, and will have a plain signification. When we no longer look at an organic being as a savage looks at a ship, as something wholly beyond his comprehension; when we regard every production of nature as one which has had a long history; when we contemplate every complex structure and instinct as the summing up of many contrivances, each useful to the possessor, in the same way as any great mechanical invention is the summing up of the labour, the experience, the reason, and even the blunders of numerous workmen; when we thus view each organic being, how far more interesting—I speak from experience—does the study of natural history become!

A grand and almost untrodden field of inquiry will be opened, on the causes and laws of variation, on correlation, on the effects of use and disuse, on the direct action of external conditions, and so forth. The study of domestic productions will rise immensely in value. A new variety raised by man will be a more important and interesting subject for study than one more species added to the infinitude of already recorded species. Our classifications will come to be, as far as they can be so made, genealogies; and will then truly give what may be called the plan of creation. The rules for classifying will no doubt become simpler when we have a definite object in view. We possess no pedigrees or armorial bearings; and we have to discover and trace the many diverging lines of descent in our natural genealogies, by characters of any kind which have long been inherited. Rudimentary organs will speak infallibly with respect to the nature of long-lost structures. Species and groups of species which are called aberrant, and which may fancifully be called living fossils, will aid us in forming a picture of the ancient forms of life. Embryology will often reveal to us the structure, in some degree obscured, of the prototype of each great class.

When we feel assured that all the individuals of the same species, and all the closely allied species of most genera, have within a not very remote period descended from one parent, and have migrated from some one birth-place; and when we better know the many means of migration, then, by the light which geology now throws, and will continue to throw, on former changes of climate and of the level of the land, we shall surely be enabled to trace in an admirable manner the former migrations of the inhabitants of the whole world. Even at present, by comparing the differences between the inhabitants of the sea on the opposite sides of a continent, and the nature of the various inhabitants on that continent, in relation to their apparent means of immigration, some light can be thrown on ancient geography.

The noble science of Geology loses glory from the extreme imperfection of the record. The crust of the earth with its imbedded remains must not be looked at as a well-filled museum, but as a poor collection made at hazard and at rare intervals. The accumulation of each great fossiliferous formation will be recognised as having depended on an unusual concurrence of favourable circumstances, and the blank intervals between the successive stages as having been of vast duration. But we shall be able to gauge with some security the duration of these intervals by a comparison of the preceding and succeeding organic forms. We must be cautious in attempting to correlate as strictly contemporaneous two formations, which do not include many identical species, by the general succession of the forms of life. As species are produced and exterminated by slowly acting and still existing causes, and not by miraculous acts of creation; and as the most important of all causes of organic change is one which is almost independent of altered and perhaps suddenly altered physical conditions, namely, the mutual relation of organism to organism,—the improvement of one organism entailing the improvement or the extermination of others; it follows, that the amount of organic change in the fossils of consecutive formations probably serves as a fair measure of the relative though not actual lapse of time. A number of species, however, keeping in a body might remain for a long period unchanged, whilst within the same period several of these species by migrating into new countries and coming into competition with foreign associates, might become modified; so that we must not overrate the accuracy of organic change as a measure of time.

In the future I see open fields for far more important researches. Psychology will be securely based on the foundation already well laid by Mr. Herbert Spencer, that of the necessary acquirement of each mental power and capacity by gradation. Much light will be thrown on the origin of man and his history.

Authors of the highest eminence seem to be fully satisfied with the view that each species has been independently created. To my mind it accords better with what we know of the laws impressed on matter by the Creator, that the production and extinction of the past and present inhabitants of the world should have been due to secondary causes, like those determining the birth and death of the individual. When I view all beings not as special creations, but as the lineal descendants of some few beings which lived long before the first bed of the Cambrian system was deposited, they seem to me to become ennobled. Judging from the past, we may safely infer that not one living species will transmit its unaltered likeness to a distant futurity. And of the species now living very few will transmit progeny of any kind to a far distant futurity; for the manner in which all organic beings are grouped, shows that the greater number of species in each genus, and all the species in many genera, have left no descendants, but have become utterly extinct. We can so far take a prophetic glance into futurity as to foretell that it will be the common and widely-spread species, belonging to the larger and dominant groups within each class, which will ultimately prevail and procreate new and dominant species. As all the living forms of life are the lineal descendants of those which lived long before the Cambrian epoch, we may feel certain that the ordinary succession by generation has never once been broken, and that no cataclysm has desolated the whole world. Hence we may look with some confidence to a secure future of great length. And as natural selection works solely by and for the good of each being, all corporeal and mental endowments will tend to progress towards perfection.

It is interesting to contemplate a tangled bank, clothed with many plants of many kinds, with birds singing on the bushes, with various insects flitting about, and with worms crawling through the damp earth, and to reflect that these elaborately constructed forms, so different from each other, and dependent upon each other in so complex a manner, have all been produced by laws acting around us. These laws, taken in the largest sense, being Growth with Reproduction; Inheritance which is almost implied by reproduction; Variability from the indirect and direct action of the conditions of life, and from use and disuse: a Ratio of Increase so high as to lead to a Struggle for Life, and as a consequence to Natural Selection, entailing Divergence of Character and the Extinction of less-improved forms. Thus, from the war of nature, from famine and death, the most exalted object which we are capable of conceiving, namely, the production of the higher animals, directly follows. There is grandeur in this view of life, with its several powers, having been originally breathed by the Creator into a few forms or into one; and that, whilst this planet has gone cycling on according to the fixed law of gravity, from so simple a beginning endless forms most beautiful and most wonderful have been, and are being evolved.

CHARLES DARWIN

The Descent of Man (1871) †

Introduction

The nature of the following work will be best understood by a brief account of how it came to be written. During many years I collected notes on the origin or descent of man, without any intention of publishing on the subject, but rather with the determination not to publish, as I thought that I should thus only add to the prejudices against my views. It seemed to me sufficient to indicate, in the first edition of my 'Origin of Species,' that by this work "light would be thrown on the origin of man and his history;" and this implies that man must be included with other organic beings in any general conclusion respecting his manner of appearance on this earth. Now the case wears a wholly different aspect. When a naturalist like Carl Vogt ventures to say in his address as President of the National Institution of Geneva (1869), "personne, en Europe au moins, n'ose plus soutenir la création indépendante et de toutes pièces, des espèces," it is manifest that at least a large number of naturalists must admit that species are the modified descendants of other species; and this especially holds good with the younger and rising naturalists. The greater number accept the agency of natural selection; though some urge, whether with justice the future must decide, that I have greatly overrated its importance. Of the older and honoured chiefs in natural science, many unfortunately are still opposed to evolution in every form.

In consequence of the views now adopted by most naturalists, and which will ultimately, as in every other case, be followed by others who are not scientific, I have been led to put together my notes, so as to see how far the general conclusions arrived at in my former works were applicable to man. This seemed all the more desirable, as I had never deliberately applied these views to a species taken singly. When we confine our attention to any one form, we are deprived of the weighty arguments derived from the nature of the affinities which connect together whole groups of organisms —their geographical distribution in past and present times, and their geological succession. The homological structure, embryological development, and rudimentary organs of a species remain to be considered, whether it be man or any other animal, to which our attention may be directed; but these great classes of facts afford, as

---

† The present text is excerpted from the second edition (1874), an extensive revision which contains a note by T. H. Huxley on the brains of humans and apes.

it appears to me, ample and conclusive evidence in favour of the principle of gradual evolution. The strong support derived from the other arguments should, however, always be kept before the mind.

The sole object of this work is to consider, firstly, whether man, like every other species, is descended from some pre-existing form; secondly, the manner of his development; and thirdly, the value of the differences between the so-called races of man. As I shall confine myself to these points, it will not be necessary to describe in detail the differences between the several races—an enormous subject which has been fully discussed in many valuable works. The high antiquity of man has recently been demonstrated by the labours of a host of eminent men, beginning with M. Boucher de Perthes; and this is the indispensable basis for understanding his origin. I shall, therefore, take this conclusion for granted, and may refer my readers to the admirable treatises of Sir Charles Lyell, Sir John Lubbock, and others. Nor shall I have occasion to do more than to allude to the amount of difference between man and the anthropomorphous apes; for Prof. Huxley, in the opinion of most competent judges, has conclusively shewn that in every visible character man differs less from the higher apes, than these do from the lower members of the same order of Primates.

This work contains hardly any original facts in regard to man; but as the conclusions at which I arrived, after drawing up a rough draft, appeared to me interesting, I thought that they might interest others. It has often and confidently been asserted, that man's origin can never be known: but ignorance more frequently begets confidence than does knowledge: it is those who know little, and not those who know much, who so positively assert that this or that problem will never be solved by science. The conclusion that man is the co-descendant with other species of some ancient, lower, and extinct form, is not in any degree new. Lamarck long ago came to this conclusion, which has lately been maintained by several eminent naturalists and philosophers; for instance, by Wallace, Huxley, Lyell, Vogt, Lubbock, Büchner, Rolle, &c.,[1] and especially by Häckel. This last naturalist, besides his great work, 'Generelle Morphologie' (1866), has recently (1868, with a second edit. in 1870), published his 'Natürliche Schöpfungsgeschichte,' in

1. As the works of the first-named authors are so well known, I need not give the titles; but as those of the latter are less well known in England, I will give them:—'Sechs Vorlesungen über die Darwin'sche Theorie:' zweite Auflage, 1868, von Dr. L. Büchner; translated into French under the title 'Conférences sur la Théorie Darwinienne,' 1869. 'Der Mensch, im Lichte der Darwin'sche Lehre,' 1865, von Dr. F. Rolle. I will not attempt to give references to all the authors who have taken the same side of the question. Thus G. Canestrini has published ('Annuario della Soc. d. Nat.,' Modena, 1867, p. 81) a very curious paper on rudimentary characters, as bearing on the origin of man. Another work has (1869) been published by Dr. Francesco Barrago, bearing in Italian the title of "Man, made in the image of God, was also made in the image of the ape."

which he fully discusses the genealogy of man. If this work had appeared before my essay had been written, I should probably never have completed it. Almost all the conclusions at which I have arrived I find confirmed by this naturalist, whose knowledge on many points is much fuller than mine. Wherever I have added any fact or view from Prof. Häckel's writings, I give his authority in the text; other statements I leave as they originally stood in my manuscript, occasionally giving in the foot-notes references to his works, as a confirmation of the more doubtful or interesting points.

During many years it has seemed to me highly probable that sexual selection has played an important part in differentiating the races of man; but in my 'Origin of Species' (first edition, p. 199) I contented myself by merely alluding to this belief. When I came to apply this view to man, I found it indispensable to treat the whole subject in full detail.[2] Consequently the second part of the present work, treating of sexual selection, has extended to an inordinate length, compared with the first part; but this could not be avoided.

I had intended adding to the present volumes an essay on the expression of the various emotions by man and the lower animals. My attention was called to this subject many years ago by Sir Charles Bell's admirable work. This illustrious anatomist maintains that man is endowed with certain muscles solely for the sake of expressing his emotions. As this view is obviously opposed to the belief that man is descended from some other and lower form, it was necessary for me to consider it. I likewise wished to ascertain how far the emotions are expressed in the same manner by the different races of man. But owing to the length of the present work, I have thought it better to reserve my essay for separate publication.

Chapter I

THE EVIDENCE OF THE DESCENT OF MAN FROM SOME LOWER FORM

Nature of the evidence bearing on the origin of man—Homologous structures in man and the lower animals—Miscellaneous points of correspondence—Development—Rudimentary structures, muscles, sense-organs, hair, bones, reproductive organs, &c.—The bearing of these three great classes of facts on the origin of man.

2. Prof. Häckel was the only author who, at the time when this work first appeared, had discussed the subject of sexual selection, and had seen its full importance, since the publication of the 'Origin'; and this he did in a very able manner in his various works.

He who wishes to decide whether man is the modified descendant of some pre-existing form, would probably first enquire whether man varies, however slightly, in bodily structure and in mental faculties; and if so, whether the variations are transmitted to his offspring in accordance with the laws which prevail with the lower animals. Again, are the variations the result, as far as our ignorance permits us to judge, of the same general causes, and are they governed by the same general laws, as in the case of other organisms; for instance, by correlation, the inherited effects of use and disuse, &c.? Is man subject to similar malconformations, the result of arrested development, of reduplication of parts, &c., and does he display in any of his anomalies reversion to some former and ancient type of structure? It might also naturally be enquired whether man, like so many other animals, has given rise to varieties and sub-races, differing but slightly from each other, or to races differing so much that they must be classed as doubtful species? How are such races distributed over the world; and how, when crossed, do they react on each other in the first and succeeding generations? And so with many other points.

The enquirer would next come to the important point, whether man tends to increase at so rapid a rate, as to lead to occasional severe struggles for existence; and consequently to beneficial variations, whether in body or mind, being preserved, and injurious ones eliminated. Do the races or species of men, whichever term may be applied, encroach on and replace one another, so that some finally become extinct? We shall see that all these questions, as indeed is obvious in respect to most of them, must be answered in the affirmative, in the same manner as with the lower animals. But the several considerations just referred to may be conveniently deferred for a time: and we will first see how far the bodily structure of man shows traces, more or less plain, of his descent from some lower form. In succeeding chapters the mental powers of man, in comparison with those of the lower animals, will be considered.

THE BODILY STRUCTURE OF MAN

It is notorious that man is constructed on the same general type or model as other mammals. All the bones in his skeleton can be compared with corresponding bones in a monkey, bat, or seal. So it is with his muscles, nerves, blood-vessels and internal viscera. The brain, the most important of all the organs, follows the same law, as shewn by Huxley and other anatomists. Bischoff,[1] who is a hostile witness, admits that every chief fissure and fold in the brain of man

---

1. 'Grosshirnwindungen des Menschen,' 1868, s. 96. The conclusions of this author, as well as those of Gratiolet and Aeby, concerning the brain, will be discussed by Prof. Huxley in the Appendix alluded to in the Preface to this edition.

has its analogy in that of the orang; but he adds that at no period of development do their brains perfectly agree; nor could perfect agreement by expected, for otherwise their mental powers would have been the same. Vulpian [2] remarks: "Les différences réelles qui existent entre l'encéphale de l'homme et celui des singes supérieurs, sont bien minimes. Il ne faut pas se faire d'illusions à cet égard. L'homme est bien plus près des singes anthropomorphes par les caractères anatomiques de son cerveau que ceux-ci ne le sont non seulement des autres mammifères, mais même de certains quadrumanes, des guenons et des macaques." But it would be superfluous here to give further details on the correspondence between man and the higher mammals in the structure of the brain and all other parts of the body.

It may, however, be worth while to specify a few points, not directly or obviously connected with structure, by which this correspondence or relationship is well shewn.

Man is liable to receive from the lower animals, and to communicate to them, certain diseases, as hydrophobia, variola, the glanders, syphilis, cholera, herpes, &c.;[3] and this fact proves the close similarity[4] of their tissues and blood, both in minute structure and composition, far more plainly than does their comparison under the best microscope, or by the aid of the best chemical analysis. Monkeys are liable to many of the same non-contagious diseases as we are; thus Rengger,[5] who carefully observed for a long time the *Cebus Azaræ* in its native land, found it liable to catarrh, with the usual symptoms, and which, when often recurrent, led to consumption. These monkeys suffered also from apoplexy, inflammation of the bowels, and cataract in the eye. The younger ones when shedding their milk-teeth often died from fever. Medicines produced the same effect on them as on us. Many kinds of monkeys have a strong taste for tea, coffee, and spirituous liquors: they will also, as I have myself seen, smoke tobacco with pleasure.[6] Brehm asserts that the natives of north-eastern Africa catch the wild baboons by exposing vessels with strong beer, by which they are made drunk.

2. 'Leç. sur la Phys.' 1866, p. 890, as quoted by M. Dally, 'L'Ordre des Primates et le Transformisme,' 1868, p. 29.
3. Dr. W. Lauder Lindsay has treated this subject at some length in the 'Journal of Mental Science,' July 1871; and in the 'Edinburgh Veterinary Review,' July 1858.
4. A Reviewer has criticised ('British Quarterly Review,' Oct. 1st, 1871, p. 472) what I have here said with much severity and contempt; but as I do not use the term identity, I cannot see that I am greatly in error. There appears to me a strong analogy between the same infection or contagion producing the same result, or one closely similar, in two distinct animals, and the testing of two distinct fluids by the same chemical reagent.
5. 'Naturgeschichte der Säugethiere von Paraguay,' 1830, s. 50.
6. The same tastes are common to some animals much lower in the scale. Mr. A. Nicols informs me that he kept in Queensland, in Australia, three individuals of the *Phaseolarctus cinereus;* and that, without having been taught in any way, they acquired a strong taste for rum, and for smoking tobacco.

He has seen some of these animals, which he kept in confinement, in this state; and he gives a laughable account of their behaviour and strange grimaces. On the following morning they were very cross and dismal; they held their aching heads with both hands, and wore a most pitiable expression: when beer or wine was offered them, they turned away with disgust, but relished the juices of lemons.[7] An American monkey, an Ateles, after getting drunk on brandy, would never touch it again, and thus was wiser than many men. These trifling facts prove how similar the nerves of taste must be in monkeys and man, and how similarly their whole nervous system is affected.

Man is infested with internal parasites, sometimes causing fatal effects; and is plagued by external parasites, all of which belong to the same genera or families as those infesting other mammals, and in the case of scabies to the same species.[8] Man is subject, like other mammals, birds, and even insects,[9] to that mysterious law, which causes certain normal processes, such as gestation, as well as the maturation and duration of various diseases, to follow lunar periods. His wounds are repaired by the same process of healing; and the stumps left after the amputation of his limbs, especially during an embryonic period, occasionally possess some power of regeneration, as in the lowest animals.[1]

The whole process of that most important function, the reproduction of the species, is strikingly the same in all mammals, from the first act of courtship by the male,[2] to the birth and nurturing of the young. Monkeys are born in almost as helpless a condition as our own infants; and in certain genera the young differ fully as much in appearance from the adults, as do our children from their full-grown parents.[3] It has been urged by some writers, as an important distinction, that with man the young arrive at maturity at a much later age than with any other animal: but if we look to the races of mankind which inhabit tropical countries the difference is

7. Brehm, 'Thierleben,' B. i. 1864, s. 75, 86. On the Ateles, s. 105. For other analogous statements, see s. 25, 107.
8. Dr. W. Lauder Lindsay, 'Edinburgh Vet. Review,' July 1858, p. 13.
9. With respect to insects see Dr. Laycock, "On a General Law of Vital Periodicity," 'British Association,' 1842. Dr. Macculloch, 'Silliman's North American Journal of Science,' vol. xvii. p. 305, has seen a dog suffering from tertian ague. Hereafter I shall return to this subject.
1. I have given the evidence on this head in my 'Variation of Animals and Plants under Domestication,' vol. ii. p. 15, and more could be added.
2. Mares e diversis generibus Quadrumanorum sine dubio dignoscunt feminas humanas a maribus. Primum, credo, odoratu, postea aspectu. Mr. Youatt, qui diu in Hortis Zoologicis (Bestiariis) medicus animalium erat, vir in rebus observandis cautus et sagax, hoc mihi certissime probavit, et curatores ejusdem loci et alii e ministris confirmaverunt. Sir Andrew Smith et Brehm notabant idem in Cynocephalo. Illustrissimus Cuvier etiam narrat multa de hâc re, quâ ut opinor, nihil turpius potest indicari inter omnia hominibus et Quadrumanis communia. Narrat enim Cynocephalum quendam in furorem incidere aspectu feminarum aliquarem, sed nequaquam accendi tanto furore ab omnibus. Semper eligebat juniores, et dignoscebat in turbâ, et advocabat voce gestûque.

not great, for the orang is believed not to be adult till the age of from ten to fifteen years.[4] Man differs from woman in size, bodily strength, hairiness, &c., as well as in mind, in the same manner as do the two sexes of many mammals. So that the correspondence in general structure, in the minute structure of the tissues, in chemical composition and in constitution, between man and the higher animals, especially the anthropomorphous apes, is extremely close.

EMBRYONIC DEVELOPMENT

Man is developed from an ovule, about the 125th of an inch in diameter, which differs in no respect from the ovules of other animals. The embryo itself at a very early period can hardly be distinguished from that of other members of the vertebrate kingdom. At this period the arteries run in arch-like branches, as if to carry the blood to branchiæ which are not present in the higher vertebrate, though the slits on the sides of the neck still remain (*f, g*, fig. 1), marking their former position. At a somewhat later period, when the extremities are developed, "the feet of lizards and mammals," as the illustrious Von Baer remarks, "the wings and feet of birds, no less than the hands and feet of man, all arise from the same fundamental form." It is, says Prof. Huxley,[5] quite in the later stages of development that the young human being presents marked differences from the young ape, while the latter departs as much from the dog in its developments, as the man does. Startling as this last assertion may appear to be, it is demonstrably true."

As some of my readers may never have seen a drawing of an embryo, I have given one of man and another of a dog, at about the same early stage of development, carefully copied from two works of undoubted accuracy.[6]

After the foregoing statements made by such high authorities, it would be superfluous on my part to give a number of borrowed details, shewing that the embryo of man closely resembles that of other mammals. It may, however, be added, that the human embryo likewise resembles certain low forms when adult in various points of structure. For instance, the heart at first exists as a simple pulsating vessel; the excreta are voided through a cloacal passage;

3. This remark is made with respect to Cynocephalus and the anthropomorphous apes by Geoffroy Saint-Hilaire and F. Cuvier, 'Hist. Nat. des Mammifères,' tom. i. 1824.
4. Huxley, 'Man's Place in Nature,' 1863, p. 34.
5. 'Man's Place in Nature,' 1863, p. 67.
6. The human embryo (upper fig.) is from Ecker, 'Icones Phys.,' 1851–1859, tab. xxx. fig. 2. This embryo was ten lines in length, so that the drawing is much magnified. The embryo of the dog is from Bischoff, 'Entwicklungsgeschichte des Hunde-Eies,' 1845, tab. xi. fig. 42 B. This drawing is five times magnified, the embryo being twenty-five days old. The internal viscera have been omitted, and the uterine appendages in both drawings removed. I was directed to these figures by Prof. Huxley, from whose work, 'Man's Place in Nature,' the idea of giving them was taken. Häckel has also given analogous drawings in his 'Schöpfungsgeschichte.'

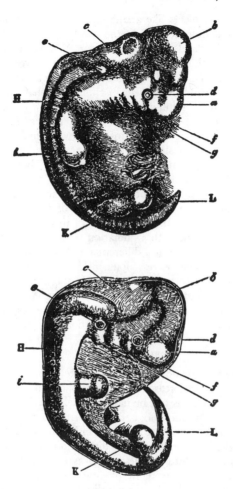

FIG. I.—Upper figure human embryo, from Ecker. Lower figure that of a dog, from Bischoff.

a. Fore-brain, cerebral hemispheres, &c.
b. Mid-brain, corpora, quadrigemina.
c. Hind-brain, cerebellum, medulla oblongata.
d. Eye. *e.* Ear. *f.* First visceral arch. *g.* Second visceral arch.
H. Vertebral columns and muscles in process of development.
i. Anterior ⎱
K. Posterior ⎰ extremities.
L. Tail or os coccyx.

and the os coccyx projects like a true tail, "extending considerably beyond the rudimentary legs." [7] In the embryos of all air-breathing vertebrates, certain glands, called the corpora Wolffiana, correspond with, and act like the kidneys of mature fishes.[8] Even at a later embryonic period, some striking resemblances between man and the lower animals may be observed. Bischoff says "that the convolutions of the brain in a human fœtus at the end of the seventh month reach about the same stage of development as in a baboon when adult." [9] The great toe, as Professor Owen remarks,[1] "which forms the fulcrum when standing or walking, is perhaps the most characteristic peculiarity in the human structure;" but in an embryo, about an inch in length, Prof. Wyman [2] found "that the great toe was shorter than the others; and, instead of being parallel to them, projected at an angle from the side of the foot, thus corresponding with the permanent condition of this part in the quadrumana." I will conclude with a quotation from Huxley,[3] who after asking, does man originate in a different way from a dog, bird, frog or fish? says, "the reply is not doubtful for a moment; without question, the mode of origin, and the early stages of the development of man, are identical with those of the animals immediately below him in the scale: without a doubt in these respects, he is far nearer to apes than the apes are to the dog."

RUDIMENTS

This subject, though not intrinsically more important than the two last, will for several reasons be treated here more fully.[4] Not one of the higher animals can be named which does not bear some part in a rudimentary condition; and man forms no exception to the rule. Rudimentary organs must be distinguished from those that are nascent; though in some cases the distinction is not easy. The former are either absolutely useless, such as the mammæ of male quadrupeds, or the incisor teeth of ruminants which never cut through the gums; or they are of such slight service to their present possessors, that we can hardly suppose that they were developed under the conditions which now exist. Organs in this latter state are not strictly rudimentary, but they are tending in this direction.

7. Prof. Wyman in 'Proc. of American Acad. of Sciences,' vol. iv. 1860, p. 17.
8. Owen, 'Anatomy of Vertebrates,' vol. i. p. 533.
9. 'Die Grosshirnwindungen des Menschen,' 1868, s. 95.
1. 'Anatomy of Vertebrates,' vol. ii. p. 553.
2. 'Proc. Soc. Nat. Hist.' Boston; 1863, vol. ix. p. 185.
3. 'Man's Place in Nature,' p. 65.

4. I had written a rough copy of this chapter before reading a valuable paper, "Caratteri rudimentali in ordine all' origine dell' uomo" ('Annuario della Soc. d. Nat.,' Modena, 1867, p. 81), by G. Canestrini, to which paper I am considerably indebted. Häckel has given admirable discussions on this whole subject, under the title of Dysteleology, in his 'Generelle Morphologie' and 'Schöpfungsgeschichte.'

Nascent organs, on the other hand, though not fully developed, are of high service to their possessors, and are capable of further development. Rudimentary organs are eminently variable; and this is partly intelligible, as they are useless, or nearly useless, and consequently are no longer subjected to natural selection. They often become wholly suppressed. When this occurs, they are nevertheless liable to occasional reappearance through reversion—a circumstance well worthy of attention.

The chief agents in causing organs to become rudimentary seem to have been disuse at that period of life when the organ is chiefly used (and this is generally during maturity), and also inheritance at a corresponding period of life. The term "disuse" does not relate merely to the lessened action of muscles, but includes a diminished flow of blood to a part or organ, from being subjected to fewer alterations of pressure, or from becoming in any way less habitually active. Rudiments, however, may occur in one sex of those parts which are normally present in the other sex; and such rudiments, as we shall hereafter see, have often originated in a way distinct from those here referred to. In some cases, organs have been reduced by means of natural selection, from having become injurious to the species under changed habits of life. The process of reduction is probably often aided through the two principles of compensation and economy of growth; but the later stages of reduction, after disuse has done all that can fairly be attributed to it, and when the saving to be effected by the economy of growth would be very small,[5] are difficult to understand. The final and complete suppression of a part, already useless and much reduced in size, in which case neither compensation nor economy can come into play, is perhaps intelligible by the aid of the hypothesis of pangenesis. But as the whole subject of rudimentary organs has been discussed and illustrated in my former works,[6] I need here say no more on this head.

Rudiments of various muscles have been observed in many parts of the human body;[7] and not a few muscles, which are regularly present in some of the lower animals can occasionally be detected in man in a greatly reduced condition. Every one must have noticed the power which many animals, especially horses, possess of moving or twitching their skin; and this is effected by the *panniculus*

5. Some good criticisms on this subject have been given by Messrs. Murie and Mivart, in 'Transact. Zoolog. Soc.' 1869, vol. vii p. 92.
6. 'Variation of Animals and Plants under Domestication,' vol. ii. pp. 317 and 397. See also 'Origin of Species,' fifth edition, p. 535.
7. For instance, M. Richard ('Annales des Sciences Nat.,' 3d series, Zoolog. 1852, tom. xviii. p. 13) describes and figures rudiments of what he calls the "muscle pédieux de la main," which he says is sometimes "infiniment petit." Another muscle, called "le tibial postérieur," is generally quite absent in the hand, but appears from time to time in a more or less rudimentary condition.

carnosus. Remnants of this muscle in an efficient state are found in various parts of our bodies; for instance, the muscle on the forehead, by which the eyebrows are raised. The *platysma myoides,* which is well developed on the neck, belongs to this system. Prof. Turner, of Edinburgh, has occasionally detected, as he informs me, muscular fasciculi in five different situations, namely in the axillæ, near the scapulæ, &c., all of which must be referred to the system of the *panniculus.* He has also shewn [8] that the *musculus sternalis* or *sternalis brutorum,* which is not an extension of the *rectus abdominalis,* but is closely allied to the *panniculus,* occurred in the proportion of about three percent. in upward of 600 bodies: he adds, that this muscle affords "an excellent illustration of the statement that occasional and rudimentary structures are especially liable to variation in arrangement."

Some few persons have the power of contracting the superficial muscles on their scalps; and these muscles are in a variable and partially rudimentary condition. M. A. de Candolle has communicated to me a curious instance of the long-continued persistence or inheritance of this power, as well as of its unusual development. He knows a family, in which one member, the present head of the family, could, when a youth, pitch several heavy books from his head by the movement of the scalp alone; and he won wagers by performing this feat. His father, uncle, grandfather, and his three children possess the same power to the same unusual degree. This family became divided eight generations ago into two branches; so that the head of the above-mentioned branch is cousin in the seventh degree to the head of the other branch. This distant cousin resides in another part of France; and on being asked whether he possessed the same faculty, immediately exhibited his power. This case offers a good illustration how persistent may be the transmission of an absolutely useless faculty, probably derived from our remote semi-human progenitors; since many monkeys have, and frequently use the power, of largely moving their scalps up and down.[9]

The extrinsic muscles which serve to move the external ear, and the intrinsic muscles which move the different parts, are in a rudimentary condition in man, and they all belong to the system of the *panniculus;* they are also variable in development, or at least in function. I have seen one man who could draw the whole ear forwards; other men can draw it upwards; another who could draw it backwards; [1] and from what one of these persons told me, it is

8. Prof. W. Turner, 'Proc. Royal Soc. Edinburgh,' 1866–67, p. 65.
9. See my 'Expression of the Emotions in Man and Animals,' 1872, p. 144.

1. Canestrini quotes Hyrtl. ('Annuario della Soc. dei Naturalisti,' Modena, 1897, p. 97) to the same effect.

probable that most of us, by often touching our ears, and thus directing our attention towards them, could recover some power of movement by repeated trials. The power of erecting and directing the shell of the ears to the various points of the compass, is no doubt of the highest service to many animals, as they thus perceive the direction of danger; but I have never heard, on sufficient evidence, of a man who possessed this power, the one which might be of use to him. The whole external shell may be considered a rudiment, together with the various folds and prominences (helix and anti-helix, tragus and anti-tragus, &c.) which in the lower animals strengthen and support the ear when erect, without adding much to its weight. Some authors, however, suppose that the cartilage of the shell serves to transmit vibrations to the acoustic nerve; but Mr. Toynbee,[2] after collecting all the known evidence on this head, concludes that the external shell is of no distinct use. The ears of the chimpanzee and orang are curiously like those of man, and the proper muscles are likewise but very slightly developed.[3] I am also assured by the keepers in the Zoological Gardens that these animals never move or erect their ears; so that they are in an equally rudimentary condition with those of man, as far as function is concerned. Why these animals, as well as the progenitors of man, should have lost the power of erecting their ears, we can not say. It may be, though I am not satisfied with this view, that owing to their arboreal habits and great strength they were but little exposed to danger, and so during a lengthened period moved their ears but little, and thus gradually lost the power of moving them. This would be a parallel case with that of those large and heavy birds, which, from inhabiting oceanic islands, have not been exposed to the attacks of beasts of prey, and have consequently lost the power of using their wings for flight. The inability to move the ears in man and several apes is, however, partly compensated by the freedom with which they can move the head in a horizontal plane, so as to catch sounds from all directions. It has been asserted that the ear of man alone possesses a lobule; but "a rudiment of it is found in the gorilla;"[4] and, as I hear from Prof. Preyer, it is not rarely absent in the negro.

The celebrated sculptor, Mr. Woolner, informs me of one little peculiarity in the external ear, which he has often observed both in men and women, and of which he perceived the full significance. His attention was first called to the subject whilst at work on his

---

2. 'The Diseases of the Ear,' by J. Toynbee, F. R. S., 1860, p. 12. A distinguished physiologist, Prof. Preyer, informs me that he had lately been experimenting on the function of the shell of the ear, and has come to nearly the same conclusion as that given here.

3. Prof. A. Macalister, 'Annals and Mag. of Nat. History,' vol. vii., 1871, p. 342.

4. Mr. St. George Mivart, 'Elementary Anatomy,' 1873, p. 396.

figure of Puck, to which he had given pointed ears. He was thus led
to examine the ears of various monkeys, and subsequently more
carefully those of man. The peculiarity consists in a little blunt
point, projecting from the inwardly folded margin, or helix. When
present, it is developed at birth, and according to Prof. Ludwig
Meyer, more frequently in man than in woman. Mr. Woolner
made an exact model of one such case, and sent me the accompanying drawing. (Fig. 2.) These points not only project inwards towards
the centre of the ear, but often a little outwards from its plane, so
as to be visible when the head is viewed from directly in front or
behind. They are variable in size, and somewhat in position, standing either a little higher or lower; and they sometimes occur on
one ear and not on the other. They are not confined to mankind,
for I observed a case in one of the spider-monkeys (*Ateles beelze-
buth*) in our Zoological Gardens; and Mr. E. Ray Lankester informs
me of another case in a chimpanzee in the gardens at Hamburg.
The helix obviously consists of the extreme margin of the ear
folded inwards; and this folding appears to be in some manner
connected with the whole external ear being permanently pressed
backwards. In many monkeys, which do not stand high in the

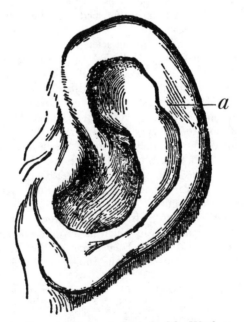

FIG. 2.—Human Ear, modelled and drawn by Mr. Woolner.
   a. The projecting point.

order, as baboons and some species of macacus,[5] the upper portion
of the ear is slightly pointed, and the margin is not at all folded
inwards; but if the margin were to be thus folded, a slight point
would necessarily project inwards towards the centre, and probably
a little outwards from the plane of the ear; and this I believe to be
their origin in many cases. On the other hand, Prof. L. Meyer, in
an able paper recently published,[6] maintains that the whole case
is one of mere variability; and that the projections are not real
ones, but are due to the internal cartilage on each side of the points
not having been fully developed. I am quite ready to admit that
this is the correct explanation in many instances, as in those figured
by Prof. Meyer, in which there are several minute points, or the
whole margin is sinuous. I have myself seen, through the kindness
of Dr. L. Down, the ear of a microcephalous idiot, on which there
is a projection on the outside of the helix, and not on the inward
folded edge, so that this point can have no relation to a former apex
of the ear. Nevertheless in some cases, my original view, that the
points are vestiges of the tips of formerly erect and pointed ears,
still seems to me probable. I think so from the frequency of their
occurrence, and from the general correspondence in position with
that of the tip of a pointed ear. In one case, of which a photograph
has been sent me, the projection is so large, that supposing, in
accordance with Prof. Meyer's view, the ear to be made perfect by
the equal development of the cartilage throughout the whole extent
of the margin, it would have covered fully one-third of the whole
ear. Two cases have been communicated to me, one in North America, and the other in England, in which the upper margin is not at
all folded inwards, but is pointed, so that it closely resembles the
pointed ear of an ordinary quadruped in outline. In one of these
cases, which was that of a young child, the father compared the ear
with the drawing which I have given [7] of the ear of a monkey, the
Cynopithecus niger, and says that their outlines are closely similar.
If, in these two cases, the margin had been folded inwards in the
normal manner, an inward projection must have been formed. I
may add that in two other cases the outline still remains somewhat
pointed, although the margin of the upper part of the ear is normally folded inwards—in one of them, however, very narrowly. The
following woodcut (No. 3) is an accurate copy of a photograph of
the fœtus of an orang (kindly sent me by Dr. Nitsche), in which it
may be seen how different the pointed outline of the ear is at this
period from its adult condition, when it bears a close general re-

5. See also some remarks, and the drawings of the ears of the Lemuroidea, in
Messrs. Murie and Mivart's excellent
paper in 'Transact. Zoolog. Soc.' vol. vii.
1869, pp. 6 and 90.

6. Ueber das Darwin'sche Spitzohr,
Archiv für Path. Anat. und Phys. 1871,
p. 485.
7. 'The Expression of the Emotions,'
p. 136.

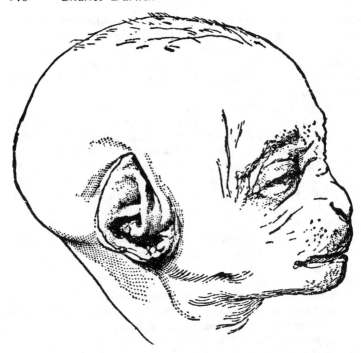

FIG. 3.—Fœtus of an Orang. Exact copy of a photograph, showing tne form of the ear at this early age.

semblance to that of man. It is evident that the folding over of the tip of such an ear, unless it changed greatly during its further development, would give rise to a point projecting inwards. On the whole, it still seems to me probable that the points in question are in some cases, both in man and apes, vestiges of a former condition.

The nictitating membrane, or third eyelid, with its accessory muscles and other structures, is especially well developed in birds, and is of much functional importance to them, as it can be rapidly drawn across the whole eye-ball. It is found in some reptiles and amphibians, and in certain fishes, as in sharks. It is fairly well developed in the two lower divisions of the mammalian series, namely, in the monotremata and marsupials, and in some few of the higher mammals, as in the walrus. But in man, the quadrumana, and most other mammals, it exists, as is admitted by all anatomists, as a mere rudiment, called the semilunar fold.[8]

8. Müller's 'Elements of Physiology,' Eng. translat., 1842, vol. ii. p. 1117. Owen, 'Anatomy of Vertebrates,' vol. iii. p. 260; ibid. on the Walrus, 'Proc. Zoolog. Soc.' November 8th, 1854. See also R. Knox, 'Great Artists and Anatomists,' p. 106. This rudiment apparently is somewhat larger in Negroes and Australians than in Europeans, see Carl Vogt, 'Lectures on Man,' Eng. translat. p. 129.

The sense of smell is of the highest importance to the greater number of mammals—to some, as the ruminants, in warning them of danger; to others, as the carnivora, in finding their prey; to others, again, as the wild boar, for both purposes combined. But the sense of smell is of extremely slight service, if any, even to the dark coloured races of men, in whom it is much more highly developed than in the white and civilised races.[9] Nevertheless it does not warn them of danger, nor guide them to their food; nor does it prevent the Esquimaux from sleeping in the most fetid atmosphere, nor many savages from eating half-putrid meat. In Europeans the power differs greatly in different individuals, as I am assured by an eminent naturalist who possesses this sense highly developed, and who has attended to the subject. Those who believe in the principle of gradual evolution, will not readily admit that the sense of smell in its present state was originally acquired by man, as he now exists. He inherits the power in an enfeebled and so far rudimentary condition, from some early progenitor, to whom it was highly serviceable, and by whom it was continually used. In those animals which have this sense highly developed, such as dogs and horses, the recollection of persons and of places is strongly associated with their odour; and we can thus perhaps understand how it is, as Dr. Maudsley has truly remarked,[1] that the sense of smell in man "is singularly effective in recalling vividly the ideas and images of forgotten scenes and places."

Man differs conspicuously from all the other Primates in being almost naked. But a few short straggling hairs are found over the greater part of the body in the man, and fine down on that of a woman. The different races differ much in hairiness; and in the individuals of the same race the hairs are highly variable, not only in abundance, but likewise in position: thus in some Europeans the shoulders are quite naked, whilst in others they bear thick tufts of hair.[2] There can be little doubt that the hairs thus scattered over the body are the rudiments of the uniform hairy coat of the lower animals. This view is rendered all the more probable, as it is known that fine, short, and pale-coloured hairs on the limbs and

9. The account given by Humboldt of the power of smell possessed by the natives of South America is well known, and has been confirmed by others. M. Houzeau ('Études sur les Facultés Mentales,' &c., tom. i. 1872, p. 91) asserts that he repeatedly made experiments, and proved that Negroes and Indians could recognise persons in the dark by their odour. Dr. W. Ogle has made some curious observations on the connection between the power of smell and the colouring matter of the membrane of the olfactory region as well as of the skin of the body. I have, therefore, spoken in the text of the dark-coloured races having a finer sense of smell than the white races. See his paper, 'Medico-Chirurgical Transactions,' London, vol. liii., 1870, p. 276.
1. 'The Physiology and Pathology of Mind,' 2nd edit. 1868, p. 134.
2. Eschricht, Ueber die Richtung der Haare am menschlichen Körper, 'Müller's Archiv für Anat. und Phys. 1837, s. 47. I shall often have to refer to this very curious paper.

other parts of the body, occasionally become developed into "thickset, long, and rather coarse dark hairs," when abnormally nourished near old-standing inflamed surfaces.[3]

I am informed by Sir James Paget that often several members of a family have a few hairs in their eyebrows much longer than the others; so that even this slight peculiarity seems to be inherited. These hairs, too, seem to have their representatives; for in the chimpanzee, and in certain species of Macacus, there are scattered hairs of considerable length rising from the naked skin above the eyes, and corresponding to our eyebrows; similar long hairs project from the hairy covering of the superciliary ridges in some baboons.

The fine wool-like hair, or so-called lanugo, with which the human fœtus during the sixth month is thickly covered, offers a more curious case. It is first developed, during the fifth month, on the eyebrows and face, and especially round the mouth, where it is much longer than that on the head. A moustache of this kind was observed by Eschricht [4] on a female fœtus; but this is not so surprising a circumstance as it may at first appear, for the two sexes generally resemble each other in all external characters during an early period of growth. The direction and arrangement of the hairs on all parts of the fœtal body are the same as in the adult, but are subject to much variability. The whole surface, including even the forehead and ears, is thus thickly clothed; but it is a significant fact that the palms of the hands and the soles of the feet are quite naked, like the inferior surfaces of all four extremities in most of the lower animals. As this can hardly be an accidental coincidence, the woolly covering of the fœtus probably represents the first permanent coat of hair in those mammals which are born hairy. Three or four cases have been recorded of persons born with their whole bodies and faces thickly covered with fine long hairs; and this strange condition is strongly inherited, and is correlated with an abnormal condition of the teeth.[5] Prof. Alex. Brandt informs me that he has compared the hair from the face of a man thus characterised, aged thirty-five, with the lanugo of a fœtus, and finds it quite similar in texture; therefore, as he remarks, the case may be attributed to an arrest of development in the hair, together with its continued growth. Many delicate children, as I have been assured by a surgeon to a hospital for children, have their backs covered by rather long silky hairs; and such cases probably come under the same head.

3. Paget, 'Lectures on Surgical Pathology,' 1853, vol. i. p. 71.
4. Eschricht, ibid. s. 40, 47.
5. See my 'Variation of Animals and Plants under Domestication,' vol. ii. p. 327. Prof. Alex Brandt has recently sent me an additional case of a father and son, born in Russia, with these peculiarities. I have received drawings of both from Paris.

It appears as if the posterior molar or wisdom-teeth were tending to become rudimentary in the more civilised races of man. These teeth are rather smaller than the other molars, as is likewise the case with the corresponding teeth in the chimpanzee and orang; and they have only two separate fangs. They do not cut through the gums till about the seventeenth year, and I have been assured that they are much more liable to decay, and are earlier lost than the other teeth; but this is denied by some eminent dentists. They are also much more liable to vary, both in structure and in the period of their development, than the other teeth.[6] In the Melanian races, on the other hand, the wisdom-teeth are usually furnished with three separate fangs, and are generally sound; they also differ from the other molars in size, less than in the Caucasian races.[7] Prof. Schaaffhausen accounts for this difference between the races by "the posterior dental portion of the jaw being always shortened" in those that are civilised,[8] and this shortening may, I presume, be attributed to civilised men habitually feeding on soft, cooked food, and thus using their jaws less. I am informed by Mr. Brace that it is becoming quite a common practice in the United States to remove some of the molar teeth of children, as the jaw does not grow large enough for the perfect development of the normal number.[9]

With respect to the alimentary canal, I have met with an account of only a single rudiment, namely the vermiform appendage of the cæcum. The cæcum is a branch or diverticulum of the intestine, ending in a cul-de-sac, and is extremely long in many of the lower vegetable-feeding mammals. In the marsupial koala it is actually more than thrice as long as the whole body.[1] It is sometimes produced into a long gradually-tapering point, and is sometimes constricted in parts. It appears as if, in consequence of changed diet or habits, the cæcum had become much shortened in various animals, the vermiform appendage being left as a rudiment of the shortened part. That this appendage is a rudiment, we may infer from its small size, and from the evidence which Prof. Canestrini[2] has collected of its variability in man. It is occasionally quite absent, or again is largely developed. The passage is sometimes completely closed for half or two-thirds of its length, with the terminal part consisting of a flattened solid expansion. In the orang this append-

6. Dr. Webb, 'Teeth in Man and the Anthropoid Apes,' as quoted by Dr. C. Carter Blake in 'Anthropological Review,' July 1867, p. 299.
7. Owen, 'Anatomy of Vertebrates,' vol. iii. pp. 320, 321, and 325.
8. 'On the Primitive Form of the Skull,' Eng. translat. in 'Anthropological Review,' Oct. 1868, p. 426.
9. Prof. Montegazza writes to me from Florence, that he has lately been study-

ing the last molar teeth in the different races of man, and has come to the same conclusion as that given in my text, viz., that in the higher or civilized races they are on the road towards atrophy or elimination.

1. Owen, 'Anatomy of Vertebrates,' vol. iii. pp. 416, 434, 441.
2. 'Annuario della Soc. d. Nat.' Modena, 1867, p. 94.

age is long and convoluted: in man it arises from the end of the short cæcum, and is commonly from four to five inches in length, being only about the third of an inch in diameter. Not only is it useless, but it is sometimes the cause of death, of which fact I have lately heard two instances: this is due to small hard bodies, such as seeds, entering the passage, and causing inflammation.[3]

In some of the lower Quadrumana, in the Lemuridæ and Carnivora, as well as in many marsupials, there is a passage near the lower end of the humerus, called the supra-condyloid foramen, through which the great nerve of the fore limb and often the great artery pass. Now in the humerus of man, there is generally a trace of this passage, which is sometimes fairly well developed, being formed by a depending hook-like process of bone, completed by a band of ligament. Dr. Struthers,[4] who has closely attended to the subject, has now shewn that this peculiarity is sometimes inherited, as it has occurred in a father, and in no less than four out of his seven children. When present, the great nerve invariably passes through it; and this clearly indicates that it is the homologue and rudiment of the supra-condyloid foramen of the lower animals. Prof. Turner estimates, as he informs me, that it occurs in about one per cent. of recent skeletons. But if the occasional development of this structure in man is, as seems probable, due to reversion, it is a return to a very ancient state of things, because in the higher Quadrumana it is absent.

There is another foramen or perforation in the humerus, occasionally present in man, which may be called the inter-condyloid. This occurs, but not constantly, in various anthropoid and other apes,[5] and likewise in many of the lower animals. It is remarkable that this perforation seems to have been present in man much more frequently during ancient times than recently. Mr. Busk [6] has collected the following evidence on this head: Prof. Broca "noticed the perforation in four and a half per cent. of the arm-bones collected in the 'Cimetière du Sud,' at Paris; and in the Grotto of Orrony, the contents of which are referred to the Bronze period, as

3. M. C. Martins ("De l'Unité Organique," in 'Revue des Deux Mondes,' June 15, 1862, p. 16), and Häckel ("Generelle Morphologie,' B. ii. s. 278), have both remarked on the singular fact of this rudiment sometimes causing death.
4. With respect to inheritance, see Dr. Struthers in the 'Lancet,' Feb. 15, 1873, and another important paper, ibid., Jan. 24, 1863, p. 83. Dr. Knox, as I am informed, was the first anatomist who drew attention to this peculiar structure in man; see his 'Great Artists and Anatomists,' p. 63. See also an important

memoir on this process by Dr. Gruber, in the 'Bulletin de l'Acad. Imp. de St. Pétersbourg,' tom xii. 1867, p. 448.
5. Mr. St. George Mivart, 'Transact. Phil. Soc.' 1867, p. 310.
6. "On the Caves of Gibraltar," 'Transact. Internat. Congress of Prehist. Arch.' Third Session, 1869, p. 159. Prof. Wyman has lately shown (Fourth Annual Report, Peabody Museum, 1871, p. 20), that this perforation is present in thirty-one per cent. of some human remains from ancient mounds in the Western United States, and in Florida. It frequently occurs in the negro.

many as eight humeri out of thirty-two were perforated; but this extraordinary proportion, he thinks, might be due to the cavern having been a sort of 'family vault.' Again, M. Dupont found thirty per cent. of perforated bones in the caves of the Valley of the Lesse, belonging to the Reindeer period; whilst M. Leguay, in a sort of *dolmen* at Argenteuil, observed twenty-five per cent. to be perforated; and M. Pruner-Bey found twenty-six per cent. in the same condition in bones from Vauréal. Nor should it be left unnoticed that M. Pruner-Bey states that this condition is common in Guanche skeletons." It is an interesting fact that ancient races, in this and several other cases, more frequently present structures which resemble those of the lower animals than do the modern. One chief cause seems to be that the ancient races stand somewhat nearer in the long line of descent to their remote animal-like progenitors.

In man, the os coccyx, together with certain other vertebræ hereafter to be described, though functionless as a tail, plainly represent this part in other vertebrate animals. At an early embryonic period it is free, and projects beyond the lower extremities; as may be seen in the drawing (Fig. 1.) of a human embryo. Even after birth it has been known, in certain rare and anomalous cases,[7] to form a small external rudiment of a tail. The os coccyx is short, usually including only four vertebræ, all anchylosed together: and these are in a rudimentary condition, for they consist, with the exception of the basal one, of the centrum alone.[8] They are furnished with some small muscles; one of which, as I am informed by Prof. Turner, has been expressly described by Theile as a rudimentary repetition of the extensor of the tail, a muscle which is so largely developed in many mammals.

The spinal cord in man extends only as far downwards as the last dorsal or first lumbar vertebra; but a thread-like structure (the *filum terminale*) runs down the axis of the sacral part of the spinal canal, and even along the back of the coccygeal bones. The upper part of this filament, as Prof. Turner informs me, is undoubtedly homologous with the spinal cord; but the lower part apparently consists merely of the *pia mater*, or vascular investing membrane. Even in this case the os coccyx may be said to possess a vestige of so important a structure as the spinal cord, though no longer enclosed within a bony canal. The following fact, for which I am also

7. Quatrefages has lately collected the evidence on this subject. 'Revue des Cours Scientifiques,' 1867–1868, p. 625. In 1840 Fleischmann exhibited a human fœtus bearing a free tail, which, as is not always the case, included vertebral bodies; and this tail was critically examined by the many anatomists present at the meeting of naturalists at Erlangen (see Marshall in Niederländischen Archiv Für Zoologie, December 1871).
8. Owen, 'On the Nature of Limbs,' 1849, p. 114.

indebted to Prof. Turner, shews how closely the os coccyx corresponds with the true tail in the lower animals: Luschka has recently discovered at the extremity of the coccygeal bones a very peculiar convoluted body, which is continuous with the middle sacral artery; and this discovery led Krause and Meyer to examine the tail of a monkey (Macacus), and of a cat, in both of which they found a similarly convoluted body, though not at the extremity.

The reproductive system offers various rudimentary structures; but these differ in one important respect from the foregoing cases. Here we are not concerned with the vestige of a part which does not belong to the species in an efficient state, but with a part efficient in the one sex, and represented in the other by a mere rudiment. Nevertheless, the occurrence of such rudiments is as difficult to explain, on the belief of the separate creation of each species, as in the foregoing cases. Hereafter I shall have to recur to these rudiments, and shall shew that their presence generally depends merely on inheritance, that is, on parts acquired by one sex having been partially transmitted to the other. I will in this place only give some instances of such rudiments. It is well known that in the males of all mammals, including man, rudimentary mammæ exist. These in several instances have become well developed, and have yielded a copious supply of milk. Their essential identity in the two sexes is likewise shewn by their occasional sympathetic enlargement in both during an attack of the measles. The *vesicula prostatica*, which has been observed in many male mammals, is now universally acknowledged to be the homologue of the female uterus, together with the connected passage. It is impossible to read Leuckart's able description of this organ, and his reasoning, without admitting the justness of his conclusion. This is especially clear in the case of those mammals in which the true female uterus bifurcates, for in the males of these the vesicula likewise bifurcates.[9] Some other rudimentary structures belonging to the reproductive system might have been here adduced.[1]

The bearing of the three great classes of facts now given is unmistakable. But it would be superfluous fully to recapitulate the line of argument given in detail in my 'Origin of Species.' The homological construction of the whole frame in the members of the same class is intelligible, if we admit their descent from a common progenitor, together with their subsequent adaptation to diversified conditions. On any other view, the similarity of pattern between the hand of a man or monkey, the foot of a horse, the

9. Leuckart, in Todd's 'Cyclop. of Anat.' 1849-52, vol. iv. p. 1415. In man this organ is only from three to six lines in length, but, like so many other rudimentary parts, it is variable in development as well as in other characters.
1. See, on this subject, Owen, 'Anatomy of Vertebrates,' vol. iii. pp. 675, 676, 706.

flipper of a seal, the wing of a bat, &c., is utterly inexplicable.[2] It is no scientific explanation to assert that they have all been formed on the same ideal plan. With respect to development, we can clearly understand, on the principle of variation supervening at a rather late embryonic period, and being inherited at a corresponding period, how it is that the embryos of wonderfully different forms should still retain, more or less perfectly, the structure of their common progenitor. No other explanation has ever been given of the marvellous fact that the embryos of a man, dog, seal, bat, reptile, &c., can at first hardly be distinguished from each other. In order to understand the existence of rudimentary organs, we have only to suppose that a former progenitor possessed the parts in question in a perfect state, and that under changed habits of life they became greatly reduced, either from simple disuse, or through the natural selection of those individuals which were least encumbered with a superfluous part, aided by the other means previously indicated.

Thus we can understand how it has come to pass that man and all other vertebrate animals have been constructed on the same general model, why they pass through the same early stages of development, and why they retain certain rudiments in common. Consequently we ought frankly to admit their community of descent; to take any other view, is to admit that our own structure, and that of all the animals around us, is a mere snare laid to entrap our judgment. This conclusion is greatly strengthened, if we look to the members of the whole animal series, and consider the evidence derived from their affinities or classification, their geographical distribution and geological succession. It is only our natural prejudice, and that arrogance which made our forefathers declare that they were descended from demi-gods, which leads us to demur to this conclusion. But the time will before long come, when it will be thought wonderful that naturalists, who were well acquainted

2. Prof. Bianconi, in a recently published work, illustrated by admirable engravings ('La Théorie Darwinienne et la création dite indépendante,' 1874), endeavours to show that homological structures, in the above and other cases, can be fully explained on mechanical principles, in accordance with their uses. No one has shewn so well, how admirably such structures are adapted for their final purpose; and this adaptation can, as I believe, be explained through natural selection. In considering the wing of a bat, he brings forward (p. 218) what appears to me (to use Auguste Comte's words) a mere metaphysical principle, namely, the preservation "in its integrity of the mammalian nature of the animal." In only a few cases does he discuss rudiments, and then only those parts which are partially rudimentary, such as the little hoofs of the pig and ox, which do not touch the ground; these he shows clearly to be of service to the animal. It is unfortunate that he did not consider such cases as the minute teeth, which never cut through the jaw in the ox, or the mammæ of male quadrupeds, or the wings of certain beetles, existing under the soldered wing-covers, or the vestiges of the pistil and stamens in various flowers, and many other such cases. Although I greatly admire Prof. Bianconi's work, yet the belief now held by most naturalists seems to me left unshaken, that homological structures are inexplicable on the principle of mere adaptation.

with the comparative structure and development of man, and other mammals, should have believed that each was the work of a separate act of creation.

Chapter II

ON THE MANNER OF DEVELOPMENT OF MAN FROM SOME LOWER FORM

Variability of body and mind in man—Inheritance—Causes of variability—Laws of variation the same in man as in the lower animals—Direct action of the conditions of life—Effects of the increased use and disuse of parts—Arrested development—Reversion—Correlated variation—Rate of increase—Checks to increase—Natural selection—Man the most dominant animal in the world—Importance of his corporeal structure—The causes which have led to his becoming erect—Consequent changes of structure—Decrease in size of the canine teeth—Increased size and altered shape of the skull—Nakedness—Absence of a tail—Defenceless condition of man.

It is manifest that man is now subject to much variability. No two individuals of the same race are quite alike. We may compare millions of faces, and each will be distinct. There is an equally great amount of diversity in the proportions and dimensions of the various parts of the body; the length of the legs being one of the most variable points.[1] Although in some quarters of the world an elongated skull, and in other quarters a short skull prevails, yet there is great diversity of shape even within the limits of the same race, as with the aborigines of America and South Australia—the latter a race "probably as pure and homogeneous in blood, customs, and language as any in existence"—and even with the inhabitants of so confined an area as the Sandwich Islands.[2] An eminent dentist assures me that there is nearly as much diversity in the teeth as in the features. The chief arteries so frequently run in abnormal courses, that it has been useful for surgical purposes to calculate from 1040 corpses how often each course prevails.[3] The muscles are eminently variable: thus those of the foot were found by Prof. Turner [4] not to be strictly alike in any two out of fifty bodies; and in some the deviations were considerable. He adds, that the power

1. Investigations in Military and Anthropolog. Statistics of American Soldiers,' by B. A. Gould, 1869, p. 256.
2. With respect to the "Cranial forms of the American aborigines," see Dr. Aitken Meigs in 'Proc. Acad. Nat. Sci.' Philadelphia, May, 1868. On the Australians, see Huxley, in Lyell's 'Antiquity of Man,' 1863, p. 87. On the Sandwich Islanders, Prof. J. Wyman, 'Observations on Crania,' Boston, 1868, p. 18.
3. 'Anatomy of the Arteries,' by R. Quain. Preface, vol. i. 1844.

of performing the appropriate movements must have been modified in accordance with the several deviations. Mr. J. Wood has recorded [5] the occurrence of 295 muscular variations in thirty-six subjects, and in another set of the same number no less than 558 variations, those occurring on both sides of the body being only reckoned as one. In the last set, not one body out of the thirty-six was "found totally wanting in departures from the standard descriptions of the muscular system given in anatomical text books." A single body presented the extraordinary number of twenty-five distinct abnormalities. The same muscle sometimes varies in many ways: thus Prof. Macalister describes [6] no less than twenty distinct variations in the *palmaris accessorius*.

The famous old anatomist, Wolff,[7] insists that the internal viscera are more variable than the external parts: *Nulla particula est quæ non aliter et aliter in aliis se habeat hominibus*. He has even written a treatise on the choice of typical examples of the viscera for representation. A discussion on the beau-ideal of the liver, lungs, kidneys, &c., as of the human face divine, sounds strange in our ears.

The variability or diversity of the mental faculties in men of the same race, not to mention the greater differences between the men of distinct races, is so notorious that not a word need here be said. So it is with the lower animals. All who have had charge of menageries admit this fact, and we see it plainly in our dogs and other domestic animals. Brehm especially insists that each individual monkey of those which he kept tame in Africa had its own peculiar disposition and temper: he mentions one baboon remarkable for its high intelligence; and the keepers in the Zoological Gardens pointed out to me a monkey, belonging to the New World division, equally remarkable for intelligence. Rengger, also, insists on the diversity in the various mental characters of the monkeys of the same species which he kept in Paraguay; and this diversity, as he adds, is partly innate, and partly the result of the manner in which they have been treated or educated.[8]

I have elsewhere [9] so fully discussed the subject of Inheritance, that I need here add hardly anything. A greater number of facts have been collected with respect to the transmission of the most trifling, as well as of the most important characters in man, than in any of the lower animals; though the facts are copious enough

4. 'Transact. Royal Soc. Edinburgh,' vol. xxiv. pp. 175, 189.
5. 'Proc. Royal Soc.' 1867, p. 544; also 1868, pp. 483, 524. There is a previous paper, 1866, p. 229.
6. 'Proc. R. Irish Academy,' vol. x. 1868, p. 141.
7. 'Act. Acad. St. Petersburg,' 1778, part ii. p. 217.

8. Brehm, 'Thierleben,' B. i. s. 58, 87. Rengger, 'Säugethiere von Paraguay,' s. 57.
9. Variation of Animals and Plants under Domestication,' vol. ii. chap. xii.
1. 'Hereditary Genius: an Inquiry into its Laws and Consequences, 1869.

with respect to the latter. So in regard to mental qualities, their transmission is manifest in our dogs, horses, and other domestic animals. Besides special tastes and habits, general intelligence, courage, bad and good temper, &c., are certainly transmitted. With man we see similar facts in almost every family; and we now know, through the admirable labours of Mr. Galton,[1] that genius which implies a wonderfully complex combination of high faculties, tends to be inherited; and, on the other hand, it is too certain that insanity and deteriorated mental powers likewise run in families.

With respect to the causes of variability, we are in all cases very ignorant; but we can see that in man as in the lower animals, they stand in some relation to the conditions to which each species has been exposed, during several generations. Domesticated animals vary more than those in a state of nature; and this is apparently due to the diversified and changing nature of the conditions to which they have been subjected. In this respect the different races of man resemble domesticated animals, and so do the individuals of the same race, when inhabiting a very wide area, like that of America. We see the influence of diversified conditions in the more civilised nations; for the members belonging to different grades of rank, and following different occupations, present a greater range of character than do the members of barbarous nations. But the uniformity of savages has often been exaggerated, and in some cases can hardly be said to exist.[2] It is, nevertheless, an error to speak of man, even if we look only to the conditions to which he has been exposed, as "far more domesticated"[3] than any other animal. Some savage races, such as the Australians, are not exposed to more diversified conditions than are many species which have a wide range. In another and much more important respect, man differs widely from any strictly domesticated animal; for his breeding has never long been controlled, either by methodical or unconscious selection. No race or body of men has been so completely subjugated by other men, as that certain individuals should be preserved, and thus unconsciously selected, from somehow excelling in utility to their masters. Nor have certain male and female individuals been intentionally picked out and matched, except in the well-known case of the Prussian grenadiers; and in this case man obeyed, as might have been expected, the law of methodical selection; for it is asserted that many tall men were reared in the villages inhabited by the grenadiers and their tall wives. In Sparta, also, a

2. Mr. Bates remarks ('The Naturalist on the Amazons,' 1863, vol. ii. p. 159), with respect to the Indians of the same South American tribe, "no two of them were at all similar in the shape of the head; one man had an oval visage with fine features, and another was quite Mongolian in breadth and prominence of cheek, spread of nostrils, and obliquity of eyes."
3. Blumenbach, 'Treatises on Anthropolog.' Eng. translat., 1865, p. 205.

form of selection was followed, for it was enacted that all children should be examined shortly after birth; the well-formed and vigorous being preserved, the others left to perish.[4]

If we consider all the races of man as forming a single species, his range is enormous; but some separate races, as the Americans and Polynesians, have very wide ranges. It is a well-known law that widely-ranging species are much more variable than species with restricted ranges; and the variability of man may with more truth be compared with that of widely-ranging species, than with that of domesticated animals.

Not only does variability appear to be induced in man and the lower animals by the same general causes, but in both the same parts of the body are effected in a closely analogous manner. This has been proved in such full detail by Godron and Quatrefages, that I need here only refer to their works.[5] Monstrosities, which graduate into slight variations, are likewise so similar in man and the lower animals, that the same classification and the same terms can be used for both, as has been shewn by Isidore Geoffroy St.-Hilaire.[6] In my work on the variation of domestic animals, I have attempted to arrange in a rude fashion the laws of variation under the following heads:—The direct and definite action of changed conditions, as exhibited by all or nearly all the individuals of the same species, varying in the same manner under the same circumstances. The effects of the long-continued use or disuse of parts. The cohesion of homologous parts. The variability of multiple parts. Compensation of growth; but of this law I have found no good instance in the case of man. The effects of the mechanical pressure of one part on another; as of the pelvis on the cranium of the infant in the womb. Arrests of development, leading to the diminution or suppression of parts. The reappearance of long-lost characters through reversion. And lastly, correlated variation. All these so-called laws apply equally to man and the lower animals; and most of them even to plants. It would be superfluous here to

4. Mitford's 'History of Greece,' vol. i. p. 282. It appears also from a passage in Xenophon's 'Memorabilia,' B. ii. 4 (to which my attention has been called by the Rev. J. N. Hoare), that it was a well recognised principle with the Greeks, that men ought to select their wives with a view to the health and vigour of their children. The Grecian poet, Theognis, who lived 550 B. C., clearly saw how important selection, if carefully applied, would be for the improvement of mankind. He saw, likewise, that wealth often checks the proper action of sexual selection. He thus writes:

"With kine and horses, Kurnus! we proceed
By reasonable rules, and choose a breed
For profit and increase, at any price:
Of a sound stock, without defect or vice.

5. Godron, 'De l'Espèce,' 1859, tom. ii. livre 3. Quatrefages, 'Unité de l'Espèce Humaine,' 1861. Also Lectures on Anthropology, given in the 'Revue des Cours Scientifiques,' 1866–1868.
6. 'Hist. Gén. et Part. des Anomalies de l'Organisation,' in three volumes, tom. i. 1832.

discuss all of them; [7] but several are so important, that they must be treated at considerable length. * * *

Civilised populations have been known under favourable conditions, as in the United States, to double their numbers in twenty-five years; and, according to a calculation, by Euler, this might occur in a little over twelve years.[8] At the former rate, the present population of the United States (thirty millions), would in 657 years cover the whole terraqueous globe so thickly, that four men would have to stand on each square yard of surface. The primary or fundamental check to the continued increase of man is the difficulty of gaining subsistence, and of living in comfort. We may infer that this is the case from what we see, for instance, in the United States, where subsistence is easy, and there is plenty of room. If such means were suddenly doubled in Great Britain, our number would be quickly doubled. With civilised nations, this primary check acts chiefly by restraining marriages. The greater death-rate of infants in the poorest classes is also very important; as well as the greater mortality, from various diseases, of the inhabitants of crowded and miserable houses, at all ages. The effects of severe epidemics and wars are soon counterbalanced, and more than counterbalanced, in nations placed under favourable conditions. Emigration also comes in aid as a temporary check, but, with the extremely poor classes, not to any great extent.

There is great reason to suspect, as Malthus has remarked, that the reproductive power is actually less in barbarous, than in civilised races. We know nothing positively on this head, for with savages no census has been taken; but from the concurrent testimony of missionaries, and of others who have long resided with such people, it appears that their families are usually small, and large ones rare. This may be partly accounted for, as it is believed, by the women suckling their infants during a long time; but it is highly probable that savages, who often suffer much hardships, and who do not obtain so much nutritious food as civilised men, would be actually less prolific. I have shewn in a former work,[9] that all our domesticated quadrupeds and birds, and all our cultivated plants, are more fertile than the corresponding species in a state of nature. It is no valid objection to this conclusion that animals suddenly supplied with an excess of food, or when grown very fat; and that most

7. I have fully discussed these laws in my 'Variation of Animals and Plants under Domestication,' vol. ii. chap. xxii. and xxiii. M. J. P. Durand has lately (1868) published a valuable essay 'De l'Influence des Milieux,' &c. He lays much stress, in the case of plants, on the nature of the soil.
8. See the ever memorable 'Essay on the Principle of Population,' by the Rev. T. Malthus, vol. i. 1826, pp. 6, 517.
9. 'Variation of Animals and Plants under Domestication,' vol. ii. pp. 111–113, 163.

plants on sudden removal from very poor to very rich soil, are rendered more or less sterile. We might, therefore, expect that civilised men, who in one sense are highly domesticated, would be more prolific than wild men. It is also probable that the increased fertility of civilised nations would become, as with our domestic animals, an inherited character: it is at least known that with mankind a tendency to produce twins runs in families.[1]

Notwithstanding that savages appear to be less prolific than civilised people, they would no doubt rapidly increase if their numbers were not by some means rigidly kept down. The Santali, or hill-tribes of India, have recently afforded a good illustration of this fact; for, as shewn by Mr. Hunter,[2] they have increased at an extraordinary rate since vaccination has been introduced, other pestilences mitigated, and war sternly repressed. This increase, however, would not have been possible had not these rude people spread into the adjoining districts, and worked for hire. Savages almost always marry; yet there is some prudential restraint, for they do not commonly marry at the earliest possible age. The young men are often required to shew that they can support a wife; and they generally have first to earn the price with which to purchase her from her parents. With savages the difficulty of obtaining subsistence occasionally limits their number in a much more direct manner than with civilised people, for all tribes periodically suffer from severe famines. At such times savages are forced to devour much bad food, and their health can hardly fail to be injured. Many accounts have been published of their protruding stomachs and emaciated limbs after and during famines. They are then, also, compelled to wander much, and, as I was assured in Australia, their infants perish in large numbers. As famines are periodical, depending chiefly on extreme seasons, all tribes must fluctuate in number. They cannot steadily and regularly increase, as there is no artificial increase in the supply of food. Savages, when hard pressed, encroach on each other's territories, and war is the result; but they are indeed almost always at war with their neighbours. They are liable to many accidents on land and water in their search for food; and in some countries they suffer much from the larger beasts of prey. Even in India, districts have been depopulated by the ravages of tigers.

Malthus has discussed these several checks, but he does not lay stress enough on what is probably the most important of all, namely infanticide, especially of female infants and the habit of procuring abortion. These practices now prevail in many quarters of the

1. Mr. Sedgwick, 'British and Foreign Medico-Chirurg. Review,' July, 1863, p. 170.

2. 'The Animals of Rural Bengal,' by W. W. Hunter, 1868, p. 259.

world; and infanticide seems formerly to have prevailed, as Mr. M'Lennan[3] has shewn on a still more extensive scale. These practices appear to have originated in savages recognising the difficulty, or rather the impossibility of supporting all the infants that are born. Licentiousness may also be added to the foregoing checks; but this does not follow from failing means of subsistence; though there is reason to believe that in some cases (as in Japan) it has been intentionally encouraged as a means of keeping down the population.

If we look back to an extremely remote epoch, before man had arrived at the dignity of manhood, he would have been guided more by instinct and less by reason than are the lowest savages at the present time. Our early semi-human progenitors would not have practised infanticide or polyandry; for the instincts of the lower animals are never so perverted[4] as to lead them regularly to destroy their own offspring, or to be quite devoid of jealousy. There would have been no prudential restraint from marriage, and the sexes would have freely united at an early age. Hence the progenitors of man would have tended to increase rapidly; but checks of some kind, either periodical or constant, must have kept down their numbers, even more severely than with existing savages. What the precise nature of these checks were, we cannot say, any more than with most other animals. We know that horses and cattle, which are not extremely prolific animals, when first turned loose in South America, increased at an enormous rate. The elephant, the slowest breeder of all known animals, would in a few thousand years stock the whole world. The increase of every species of monkey must be checked by some means; but not, as Brehm remarks, by the attacks of beasts of prey. No one will assume that the actual power of reproduction in the wild horses and cattle of America, was at first in any sensible degree increased; or that, as each district became fully stocked, this same power was diminished. No doubt in this case, and in all others, many checks concur, and different checks under different circumstances; periodical dearths, depending on unfavourable seasons, being probably the most important of all. So it will have been with the early progenitors of man.

---

3. 'Primitive Marriage,' 1865.
4. A writer in the 'Spectator' (March 12th, 1871, p. 320) comments as follows on this passage:—"Mr. Darwin finds himself compelled to reintroduce a new doctrine of the fall of man. He shews that the instincts of the higher animals are far nobler than the habits of savage races of men, and he finds himself, therefore, compelled to re-introduce,—in a form of the substantial orthodoxy of which he appears to be quite unconscious,—and to introduce as a scientific hypothesis the doctrine that man's gain of *knowledge* was the cause of a temporary but long-enduring moral deterioration as indicated by the many foul customs, especially as to marriage, of savage tribes. What does the Jewish tradition of the moral degeneration of man through his snatching at a knowledge forbidden him by his highest instinct assert beyond this?"

NATURAL SELECTION

We have now seen that man is variable in body and mind; and that the variations are induced, either directly or indirectly, by the same general causes, and obey the same general laws, as with the lower animals. Man has spread widely over the face of the earth, and must have been exposed, during his incessant migration,[5] to the most diversified conditions. The inhabitants of Tierra del Fuego, the Cape of Good Hope, and Tasmania in the one hemisphere, and of the Arctic regions in the other, must have passed through many climates, and changed their habits many times, before they reached their present homes.[6] The early progenitors of man must also have tended, like all other animals, to have increased beyond their means of subsistence; they must, therefore, occasionally have been exposed to a struggle for existence, and consequently to the rigid law of natural selection. Beneficial variations of all kinds will thus, either occasionally or habitually, have been preserved and injurious ones eliminated. I do not refer to strongly-marked deviations of structure, which occur only at long intervals of time, but to mere individual differences. We know, for instance, that the muscles of our hands and feet, which determine our powers of movement, are liable, like those of the lower animals,[7] to incessant variability. If then the progenitors of man inhabiting any district, especially one undergoing some change in its conditions, were divided into two equal bodies, the one half which included all the individuals best adapted by their powers of movement for gaining subsistence, or for defending themselves, would on an average survive in greater numbers, and procreate more offspring than the other and less well endowed half.

Man in the rudest state in which he now exists is the most dominant animal that has ever appeared on this earth. He has spread more widely than any other highly organised form: and all others have yielded before him. He manifestly owes this immense superiority to his intellectual faculties, to his social habits, which lead him to aid and defend his fellows, and to his corporeal structure. The supreme importance of these characters has been proved by the final arbitrament of the battle for life. Through his powers of intellect, articulate language has been evolved; and on this his wonderful advancement has mainly depended. As Mr. Chauncey

---

5. See some good remarks to this effect by W. Stanley Jevons, "A Deduction from Darwin's Theory," 'Nature,' 1869, p. 231.
6. Latham, 'Man and his Migrations,' 1851, p. 135.
7. Messrs. Murie and Mivart in their 'Anatomy of the Lemuroidea' ('Transact. Zoolog. Soc.' vol. vii. 1869, pp. 96–98) say, "some muscles are so irregular in their distribution that they cannot be well classed in any of the above groups." These muscles differ even on the opposite sides of the same individual.

Wright remarks: [8] "a psychological analysis of the faculty of language shews, that even the smallest proficiency in it might require more brain power than the greatest proficiency in any other direction." He has invented and is able to use various weapons, tools, traps, &c. with which he defends himself, kills or catches prey, and otherwise obtains food. He has made rafts or canoes for fishing or crossing over to neighbouring fertile islands. He has discovered the art of making fire, by which hard and stringy roots can be rendered digestible, and poisonous roots or herbs innocuous. This discovery of fire, probably the greatest ever made by man, excepting language, dates from before the dawn of history. These several inventions, by which man in the rudest state has become so pre-eminent, are the direct results of the development of his powers of observation, memory, curiosity, imagination, and reason. I cannot, therefore, understand how it is that Mr. Wallace [9] maintains, that "natural selection could only have endowed the savage with a brain a little superior to that of an ape."

Although the intellectual powers and social habits of man are of paramount importance to him, we must not underrate the importance of his bodily structure, to which subject the remainder of this chapter will be devoted; the development of the intellectual and social or moral faculties being discussed in a later chapter.

Even to hammer with precision is no easy matter, as every one who has tried to learn carpentry will admit. To throw a stone with as true an aim as a Fuegian in defending himself, or in killing birds, requires the most consummate perfection in the correlated action of the muscles of the hand, arm, and shoulder, and, further, a fine sense of touch. In throwing a stone or spear, and in many other actions, a man must stand firmly on his feet; and this again demands the perfect co-adaptation of numerous muscles. To chip a flint into the rudest tool, or to form a barbed spear or hook from a bone, demands the use of a perfect hand; for, as a most capable judge, Mr. Schoolcraft,[1] remarks, the shaping fragments of stone

8. Limits of Natural Selection, 'North American Review,' Oct. 1870, p. 295.
9. 'Quarterly Review,' April 1869, p. 392. This subject is more fully discussed in Mr. Wallace's 'Contributions to the Theory of Natural Selection,' 1870, in which all the essays referred to in this work are republished. The 'Essay on Man,' has been ably criticised by Prof. Claparède, one of the most distinguished zoologists in Europe, in an article published in the 'Bibliothèque Universelle,' June 1870. The remark quoted in my text will surprise every one who has read Mr. Wallace's celebrated paper on 'The origin of Human Races deduced from the Theory of Natural Selection,' originally published in the 'Anthropological Review,' May 1864, p. clviii. I cannot here resist quoting a most just remark by Sir J. Lubbock ('Prehistoric Times,' 1865, p. 479) in reference to this paper, namely, that Mr. Wallace, "with characteristic unselfishness, ascribes it (i. e. the idea of natural selection) unreservedly to Mr. Darwin, although, as is well known, he struck out the idea independently, and published it, though not with the same elaboration, at the same time."
1. Quoted by Mr. Lawson Tait in his 'Law of Natural Selection,'—'Dublin Quarterly Journal of Medical Science,' Feb. 1869. Dr. Keller is likewise quoted to the same effect.

into knives, lances, or arrow-heads, shews "extraordinary ability and long practice." This is to a great extent proved by the fact that primeval men practised a division of labour; each man did not manufacture his own flint tools or rude pottery, but certain individuals appear to have devoted themselves to such work, no doubt receiving in exchange the produce of the chase. Archæologists are convinced that an enormous interval of time elapsed before our ancestors thought of grinding chipped flints into smooth tools. One can hardly doubt, that a man-like animal who possessed a hand and arm sufficiently perfect to throw a stone with precision, or to form a flint into a rude tool, could, with sufficient practice, as far as mechanical skill alone is concerned, make almost anything which a civilised man can make. The structure of the hand in this respect may be compared with that of the vocal organs, which in the apes are used for uttering various signal-cries, as in one genus, musical cadences; but in man the closely similar vocal organs have become adapted through the inherited effects of use for the utterance of articulate language.

Turning now to the nearest allies of man, and therefore to the best representatives of our early progenitors, we find that the hands of the Quadrumana are constructed on the same general pattern as our own, but are far less perfectly adapted for diversified uses. Their hands do not serve for locomotion so well as the feet of a dog; as may be seen in such monkeys as the chimpanzee and orang, which walk on the outer margins of the palms, or on the knuckles.[2] Their hands, however, are admirably adapted for climbing trees. Monkeys seize thin branches or ropes, with the thumb on one side and the fingers and palm on the other, in the same manner as we do. They can thus also lift rather large objects, such as the neck of a bottle, to their mouths. Baboons turn over stones, and scratch up roots with their hands. They seize nuts, insects, or other small objects with the thumb in opposition to the fingers, and no doubt they thus extract eggs and young from the nests of birds. American monkeys beat the wild oranges on the branches until the rind is cracked, and then tear it off with the fingers of the two hands. In a wild state they break open hard fruits with stones. Other monkeys open mussel-shells with the two thumbs. With their fingers they pull out thorns and burs, and hunt for each other's parasites. They roll down stones, or throw them at their enemies: nevertheless, they are clumsy in these various actions, and, as I have myself seen, are quite unable to throw a stone with precision.

It seems to me far from true that because "objects are grasped clumsily" by monkeys, "a much less specialised organ of prehen-

2. Owen, 'Anatomy of Vertebrates,' vol. iii. p. 71.

sion" would have served them [3] equally well with their present hands. On the contrary, I see no reason to doubt that more perfectly constructed hands would have been an advantage to them, provided that they were not thus rendered less fitted for climbing trees. We may suspect that a hand as perfect as that of man would have been disadvantageous for climbing; for the most arboreal monkeys in the world, namely, Ateles in America, Colobus in Africa, and Hylobates in Asia, are either thumbless, or their toes partially cohere, so that their limbs are converted into mere grasping hooks.[4]

As soon as some ancient member in the great series of the Primates came to be less aboreal, owing to a change in its manner of procuring subsistence, or to some change in the surrounding conditions, its habitual manner of progression would have been modified: and thus it would have been rendered more strictly quadrupedal or bipedal. Baboons frequent hilly and rocky districts, and only from necessity climb high trees;[5] and they have acquired almost the gait of a dog. Man alone has become a biped; and we can, I think, partly see how he has come to assume his erect attitude, which forms one of his most conspicuous characters. Man could not have attained his present dominant position in the world without the use of his hands, which are so admirably adapted to act in obedience to his will. Sir C. Bell [6] insists that "the hand supplies all instruments, and by its correspondence with the intellect gives him universal dominion." But the hands and arms could hardly have become perfect enough to have manufactured weapons, or to have hurled stones and spears with a true aim, as long as they were habitually used for locomotion and for supporting the whole weight of the body, or, as before remarked, so long as they were especially fitted for climbing trees. Such rough treatment would also have blunted the sense of touch, on which their delicate use largely depends. From these causes alone it would have been an advantage to man to become a biped; but for many actions it is indispensable that the arms and whole upper part of the body should be free; and he must for this end stand firmly on his feet. To gain this great advantage, the feet have been rendered flat; and the great toe has been peculiarly modified, though this has entailed the almost complete loss of its power of prehension. It accords with the principle of the division of physiological labour, prevailing

3. 'Quarterly Review,' April 1869, p. 392.
4. In *Hylobates syndactylus*, as the name expresses, two of the toes regularly cohere; and this, as Mr. Blyth informs me, is occasionally the case with the toes of *H. agilis, lar,* and *leuciscus*. Colobus is strictly arboreal and extraordinarily active (Brehm,

'Thierleben,' B. i. s. 50), but whether a better climber than the species of the allied genera, I do not know. It deserves notice that the feet of the sloths, the most arboreal animals in the world, are wonderfully hook-like.
5. Brehm, 'Thierleben,' B. i. s. 80.
6. "The Hand," &c. 'Bridgewater Treatise,' 1833, p. 38.

throughout the animal kingdom, that as the hands became perfected for prehension, the feet should have become perfected for
support and locomotion. With some savages, however, the foot has
not altogether lost its prehensile power, as shewn by their manner
of climbing trees, and of using them in other ways.[7]

If it be an advantage to man to stand firmly on his feet and to
have his hands and arms free, of which, from his pre-eminent success in the battle of life, there can be no doubt, then I can see no
reason why it should not have been advantageous to the progenitors
of man to have become more and more erect or bipedal. They
would thus have been better able to defend themselves with stones
or clubs, to attack their prey, or otherwise to obtain food. The best
built individuals would in the long run have succeeded best, and
have survived in large numbers. If the gorilla and a few allied
forms had become extinct, it might have been argued, with great
force and apparent truth, that an animal could not have been
gradually converted from a quadruped into a biped, as all the
individuals in an intermediate condition would have been miserably
ill-fitted for progression. But we know (and this is well worthy of
reflection) that the anthropomorphous apes are now actually in an
intermediate condition; and no one doubts that they are on the
whole well adapted for their conditions of life. Thus the gorilla
runs with a sidelong shambling gait, but more commonly progresses
by resting on its bent hands. The long-armed apes occasionally use
their arms like crutches, swinging their bodies forward between
them, and some kinds of Hylobates, without having been taught,
can walk or run upright with tolerable quickness; yet they move
awkwardly, and much less securely than man. We see, in short, in
existing monkeys a manner of progression intermediate between
that of a quadruped and a biped; but, as an unprejudiced judge [8]
insists, the anthropomorphous apes approach in structure more
nearly to the bipedal than to the quadrupedal type.

As the progenitors of man became more and more erect, with
their hands and arms more and more modified for prehension and
other purposes, with their feet and legs at the same time transformed for firm support and progression, endless other changes of
structure would have become necessary. The pelvis would have to
be broadened, the spine peculiarly curved, and the head fixed in an
altered position, all which changes have been attained by man.

7. Häckel has an excellent discussion
on the steps by which man became a biped: 'Natürliche Schöpfungsgeschichte,'
1868, s. 507. Dr. Büchner ('Conférences
sur la Théorie Darwinienne,' 1869, p.
135) has given good cases of the use of
the foot as a prehensile organ by man;
and has also written on the manner of
progression of the higher apes, to which
I allude in the following paragraph: see
also Owen ('Anatomy of Vertebrates,'
vol. iii. p. 71) on this latter subject.
8. Prof. Broca, La Constitution des
Vertèbres caudales; 'La Revue d'Anthropologie,' 1872, p. 26, (separate
copy).

Prof. Schaaffhausen [9] maintains that "the powerful mastoid processes of the human skull are the result of his erect position;" and these processes are absent in the orang, chimpanzee, &c., and are smaller in the gorilla than in man. Various other structures, which appear connected with man's erect position, might here have been added. It is very difficult to decide how far these correlated modifications are the result of natural selection, and how far of the inherited effects of the increased use of certain parts, or of the action of one part on another. No doubt these means of change often co-operate: thus when certain muscles, and the crests of bone to which they are attached, become enlarged by habitual use, this shews that certain actions are habitually performed and must be serviceable. Hence the individuals which performed them best, would tend to survive in greater numbers.

The free use of the arms and hands, partly the cause and partly the result of man's erect position, appears to have led to an indirect manner to other modifications of structure. The early male forefathers of man were, as previously stated, probably furnished with great canine teeth; but as they gradually acquired the habit of using stones, clubs, or other weapons, for fighting with their enemies or rivals, they would use their jaws and teeth less and less. In this case, the jaws, together with the teeth, would become reduced in size, as we may feel almost sure from innumerable analogous cases. In a future chapter we shall meet with a closely parallel case, in the reduction or complete disappearance of the canine teeth in male ruminants, apparently in relation with the development of their horns; and in horses, in relation to their habit of fighting with their incisor teeth and hoofs.

In the adult male anthropomorphous apes, as Rütimeyer,[1] and others, have insisted, it is the effect on the skull of the great development of the jaw-muscles that causes it to differ so greatly in many respects from that of man, and has given to these animals "a truly frightful physiognomy." Therefore, as the jaws and teeth in man's progenitors gradually become reduced in size, the adult skull would have come to resemble more and more that of existing man. As we shall hereafter see, a great reduction of the canine teeth in the males would almost certainly affect the teeth of the females through inheritance.

As the various mental faculties gradually developed themselves the brain would almost certainly become larger. No one, I presume, doubts that the large proportion which the size of man's brain bears to his body, compared to the same proportion in the gorilla or

9. 'On the Primitive Form of the Skull,' translated in 'Anthropological Review,' Oct. 1868, p. 428. Owen ('Anatomy of Vertebrates,' vol. ii. 1866, p. 551) on the mastoid processes in the higher apes.
1. 'Die Grenzen der Thierwelt, eine Betrachtung zu Darwin's Lehre,' 1868, s. 51.

orang, is closely connected with his higher mental powers. We meet with closely analogous facts with insects, for in ants the cerebral ganglia are of extraordinary dimensions, and in all the Hymenoptera these ganglia are many times larger than in the less intelligent orders, such as beetles.[2] On the other hand, no one supposes that the intellect of any two animals or of any two men can be accurately gauged by the cubic contents of their skulls. It is certain that there may be extraordinary mental activity with an extremely small absolute mass of nervous matter: thus the wonderfully diversified instincts, mental powers, and affections of ants are notorious, yet their cerebral ganglia are not so large as the quarter of a small pin's head. Under this point of view, the brain of an ant is one of the most marvellous atoms of matter in the world, perhaps more so than the brain of a man.

The belief that there exists in man some close relation between the size of the brain and the development of the intellectual faculties is supported by the comparison of the skulls of savage and civilised races, of ancient and modern people, and by the analogy of the whole vertebrate series. Dr. J. Bernard Davis has proved,[3] by many careful measurements, that the mean internal capacity of the skull in Europeans is 92.3 cubic inches; in Americans 87.5; in Asiatics 87.1; and in Australians only 81.9 cubic inches. Professor Broca[4] found that the nineteenth century skulls from graves in Paris were larger than those from vaults of the twelfth century, in the proportion of 1484 to 1426; and that the increased size, as ascertained by measurements, was exclusively in the frontal part of the skull—the seat of the intellectual faculties. Prichard is persuaded that the present inhabitants of Britain have "much more capacious braincases" than the ancient inhabitants. Nevertheless, it must be admitted that some skulls of very high antiquity, such as the famous one of Neanderthal, are well developed and capacious.[5] With respect to the lower animals, M. E. Lartet,[6] by comparing the crania of tertiary and recent mammals belonging to the same

2. Dujardin, 'Annales des Sc. Nat.' 3rd series Zoolog. tom. xiv. 1850. p. 203. See also Mr. Lowne, 'Anatomy and Phys. of the *Musca vomitoria*,' 1870, p. 14. My son, Mr. F. Darwin, dissected for me the cerebral ganglia of the *Formica rufa*.

3. 'Philosophical Transactions,' 1869, p. 513.

4. 'Les Sélections,' M. P. Broca, 'Revue d'Anthropologies,' 1873; see also, as quoted in C. Vogt's 'Lectures on Man,' Eng. Translat. 1864, pp. 88, 90. Prichard, 'Phys. Hist. of Mankind,' vol. i. 1838, p. 305.

5. In the interesting article just referred to, Prof. Broca has well remarked, that in civilised nations, the average capacity of the skull must be lowered by the preservation of a considerable number of individuals, weak in mind and body, who would have been promptly eliminated in the savage state. On the other hand, with savages, the average includes only the more capable individuals, who have been able to survive under extremely hard conditions of life. Broca thus explains the otherwise inexplicable fact, that the mean capacity of the skull of the ancient Troglodytes of Lozère is greater than that of modern Frenchmen.

6. 'Comptes-rendus des Sciences,' &c., June 1, 1868.

groups, has come to the remarkable conclusion that the brain is generally larger and the convolutions are more complex in the more recent forms. On the other hand, I have shewn [7] that the brains of domestic rabbits are considerably reduced in bulk, in comparison with those of the wild rabbit or hare; and this may be attributed to their having been closely confined during many generations, so that they have exerted their intellect, instincts, senses, and voluntary movements but little.

The gradually increasing weight of the brain and skull in man must have influenced the development of the supporting spinal column, more especially whilst he was becoming erect. As this change of position was being brought about, the internal pressure of the brain will also have influenced the form of the skull; for many facts shew how easily the skull is thus affected. Ethnologists believe that it is modified by the kind of cradle in which infants sleep. Habitual spasms of the muscles, and a cicatrix from a severe burn, have permanently modified the facial bones. In young persons whose heads have become fixed either sideways or backwards, owing to disease, one of the two eyes has changed its position, and the shape of the skull has been altered apparently by the pressure of the brain in a new direction.[8] I have shewn that with long-eared rabbits even so trifling a cause as the lopping forward of one ear drags forward almost every bone of the skull on that side; so that the bones on the opposite side no longer strictly correspond. Lastly, if any animal were to increase or diminish much in general size, without any change in its mental powers, or if the mental powers were to be much increased or diminished, without any great change in the size of the body, the shape of the skull would almost certainly be altered. I infer this from my observations on domestic rabbits, some kinds of which have become very much larger than the wild animal, whilst others have retained nearly the same size, but in both cases the brain has been much reduced relatively to the size of the body. Now I was at first much surprised on finding that in all these rabbits the skull had become elongated or dolichocephalic; for instance, of two skulls of nearly equal breadth, the one from a wild rabbit and the other from a large domestic kind, the former was 3.15 and the latter 4.3 inches in length.[9]

7. 'The Variation of Animals and Plants under Domestication,' vol. i. pp. 124–129.
8. Schaaffhausen gives from Blumenbach and Busch, the cases of the spasms and cicatrix, in 'Anthropolog. Review,' Oct. 1868, p. 420. Dr. Jarrold ('Anthropologia,' 1808, pp. 115, 116) adduces from Camper and from his own observations, cases of the modification of the skull from the head being fixed in an unnatural position. He believes that in certain trades, such as that of a shoemaker, where the head is habitually held forward, the forehead becomes more rounded and prominent.
9. 'Variation of Animals,' &c., vol. i. p. 117, on the elongation of the skull; p. 119, on the effect of the lopping of one ear.

One of the most marked distinctions in different races of men is that the skull in some is elongated, and in others rounded; and here the explanation suggested by the case of the rabbits may hold good; for Welcker finds that short "men incline more to brachycephaly, and tall men to dolichocephaly;" [1] and tall men may be compared with the larger and longer-bodied rabbits, all of which have elongated skulls, or are dolichocephalic.

From these several facts we can understand, to a certain extent, the means by which the great size and more or less rounded form of the skull have been acquired by man; and these are characters eminently distinctive of him in comparison with the lower animals.

Another most conspicuous difference between man and the lower animals is the nakedness of his skin. Whales and porpoises (Cetacea), dugongs (Sirenia) and the hippopotamus are naked; and this may be advantageous to them for gliding through the water; nor would it be injurious to them from the loss of warmth, as the species, which inhabit the colder regions, are protected by a thick layer of blubber, serving the same purpose as the fur of seals and others. Elephants and rhinoceroses are almost hairless; and as certain extinct species, which formerly lived under an Arctic climate, were covered with long wool or hair, it would almost appear as if the existing species of both genera had lost their hairy covering from exposure to heat. This appears the most probable, as the elephants in India which live on elevated and cool districts are more hairy [2] than those on the lowlands. May we then infer that man became divested of hair from having aboriginally inhabited some tropical land? That the hair is chiefly retained in the male sex on the chest and face, and in both sexes at the junction of all four limbs with the trunk, favours this inference—on the assumption that the hair was lost before man became erect; for the parts which now retain most hair would then have been most protected from the heat of the sun. The crown of the head, however, offers a curious exception, for at all times it must have been one of the most exposed parts, yet it is thickly clothed with hair. The fact, however, that the other members of the order of Primates, to which man belongs, although inhabiting various hot regions, are well clothed with hair, generally thickest on the upper surface,[3] is opposed to the supposition that man became

1. Quoted by Schaaffhausen, in 'Anthropolog. Review,' Oct. 1868, p. 419.
2. Owen, 'Anatomy of Vertebrates,' vol. iii. p. 619.
3. Isidore Geoffroy St.-Hilaire remarks ('Hist. Nat. Générale,' tom. ii. 1859, pp. 215–217) on the head of man being covered with long hair; also on the upper surfaces of monkeys and of other mammals being more thickly clothed than the lower surfaces. This has likewise been observed by various authors. Prof. P. Gervais ('Hist. Nat. des Mammifères,' tom. i. 1854, p. 28), however, states that in the Gorilla the hair is thinner on the back, where it is partly rubbed off, than on the lower surface.

naked through the action of the sun. Mr. Belt believes [4] that within the tropics it is an advantage to man to be destitute of hair, as he is thus enabled to free himself of the multitude of ticks (acari) and other parasites, with which he is often infested, and which sometimes cause ulceration. But whether this evil is of sufficient magnitude to have led to the denudation of his body through natural selection, may be doubted, since none of the many quadrupeds inhabiting the tropics have, as far as I know, acquired any specialised means of relief. The view which seems to me the most probable is that man, or rather primarily woman, became divested of hair for ornamental purposes, as we shall see under Sexual Selection; and, according to this belief, it is not surprising that man should differ so greatly in hairiness from all other Primates, for characters, gained through sexual selection, often differ to an extraordinary degree in closely related forms.

According to a popular impression, the absence of a tail is eminently distinctive of man; but as those apes which come nearest to him are destitute of this organ, its disappearance does not relate exclusively to man. The tail often differs remarkably in length within the same genus: thus in some species of Macacus it is longer than the whole body, and is formed of twenty-four vertebræ; in others it consists of a scarcely visible stump, containing only three or four vertebræ. In some kinds of baboons there are twenty-five, whilst in the mandrill there are ten very small stunted caudal vertebræ, or, according to Cuvier,[5] sometimes only five. The tail, whether it be long or short, almost always tapers toward the end; and this, I presume, results from the atrophy of the terminal muscles, together with their arteries and nerves, through disuse, leading to the atrophy of the terminal bones. But no explanation can at present be given of the great diversity which often occurs in its length. Here, however, we are more specially concerned with the complete external disappearance of the tail. Professor Broca has recently shewn [6] that the tail in all quadrupeds consists of two portions, generally separated abruptly from each other; the basal portion consists of vertebræ, more or less perfectly channelled and furnished with apophyses like ordinary vertebræ; whereas those of the terminal portion are not channelled, are almost smooth, and scarcely resemble true vertebræ. A tail, though not externally visible, is really present in man and the anthropomorphous apes, and is constructed on exactly the same pattern in both. In the terminal portion the verte-

---

4. The 'Naturalist in Nicaragua,' 1874, p. 209. As some confirmation of Mr. Belt's view, I may quote the following passage from Sir W. Denison ('Varieties of Vice-Regal Life,' vol. i. 1870, p. 440): "It is said to be a practice with the Australians, when the vermin get troublesome, to singe themselves."

5. Mr. St. George Mivart, 'Proc. Zoolog. Soc.' 1865, pp. 562, 583. Dr. J. E. Gray, 'Cat. Brit. Mus.: Skeletons.' Owen, 'Anatomy of Vertebrates,' vol. ii. p. 517. Isidore Geoffroy, 'Hist. Nat. Gén.' tom. ii. p. 244.
6. 'Revue d'Anthropologie,' 1872; 'La Constitution des Vertèbres caudales.'

bræ, constituting the *os coccyx*, are quite rudimentary, being much reduced in size and number. In the basal portion, the vertebræ are likewise few, are united firmly together, and are arrested in development; but they have been rendered much broader and flatter than the corresponding vertebræ in the tails of other animals: they constitute what Broca calls the accessory sacral vertebræ. These are of functional importance by supporting certain internal parts and in other ways; and their modification is directly connected with the erect or semi-erect attitude of man and the anthropomorphous apes. This conclusion is the more trustworthy, as Broca formerly held a different view, which he has now abandoned. The modification, therefore, of the basal caudal vertebræ in man and the higher apes may have been effected, directly or indirectly, through natural selection.

But what are we to say about the rudimentary and variable vertebræ of the terminal portion of the tail, forming the *os coccyx?* A notion which has often been, and will no doubt again be ridiculed, namely, that friction has had something to do with the disappearance of the external portion of the tail, is not so ridiculous as it at first appears. Dr. Anderson [7] states that the extremely short tail of *Macacus brunneus* is formed of eleven vertebræ, including the imbedded basal ones. The extremity is tendonous and contains no vertebræ; this is succeeded by five rudimentary ones, so minute that together they are only one line and a half in length, and these are permanently bent to one side in the shape of a hook. The free part of the tail, only a little above an inch in length, includes only four more small vertebræ. This short tail is carried erect; but about a quarter of its total length is doubled on to itself to the left; and this terminal part, which includes the hook-like portion, serves "to fill up the interspace between the upper divergent portion of the callosities;" so that the animal sits on it, and thus renders it rough and callous. Dr. Anderson thus sums up his observations: "These facts seem to me to have only one explanation; this tail, from its short size, is in the monkey's way when it sits down, and frequently becomes placed under the animal while it is in this attitude; and from the circumstance that it does not extend beyond the extremity of the ischial tuberosities, it seems as if the tail originally had been bent round by the will of the animal, into the interspace between the callosities, to escape being pressed between them and the ground, and that in time the curvature became permanent, fitting in of itself when the organ happens to be sat upon." Under these circumstances it is not surprising that the surface of the tail should have been roughened and rendered callous, and Dr. Murie,[8] who carefully observed this species in the

7. 'Proc. Zoolog. Soc.,' 1872, p. 210.   8. 'Proc. Zoolog. Soc.,' 1872, p. 786.

172 · Charles Darwin

Zoological Gardens, as well as three other closely allied forms with slightly longer tails, says that when the animal sits down, the tail "is necessarily thrust to one side of the buttocks; and whether long or short its root is consequently liable to be rubbed or chafed." As we now have evidence that mutilations occasionally produce an inherited effect,[9] it is not very improbable that in short-tailed monkeys, the projecting part of the tail, being functionally useless, should after many generations have become rudimentary and distorted, from being continually rubbed and chafed. We see the projecting part in this condition in the *Macacus brunneus,* and absolutely aborted in the *M. ecaudatus* and in several of the higher apes. Finally, then, as far as we can judge, the tail has disappeared in man and the anthropomorphous apes, owing to the terminal portion having been injured by friction during a long lapse of time; the basal and embedded portion having been reduced and modified, so as to become suitable to the erect or semi-erect position.

I have now endeavoured to shew that some of the most distinctive characters of man have in all probability been acquired, either directly, or more commonly indirectly, through natural selection. We should bear in mind that modifications in structure or constitution which do not serve to adapt an organism to its habits of life, to the food which it consumes, or passively to the surrounding conditions, cannot have been thus acquired. We must not, however, be too confident in deciding what modifications are of service to each being: we should remember how little we know about the use of many parts, or what changes in the blood tissues may serve to fit an organism for a new climate or new kinds of food. Nor must we forget the principle of correlation, by which, as Isidore Geoffroy has shewn in the case of man, many strange deviations of structure are tied together. Independently of correlation, a change in one part often leads, through the increased or decreased use of other parts, to other changes of a quite unexpected nature. It is also well to reflect on such facts, as the wonderful growth of galls on plants caused by the poison of an insect, and on the remarkable changes of colour in the plumage of parrots when fed on certain fishes, or inoculated with the poison of toads;[1] for we can thus see that the fluids of the system, if altered for some special purpose, might induce other changes. We should especially bear in mind that modifications acquired and continually used during past ages for some

9. I allude to Dr. Brown-Séquard's observations on the transmitted effect of an operation causing epilepsy in guinea-pigs, and likewise more recently on the analogous effects of cutting the sympathetic nerve in the neck. I shall hereafter have occasion to refer to Mr. Salvin's interesting case of the apparently inherited effects of motmots biting off the barbs of their own tail-feathers. See also on the general subject 'Variation of Animals and Plants under Domestication,' vol. ii. pp. 22–24.
1. "The Variation of Animals and Plants under Domestication,' vol. ii. pp. 280, 282.

useful purpose, would probably become firmly fixed, and might be long inherited.

Thus a large yet undefined extension may safely be given to the direct and indirect results of natural selection; but I now admit, after reading the essay by Nägeli on plants, and the remarks by various authors with respect to animals, more especially those recently made by Professor Broca, that in the earlier editions of my 'Origins of Species' I perhaps attributed too much to the action of natural selection or the survival of the fittest. I have altered the fifth edition of the 'Origin' so as to confine my remarks to adaptive changes of structure; but I am convinced, from the light gained during even the last few years, that very many structures which now appear to us useless, will hereafter be proved to be useful, and will therefore come within the range of natural selection. Nevertheless, I did not formerly consider sufficiently the existence of structures, which, as far as we can at present judge, are neither beneficial nor injurious; and this I believe to be one of the greatest oversights as yet detected in my work. I may be permitted to say, as some excuse, that I had two distinct objects in view; firstly, to shew that species had not been separately created, and secondly, that natural selection had been the chief agent of change, though largely aided by the inherited effects of habit, and slightly by the direct action of the surrounding conditions. I was not, however, able to annul the influence of my former belief, then almost universal, that each species had been purposely created; and this led to my tacit assumption that every detail of structure, excepting rudiments, was of some special, though unrecognised, service. Any one with this assumption in his mind would naturally extend too far the action of natural selection, either during past or present times. Some of those who admit the principle of evolution, but reject natural selection, seem to forget, when criticising my book, that I had the above two objects in view; hence if I have erred in giving to natural selection great power, which I am very far from admitting, or in having exaggerated its power, which is in itself probable, I have at least, as I hope, done good service in aiding to overthrow the dogma of separate creations.

It is, as I can now see, probable that all organic beings, including man, possess peculiarities of structure, which neither are now, nor were formerly of any service to them, and which, therefore, are of no physiological importance. We know not what produces the numberless slight differences between the individuals of each species, for reversion only carries the problem a few steps backwards, but each peculiarity must have had its efficient cause. If these causes, whatever they may be, were to act more uniformly and energetically during a lengthened period (and against this no reason can be assigned), the result would probably be not a mere slight individual difference, but a well-marked and constant modification, though one of no physiological importance. Changed structures, which are in no way beneficial, cannot be kept uniform through natural selection, though the injurious will be thus eliminated. Uniformity of character would, however, naturally follow from the assumed uniformity of the exciting causes, and likewise from the free intercrossing of many individuals. During successive periods, the same organism might in this manner acquire successive modifications, which would be transmitted in a nearly uniform state as long as the exciting causes remained the same and there was free intercrossing. With respect to the exciting causes we can only say, as when speaking of so-called spontaneous variations, that they relate much more closely to the constitution of the varying organism, than to the nature of the conditions to which it has been subjected.

CONCLUSION

In this chapter we have seen that as man at the present day is liable, like every other animal, to multiform individual differences or slight variations, so no doubt were the early progenitors of man; the variations being formerly induced by the same general causes, and governed by the same general and complex laws as at present. As all animals tend to multiply beyond their means of subsistence, so it must have been with the progenitors of man; and this would inevitably lead to a struggle for existence and to natural selection. The latter process would be greatly aided by the inherited effects of the increased use of parts, and these two processes would incessantly react on each other. It appears, also, as we shall hereafter see, that various unimportant characters have been acquired by man through sexual selection. An unexplained residuum of change must be left to the assumed uniform action of those unknown agencies, which occasionally induce strongly marked and abrupt deviations of structure in our domestic productions.

Judging from the habits of savages and of the greater number of the Quadrumana, primeval men, and even their ape-like progenitors, probably lived in society. With strictly social animals, natural selection sometimes acts on the individual, through the preservation of variations which are beneficial to the community. A community which includes a large number of well-endowed individuals increases in number, and is victorious over other less favoured ones; even although each separate member gains no advantage over the others of the same community. Associated insects have thus acquired many remarkable structures, which are of little or no service to the individual, such as the pollen-collecting apparatus, or the sting of the worker-bee, or the great jaws of soldier-ants. With the higher social animals, I am not aware that any structure has been modified solely for the good of the community, though some are of secondary service to it. For instance, the horns of ruminants and the great canine teeth of baboons appear to have been acquired by the males as weapons for sexual strife, but they are used in defence of the herd or troop. In regard to certain mental powers the case, as we shall see in the fifth chapter, is wholly different; for these faculties have been chiefly, or even exclusively, gained for the benefit of the community, and the individuals thereof have at the same time gained an advantage indirectly.

It has often been objected to such views as the foregoing, that man is one of the most helpless and defenceless creatures in the world; and that during his early and less well-developed condition, he would have been still more helpless. The Duke of Argyll, for instance, insists [2] that "the human frame has diverged from the structure of brutes, in the direction of greater physical helplessness and weakness. That is to say, it is a divergence which of all others it is most impossible to ascribe to mere natural selection." He adduces the naked and unprotected state of the body, the absence of great teeth or claws for defence, the small strength and speed of man, and his slight power of discovering food or of avoiding danger by smell. To these deficiencies there might be added one still more serious, namely, that he cannot climb quickly, and so escape from enemies. The loss of hair would not have been a great injury to the inhabitants of a warm country. For we know that the unclothed Fuegians can exist under a wretched climate. When we compare the defenceless state of man with that of apes, we must remember that the great canine teeth with which the latter are provided, are possessed in their full development by the males alone, and are chiefly used by them for fighting with their rivals; yet the females, which are not thus provided, manage to survive.

In regard to bodily size or strength, we do not know whether man is descended from some small species, like the chimpanzee, or from one as powerful as the gorilla; and, therefore, we cannot say whether man has become larger and stronger, or smaller and weaker, than his ancestors. We should, however, bear in mind that an animal possessing great size, strength, and ferocity, and which, like the gorilla, could defend itself from all enemies, would not perhaps have become social: and this would most effectually have checked the acquirement of the higher mental qualities, such as sympathy and the love of his fellows. Hence it might have been an immense advantage to man to have sprung from some comparatively weak creature.

The small strength and speed of man, his want of natural weap-

---

2. 'Primeval Man,' 1869, p. 66.

ons, &c., are more than counterbalanced, firstly, by his intellectual powers, through which he has formed for himself weapons, tools, &c., though still remaining in a barbarous state, and secondly, by his social qualities which lead him to give and receive aid from his fellow-men. No country in the world abounds in a greater degree with dangerous beasts than Southern Africa; no country presents more fearful physical hardships than the Arctic regions; yet one of the puniest of races, that of the Bushmen, maintains itself in Southern Africa, as do the dwarfed Esquimaux in the Arctic regions. The ancestors of man were, no doubt, inferior in intellect, and probably in social disposition, to the lowest existing savages; but it is quite conceivable that they might have existed, or even flourished, if they had advanced in intellect, whilst gradually losing their brute-like powers, such as that of climbing trees, &c. But these ancestors would not have been exposed to any special danger, even if far more helpless and defenceless than any existing savages, had they inhabited some warm continent or large island, such as Australia, New Guinea, or Borneo, which is now the home of the orang. And natural selection arising from the competition of tribe with tribe, in some large area as one of these, together with the inherited effects of habit, would, under favourable conditions, have sufficed to raise man to his present high position in the organic scale.

Chapter III

COMPARISON OF THE MENTAL POWERS OF MAN AND THE LOWER ANIMALS

The difference in mental power between the highest ape and the lowest savage, immense—Certain instincts in common—The emotions—Curiosity—Imitation—Attention—Memory—Imagination—Reason—Progressive improvement—Tools and weapons used by animals—Abstraction, self-consciousness—Language—Sense of Beauty—Belief in God, spiritual agencies, superstitions.

We have seen in the last two chapters that man bears in his bodily structure clear traces of his descent from some lower form; but it may be urged that, as man differs so greatly in his mental power from all other animals, there must be some error in this conclusion. No doubt the difference in this respect is enormous, even if we compare the mind of one of the lowest savages, who has no words to express any number higher than four, and who uses hardly any abstract terms for common objects or for the affections,[1]

---

1. See the evidence on those points, as given by Lubbock, 'Prehistoric Times,' p. 354, &c.

with that of the most highly organised ape. The difference would, no doubt, still remain immense, even if one of the higher apes had been improved or civilised as much as a dog has been in comparison with its parent-form, the wolf or jackal. The Fuegians rank amongst the lowest barbarians; but I was continually struck with surprise how closely the three natives on board H. M. S. "Beagle," who had lived some years in England, and could talk a little English, resembled us in disposition and in most of our mental faculties. If no organic being excepting man had possessed any mental power, or if his powers had been of a wholly different nature from those of the lower animals, then we should never have been able to convince ourselves that our high faculties had been gradually developed. But it can be shewn that there is no fundamental difference of this kind. We must also admit that there is a much wider interval in mental power between one of the lowest fishes, as a lamprey or lancelet, and one of the higher apes, than between an ape and man; yet this interval is filled up by numberless gradations.

Nor is the difference slight in moral disposition between a barbarian, such as the man described by the old navigator Byron, who dashed his child on the rocks for dropping a basket of sea-urchins, and a Howard or Clarkson; and in intellect, between a savage who uses hardly any abstract terms, and a Newton or Shakespeare. Differences of this kind between the highest men of the highest races and the lowest savages, are connected by the finest gradations. Therefore it is possible that they might pass and be developed into each other.

My object in this chapter is to shew that there is no fundamental difference between man and the higher mammals in their mental faculties. Each division of the subject might have been extended into a separate essay, but must here be treated briefly. As no classification of the mental powers has been universally accepted, I shall arrange my remarks in the order most convenient for my purpose; and will select those facts which have struck me most, with the hope that they may produce some effect on the reader.

* * * The lower animals, like man, manifestly feel pleasure and pain, happiness and misery. Happiness is never better exhibited than by young animals, such as puppies, kittens, lambs, &c., when playing together, like our own children. Even insects play together, as has been described by that excellent observer, P. Huber,[2] who saw ants chasing and pretending to bite each other, like so many puppies.

The fact that the lower animals are excited by the same emotions as ourselves is so well established, that it will not be necessary to

2. 'Recherches sur les Mœurs des Fourmis,' 1810, p. 173.

weary the reader by many details. Terror acts in the same manner on them as on us, causing the muscles to tremble, the heart to palpitate, the sphincters to be relaxed, and the hair to stand on end. Suspicion, the offspring of fear, is eminently characteristic of most wild animals. It is, I think, impossible to read the account given by Sir E. Tennent, of the behaviour of the female elephants, used as decoys, without admitting that they intentionally practise deceit, and well know what they are about. Courage and timidity are extremely variable qualities in the individuals of the same species, as is plainly seen in our dogs. Some dogs and horses are illtempered, and easily turn sulky; others are good-tempered; and these qualities are certainly inherited. Every one knows how liable animals are to furious rage, and how plainly they shew it. Many, and probably true, anecdotes have been published on the long-delayed and artful revenge of various animals. The accurate Rengger, and Brehm[3] state that the American and African monkeys which they kept tame, certainly revenged themselves. Sir Andrew Smith, a zoologist whose scrupulous accuracy was known to many persons, told me the following story of which he was himself an eye-witness; at the Cape of Good Hope an officer had often plagued a certain baboon, and the animal, seeing him approaching one Sunday for parade, poured water into a hole and hastily made some thick mud, which he skilfully dashed over the officer as he passed by, to the amusement of many bystanders. For long afterwards the baboon rejoiced and triumphed whenever he saw his victim.

The love of a dog for his master is notorious; as an old writer quaintly says,[4] "A dog is the only thing on this earth that luvs you more than he luvs himself."

In the agony of death a dog has been known to caress his master, and every one has heard of the dog suffering under vivisection, who licked the hand of the operator; this man, unless the operation was fully justified by an increase of our knowledge, or unless he had a heart of stone, must have felt remorse to the last hour of his life.

As Whewell[5] has well asked, "who that reads the touching instances of maternal affection, related so often of the women of all nations, and of the females of all animals, can doubt that the principle of action is the same in the two cases?" We see maternal affection exhibited in the most trifling details; thus Rengger observed an American monkey (a Cebus) carefully driving away the flies which plagued her infant; and Duvaucel saw a Hylobates

3. All the following statements, given on the authority of these two naturalists, are taken from Rengger's 'Naturgesch. der Säugethiere von Paraguay,' 1830, s. 41–57, and from Brehm's 'Thierleben,' B. i. s. 10–87.

4. Quoted by Dr. Lauder Lindsay, in his 'Physiology of Mind in the Lower Animals;' 'Journal of Mental Science,' April 1871, p. 38.
5. 'Bridgewater Treatise,' p. 263.

washing the faces of her young ones in a stream. So intense is the grief of female monkeys for the loss of their young, that it invariably caused the death of certain kinds kept under confinement by Brehm in N. Africa. Orphan monkeys were always adopted and carefully guarded by the other monkeys, both males and females. One female baboon had so capacious a heart that she not only adopted young monkeys of other species, but stole young dogs and cats, which she continually carried about. Her kindness, however, did not go so far as to share her food with her adopted offspring, at which Brehm was surprised, as his monkeys always divided everything quite fairly with their own young ones. An adopted kitten scratched this affectionate baboon, who certainly had a fine intellect, for she was much astonished at being scratched, and immediately examined the kitten's feet, and without more ado bit off the claws.[6] In the Zoological Gardens, I heard from the keeper that an old baboon (*C. chacma*) had adopted a Rhesus monkey; but when a young drill and mandrill were placed in the cage, she seemed to perceive that these monkeys, though distinct species, were her nearer relatives, for she at once rejected the Rhesus and adopted both of them. The young Rhesus, as I saw, was greatly discontented at being thus rejected, and it would, like a naughty child, annoy and attack the young drill and mandrill whenever it could do so with safety; this conduct exciting great indignation in the old baboon. Monkeys will also, according to Brehm, defend their master when attacked by any one, as well as dogs to whom they are attached, from the attacks of other dogs. But we here trench on the subjects of sympathy and fidelity, to which I shall recur. Some of Brehm's monkeys took much delight in teasing a certain old dog whom they disliked, as well as other animals, in various ingenious ways.

Most of the more complex emotions are common to the higher animals and ourselves. Every one has seen how jealous a dog is of his master's affection, if lavished on any other creature; and I have observed the same fact with monkeys. This shews that animals not only love, but have desire to be loved. Animals manifestly feel emulation. They love approbation or praise; and a dog carrying a basket for his master exhibits in a high degree self-complacency or pride. There can, I think, be no doubt that a dog feels shame, as distinct from fear, and something very like modesty when begging too often for food. A great dog scorns the snarling of a little dog, and this may be called magnanimity. Several observers have stated that monkeys certainly dislike being laughed at; and they sometimes

6. A critic, without any grounds ('Quarterly Review,' July, 1871, p. 72), disputes the possibility of this act as described by Brehm, for the sake of discrediting my work. Therefore I tried, and found that I could readily seize with my own teeth the sharp little claws of a kitten nearly five weeks old.

invent imaginary offences. In the Zoological Gardens I saw a baboon who always got into a furious rage when his keeper took out a letter or book and read it aloud to him; and his rage was so violent that, as I witnessed on one occasion, he bit his own leg till the blood flowed. Dogs shew what may be fairly called a sense of humour, as distinct from mere play; if a bit of stick or other such object be thrown to one, he will often carry it away for a short distance; and then squatting down with it on the ground close before him, will wait until his master comes quite close to take it away. The dog will then seize it and rush away in triumph, repeating the same manœuvre, and evidently enjoying the practical joke.

We will now turn to the more intellectual emotions and faculties, which are very important, as forming the basis for the development of the higher mental powers. Animals manifestly enjoy excitement, and suffer from ennui, as may be seen with dogs, and, according to Rengger, with monkeys. All animals feel Wonder, and many exhibit Curiosity. They sometimes suffer from this latter quality, as when the hunter plays antics and thus attracts them; I have witnessed this with deer, and so it is with the wary chamois, and with some kinds of wild-ducks. Brehm gives a curious account of the instinctive dread, which his monkeys exhibited, for snakes; but their curiosity was so great that they could not desist from occasionally satiating their horror in a most human fashion, by lifting up the lid of the box in which the snakes were kept. I was so much surprised at this account, that I took a stuffed and coiled-up snake into the monkey-house at the Zoological Gardens, and the excitement thus caused was one of the most curious spectacles which I ever beheld. Three species of Cercopithecus were the most alarmed; they dashed about their cages, and uttered sharp signal cries of danger, which were understood by the other monkeys. A few young monkeys and one old Anubis baboon alone took no notice of the snake. I then placed the stuffed specimen on the ground in one of the larger compartments. After a time all the monkeys collected round it in a large circle, and staring intently, presented a most ludicrous appearance. They became extremely nervous; so that when a wooden ball, with which they were familiar as a plaything, was accidentally moved in the straw, under which it was partly hidden, they all instantly started away. These monkeys behaved very differently when a dead fish, a mouse,[7] a living turtle, and other new objects were placed in their cages; for though at first frightened, they soon approached, handled and examined them. I then placed a live snake in a paper bag, with the mouth loosely closed, in one of the larger compartments. One of the monkeys

7. I have given a short account of their behaviour on this occasion in my "Expression of the Emotions,' p. 43.

immediately approached, cautiously opened the bag a little, peeped in, and instantly dashed away. Then I witnessed what Brehm has described, for monkey after monkey, with head raised high and turned on one side, could not resist taking a momentary peep into the upright bag, at the dreadful object lying quietly at the bottom. It would almost appear as if monkeys had some notion of zoological affinities, for those kept by Brehm exhibited a strange, though mistaken, instinctive dread of innocent lizards and frogs. An orang, also, has been known to be much alarmed at the first sight of a turtle.[8]

The principle of Imitation is strong in man, and especially, as I have myself observed, with savages. In certain morbid states of the brain this tendency is exaggerated to an extraordinary degree: some hemiplegic patients and others, at the commencement of inflammatory softening of the brain, unconsciously imitate every word which is uttered, whether in their own or in a foreign language, and every gesture or action which is performed near them.[9] Desor[1] has remarked that no animal voluntarily imitates an action performed by man, until in the ascending scale we come to monkeys, which are well known to be ridiculous mockers. Animals, however, sometimes imitate each other's actions: thus two species of wolves, which had been reared by dogs, learned to bark, as does sometimes the jackal,[2] but whether this can be called voluntary imitation is another question. Birds imitate the songs of their parents, and sometimes of other birds; and parrots are notorious imitators of any sound which they often hear. Dureau de la Malle gives an account [3] of a dog reared by a cat, who learnt to imitate the well-known action of a cat licking her paws, and thus washing her ears and face; this was also witnessed by the celebrated naturalist Audouin. I have received several confirmatory accounts; in one of these, a dog had not been suckled by a cat, but had been brought up with one, together with kittens, and had thus acquired the above habit, which he ever afterwards practised during his life of thirteen years. Dureau de la Malle's dog likewise learnt from the kittens to play with a ball by rolling it about with his fore paws, and springing on it. A correspondent assures me that a cat in his house used to put her paws into jugs of milk having too narrow a mouth for her head. A kitten of this cat soon learned the same trick, and practised it ever afterwards, whenever there was an opportunity.

The parents of many animals, trusting to the principle of imitation in their young, and more especially to their instinctive or in-

8. W. C. L. Martin, 'Nat. Hist. of Mammalia,' 1841, p. 405.
9. Dr. Bateman 'On Aphasia,' 1870, p. 110.
1. Quoted by Vogt, 'Mémoire sur les Microcéphales,' 1867, p. 168.
2. 'The Variation of Animals and Plants under Domestication,' vol. i. p. 27.
3. 'Annales des Sc. Nat.' (1st Series), tom. xxii. p. 397.

herited tendencies, may be said to educate them. We see this when a cat brings a live mouse to her kittens; and Dureau de la Malle has given a curious account (in the paper above quoted) of his observations on hawks which taught their young dexterity, as well as judgment of distances, by first dropping through the air dead mice and sparrows, which the young generally failed to catch, and then bringing them live birds and letting them loose.

Hardly any faculty is more important for the intellectual progress of man than Attention. Animals clearly manifest this power, as when a cat watches by a hole and prepares to spring on its prey. Wild animals sometimes become so absorbed when thus engaged, that they may be easily approached. Mr. Bartlett has given me a curious proof how variable this faculty is in monkeys. A man who trains monkeys to act in plays, used to purchase common kinds from the Zoological Society at the price of five pounds for each; but he offered to give double the price, if he might keep three or four of them for a few days, in order to select one. When asked how he could possibly learn so soon, whether a particular monkey would turn out a good actor, he answered that it all depended on their power of attention. If when he was talking and explaining anything to a monkey, its attention was easily distracted, as by a fly on the wall or other trifling object, the case was hopeless. If he tried by punishment to make an inattentive monkey act, it turned sulky. On the other hand, a monkey which carefully attended to him could always be trained.

It is almost superfluous to state that animals have excellent Memories for persons and places. A baboon at the Cape of Good Hope, as I have been informed by Sir Andrew Smith, recognised him with joy after an absence of nine months. I had a dog who was savage and averse to all strangers, and I purposely tried his memory after an absence of five years and two days. I went near the stable where he lived, and shouted to him in my old manner; he shewed no joy, but instantly followed me out walking, and obeyed me, exactly as if I had parted with him only half an hour before. A train of old associations, dormant during five years, had thus been instantaneously awakened in his mind. Even ants, as P. Huber [4] has clearly shewn, recognised their fellow-ants belonging to the same community after a separation of four months. Animals can certainly by some means judge of the intervals of time between recurrent events.

The Imagination is one of the highest prerogatives of man. By this faculty he unites former images and ideas, independently of the will, and thus creates brilliant and novel results. A poet, as Jean

4. 'Les Mœurs des Fourmis,' 1810, p. 150.

Paul Richter remarks,[5] "who must reflect whether he shall make a character say yes or no—to the devil with him; he is only a stupid corpse." Dreaming gives us the best notion of this power; as Jean Paul again says, "The dream is an involuntary art of poetry." The value of the products of our imagination depends of course on the number, accuracy, and clearness of our impressions, on our judgment and taste in selecting or rejecting the involuntary combinations, and to a certain extent on our power of voluntarily combining them. As dogs, cats, horses, and probably all the higher animals, even birds [6] have vivid dreams, and this is shewn by their movements and the sounds uttered, we must admit that they possess some power of imagination. There must be something special, which causes dogs to howl in the night, and especially during moonlight, in that remarkable and melancholy manner called baying. All dogs do not do so; and, according to Houzeau,[7] they do not then look at the moon, but at some fixed point near the horizon. Houzeau thinks that their imaginations are disturbed by the vague outlines of the surrounding objects, and conjure up before them fantastic images: if this be so, their feelings may almost be called superstitious.

Of all the faculties of the human mind, it will, I presume, be admitted that Reason stands at the summit. Only a few persons now dispute that animals possess some power of reasoning. Animals may constantly be seen to pause, deliberate, and resolve. It is a significant fact, that the more the habits of any particular animal are studied by a naturalist, the more he attributes to reason and the less to unlearnt instincts.[8] In future chapters we shall see that some animals extremely low in the scale apparently display a certain amount of reason. No doubt it is often difficult to distinguish between the power of reason and that of instinct. For instance, Dr. Hayes, in his work on 'The Open Polar Sea,' repeatedly remarks that his dogs, instead of continuing to draw the sledges in a compact body, diverged and separated when they came to thin ice, so that their weight might be more evenly distributed. This was often the first warning which the travellers received that the ice was becoming thin and dangerous. Now, did the dogs act thus from the experience of each individual, or from the example of the older and wiser dogs, or from an inherited habit, that is from instinct? This instinct, may possibly have arisen since the time, long ago, when

5. Quoted in Dr. Maudsley's 'Physiology and Pathology of Mind,' 1868, pp. 19, 220.
6. Dr. Jerdon, 'Birds of India,' vol. i. 1862, p. xxi. Houzeau says that his parokeets and canary-birds dreamt: 'Facultés Mentales,' tom. ii. p. 136.

7. 'Facultés Mentales des Animaux,' 1872, tom. ii. p. 181.
8. Mr. L. H. Morgan's work on 'The American Beaver,' 1868, offers a good illustration of this remark. I cannot help thinking, however, that he goes too far in underrating the power of instinct.

dogs were first employed by the natives in drawing their sledges; or the Arctic wolves, the parent-stock of the Esquimaux dog, may have acquired an instinct impelling them not to attack their prey in a close pack, when on thin ice.

We can only judge by the circumstances under which actions are performed, whether they are due to instinct, or to reason, or to the mere association of ideas: this latter principle, however, is intimately connected with reason. A curious case has been given by Prof. Möbius,[9] of a pike, separated by a plate of glass from an adjoining aquarium stocked with fish, and who often dashed himself with such violence against the glass in trying to catch the other fishes, that he was sometimes completely stunned. The pike went on thus for three months, but at last learnt caution, and ceased to do so. The plate of glass was then removed, but the pike would not attack these particular fishes, though he would devour others which were afterwards introduced; so strongly was the idea of a violent shock associated in his feeble mind with the attempt on his former neighbours. If a savage, who had never seen a large plate-glass window, were to dash himself even once against it, he would for a long time afterwards associate a shock with a window-frame; but very differently from the pike, he would probably reflect on the nature of the impediment, and be cautious under analogous circumstances. Now with monkeys, as we shall presently see, a painful or merely a disagreeable impression, from an action once performed, is sometimes sufficient to prevent the animal from repeating it. If we attribute this difference between the monkey and the pike solely to the association of ideas being so much stronger and more persistent in the one than the other, though the pike often received much the more severe injury, can we maintain in the case of man that a similar difference implies the possession of a fundamentally different mind?

Houzeau relates [1] that, whilst crossing a wide and arid plain in Texas, his two dogs suffered greatly from thirst, and that between thirty and forty times they rushed down the hollows to search for water. These hollows were not valleys, and there were no trees in them, or any other difference in the vegetation, and as they were absolutely dry there could have been no smell of damp earth. The dogs behaved as if they knew that a dip in the ground offered them the best chance of finding water, and Houzeau has often witnessed the same behaviour in other animals.

I have seen, as I daresay have others, that when a small object is thrown on the ground beyond the reach of one of the elephants in the Zoological Gardens, he blows through his trunk on the ground

---

9. 'Die Bewegungen der Thiere,' &c., 1873, p. 11.

1. 'Facultés Mentales des Animaux,' 1872, tom. ii. p. 265.

beyond the object, so that the current reflected on all sides may drive the object within his reach. Again a well-known ethnologist, Mr. Westropp, informs me that he observed in Vienna a bear deliberately making with his paw a current in some water, which was close to the bars of his cage, so as to draw a piece of floating bread within his reach. These actions of the elephant and bear can hardly be attributed to instinct or inherited habit, as they would be of little use to an animal in a state of nature. Now, what is the difference between such actions, when performed by an uncultivated man, and by one of the higher animals?

The savage and the dog have often found water at a low level, and the coincidence under such circumstances has become associated in their minds. A cultivated man would perhaps make some general proposition on the subject; but from all that we know of savages it is extremely doubtful whether they would do so, and a dog certainly would not. But a savage, as well as a dog, would search in the same way, though frequently disappointed; and in both it seems to be equally an act of reason, whether or not any general proposition on the subject is consciously placed before the mind.[2] The same would apply to the elephant and the bear making currents in the air or water. The savage would certainly neither know nor care by what law the desired movements were effected; yet his act would be guided by a rude process of reasoning, as surely as would a philosopher in his longest chain of deductions. There would no doubt be this difference between him and one of the higher animals, that he would take notice of much slighter circumstances and conditions, and would observe any connection between them after much less experience and this would be of paramount importance. I kept a daily record of the actions of one of my infants, and when he was about eleven months old, and before he could speak a single word, I was continually struck with the greater quickness, with which all sorts of objects and sounds were associated together in his mind, compared with that of the most intelligent dogs I ever knew. But the higher animals differ in exactly the same way in this power of association from those low in the scale, such as the pike, as well as in that of drawing inferences and of observation.

The promptings of reason, after very short experience, are well shewn by the following actions of American monkeys, which stand low in their order. Rengger, a most careful observer, states that when he first gave eggs to his monkeys in Paraguay, they smashed

---

2. Prof. Huxley has analysed with admirable clearness the mental steps by which a man, as well as a dog, arrives at a conclusion in a case analogous to that given in my text. See his article, 'Mr. Darwin's Critics,' in the 'Contemporary Review,' Nov. 1871, p. 462, and in his 'Critques and Essays,' 1873, p. 279.

them, and thus lost much of their contents; afterwards they gently hit one end against some hard body, and picked off the bits of shell with their fingers. After cutting themselves only *once* with any sharp tool, they would not touch it again, or would handle it with the greatest caution. Lumps of sugar were often given them wrapped up in paper; and Rengger sometimes put a live wasp in the paper, so that in hastily unfolding it they got stung; after this had *once* happened, they always first held the packet to their ears to detect any movement within.[3]

The following cases relate to dogs. Mr. Colquhoun [4] winged two wild-ducks, which fell on the further side of a stream; his retriever tried to bring over both at once, but could not succeed; she then, though never before known to ruffle a feather, deliberately killed one, brought over the other, and returned for the dead bird. Col. Hutchinson relates that two partridges were shot at once, one being killed, the other wounded; the latter ran away, and was caught by the retriever, who on her return came across the dead bird; "she stopped, evidently greatly puzzled, and after one or two trials, finding she could not take it up without permitting the escape of the winged bird, she considered a moment, then deliberately murdered it by giving it a severe crunch, and afterwards brought away both together. This was the only known instance of her ever having wilfully injured any game." Here we have reason though not quite perfect, for the retriever might have brought the wounded bird first and then returned for the dead one, as in the case of the two wild-ducks. I give the above cases, as resting on the evidence of two independent witnesses, and because in both instances the retrievers, after deliberation, broke through a habit which is inherited by them (that of not killing the game retrieved), and because they shew how strong their reasoning faculty must have been to overcome a fixed habit.

I will conclude by quoting a remark by the illustrious Humboldt.[5] "The muleteers in S. America say, 'I will not give you the mule whose step is easiest, but *la mas racional*,—the one that reasons best;' " and as he adds, "this popular expression, dictated by long experience, combats the system of animated machines, better perhaps than all the arguments of speculative philosophy." Nevertheless some writers even yet deny that the higher animals possess

3. Mr. Belt, in his most interesting work, 'The Naturalist in Nicaragua,' 1874 (p. 119), likewise describes various actions of a tamed Cebus, which, I think, clearly shew that this animal possessed some reasoning power.

4. 'The Moor and the Loch,' p. 45. Col. Hutchinson on 'Dog Breaking,' 1850, p. 46.

5. 'Personal Narrative,' Eng. translat., vol. iii. p. 106.

a trace of reason; and they endeavor to explain away, by what appears to be mere verbiage,[6] all such facts as those above given.

It has, I think, now been shewn that man and the higher animals, especially the Primates, have some few instincts in common. * * *

Chapter VI

ON THE AFFINITIES AND GENEALOGY OF MAN

Position of man in the animal series—The natural system genealogical—Adaptive characters of slight value—Various small points of resemblance between man and the Quadrumana—Rank of man in the natural system—Birthplace and antiquity of man—Absence of fossil connecting links—Lower stages in the genealogy of man, as inferred, firstly from his affinities and secondly from his structure—Early androgynous condition of the Vertebrata—Conclusion.

Even if it be granted that the difference between man and his nearest allies is as great in corporeal structure as some naturalists maintain, and although we must grant that the difference between them is immense in mental power, yet the facts given in the earlier chapters appear to declare, in the plainest manner, that man is descended from some lower form, notwithstanding that connecting-links have not hitherto been discovered.

Man is liable to numerous, slight, and diversified variations, which are induced by the same general causes, are governed and transmitted in accordance with the same general laws, as in the lower animals. Man has multiplied so rapidly, that he has necessarily been exposed to struggle for existence, and consequently to natural selection. He has given rise to many races, some of which differ so much from each other, that they have often been ranked by naturalists as distinct species. His body is constructed on the same homological plan as that of other mammals. He passes through the same phases of embryological development. He retains many rudimentary and useless structures, which no doubt were once serviceable. Characters occasionally make their re-appearance in him, which we have reason to believe were possessed by his early progenitors. If the origin of man had been wholly different from that

6. I am glad to find that so acute a reasoner as Mr. Leslie Stephen ('Darwinism and Divinity, Essays on Free-thinking,' 1873, p. 80), in speaking of the supposed impassable barrier between the minds of man and the lower animals, says, "The distinctions, indeed, which have been drawn, seem to us to rest upon no better foundation than a great many other metaphysical distinctions; that is, the assumption that because you can give two things different names, they must therefore have different natures. It is difficult to understand how anybody who has ever kept a dog, or seen an elephant, can have any doubt as to an animal's power of performing the essential processes of reasoning."

of all other animals, these various appearances would be mere empty deceptions; but such an admission is incredible. These appearances, on the other hand, are intelligible, at least to a large extent, if man is the co-descendant with other mammals of some unknown and lower form.

Some naturalists, from being deeply impressed with the mental and spiritual powers of man, have divided the whole organic world into three kingdoms, the Human, the Animal, and the Vegetable, thus giving to man a separate kingdom.[1] Spiritual powers cannot be compared or classed by the naturalist: but he may endeavour to shew, as I have done, that the mental faculties of man and the lower animals do not differ in kind, although immensely in degree. A difference in degree, however great, does not justify us in placing man in a distinct kingdom, as will perhaps be best illustrated by comparing the mental powers of two insects, namely, a coccus or scale-insect and an ant, which undoubtedly belong to the same class. The difference is here greater than, though of a somewhat different kind from, that between man and the highest mammal. The female coccus, whilst young, attaches itself by its proboscis to a plant; sucks the sap, but never moves again; is fertilised and lays eggs; and this is its whole history. On the other hand, to describe the habits and mental powers of worker-ants, would require, as Pierre Huber has shewn, a large volume; I may, however, briefly specify a few points. Ants certainly communicate information to each other, and several unite for the same work, or for games of play. They recognise their fellow-ants after months of absence, and feel sympathy for each other. They build great edifices, keep them clean, close the doors in the evening, and post sentries. They make roads as well as tunnels under rivers, and temporary bridges over them, by clinging together. They collect food for the community, and when an object, too large for entrance, is brought to the nest, they enlarge the door, and afterwards build it up again. They store up seeds, of which they prevent the germination, and which, if damp, are brought up to the surface to dry. They keep aphides and other insects as milch-cows. They go out to battle in regular bands, and freely sacrifice their lives for the common weal. They emigrate according to a preconcerted plan. They capture slaves. They move the eggs of their aphides, as well as their own eggs and cocoons, into warm parts of the nest, in order that they may be quickly hatched; and endless similar facts could be given.[2] On the whole,

---

1. Isidore Geoffroy St.-Hilaire gives a detailed account of the position assigned to man by various naturalists in their classifications: 'Hist. Nat. Gén.', tom. ii. 1859, pp. 170–189.
2. Some of the most interesting facts ever published on the habits of ants are given by Mr. Belt, in his 'Naturalist in Nicaragua,' 1874. See also Mr. Moggridge's admirable work, 'Harvesting Ants,' &c., 1873, also L'Instinct chez les Insectes,' by M. George Pouchet, 'Revue des Deux Mondes,' Feb. 1870, p. 682.

the difference in mental power between an ant and a coccus is immense; yet no one has ever dreamed of placing these insects in distinct classes, much less in distinct kingdoms. No doubt the difference is bridged over by other insects; and this is not the case with man and the higher apes. But we have every reason to believe that the breaks in the series are simply the results of many forms having become extinct.

Professor Owen, relying chiefly on the structure of the brain, has divided the mammalian series into four sub-classes. One of these he devotes to man; in another he places both the Marsupials and the Monotremata; so that he makes man as distinct from all other mammals as are these two latter groups conjoined. This view has not been accepted, as far as I am aware, by any naturalist capable of forming an independent judgment and therefore need not here be further considered.

We can understand why a classification founded on any single character or organ—even an organ so wonderfully complex and important as the brain—or on the high development of the mental faculties, is almost sure to prove unsatisfactory. This principle has indeed been tried with hymenopterous insects; but when thus classed by their habits or instincts, the arrangement proved thoroughly artificial.[3] Classifications may, of course, be based on any character whatever, as on size, colour, or the element inhabited; but naturalists have long felt a profound conviction that there is a natural system. This system, it is now generally admitted, must be, as far as possible, genealogical in arrangement,—that is the co-descendants of the same form must be kept together in one group, apart from the co-descendants of any other form; but if the parent-forms are related, so will be their descendants, and the two groups together will form a larger group. The amount of difference between the several groups—that is the amount of modification which each has undergone—is expressed by such terms as genera, families, orders, and classes. As we have no record of the lines of descent, the pedigree can be discovered only by observing the degrees of resemblance between the beings which are to be classed. For this object numerous points of resemblance are of much more importance than the amount of similarity or dissimilarity in a few points. If two languages were found to resemble each other in a multitude of words and points of construction, they would be universally recognised as having sprung from a common source, notwithstanding that they differed greatly in some few words or points of construction. But with organic beings the points of resemblance must not consist of adaptations to similar habits of life: two animals may, for instance, have had their whole frames modified for living in the

3. Westwood, 'Modern Class of Insects,' vol. ii. 1840, p. 87.

water, and yet they will not be brought any nearer to each other in the natural system. Hence we can see how it is that resemblances in several unimportant structures, in useless and rudimentary organs, or not now functionally active, or in an embryological condition, are by far the most serviceable for classification; for they can hardly be due to adaptations within a late period; and thus they reveal the old lines of descent or of true affinity.

We can further see why a great amount of modification in some one character ought not to lead us to separate widely any two organisms. A part which already differs much from the same part in other allied forms has already, according to the theory of evolution, varied much; consequently it would (as long as the organism remained exposed to the same exciting conditions) be liable to further variations of the same kind; and these, if beneficial, would be preserved, and thus be continually augmented. In many cases the continued development of a part, for instance, of the beak of a bird, or of the teeth of a mammal, would not aid the species in gaining its food, or for any other object; but with man we can see no definite limit to the continued development of the brain and mental faculties, as far as advantage is concerned. Therefore in determining the position of man in the natural or genealogical system, the extreme development of his brain ought not to outweigh a multitude of resemblances in other less important or quite unimportant points.

The greater number of naturalists who have taken into consideration the whole structure of man, including his mental faculties, have followed Blumenbach and Cuvier, and have placed man in a separate Order, under the title of the Bimana, and therefore on an equality with the orders of the Quadrumana, Carnivora, &c. Recently many of our best naturalists have recurred to the view first propounded by Linnæus, so remarkable for his sagacity, and have placed man in the same Order with the Quadrumana, under the title of the Primates. The justice of this conclusion will be admitted: for in the first place, we must bear in mind the comparative insignificance for classification of the great development of the brain in man, and that the strongly-marked differences between the skulls of man and the Quadrumana (lately insisted upon by Bischoff, Aeby, and others) apparently follow from their differently developed brains. In the second place, we must remember that nearly all the other and more important differences between man and the quadrumana are manifestly adaptive in their nature, and relate chiefly to the erect position of man; such as the structure of his hand, foot, and pelvis, the curvature of his spine, and the position of his head. The family of Seals offers a good illustration of the small importance of adaptive characters for classification. These animals differ from all other Carnivora in the form of their bodies and in the structure of their limbs, far more than does man from the higher apes; yet in most systems, from that of Cuvier to the most recent one by Mr. Flower,[4] seals are ranked as a mere family in the Order of the Carnivora. If man had not been his own classifier, he would never have thought of founding a separate order for his own reception.

It would be beyond my limits, and quite beyond my knowledge, even to name the innumerable points of structure in which man agrees with the other Primates. Our great anatomist and philosopher, Prof. Huxley, has fully discussed this subject,[5] and concludes that man in all parts of his organization differs less from the higher apes, than these do from the lower members of the same group. Consequently there "is no justification for placing man in a distinct order." * * *

LOWER STAGES IN THE GENEALOGY OF MAN

* * * We have thus far endeavoured rudely to trace the genealogy of the Vertebrata by the aid of their mutual affinities. We will now look to man as he exists; and we shall, I think, be able partially to restore the structure of our early progenitors, during successive periods, but not in due order of time. This can be effected by means of the rudiments which man still retains, by the characters which occasionally make their appearance in him through reversion, and by the aid of the principles of morphology and embryology. The various facts, to which I shall here allude, have been given in the previous chapters.

The early progenitors of man must have been once covered with hair, both sexes having beards; their ears were probably pointed, and capable of movement; and their bodies were provided with a tail, having the proper muscles. Their limbs and bodies were also acted on by many muscles which now only occasionally reappear, but are normally present in the Quadrumana. At this or some earlier period, the great artery and nerve of the humerus ran through a supra-condyloid foramen. The intestine gave forth a much larger diverticulum or cæcum than that now existing. The foot was then prehensile, judging from the condition of the great toe in the fœtus; and our progenitors, no doubt, were arboreal in their habits, and frequented some warm, forest-clad land. The males had great canine teeth, which served them as formidable weapons. At a much earlier period the uterus was double; the excreta were voided through a cloaca; and the eye was protected by a third eyelid or nictitating membrane. At a still earlier period the progenitors of man must have been aquatic in their habits; for morphology plainly tells us that our lungs consist of a modified swim-bladder,

---

4. 'Proc. Zoolog. Soc.' 1863, p. 4. 5. 'Evidence as to Man's Place in Nature,' 1863, p. 70, *et passim.*

which once served as a float. The clefts on the neck in the embryo of man show where the branchiæ once existed. In the lunar or weekly recurrent periods of some of our functions we apparently still retain traces of our primordial birthplace, a shore washed by the tides. At about this same early period the true kidneys were replaced by the corpora wolffiana. The heart existed as a simple pulsating vessel; and the chorda dorsalis took the place of a vertebral column. These early ancestors of man, thus seen in the dim recesses of time, must have been as simply, or even still more simply organised than the lancelet or amphioxus.

There is one other point deserving a fuller notice. It has long been known that in the vertebrate kingdom one sex bears rudiments of various accessory parts, appertaining to the reproductive system, which properly belongs to the opposite sex; and it has now been ascertained that at a very early embryonic period both sexes possess true male and female glands. Hence some remote progenitor of the whole vertebrate kingdom appears to have been hermaphrodite or androgynous.[6] But here we encounter a singular difficulty. In the mammalian class the males possess rudiments of a uterus with the adjacent passage, in their vesiculæ prostaticæ; they bear also rudiments of mammæ, and some male Marsupials have traces of a marsupial sack.[7] Other analogous facts could be added. Are we, then, to suppose that some extremely ancient mammal continued androgynous, after it had acquired the chief distinctions of its class, and therefore after it had diverged from the lower classes of the vertebrate kingdom? This seems very improbable, for we have to look to fishes, the lowest of all the classes, to find any still existent androgynous forms.[8] That various accessory parts, proper to each sex, are found in a rudimentary condition in the opposite sex, may be explained by such organs having been gradually acquired by the one sex, and then transmitted in a more or less imperfect state to the other. When we treat of sexual selection, we shall meet with innumerable instances of this form of transmission,—as in the case

6. This is the conclusion of Prof. Gegenbaur, one of the highest authorities in comparative anatomy: see 'Grundzüge der vergleich. Anat.' 1870, s. 876. The result has been arrived at chiefly from the study of the Amphibia; but it appears from the researches of Waldeyer (as quoted in 'Journal of Anat. and Phys.' 1869, p. 161), that the sexual organs of even "the higher vertebrata are, in their early condition, hermaphrodite." Similar views have long been held by some authors, though until recently without a firm basis.
7. The male Thylacinus offers the best instance. Owen, 'Anatomy of Vertebrates,' vol. iii. p. 771.

8. Hermaphroditism has been observed in several species of Serranus, as well as in some other fishes, where it is either normal and symmetrical, or abnormal and unilateral. Dr. Zouteveen has given me references on this subject, more especially to a paper by Prof. Halbertsma, in the 'Transact. of the Dutch Acad. of Sciences,' vol. xvi. Dr. Günther doubts the fact, but it has now been recorded by too many good observers to be any longer disputed. Dr. M. Lessona writes to me, that he has verified the observations made by Cavolini on Serranus. Prof. Ercolani has recently shewn ('Acad. delle Scienze,' Bologna, Dec. 28, 1871) that eels are androgynous.

of the spurs, plumes, and brilliant colours, acquired for battle or ornament by male birds, and inherited by the females in an imperfect or rudimentary condition.

The possession by male mammals of functionally imperfect mammary organs is, in some respects, especially curious. The Monotremata have the proper milk-secreting glands with orifices, but no nipples; and as these animals stand at the very base of the mammalian series, it is probable that the progenitors of the class also had milk-secreting glands, but no nipples. This conclusion is supported by what is known of their manner of development; for Professor Turner informs me, on the authority of Kölliker and Langer, that in the embryo the mammary glands can be distinctly traced before the nipples are in the least visible; and the development of successive parts in the individual generally represents and accords with the development of successive beings in the same line of descent. The Marsupials differ from the Monotremata by possessing nipples; so that probably these organs were first acquired by the Marsupials, after they had diverged from, and risen above, the Monotremata, and were then transmitted to the placental mammals.[9] No one will suppose that the Marsupials still remained androgynous, after they had approximately acquired their present structure. How then are we to account for male mammals possessing mammæ? It is possible that they were first developed in the females and then transferred to the males, but from what follows this is hardly probable.

It may be suggested, as another view, that long after the progenitors of the whole mammalian class had ceased to be androgynous, both sexes yielded milk, and thus nourished their young; and in the case of the Marsupials, that both sexes carried their young in marsupial sacks. This will not appear altogether improbable, if we reflect that the males of existing syngnathous fishes receive the eggs of the females in their abdominal pouches, hatch them, and afterwards, as some believe, nourish the young;[1]—that certain other male fishes hatch the eggs within their mouths or branchial cavities;— that certain male toads take the chaplets of eggs from the females, and wind them round their own thighs, keeping them there until

9. Prof. Gegenbaur has shewn ('Jenaische Zeitschrift,' Bd. vii. p. 212) that two distinct types of nipples prevail throughout the several mammalian orders, but that it is quite intelligible how both could have been derived from the nipples of the Marsupials, and the latter from those of the Monotremata. See, also, a memoir by Dr. Max Huss, on the mammary glands, ibid. B. viii. p. 176.

1. Mr. Lockwood believes (as quoted in 'Quart. Journal of Science,' April, 1868, p. 269), from what he has observed of the development of Hippocampus, that the walls of the abdominal pouch of the male in some way afford nourishment. On male fishes hatching the ova in their mouths, see a very interesting paper by Prof. Wyman, in 'Proc. Boston Soc. of Nat. Hist.' Sept. 15, 1857; also Prof. Turner, in 'Journal of Anat. and Phys.' Nov. 1, 1866, p. 78. Dr. Günther has likewise described similar cases.

the tadpoles are born;—that certain male birds undertake the whole duty of incubation, and that male pigeons, as well as the females, feed their nestlings with a secretion from their crops. But the above suggestion first occurred to me from mammary glands of male mammals being so much more perfectly developed than the rudiments of the other accessory reproductive parts, which are found in the one sex though proper to the other. The mammary glands and nipples, as they exist in male mammals, can indeed hardly be called rudimentary; they are merely not fully developed, and not functionally active. They are sympathetically affected under the influence of certain diseases, like the same organs in the female. They often secrete a few drops of milk at birth and at puberty: this latter fact occurred in the curious case before referred to, where a young man possessed two pairs of mammæ. In man and some other male mammals these organs have been known occasionally to become so well developed during maturity as to yield a fair supply of milk. Now if we suppose that during a former prolonged period male mammals aided the females in nursing their offspring,[2] and that afterwards from some cause (as from the production of a smaller number of young) the males ceased to give this aid, disuse of the organs during maturity would lead to their becoming inactive; and from two well-known principles of inheritance, this state of inactivity would probably be transmitted to the males at the corresponding age of maturity. But at an earlier age these organs would be left unaffected, so that they would be almost equally well developed in the young of both sexes.

CONCLUSION

Von Baer has defined advancement or progress in the organic scale better than any one else, as resting on the amount of differentiation and specialisation of the several parts of a being,—when arrived at maturity, as I should be inclined to add. Now as organisms have become slowly adapted to diversified lines of life by means of natural selection, their parts will have become more and more differentiated and specialised for various functions from the advantage gained by the division of physiological labour. The same part appears often to have been modified first for one purpose, and then long afterwards for some other and quite distinct purpose; and thus all the parts are rendered more and more complex. But each organism still retains the general type of structure of the progenitor from which it was aboriginally derived. In accordance with this view it seems, if we turn to geological evidence, that organisation on the whole has advanced throughout the world by slow and inter-

2. Maddle. C. Royer has suggested a   l'Homme,' &c., 1870.
similar   view   in   her   'Origine   de

rupted steps. In the great kingdom of the Vertebrata it has culminated in man. It must not, however, be supposed that groups of organic beings are always supplanted, and disappear as soon as they have given birth to other and more perfect groups. The latter, though victorious over their predecessors, may not have become better adapted for all places in the economy of nature. Some old forms appear to have survived from inhabiting protected sites, where they have not been exposed to very severe competition; and these often aid us in constructing our genealogies, by giving us a fair idea of former and lost populations. But we must not fall into the error of looking at the existing members of any lowly-organised group as perfect representatives of their ancient predecessors.

The most ancient progenitors in the kingdom of the Vetebrata, at which we are able to obtain an obscure glance, apparently consisted of a group of marine animals,[3] resembling the larvæ of existing Ascidians. These animals probably gave rise to a group of fishes, as lowly organised as the lancelet; and from these the Ganoids, and other fishes like the Lepidosiren, must have been developed. From such fish a very small advance would carry us on to the Amphibians. We have seen that birds and reptiles were once intimately connected together; and the Monotremata now connect mammals with reptiles in a slight degree. But no one can at present say by what line of descent the three higher and related classes, namely, mammals, birds, and reptiles, were derived from the two lower vertebrate classes, namely, amphibians and fishes. In the class of mammals the steps are not difficult to conceive which led from the ancient Monotremata to the ancient Marsupials; and from these to the early progenitors of the placental mammals. We may thus ascend to the Lemuridæ; and the interval is not very wide from these to the Simiadæ. The Simiadæ then branched off into two

3. The inhabitants of the seashore mus* be greatly affected by the tides; animais living either about the *mean* high-water mark, or about the *mean* low-water mark, pass through a complete cycle of tidal changes in a fortnight. Consequently, their food supply will undergo marked changes week by week. The vital functions of such animals, living under these conditions for many generations, can hardly fail to run their course in regular weekly periods. Now it is a mysterious fact that in the highest and now terrestrial Vertebrata, as well as in other classes, many normal and abnormal processes have one or more whole weeks as their periods; this would be rendered intelligible if the Vetebrata are descended from an animal allied to the existing tidal Ascidians. Many instances of such periodic processes might be given, as the gestation of mammals, the duration of fevers, &c. The hatching of eggs affords also a good example, for, according to Mr. Bartlett ('Land and Water,' Jan. 7, 1871), the eggs of the pigeon are hatched in two weeks; those of the fowl in three; those of the duck in four; those of the goose in five; and those of the ostrich in seven weeks. As far as we can judge, a recurrent period, if approximately of the right duration for any process or function, would not, when once gained, be liable to change; consequently it might be thus transmitted through almost any number of generations. But if the function changed, the period would have to change, and would be apt to change almost abruptly by a whole week. This conclusion, if sound, is highly remarkable; for the period of gestation in each mammal, and the hatching of each bird's eggs, and many other vital processes, thus betray to us the primordial birthplace of these animals.

great stems, the New World and Old World monkeys; and from the latter, at a remote period, Man, the wonder and glory of the Universe, proceeded.

Thus we have given to man a pedigree of prodigious length, but not, it may be said, of noble quality. The world, it has often been remarked, appears as if it had long been preparing for the advent of man: and this, in one sense is strictly true, for he owes his birth to a long line of progenitors. If any single link in this chain had never existed, man would not have been exactly what he now is. Unless we wilfully close our eyes, we may, with our present knowledge, approximately recognise our parentage; nor need we feel ashamed of it. The most humble organism is something much higher than the inorganic dust under our feet; and no one with an unbiased mind can study any living creature, however humble, without being struck with enthusiasm at its marvellous structure and properties.

Chapter XXI

GENERAL SUMMARY AND CONCLUSION

Main conclusion that man is descended from some lower form—Manner of development—Genealogy of man—Intellectual and moral faculties—Sexual Selection—Concluding remarks.

A brief summary will be sufficient to recall to the reader's mind the more salient points in this work. Many of the views which have been advanced are highly speculative, and some no doubt will prove erroneous; but I have in every case given the reasons which have led me to one view rather than to another. It seemed worth while to try how far the principle of evolution would throw light on some of the more complex problems in the natural history of man. False facts are highly injurious to the progress of science, for they often endure long; but false views, if supported by some evidence, do little harm, for every one takes a salutary pleasure in proving their falseness and when this is done, one path towards error is closed and the road to truth is often at the same time opened.

The main conclusion here arrived at, and now held by many naturalists who are well competent to form a sound judgment, is that man is descended from some less highly organised form. The grounds upon which this conclusion rests will never be shaken, for the close similarity between man and the lower animals in embryonic development, as well as in innumerable points of structure and constitution, both of high and of the most trifling importance,—the rudiments which he retains, and the abnormal reversions to which he is occasionally liable,—are facts which cannot be disputed. They have long been known, but until recently they told us nothing with respect to the origin of man. Now when viewed by the light of our knowledge of the whole organic world, their meaning is unmistakable. The great principle of evolution stands up clear and firm, when these groups or facts are considered in connection with others, such as the mutual affinities of the members of the same group, their geographical distribution in past and present times, and their geological succession. It is incredible that all these facts should speak falsely. He who is not content to look, like a savage, at the phenomena of nature as disconnected, cannot any longer believe that man is the work of a separate act of creation. He will be forced to admit that the close resemblance of the embryo of man to that, for instance, of a dog—the construction of his skull, limbs and whole frame on the same plan with that of other mammals, independently of the uses to which the parts may be put—the occasional re-appearance of various structures, for instance of several muscles, which man does not normally possess, but which are common to the Quadrumana—and a crowd of analogous facts—all point in the plainest manner to the conclusion that man is the co-descendant with other mammals of a common progenitor.

We have seen that man incessantly presents individual differences in all parts of his body and in his mental faculties. These differences or variations seem to be induced by the same general causes, and to obey the same laws as with the lower animals. In both cases similar laws of inheritance prevail. Man tends to increase at a greater rate than his means of subsistence; consequently he is occasionally subjected to a severe struggle for existence, and natural selection will have effected whatever lies within its scope. A succession of strongly-marked variations of a similar nature is by no means requisite; slight fluctuating differences in the individual suffice for the work of natural selection; not that we have any reason to suppose that in the same species, all parts of the organisation tend to vary to the same degree. We may feel assured that the inherited effects of the long-continued use or disuse of parts will have done much in the same direction with natural selection. Modifications formerly of importance, though no longer of any special use, are long-inherited. When one part is modified, other parts change through the principle of correlation, of which we have instances in many curious cases of correlated monstrosities. Something may be attributed to the direct and definite action of the surrounding conditions of life, such as abundant food, heat or moisture; and lastly, many characters of slight physiological importance, some indeed of considerable importance, have been gained through sexual selection.

No doubt man, as well as every other animal, presents structures, which seem to our limited knowledge, not to be now of any service to him, nor to have been so formerly, either for the general conditions of life, or in the relations of one sex to the other. Such structures cannot be accounted for by any form of selection, or by the inherited effects of the use and disuse of parts. We know, however, that many strange and strongly-marked peculiarities of structure occasionally appear in our domesticated productions, and if their unknown causes were to act more uniformly, they would probably become common to all the individuals of the species. We may hope hereafter to understand something about the causes of such occasional modifications, especially through the study of monstrosities: hence the labours of experimentalists such as those of M. Camille Dareste, are full of promise for the future. In general we can only say that the cause of each slight variation and of each monstrosity lies much more in the constitution of the organism, than in the nature of the surrounding conditions; though new and changed conditions certainly play an important part in exciting organic changes of many kinds.

Through the means just specified, aided perhaps by others as yet undiscovered, man has been raised to his resent state. But since he attained to the rank of manhood, he has diverged into distinct races, or as they may be more fitly called, sub-species. Some of these, such as the Negro and European, are so distinct that, if specimens had been brought to a naturalist without any further information, they would undoubtedly have been considered by him as good and true species. Nevertheless all the races agree in so many unimportant details of structure and in so many mental peculiarities that these can be accounted for only by inheritance from a common progenitor; and a progenitor thus characterised would probably deserve to rank as man.

It must not be supposed that the divergence of each race from the other races, and of all from a common stock, can be traced back to any one pair of progenitors. On the contrary, at every stage in the process of modification, all the individuals which were in any way better fitted for their conditions of life, though in different degrees, would have survived in greater numbers than the less well-fitted. The process would have been like that followed by man, when he does not intentionally select particular individuals, but breeds from all the superior individuals, and neglects the inferior. He thus slowly but surely modifies his stock, and unconciously forms a new strain. So with respect to modifications acquired independently of selection, and due to variations arising from the nature of the organism and the action of the surrounding conditions, or from changed habits of life, no single pair will have been modified much more than the other pairs inhabiting the same country, for all will have been continually blended through free intercrossing.

By considering the embryological structure of man,—the homologies which he presents with the lower animals,—the rudiments which he retains,—and the reversions to which he is liable, we can partly recall in imagination the former condition of our early progenitors; and can approximately place them in their proper place in the zoological series. We thus learn that man is descended from a hairy, tailed quadruped, probably arboreal in its habits, and an inhabitant of the Old World. This creature, if its whole structure had been examined by a naturalist, would have been classed amongst the Quadrumana, as surely as the still more ancient progenitor of the Old and New World monkeys. The Quadrumana and all the higher mammals are probably derived from an ancient marsupial animal, and this through a long series of diversified forms, from some amphibian-like creature, and this again from some fish-like animal. In the dim obscurity of the past we can see that the early progenitor of all the Vertebrata must have been an aquatic animal provided with branchiæ, with the two sexes united in the same individual, and with the most important organs of the body (such as the brain and heart) imperfectly or not at all developed. This animal seems to have been more like the larvæ of the existing marine Ascidians than any other known form.

The high standard of our intellectual powers and moral disposition is the greatest difficulty which presents itself, after we have been driven to this conclusion on the origin of man. But every one who admits the principle of evolution, must see that the mental powers of the higher animals, which are the same in kind with those of man, though so different in degree, are capable of advancement. Thus the interval between the mental powers of one of the higher apes and of a fish, or between those of an ant and scale-insect, is immense; yet their development does not offer any special difficulty; for with our domesticated animals, the mental faculties are certainly variable, and the variations are inherited. No one doubts that they are of the utmost importance to animals in a state of nature. Therefore the conditions are favourable for their development through natural selection. The same conclusion may be extended to man; the intellect must have been all-important to him, even at a very remote period, as enabling him to invent and use language, to make weapons, tools, traps, &c., whereby with the aid of his social habits, he long ago became the most dominant of all living creatures.

A great stride in the development of the intellect will have followed, as soon as the half-art and half-instinct of language came into use; for the continued use of language will have reacted on the brain and produced an inherited effect; and this again will have reacted on the improvement of language. As Mr. Chauncey Wright [1] has

1. 'On the Limits of Natural Selection,' in the 'North American Review,' Oct. 1870, p. 295.

well remarked, the largeness of the brain in man relatively to his body, compared with the lower animals, may be attributed in chief part to the early use of some simple form of language,—that wonderful engine which affixes signs to all sorts of objects and qualities, and excites trains of thought which would never arise from the mere impression of the senses, or if they did arise could not be followed out. The higher intellectual powers of man, such as those of ratiocination, abstraction, self-consciousness, &c., probably follow from the continued improvement and exercise of the other mental faculties.

The development of the moral qualities is a more interesting problem. The foundation lies in the social instincts, including under this term the family ties. These instincts are highly complex, and in the case of the lower animals give special tendencies towards certain definite actions; but the more important elements are love, and the distinct emotion of sympathy. Animals endowed with the social instincts take pleasure in one another's company, warn one another of danger, defend and aid one another in many ways. These instincts do not extend to all the individuals of the species, but only to those of the same community. As they are highly beneficial to the species, they have in all probability been acquired through natural selection.

A moral being is one who is capable of reflecting on his past actions and their motives—of approving of some and disapproving of others; and the fact that man is the one being who certainly deserves this designation, is the greatest of all distinctions between him and the lower animals. But in the fourth chapter I have endeavoured to shew that the moral sense follows, firstly, from the enduring and ever-present nature of the social instincts; secondly, from man's appreciation of the approbation and disapprobation of his fellows; and thirdly, from the high activity of his mental faculties, with past impressions extremely vivid; and in these latter respects he differs from the lower animals. Owing to this condition of mind, man cannot avoid looking both backwards and forwards, and comparing past impressions. Hence after some temporary desire or passion has mastered his social instincts, he reflects and compares the now weakened impression of such past impulses with the ever-present social instincts; and he then feels that sense of dissatisfaction which all unsatisfied instincts leave behind them, he therefore resolves to act differently for the future,—and this is conscience. Any instinct, permanently stronger or more enduring than another, gives rise to a feeling which we express by saying that it ought to be obeyed. A pointer dog, if able to reflect on his past conduct, would say to himself, I ought (as indeed we say of him) to have pointed at that hare and not have yielded to the passing temptation of hunting it.

Social animals are impelled partly by a wish to aid the members of their community in a general manner, but more commonly to perform certain definite actions. Man is impelled by the same general wish to aid his fellows; but has few or no special instincts. He differs also from the lower animals in the power of expressing his desires by words, which thus become a guide to the aid required and bestowed. The motive to give aid is likewise much modified in man: it no longer consists solely of a blind instinctive impulse, but is much influenced by the praise or blame of his fellows. The appreciation and the bestowal of praise and blame both rest on sympathy; and this emotion, as we have seen, is one of the most important elements of the social instincts. Sympathy, though gained as an instinct, is also much strengthened by exercise or habit. As all men desire their own happiness, praise or blame is bestowed on actions and motives, according as they lead to this end; and as happiness is an essential part of the general good, the greatest-happiness principle indirectly serves as a nearly safe standard of right and wrong. As the reasoning powers advance and experience is gained, the remoter effects of certain lines of conduct on the character of the individual, and on the general good, are perceived; and then the self-regarding virtues come within the scope of public opinion, and receive praise, and their opposites blame. But with the less civilised nations reason often errs, and many bad customs and base superstitions come within the same scope, and are then esteemed as high virtues, and their breach as heavy crimes.

The moral faculties are generally and justly esteemed as of higher value than the intellectual powers. But we should bear in mind that the activity of the mind in vividly recalling past impressions is one of the fundamental though secondary bases of conscience. This affords the strongest argument for educating and stimulating in all possible ways the intellectual faculties of every human being. No doubt a man with a torpid mind, if his social affections and sympathies are well developed, will be led to good actions, and may have a fairly sensitive conscience. But whatever renders the imagination more vivid and strengthens the habit of recalling and comparing past impressions, will make the conscience more sensitive, and may even somewhat compensate for weak social affections and sympathies.

The moral nature of man has reached its present standard, partly through the advancement of his reasoning powers and consequently of a just public opinion, but especially from his sympathies having been rendered more tender and widely diffused through the effects of habit, example, instruction, and reflection. It is not improbable that after long practice virtuous tendencies may be inherited. With the more civilised races, the conviction of the existence of an all-seeing Deity has had a potent influence on the advance of morality. Ultimately man does not accept the praise or blame of his fellows as his sole guide, though few escape this influence, but his habitual convictions, controlled by reason, afford him the safest rule. His conscience then becomes the supreme judge and monitor. Nevertheless the first foundation or origin of the moral sense lies in the social instincts, including sympathy; and these instincts no doubt were primarily gained, as in the case of the lower animals, through natural selection.

The belief in God has often been advanced as not only the greatest, but the most complete of all the distinctions between man and the lower animals. It is however impossible, as we have seen, to maintain that this belief is innate or instinctive in man. On the other hand a belief in all-pervading spiritual agencies seems to be universal; and apparently follows from a considerable advance in man's reason, and from a still greater advance in his faculties of imagination, curiosity and wonder. I am aware that the assumed instinctive belief in God has been used by many persons as an argument for His existence. But this is a rash argument, as we should thus be compelled to believe in the existence of many cruel and malignant spirits, only a little more powerful than man; for the belief in them is far more general than in a beneficent Deity. The idea of a universal and beneficent Creator does not seem to arise in the mind of man, until he has been elevated by long-continued culture.

He who believes in the advancement of man from some low organised form, will naturally ask how does this bear on the belief in the immortality of the soul. The barbarous races of man, as Sir J. Lubbock has shewn, possess no clear belief of this kind; but arguments derived from the primeval beliefs of savages are, as we have just seen, of little or no avail. Few persons feel any anxiety from the impossibility of determining at what precise period in the development of the individual, from the first trace of a minute germinal vesicle, man becomes an immortal being; and there is no greater cause for anxiety because the period cannot possibly be determined in the gradually ascending organic scale.[2]

I am aware that the conclusions arrived at in this work will be denounced by some as highly irreligious; but he who denounces them is bound to shew why it is more irreligious to explain the origin of man as a distinct species by descent from some lower form, through the laws of variation and natural selection, than to explain the birth of the individual through the laws of ordinary reproduction. The birth both of the species and of the individual are equally parts of that grand sequence of events, which our minds refuse to

2. The Rev. J. A. Picton gives a discussion to this effect in his 'New Theories and the Old Faith,' 1870.

accept as the result of blind chance. The understanding revolts at such a conclusion, whether or not we are able to believe that every slight variation of structure,—the union of each pair in marriage,—the dissemination of each seed,—and other such events, have all been ordained for some special purpose.

Sexual selection has been treated at great length in this work; for, as I have attempted to shew, it has played an important part in the history of the organic world. I am aware that much remains doubtful, but I have endeavoured to give a fair view of the whole case. In the lower divisions of the animal kingdom, sexual selection seems to have done nothing: such animals are often affixed for life to the same spot, or have the sexes combined in the same individual, or what is still more important, their perceptive and intellectual faculties are not sufficiently advanced to allow of the feelings of love and jealousy, or of the exertion of choice. When, however, we come to the Arthropoda and Vertebrata, even to the lowest classes in these two great Sub-Kingdoms, sexual selection has effected much.

In the several great classes of the animal kingdom,—in mammals, birds, reptiles, fishes, insects, and even crustaceans,—the differences between the sexes follow nearly the same rules. The males are almost always the wooers; and they alone are armed with special weapons for fighting with their rivals. They are generally stronger and larger than the females, and are endowed with the requisite qualities of courage and pugnacity. They are provided, either exclusively or in a much higher degree than the females, with organs for vocal or instrumental music, and with odoriferous glands. They are ornamental with infinitely diversified appendages, and with the most brilliant or conspicuous colours, often arranged in elegant patterns, whilst the females are unadorned. When the sexes differ in more important structures, it is the male which is provided with special sense-organs for discovering the female, with locomotive organs for reaching her, and often with prehensile organs for holding her. These various structures for charming or securing the female are often developed in the male during only part of the year, namely the breeding-season. They have in many cases been more or less transferred to the females; and in the latter case they often appear in her as mere rudiments. They are lost or never gained by the males after emasculation. Generally they are not developed in the male during early youth, but appear a short time before the age for reproduction. Hence in most cases the young of both sexes resemble each other; and the female somewhat resembles her young offspring throughout life. In almost every great class a few anomalous cases occur, where there has been an almost complete transposition of the characters proper to the two sexes; the females assuming characters which properly belong to the males. This surprising uniformity in the laws regulating the differences between the sexes in so many and such widely separated classes, is intelligible if we admit the action of one common cause, namely sexual selection.

Sexual selection depends on the success of certain individuals over others of the same sex, in relation to the propagation of the species; whilst natural selection depends on the success of both sexes, at all ages, in relation to the general conditions of life. The sexual struggle is of two kinds; in the one it is between individuals of the same sex, generally the males, in order to drive away or kill their rivals, the females remaining passive; whilst in the other, the struggle is likewise between the individuals of the same sex, in order to excite or charm those of the opposite sex, generally the females, which no longer remain passive, but select the more agreeable partners. This latter kind of selection is closely analogous to that which man unintentionally, yet effectually, brings to bear on his domesticated productions, when he preserves during a long period the most pleasing or useful individuals, without any wish to modify the breed.

The laws of inheritance determine whether characters gained through sexual selection by either sex shall be transmitted to the same sex, or to both; as well as the age at which they shall be developed. It appears that variations arising late in life are commonly transmitted to one and the same sex. Variability is the necessary basis for the action of selection, and is wholly independent of it. It follows from this, that variations of the same general nature have often been taken advantage of and accumulated through sexual selection in relation to the propagation of the species, as well as through natural selection in relation to the general purposes of life. Hence secondary sexual characters, when equally transmitted to both sexes can be distinguished from ordinary specific characters only by the light of analogy. The modifications acquired through sexual selection are often so strongly pronounced that the two sexes have frequently been ranked as distinct species, or even as distinct genera. Such strongly-marked differences must be in some manner highly important; and we know that they have been acquired in some instances at the cost not only of inconvenience, but of exposure to actual danger.

The belief in the power of sexual selection rests chiefly on the following considerations. Certain characters are confined to one sex; and this alone renders it probable that in most cases they are connected with the act of reproduction. In innumerable instances these characters are fully developed only at maturity, and often during only a part of the year, which is always the breeding-season.

The males (passing over a few exceptional cases) are the more active in courtship; they are the better armed, and are rendered the more attractive in various ways. It is to be especially observed that the males display their attractions with elaborate care in the presence of the females; and that they rarely or never display them excepting during the season of love. It is incredible that all this should be purposeless. Lastly we have distinct evidence with some quadrupeds and birds, that the individuals of one sex are capable of feeling a strong antipathy or preference for certain individuals of the other sex.

Bearing in mind these facts, and the marked results of man's unconscious selection, when applied to domesticated animals and cultivated plants, it seems to me almost certain that if the individuals of one sex were during a long series of generations to prefer pairing with certain individuals of the other sex, characterised in some peculiar manner, the offspring would slowly but surely become modified in this same manner. I have not attempted to conceal that, excepting when the males are more numerous than the females, or when polygamy prevails, it is doubtful how the more attractive males succeed in leaving a large number of offspring to inherit their superiority in ornaments or other charms than the less attractive males; but I have shewn that this would probably follow from the females,—especially the more vigorous ones, which would be the first to breed,—preferring not only the more attractive but at the same time the more vigorous and victorious males.

Although we have some positive evidence that birds appreciate bright and beautiful objects, as with the bower-birds of Australia, and although they certainly appreciate the power of song, yet I fully admit that it is astonishing that the females of many birds and some mammals should be endowed with sufficient taste to appreciate ornaments, which we have reason to attribute to sexual selection; and this is even more astonishing in the case of reptiles, fish, and insects. But we really know little about the minds of the lower animals. It cannot be supposed, for instance, that male birds of paradise or peacocks should take such pains in erecting, spreading, and vibrating their beautiful plumes before the females for no purpose. We should remember the fact given on excellent authority in a former chapter, that several peahens, when debarred from an admired male, remained widows during a whole season rather than pair with another bird.

Nevertheless I know of no fact in natural history more wonderful than that of the female Argus pheasant should appreciate the exquisite shading of the ball-and-socket ornaments and the elegant patterns on the wing-feathers of the male. He who thinks that the male was created as he now exists must admit that the great plumes, which prevent the wings from being used for flight, and which are displayed during courtship and at no other time in a manner quite peculiar to this one species, were given to him as an ornament. If so, he must likewise admit that the female was created and endowed with the capacity of appreciating such ornaments. I differ only in the conviction that the male Argus pheasant acquired his beauty gradually, through the preference of the females during many generations for the more highly ornamented males; the æsthetic capacity of the females having been advanced through exercise or habit, just as our own taste is gradually improved. In the male through the fortunate chance of a few feathers being left unchanged, we can distinctly trace how simple spots with a little fulvous shading on one side may have been developed by small steps into the wonderful ball-and-socket ornaments; and it is probable that they were actually thus developed.

Everyone who admits the principle of evolution, and yet feels great difficulty in admitting that female mammals, birds, reptiles, and fish, could have acquired the high taste implied by the beauty of the males, and which generally coincides with our own standard, should reflect that the nerve-cells of the brain in the highest as well as in the lowest members of the Vertebrate series, are derived from those of the common progenitor of this great Kingdom. For we can thus see how it has come to pass that certain mental faculties, in various and widely distinct groups of animals, have been developed in nearly the same manner and to nearly the same degree.

The reader who has taken the trouble to go through the several chapters devoted to sexual selection, will be able to judge how far the conclusions at which I have arrived are supported by sufficient evidence. If he accepts these conclusions he may, I think, safely extend them to mankind; but it would be superfluous here to repeat what I have so lately said on the manner in which sexual selection apparently has acted on man, both on the male and female side, causing the two sexes to differ in body and mind, and the several races to differ from each other in various characters, as well as from their ancient and lowly-organised progenitors.

He who admits the principle of sexual selection will be led to the remarkable conclusion that the nervous system not only regulates most of the existing functions of the body, but has indirectly influenced the progressive development of various bodily structures and of certain mental qualities. Courage, pugnacity, perseverance, strength and size of body, weapons of all kinds, musical organs, both vocal and instrumental, bright colours and ornamental appendages, have all been indirectly gained by the one sex or the other, through the exertion of choice, the influence of love and jealousy, and the appreciation of the beautiful in sound, colour or form; and these powers of the mind manifestly depend on the development of the brain.

Man scans with scrupulous care the character and pedigree of his horses, cattle, and dogs before he matches them; but when he comes to his own marriage he rarely, or never, takes any such care. He is impelled by nearly the same motives as the lower animals, when they are left to their own free choice, though he is in so far superior to them that he highly values mental charms and virtues. On the other hand he is strongly attracted by mere wealth or rank. Yet he might by selection do something not only for the bodily constitution and frame of his offspring, but for their intellectual and moral qualities. Both sexes ought to refrain from marriage if they are in any marked degree inferior in body or mind; but such hopes are Utopian and will never be even partially realised until the laws of inheritance are thoroughly known. Everyone does good service, who aids toward this end. When the principles of breeding and inheritance are better understood, we shall not hear ignorant members of our legislature rejecting with scorn a plan for ascertaining whether or not consanguineous marriages are injurious to man.

The advancement of the welfare of mankind is a most intricate problem: all ought to refrain from marriage who cannot avoid abject poverty for their children; for poverty is not only a great evil, but tends to its own increase by leading to recklessness in marriage. On the other hand, as Mr. Galton has remarked, if the prudent avoid marriage, whilst the reckless marry, the inferior members tend to supplant the better members of society. Man, like every other animal, has no doubt advanced to his present high condition through a struggle for existence consequent on his rapid multiplication; and if he is to advance still higher, it is to be feared that he must remain subject to a severe struggle. Otherwise he would sink into indolence, and the more gifted men would not be more successful in the battle of life than the less gifted. Hence our natural rate of increase, though leading to many and obvious evils, must not be greatly diminished by any means. There should be open competition for all men; and the most able should not be prevented by laws or customs from succeeding best and rearing the largest number of offspring. Important as the struggle for existence has been and even still is, yet as far as the highest part of man's nature is concerned there are other agencies more important. For the moral qualities are advanced, either directly or indirectly, much more through the effects of habit, the reasoning powers, instruction, religion, &c., than through natural selection; though to this latter agency may be safely attributed the social instincts, which afforded the basis for the development of the moral sense.

The main conclusion arrived at in this work, namely, that man is descended from some lowly organised form, will, I regret to think, be highly distasteful to many. But there can hardly be a doubt that we are descended from barbarians. The astonishment which I felt on first seeing a party of Fuegians on a wild and broken shore will never be forgotten by me, for the reflection at once rushed into my mind—such were our ancestors. These men were absolutely naked and bedaubed with paint, their long hair was tangled, their mouths, frothed with excitement, and their expression was wild, startled, and distrustful. They possessed hardly any arts, and like wild animals lived on what they could catch; they had no government, and were merciless to every one not of their own small tribe. He who has seen a savage in his native land will not feel much shame, if forced to acknowledge that the blood of some more humble creature flows in his veins. For my own part I would as soon be descended from that heroic little monkey, who braved his dreaded enemy in order to save the life of his keeper, or from that old baboon, who descending from the mountains, carried away in triumph his young comrade from a crowd of astonished dogs—as from a savage who delights to torture his enemies, offers up bloody sacrifices, practises infanticide without remorse, treats his wives like slaves, knows no decency, and is haunted by the grossest superstitions.

Man may be excused for feeling some pride at having risen, though not through his own exertions, to the very summit of the organic scale; and the fact of his having thus risen, instead of having been aboriginally placed there, may give him hope for a still higher destiny in the distant future. But we are not here concerned with hopes or fears, only with the truth as far as our reason permits us to discover it; and I have given the evidence to the best of my ability. We must, however, acknowledge, as it seems to me, that man with all his noble qualities, with sympathy which feels for the most debased, with benevolence which extends not only to other men but to the humblest living creature, with his god-like intellect which has penetrated into the movements and constitution of the solar system—with all these exalted powers—Man still bears in his bodily frame the indelible stamp of his lowly origin.

PART III

Darwin
and Science

I do not expect my ideas to be adopted all at once. The human mind gets creased into a way of seeing things. Those who have envisaged nature according to a certain point of view during much of their career, rise only with difficulty to new ideas.
—Lavoisier, 1785

It is manifest that at least a large number of naturalists must admit that species are the modified descendants of other species; and this especially holds good with the younger and rising naturalists. * * * Of the older and honoured chiefs in natural science, many unfortunately are still opposed to evolution in every form.
—Darwin, 1871

Neo-Darwinism, as we may call the modern theory of gradual transformation operated by natural selection upon a Mendelian genetic outfit of self-reproducing and self-varying genes, is fully accepted by the great majority of students of evolution.
—Sir Julian Huxley, 1958

Introduction

BERT JAMES LOEWENBERG

The Mosaic of Darwinian Thought (1959) †

The Darwinian revolution established the hypothesis of transmutation; the establishment of the hypothesis of transmutation of
species widened the scope of scientific method and absorbed biology within the realm of objective science. Darwin, in Kant's prophetic phrase, was "the Newton of the grass blades," for Darwin
accomplished for biology what Galileo and Newton had already
accomplished for mechanics and physics. The revolution in biology, spurred by Darwinism, was premised on a new way of looking
at nature and a new way of looking at life. It was likewise premised
on newer concepts of man which remolded the profile of humanity
and therefore the cast of society. New views of life, of nature, and
of society reshaped the metaphysics of the ultimate and reformed
the philosophy of the temporal. The mosaic of Darwinian
thought transcends Charles Darwin. The implications of Darwinian
thought are wedged into a pattern which goes back to the Greeks
and stretches into the future. * * *

Darwin's data was actually overwhelming. The *Origin of Species*
was crammed with data and the evidence was expanded, refined,
and elaborated in later editions of the *Origin* and in Darwin's subsequent works. The facts, often new and rare, were garnered from
innumerable sources and covered virtually the entire range of
natural history. Old and familiar facts were placed in startlingly
novel perspective.

But the genius of the *Origin of Species* and the *Descent of Man*
resides in its conceptual organization, the hypotheses of descent,
natural selection, struggle, isolation, sexual selection, heredity, and
kindred theories. The genius of Darwin lies in the capacity for
marshalling the data, new and old, in a framework of theoretical
analysis. Darwin ferreted data out of horticultural journals and
breeders' records. He observed seedlings, insects, and birds with
unbelievable patience. Monographs of research gave him what he

† *Victorian Studies*, III (1959), 3–18.
Bert James Loewenberg (1905–1974) was professor of history at Sarah
Lawrence College.

called a harvest of facts and he extracted additional facts and additional ideas from his friends and coworkers. He discovered data as the result of his experiments with animals, with orchids, and with climbing plants; with volcanoes, coral reefs, and barnacles. Darwin's data were varied and magnificent, but the validity of the evidence for the Darwinian doctrine of descent by modification rested on the validity of the Darwinian hypothesis of development. And the validity of the hypothesis of evolution depended on the validity of the special hypotheses that explained its operation. Both depended on concepts of scientific method which were in turn rooted in a logic justifying its principles and its philosophy. Darwin's greatest contribution was to weld these elements together. He merged the evidence, the hypotheses, and the method in a grand analytical synthesis. As a consequence he legitimized the methodology by which the evidence was clarified and by which the hypotheses were validated.

While the evidence, to use a favorite Darwinian word, was truly "staggering," the hypothesis of natural selection was more important than the data. The hypothesis of natural selection, crucial to the establishment of the concept of evolution, is historically less vital than the mode of its establishment. It is the method which constitutes Darwin's claim to enduring greatness. Darwin's greatness rests on his total contribution, but the refinement of the evidence of transmutation taken alone is no more than a detail in the history of science. The expansion of the method of science exemplified by Darwin in establishing the doctrine of evolution constitutes an epoch in the history of science and a landmark in the history of thought.

Whether old or new, Darwin's evidence concentrated on difficulties, difficulties hard to explain on any current biological theory. How could conventional arguments receive so wide an acceptance when they failed to eliminate stark exceptions or to explain away incongruities with other bodies of fact? Genetic derivation, he repeatedly urged, at least offered a plausible explanation. Evolution by descent, moreover, provided an hypothesis which explained many apparently diverse facts and offered a unifying interpretation of the variety and alternations of living forms. Darwin did not generally encounter opposition to his specific data; it was his interpretation of the data which was suspect. The facts of geology were as rarely in dispute as the facts of embryology. No one doubted the existence of rudimentary organs, but Darwin's explanation of them was frequently spurned. That different plants and animals were distributed over the earth was an elementary principle; but Darwin's theories of geographical distribution were hardly elementary and were not universally accepted as principles. Darwin's hypotheses were criticized because Darwin's method and its logic defied regnant philosophical views.

Darwin's exposition of classification as of embryology and taxonomy was a calculated refutation of contemporary postulates.[1] He not only set forth the evidence in evolutionary categories but he also challenged accepted maxims of interpretation and method. When discussing the natural system he remarked that "scarcely two naturalists will give the same answer" when seeking to define it. Charles Darwin was invariably temperate and polite, but his queries and comments were not on that account less devastating: "How it comes, that certain facts of the structure, by which the habits and functions of the species are settled, are of no use in classification, whilst, other parts, formed at the same time, are of the greatest, it would be difficult to say, on the theory of separate creations" (*Foundations* [1844], p. 199).

To a Richard Owen or a Louis Agassiz it must have seemed that Darwin was deliberately irritating. He was forever accenting the negative, probing into difficulties that had long agonized his adversaries. He was purposely exposing the weaknesses of the opposition case. That there was no other way of making his own was beside the point. And Darwin was bent on making it. Certain naturalists, he commented, "believe that the degree of affinity on the natural system depends on the degrees of resemblance in organs more or less physiologically important for the preservation of life" (*Foundations* [1844], p. 200). To discover a scale of importance was unquestionably difficult. Nevertheless, the general proposition, said Darwin, "must be rejected as false; though it may be partially true." The reasons for so blunt a statement were not abstruse. Classification as interpreted by Owen or Agassiz did not work in Darwinian terms. Such systems of classification failed to work because they bore little resemblance to the conditions of life in which the organs actually functioned. Darwin was not seeking a universal plan of nature; he was seeking specific causal explanations, explanations of functioning organs in organic life and in a series of changing environments. Regardless of the particular Darwinian argument, the contention was always the same: what was the explanation of specific change? Regardless of the particular Darwinian contention, men were asked to see familiar data in new relations and the new relations were conceptual, constructs based upon methodological principles which many felt were invalid and inappropriate.

Darwin's search took him to the most unexpected places and in-

1. Charles Darwin, *The Foundations of the Origin of Species, Two Essays Written in 1842 and 1844*, Francis Darwin, ed. (1909), pp. 198, 199; George John Romanes, *Darwin, and After Darwin* 3 vols. (1892, 1895, 1897), I, 24 ff.

duced him to ask all manner of unorthodox questions. "If you knew," he wrote Hooker, "some of the experiments (if they may be so called) which I am trying, you would have a good right to sneer, for they are so *absurd* even in *my* opinion that I dare not tell you." [2] Darwin's efforts to extract fresh meanings from established convictions taught him to suspect definitive solutions and to abjure the ideal of finality. He urged Hooker, who slashed at difficulties with a candor only friendship permitted, to do his worst, but he admonished him to remember that "you cannot have thought so freely on the subject as I have." [3] In making this point Darwin made an essential point about himself and about scientific method. Darwin's free-ranging explorations disposed him to regard all questions as open, to accept no conclusions drained from observed facts as beyond further extension by hypothesis. But it was just this tendency which invited dissent, for such queries as Darwin asked were exactly the queries which had been definitely settled. Yet Darwin was simply exemplifying another facet of scholarship: the determination to reject provisionally all prescribed formulations while examining competing formulations. The principle of exclusion possesses the advantage of apparent finality but it is bought at the price of ruling out probabilities. "This is experiment after my own heart," Darwin once wrote illustrating the principle, "with chances 1000 to 1 against its success." [4]

Darwin was rarely inhibited by epistemological reservations. Darwin accepted the facts of nature as provisionally given; he did not begin his inquiry with the problems of knowledge. He was in no sense an aggressive empiricist; he simply was not concerned with metaphysics.[5] If variations were accepted as given for purposes of further analysis, then subsequent changes or further variations occurred as the result of natural causes, the interactivities of the total environments. The word "origin" was never used in its sense of "beginning"; it always implied changes in the development of life-forms already in existence.

Criticisms levelled at Darwin's theory of variation have confounded his own conception of it. Whatever inferences are latent in the text of the *Origin* and other Darwin writings, Darwin's own thinking was unambiguous. "I imagine," he once wrote to Hooker, successfully restraining his irritation, "that you look at variability as some necessary contingency" within the organism, "that there is some necessary tendency in the variability to go on diverging in

2. Darwin to Hooker, 14 Apr., 1855, in Francis Darwin, ed., *The Life and Letters of Charles Darwin*, 3 vols. (1887), II, 55 (italics in original).
3. Darwin to Hooker, 12 Oct., 1858, *Life*, II, 138, and Oct., 1856, p. 85.

4. Darwin to Hooker [1855], *Life*, II, 57.
5. *Life*, I, 69. But see Robert E. Fitch, "Charles Darwin: Science and the Saintly Sentiments," *Columbia University Forum*, II (1959), 7–12.

character or degree." "I do not agree," he said simply.[6] "The formation of a strong variety or species I look at as almost wholly due to the selection of what may be incorrectly called *chance* variations or variability." "No doubt . . . variability is governed by laws, some of which I am endeavouring very obscurely to trace." [7] They were incorrectly called chance variations because factors as yet unknown doubtless explained them, but they were none the less random in the sense that they were unwilled and unplanned. Wallace, as so often happened, was even clearer. Variation, after all, was no more than *"the absence of identity,"* [8] and required no additional elaboration. To Darwin he wrote: "variations of every kind are always occurring in every part of every species, and . . . favourable variations are always ready when wanted." [9]

Darwin was employing the objective method of science. He was seeking to define "natural laws," by which he meant the identification of sequences occurring in nature. These sequences expressed relations among phenomena and offered explanations of their behavior without reference to ultimate causes exterior to the phenomena under review. Darwin did not seek to explain the quality or essence of a prehistoric barnacle or to assign a primary cause for the existence of the varieties of Alpine flora. He observed, compared, and measured varieties in historical and contemporary contexts, and sought to discover connections within the economy of the individual organism as well as within the economy of nature. Darwin did not seek for final causes of gill, fin, wing, or bone. He always asked what these organs did, how they changed, what purposes they served under one set of conditions or under another.

Darwin held universal theories in abeyance. "I find," he wrote the cosmic philosopher, John Fiske, "that my mind is so fixed by the inductive method, that I cannot appreciate deductive reasoning." He did not deny Fiske's right to construct a cosmic philosophy, he simply explained why he was unable to do so. "I must begin with a good body of facts, and not from principle (in which I always suspect some fallacy), and then as much deduction as you please." [1] Darwin understood by deduction not only reasoning from the general to the particular, from a principle or law to a particular fact, but deducing facts from principles which were fixed beyond investigation. "I have no faith in anything," he once remarked, "short of actual measurement and the Rule of Three." [2]

6. Darwin to Hooker, 11 May [1859], *Life*, II, 158; Darwin to Lyell, 25 Oct. [1859], pp. 176–177.
7. Darwin to Hooker, 23 Nov. [1856], *Life*, II, 87.
8. Alfred Russel Wallace, "The Origin of Species and Genera," *Studies Scientific and Social* (1900), I, 302 (italics in original).

9. Wallace to Darwin, 2 July [1866], in Francis Darwin and A. C. Seward, eds., *More Letters of Charles Darwin*, 2 vols. (1903), I, 270; Darwin, *Foundations* [1842], pp. 1–2.
1. Darwin to Fiske, 8 Dec. [1874], *Life*, III, 193–194.
2. *Life*, II, 51 [1855].

Darwin stuck to his scientific guns and often fired broadsides at his detractors. "It is mere rubbish," he exploded in a letter to Hooker, "thinking at present of the origin of life; one might as well think of the origin of matter." [3] "What," he asked in the 1842 Sketch, "would the Astronomer say to the doctrine that the planets moved [not] according to the laws of gravitation, but from the Creator having willed each separate planet to move in its particular orbit?" (*Foundations*, p. 22). Darwin was unequivocal. In an early criticism of the manuscript that was to become the *Origin*, Lyell unravelled his reservations. Darwin gratefully acknowledged them, but he had already outdistanced his master in refining a philosophy of science. Lyell propounded what for him was a fundamental question: "*must you not assume a primordial creative power which does not act with uniformity, or how else could man supervene?*" [4] To this question Darwin replied: "under present knowledge [we must assume] the creation of one or a few new forms in the same manner as philosophers assume a power of attraction without any explanation." The remainder of Darwin's answer is an excellent statement of his own position and one of the best statements of the philosophy of scientific method.

I entirely reject, as in my judgment quite unnecessary, any subsequent addition of "new powers and attributes and forces": or of any "principle of improvement", except in so far as every character which is naturally selected or preserved is in some way an advantage or improvement, otherwise it would not have been selected. If I were convinced that I required such additions to the theory of natural selection, I would reject it as rubbish, but I have firm faith in it, as I cannot believe, that if false, it would explain so many whole classes of facts, which, if I am in my senses, it seems to explain. . . . I would give absolutely nothing for the theory of Natural Selection, if it requires miraculous additions at any one stage or descent. I think Embryology, Homology, Classification, &c., &c., show us that all vertebrata have descended from one parent; how that parent appeared we know not. If you admit in ever so little a degree . . . you will find it difficult to say: thus far the explanation holds good, but no further; here we must call in "the addition of new creative forces." I think you will be driven to reject all or admit all: I fear by your letter it will be the former alternative; and in that case I shall feel sure it is my fault, and not the theory's fault, and this will certainly comfort me.[5]

The Darwinian theory of evolution itself was Darwin's most impressive witness. Darwinian evolution was an hypothesis. As such

3. Darwin to Hooker [29 Mar. 1863], *Life*, III, 18.
4. Darwin to Lyell, 11 Oct. [1859],
Life, II, 210 (italics in original).
5. *Life*, II, 210–211.

it was a theoretical instrument devised to organize and test the data. There were no incontrovertible facts attesting that one variety had been transmuted into another. There was no concrete evidence to establish that random variations, basic to the operation of natural selection, existed in nature and had always so existed. Darwin could not even demonstrate concretely the process by which altered physical characters in a given organism were transmitted to succeeding generations. General critics flayed the theory as "mere hypothesis," hypothesis in the sense of unsubstantial speculation. That Darwin's theory was "vain" was underscored by the popular notion of the role of the scientist as a collector of facts. When the facts were collected and organized, they then spoke for themselves. Scholars—philosophers, scientists, and theologians— rejected Darwin's theory on more sophisticated grounds. For them the hypothesis violated the logic of hypothesis. It constituted a perversion of the canons of induction, for assumptions, not facts, were offered as the ground of its credibility. The learned William Whewell's critique of Hume applied with equal force to Darwin: "Our inference from Hume's observations is, not the truth of his conclusions, but the falsehood of his premises: not that, therefore, we can know nothing of natural connexion, but that, therefore, we have some other source of knowledge than experience." The philosophy of induction derived from the philosophy of causation. "Cause is to be conceived as some abstract quality, power, or efficacy, by which change is produced; a quality not identical with the events, but disclosed by means of them." [6]

With Lyell, constantly concerned about the ultimate, Darwin conducted a running debate, a debate Darwin called "our quasi-theological controversy about natural selection." "Do you consider," he asked Lyell, "the successive variations in the size of the crop of a Pouter Pigeon, which man has accumulated to please his caprice, . . . due to the creative and sustaining powers of Brahma?" [7] Darwin could not accept this inference. Since he could not imagine that Lyell would think otherwise, he wondered how any logical difference could be established between selection produced by the breeder under domestication and the result of selection in a state of nature.

If Darwin's debate with Lyell was quasi-theological, his debate with Asa Gray was frankly theological. He was, he confessed, "in an

6. William Whewell, *The Philosophy of the Inductive Sciences* (1840), I, 72; Alvar Ellegård, "Darwin's Theory and Nineteenth Century Philosophy of Science," in *Roots of Scientific Thought*, pp. 537–568; C. J. Ducasse, "Whewell's Philosophy of Scientific Discovery," *Philosophical Review*, LX (1951), 56–69, 213–234; E. W. Strong, "William Whewell and John Stuart Mill: Their Controversy About Scientific Knowledge," *Journal of the History of Ideas*, XVI (1955), 209–231.
7. Darwin to Lyell, Apr. [1860], *Life*, II, 303–304.

218 · Bert James Loewenberg

utterly hopeless muddle." Yet he could not endorse Gray's resolute faith in design: "I cannot look at each separate thing as the result of Design." [8] However, he was not sufficiently muddled to be without a point of view. Questions of ultimate purpose, he told Lyell, are "beyond the human intellect, like 'predestination' and 'free will,' or the 'origin of evil'." [9] Darwin entertained wistful thoughts about ultimate meanings, but he never permitted such thoughts to interfere with his operations. He did not know, to be sure, where he was coming out, but he struggled conscientiously to suspend judgment about the purpose of the universe while he was engaged in the scientific examination of its terrestrial parts. "I am inclined," he admitted to Gray, certain his admission would not please him, "to look at everything as resulting from designed laws, with the details, whether good or bad, left to the working out of what we call chance. Not that this notion *at all* satisfies me. I feel most deeply that the whole subject is too profound for the human intellect. A dog might as well speculate on the mind of a Newton. Let each man hope and believe what he can." [1]

Darwin's attitude toward cosmic purpose resembles the attitude of Chauncey Wright. "When it was objected to him," William James recalled, "that there must be some principle of oneness in the diversity of phenomena—some *glue* to hold them together . . . he would reply that there is no need of a glue to join things unless we apprehend some reason why they should fall asunder. Phenomena *are* grouped—more we cannot say of them." [2]

Darwin and Chauncey Wright were in general accord. Both were advocates of the neutrality of science. "True science," wrote the American logician, "should approach . . . questions, avoiding . . . the terms which have attached to them *good* and *bad* meanings in place of scientific distinctness,—terms which have a moral connotation as well as a scientific one . . .Words have 'reputations' as well as other authorities, and there is a tyranny in their reputations even more fatal to freedom of thought. True science deals with nothing but questions of facts—and in terms, if possible, which shall not determine beforehand how we ought to feel about the facts; for this is one of the most certain and fatal means of corrupting evidence." [3]

Darwin granted special weight to no category of probable meanings. Neither Cause, Being, Life, or Design was accorded any special prior significance. Darwin accounted life a given of nature. If

8. Darwin to Gray, 26 Nov. 1860, *Life*, II, 353.
9. Darwin to Lyell, 25 Apr. [1860], *Life*, II, 304.
1. Darwin to Gray, 22 May [1860], *Life*, II, 310–311, 312.
2. William James, "Chauncey Wright," *Nation*, XXI (1875), 194.
3. Cited from the Wright papers by Philip P. Wiener, *Evolution and the Founders of Pragmatism* (Cambridge, Mass., 1949), pp. 44–45.

The Victorian Opposition
to Darwin

ADAM SEDGWICK

Objections to Mr. Darwin's Theory of the Origin of Species (1860) †

[The Archbishop of Dublin has received the following remarks, in answer to an inquiry he had made of a friend (eminent
in the world of science) on the subject of Darwin's theory of the origin of species.]

* * * I must in the first place observe that Darwin's theory is
not *inductive*,—not based on a series of acknowledged facts pointing
to a *general* conclusion,—not a proposition evolved out of the facts,
logically, and of course including them. To use an old figure, I look
on the theory as a vast pyramid resting on its apex, and that apex a
mathematical point. The only facts he pretends to adduce, as true
elements of proof, are the *varieties* produced by domestication, or
the *human artifice* of cross-breeding. We all admit the varieties,
and the very wide limits of variation, among domestic animals. How
very unlike are poodles and greyhounds. Yet they are of one
species. And how nearly alike are many animals,—allowed to be of
distinct species, on any acknowledged views of species. Hence there
may have been very many blunders among naturalists, in the discrimination and enumeration of species. But this does not under-
mine the grand truth of nature, and the continuity of species.
Again, the varieties, built upon by Mr. Darwin, are varieties of
domestication and human *design*. Such varieties could have no
existence in the old world. Something may be done by cross-breeding; but mules are generally sterile, or the progeny (in some rare
instances) passes into one of the original crossed forms. The Author
of Nature will not permit His work to be spoiled by the wanton

† Adam Sedgwick (1785–1873) was
Woodwardian Professor of Geology at
Cambridge and president of the Geological Society and of the British Association. His review appeared anonymously
in *The Spectator*, XXXIII (March 24,
1860), 285–286.

it had larger meanings, those meanings were yet to be determined. Ultimate meanings were not within the scope of science. Wright, following Kant, distinguished between science and ethics, and Darwin in practice agreed with both. "If the facts are determined, and, as far as may be, free from moral biases, then practical science comes in to determine what, in view of the facts, our feelings and rules of conduct ought to be; but practical science has no inherent postulates any more than speculative science. Its ultimate grounds are the particular goods or ends of human life." [4]

A vital aspect of the Darwinian revolution consists in Darwin's contribution to the method and philosophy of science. The nature of the Darwinian revolution is the revolution in man's conception of nature. Copernicus brought astronomy within the domain of science. Darwin brought zoology within the domain of science. Darwin made the biological sciences objective, experimental, phenomenal, and empirical. As Darwin viewed the world of Reality, Being possessed no antecedent priority. Being, if Being there was, was to be found in the process of natural exploration. Darwin contributed to reverse the order of Being and process. Being and permanence were conceived, not as ultimate coordinates of temporal change within an antecedent transcendental system. They were conceived as logical coordinates emergent in the study of natural parts. Historically, the question is not whether Parmenides was wrong and Darwin and his successors right. Significant is the fact that Darwin separated the study of process from the concept of Being. The impact of Darwin is the impact of scientific method on the life sciences and on the sciences of human life. The laws of moral "harmony," Chauncey Wright is reported to have said, "are of a wholly different order, *different in meaning* . . . neither contradictory to nor in conformity with those of the scientific cosmos." [5]

4. Wiener, pp. 44–45; A. D. Lindsay, *Kant* (London, 1934), pp. 163–164.
5. Wiener, p. 36 (italics in original);

Charles C. Gillispie, "Lamarck and Darwin in the History of Science," in *Forerunners of Darwin*, pp. 265–291.

curiosity of Man. And in a state of nature (such as that of the old world before Man came upon it) wild animals of different species do not desire to cross and unite.

Species have been constant for thousands of years; and time (so far as I see my way) though multiplied by millions and billions would never change them, so long as the conditions remained constant. Change the conditions, and old species would disappear; and new species *might* have room to come in and flourish. But how, and by what causation? I say by *creation*. But, what do I mean by creation? I reply, the operation of a power quite beyond the powers of a pigeon-fancier, a cross-breeder, or hybridizer; a power I cannot imitate or comprehend; but in which I can believe, by a legitimate conclusion of sound reason drawn from the laws and harmonies of Nature,—proving in all around me, a design and purpose, and a mutual adaptation of parts, which I *can* comprehend,— and which prove that there is exterior to, and above, the mere phenomena of Nature a great prescient and designing cause. Believing this, I have no difficulty in the repetition of new species.

But Darwin would say that I am introducing a *miracle* by the supposition. In one sense I am; in another I am not. The hypothesis does not suspend or interrupt an established law of Nature. It does suppose the introduction of a new phenomenon unaccounted for by the operation of any *known* law of Nature; and it appeals to a power above established laws, and yet acting in conformity with them. * * *

I place the theory against facts viewed collectively. 1st. I see no proofs of enormous *gaps* of geological time, (I say nothing of years or centuries,) in those cases where there is a sudden change in the ancient fauna and flora. I am willing, out of the stock of past time, to lavish millions or billions upon each epoch, if thereby we can gain rational results from the operation of *true causes*. But time and "natural selection" can do nothing if there be not a vera causa working in them. [Note—see remark on *Time*, in the *Annotations on Bacon's Essays*.] I must confine myself to a few of the collective instances.

2d. Towards the end of the carboniferous period, there was a vast extinction of animal and vegetable life. We can, I think, account for this extinction mechanically. The old crust was broken up. The sea bottom underwent a great change. The old flora and fauna went out; a new flora and fauna appeared, in the ground now called Permian, at the base of the new red sandstone, which overlie the carboniferous. I take the fact as it *is*, and I have no difficulty. The time in which all this was brought *may* have been very long, even upon a geological scale of time. But where do the *intervening* and connecting types exist, which are to mark the *work of natural*

222 · *Adam Sedgwick*

selection? We do not find them. Therefore the step onwards gives no true resting-place to a baseless theory; and is, in fact, a stumbling-block in its way.

3d. Before we rise through the new red sandstone, we find the muschel-kalk (wanting in England, though its place on the scale is well-known) with *an entirely new* fauna: where have we a proof of any enormous lapse of geological time to account for the change? We have no proof in the deposits themselves: the presumption they offer to our senses is of a contrary kind.

4th. If we rise from the muschel-kalk to the Lias, we find again a new fauna. All the anterior species are gone. Yet the passage through the upper members of the new red sandstone to the Lias is by insensible gradation, and it is no easy matter to fix the physical line of their demarcation. I think it would be a very rash assertion to affirm that a great interval took place between the formation of the upper part of the new red sandstone and the Lias. Physical evidence is against it. To support a baseless theory, Darwin would require a countless lapse of ages of which we have *no* commensurate physical monuments; and he is unable to supply any of the connecting organic links that ought to bind together the older fauna with that of the Lias.

I need hardly go on any further with these objections. But I cannot conclude without expressing my detestation of the theory, because of its unflinching materialism;—because it has deserted the inductive track, the only track that leads to physical truth;—because it utterly repudiates final causes, and thereby indicates a demoralized understanding on the part of its advocates. In some rare instances it shows a wonderful credulity. Darwin seems to believe that a white bear, by being confined to the slops floating in the Polar basin, might be turned into a whale; that a Lemur might easily be turned into a bat; that a three-toed Tapir might be the great grandfather of a horse! or the progeny of a horse may (in America) have gone back to the tapir.

But any startling and (supposed) novel paradox, maintained very boldly and with something of imposing plausibility, produces, in some minds, a kind of pleasing excitement, which predisposes them in its favour; and if they are unused to careful reflection, and averse to the labour of accurate investigation, they will be likely to conclude that what is (apparently) *original,* must be a production of original *genius,* and that anything very much opposed to prevailing notions must be a grand *discovery,*—in short, that whatever comes from "the bottom of a well" must be the "truth" supposed to be hidden there.

SIR RICHARD OWEN

Darwin on the Origin of Species (1860) †

* * * Mr. Darwin refers to the multitude of the individuals of
every species, which, from one cause or another, perish either before,
or soon after attaining maturity.

'Owing to this struggle for life, any variation, however slight
and from whatever cause proceeding, if it be in any degree profitable to an individual of any species, in its infinitely complex relations to other organic beings and to external nature, will tend to
the preservation of that individual, and will generally be inherited by its offspring. The offspring, also, will thus have a better
chance of surviving, for, of the many individuals of any species
which are periodically born, but a small number can survive. I
have called this principle, by which each slight variation, if useful, is preserved, by the term of Natural Selection, in order to mark
its relation to man's power of selection. We have seen that man
by selection can certainly produce great results, and can adapt
organic beings to his own uses, through the accumulation of
slight but useful variations, given to him by the hand of Nature.
But Natural Selection, as we shall hereafter see, is a power incessantly ready for action, and is as immeasurably superior to man's
feeble efforts, as the works of Nature are to those of Art.' (P. 61.)

The scientific world has looked forward with great interest to the
facts which Mr. Darwin might finally deem adequate to the support
of his theory on this supreme question in biology, and to the course
of inductive original research which might issue in throwing light
on 'that mystery of mysteries.' But having now cited the chief, if
not the whole, of the original observations adduced by its author in
the volume now before us, our disappointment may be conceived.
Failing the adequacy of such observations, not merely to carry conviction, but to give a colour to the hypothesis, we were then left to
confide in the superior grasp of mind, strength of intellect, clearness
and precision of thought and expression, which might raise one man
so far above his contemporaries, as to enable him to discern in the
common stock of facts, of coincidences, correlations and analogies
in Natural History, deeper and truer conclusions than his fellow-
labourers had been able to reach.

† Sir Richard Owen (1804–1892), superintendent of the Natural History Department of the British Museum, was a
distinguished comparative anatomist and
a pioneer in vertebrate paleontology.
His review of the *Origin of Species* appeared anonymously in the *Edinburgh
Review*, CXI (1860), 487–532.

These expectations, we must confess, received a check on perusing the first sentence in the book.

> 'When on board H.M.S "Beagle," as naturalist, I was much struck with certain facts in the distribution of the inhabitants of South America, and in the geological relations of the present to the past inhabitants of that continent. These facts seemed to me to throw some light on the origin of species—that mystery of mysteries, as it has been called by some of our greatest philosophers.' (P. 1.)

What is there, we asked ourselves, as we closed the volume to ponder on this paragraph,—what can there possibly be in the inhabitants, we suppose he means aboriginal inhabitants, of South America, or in their distribution on that continent, to have suggested to any mind that man might be a transmuted ape, or to throw any light on the origin of the human or other species? Mr. Darwin must be aware of what is commonly understood by an 'uninhabited island;' he may, however, mean by the inhabitants of South America, not the human kind only, whether aboriginal or otherwise, but all the lower animals. Yet again, why are the freshwater polypes or sponges to be called 'inhabitants' more than the plants? Perhaps what was meant might be, that the distribution and geological relations of the organised beings generally in South America, had suggested transmutational views. They have commonly suggested ideas as to the independent origin of such localized kinds of plants and animals. But what the 'certain facts' were, and what may be the nature of the light which they threw upon the mysterious beginning of species, is not mentioned or further alluded to in the present work. * * *

'Isolation also,' says Mr. Darwin, 'is an important element in the process of natural selection.' But how can one select if a thing be 'isolated'? Even using the word in the sense of a confined area, Mr. Darwin admits that the conditions of life 'throughout such area, will tend to modify all the individuals of a species in the same manner, in relation to the same conditions.' (P. 104.) No evidence, however, is given of a species having ever been created in that way; but granting the hypothetical influence and transmutation, there is no selection here. The author adds, 'Although I do not doubt that isolation is of considerable importance in the production of new species, on the whole, I am inclined to believe, that largeness of area is of more importance in the production of species capable of spreading widely.' (P. 105.)

Now, on such a question as the origin of species, and in an express, formal, scientific treatise on the subject, the expression of a belief, where one looks for a demonstration, is simply provoking.

We are not concerned in the author's beliefs or inclinations to believe. Belief is a state of mind short of actual knowledge. It is a state which may govern action, when based upon a tacit admission of the mind's incompetency to prove a proposition, coupled with submissive acceptance of an authoritative dogma, or worship of a favourite idol of the mind. We readily concede, and it needs, indeed, no ghost to reveal the fact, that the wider the area in which a species may be produced, the more widely it will spread. But we fail to discern its import in respect of the great question at issue.

We have read and studied with care most of the monographs conveying the results of close investigations of particular groups of animals, but have not found, what Darwin asserts to be the fact, at least as regards all those investigators of particular groups of animals and plants whose treatises he has read, viz., that their authors 'are one and all firmly convinced that each of the well-marked forms or species was at the first independently created.' Our experience has been that the monographers referred to have rarely committed themselves to any conjectural hypothesis whatever, upon the origin of the species which they have closely studied.

Darwin appeals from the 'experienced naturalists whose minds are stocked with a multitude of facts' which he assumes to have been 'viewed from a point of view opposite to his own,' to the 'few naturalists endowed with much flexibility of mind,' for a favourable reception of his hypothesis. We must confess that the minds to whose conclusions we incline to bow belong to that truth-loving, truth-seeking, truth-imparting class, which Robert Brown [1], Bojanus [2], Rudolphi, Cuvier [3], Ehrenberg [4], Herold [4], Kölliker [5], and Siebold, [6] worthily exemplify. The rightly and sagaciously generalising intellect is associated with the power of endurance of continuous and laborious research, exemplarily manifested in such monographs as we have quoted below. Their authors are the men who trouble the intellectual world little with their beliefs, but enrich it greatly with their proofs. If close and long-continued research, sustained by the determination to get accurate results, blunted, as Mr. Darwin seems to imply, the far-seeing discovering faculty, then are we driven to this paradox, viz., that the elucidation of the higher problems, nay the highest, in Biology, is to be sought for or expected in the lucubrations of those naturalists whose minds are not weighed or troubled with more than a discursive and superficial knowledge of nature.

Lasting and fruitful conclusions have, indeed, hitherto been based

1. Prodromus Floræ Novæ Hollandiæ.
2. Anatome Testudinis Europæ.
3. Mémoires pour servir à l'Anatomie des Mollusques.
4. Die Infusionsthierchen, als vollkommene Organismen.
5. Disquisitiones de Animalium vertebris carentium, &c.
6. Entwickelungsgeschichte des Cephalopoden.

only on the possession of knowledge; now we are called upon to accept an hypothesis on the plea of want of knowledge. The geological record, it is averred, is so imperfect! But what human record is not? Especially must the record of past organisms be must less perfect than of present ones. We freely admit it. But when Mr. Darwin, in reference to the absence of the intermediate fossil forms required by his hypothesis—and only the zootomical zoologist can approximatively appreciate their immense numbers—the countless hosts of transitional links which, on 'natural selection,' must certainly have existed at one period or another of the world's history —when Mr. Darwin exclaims what may be, or what may not be, the forms yet forthcoming out of the graveyards of strata, we would reply, that our only ground for prophesying of what may come, is by the analogy of what has come to light. We may expect, e.g., a chambered-shell from a secondary rock; but not the evidence of a creature linking on the cuttle-fish to the lump-fish.

Mr. Darwin asks, 'How is it that varieties, which I have called incipient species, become ultimately good and distinct species?' To which we rejoin with the question:—Do they become good and distinct species? Is there any one instance proved by observed facts of such transmutation? We have searched the volume in vain for such. When we see the intervals that divide most species from their nearest congeners, in the recent and especially the fossil series, we either doubt the fact of progressive conversion, or, as Mr. Darwin remarks in his letter to Dr. Asa Gray [7], one's 'imagination must fill up very wide blanks.' * * *

The essential element in the complex idea of species, as it has been variously framed and defined by naturalists, viz., the blood-relationship between all the individuals of such species, is annihilated on the hypothesis of 'natural selection.' According to this view a genus, a family, an order, a class, a sub-kingdom,—the individuals severally representing these grades of difference or relationship,— now differ from individuals of the same species only in degree: the species, like every other group, is a mere creature of the brain; it is no longer from nature. With the present evidence from form, structure, and procreative phenomena, of the truth of the opposite proposition, that 'classification is the task of science, but species the work of nature,' we believe that this aphorism will endure; we are certain that it has not yet been refuted; and we repeat in the words of Linnæus, '*Classis et Ordo* est sapientiæ, *Species* naturæ opus.' [8]

---

7. Proceedings of the Linnæan Society, 1858, p. 61.
8. For Darwin's response to Owen, see the "Historical Sketch" above, pp. 32–33.

Victorian Supporters of Darwin

SIR JOSEPH DALTON HOOKER

Flora Tasmaniae (1859) †

* * * In the Introductory Essay to the New Zealand Flora, I advanced certain general propositions as to the origin of species, which I refrained from endorsing as articles of my own creed: amongst others was the still prevalent doctrine that these are, in the ordinary acceptation of the term, created as such, and are immutable. In the present Essay I shall advance the opposite hypothesis, that species are derivative and mutable; and this chiefly because, whatever opinions a naturalist may have adopted with regard to the origin and variation of species, every candid mind must admit that the facts and arguments upon which he has grounded his convictions require revision since the recent publication by the Linnean Society of the ingenious and original reasonings and theories of Mr. Darwin and Mr. Wallace. * * *

With regard to my own views on the subjects of the variability of existing species and the fallacy of supposing we can ascertain anything through these alone of their ancestry or of originally created types, they are, in so far as they are liable to influence my estimate of the value of the facts collected for the analysis of the Australian Flora, unaltered from those which I maintained in the 'Flora of New Zealand:' on such theoretical questions, however, as the origin and ultimate permanence of species, they have been greatly influenced by the views and arguments of Mr. Darwin and Mr. Wallace above alluded to, which incline me to regard more favourably the hypothesis that it is to variation that we must look as the means which Nature has adopted for peopling the globe with those diverse existing forms which, when they tend to transmit their characters unchanged through many generations, are called species. * * *

† Hooker and Thomas Henry Huxley were two of the earliest of Victorian scientists to rally to Darwin's support. This excerpt is from the "Introductory Essay" to the *Flora Tasmaniae*, Volume III of *The Botany of the Antarctic Voyage of H. M. Discovery Ships Erebus and Terror, in the Years 1839–* *1843* (London, 1859). It appeared in December, 1859, thus putting Hooker in public support of Darwin almost at the moment the *Origin* was published. Compare Hooker's earlier position in *Flora Nova-Zelandiae* (1853), pp. 19–23, above.

In conformity with my plan of starting from the variable and not the fixed aspect of Nature, I have now set down the prominent features of the Vegetable Kingdom, as surveyed from this point of view. From the preceding paragraphs the evidence appears to be certainly in favour of proneness to change in individuals, and of the power to change ceasing only with the life of the individual; and we have still to account for the fact that there are limits to these mutations, and laws that control the changes both as to degree and kind; that species are neither visionary nor even arbitrary creations of the naturalist; that they are, in short, realities, whether only temporarily so or not.

13. Granting then that the tendency of Nature is first to multiply forms of existing plants by graduated changes, and next by destroying some to isolate the rest in area and in character, we are now in a condition to seek some theory of the *modus operandi* of Nature that will give temporary permanence of character to these changelings. And here we must appeal to theory or speculation; for our knowledge of the history of species in relation to one another, and to the incessant mutations of their environing physical conditions, is far too limited and incomplete to afford data for demonstrating the effects of these in the production of any one species in a native state.

Of these speculations by far the most important and philosophical is that of the delimitation of species by natural selection, for which we are indebted to two wholly independent and original thinkers, Mr. Darwin and Mr. Wallace.[1] These authors assume that all animal and vegetable forms are variable, that the average amount of space and annual supply of food for each species (or other group of individuals) is limited and constant, but that the increase of all organisms tends to proceed annually in a geometrical ratio; and that, as the sum of organic life on the surface of the globe does not increase, the individuals annually destroyed must be incalculably great; also that each species is ever warring against many enemies, and only holding its own by a slender tenure. In the ordinary course of nature this annual destruction falls upon the eggs or seeds and young of the organisms, and as it is effected by a multitude of antagonistic, ever-changing natural causes, each more destructive of one organism than of any other, it operates with different effect on each group of individuals, in every locality, and at every returning season. Here then we have an infinite number of varying conditions, and a superabundant supply of variable organisms, to accommodate themselves to these conditions. Now the organisms can have no power of surviving any change in these conditions, except they are endowed with the means of accommodating themselves to it. The exercise of this power may be accompanied by a

1. Journal of the Linnean Society of London, Zoology, vol. iii. p. 45.

visible (morphological) change in the form or structure of the individual, or it may not, in which case there is still a change, but a physiological one, not outwardly manifested; but there is always a morphological change if the change of conditions be sudden, or when, through lapse of time, it becomes extreme. The new form is necessarily that best suited to the changed condition, and as its progeny are henceforth additional enemies to the old, they will eventually tend to replace their parent form in the same locality. Further, a greater proportion of the seeds and young of the old will annually be destroyed than of the new, and the survivors of the old, being less well adapted to the locality, will yield less seed, and hence have fewer descendants. * * *

35. From the sum then of our theories, as arranged in accordance with ascertained facts, we may make the following assumptions:— That the principal recognized families of plants which inhabited the globe at and since the Palæozoic period still exist, and therefore have as families survived all intervening geological changes. That of these types some have been transferred, or have migrated, from one hemisphere to another. That it is not unreasonable to suppose that further evidence may be forthcoming which will show that all existing species may have descended genealogically from fewer pre-existing ones; that we owe their different forms to the variation of individuals, and the power of limiting them into genera and species to the destruction of some of these varieties, etc., and the increase in individuals of others. Lastly, that the fact of species being with so much uniformity the ultimate and most definable group (the leaves as it were of the family tree), may possibly be owing to the tendency to vary being checked, partly by the ample opportunities each brood of a variety possesses of being fertilized by the pollen of its nearest counterpart, partly by the temporary stability of its surrounding physical conditions, and partly by the superabundance of seeds shed by each individual, those only vegetating which are well suited to existing conditions: an appearance of stability is also, in the case of many perennials, due to the fact that the individuals normally attain a great age,[2] and thus survive many generations of other species, of which generations some present characters foreign to their parents. * * *

2. In considering the relative amount and rate at which different plants vary, it should be remembered that we habitually estimate them not only loosely but falsely. We assume annuals to be more variable than perennials, but we probably greatly overrate the amount to which they really are so, because a brief personal experience enables us to study many generations of an annual under many combinations of physical conditions; whereas the same experience embraces but a fractional period of the duration of (comparatively) very few perennials. It has also been well shown by Bentham (in his paper on the British Flora, read (1858) before the Linnæan Society) that an appearance of stability is given to many varieties of perennials, through their habitual increase by buds, offsets, etc., which propagate the individual; and in the case of *Rubi*, which comparatively seldom propagate by seed, a large tract of ground may be peopled by parts of a single individual.

37. Again, it is argued by both Mr. Darwin and Mr. Wallace that the general effects of variation by selection must be to establish a general progressive development of the whole animal kingdom. But here again in botany we are checked by the question, What is the standard of progression? Is it physiological or morphological? Is it evidenced by the power of overcoming physical obstacles to dispersion or propagation, or by a nice adaptation of structure or constitution to very restricted or complex conditions? Are cosmopolites to be regarded as superior to plants of restricted range, hermaphrodite plants to unisexual, parasites to self-sustainers, albuminous-seeded to exalbuminous, gymnosperms to angiosperms, water plants to land, trees to herbs, perennials to annuals, insular plants to continental? and, in fine, what is the significance of the multitudinous differences in point of structure and complexity, and powers of endurance, presented by the members of the Vegetable Kingdom, and which have no recognized physiological end and interpretation, nor importance in a classificatory point of view? It is extremely easy to answer any of these questions, and to support the opinion by a host of arguments, morphological, physiological, and teleological; but any one gifted with a quick perception of relations, and whose mind is stored with a sufficiency of facts, will turn every argument to equal advantage for both sides of the question.

To my mind, however, the doctrine of progression, if considered in connection with the hypothesis of the origin of species being by variation, is by far the most profound of all that have ever agitated the schools of Natural History, and I do not think that it has yet been treated in the unprejudiced spirit it demands. The elements for its study are the vastest and most complicated which the naturalist can contemplate, and reside in the comprehension of the reciprocal action of the so-called inorganic on the organic world. Granting that multiplication and specialization of organs is the evidence and measure of progression, that variation explains the *rationale* of the operation which results in this progression, the question arises, What are the limits to the combinations of physical causes which determine this progrecssion, and how can the specializing power of Nature stop short of causing every race or family ultimately to represent a species? While the psychological philosophers persuade us that we see the tendency to specialize pervading every attribute of organic life, mental and physical; and the physicists teach that there are limits to the amount and duration of heat, light, and every other manifestation of physical force which our senses present or our intellects perceive, and which are all in process of consumption; the reflecting botanist, knowing that his ultimate results must accord with these facts, is perplexed at feeling that he has failed to establish on independent evidence the doctrines of variation and progressive specialization, or to co-ordinate his attempts to do so with the successive discoveries in physical science. * * *

The arguments deduced from genetic resemblance being (in the present state of science), as far as I can discover, exhausted, I have felt it my duty to re-examine the phenomena of variation in reference to the origin of existing species; these phenomena I have long studied independently of this question, and when treating either of whole Floras or of species, I have made it my constant aim to demonstrate how much more important and prevalent this element of variability is than is usually admitted, as also how deep it lies beneath the foundations of all our facts and reasonings concerning classification and distribution. I have hitherto endeavoured to keep my ideas upon variation in subjection to the hypothesis of species being immutable, both because a due regard to that theory checks any tendency to careless observation of minute facts, and because the opposite one is apt to lead to a precipitate conclusion that slight differences have no significance; whereas, though not of specific importance, they may be of high structural and physiological value, and hence reveal affinities that might otherwise escape us. I have already stated how greatly I am indebted to Mr. Darwin's [3] *rationale* of the phenomena of variation and natural selection in the production of species; and though it does not positively establish the doctrine of creation by variation, I expect that every additional fact and observation relating to species will gain great additional value from being viewed in reference to it, and that it will materially assist in developing the principles of classification and distribution.

THOMAS HENRY HUXLEY

On the Relations of Man to the Lower Animals (1863) †

* * * The question of questions for mankind—the problem which underlies all others, and is more deeply interesting than any

3. In this Essay I refer to the brief abstract only (Linn. Journ.) of my friend's views, not to his work now in the press, a deliberate study of which may modify my opinion on some points whereon we differ. Matured conclusions on these subjects are very slowly developed.

† Thomas Henry Huxley (1825–1895) studied medicine as a young man and matured as a naturalist during a voyage of discovery aboard H.M.S. *Rattlesnake,* at the end of which he was elected a Fellow of the Royal Society. His review of the *Origin* in the London *Times* was an important contribution to public understanding of the book, and for years Huxley was Darwin's ablest advocate, "Darwin's bulldog." The present excerpts are from Chapter 2 of *Man's Place in Nature* (London, 1863).

other—is the ascertainment of the place which Man occupies in nature and of his relations to the universe of things. Whence our race has come; what are the limits of our power over nature, and of nature's power over us; to what goal we are tending; are the problems which present themselves anew and with undiminished interest to every man born into the world. * * *

As if to demonstrate, by a striking example, the impossibility of erecting any cerebral barrier between man and the apes, Nature has provided us, in the latter animals, with an almost complete series of gradations from brains little higher than that of a Rodent, to brains little lower than that of Man. And it is a remarkable circumstance that though, so far as our present knowledge extends, there *is* one true structural break in the series of forms of Simian brains, this hiatus does not lie between Man and the man-like apes, but between the lower and the lowest Simians; or, in other words, between the old and new world apes and monkeys, and the Lemurs. Every Lemur which has yet been examined, in fact, has its cerebellum partially visible from above, and its posterior lobe, with the contained posterior cornu and hippocampus minor, more or less rudimentary. Every Marmoset, American monkey, old world monkey, Baboon, or Man-like ape, on the contrary, has its cerebellum entirely hidden, posteriorly, by the cerebral lobes, and possesses a large posterior cornu, with a well-developed hippocampus minor. * * *

As to the convolutions, the brains of the apes exhibit every stage of progress, from the almost smooth brain of the Marmoset, to the Orang and the Chimpanzee, which fall but little below Man. And it is most remarkable that, as soon as all the principal sulci appear, the pattern according to which they are arranged is identical with that of the corresponding sulci of man. The surface of the brain of a monkey exhibits a sort of skeleton map of man's, and in the man-like apes the details become more and more filled in, until it is only in minor characters, such as the greater excavation of the anterior lobes, the constant presence of fissures usually absent in man, and the different disposition and proportions of some convolutions, that the Chimpanzee's or the Orang's brain can be structurally distinguished from Man's.

So far as cerebral structure goes, therefore, it is clear that Man differs less from the Chimpanzee or the Orang, than these do even from the Monkeys, and that the difference between the brains of the Chimpanzee and of Man is almost insignificant, when compared with that between the Chimpanzee brain and that of a Lemur.

It must not be overlooked, however, that there is a very striking difference in the absolute mass and weight between the lowest human brain and that of the highest ape—a difference which is all

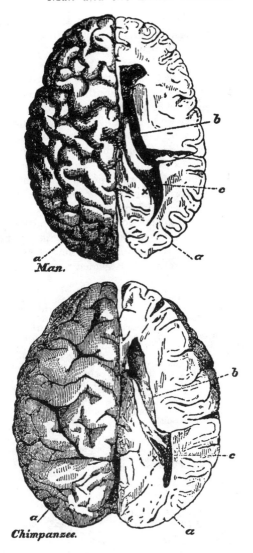

Drawings of the cerebral hemispheres of a Man and of a Chimpanzee of the same length, in order to show the relative proportions of the parts: the former taken from a specimen, which Mr. Flower, Conservator of the Museum of the Royal College of Surgeons, was good enough to dissect for me; the latter, from the photograph of a similarly dissected Chimpanzee's brain, given in Mr. Marshall's paper above referred to. *a*, posterior lobe; *b*, lateral ventricle; *c*, posterior cornu; *x*, the hippocampus minor.

the more remarkable when we recollect that a full grown Gorilla is probably pretty nearly twice as heavy as a Bosjes man, or as many an European woman. It may be doubted whether a healthy human adult brain ever weighed less than thirty-one or two ounces, or that the heaviest Gorilla brain has exceeded twenty ounces.

This is a very noteworthy circumstance, and doubtless will one day help to furnish an explanation of the great gulf which intervenes between the lowest man and the highest ape in intellectual power;[1] but it has little systematic value, for the simple reason that, as may be concluded from what has been already said respecting cranial capacity, the difference in weight of brain between the highest and the lowest men is far greater, both relatively and absolutely, than that between the lowest man and the highest ape. The latter, as has been seen, is represented by, say twelve, ounces of cerebral substance absolutely, or by 32 : 20 relatively; but as the largest recorded human brain weighed between 65 and 66 ounces, the former difference is represented by more than 33 ounces absolutely, or by 65 : 32 relatively. Regarded systematically the cerebral

---

1. I say *help* to furnish: for I by no means believe that it was any original difference of cerebral quality, or quantity, which caused that divergence between the human and the pithecoid stirpes, which has ended in the present enormous gulf between them. It is no doubt perfectly true, in a certain sense, that all difference of function is a result of difference of structure; or, in other words, of difference in the combination of the primary molecular forces of living substance; and, starting from this undeniable axiom, objectors occasionally, and with much seeming plausibility, argue that the vast intellectual chasm between the Ape and Man implies a corresponding structural chasm in the organs of the intellectual functions; so that, it is said, the non-discovery of such vast differences proves, not that they are absent, but that Science is incompetent to detect them. A very little consideration, however, will, I think, show the fallacy of this reasoning. Its validity hangs upon the assumption, that intellectual power depends altogether on the brain—whereas the brain is only one condition out of many on which intellectual manifestations depend; the others being, chiefly, the organs of the senses and the motor apparatuses, especially those which are concerned in prehension and in the production of articulate speech.

A man born dumb, notwithstanding his great cerebral mass and his inheritance of strong intellectual instincts, would be capable of few higher intellectual manifestations than an Orang or a Chimpanzee, if he were confined to the society of dumb associates. And yet there might not be the slightest discernible difference between brain and that of a highly intelligent and cultivated person. The dumbness might be the result of a defective structure of the mouth, or of the tongue, or a mere defective innervation of these parts; or it might result from congenital deafness, caused by some minute defect of the internal ear, which only a careful anatomist could discover.

The argument, that because there is an immense difference between a Man's intelligence and an Ape's, therefore, there must be an equally immense difference between their brains, appears to me to be about as well based as the reasoning by which one should endeavour to prove that, because there is a "great gulf" between a watch that keeps accurate time and another that will not go at all, there is therefore a great structural hiatus between the two watches. A hair in the balance-wheel, a little rust on a pinion, a bend in a tooth of the escapement, a something so slight that only the practised eye of the watchmaker can discover it, may be the source of all the difference.

And believing, as I do, with Cuvier, that the possession of articulate speech is the grand distinctive character of man (whether it be absolutely peculiar to him or not), I find it very easy to comprehend, that some equally inconspicuous structural difference may have been the primary cause of the immeasurable and practically infinite divergence of the Human from the Simian Stirps.

differences, of man and apes, are not of more than generic value
—his Family distinction resting chiefly on his dentition, his pelvis,
and his lower limbs.

Thus, whatever system of organs be studied, the comparison of
their modifications in the ape series leads to one and the same result—that the structural differences which separate Man from the
Gorilla and the Chimpanzee are not so great as those which separate the Gorilla from the lower apes.

But in enunciating this important truth I must guard myself
against a form of misunderstanding, which is very prevalent. I find,
in fact, that those who endeavour to teach what nature so clearly
shows us in this matter, are liable to have their opinions misrepresented and their phraseology garbled, until they seem to say that
the structural differences between man and even the highest apes
are small and insignificant. Let me take this opportunity then of
distinctly asserting, on the contrary, that they are great and significant; that every bone of a Gorilla bears marks by which it might
be distinguished from the corresponding bone of a Man; and that,
in the present creation, at any rate, no intermediate link bridges
over the gap between *Homo* and *Troglodytes*.

It would be no less wrong than absurd to deny the existence of
this chasm; but it is at least equally wrong and absurd to exaggerate
its magnitude, and, resting on the admitted fact of its existence, to
refuse to inquire whether it is wide or narrow. Remember, if you
will, that there is no existing link between Man and the Gorilla,
but do not forget that there is no less sharp line of demarcation, a
no less complete absence of any transitional form, between the
Gorilla and the Orang, or the Orang and the Gibbon. I say, not
less sharp, though it is somewhat narrower. The structural differences beween Man and the Man-like apes certainly justify our
regarding him as constituting a family apart from them; though,
inasmuch as he differs less from them than they do from other
families of the same order, there can be no justification for placing
him in a distinct order.

And thus the sagacious foresight of the great lawgiver of systematic zoology, Linnæus, becomes justified, and a century of anatomical research brings us back to his conclusion, that man is a
member of the same order (for which the Linnæan term PRIMATES
ought to be retained) as the Apes and Lemurs. This order is now
divisible into seven families, of about equal systematic value: the
first, the ANTHROPINI, contains Man alone; the second, the CATA-
RHINI, embraces the old world apes; the third, the PLATYRHINI,
all new world apes, except the Marmosets; the fourth, the ARC-
TOPITHECINI, contains the Marmosets; the fifth, the LEMURINI, the

Lemurs—from which *Cheiromys* should probably be excluded to form a sixth distinct family, the CHEIROMYINI; while the seventh, the GALEOPITHECINI, contains only the flying Lemur *Galeopithecus*, —a strange form which almost touches on the Bats, as the *Cheiromys* puts on a rodent clothing, and the Lemurs simulate Insectivora.

Perhaps no order of mammals presents us with so extraordinary a series of gradations as this—leading us insensibly from the crown and summit of the animal creation down to creatures, from which there is but a step, as it seems, to the lowest, smallest, and least intelligent of the placental Mammalia. It is as if nature herself had foreseen the arrogance of man, and with Roman severity had provided that his intellect, by its very triumphs, should call into prominence the slaves, admonishing the conqueror that he is but dust.

These are the chief facts, this the immediate conclusion from them to which I adverted the commencement of this Essay. The facts, I believe, cannot be disputed; and if so, the conclusion appears to me to be inevitable.

But if Man be separated by no greater structural barrier, from the brutes than they are from one another—then it seems to follow that if any process of physical causation can be discovered by which the genera and families of ordinary animals have been produced, that process of causation is amply sufficient to account for the origin of Man. In other words, if it could be shown that the Marmosets, for example, have arisen by gradual modification of the ordinary Platyrhini, or that both Marmosets and Platyrhini are modified ramifications of a primitive stock—then, there would be no rational ground for doubting that man might have originated, in the one case, by the gradual modification of a man-like ape; or, in the other case, as a ramification of the same primitive stock as those apes.

At the present moment, but one such process of physical causation has any evidence in its favour; or, in other words, there is but one hypothesis regarding the origin of species of animals in general which has any scientific existence—that propounded by Mr. Darwin. For Lamarck, sagacious as many of his views were, mingled them with so much that was crude and even absurd, as to neutralize the benefit which his originality might have effected, had he been a more sober and cautious thinker; and though I have heard of the announcement of a formula touching "the ordained continuous becoming of organic forms," it is obvious that it is the first duty of a hypothesis to be intelligible, and that a qua-quâ-versal proposition of this kind, which may be read backwards, or forwards, or sideways, with exactly the same amount of signification, does not really exist, though it may seem to do so.

At the present moment, therefore, the question of the relation of man to the lower animals resolves itself, in the end, into the larger question of the tenability or untenability of Mr. Darwin's views. But here we enter upon difficult ground, and it behoves us to define our exact position with the greatest care.

It cannot be doubted, I think, that Mr. Darwin has satisfactorily proved that what he terms selection, or selective modification, must occur, and does occur, in nature; and he has also proved to superfluity that such selection is competent to produce forms as distinct structurally, as some genera even are. If the animated world presented us with none but structural differences, I should have no hesitation in saying that Mr. Darwin had demonstrated the existence of a true physical cause, amply competent to account for the origin of living species, and of man among the rest.

But, in addition to their structural distinctions, the species of animals and plants, or at least a great number of them, exhibit physiological characters—what are known as distinct species, structurally, being for the most part either altogether incompetent to breed one with another; or if they breed, the resulting mule, or hybrid, is unable to perpetuate its race with another hybrid of the same kind.

A true physical cause is, however, admitted to be such only on one condition—that it shall account for all the phenomena which come within the range of its operation. If it is inconsistent with any one phenomenon, it must be rejected; if it fails to explain any one phenomenon, it is so far weak, so far to be suspected; though it may have a perfect right to claim provisional acceptance.

Now, Mr. Darwin's hypothesis is not, so far as I am aware, inconsistent with any known biological fact; on the contrary, if admitted, the facts of Development, of Comparative Anatomy, of Geographical Distribution, and of Palæontology, become connected together, and exhibit a meaning such as they never possessed before; and I, for one, am fully convinced, that if not precisely true, that hypothesis is as near an approximation to the truth as, for example, the Copernican hypothesis was to the true theory of the planetary motions.

But, for all this, our acceptance of the Darwinian hypothesis must be provisional so long as one link in the chain of evidence is wanting; and so long as all the animals and plants certainly produced by selective breeding from a common stock are fertile, and their progeny are fertile with one another, that link will be wanting. For, so long, selective breeding will not be proved to be competent to do all that is required of it to produce natural species.

I have put this conclusion as strongly as possible before the reader, because the last position in which I wish to find myself is that of an advocate for Mr. Darwin's, or any other views—if by

238 · *Thomas Henry Huxley*

an advocate is meant one whose business it is to smooth over real difficulties, and to persuade where he cannot convince.

In justice to Mr. Darwin, however, it must be admitted that the conditions of fertility and sterility are very ill understood, and that every day's advance in knowledge leads us to regard the hiatus in his evidence as of less and less importance, when set against the multitude of facts which harmonize with, or receive an explanation from, his doctrines.

I adopt Mr. Darwin's hypothesis, therefore, subject to the production of proof that physiological species may be produced by selective breeding; just as a physical philosopher may accept the undulatory theory of light, subject to the proof of the existence of the hypothetical ether; or as the chemist adopts the atomic theory, subject to the proof of the existence of atoms; and for exactly the same reasons, namely, that it has an immense amount of primâ facie probability; that it is the only means at present within reach of reducing the chaos of observed facts to order; and lastly, that it is the most powerful instrument of investigation which has been presented to naturalists since the invention of the natural system of classification, and the commencement of the systematic study of embryology.

But even leaving Mr. Darwin's views aside, the whole analogy of natural operations furnishes so complete and crushing an argument against the intervention of any but what are termed secondary causes, in the production of all the phenomena of the universe; that, in view of the intimate relations between Man and the rest of the living world; and between the forces exerted by the latter and all other forces, I can see no excuse for doubting that all are co-ordinated terms of Nature's great progression, from the formless to the formed—from the inorganic to the organic—from blind force to conscious intellect and will.

Science has fulfilled her function when she has ascertained and enunciated truth; and were these pages addressed to men of science only, I should now close this essay, knowing that my colleagues have learned to respect nothing but evidence, and to believe that their highest duty lies in submitting to it, however it may jar against their inclinations.

But desiring, as I do, to reach the wider circle of the intelligent public, it would be unworthy cowardice were I to ignore the repugnance with which the majority of my readers are likely to meet the conclusions to which the most careful and conscientious study I have been able to give to this matter, has led me.

On all sides I shall hear the cry—"We are men and women, not a mere better sort of apes, a little longer in the leg, more compact in the foot, and bigger in brain than your brutal Chimpanzees and

Gorillas. The power of knowledge—the conscience of good and evil—the pitiful tenderness of human affections, raise us out of all real fellowship with the brutes, however closely they may seem to approximate us."

To this I can only reply that the exclamation would be most just and would have my own entire sympathy, if it were only relevant. But, it is not I who seek to base Man's dignity upon his great toe, or insinuate that we are lost if an Ape has a hippocampus minor. On the contrary, I have done my best to sweep away this vanity. I have endeavoured to show that no absolute structural line of demarcation, wider than that between the animals which immediately succeed us in the scale, can be drawn between the animal world and ourselves; and I may add the expression of my belief that the attempt to draw a psychical distinction is equally futile, and that even the highest faculties of feeling and of intellect begin to germinate in lower forms of life.[2] At the same time, no one is more strongly convinced than I am of the vastness of the gulf between civilized man and the brutes; or is more certain that whether *from* them or not, he is assuredly not *of* them. No one is less disposed to think lightly of the present dignity, or despairingly of the future hopes, of the only consciously intelligent denizen of this world.

We are indeed told by those who assume authority in these matters, that the two sets of opinions are incompatible, and that the belief in the unity of origin of man and brutes involves the brutalization and degradation of the former. But is this really so? Could not a sensible child confute, by obvious arguments, the shallow rhetoricians who would force this conclusion upon us? Is it, indeed, true, that the Poet, or the Philosopher, or the Artist whose genius is the glory of his age, is degraded from his high estate by the undoubted historical probability, not to say certainty, that he is the direct descendant of some naked and bestial savage, whose intelligence was just sufficient to make him a little more cunning

2. It is so rare a pleasure for me to find Professor Owen's opinions in entire accordance with my own, that I cannot forbear from quoting a paragraph which appeared in his Essay "On the Characters, &c., of the Class Mammalia," in the 'Journal of the Proceedings of the Linnean Society of London' for 1857, but is unaccountably omitted in the "Reade Lecture" delivered before the University of Cambridge two years later, which is otherwise nearly a reprint of the paper in question. Prof. Owen writes: "Not being able to appreciate or conceive of the distinction between the psychical phenomena of a Chimpanzee and of a Boschisman or of an Aztec, with arrested brain growth, as being of a nature so essential as to preclude a comparison between them, or as being other than a difference of degree, I cannot shut my eyes to the significance of that all-pervading similitude of structure—every tooth, every bone, strictly homologous—which makes the determination of the difference between *Homo* and *Pithecus* the anatomist's difficulty."

Surely it is a little singular that the 'anatomist,' who finds it 'difficult' to 'determine the difference' between *Homo* and *Pithecus*, should yet range them on anatomical grounds, in distinct sub-classes!

than the Fox, and by so much more dangerous than the Tiger? Or is he bound to howl and grovel on all fours because of the wholly unquestionable fact, that he was once an egg, which no ordinary power of discrimination could distinguish from that of a Dog? Or is the philanthropist or the saint to give up his endeavours to lead a noble life, because the simplest study of man's nature reveals, at its foundations, all the selfish passions and fierce appetites of the merest quadruped? Is mother-love vile because a hen shows it, or fidelity base because dogs possess it?

The common sense of the mass of mankind will answer these questions without a moment's hesitation. Healthy humanity, finding itself hard pressed to escape from real sin and degradation, will leave the brooding over speculative pollution to the cynics and the 'righteous overmuch' who, disagreeing in everything else, unite in blind insensibility to the nobleness of the visible world, and in inability to appreciate the grandeur of the place Man occupies therein.

Nay more, thoughtful men, once escaped from the blinding influences of traditional prejudice, will find in the lowly stock whence man has sprung, the best evidence of the splendour of his capacities; and will discern in his long progress through the Past, a reasonable ground of faith in his attainment of a nobler Future.

They will remember that in comparing civilized man with the animal world, one is as the Alpine traveller, who sees the mountains soaring into the sky and can hardly discern where the deep shadowed crags and roseate peaks end, and where the clouds of heaven begin. Surely the awe-struck voyager may be excused if, at first, he refuses to believe the geologist, who tells him that these glorious masses are, after all, the hardened mud of primeval seas, or the cooled slag of subterranean furnaces—of one substance with the dullest clay, but raised by inward forces to that place of proud and seemingly inaccessible glory.

But the geologist is right; and due reflection on his teachings, instead of diminishing our reverence and our wonder, adds all the force of intellectual sublimity to the mere esthetic intuition of the uninstructed beholder.

And after passion and prejudice have died away, the same result will attend the teachings of the naturalist respecting that great Alps and Andes of the living world—Man. Our reverence for the nobility of manhood will not be lessened by the knowledge, that Man is, in substance and in structure, one with the brutes; for, he alone possesses the marvellous endowment of intelligible and rational speech, whereby, in the secular period of his existence, he has slowly accumulated and organized the experience which is almost wholly lost with the cessation of every individual life in other animals; so that now he stands raised upon it as on a mountain top, far above the level of his humble fellows, and transfigured from his grosser nature by reflecting, here and there, a ray from the infinite source of truth.

SIR CHARLES LYELL

Principles of Geology (1867) †

* * * In former editions of this work from 1832 to 1853, I did not venture to differ from the opinion of Linnæus, that each species had remained from its origin such as we now see it, being variable, but only within certain fixed limits. The mystery in which the origin of each species was involved seemed to me no greater than that in which the beginning of all vital phenomena on the earth is shrouded. * * *

* * * Mr. Charles Darwin * * * had been for many years busily engaged in collecting materials for a great work on the origin of species; having made for that purpose a vast series of original observations and experiments on domesticated animals and cultivated plants, and having reflected profoundly on those problems in geology and biology which were calculated to throw most light on that question. For eighteen years these researches had all been pointing to the same conclusion, namely, that the species now living had been derived by variation and generation from those which had pre-existed, and these again from others of still older date. Several of his MS. volumes on this subject had been read by Dr. Hooker as long ago as 1844, and how long the ever-accumulating store of facts and reasonings might have remained unknown to the general public, had no one else attempted to work out the same problem, it is impossible to say. But at length Mr. Darwin received a communication, dated February 1858, from Mr. Wallace, then residing at Ternate in the Malay Archipelago, entitled 'On the Tendency of Varieties to depart indefinitely from the Original Type.'

The Author requested Mr. Darwin to show this essay to me should he think it sufficiently novel and interesting. It was brought to me by Dr. Hooker, who remarked how complete was the coincidence of Mr. Wallace's new views and those contained in one of

† Lyell was the most reluctant of Darwin's several confidants to come out publicly in support of evolution. (See Lyell's earlier antievolutionary position, above, pp. 10–15.) His remarks on the subject in *The Antiquity of Man* (1863) were deeply disappointing to Darwin, and there was no new edition of the *Principles* until 1867, in which the present passage occurred. The text given here is from Chapter 35 of the eleventh edition (New York, 1883).

the chapters of Mr. Darwin's unpublished work. Accordingly, he suggested that it would be unfair to let Mr. Wallace's essay go to press unaccompanied by the older memoir on the same subject. Although, therefore, Mr. Darwin was willing to waive his claim to priority, the two papers were read on the same evening to the Linnæan Society and published in their Proceedings for 1858. The title of the chapter extracted from Mr. Darwin's MS. ran as follows: 'On the Tendency of Species to form Varieties, and on the Perpetuation of Species and Varieties by Natural Means of Selection.'

Already in the previous year, September 1857, Mr. Darwin had sent to Professor Asa Gray, the celebrated American botanist, a brief sketch of his forthcoming treatise on what he then termed 'Natural Selection.' This letter, also printed by the Linnæan Society together with the papers above alluded to, contained an outline of the leading features of his theory of selection as since explained, showing how new races were formed by the breeder, and how analogous results might or must occur in nature under changed conditions in the animate and inanimate world. Reference was made in the same letter to the law of human population first enunciated by Malthus, or the tendency in man to increase in a geometrical ratio, while the means of subsistence cannot be made to augment in the same ratio. We were reminded that in some countries the human population has doubled in twenty-five years, and would have multiplied faster if food could have been supplied. In like manner every animal and plant is capable of increasing so rapidly, that if it were unchecked by other species, it would soon occupy the greater part of the habitable globe; but in the general struggle for life few only of those which are born into the world can obtain subsistence and arrive at maturity. In any given species those alone survive which have some advantage over others, and this is often determined by a slight peculiarity capable in a severe competition of turning the scale in their favour. Notwithstanding the resemblance to each other and to their parents of all the individuals of the same family, no two of them are exactly alike. The breeder chooses out from among the varieties presented to him those best suited to his purpose, and the divergence from the original stock is more and more increased by breeding in each successive generation from individuals which possess the desired characters in the most marked degree. In this manner Mr. Darwin suggests that as the surrounding conditions in the organic and inorganic world slowly alter in the course of geological periods, new races which are more in harmony with the altered state of things must be formed in a state of nature, and must often supplant the parent type.

Although this law of natural selection constituted one only of the grounds on which Mr. Darwin relied for establishing his views as to the origin of species by variation, yet it formed so original and prominent a part of his theory that the fact of Mr. Wallace having independently thought out the same principle and illustrated it by singularly analogous examples, is remarkable. It raises at the same time a strong presumption in favour of the truth of the doctrine. * * *

After the publication of the detached chapter of his book in the Linnæan Proceedings, Mr. Darwin was persuaded by his friends that he ought no longer to withhold from the world the result of his investigations on the nature and origin of species, and his theory of Natural Selection. Great was the sensation produced in the scientific world by the appearance of the abridged and condensed statement of his views comprised in his work entitled 'On the Origin of Species by means of Natural Selection, or the Preservation of Favoured Races in the Struggle for Life.' From the hour of its appearance it gave, as Professor Huxley truly said, 'a new direction to biological speculation,' for even where it failed to make proselytes, it gave a shock to old and time-honoured opinions from which they have never since recovered. It effected this not merely by the manner in which it explained how new races and species might be formed by Natural Selection, but also by showing that, if we assume this principle, much light is thrown on many very distinct and otherwise unconnected classes of phenomena, both in the present condition and past history of the organic world. * * *

Darwin and Modern Science

SIR JULIAN HUXLEY

Evolution: The Modern Synthesis (1942, 1963) †

I. The Theory of Natural Selection

Evolution may lay claim to be considered the most central and the most important of the problems of biology. For an attack upon it we need facts and methods from every branch of the science—ecology, genetics, paleontology, geographical distribution, embryology, systematics, comparative anatomy—not to mention reinforcements from other disciplines such as geology, geography, and mathematics.

Biology at the present time is embarking upon a phase of synthesis after a period in which new disciplines were taken up in turn and worked out in comparative isolation. Nowhere is this movement towards unification more likely to be valuable than in this many-sided topic of evolution; and already we are seeing the first-fruits in the re-animation of Darwinism.

By Darwinism I imply that blend of induction and deduction which Darwin was the first to apply to the study of evolution. He was concerned both to establish the fact of evolution and to discover the mechanism by which it operated; and it was precisely because he attacked both aspects of the problem simultaneously, that he was so successful.[1] On the one hand he amassed enormous quantities of facts from which inductions concerning the evolutionary process could be drawn; and on the other, starting from a few general principles, he deduced the further principle of natural selection.

It is as well to remember the strong deductive element in Darwinism. Darwin based his theory of natural selection on three observable facts of nature and two deductions from them. The first fact is the tendency of all organisms to increase in a geometrical

† The following selections comprise Chapter 1 of the first edition (1942) and excerpts from the Introduction to the second edition (1963) of *Evolution: The Modern Synthesis*. Sir Julian Huxley (1887–1975), the grandson of Thomas Henry Huxley, was a distin-guished zoologist and man of letters.

1. This method is not, as has sometimes been asserted, a circular argument. See discussion in J. S. Huxley, "Darwin's Theory of Sexual Selection . . . ," *American Naturalist*, LXXII (1938), 416.

ratio. The tendency of all organisms to increase is due to the fact that offspring, in the early stages of their existence, are always more numerous than their parents; this holds good whether reproduction is sexual or asexual, by fission or by budding, by means of seeds, spores, or eggs.[2] The second fact is that, in spite of this tendency to progressive increase, the numbers of a given species actually remain more or less constant.

The first deduction follows. From these two facts he deduced the struggle for existence. For since more young are produced than can survive, there must be competition for survival. In amplifying his theory, he extended the concept of the struggle for existence to cover reproduction. The struggle is in point of fact for survival of the stock; if its survival is aided by greater fertility, an earlier breeding season, or other reproductive function, these should be included under the same head.

Darwin's third fact of nature was variation: all organisms vary appreciably. And the second and final deduction, which he deduced from the first deduction and the third fact, was Natural Selection. Since there is a struggle for existence among individuals, and since these individuals are not all alike, some of the variations among them will be advantageous in the struggle for survival, others unfavourable. Consequently, a higher proportion of individuals with favourable variations will on the average survive, a higher proportion of those with unfavourable variations will die or fail to reproduce themselves. And since a great deal of variation is transmitted by heredity, these effects of differential survival will in large measure accumulate from generation to generation. Thus natural selection will act constantly to improve and to maintain the adjustment of animals and plants to their surroundings and their way of life.

A few comments on these points in the light of the historical development of biology since Darwin's day will clarify both his statement of the theory and the modern position in regard to it.

His first fact has remained unquestioned. All organisms possess the potentiality of geometric increase. We had better perhaps say *increase of geometric type*, since the ratio of offspring to parents may vary considerably from place to place, and from season to season. In all cases, however, the tendency or potentiality is not merely to a progressive increase, but to a multiplicative and not to an additive increase.

Equally unquestioned is his second fact, the general constancy of numbers of any species. As he himself was careful to point out, the constancy is only approximate. At any one time, there will

---

2. The only exception, so far as I am aware, is to be found in certain human populations which fall far short of replacing themselves.

always be some species that are increasing in their numbers, others that are decreasing. But even when a species is increasing, the actual increase is never as great as the potential: some young will fail to survive. Again, with our much greater knowledge of ecology, we know to-day that many species undergo cyclical and often remarkably regular fluctuations, frequently of very large extent, in their numbers.[3] But this fact, although it has certain interesting evolutionary consequences, does not invalidate the general principle.

The first two facts being accepted, the deduction from them also holds: a struggle for existence, or better, a struggle for survival, must occur.

The difficulties of the further bases of the theory are greater, and it is here that the major criticisms have fallen. In the first place, Darwin assumed that the bulk of variations were inheritable. He expressly stated that any which were not inheritable would be irrelevant to the discussion; but he continued in the assumption that those which are inheritable provide an adequate reservoir of potential improvement.[4]

As Haldane [5] has pointed out, the decreased interest in England in plant-breeding, caused by the repeal of the Corn Laws, led Darwin to take most of his evidence from animal-breeders. This was much more obscure than what the plant-breeders in France had obtained: in fact Vilmorin, before Darwin wrote, had fully established the roles of heritable and non-heritable variation in wheat.

Thus in Darwin's time, and still more in England than in France, the subject of inheritance was still very obscure. In any case the basic laws of heredity, or, as we should now say, the principles of genetics, had not yet emerged. In a full formulation of the theory of Natural Selection, we should have to add a further fact and a further deduction. We should begin, as he did, with the fact of variation, and deduce from it and our previous deduction of the struggle for existence that there must be a *differential survival* of different types of offspring in each generation. We should then proceed to the fact of inheritance. *Some* variation is inherited: and that fraction will be available for transmission to later generations. Thus our final deduction is that the result will be a differential transmission of inherited variation. The term Natural Selection is

3. See C. S. Elton, *Animal Ecology* (London, 1927), p. 110.
4. *The Origin of Species* (6th. ed., one vol. ed., p. 9): ". . . any variation which is not inherited is unimportant for us. But the number and diversity of inheritable deviations of structure, both those of slight and those of considerable physiological importance, are endless. No breeder doubts how strong is the tendency to inheritance: that like produces like is his fundamental belief." And so on.
5. J. B. S. Haldane, *The Marxist Philosophy and the Sciences* (London, 1938), p. 107.

thus seen to have two rather different meanings. In a broad sense it covers all cases of differential survival: but from the evolutionary point of view it covers only the differential transmission of inheritable variations.

Mendelian analysis has revealed the further fact, unsuspected by Darwin, that recombination of existing genetic units may both produce and modify new inheritable variations. And this, as we shall see later, has important evolutionary consequences.

Although both the principle of differential survival and that of its evolutionary accumulation by Natural Selection were for Darwin essentially deductions, it is important to realize that, if true, they are also facts of nature capable of verification by observation and experiment. And in point of fact differential mortality, differential survival, and differential multiplication among variants of the same species are now known in numerous cases.

The criticism, however, was early made that a great deal of the mortality found in nature appeared to be accidental and non-selective. This would hold for the destruction of the great majority of eggs and larvae of prolific marine animals, or the death of seeds which fell on stony ground or other unsuitable habitats. It remains true that we require many more quantitative experiments on the subject before we can know accurately the extent of non-selective elimination. Even a very large percentage of such elimination, however, in no way invalidates the selection principle from holding for the remaining fraction. The very fact that it is accidental and non-selective ensures that the residue shall be a random sample, and will therefore contain any variation of selective value in the same proportions as the whole population. It is, I think, fair to say that the fact of differential survival of different variations is generally accepted, although it still requires much clarification, especially on the quantitative side. In other words, natural selection within the bounds of the single generation is an active factor in biology.

2. *The Nature of Variation*

The really important criticisms have fallen upon Natural Selection as an evolutionary principle, and have centred round the nature of inheritable variation.

Darwin, though his views on the subject did not remain constant, was always inclined to allow some weight to Lamarckian principles, according to which the effects of use and disuse and of environmental influences were supposed to be in some degree inherited. However, later work has steadily reduced the scope that can be allowed to such agencies: Weismann drew a sharp distinction between soma and germplasm, between the individual body which was not concerned in reproduction, and the hereditary constitution contained in the germ-cells, which alone was transmitted in heredity. Purely somatic effects, according to him, could not be passed on: the sole inheritable variations were variations in the hereditary constitution.

Although the distinction between soma and germplasm is not always so sharp as Weismann supposed, and although the principle of Baldwin and Lloyd Morgan, usually called Organic Selection, shows how Lamarckism may be simulated by the later replacement of adaptive modifications by adaptive mutations, Weismann's conceptions resulted in a great clarification of the position. It is owing to him that we to-day classify variations into two fundamentally distinct cagetories—modifications and mutations (together with new arrangements of mutations, or recombinations; see below, p. 331). Modifications are produced by alterations in the environment (including modifications of the internal environment such as are brought about by use and disuse), mutations by alterations in the substance of the hereditary constitution. The distinction may be put in a rather different but perhaps more illuminating way. Variation is a study of the differences between organisms. On analysis, these differences may turn out to be due to differences in environment (as with an etiolated plant growing in a cellar as against a green one in light; or a sun-tanned sailor as against a pale slum-dweller); or they may turn out to be due to differences in hereditary constitution (as between an albino and a green seedling in the same plot, or a negro and a white man in the same city); or of course to a simultaneous difference both in environment and in constitution (as with the difference in stature between an undernourished pigmy and a well-nourished negro). Furthermore, only the second are inherited. We speak of them as genetic differences: at their first origin they appear to be due to mutations in the hereditary constitution. The former we call modifications, and are not inheritable.

The important fact is that only experiment can decide between the two. Both in nature and in the laboratory, one of two indistinguishable variants may turn out to be due to environment, the other to genetic peculiarity. A particular shade of human complexion may be due to genetic constitution making for fair complexion plus considerable exposure to the sun, or to a genetically dark complexion plus very little tanning: and similarly for stature, intelligence, and many other characters.

This leads to a further important conclusion: characters as such are not and cannot be inherited. For a character is always the joint product of a particular genetic composition and a particular set of environmental circumstances. Some characters are much more stable in regard to the normal range of environmental variation than are others—for instance, human eye-colour or hair-form as against skin-colour or weight. But these too are in principle similar. Alter the environment of the embryo sufficiently, and eyeless monsters with markedly changed brain-development are produced.

In the early days of Mendelian research, phrases such as "in fowls, the character rose-comb is inherited as a Mendelian dominant" were current. So long as such phrases are recognized as mere convenient shorthand, they are harmless; but when they are taken to imply the actual genetic transmission of the characters, they are wholly incorrect.

Even as shorthand, they may mislead. To say that rose-comb is inherited as a dominant, even if we know that we mean the genetic factor for rose-comb, is likely to lead to what I may call the one-to-one or billiard-ball view of genetics. There are assumed to be a large number of characters in the organism, each one represented in a more or less invariable way by a particular factor or gene, or a combination of a few factors. This crude particulate view is a mere restatement of the preformation theory of development: granted the rose-comb factor, the rose-comb character, nice and clear-cut, will always appear. The rose-comb factor, it is true, is not regarded as a sub-microscopic replica of the actual rose-comb, but is taken to represent it by some form of unanalysed but inevitable correspondence.

The fallacy in this view is again revealed by the use of the difference method. In asserting that rose-comb is a dominant character, we are merely stating in a too abbreviated form the results of experiments to determine what constitutes the difference between fowls with rose-combs and fowls with single combs. In reality, what is inherited as a Mendelian dominant is the gene in the rose-combed stock which differentiates it from the single-combed stock: we have no right to assert anything more as a result of our experiments than the existence of such a differential factor.

Actually, every character is dependent on a very large number (possibly all) of the genes in the hereditary constitution: but some of these genes exert marked differential effects upon the visible appearance. Both rose- and single-comb fowls contain all the genes needed to build up a full-sized comb: but "rose" genes build it up according to one growth-pattern, "single" genes according to another.

This principle is of great importance. For instance, up till very recently the chief data in human genetics have been pedigrees of abnormalities or diseases collected by medical men. And in collecting these data, medical men have usually been obsessed with the implications of the ideas of "character-inheritance". When the character has not appeared in orthodox and classical Mendelian fashion they have tended to dismiss it with some such phrase as "inheritance irregular", whereas further analysis might have shown a perfectly normal *inheritance* of the gene concerned, but an irregular *expression* of the character, dependent on the other genes with which it was associated and upon differences in environment.[6]

This leads on to a further and very vital fact, namely, the existence of a type of genetic process undreamt of until the Mendelian epoch. In Darwin's day biological inheritance meant the reappearance of similar characters in offspring and parent, and implied the physical transmission of some material basis for the characters. What would Darwin or any nineteenth-century biologist say to facts such as the following, which now form part of any elementary course in genetics? A black and an albino mouse are mated. All their offspring are grey, like wild mice: but in the second generation greys, blacks, and albinos appear in the ratio 9:3:4. Or again, fowls with rose-comb and pea-comb mated together produce nothing but so-called walnut combs: but in the next generation, in addition to walnut, rose, and pea, some single combs are produced.

To the biologist of the Darwinian period the production of the grey mice would have been not inheritance, but "reversion" to the wild type, and the reappearance of the blacks and whites in the next generation would have been "atavism" or "skipping a generation". Similarly the appearance of single combs in the fowl cross would have been described as reversion, while the production of walnut combs would have been regarded as some form of "sport."

In reality, the results are in both cases immediately explicable on the assumption of two pairs of genes, each transmitted from parent to offspring by the same fundamental genetic mechanism. The "reversions", "atavisms", and "sports" are all due to new combinations of old genes. Thus, although all the facts are in one sense phenomena of inheritance, it is legitimate and in some ways desirable to distinguish those in which the same characters reappear generation after generation from those in which new characters are generated. As Haldane has put it, modern genetics deals not only with inheritance, but with recombination.

Thus the raw material available for evolution by natural selection falls into two categories—mutation and recombination. Mutation is the only begetter of intrinsic change in the separate units of the hereditary constitution: it alters the nature of genes.[7]

Recombination, on the other hand, though it may produce quite

6. See discussion in L. T. Hogben, *Nature and Nurture* (London, 1933).
7. Strictly speaking, this applies only to gene-mutation. Chromosome-mutation, whether it adds or subtracts chromosome-sets, whole chromosomes, or parts of chromosomes, or inverts sections of chromosomes, merely provides new quantitative or positional combinations of old genes. However, chromosomes-mutation may alter the *effects* of genes. Thus we are covered if we say that mutation alters either the qualitative nature or the effective action (including the mode of transmission) of the hereditary constitution.

new combinations with quite new effects on characters, only juggles with existing genes. It is, however, almost as important for evolution. It cannot occur without sexual reproduction: and its importance in providing the possibility of speedily combining several favourable mutations doubtless accounts for the all-but-universal presence of the sexual process in the life-cycle of organisms. We shall in later chapters see its importance for adjusting mutations to the needs of the organism.

Darwinism to-day thus still contains an element of deduction, and is none the worse for that as a scientific theory. But the facts available in relation to it are both more precise and more numerous, with the result that we are able to check our deductions and to make quantitative prophecies with much greater fullness than was possible to Darwin. This has been especially notable as regards the mathematical treatment of the problem, which we owe to R. A. Fisher, J. B. S. Haldane, Sewall Wright, and others. We can now take mutation-rates and degrees of advantage of one mutation or combination over another, which are within the limits actually found in genetic experiments, and can calculate the rates of evolution which will then occur.

If mutation had a rate that was very high it would neutralize or over-ride selective effects: if one that was very low, it would not provide sufficient raw material for change; if it were not more or less at random in many directions, evolution would run in orthogenetic grooves. But mutation being in point of fact chiefly at random, and the mutation-rate being always moderately low, we can deduce that the struggle for existence will be effective in producing differential survival and evolutionary change.

3. *The Eclipse of Darwinism*

The death of Darwinism has been proclaimed not only from the pulpit, but from the biological laboratory; but, as in the case of Mark Twain, the reports seem to have been greatly exaggerated, since to-day Darwinism is very much alive.

The reaction against Darwinism set in during the nineties of last century. The younger zoologists of that time were discontented with the trends of their science. The major school still seemed to think that the sole aim of zoology was to elucidate the relationship of the larger groups. Had not Kovalevsky demonstrated the vertebrate affinities of the sea-squirts, and did not comparative embryology prove the common ancestry of groups so unlike as worms and molluscs? Intoxicated with such earlier successes of evolutionary phylogeny, they proceeded (like some Forestry Commission of science) to plant wildernesses of family trees over the beauty-spots of biology.

A related school, a little less prone to speculation, concentrated on the pursuit of comparative morphology within groups. This provides one of the most admirable of intellectual trainings for the student, and has yielded extremely important results for science. But if pursued too exclusively for its own sake, it leads, as Radl has pithily put it in his *History of Biological Theories*, to spending one's time comparing one thing with another without ever troubling about what either of them really is. In other words, zoology, becoming morphological, suffered divorce from physiology. And finally Darwinism itself grew more and more theoretical. The paper demonstration that such and such a character was or might be adaptive was regarded by many writers as sufficient proof that it must owe its origin to Natural Selection. Evolutionary studies became more and more merely case-books of real or supposed adaptations. Late nineteenth-century Darwinism came to resemble the early nineteenth-century school of Natural Theology. Paley *redivivus*, one might say, but philosophically upside down, with Natural Selection instead of a Divine Artificer as the *Deus ex machina*. There was little contact of evolutionary speculation with the concrete facts of cytology and heredity, or with actual experimentation.

A major symptom of revolt was the publication of William Bateson's *Materials for the Study of Variation* in 1894. Bateson had done valuable work on the embryology of *Balanoglossus*; but his sceptical and concrete mind found it distasteful to spend itself on speculations on the ancestry of the vertebrates, which was then regarded as the outstanding topic of evolution, and he turned to a task which, however different it might seem, he rightly regarded as piercing nearer to the heart of the evolutionary problems. Deliberately he gathered evidence of variation which was discontinuous, as opposed to the continuous variation postulated by Darwin and Weismann. The resultant volume of material, though its gathering might fairly be called biassed, was impressive in quantity and range, and deeply impressed the more active spirits in biology. It was the first symptom of what we may call the period of mutation theory, which postulated that large mutations, and not small "continuous variations", were the raw material of evolution, and actually determined most of its course, selection being relegated to a wholly subordinate position.

This was first formally promulgated by de Vries [8] as a result of his work with the evening primroses, *Oenothera*, and was later adopted by various other workers, notably T. H. Morgan, in his first genetical phase. The views of the early twentieth-century

8. H. de Vries, *Die Mutationstheorie* (Leipzig, 1901); *Species and Varieties; their Origin by Mutation* (Chicago, 1905).

geneticists, moreover, were coloured by the rediscovery of Mendel's laws by Correns, de Vries, and Tschermak in the spring of 1900, and the rapid generalization of them, notably by Bateson.

Naturally, the early Mendelians worked with clear-cut differences of large extent. As it became clearer that mendelian inheritance was universal, it was natural to suppose all mendelian factors produced large effects, that therefore mutation was sharp and discontinuous, and that the continuous variation which is obviously widespread in nature is not heritable.

Bateson did not hesitate to draw the most devastating conclusions from his reading of the mendelian facts. In his Presidential Address to the British Association in 1914, assuming first that change in the germplasm is always by large mutation and secondly that all mutation is loss, from a dominant something to a recessive nothing, he concluded that the whole of evolution is merely an unpacking. The hypothetical ancestral amoeba contained—actually and not just potentially—the entire complex of life's hereditary factors. The jettisoning of different portions of this complex released the potentialities of this, that, and the other group and form of life. Selection and adaptation were relegated to an unconsidered background.

Meanwhile the true-blue Darwinian stream, leaving Weismannism behind, had reached its biometric phase. Tracing its origin to Galton, biometry blossomed under the guidance of Karl Pearson and Weldon. Unfortunately this, the first thorough application of mathematics to evolution, though productive of many important results and leading to still more important advances in method, was for a considerable time rendered sterile by its refusal to acknowledge the genetic facts discovered by the Mendelians. Both sides, indeed, were to blame. The biometricians stuck to hypothetical modes of inheritance and genetic variation on which to exercise their mathematical skill; the Mendelians refused to acknowledge that continuous variation could be genetic, or at any rate dependent on genes, or that a mathematical theory of selection could be of any real service to the evolutionary biologist.

It was in this period, immediately prior to the war, that the legend of the death of Darwinism acquired currency. The facts of mendelism appeared to contradict the facts of paleontology; the theories of the mutationists would not square with the Weismannian views of adaptation, the discoveries of experimental embryology seemed to contradict the classical recapitulatory theories of development. Zoologists who clung to Darwinian views were looked down on by the devotees of the newer disciplines, whether cytology or genetics, *Entwicklungsmechanik* or comparative physiology, as old-fashioned theorizers; and the theological and philosophical antipathy to Darwin's great mechanistic generalization could once more raise its head without fearing too violent a knock.

But the old-fashioned selectionists were guided by a sound instinct. The opposing factions became reconciled as the younger branches of biology achieved a synthesis with each other and with the classical disciplines: and the reconciliation converged upon a Darwinian centre.

It speedily became apparent that mendelism applied to the heredity of all many-celled and many single-celled organisms, both animals and plants. The mendelian laws received a simple and general interpretation: they were due in the first place to inheritance being particulate, and in the second place to the particles being borne on the chromosomes, whose behaviour could be observed under the microscope. Many apparent exceptions to mendelian rules turned out to be due to aberrations of chromosome-behaviour. Segregation and recombination, the fundamental mendelian facts, are all but universal, being co-extensive with sexual reproduction; and mutation, the further corollary of the particulate theory of heredity, was found to occur even more widely, in somatic tissues and in parthenogenetic and sexually-reproducing strains as well as in the germtrack of bisexual species. Blending inheritance as originally conceived was shown not to occur, and cytoplasmic inheritance to play an extremely subsidiary role.

The Mendelians also found that mutations could be of any extent, and accordingly that apparently continuous as well as obviously discontinuous variation had to be taken into account in discussing heredity and evolution. The mathematicians found that biometric methods could be applied to neo-mendelian postulates, and then become doubly fruitful. Cytology became intimately linked with genetics. Experimental embryology and the study of growth illuminated heredity, recapitulation, and paleontology. Ecology and systematics provided new data and new methods of approach to the evolutionary problem. Selection, both in nature and in the laboratory, was studied quantitatively and experimentally. Mathematical analysis showed that only particulate inheritance would permit evolutionary change: blending inheritance, as postulated by Darwin, was shown by R. A. Fisher[9] to demand mutation-rates enormously higher than those actually found to occur. Thus, though it may still be true in a formal sense that, as such an eminent geneticist as Miss E. R. Saunders said at the British Association meeting in 1920, "Mendelism is a theory of heredity: it is not a theory of evolution", yet the assertion is purely formal. Mendelism is now seen as an essential part of the theory of evolution. Mendelian analysis does not merely explain the distribu-

9. R. A. Fisher, *The Genetical Theory of Natural Selection* (Oxford, 1930).

tive hereditary mechanism: it also, together with selection, explains the progressive mechanism of evolution.

Biology in the last twenty years, after a period in which new disciplines were taken up in turn and worked out in comparative isolation, has become a more unified science. It has embarked upon a period of synthesis, until to-day it no longer presents the spectacle of a number of semi-independent and largely contradictory sub-sciences, but is coming to rival the unity of older sciences like physics, in which advance in any one branch leads almost at once to advance in all other fields, and theory and experiment march hand-in-hand. As one chief result, there has been a rebirth of Darwinism. The historical facts concerning this trend are summarized by Shull in a recent book.[1] It is noteworthy that T. H. Morgan, after having been one of the most extreme critics of selectionist doctrine, has recently, as a result of modern work in genetics (to which he has himself so largely contributed), again become an upholder of the Darwinian point of view;[2] while his younger colleagues, notably Muller and Sturtevant, are strongly selectionist in their evolutionary views.

The Darwinism thus reborn is a modified Darwinism, since it must operate with facts unknown to Darwin; but it is still Darwinism in the sense that it aims at giving a naturalistic interpretation of evolution, and that its upholders, while constantly striving for more facts and more experimental results, do not, like some cautious spirits, reject the method of deduction.

Hogben[3] disagrees with this conclusion. He accepts the findings of neo-Mendelism and the mathematical conclusions to be drawn from them; but, to use his own words, "the essential difference between the theory of natural selection expounded by such contemporary writers as J. B. S. Haldane, Sewall Wright, and R. A. Fisher, as contrasted with that of Darwin, resides in the fact that Darwin interpreted the process of artificial selection in terms of a theory of 'blending inheritance' universally accepted by his own generation, whereas the modern view is based on the Theory of Particulate Inheritance. The consequences of the two views are very different. According to the Darwinian doctrine, evolution is an essentially continuous process, and selection is essentially creative in the sense that no change would occur if selection were removed. According to the modern doctrine, evolution is discontinuous. The differentiation of varieties or species may suffer periods of stagnation. Selection is a destructive agency."

Accordingly, Hogben would entirely repudiate the title of Dar-

1. A. F. Shull, *Evolution* (New York and London, 1936).
2. T. H. Morgan, *Evolution and Genetics* (Princeton, 1925); and later writings.
3. L. T. Hogben, *Genetic Principles in Medicine and Social Science* (London, 1931), pp. 145 ff.

winism for the modern outlook, and would prefer to see the term Natural Selection replaced by another to mark the new connotations it has acquired, although on this latter point he is prepared to admit the convenience of retention.

These objections, coming from a biologist of Hogben's calibre, must carry weight. On the other hand we shall see reason in later chapters for finding them ungrounded. In the first place, evolution, as revealed in fossil trends, *is* "an essentially continuous process". The building-blocks of evolution, in the shape of mutations, are, to be sure, discrete quanta of change. But firstly, the majority of them (and the very great majority of those which survive to become incorporated in the genetic constitution of living things) appear to be of small extent; secondly, the effect of a given mutation will be different according to the combinations of modifying genes present; and thirdly, its effect may be masked or modified by environmental modification. The net result will be that, for all practical purposes, most of the variability of a species at any given moment will be continuous, however accurate are the measurements made; and that most evolutionary change will be gradual, to be detected by a progressive shifting of a mean value from generation to generation.

In the second place, the statement that selection is a destructive agency is not true, if it is meant to imply that it is *merely* destructive. It is also directive, and because it is directive, it has a share in evolutionary creation. Neither mutation nor selection alone is creative of anything important in evolution; but the two in conjunction are creative.

Hogben is perfectly right in stressing the fact of the important differences in content and implication between the Darwinism of Darwin or Weismann and that of Fisher or Haldane. We may, however, reflect that the term *atom* is still in current use and the atomic theory not yet rejected by physicists, in spite of the supposedly indivisible units having been divided. This is because modern physicists still find that the particles called atoms by their predecessors do play an important role, even if they are compound and do occasionally lose or gain particles and even change their nature. If this is so, biologists may with a good heart continue to be Darwinians and to employ the term Natural Selection, even if Darwin knew nothing of mendelizing mutations, and if selection is by itself incapable of changing the constitution of a species or a line.[4]

4. It should be added that Hogben was in 1931 concerned to stress mutation-pressure as an agency of change—then a new and not generally accepted conception. Since then he has allowed much more weight to the joint role of selection and mutation in producing adaptive change. See Hogben, "Problems of the Origin of Species," in *The New Systematics*, J. S. Huxley, ed. (Oxford, 1940).

Introduction to the Second Edition

* * * In the twenty years since this book was first published, there has been an enormous volume of new work and new ideas on the subject of evolution. * * *

The main fact to note is that the neo-Darwinian, synthetic, or integrative theory of evolution that I maintained in 1942 has gained many new adherents and may now be regarded as the established view. It has been supported by Rensch in his *Evolution above the Species Level* (1959a); by G. G. Simpson in *Tempo and Mode in Evolution* (1944) and *Major Factors in Evolution* (1953), by Ernst Mayr in *Systematics and the Origin of Species* (1942), by Dobhansky in *Genetics and the Origin of Species* (1951) and in *Mankind Evolving* (1962), by Stebbins in *Variation and Evolution in Plants* (1954), by Carter in *A Hundred Years of Evolution* (1957): also by the mass of the contributors to *The Evolution of Life*, Vol. 1 of the University of Chicago centennial on *Evolution after Darwin* (1960), to the Society of Experimental Biology's Symposium on *Evolution* (1953), to *Hundert Jahre Evolutionsforschung*, edited by Heberer and Schwanitz (1960), to *Darwin's Biological Work*, edited by P. R. Bell (1959), and to *A Century of Darwin*, edited by S. A. Barnett (1958). See also Waddington's *The Nature of Life* (1961) and Moody's *Introduction to Evolution* (1953).

It underlies most recent works on genetics, like L. C. Dunn's symposium on *Genetics in the 20th Century* (1951) Srb and Owen's text-book of *General Genetics* (1952) or King's up-to-date *Genetics* (1962), and modern treatments of major animal groups such as J. Z. Young's remarkable *The Life of Vertebrates* (1950). Finally, it has been adopted or assumed by the great majority of the contributors to *Evolution*, the first scientific journal devoted to the subject, whose successful launching in 1947 marked a major step in the progress of evolutionary biology.

Darwin's original contention, that biological evolution is a nattural process, effected primarily by natural selection, has thus become increasingly confirmed, and all other theories of evolution requiring a supernatural or vitalistic force or mechanism, such as Bergson's creative evolution, and all "autogenetic" theories (Dobzhansky) such as Berg's nomogenesis, Osborn's aristogenesis, and orthogenesis in the strict sense, together with all Lamarckian theories involving the inheritance of acquired characters, have become increasingly untenable.

Only in the U.S.S.R. has Lamarckism found favour. Here, under the influence of Lysenko, the peculiar brand of Lamarckism styled Michurinism was given official sanction, and extravagant and ill-founded claims were made on its behalf, while neo-Mendelian genetics, which everywhere else was advancing in a spectacular way, was officially condemned as bourgeois or capitalist "Morganist-Mendelist," and Soviet geneticists were exiled or lost their jobs. See J. S. Huxley, *Soviet Genetics and World Science*, 1949; and C. Zirkle, *Evolution, Marxian Biology and the Social Scene*, 1959.

The Soviet opposition to genetical science was particularly strong in the field of human genetics, since the orthodox Marxists believed or wanted to believe that a few generations of socialism would improve the genetic quality of the population. Eventually Lysenko lost his dominant position. But though orthodox genetics is now once more permitted, some official encouragement is given to an uneasy mixture of Mendelism and Michurinism.

Meanwhile in Britain, Waddington [1] has made a notable contribution to evolutionary theory by his discovery that Lamarckian inheritance may be simulated by a purely neo-Darwinian mechanism. This he called *genetic assimilation*. It operates through the natural selection of genes which dispose the developing organism to become modified in reaction to some environmental stimulus. Waddington showed experimentally that after a number of generations of selection for individuals which showed the most pronounced reaction, a strain could be obtained which developed the modified character in the absence of the environmental stimulus. This applies to adaptive as well as to non-adaptive modifications, and, as Haldane [2] points out, could clearly be effective in regard to the origin of various types of instinctive behaviour, by the genetic assimilation of behavioural modifications.[3]

The upholders of orthogenetic evolution had claimed that good fossil series showed unvarying evolutionary trends in one definite direction, and that this could not be explained except by postulating some inherent directive force. Their standard example was the evolution of the horse. However, G. G. Simpson in his book *Horses* (1951) conclusively demonstrated that the facts are otherwise: not only are trends sometimes reversed in single branches of the group, but the main trend shows definite changes of direction during its course. This is consonant with the view that natural selection is "opportunistic" in its operations, a view especially championed by G. G. Simpson and accepted by most other modern authorities, such as Dobzhansky and Mayr.

Sheppard in his book *Natural Selection and Heredity* (1958) has

---

1. C. H. Waddington, *The Strategy of the Genes* (London, 1957); "Evolutionary Adaptation," in *Evolution after Darwin*, I, Sol Tax, ed. (Chicago, 1960).
2. J.B.S. Haldane, "Natural Selection" in P. R. Bell, ed., *Darwin's Biological Work* (Cambridge, 1959), p. 146.
3. See also C. Stern, "Genetic Assimilation," Proceedings of the American Philosophical Society, CIII (1959), 183.

analysed the operation of natural selection in detail, especially in relation to population genetics, speciation, and adaptations such as mimicry.

The most comprehensive and up-to-date exposition of the synthetic theory of evolution has just been given by Ernst Mayr in his magistral book *Animal Species and Evolution* (1963). As he points out, a radical change in recent evolutionary theory has been "the replacement of typologic thinking by population thinking." However, the modern synthetic theory still retains the combination of induction and deduction that underlay Darwin's original theory of evolution by natural selection.

His main point is that the species is a highly organised unit of evolution, based on an integrated pattern of co-operative genes co-adapted to produce an optimal phenotype, highly homeostatic and resistant to major change. This results in what has been termed *genetic relativity*. No gene has a fixed selective value: one and the same gene may be highly advantageous on one genetic background, highly disadvantageous on another. A long-term consequence is that the range of mutations and recombinations available to any particular organism or taxon is a restricted one and its evolutionary possibilities are correspondingly limited. This presumably accounts for some so-called orthogenetic trends, and for various phenotypic tendencies of different families and orders of animals and plants.

As a further result, speciation, in the sense of the splitting of one species into two, appears to occur most frequent by divergence of isolated populations near the margins of a species' range. These, under the pressure of new selective forces and in the absence of gene-flow from the central gene-pool of the species, are able to escape from the old integration and undergo genetic reconstruction with formation of a new integrated genotypic pattern. * * *

As a result of the marked increase of interest in population genetics as against formal genetics, selection theory has undergone various changes. One striking and in my opinion undesirable innovation concerns the concept of *fitness*. It is now fashionable to define fitness solely in terms of differential reproductive advantage, without any reference to phenotypic fitness ensuring individual survival. Some authors, like Dobzhansky [4], go so far as to call differential reproductive advantage "Darwinian fitness," although Darwin never used fitness in this sense, and although it was Herbert Spencer who first introduced the term into evolutionary theory by his unfortunate phrase *The Survival of the Fittest*, which Darwin did not employ in the earlier editions of the *Origin of Species*.

4. T. Dobzhansky, "A Review of Some Fundamental Concepts and Problems of Population Genetics," *Cold Spring Harbor Symp. Quant. Biol.*, XX (1955), 1.

Dobzhansky writes that "Darwinian fitness is measurable only in terms of reproductive proficiency," and later (p.221) that "the only trend [or] direction . . . discernible in life and its evolution is the product of more life." Accordingly (p. 11) "natural selection *means* [5] *differential reproduction* of carriers of different genetic endowments . . ."

When we examine the problem more critically, we find that we must differentiate between two quite distinct modes of natural selection, leading to different types of evolutionary trend, which we may call *survival selection* and *reproductive selection*. Haldane [6] also distinguishes these two modes of natural selection, but calls them phenotypic and genotypic respectively. I prefer my terminology for natural selection, but suggest using *phenotypic* and *genotypic* for the corresponding types of social selection (see below).

In the actual processes of biological evolution, survival selection is much the more important: selection exerts its effects mainly on individual phenotypes, and operates primarily by means of their differential survival to maturity. This will produce evolutionary effects because, as Darwin saw, (a) the majority of individuals which survive to maturity will mate and leave offspring; (b) much of the phenotypic variance promoting survival has a genetic basis.

Natural selection clearly may also operate by means of the differential reproduction of mature individuals, but in point of fact this *reproductive selection* has only minor evolutionary effects. Its most general effect is to promote an optimum clutch-size, litter-size, or in general terms progeny-number. Its effect in organisms with separate sexes is to promote mechanisms for securing successful matings, from flower-colour in entomophilous plants to mating behaviour in birds.[7] Only when there is strong intra-sexual competition with a high premium on mating success, does reproductive selection promote special trends like those to striking display characters in polygamous-promiscuous birds like Birds of Paradise and Argus Pheasants; or those to large size, special weapons, and general combative character in mammals with a harem-system, like deer and Elephant Seals. Darwin recognized the basic difference between these two forms of selection when he coined the term *sexual selection* for reproductive selection operating by inter-male competition.[8]

Survival selection, on the other hand, as Darwin saw in 1859, inevitably promotes all kinds of trends leading to biological improve-

5. It would be more logical to say *operates by means of.*
6. Haldane, "Natural Selection.".
7. See Maynard Smith, *The Theory of Evolution* (London, 1958), Chapters 8 and 11.

8. For important discussions of sexual selection, see Chapter 6 of R. A. Fisher, *Genetical Theory of Natural Selection*; Maynard Smith; and S. A. Barnett, ed., *A Century of Darwin* (London, 1958).

ment, whether improvement in close adaptation to environment, in specialisation, in functional efficiency of particular organ-systems, in self-regulation, or in general organisation.

As R. A. Fisher pointed out in chapters 8 to 11 of his great book *The Genetical Theory of Natural Selection*, man is reproductively unique among organisms in showing an enormous range of individual variation in fertility, instead of a single optimum value with low variance. Man is also unique in having markedly reduced the impact of natural selection on the survival of individuals by artificial means, such as medical care and sanitation. The relative importance of differential survival and differential reproduction has thus been completely reversed in most present-day communities.

The human situation is so different from the biological that it may prove best to abandon the attempt to apply concepts like natural selection to modern human affairs. All the evolutionary differentials now operating, whether in survival or in reproduction, have their roots in the special psychosocial character of human evolution. It would seem best to accept the fact that a novel form of selection, *psychosocial selection*, or more simply *social selection*, is now operating; to attempt to define and analyse it more closely; and to see how it could be applied to produce eugenic results. Both phenotypic (survival) social selection and genotypic (reproductive) social selection are now probably dysgenic in their effects.

Thus R. A. Fisher [9] says that evolution in certain early types of society proceeds by "the social promotion of fertility," whereas in most modern societies there is a "social selection of infertility." I have coined the word *euselection* to denote deliberate selection for what are deemed desirable genetic qualities. Herbert Brewer uses *eutelgenesis* to denote eugenic improvement by means of artificial insemination from selected donors; and H. J. Muller [1] and he have pointed out how it could be rendered much more effective by the use of the recent technique of preserving mammalian sperm (and eventually ova and immature germ-cells) in a deep-frozen state.

Eugenics and the general relation of human genetics to human evolution has been much discussed recently, notably by Dobzhansky [2] by Crow, Muller and others in the first part of the symposium on *Evolution and Man's Progress*,[3] by Medawar in his Reith Lectures (1960), and by myself in my Galton Lectures (1962). It is becoming clear that social euselection (eugenic selec-

9. Fisher, p. 245.
1. H. J. Müller, "The Guidance of Human Evolution," *Persp. Biol. Med.* III (1959), 1.; and "Should We Weaken or Strengthen our Genetic Heritage?" in H. Hoagland and R. W. Burhoe, *Evolution and Man's Progress* (New York and London, 1962).
2. Dobzhansky, *Mankind Evolving* (New Haven, 1962).
3. Hoagland and Burhoe, eds., *Evolution and Man's Progress* (London, 1962).

tion for the deliberate genetic improvement of man) will differ radically from artificial selection for the deliberate genetic improvement of domesticated plants and animals; and also from natural selection, which operates automatically to produce biological improvement in natural species of groups. It is also clear that, in so far as immediate threats to human progress are overcome, such as over-population, atomic war, and over-exploitation of natural resources, eugenic improvement will become an increasingly important goal of evolving man.

Much theoretical and experimental work has been done on selection in general. In addition to survival (phenotypic) and reproductive (genotypic), sexual, and social (psychosocial) selection (see above), the following main types of natural selection are now usually distinguished [4]:

(1) *Normalizing*, centripetal, or stabilizing selection: tending to reduce variance, to promote the continuance of the "normal" type, and to prevent change in a well-adapted organisation.

(2) *Directional*, directed, or dynamic selection: tending to produce change in an adaptive direction.

(3) *Diversifying*, disruptive, or centrifugal selection: tending to separate a single population into two genetically distinct populations.

(4) *Balancing* selection: tending to produce balanced polymorphisms and heteroses in populations.

(5) Selection for variability: leading to high variance in cryptic adaptation in certain conditions (see Sheppard, 1958). To which we may perhaps add

(6) *Post hoc* selection, as when a viable new species originates suddenly by allopolyploidy.

In recent years, much attention has been paid to the effects of population-density on survival, and a careful analysis has been made of the various density-dependent and density-independent factors involved and of their selective effects.[5]

In numerically very small populations, as Sewall Wright first pointed out, change in gene-frequency may occur by chance, through random survival without the intervention of selection. When this occurs through the loss of alleles which inevitably takes place in such populations, it is termed *genetic drift*, and may ac-

4. See Dobzhansky, *Mankind Evolving*, Haldane, "Natural Selection"; P. M. Sheppard, *Natural Selection and Heredity* (London, 1958); J. M. Thoday, "Natural Selection and Biological Progress," in S. A. Barnett, *A Century of Darwin* (London, 1958); etc. Haldane in particular has helped to quantify the subject.

5. W. C. Allee et al., *Principles of Animal Ecology* (Philadelphia and London, 1949); V. C. Wynne-Edwards, *Animal Dispersion in Relation to Social Behaviour* (Edinburgh and London, 1962); Ernst Mayr, *Animal Species and Evolution* (Cambridge, Mass., 1963).

tually override selection-pressure and even lead to reduction or extinction of the population. Further, as discussed in chaps. 2 and 5 of the present work it may also occur when an isolated habitat, such as an island or a lake, is colonized by a handful of invaders. These will almost certainly not have a full complement of the alleles in the gene-complex of the species, so that the local population will be genetically distinct from the outset, and will frequently show further divergence owing to genetic drift and to local selection (see below). This has been called the *founder principle* by Mayr, who gives numerous examples of its effects. * * *

Perhaps the most important fact to emerge from research in population genetics is that in most animal species, the majority of wild populations have a surprisingly high genetic variance, but that much of it is potential, and is not manifested phenotypically unless released under the influence of selection. This capacity of the integrated genotype for storing variance is highly adaptive in relation to the evolutionary survival of species. On the other hand, the species has to pay a considerable price for this capacity, in the shape of the genetic load of disadvantageous variations which may be released by recombination.

Most such populations are not even approximately homozygous, but are heterozygous for a large proportion, perhaps a majority, of their genes. There is considerable dispute as to how much of this heterozygosity is maintained through selectively balanced morphisms, through straight heterozygote advantage in single genes, through traditional heterosis due to the co-operation of complementary genes, through the establishment of complementary linked polygenic systems as described by Mather, or through that of complementary chromosomal types (chromosome morphisms) as found by Dobzhansky in wild Drosophila. In any case, the widespread existence of heterozygosity will lock up a great deal of the variance of a natural population in potential form. Linked polygenic systems are normally balanced so as to secure an optimum mean effect on a given character (or on a pair or set of balanced morphic characters; see below). Long-continued selection can change the manifestation of the character, by a slow but stepwise release of their latent (stored) variance, as shown for instance, by the work of Mather [6] and Thoday.[7]

In this and other ways high heterozygosity confers a marked degree of stability on a population, but it also ensures a large store of potential variance, which can be released by selection if circum-

6. K. Mather, "The Genetical Structure of Populations," in *Symp. Soc. Exp. Biol.* VII (Cambridge, England, 1953); and discussion of heterosis in *Proc. Roy. Soc.* (B) CXLIV (1956), 143.

7. J. M. Thoday, "Components of Fitness," *Symp. Soc. Exp. Biol.;* VII, Evolution, p. 96; and "Natural Selection and Biological Progress," in S. A. Barnett, *A Century of Darwin.*

stances demand it. Darwin's postulate that long-term and major evolution by natural selection is normally slow and manifested by gradual trends of change, largely in quantitative characters, has thus been confirmed, though modern population-genetics has shown that short-term minor changes may occur with surprising rapidity, under the influence of unexpectedly high selective pressures. * * *

I have left to the end the most important scientific event of our times—the discovery by Watson and Crick that the deoxyribonucleic acids—DNA for short—are the true physical basis of life, and provide the mechanism of heredity and evolution.[8] Their chemical structure, combining two elongated linear sequences in a linked double spiral or bihelix, makes them self-reproducing, and ensures that they can act as a code, providing an immense amount of genetical "information," together with occasional variations of information (mutations) which also reproduce themselves. Linear constructions of DNA are, of course, the primary structures in the genetic organelles we call chromosomes. In some primitive organisms there is only a single chromosome, including the species' entire apparatus of DNA.[9]

Specific DNA also plays the key role in determining the specific proteins, including enzymes, in living cells, through the intermediary of specific forms of RNA (ribose nucleic acid). The particular DNA code of each species thus provides epigenetic "instruction" as well as phylogenetic "information." Mayr[1] makes the same distinction in slightly different terms. In his formulation, the phenomena of ontogeny and physiology are manifestations of the decoding of the information provided by the genotypic DNA, while those of evolutionary change are the result of the provision of ever-new codes of genetic information.

It may well prove that DNA structure has the further intrinsic property of ensuring recombination of mutants by interchange between separate homologous sections of DNA (chromosomes). Even if this essentially sexual process were not intrinsic *ab origine*, it confers such a high degree of evolutionary advantage that it must have been incorporated into the stream of life very early in its evolution. * * *

The various properties of DNA which I have mentioned make evolution inevitable. The existence of an elaborate self-reproducing code of genetical information ensures continuity and specificity; the intrinsic capacity for mutation provides varability; the capacity for self-reproduction ensures potentially geometric increase and there-

8. For a brief account, see Davidson, 1960, and for a general discussion, see New Biology, No. 31, *Biological Replication*, 1960.

9. E. Chargaff and J. N. Davidson, eds., *The Nucleic Acids* (New York, 1955–1960).

1. *Animal Species and Evolution*.

fore a struggle for existence; the existence of genetic variability ensures differential survival of variants and therefore natural selection; and this results in evolutionary transformation.

Our detailed knowledge of the constitution and operation of DNA and RNA will help in the unravelling of many particular genetic-evolutionary problems. Among these may be mentioned the relation of genes to developmental processes, the interaction of different genes, and the relations of genes to immunology via antigens and antibodies. Light is already being shed on the fine structure of genes, which are proving to be far more complex than was originally supposed.[2]

It would also seem certain that more detailed knowledge about DNA will give us fuller understanding of mutation and the ways in which it depends on chemical structure, with the eventual possibility of influencing the type and direction of mutation by artificial means. In general, however, the discovery of DNA and its properties has not led to important new developments or significant modifications in evolutionary theory or in our understanding of the course of biological evolution. What it has done is to reveal the physical basis underlying the evolutionary mechanisms which Darwin's genius deduced must be operative in nature, and to open up new possibilities of detailed genetic analysis and of experimental control of the genetic-evolutionary process. The edifice of evolutionary theory is still essentially Darwinian after the incorporation of all our new knowledge of mendelian (particulate) genetics; it will remain so long after the incorporation of our knowledge of its detailed chemical basis.

THEODOSIUS DOBZHANSKY

The Nature of Heredity (1964) †

* * *

Chromosome Chemistry

The work of the Morgan school on Drosophila genetics and cytogenetics attained such a degree of refinement that after it the next development in the understanding of the physical basis of heredity could only come, and it did come, from the study of the

2. C. Pontecorvo, *Trends in Genetic Analysis* (New York and Oxford, 1959).
† From Chapter 1 of *Heredity and the Nature of Man* (New York, 1964).

Theodosius Dobzhansky (1900–1975) was professor of genetics at Rockefeller University.

chemistry of chromosomes. The two classes of chemical compounds that account for most of the material composing a chromosome are deoxyribonucleic acids (abbreviated as DNA) and proteins, loosely joined to form nucleoproteins. The question naturally arises, what makes one gene different from another? A human sex cell contains probably no fewer than 10,000 different genes, and there may be millions and millions of kinds of genes in different organisms in the living world.

Until fairly recently, say twenty years ago, most biologists were inclined to regard the proteins as probably responsible for the specific qualities of each gene. At present, it is considered extremely probable that heredity, genetic information, to use a now-fashionable phrase, is stored chiefly in the chromosomal DNA. Let us see what has led to this change of opinion. The nucleic acids are seemingly rather too simple and too uniform in chemical composition in most diverse organisms to produce a variety of structures at least equal to the variety of genes that exist in the living world. Proteins are, on the contrary, large, some of them being enormous, molecules; they exist in a great variety of forms, and they can be envisaged to produce almost infinite variety.

Facts began, however, to come to light that argued for the nucleic acids being the chief carriers of genetic information. A. E. Mirsky in the United States, R. Vendrely in France, and others found that the amount of DNA per cell doubles in the interval between successive cell divisions, and is reduced by half when the cell divides. However, this amount is remarkably constant in body cells of a given species of organism, except that the sex cells contain only half as much DNA and half as many chromosomes as do body cells. The chromosomal proteins are, on the contrary, quite variable, both in amount and in composition in different cells of the same body.

O. T. Avery, C. M. MacLeod, and M. McCarty discovered in 1944 that hereditary characteristics can be transferred from one strain of bacteria to other strains, causing pneumonia (*Pneumococcus*) by means of a transforming principle extracted from the donor strain. This "transforming principle" was identified as a nucleic acid. Such transformations of the hereditary endowment are now known in several species of bacteria; whether this is also possible in higher organisms remains to be seen. A. D. Hershey secured a very elegant demonstration of the importance of DNA in the transmission of heredity in his study of the bacteriophages (bacterial viruses). A bacteriophage is an organism too small to be seen in an ordinary light microscope but visible in electron microscopes; it enters living bacterial cells, multiplies therein, and causes the bacteria to disintegrate, releasing numerous new bacteriophages.

Now, the body of a bacteriophage consists of a DNA core and a protein envelope; Hershey showed that only the DNA enters the host bacterial cell, while the protein is left outside.

The amounts of the DNA involved in the transmission of heredity are actually remarkably small, even in higher organisms. For example, the nucleus of the spermatozoon of a fish (carp) contains about 1.6 billionths of a milligram (1.6×10^{-12} of a gram) of DNA, while the nuclei of the body cells (red blood cells) contain 3.0 to 3.3 billionths. (This variation is probably a matter of imprecision in measurement.) Another fish (trout) has 2.45 of the same units of DNA in a spermatozoon, and 4.9 in a bodycell nucleus. Spermatozoa of a bull have 3.3 units, body cells some 6.4 to 6.8. Human body cells contain 6.0 to 6.8 units; the amount in human sex cells does not seem to have been measured.

One can make an interesting calculation of the total amount of DNA that has contained and has transmitted the genetic endowment of mankind. Take three billion (3×10^9) as the number of human beings now living; each of them arose from a fertilized egg cell, the nucleus of which had between 6 and 7×10^{-12} gram of DNA; all these egg cells had, then, between 0.018 and 0.021 of a gram, roughly 20 milligrams of DNA. Truly, the powers concealed in this extraordinary substance exceed by far anything in the atomic and other bombs yet invented!

Lower organisms generally have less DNA than higher ones. Thus, a bacteriophage (bacterial virus) has only 0.0002×10^{-12} of a gram; a colon bacterium (*Escherichia coli*), 0.01; the nucleus of a cell of a sponge, 0.1; of a sea urchin, 1.97; of a mouse, 5; of a man, as stated above, between 6 and 7. Man is, however, far from the top of the series. More DNA than in human cells is contained in a cell nucleus of the amphibians, such as a toad (7.3), a frog (15.0), *Necturus* (48), and *Amphiuma* (168). The meaning of this is obscure—in our pride we would not like to entertain the notion that toads, frogs, and salamanders need either more numerous or more complicated genes than man does. One possible but unconfirmed explanation might be that in some organisms the chromosomes of the cell nuclei contain the set of genes each represented only once, while in other organisms each gene of the set is repeated several times.

The chemical structure of DNA is a fascinating story in its own right. Many outstanding investigators in different parts of the world have been working on it in recent years, and with outstanding success. The results obtained are of the greatest importance; so much so, that it seems in the highest degree likely that our time will stand, in the history of biology, as that of the discovery of the chemical basis of heredity. Furthermore, it is sometimes said that truly great discoveries in science are beautifully simple; I am not sure that this proposition can always be sustained, but it certainly applies to the DNA story. Its essentials can be stated briefly and simply, without going into chemical details. DNA (Figures 4 and 5) extracted from the chromosomes of cell nuclei can be broken down to a fairly small number of constituents. These are a kind of sugar called deoxyribose, a phosphoric acid, and four so-called nucleotide bases, namely adenine, guanine, cytosine, and thymine. We shall not discuss the chemical structure and chemical formulae

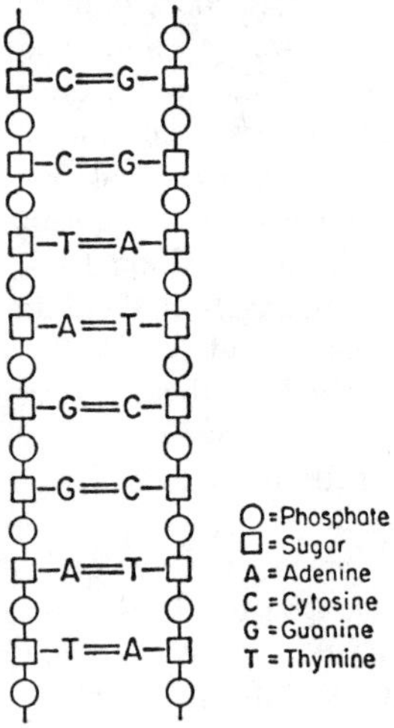

Figure 4. The comparison of the DNA (deoxyribonucleic acid), the substance which carries the master blueprints of heredity in the form of a genetic "code." Two chains of sugars and phosphates are cross-linked by pairs of nucleotide bases, C-G or A-T.

of these constituents; furthermore, we shall take the liberty of denoting the adenine, guanine, cytosine, and thymine nucleotide bases simply by their initial letters, A, G, C, and T. Only rarely, in some exceptional organisms, is one of the bases replaced by a closely related chemical compound. This uniformity is, of course, in itself a most remarkable fact, attesting the fundamental unity of all that lives.

The DNA obtained from a series of quite diverse organisms has been submitted to chemical analysis. A suggestive regularity has emerged: namely, the content of A always equals, within limits of analytical error, that of T, and the content of G is the same as C. By contrast, the amount of A + T in relation to that of G + C

ORGANISM	A : T	G : C	(A + T) : (G + C)
BACTERIOPHAGE	1.00	1.09	1.87
COLON BACTERIA	1.09	0.99	1.00
YEAST	0.96	1.08	1.80
SEA URCHIN	1.02	1.01	1.85
SALMON	1.02	1.01	1.43
CATTLE	0.99	1.00	1.37
MAN	1.00	1.00	1.54

TABLE 1. The relative amounts of the nucleotide bases adenine (A), cytosine (C), guanine (G), and thymine (T) in the deoxyribonucleic acids (DNA) extracted from different organisms.

is variable, some organisms being relatively richer in A + T and others in G + C (Table 1). This suggests that in the intact DNA, as it exists in the chromosomes, every A component is somehow paired with a T, and a G is paired with a C.

Two biochemists, J. D. Watson, in the United States, and F. H. C. Crick, in England, derived from these data a brilliant hypothesis. They envisaged how the component parts are put together to give a DNA molecule. Their celebrated model of the DNA structure shows something like a rope ladder wound up in a spiral (represented in Figures 4 and 5). The vertical part of the "ladder" is a monotonous sequence of the deoxyribose sugars and phosphates. The "rungs" of the "ladder" consist of the A, G, C, and T residues; there are two kinds of "rungs"—in one of them, A is coupled with T; in the other kind, G is coupled with C. Here, then, is an explanation of the fact that the DNA's obtained from most diverse organisms contain as many A's as T's and as many C's as G's, so that the ratios of their amount are always close to unity; the members of these pairs are the necessary complements of each other.

The Watson-Crick model provides a solution to the problem mentioned above, namely, how can there be so many kinds of genes if all of them have their distinctive properties specified by their DNA? This solution is best explained by means of an analogy. There are some 400,000 words in the English language, yet all these words can be spelled with only twenty-six letters of the alphabet. In fact, all of them can also be spelled with only three "letters" —in the Morse telegraphic code's dot, dash, and gap. A line in a printed page consists of words; words contain different letters, or the same letters differently arranged. The genetic "alphabet" consists of the four "letters" A, T, G, C; different combinations of them can give a virually infinite variety of genetic "words" or "messages." The matter may also be looked at in another light— in the light of evolution. The evolutionary development of the living world has evidently taken place on the levels of the genetic words and messages, while the genetic alphabet has remained virtually unaltered throughout. Man differs from a Drosophila fly, a corn plant, or a bacteriophage by virtue of the fact that his gene endowment contains different messages, but these messages are conveyed by means of the same alphabet.

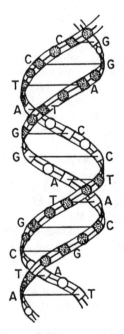

Figure 5. A representation of the Watson-Crick model of the structure of the DNA (deoxyribonucleic acid). The two cross-linked chains shown in Figure 4 are wound in a double helical spiral.

The genes are, then, sections of the DNA ladder-like molecules; different genes are different because they contain different sequences of the "letters" A, T, G, and C. It can be said that heredity is "coded" in the genes, or in the DNA of the chromosomes, in a manner similar to a message written in Morse code or in some secret code used by diplomats, generals, or spies. The day may not be far away when the sequences of the genetic "letters" in the various genes in man and in other organisms may become known. It is, however, a tremendous achievement to have understood the method of construction of the genetic messages, even if, for the time being, we cannot spell many of them out ourselves in the laboratory.

How Genes Make Their Own Copies

The Watson-Crick model has suggested a solution for another knotty biological problem. When a cell divides, its chromosomes split in equal halves, so that the daughter cells receive the same chromosomes, and presumably the same genes, the mother cell had. To say that a gene "splits" suggests, however, a crude and inaccurate picture of what actually happens. What a gene in fact appears to do is to manufacture its own copy, another gene just like itself. The self-copying, or replication, of the genes has to be very precise and accurate if the heredity is to be maintained and the progeny is to resemble the parents. Let us, then, represent a portion of the DNA "ladder" lying horizontally, like this:

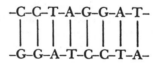

Now suppose that the "rungs" of the "ladder" break, and that each C attracts to itself a G and vice versa, and that each A attracts a T and vice versa. The result would then be two "ladders" similar to each other and to the original one. (The capital letters stand for the original components and the small ones for the new components.)

An individual receives, then, his heredity in the form of the two genetic "messages" encoded in the DNA of the two sex cells, the egg cell from the mother and the spermatozoon from the father.

These two cells unite at fertilization, and initiate the long and complex series of processes in the development of the individual. The fertilized egg is a single cell; it divides in two, four, eight, and finally billions of cells; the cells form an embryo, then a fetus, an infant, a child, an adolescent, an adult, an oldster. An individual develops as long as he lives. Growth and maturation, as well as senescence and old-age decrepitude, are parts of the sequence of the developmental process. Looked at from the standpoint of genetics, the development of an individual may be said to represent a translation, or a decoding, of the genetic messages this individual received from his parents. Little is known at present, and much is to be learned, about the precise ways in which this translation of the genetic messages really takes place in the growing and developing organism when its organs are formed and its cells differentiate. The physiology of the development is a field of study rapidly developing at present.

Genes and Proteins

Some of the most important constituents of all living bodies belong to the class of chemical compounds known as proteins. The hemoglobin of red blood cells, the myosin of the muscles, the pepsin and trypsin so essential for the digestion of food, and numerous enzymes indispensable to the life of body cells, all are proteins. The human body contains no fewer than 10,000 and possibly as many as 100,000 different kinds of proteins. Mention has already been made that proteins are large, some of them enormous, chemical molecules. Chemists discovered, however, that under the influence of acids or alkalis, proteins can be broken up into much smaller constituents. These constituents are amino acids. There is no need to describe here the chemical structure of the amino acids. What is important for us is that there are about twenty different kinds of amino acids which are the constituents of most known proteins. The proteins consist of long chains of amino-acid residues; these chains may be linked together by cross-connections, and may be coiled in various complicated but specific ways. Protein molecules may be long and slender fibers, or more or less spherical or globular in shape. Different proteins contain different sets and proportions of the twenty known amino acids. Moreover, the properties of a protein depend upon the exact alignment of the amino-acid residues in the chains.

One may say that the protein "alphabet" consists of about twenty "letters," the different amino acids. By analogy with the DNA nucleic acids, with their four genetic "letters," one may attempt to represent the structure of the proteins in terms of the twenty amino-acid "letters." The difficulty here is that, as indicated, a protein molecule may contain several different amino-acid chains with various cross-links and convolutions. In other words, the "letters" in a protein are not necessarily all disposed in a single line; they may form a complicated three-dimensional structure consisting of several amino-acid chains. The analogy with DNA is nevertheless a useful one, because the chief function the genes play in the development is to direct the synthesis of the proteins. Some authorities consider it probable that every gene specifies the sequence of the amino acids in just one chain composing a certain enzyme or some other protein the body must contain. To put it differently, the genetic message encoded in the DNA of the gene in the form of the sequence of the letters A, T, G, C is translated into the sequence of the amino-acid "letters" in a chain composing a certain protein.

In recent years, biochemists have obtained some very valuable information concerning the ways and means whereby this "translation" of the DNA four-letter code into the twenty-letter amino-acid code is actually accomplished (Figure 6). It appears that the "translators" are still-different substances, the ribonucleic acids, abbreviated RNA. RNA differs from DNA in several respects. It contains a different kind of sugar, a ribose instead of deoxyribose. It is at least usually single-stranded, instead of double-stranded with "rungs" like a ladder. It contains the base called uracil instead of thymine. The four-letter alphabet of RNA thus differs in one letter from DNA—it is A, U, G, C, instead of A, T, G, C.

The process of translation of the DNA message into the amino-acids sequence in the protein happens in the following way (Figure 6). First, a strand of RNA is formed, in which the sequence of the "letters" in a section of the DNA strand is impressed in a corresponding sequence of the RNA. The result is called the messenger RNA. It comes out from the cell nucleus into the cell cytoplasm, and attaches itself to the surface of very tiny bodies called ribosomes, visible only with the aid of electron microscopes. A series of amino acids then becomes arranged in a chain characteristic of a given protein and corresponding to the sequence of the "letters" in a given messenger RNA. Each amino acid in the protein is specified by a sequence of three "letters" in the RNA and the DNA. Successful attempts have been made in recent years to break this "triplet Code," that is, to determine just which groups of three "letters" in RNA and DNA correspond to each one of the twenty amino acids. So spectacularly rapid has been the progress in this line of endeavor that the code is now well on the way to being deciphered, although some problems still await solution. One, perhaps rather unexpected, feature is that the code proved to be a degenerate one. "Degeneracy" (the word here does not imply that the code was in the past somehow better or more efficient than it is now) means that instead of a strict one-to-one correspondence between an RNA triplet and an amino acid, some amino acids can be specified by two or more different triplets.

Origin of Life

The foregoing pages have attempted to outline, of necessity in a very condensed and even superficial manner, the remarkable progress the study of heredity has made since the pioneer microscopists first sighted the sex cells. The remainder of the present chapter will deal with a frankly speculative matter: the origin of life on earth. Man has discovered that he is a product of evolution of living matter, and he cannot refrain from asking whence he, together with everything that lives, ultimately came.

The development of ideas about the origin of life went through at least three phases. To those unfamiliar with biology, the problem appeared to be very simple, or, rather, the problem did not seem to exist at all. Primitive man was an animist, believing that all natural objects possess some sort of life or vitality. He was ready to assume that living beings arise from nonliving materials all the time. Countless legends and myths relate, often with great poetic elegance, how diverse animals and even men appeared out of stones, earth, or simply from the air. More prosaically, it was generally credited that fly maggots arise from putrid meat, lice from dirty clothing, and mice from old rags. As a cheeky youth, I remember having angered a dear old lady by refusing to believe that clothes moths will appear in the stored woolens if no moth comes in from the outside. She did not know, or care to know, that Francesco Redi and Spallanzani had already proved, in the seventeenth and eighteenth centuries, that spontaneous generation of life does not occur—an example, I suppose, of what is politely called the "academic lag."

After Louis Pasteur's classical work of 1862, the principle *omne vivum ex vivo* (all life arises from life) became the fundamental tenet of biology. Darwin's theory of evolution, of "descent with modification," was taken to explain the development of the living world, from the lowest to the highest forms, from "amoeba to man," as it used to be formulated. This theory did not, however, pretend to explain how the lowest organisms arose in the first place. Biological evolution was supposed to start with an "amoeba"; nowadays, we prefer to start with some primordial virus, since the amoeba is much too complicated an organism already. The Swedish astronomer S. A. Arrhenius in 1907 proposed an escape: Life is

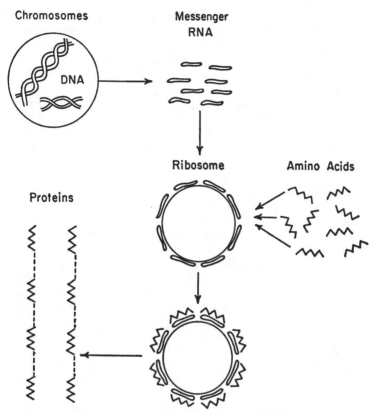

Figure 6. A schematic representation of how the genes act to build proteins, some of which act as enzymes. The DNA of the genes in the chromosomes impresses its specificity on another substance, the messenger RNA. This "messenger" passes from the cell nucleus to the cytoplasm, and settles on the surface of very minute bodies called ribosomes. Amino acids then become linked together in orders specified by the messenger RNA, to form different proteins.

present in many parts of the universe, and its seeds were introduced on our planet with some sort of cosmic dust. Nobody has ever found any such seeds coming in from cosmic space. This is not the only flaw in Arrhenius' hypothesis. The problem is merely pushed back in time, and the question immediately arises: How did life start in the cosmos?

The spectacular recent advances of biochemistry and genetics have imbued biologists with enough self-confidence to face again the problem that for so long seemed beyond reach, namely, creating life in the laboratory from nonliving constituents. Such a feat is yet to be achieved. It is, however, interesting to consider briefly some experiments that come nearest, to date, to this achievement. A. Kornberg (now at Stanford University) prepared a mixture of the component parts of DNA, that is, of the "letters" A, T, C, and G. His preparation actually contained them in the form of deoxynucleoside triphosphates of adenine, thymine, cytosine, and guanine. The problem was, of course, how to link these components together as they are linked in the DNA.

Kornberg extracted from the colon bacterium an enzyme that can mediate the reaction of linking. The addition of the enzyme to the mixture of the triphosphates of A, T, C, and G did not, however, suffice to accomplish the synthesis of DNA. What was missing was a "primer." Kornberg, in 1956, found that a small amount of DNA extracted from some living organism could serve as such a primer. The addition of a primer caused the appearance in the preparation of DNA molecules. Most important of all, the DNA synthesized was identical in the proportions of the different nucleotides (the "letters") not to the DNA of the organism furnishing the enzyme, in this case the colon bacterium, but to that furnishing the primer. Kornberg was able to induce the synthesis of the DNA characteristic of a bacteriophage, of at least two species of bacteria, and of cattle by using as primers DNA extracted from these organisms.

In Kornberg's experiments, the molecules of the primer DNA "reproduced" themselves. Or, to be more precise, they served as models, or templates, for the synthesis of their copies. The genes in the chromosomes of living cells reproduce themselves probably by means of a priming mechanism of the same kind that operated in Kornberg's experiments. One would, of course, like to see an experiment performed with a synthetic primer, instead of with a primer taken from a living cell. Is this a possible goal? In a recently published work, Kornberg and his colleagues L. L. Bertsch, J. F. Jackson, and H. G. Khorana seem to be well on the way to this achievement. When it is finally achieved, one will have to face a tough question: Does this mean that life has been created artificially? It must at the very least be admitted that this would give us a good model of life, even though it may not re-create a facsimile of any actually existing life.

At the base of it all there is, just the same, a real problem: What was the origin on earth, or anywhere in the universe, of the first "primer," which initiated the process of self-copying, the fundamental characteristic of life. For the time being this remains an unsolved riddle. But the problem is a meaningful one, and it is within this larger context that many biologists, chemists, astronomers, and geologists have been doing some interesting experiments, and a great deal of speculative writing. The results obtained by A. I. Oparin, in Russia, J. D. Bernal, in England, and Harold Urey, Stanley Miller, M. Calvin, S. W. Fox, and Harlow Shapley, in the United States, are in general agreement on one basic point: the primeval conditions on earth, which existed before there was any life, permitted the formation of certain chemical compounds that are now formed, exclusively or at least principally, in living bodies.

The atmosphere of the young planet Earth was very different from the one we breathe; it had little or no free oxygen, but it did contain, in addition to water vapor, the hydrocarbon methane (CH_4) and ammonia (NH_3). The chemical reactions that could take place in such an atmosphere have been explored by Stanley Miller and others. In Miller's classical experiment of 1953, at least two amino acids, alanine and glutamic acid, were obtained in a vessel containing water, hydrogen, methane, and ammonia under the influence of electric discharges. There is now good evidence that a number of organic compounds, formaldehyde, acetic and several other organic acids, as well as five amino acids, can be formed in a mixture of gases resembling the atmosphere of the primordial earth under the influence of high-energy ultraviolet radiations, electric discharges, and perhaps other agencies. The waters of the seas and oceans were probably a kind of thin "soup," a dilute solution of some of the substances now formed in living organisms. Larger and more complex organic molecules, particularly proteins and nucleic acids, could conceivably arise in such a "soup," although this has not yet been conclusively demonstrated experimentally under realistically contrived "primitive" conditions. Oparin believes that an important process was the formation of so-called coacervate droplets, simple colloidal suspensions; Bernal thinks that protein molecules may have been formed owing to absorption of amino acids on the surface of clay particles.

All this adds up to the surmise that the first life could have arisen under the conditions that once existed on earth. The critical step, the appearance of the first self-replicating molecule or a combination of molecules, still seems, however, to be an improbable event. As long as this step is not reproduced experimentally, there will exist a difference of opinion about how it occurred. Some scientists are so headstrong as to believe that the surmise is plausible enough to be accepted as a probable description of what happened in reality. Given eons of time—and our planet is known to be at least three billion years old—a highly improbable event can take place somewhere, or even in several places, in the universe. Perhaps the first spark that kindled the flame of life did occur on earth, this insignificant little speck in vast cosmic spaces. Shapley seems to be

278 · *Theodosius Dobzhansky*

convinced that life *must* exist also on some other planets, in many solar systems, and in galaxies other than our own. On the other hand, some people continue to regard the origin of life not only as an unsolved but also as an unsolvable mystery. They are as firmly convinced as ever that an act of God must have been invoked to contribute that first spark. I strongly feel that this point of view must not be ignored but must be faced honestly in a book dealing with the humanistic aspects of biology, even though it is impossible to attempt here more than an indication of the broad lines of the relevant arguments.

That there occur in living bodies many chemical and physical processes similar in principle to those observable in inert bodies is not doubted by anyone. Thus, nutrition is analogous to stoking an engine with fuel, and respiration to the combustion of that fuel. The question is whether *in addition* to such processes there are also in life other processes, forces, or agents which are not composed of physicochemical ones. Mechanists hold that such additional, irreducible, specifically vital forces do not exist. Vitalists believe that they do, and call them by a variety of names—the vital force, entelechy, psyche. Vitalism is at present a minority opinion, but it is a minority not because the mechanists have actually "explained" every one and all biological phenomena by reducing them to physics and chemistry. It will be argued in the next chapter that reductionist explanations are not always the most meaningful ones. Mechanists have achieved something perhaps better than a simple reduction. The living world is, hopefully, understandable as the outcome of the formation of progressively more and more complex and perfect compounds or patterns of physico-chemical processes in the course of biological evolution.

Biologists have rejected vitalism not because it has been proved that in no biological phenomenon may there be lurking a vital force. One cannot prove a universal negative. It is, rather, that vitalism has been shown to be unnecessary. Actually, the best argument that a vitalist can offer is that a mechanistic universe is too dull, flat, and uninteresting. Most vitalists are also theists. They are looking for gaps left between scientifically understandable events, hoping to have these gaps filled with God's interventions. The origin of life is one such gap. There are certainly innumerable others. They become, however, inexorably fewer and fewer as science progresses. Therefore, a supernatural God becomes less and less necessary. I am convinced that religion in the Age of Science cannot be sustained by the assumption of miraculous events abrogating the order of Nature. It should, rather, see acts of God in events the natural causes of which it fully understands. Then and only then nature as a whole, organic and inorganic, human and prehuman, macrocosmic and microcosmic, becomes a field for God's eternal and continuing, immanent and transcendent, natural and providential activity.

To those who ascribe the origin of life to God's special intervention it can be pointed out that this makes God simply another physico-chemical agent, but one perversely concealed from observation because it acts so very rarely. Suppose that it was God who some two billion years ago compounded the four kinds of nucleotides into the first DNA strand capable of self-replication. Was God then an enzyme of a peculiarly complex structure which no chemist can synthesize? But what if some bright chemist in the future synthesizes this enzyme, or at least figures out what chemical structure it must have had? And this predicament is not peculiar to the problem of the origin of life—it occurs every time one chooses to invoke God's intervention into natural processes. Does it make sense, for example, to think that organic evolution is guided by God's intervention? This would presumably mean that God induces from time to time some unusual mutations of a special kind, or that He directs the chromosomes to form particular gene combinations. There is certainly no compelling reason to make such assumptions. The origin of life and the emergence of human self-awareness were the crucial events of the evolutionary development of the cosmos. They certainly did take place here, on earth; we do not know whether similar events happened elsewhere in the universe. Be that as it may, creation is a process, not an act; it was not completed some five thousand or any other number of years ago; it continues now, before our eyes, and is accessible to scientific study.

RICHARD E. LEAKEY and ROGER LEWIN

The Greatest Revolution (1977) †

Any scientific meeting on our origins nowadays might be attended by archeologists (who search for stone tools), paleoanthropologists (who look for early human fossils), geologists (who study the environments of ancient living sites), taphonomists (who investigate the way bones may become buried and subsequently fossil-

† From Chapter 2 of Richard E. Leakey and Roger Lewin, *Origins* (New York, 1977). Richard Leakey (b. 1944), like his parents, Mary and Louis Leakey, has for many years searched for hominid fossils in east Africa. Roger Lewin (b. 1944) is science editor of the British magazine *New Scientist*.

ized), anthropologists (who learn the ways of contemporary 'simple' societies), animal behaviorists (who study the habits of monkeys and apes), and psychologists (who may be interested in the development of the human brain). It may seem a motley collection, but by weaving together the threads of their knowledge and expertise a more complete picture than ever before can be created about human origins. Each discipline not only contributes facts which can be incorporated into our understanding of human evolution, but because of the different way in which the varying approaches interact, new questions can be asked which previously were inconceivable.

By good fortune this new approach to human prehistory comes at a time when prehuman fossils are being discovered at an unprecedented rate. During the 1970s, sites in Ethiopia, Kenya, and Tanzania have yielded so many important fossils that it will take years before they will have been through the thorough analysis that is now accorded such specimens. But it is not simply the *number* of fossil finds that is significant and exciting, it is the *nature* of the fossils themselves that is causing so much of a stir among prehistorians. Our view of human evolution has been transformed within the past few years. It is now apparent that the ancestral line that led to modern humans stretches back five, perhaps six, million years. And it is clear that for a large part of that time our ancestors shared their environment with two types of creatures with whom they were closely related but who eventually became extinct. These evolutionary cousins are called the australopithecines, one of whom was slightly built while the other was much more robust.

The two forms of australopithecine and the *Homo* ancestor shared at least two things: first, they shared a common ancestor, a small ape-like creature called *Ramapithecus* who first appeared at least twelve million years ago and lived in Europe, Asia, and Africa; and second, they all stood and walked upright. At present we cannot be certain what evolutionary pressures allowed *Ramapithecus* to diversify into the australopithecine and *Homo* descendants, a process which, incidentally, appears to have happened only in Africa and not in any of the other continents in which it lived. But, because of the new approach to the study of mankind's past and the flood of fossil discoveries, we can begin to guess at the subtle differences in behavior which separated these three evolutionary cousins, known collectively as hominids. At first their ways of making a living would not have been dramatically different. But gradually the growing social complexity of the *Homo* stock would have driven a bigger and bigger evolutionary wedge between it and the australopithecines. The adoption of the combination of meat eating and plant-food gathering was a vital part of that upgrading in social organization, and it was a way of life that dominated human existence until a mere 10,000 years ago when people began to exploit the potential of farming.

The story since then is well known: the Agricultural Revolution was followed by the Industrial Revolution (last century), and that led to today's technological revolution. And with these dramatic changes in the lifestyle of human beings has come an explosion in world population * * *

Perhaps more prophetic than anything else in *The Descent of Man* was its suggestion that the African continent was the cradle of mankind. Darwin reasoned that 'in each great region of the world the living mammals are closely related to the extinct species of the same region. It is, therefore, probable that Africa was formerly inhabited by extinct apes closely allied to the gorilla and chimpanzee; and as these two species are now man's nearest allies, it is somewhat more than probable that our early progenitors lived on the African continent than elsewhere.' The current accumulation of fossil evidence strongly supports Darwin's hunch—whether or not it can ever be finally proved.

Meanwhile, the first pre-human skulls had been unearthed—and rejected as having nothing to do with human evolution. In the summer of 1856 workmen in the Neander valley, a steep-sided gorge not far from the German city of Düsseldorf, had blasted open a small cave some sixty feet above the waters of a tributary to the Rhine. Once inside the cave, as the men hacked through the rubble in their quest for limestone, they came upon some ancient bones. Because the workers' primary interest was in commerce, not antiquity, many of the bones were smashed, leaving only the skull cap and a few fragments from the rest of the skeleton. They belonged to what came to be known as Neanderthal Man, a member of the human family who lived between about thirty thousand and a hundred thousand years ago. * * *

In 1868 it was once again a party of workmen, this time on a railway line through the cliffs of Les Eyzies in the Vézère Valley in south-western France, who made the discovery. In a rock shelter known as Cro-Magnon they found the remains of five individuals with the unmistakable high-domed cranium and small jaw of modern humans. By late 1912, when a discovery of a peculiar sort received wide publicity, excavation in many parts of Europe began yielding up ancient bones and artifacts. Earlier (between 1891 and 1898), in Java, a young Dutchman, Eugène Dubois, had unearthed the skull cap and upper leg bone, or femur, of a creature that was definitely neither man nor ape, but something in between, which he called *Pithecanthropus erectus* * * *

As we see it, the story of human evolution some two to three million years ago involved probably four main characters. First in our list, but not necessarily first in importance at the time, was a hominid whose principal distinction was that its descendants are us, modern humans. Although no one can be sure, because there are no complete skeletons, this ancient forerunner of true humans probably stood around five feet tall; moreover it stood fully erect, just as we do today. The size of its brain was around two thirds of the average human's today. Looking not dissimilar, but more diminutive and with a smaller brain, was the second hominid in our list. Third was a much stockier individual, standing perhaps five feet tall, but with a significantly smaller brain than our direct ancestor's. Last is the smallest creature of them all, the one most shadowy in terms of the fossil record (except perhaps for one remarkably-complete skeleton discovered recently in Ethiopia).

These, then, are the actors in the story. What are their names?

* * * we can begin to put some names on our list, starting with the middle two for the best reason of all: they are easiest. Because of important similarities between them, they are both lumped into the same genus, *Australopithecus*, but the gracile individual is given the specific name of *africanus* while for the robust creature we shall stick to the specific name of *boisei*. The labels we use are at worst convenient, but without being misleading; some people argue for a different naming scheme, but that is not especially important here.

The first character in the list is more of a problem. Although anatomically not *startlingly* different from its hominid cousins there are good reasons for believing that there was a significant behavioral gulf between them. And it was behavioral sophistication that in large measure helped to propel this human ancestor along the road to mankind. In evolutionary terms the speed at which this journey was undertaken was breathtaking: biological milestones were reached and passed with great rapidity. The creature was in such a dynamic state of evolution that it is almost more trouble than it is worth to try to pin down any particular stage by attaching definite specific names. The major point, however, is that this creature was on its way to modern humans, *Homo sapiens sapiens*. For the moment we will apply the generic name of *Homo* without tying ourselves down with specific names. This may seem to be a pedantic point, but, as will become clearer as we explore the bones and stones that litter the path of human evolution, it is important for a rational view of how that path was traveled.

Last in our list is a link with the past, the most ancient human ancestor of all, *Ramapithecus*. We left *Ramapithecus*, or rather the meager collection of fossil fragments that we know him by, tentatively exploring the forest fringes some nine to twelve million years ago. There then opens up an enormous fossil void until round about four million years ago. And it is not until the two- to three-million year stage that there is anything like enough hominid fossils for anyone to have a sensible conversation about. This yawning void is particularly frustrating because on one side of it there is just one creature, *Ramapithecus*, while milling about on the other side is a menagerie of hominids. *Australopithecus africanus, Australopithecus boisei,* early *Homo,* and late *Ramapithecus.* And if we were to leap forward in time to perhaps three-quarters of a million years ago, we find that the menagerie has dwindled once again to a single representative, a creature called *Homo erectus.* The story of that initial diversification followed by a drastic pruning is the story of human evolution. * * *

Our task is not unlike attempting to assemble a three-dimensional jigsaw puzzle in which most of the pieces are missing, and those few bits that are to hand are broken! The jigsaw is multidimensional because against a background of the physical evolution of our ancestors, we are also trying to construct some semblance of their social and behavioral patterns.

The core of the problem, then, is the fossil record, the fragments of bones which survived the combined destructive activities of the environment to become preserved for later discovery by one of the many teams of fossil hunters now scouring promising sites in Africa. Just as finding a key piece in a jigsaw can help you slot into place many others that have been something of a puzzle, so the lucky discovery at the East Turkana site of a remarkable fossil at the end of 1972 proved to be an important event in the emergence of the new picture of human evolution. In many ways the fossil skull, which is usually referred to simply as 1470 after its index number at the National Museums of Kenya, merely confirmed certain earlier ideas of the path of evolution, ideas that seemed reasonable in terms of a biologically-sound scenario of human prehistory, but ones that lacked the important evidence of a reasonably complete specimen.

In terms of fossil discovery 1470 has a predecessor, an individual who was found early in 1961 in Tanzania's famous Olduvai Gorge. That find was important because, although the brain case was not complete, it was obvious from its size and shape that here was a very advanced hominid who had lived around one and three-quarter million years ago: he was eventually called *Homo habilis.* This was the first evidence that early members of the human lineage were contemporaries of the australopithecines, not descendants as was generally believed. Exciting though the discovery of *Homo habilis* was, it remained frustratingly incomplete. For the newly developing theory of human evolution to be really persuasive there needed to be a better, more complete specimen discovered. That turned out to be 1470.

* * * 1470 *was* very special—it represented an almost complete skull of *Homo habilis.*

This remarkable skull confirmed two things. First, that the human ancestral line, *Homo,* originated much earlier than most people suspected, earlier perhaps by as much as a million years. Second, because the history of *Homo* goes back that far, it means that these individuals were living at the same time as some of the earliest australopithecines, making it unlikely that our direct ancestors are evolutionary descendants of the australopithecines—cousins, yes, but descendants, no. Up to that time workers in this field believed that although the robust *Australopithecus* might be a sidetrack of the main path of human evolution, its slighter cousin, *Australopithecus africanus,* was certainly marching along the main route, eventually to give rise to the *Homo* line.

With this crucial piece of evidence now in our grasp, the newly-emerging theory of man's origins gradually gained strength. It was now possible to predict that some day fossil hunters would unearth early specimens of *Homo* individuals perhaps as old as four or five million years. The theory is that around five or six million years ago the ancestral stock, *Ramapithecus,* suddenly diversified into several different lines, probably because climatic or other environmental changes formed new habitats for exploitation. (Incidentally, there is evidence that other creatures also diversified at this time, adding weight to the notion of a general environmental change.) If this is true, it means that as one approaches closer and closer to the time of speciation it becomes increasingly difficult to distinguish the fossil remains of one hominid type from another: they will tend to all look more and more like the ancestral hominid from which they evolved, and therefore more and more like each other.

In the flood of fossil finds throughout East Africa that have all but overwhelmed us since the portentous 1972 discovery of 1470, this prediction has been borne out: spectacular fossils, found particularly by Don Johanson and his colleagues in the arid wastes of eastern Ethiopia, but also by Mary Leakey and her helpers in long-neglected fossil-bearing deposits a few miles from Olduvai Gorge, include examples of primitive *Homo* nearly four million years old! Just a few years ago no one in their right mind would have believed this possible. But it is, and the evidence is there for all to see—and to wonder at, for it is awe-inspiring to try mentally to grapple with the notion that our direct ancestors inhabited the earth so very long ago. Meanwhile, too, some quite unexpected and important fossils have been discovered and unearthed from the East Turkana deposits, discoveries that give us the most complete and probably the earliest examples of *Homo erectus,* our immediate ancestors who, for a reason we can only guess at, crossed the thin strip of land that joins Africa to Asia, thus beginning mankind's present domination of the world.

NICHOLAS WADE

The Ultimate Experiment: Man-Made Evolution (1977) †

A turning point has been reached in the study of life. A turning point of such consequence that it may make its mark not just in the history of science but perhaps even in the evolution of life itself.

The turning point is the discovery in 1973 of a technique for manipulating the stuff of life. Known at present by the awkward name of recombinant DNA research, the technique is in essence a method of chemically cutting and splicing DNA, the molecular material which the genes of living organisms are made of. It enables biologists to transfer genes from one species to another, and in doing so to create new forms of life.

All previous speculations about genetic engineering can now be forgotten. The new gene-splicing technique is far more potent and dexterous than anything the theorists contemplated. Its impact will be profound, and it will be felt almost immediately.

For the last twenty-five years molecular biology, the study of DNA, has made the fastest progress of any branch of science. A mass of pure knowledge has been accumulated, but so far with rather little practical effect. Gene splicing promises to offer a quick bridge between this vast untapped storehouse of pure knowledge and the practical world of medicine, agriculture and industry. Everything that biologists have learned in their attempt to understand nature now becomes a means to change it.

Some thirty-five years ago physicists learned how to manipulate the forces in the nucleus of the atom, and the world has been struggling to cope with the results of that discovery ever since. The ability to penetrate the nucleus of the living cell, to rearrange and transplant the nucleic acids that constitute the genetic material of all forms of life, seems a more beneficent power but one that is likely to prove at least as profound in its consequences.

It could well prove comparable to that other biological revolution in man's history, the domestication of plants and animals. That achievement, by the people of the Neolithic Age, opened a doorway

† From Chapters 1, 6, 9, and 12 of Nicholas Wade, *The Ultimate Experiment: Man-Made Evolution* (New York, 1977). Nicholas Wade (b. 1942) is a senior staff writer for *Science* and former deputy editor of *Nature*.

for man to pass from uncertain existence as a hunter and gatherer to life as a farmer, herder, and city dweller. From that beginning some seven thousand years of urban civilization have followed. Yet Neolithic man, like animal and plant breeders ever since, did not create new species; he only selected, and reinforced by breeding, the characteristics he desired from among those already within the natural genetic potential of a species.,

Scientists today cannot design entirely new genes any more than Neolithic man could (although that may eventually be possible). What the new gene-splicing technique does make possible is the transfer of genes from one species to another, regardless of the reproductive barriers that nature has built between them to isolate one species from another. It is now becoming technically possible (though practically fruitless) to intermingle the genes of man and fungus, ant and elephant, oak and cabbage. The whole gene pool of the planet, the product of three billion years of evolution, is at our disposal. The key to the living kingdom has been put into our hands.

There are occasional suggestions, made on scientific or moral grounds, that the key should be thrown away. Such abnegation of intellectual curiosity is not in man's nature, and in any case the question is moot: the door to the treasure-house is already ajar, and the only question remaining is what use will be made of the riches within.

The immediate benefit of gene splicing and the kindred techniques it generates will be pure knowledge. The technique gives biologists a handle on many fundamental problems, some of which had seemed almost insoluble by previous methods. How genes work in human and other cells, how they are switched on and off, how they obey the master plan that guides the development of each organism from egg to adult—these are some of the problems in which the pace of discovery will now appreciably quicken.

It is reasonable to suppose that the accumulating body of knowledge about the cell will eventually provide an understanding of diseases such as cancer, which in turn may perhaps (but not necessarily) lead to appropriate methods of treatment.

Such possibilities lie a long way off. Much closer at hand is the use of gene splicing to program bacteria to produce valuable proteins of use not just in research but also in medicine and industry.

The basis of the proposed method is to grow and harvest bacteria much in the manner used to produce substances such as penicillin. But instead of the bacteria producing a substance specified by their own hereditary information, a new gene is spliced into them so that they synthesize whatever substance the gene specifies.

Though not yet proved, the concept should offer a powerful

means of producing many kinds of important protein, such as insulin, interferon (the body's antiviral substance), and vaccines.

Further down the road is the possibility of using the technique to modify whole organisms. Plants, since they can be grown from a single cell, are a prime candidate for genetic engineering. Most important crop plants cannot extract nitrogen from the air; they must have it supplied to them in the costly and polluting form of nitrogen fertilizer. Were it possible to transfer to wheat the relevant genes of the nitrogen-fixing bacterium, a new agricultural revolution would be in the making.

If genes can be added to plants, why not also to humans? Many people suffer from genetic diseases, such as sickle-cell anemia. Gene therapy is the word already given to the idea that it may one day be possible to switch off the defective gene and switch on or insert the genes that specify the correct product.

Such projects are only gleams in the experimenter's eye, but they are indicative of the hopes being held out for the new technique. Applications that no one has yet thought of will doubtless turn out to be at least as significant as those now being discussed. The gene-splicing technique is only the first of a succession of technologies that will make possible ever finer control of the chemical materials of life. Other technologies developed in the course of civilization are merely extensions of man's hands or senses. The ability to manipulate the stuff of life is an art of a different order, the ultimate technology.

All technologies have their unintended and untoward side effects, and a technique of such power as gene splicing is unlikely to prove an exception.

The most immediate fears concern its possible threat to laboratory workers and, through them, to the public health. In transferring genes from one organism to another, might not a researcher unknowingly enhance the virulence of an existing microbe or perhaps create a new pathogen for which no defenses had been prepared?

Though far from likely, such a possibility is made more tangible by the fact that the standard organism of laboratory study is *Escherichia coli*, a bacterium whose natural habitat is the gut of humans and other warmblooded animals.

Moreover, many of the scientists who will be manipulating genes in laboratories throughout the world are molecular biologists, not all of whom are trained in the painstaking procedures used by microbiologists to prevent infection of themselves or others.

The gene-splicing technique thus raised from its inception a question of laboratory safety and public health. The past three years of intense debate, first among scientists and then in public forums, have focused almost exclusively on this specific problem and the means to cope with it.

More recently a second kind of doubt has been raised about gene splicing: the possibility that the technique may have long-term evolutionary consequences. Single-celled organisms like bacteria are organized on somewhat different principles from those that govern the cells of higher plants and animals. Transferring animal or plant genes into bacteria, the argument goes, might endow bacteria with the genetic signals of higher cells and render the animal and plant kingdoms vulnerable to a new mode of bacterial attack. Whatever the merits of the argument, and they are hotly disputed, it would seem in a purely general way that in shuffling genes from one organism to another, scientists are playing evolution's game without exactly knowing either the rules or what the forfeit may be for transgressing them. But many biologists believe, and they may well be right, that evolution's rule is that anything goes and that thus there is nothing to be worried about.

Accidents apart, there will always be the chance of putting so potent a technology to malign use. It was for lack of just such a technique as gene splicing that the U.S. Army's twenty-five-year program in biological warfare produced so little of military value. The United States voluntarily renounced offensive biological warfare in 1969, and both the United States and the Soviet Union are signatories of a convention that prohibits the development, production, and stockpiling of biological weapons. Though it does not preclude research, the convention is a significant barrier to the military exploitation of gene splicing, at least by these two superpowers. Whether or not it will inhibit smaller nations seeking to develop a cheap substitute for nuclear terror is another matter. As gene splicers' capabilities increase, there is no knowing what temptations may be presented to military planners or those who perceive themselves in desperate straits.

Gene splicing is so simple a technique that for most present purposes it requires only a few dollars' worth of special materials, all commercially available, and access to a standard biological laboratory. Political analysts worry about the proliferation of nuclear weapons and the vulnerability of peaceful nuclear materials to terrorist diversion. Gene splicing seems a far more beneficent technology; yet should it prove otherwise, there will be no way of preventing general access to it.

Terrorists will doubtless continue to prefer the multitude of conventional weapons at their disposal. Perhaps more to be feared is the deranged do-gooder who decides to take some unilateral action for what he conceives to be the relief of suffering humanity. Figuring that many deaths from lung cancer could be prevented by the eradication of the tobacco plant, a scientist or competent technician might use the technique to improve upon the natural virulence of the tobacco plant's viruses.

An increasingly potent art is about to be placed at the disposal of every government and several thousand biologists. Even if perverse uses are avoided, the inventions that flow from it will certainly require some hard decisions. Gene splicing is a significant first step toward making human genetic engineering technically feasible. Controlling our progress down that route will not be simple. The alluring benefits of genetic engineering, it can be envisaged, may be established first in crops, then in domestic animals, next in remedying human genetic diseases, and then in enhancing natural growth so as to ensure that each individual attains his full genetic potential. Somewhere along that route, the engineers may cross, perhaps imperceptibly, the Rubicon that everyone had supposed to be the natural stopping point, the inviolability of the human genetic constitution. The way would then be opened for *Homo sapiens* to bring to birth his finest creation: *Homo sapientissimus*.

Such a chain of events would probably be broken at an early stage by technical infeasibility or social resistance. In any case, society is far from incapable of both reaping the benefits of a technology and minimizing its risks. Yet some technologies seem to possess an inherent pace of development, which may not necessarily be as deliberate as society would prefer.

Gene splicing, at any rate, is a technique that will profoundly transform our knowledge of ourselves and our evolutionary history.
* * *

The following types of hazards—or "disaster scenarios"—are among those raised and discussed by scientists during the formulation of the NIH committee's guidelines. The interest of the scenarios is not so much that any is likely to occur—the opposite is the case—but that they influenced the NIH committee's thinking in devising its guidelines.

The most obvious class of hazards arises from the ubiquitous use of *E. coli* as the standard host for foreign genes. And the worst conceivable hazard is that man's normally peaceful microbial guest should suddenly be turned into an organism capable of causing epidemic disease.

How might this come about? A researcher, whether by design or accident, inserts into *E. coli* foreign genes that somehow convert it into a pathogenic organism. The virulent *E. coli* escapes from the laboratory by infecting a researcher or technician, who in turn infects his or her family and others, starting off the spread of the bacterium throughout the population. Establishing colonies in people's guts, just as does any other strain of *E. coli*, the escaped bacterium produces quantities of the protein specified by the foreign gene. The protein crosses the gut wall, exposing the individual to significant daily doses of the foreign protein. * * *

The third wave of critics, [Erwin] Chargaff and [Robert] Sinsheimer, may well have been responsible for some of the doubts that still linger about the approach of the NIH guidelines. Science is an elitist institution, and in certain matters scientists heed who is saying it no less than what is said. Had the call for a moratorium come from scientists less well known than those in the Academy group, it would probably have fallen on very stony ground. Similarly, when Chargaff and Sinsheimer raised objections of principle to the NIH approach, they were probably accorded a careful hearing. Both are members of the National Academy of Sciences and have made discoveries that merit mention in the basic textbooks of molecular biology.

* * * In a letter to *Science* entitled "on the Dangers of Genetic Meddling," Chargaff let slip his satirist's mask, revealing the moralist underneath:

What seems to have been disregarded completely is that we are dealing here much more with an ethical problem than with one in public health, and that the principal question to be answered is whether we have the right to put an additional fearful load on generations that are not yet born. . . . You can stop splitting the atom; you can stop visiting the moon; you can stop using aerosols; you may even decide not to kill entire populations by the use of a few bombs. But you cannot recall a new form of life. Once you have constructed a viable *E. coli* cell carrying a plasmid DNA into which a piece of eukaryotic DNA has been spliced, it will survive you and your children and your children's children. An irreversible attack on the biosphere is something so unheard of, so unthinkable to previous generations, that I could only wish that mine had not been guilty of it. The hybridization of Prometheus with Herostratus[1] is bound to give evil results. . . .

Have we the right to counteract, irreversibly, the evolutionary wisdom of millions of years, in order to satisfy the ambition and curiosity of a few scientists?

This world is given to us on loan. We come and we go; and after a time we leave earth and air and water to others who come after us. My generation, or perhaps the one preceding mine, has been the first to engage, under the leadership of the exact sciences, in a destructive colonial war against nature. The future will curse us for it.[2]

1. Prometheus stole the gift of fire from the gods and gave it to man; Herostratus burnt down the temple of Diana at Ephesus to give himself a name in history.

2. Erwin Chargaff, "On the Dangers of Genetic Meddling," *Science* 192 (4 June 1976), 938.

Most gene-spliced organisms that escape from the laboratory or factory will perish in nature, and almost all will die in the long run —most species that have ever lived are now extinct. But Chargaff is correct in the sense that a laboratory-created organism that happened to find a niche in nature could probably not be eradicated by man; the change would be irreversible. * * *

The other critic of major stature within the scientific universe is Robert Sinsheimer, chairman of the division of biology at Caltech. A member of the National Academy of Sciences and editor of its *Proceedings*, Sinsheimer's career as a biophysicist has included study of the nucleic acids of viruses and in particular of a scientifically interesting virus known as phi-X174. * * *

In a recent talk he warned of the dangers that may accompany new knowledge: " 'Know the truth and the truth shall make you free' is a credo carved on the walls and lintels of laboratories and libraries across the land." But,

> We begin to see that the truth is not enough, that the truth is necessary but not sufficient, that scientific inquiry, the revealer of truth, needs to be coupled with wisdom if our object is to advance the human condition. . . .
>
> The twentieth century has seen a cascade of magnificent scientific discoveries. Two, in particular, have extended our powers far beyond prior human scale and experience. In the nucleus of the atom we have penetrated to the core of matter and energy. In the nucleic acids of the cell we have penetrated to the core of life.
>
> When we are armed with such powers I think there are limits to the extent to which we can continue to rely upon the resilience of nature or of social institutions to protect us from our follies and our finite wisdom. Our thrusts of inquiry should not too far exceed our perception of their consequence. There are time constants and momenta in human affairs. We need to recognize that the great forces we now wield might—just might—drive us too swiftly toward some unseen chasm.[3]

For a scientist, that is some change of faith. What has converted Sinsheimer from advocate to skeptic, from enthusiasm about genetic engineering to misgivings so grave as to set him on a different path from the mass of his colleagues? * * *

On reviewing the guidelines at the NIH's request, Sinsheimer found that they had dealt reasonably well with the immediate health hazards but "had given no thought to the evolutionary question."

The oversight was not in his view surprising: "It was implicit for the guidelines committee to concern itself with health hazards—it

3. Robert Sinsheimer, "On Coupling Inquiry and Wisdom," unpublished lecture, June 1976.

simply was not constituted to cope with the larger issues." Part of the fault is that most biological research in the United States is financed by the NIH, an agency whose primary mission is health. This dependence, Sinsheimer considers, has distorted biology and biased scientists' values. For lack of an evolutionary perspective, the NIH guidelines

> reflect a view of Nature as a static and passive domain, wholly subject to our dominion. They regard our ecological niche as wholly secure, deeply insulated from potential onslaught, with no chinks or unguarded section or perimeter. I cannot be so sanguine. In simple truth just one—just one—penetration of our niche could be sufficient to produce a catastrophe.[4]

Living species, as Sinsheimer often points out, are all the product of some three billion years of evolution. The evolutionary tree that traces the development of all species of life represents the fact that evolution proceeds in a linear, branching manner to produce gradually diverging species. The cardinal feature of the tree is that its branches do not cross or interweave. Nature has so arranged matters that, by and large, genes only interact within a particular species.

The gene-splicing technique enables man to turn the tree into a network by merging genes from one species with those of another. The technique also fractures another of nature's arrangements: the measured pace by which, in a series of gradual interactions, a new species enters the quasi-equilibrium of natural ecology or an old species fades out. Man can now create a new species from nowhere and dump it into the system without notice. As Sinsheimer puts it, "Now we come, with our splendid science and our ingenuity, and we have now the power to introduce quantum jumps into the evolutionary process. But do we have the commensurate understanding to foresee the consequences to the currently established equilibria on which, quite literally, our life support systems depend?"

In a shotgun experiment, for example, the DNA from an insect or sea urchin can be cut with a restriction enzyme into some fifty thousand fragments, say, each containing an unknown cluster of genes. Using a second restriction enzyme, with an affinity for a different sequence of bases, another set of fifty thousand fragments can be produced for insertion into bacteria and cloning. Says Sinsheimer: "Somehow it is presumed that we know, *a priori*, that none of these clones will be harmful to man or to our animals or to our crops or to other microbes—on which we unthinkingly rely. I don't know that and, worse, I don't know how anyone else does."[5] * * *

4. Robert Sinsheimer, "An Evolutionary Perspective for Genetic Engineering," *New Scientist*, 20 January 1977, 150.
5. Ibid.

The ability to manipulate the stuff of life is the ultimate technology. Other technologies are merely extensions of man's hands or mind or senses, serving to amplify or project the capabilities of the user. The further improvement and refinement of these technologies will doubtless continue to be a preoccupation for long into the future. But the impending ability to turn the tools inward for the reshaping of man himself would be an event quite out of the ordinary march of technological progress. Hitherto evolution has seemed as inexorable and irreversible a process as time or entropy; now at least there lies almost within man's grasp a tool for manipulating the force that shaped him, for controlling his own creator.

PART IV

Darwin, Philosophy, and Theology

And God said, Let us make man in our image, after our likeness: and let them have dominion over the fish of the sea, and
over the fowl of the air, and over the cattle, and over all the earth,
and over every creeping thing that creepeth upon the earth.

So God created man in his own image, in the image of God
created he him; male and female created he them.

—Genesis I, 26–27

Darwin threw down a challenge to the old rigidities, and his doctrine of evolution made everything a matter of degree, obliterating
the absoluteness of white-and-black, right-and-wrong. * * * It
seemed that everything, instead of being so or not so, as in the
logic books, was only more so or less so. And in this mush of
compromise all the old splendid certainties dissolved.

—Bertrand Russell, 1949

Intellectual progress usually occurs through sheer abandonment
of questions. * * * We do not solve them; we get over them.

—John Dewey, 1909

Today we know that we are not entirely the masters of our fate,
certainly not the captains of our souls, but neither are we innocent and passive bystanders. Many factors in nature interact to
cause and direct our evolution, but our understanding of evolution has itself become one of the factors.

—Conway Zirkle, 1958

MORSE PECKHAM

Darwinism and Darwinisticism (1959) †

Everyone knows that the impact of the *Origin of Species* was immense and that it has had a profound influence upon the literature of England and of the West ever since that late November day in 1859. But when one tries to tally up the writers affected and to list the books and make an inventory of passages showing Darwinian influence and Darwinian assumptions in novels, poems, and essays, a fog seems to arise in one's mind, through which are discernible twinkles of what may or may not be bits of genuine Darwinism.

Indeed, here is the first problem. What is Darwinism? Or at least, what is the Darwinism found in the *Origin*, for that alone is the Darwinism with which I am here concerned. The name of Darwin has magnetized to itself a thousand bits and pieces of ideas which are certainly not to be found in the book itself, and some of which Darwin, had he been able to understand them, would certainly have repudiated. For example, it has been said a million times and will be said a million times more that for Darwin competition between species and members of species is the only mechanism of directive and progressive evolution. Thus he has been adulated for having revealed that in capitalism and its related and derived values was to be found the natural system of social and economic organization which assures the progress of man; and execrated for having led men to disbelieve the seemingly obvious truth that man's proper, natural, and normal mode of behavior is cooperation, harmony, and love. Again, it is always being rediscovered that in natural selection there are cooperative as well as competitive mechanisms at work. Alternatively, it is frequently stated that Darwin failed to perceive the element of cooperation because he was himself the product of a laissez-faire society: Marxists are particularly grand and imposing on the subject.

In this one example are to be found the typical confusions observable in many discussions of Darwinism carried on by nonscientists and even by scientists when they are not scientizing. First, there is by the very use of the terms an introduction of values into a descriptive construct; or the misinterpretation of descriptive terms by ascribing to the words a moral significance and to the author a moral intention. The roots of this error are to be found in

† *Victorian Studies*, III (1959), 3–40. Morse Peckham (b. 1914) is Distin- guished Professor of English at the University of South Carolina.

the ancient exhortation that Nature should be our basic model for Right Behavior. Not surprisingly it is constantly assumed that the *Origin* rests on moral assumptions: that a value statement may be verified in the same way that an empiricial or predictive statement is verified is an attitude that only a small fraction of human beings have yet outgrown, and that in only a small part of their behavior. The difficulty arose because Darwin did not have the word "ecology." He was in fact an ecological thinker, and in ecology words like "competition" and "cooperation" are too inexact, too value-weighted, too metaphorical, and too anthropomorphic to be used at all.

Second, scientific statements are continuously subjected not only to moral interpretations but also, and more subtly, to metaphysical interpretations. Hence, the unconscious ascription to the *Origin* of a metaphysic. Darwin is said to have discovered the Law of Evolution, according to which the universe is characterized by a steady growth in richness and complexity and excellence. Now Spencer formulated a Law of Evolution, but there is no such law in the *Origin*. In fact, in the fourth edition there is a brief but profoundly important passage at the beginning of Chapter Four in which Darwin specifically disclaims any knowledge of and any statements about Laws of Nature, which he clearly labels mental conveniences, or constructs. He is a scientist, not a moralist and not a metaphysician, and he knows it. Unfortunately, most humanists then and now have little notion of what a scientist is and does. They are interested in metaphysics and morals, and when a science seems to have a metaphysical and moral implication, or when a scientist assumes another role and makes metaphysical and moral statements, then only do they evince an interest and subject themselves to what they think are scientific influences.

It will be apparent from what I have said so far that the problem of the impact of the *Origin* upon the culture of the last one hundred years is a complex one. It involves, above all, the question, what is the difference between "Darwinian" and "Darwinistic" (that is, between those propositions and implied assumptions which may be properly ascribed to a source in the *Origin*, and those propositions and derived assumptions which are not properly so ascribed). I shall attempt to clear the way for future studies of the *Origin* and literature, using "literature" generally and loosely.

The question to be answered, then, is, what was the Darwinian and Darwinistic impact of the *Origin* upon Western culture? But even this is much too vague. How is the culture of the past available and what do we mean by "culture"? It is said that historical investigation is concerned with the events of the past. But of course past events are not observable, and so we are left with the question as to what in fact the historian observes. The problem may be somewhat crudely, though I think not naïvely, tackled by observing what the historian actually does. He is engaged in the manipulation (with all that the word implies) of documents and artifacts. These are his data, not past events. The empirical referent of his "History," that is, his construct which purports to refer to the events of the past, or "history," is his own operations with those documents and artifacts which he assumes to have had an existence prior to the moment he began examining them. His History is a linguistic construct, characterized by what he hopes is at least an intuitive consistence, designed to justify his work. Since internal inconsistencies are always discoverable in his construct, and since his collection of documents and artifacts is never complete, nor its degree of completeness ever known, History, like any science, is characterized by instability. (Like physics, it is always being reconstructed.) Thus the process of historiography is the consequence of a continuous interaction, manipulated by historians, between construct and data.

One particular problem remains: what is the model of the historian's construct? Such models certainly are now, and perhaps always will be, intuitive. At least I know of no mathematical or logical model for a historical narrative. But though models for battles, parliamentary debates, and assassinations are probably pretty reliable, those for cultural history are probably not. In cultural history we are involved with matters of extraordinary difficulty and subtlety. Whereas the assassination of Lincoln was eminently observable at one time (there were witnesses; a reasonably consistent construct may be created of his murder and death), a priest may lose his religious belief and nobody be the wiser (Pater thought he could have a successful career as an Anglican clergyman with no religious belief whatsoever, and he was probably right). The difficulty lies in the fact that the locus of cultural history is covert behavior. When we realize that there is no such entity as "culture" but only human beings doing something, or behaving covertly, and that such behavior may or may not leave traces in documents and artifacts, the general problem of the inaccessibility of the past is twice compounded; for cultural behavior is not necessarily observable even when it is going on in a human being who is right before the observer's eyes or even at times, when it is going on inside the observer. When we talk about "culture" in the old-fashioned way, or "high-level culture" in the modern way, we are referring somewhat vaguely to two kinds of data, first, recorded verbal behavior, sufficiently complex and highly-valued to be called literature, philosophy, or science, and recorded sign-systems of a parallel complexity which we call the visual and auditory arts, and, second, unrecorded and covert linguistic and aesthetic semiotic behavior. On the model of our own behavior, insofar as we can and have trained ourselves to observe it, aided by various admittedly inadequate personality or psychological theories, we try to write cultural history. Now, we know very little about cultural transmission and cultural innovation at any level, let alone complex high-level transmission and innovation. It is not surprising that when we undertake to write cultural history we finish feeling a bit baffled and inadequate.

At least, however, we can now see our basic problem somewhat more precisely. On the one hand there are the Darwinian and Darwinistic documents, on the other, documents and artifacts which show Darwinian and Darwinistic influences, and in between, casually, we hope or assume for constructive purposes, connecting the two categories, a doubly inaccessible process of cultural history of which we wish to make a construct. But, alas! each part of the problem consists of a set of variables. For instance, a single Darwinistic sentence might have had a profoundly revolutionary impact upon the covert behavior of an individual, with the consequence that he wrote a single poem profoundly different from anything he had written before. (Did this happen in the case of Swinburne's "Hertha"?) Or a reading of the entire *Origin* might have had a slight impact which resulted, for the moment, at least, in a fairly brief document. (Was this the case of Kingsley's famous letter which Darwin was so happy to quote in later editions in order to avert the theological lightning?) Or a very thorough reading of Darwinian and Darwinistic material might so confirm the already existing attitudes of an individual that he perceived nothing innovative. (Was this the case with Browning, whose post-*Origin* work indicates that he not only read Darwin but read him with such extreme care that frequent re-reading is implied?) * * *

In 1859 a metaphysic of goal-directed organic growth was dominant in the higher levels of Western culture. Canon Raven has pointed out that the agitation produced by Darwin can not be understood without reference to the *Essays and Reviews*, which appeared only a few months after, or to Colenso's work, which appeared in 1862. The academic difficulties of Max Müller and of Benjamin Jowett are equally inseparable from the total situation. Today it is somewhat difficult to understand why all of these books and events should have been interconnected in the covert culture of the day. But a reading of *Essays and Reviews* shows the deep penetration of metaphysical evolutionism into the minds of its authors. That was their offense: they were addressing a world of a lower cultural level which still lived by a static metaphysic. I have referred to Newman's speculation about the possibility of applying his ideas of development to the biological world, and he has been praised for his profundity in thus anticipating and understanding Darwin. But the praise has come from individuals who did not themselves understand Darwin, for in fact the *Origin* was an embarrassment to the metaphysical evolutionists.

The evolutionists were already used to having their metaphysic apparently confirmed by scientific developments. Lyell and Herschel and Nichol seemed to support them, and they took the *Vestiges of Creation* to be a scientific work. Consequently, there is no indication that the *Origin* disturbed Tennyson, for example, or Newman, or George Eliot. "Hertha," again, is a good example. Written in the latter half of the 1860's, it appears to be a perfect instance of the impact of Darwin. Yet it can just as well be thought of as a humanistic and anti-religious interpretation of the concluding speech of *Paracelsus*. It could have been written had the *Origin* never been published. That it was written as a consequence of the *Origin* seems highly probable, but as a consequence of a misunderstanding of the *Origin*. For the biologic world that Darwin revealed, if you do not read him with the assumptions of metaphysical evolutionism as instruments for understanding the book, is a world totally lacking in the organized and teleological process characteristic of evolutionary metaphysics. New species come into existence by a process which can only be described as accidental. If a species has a range of variations among its individuals such that when the environment of the species changes, hitherto non-adaptive variations are selected as means of survival, a new species will in the course of time emerge, provided that the change in environment is not so great as to cause the total extinction of the species and provided that the population of the species is sufficient to maintain itself during the period of the development of the new species out of the old. No organism, Darwin said, is as perfectly adapted as it might be. That is, it includes within its population instincts and organs which are not instrumental to its environmental adaptation, although in its ancestry at some time or other such organs and instincts were adaptive. (To be sure, Darwin was not very certain about this and proposed other reasons, particularly morphology, for non-adaptive organs.) Further, there are numerous instances not only of extinction but of total or partial regression, or regression at some stage of an organism's life-cycle. Nor is there any reason to believe that natural selection operates in a morally or metaphysically progressive fashion. Indeed, from the *Origin* it is very easy to conclude that the more complex an organism the less its chances to survive. It is impossible to find in the *Origin* a basis in the biological world for any kind of orthogenesis or goal-directed process. Consequently it has been misread or simply not read at all, though discussed by all varieties of metaphysical evolutionists from Newman to Gerald Heard and current Catholic theologians.

Thus the grand thesis of metaphysical evolutionism—from simple to complex means from good to better, infinitely or finitely, as your metaphysical taste determines—not only received no support from the *Origin* but, if the book were properly understood and if the individual involved felt that a metaphysic should and could have scientific support, was positively demolished. Hence the curious spectacle, to be found so often, of orthodox fundamentalist Christians and anti-Christian or quasi-Christian metaphysical evolutionists ranged side by side in opposition to Darwin. And hence the equally curious spectacle of other metaphysical and Christian evolutionists swallowing the book without even a catch in the throat.

But the book presented an even deeper problem of which very few were apparently aware, although it was implied in the early editions and was clearly spelled out in the fourth. In the middle of the century most scientists characteristically conceived their task as discovering the laws of nature. Newton's Law of Gravity was held to be unrepealable, and for a hundred and fifty years Law had been gradually replacing Providence at the higher cultural levels. To be sure there were exceptions. Newman preferred to believe that the weather was controlled by angels, and he has several very pretty passages on the subject. But for the most part advanced thinkers felt like Nichol, who in 1839 hailed the advent of the comprehension of Nature through discoverable Laws and rejoiced at the disappearance of the capricious ways of Providence. He felt it added greatly to the dignity of God to think that He governed the world through Laws and not through unpredictable wilfullness. It is hard not to see the influence here of political liberalism. Or perhaps it is the other way around. Certainly the two seem to be connected, for the idea of the subjection of the Crown to the rational laws of elected representatives, the progress away from capricious tyranny, is remarkably like Nichol's conception. An Enlightenment idea, it was a basic ingredient of most Romantic metaphysics and fundamental to evolutionary metaphysics. The metaphor unconsciously used seems too transparent to be missed, and yet it was missed. The notion was that just as it is possible to study the political behavior of a people and hence deduce its laws, so it is possible to study the behavior of nature and arrive at the laws which govern it. It was a notion particularly appealing to Englishmen, who, because of the peculiar and highly admired nature of the English Constitution, were in part governed by written laws and in part by laws not spelled out in a written constitution in the style of the infidel Bentham and the misguided Americans but implicit in the political structure of the nation. In Nature the laws are there, they are immanent in the natural world, and it is the will of God that in our enlightened progress we should discover them. Constant reference to such economic ideas as the Law of Supply and Demand continually reinforced such concepts; and it is typical that Ruskin's aesthetic and socio-economic writings are filled with Laws of This and Laws of That.

The *Origin* did not fit into this conception at all. Not only was an apparently accidental world revealed, but even if one insisted upon discovering an order in the apparent chaos of the biological world, the incredible intricacy of ecological relations was such that Darwin himself felt that a full comprehension was beyond him or any human being. When biology can be studied mathematically —and biologists are making progress in that direction, particularly in genetics—perhaps a few people will comprehend the biologic world, but it is too much for mathematically unorganized descriptive language.

Thus at the time there were frequent complaints that Darwin did not really reveal the Laws of Nature. The culture was still penetrated by the Baconian notion that the Laws of Nature are not only immanent, because they had been put there by God, but also were few in number and essentially simple, because God had so designed them that the human mind might understand them. The culture accepted the Baconian notion that if one assembled all the data pertinent to a line of inquiry, the true relations between the separate bits of data and the laws that governed them would reveal themselves. Again we find, metaphysically, the desire to penetrate into a world of pure order.

But Darwin's notion of scientific law was empiricistic and extraordinarily modern. He implies it in his superb discussion of the term "species" and its related words. He demonstrates that to the term there is no corresponding reality or entity in the biological world. It is essential to his argument that species should not be regarded as fixed, and he disproves their fixity not so much by aligning data as by analyzing the term to demonstrate that the attempt to find distinct species in nature is necessarily fruitless, since the term is only of convenience in creating hypotheses, or, as we should say today, constructs. Further, he spelled his notion out in additions made to the opening of Chapter Four in the fourth edition. To him a scientific law was a mental convenience. The mind organized the data into meaningful structures; it did not discover the principles of organization immanent within the data. To a certain extent his public was at least intuitively aware of this position and responded to it negatively. Nevertheless for the most part the Legalists of Nature simply derived from the *Origin* further proof of their arguments. It is yet another example of how Darwinism was converted into Darwinisticism and is comparable and related to the similar absorption of the *Origin* and natural selection into metaphysical evolutionism.

There are further variables in this part of the basic question, such as adaptation, economy, and morality. Huxley, in his Romanes lecture, and Mill, earlier, in *Three Essays on Religion*, concluded that the ancient "Follow nature" as a basis for morality was in error, and that if a genuine morality were to be developed it must be on a purely human basis, indifferent to and even opposed to the workings of evolution. The economists, as we have seen, followed a different course, and with the aid of Spencer found in the *Origin* a basis for their own morality. And in the matter of adaptation, the final basis of British empirical theology, the notion of perfect adaptation of organism to environment was washed away by the *Origin*. Consequently, as might have been expected, Darwinisticism in the field of moralized psychology has used Darwin as a basis for attempting to make perfect adaptation of the individual personality to its social environment into the criterion of psychological health. There can be located still other variables, but I have attempted to go into at least two of the problems involved in the impact of the *Origin* in order to show the profound difference between Darwinism and Darwinisticism. Darwinism is a scientific theory about the origin of biological species from pre-existent species, the mechanism of that process being an extraordinarily complex ecology which can be observed only in fairly small and artificially isolated instances. It reveals a world not of accident precisely but rather one in which "accident" becomes a meaningless problem. Darwinisticism can be an evolutionary metaphysic about the nature of reality and the universe. It can be a metaphysical and simplistic notion of natural law. It can be an economic theory, or a moral theory, or an aesthetic theory, or a psychological theory. It can be anything which claims to have support from the *Origin*, or conversely anything which claims to have really understood what Darwin inadequately and partially presented. Once one is aware of the distinction, much which is ascribed to Darwin and much which appears to be Darwinian in the cultural documents of the past one hundred years turns out not to be Darwinian at all but Darwinistic. Is it true that what Darwin said had very little impact, but that what people thought he said, that is, what they already believed and believed to have been confirmed by Darwin, had an enormous impact? * * *

JOHN DEWEY

The Influence of Darwin on Philosophy (1909) †

I

That the publication of the "Origin of Species" marked an epoch in the development of the natural sciences is well known to the layman. That the combination of the very words origin and species embodied an intellectual revolt and introduced a new intellectual temper is easily overlooked by the expert. The conceptions that had reigned in the philosophy of nature and knowledge for two thousand years, the conceptions that had become the familiar furniture of the mind, rested on the assumption of the superiority of the fixed and final; they rested upon treating change and origin as signs of defect and unreality. In laying hands upon the sacred ark of absolute permanency, in treating the forms that had been regarded as types of fixity and perfection as originating and passing away, the "Origin of Species" introduced a mode of thinking that in the end was bound to transform the logic of knowledge, and hence the treatment of morals, politics, and religion.

No wonder, then, that the publication of Darwin's book, a half century ago, precipitated a crisis. The true nature of the controversy is easily concealed from us, however, by the theological clamor that attended it. The vivid and popular features of the anti-Darwinian row tended to leave the impression that the issue was between science on one side and theology on the other. Such was not the case—the issue lay primarily within science itself, as Darwin himself early recognized. The theological outcry he discounted from the start, hardly noticing it save as it bore upon the "feelings of his female relatives." But for two decades before final publication he contemplated the possibility of being put down by his scientific peers as a fool or as crazy; and he set, as the measure of his success, the degree in which he should affect three men of science: Lyell in geology, Hooker in botany, and Huxley in zoology.

Religious considerations lent fervor to the controversy, but they did not provoke it. Intellectually, religious emotions are not creative but conservative. They attach themselves readily to the current view of the world and consecrate it. They steep and dye

† Originally a lecture given at Columbia University in 1909 by the noted American philosopher John Dewey (1859–1952), this essay was subsequently included in Dewey's *The Influence of Darwin on Philosophy and Other Essays in Contemporary Thought* (New York, 1910).

intellectual fabrics in the seething vat of emotions; they do not form their warp and woof. There is not, I think, an instance of any large idea about the world being independently generated by religion. Although the ideas that rose up like armed men against Darwinism owed their intensity to religious associations, their origin and meaning are to be sought in science and philosophy, not in religion.

II

Few words in our language foreshorten intellectual history as much as does the word species. The Greeks, in initiating the intellectual life of Europe, were impressed by characteristic traits of the life of plants and animals; so impressed indeed that they made these traits the key to defining nature and to explaining mind and society. And truly, life is so wonderful that a seemingly successful reading of its mystery might well lead men to believe that the key to the secrets of heaven and earth was in their hands. The Greek rendering of this mystery, the Greek formulation of the aim and standard of knowledge, was in the course of time embodied in the word species, and it controlled philosophy for two thousand years. To understand the intellectual face-about expressed in the phrase "Origin of Species," we must, then, understand the long dominant idea against which it is a protest.

Consider how men were impressed by the facts of life. Their eyes fell upon certain things slight in bulk, and frail in structure. To every appearance, these perceived things were inert and passive. Suddenly, under certain circumstances, these things—henceforth known as seeds or eggs or germs—begin to change, to change rapidly in size, form, and qualities. Rapid and extensive changes occur, however, in many things—as when wood is touched by fire. But the changes in the living thing are orderly; they are cumulative; they tend constantly in one direction; they do not, like other changes, destroy or consume, or pass fruitless into wandering flux; they realize and fulfil. Each successive stage, no matter how unlike its predecessor, preserves its net effect and also prepares the way for a fuller activity on the part of its successor. In living beings, changes do not happen as they seem to happen elsewhere, any which way; the earlier changes are regulated in view of later results. This progressive organization does not cease till there is achieved a true final term, a τελὸs, a completed, perfected end. This final form exercises in turn a plenitude of functions, not the least noteworthy of which is production of germs like those from which it took its own origin, germs capable of the same cycle of self-fulfilling activity.

But the whole miraculous tale is not yet told. The same drama is enacted to the same destiny in countless myriads of individuals so sundered in time, so severed in space, that they have no opportunity for mutual consultation and no means of interaction. As an old writer quaintly said, "things of the same kind go through the same formalities"—celebrate, as it were, the same ceremonial rites.

This formal activity which operates throughout a series of changes and holds them to a single course; which subordinates their aimless flux to its own perfect manifestation; which, leaping the boundaries of space and time, keeps individuals distant in space and remote in time to a uniform type of structure and function: this principle seemed to give insight into the very nature of reality itself. To it Aristotle gave the name, εἶδος. This term the scholastics translated as *species*.

The force of this term was deepened by its application to everything in the universe that observes order in flux and manifests constancy through change. From the casual drift of daily weather, through the uneven recurrence of seasons and unequal return of seed time and harvest, up to the majestic sweep of the heavens— the image of eternity in time—and from this to the unchanging pure and contemplative intelligence beyond nature lies one unbroken fulfillment of ends. Nature as a whole is a progressive realization of purpose strictly comparable to the realization of purpose in any single plant or animal.

The conception of εἶδος, species, a fixed form and final cause, was the central principle of knowledge as well as of nature. Upon it rested the logic of science. Change as change is mere flux and lapse; it insults intelligence. Genuinely to know is to grasp a permanent end that realizes itself through changes, holding them thereby within the metes and bounds of fixed truth. Completely to know is to relate all special forms to their one single end and good: pure contemplative intelligence. Since, however, the scene of nature which directly confronts us is in change, nature as directly and practically experienced does not satisfy the conditions of knowledge. Human experience is in flux, and hence the instrumentalities of sense-perception and of inference based upon observation are condemned in advance. Science is compelled to aim at realities lying behind and beyond the processes of nature, and to carry on its search for these realities by means of rational forms transcending ordinary modes of perception and inference.

There are, indeed, but two alternative courses. We must either find the appropriate objects and organs of knowledge in the mutual interactions of changing things; or else, to escape the infection of change, we *must* seek them in some transcendent and supernal region. The human mind, deliberately as it were, exhausted the logic of the changeless, the final, and the transcendent, before it essayed adventure on the pathless wastes of generation and transformation. We dispose all too easily of the efforts of the schoolmen to interpret nature and mind in terms of real essences, hidden forms, and occult faculties, forgetful of the seriousness and dignity of the ideas that lay behind. We dispose of them by laughing at the famous gentleman who accounted for the fact that opium put people to sleep on the ground it had a dormitive faculty. But the doctrine, held in our own day, that knowledge of the plant that yields the poppy consists in referring the peculiarities of an individual to a type, to a universal form, a doctrine so firmly established that any other method of knowing was conceived to be unphilosophical and unscientific, is a survival of precisely the same logic. This identity of conception in the scholastic and anti-Darwinian theory may well suggest greater sympathy for what has become unfamiliar as well as greater humility regarding the further unfamiliarities that history has in store.

Darwin was not, of course, the first to question the classic philosophy of nature and of knowledge. The beginnings of the revolution are in the physical science of the sixteenth and seventeenth centuries. When Galileo said: "It is my opinion that the earth is very noble and admirable by reason of so many and so different alterations and generations which are incessantly made therein," he expressed the changed temper that was coming over the world; the transfer of interest from the permanent to the changing. When Descartes said: "The nature of physical things is much more easily conceived when they are beheld coming gradually into existence, than when they are only considered as produced at once in a finished and perfect state," the modern world became self-conscious of the logic that was henceforth to control it, the logic of which Darwin's "Origin of Species" is the latest scientific achievement. Without the methods of Copernicus, Kepler, Galileo, and their successors in astronomy, physics, and chemistry, Darwin would have been helpless in the organic sciences. But prior to Darwin the impact of the new scientific method upon life, mind, and politics, had been arrested, because between these ideal or moral interests and the inorganic world intervened the kingdom of plants and animals. The gates of the garden of life were barred to the new ideas; and only through this garden was there access to mind and politics. The influence of Darwin upon philosophy resides in his having conquered the phenomena of life for the principle of transition, and thereby freed the new logic for application to mind and morals and life. When he said of species what Galileo had said of the earth, *e pur se muove*, he emancipated, once for all, genetic and experimental ideas as an organon of asking questions and looking for explanations.

III

The exact bearings upon philosophy of the new logical outlook are, of course, as yet, uncertain and inchoate. We live in the twilight of intellectual transition. One must add the rashness of the prophet to the stubbornness of the partizan to venture a systematic exposition of the influence upon philosophy of the Darwinian method. At best, we can but inquire as to its general bearing—the effect upon mental temper and complexion, upon that body of half-conscious, half-instinctive intellectual aversions and preferences which determine, after all, our more deliberate intellectual enterprises. In this vague inquiry there happens to exist as a kind of touchstone a problem of long historic currency that has also been much discussed in Darwinian literature. I refer to the old problem of design *versus* chance, mind *versus* matter, as the causal explanation, first or final, of things.

As we have already seen, the classic notion of species carried with it the idea of purpose. In all living forms, a specific type is present directing the earlier stages of growth to the realization of its own perfection. Since this purposive regulative principle is not visible to the senses, it follows that it must be an ideal or rational force. Since, however, the perfect form is gradually approximated through the sensible changes, it also follows that in and through a sensible realm a rational ideal force is working out its own ultimate manifestation. These inferences were extended to nature: (*a*) She does nothing in vain; but all for an ulterior purpose. (*b*) Within natural sensible events there is therefore contained a spiritual causal force, which as spiritual escapes perception, but is apprehended by an enlightened reason. (*c*) The manifestation of this principle brings about a subordination of matter and sense to its own realization, and this ultimate fulfillment is the goal of nature and of man. The design argument thus operated in two directions. Purposefulness accounted for the intelligibility of nature and the possibility of science, while the absolute or cosmic character of this purposefulness gave sanction and worth to the moral and religious endeavors of man. Science was underpinned and morals authorized by one and the same principle, and their mutual agreement was eternally guaranteed.

This philosophy remained, in spite of sceptical and polemic outbursts, the official and the regnant philosophy of Europe for over two thousand years. The expulsion of fixed first and final causes from astronomy, physics, and chemistry had indeed given the doctrine something of a shock. But, on the other hand, increased acquaintance with the details of plant and animal life operated as a counterbalance and perhaps even strengthened the argument from design. The marvelous adaptations of organisms to their environment, of organs to the organism, of unlike parts of a complex organ—like the eye—to the organ itself; the foreshadowing by lower forms of the higher; the preparation in earlier stages of growth for organs that only later had their functioning—these things were increasingly recognized with the progress of botany, zoology, paleontology, and embryology. Together, they added such prestige to the design argument that by the late eighteenth century it was, as approved by the sciences of organic life, the central point of theistic and idealistic philosophy.

The Darwinian principle of natural selection cut straight under this philosophy. If all organic adaptations are due simply to constant variation and the elimination of those variations which are harmful in the struggle for existence that is brought about by excessive reproduction, there is no call for a prior intelligent causal force to plan and preordain them. Hostile critics charged Darwin with materialism and with making chance the cause of the universe.

Some naturalists, like Asa Gray, favored the Darwinian principle and attempted to reconcile it with design. Gray held to what may be called design on the installment plan. If we conceive the "stream of variations" to be itself intended, we may suppose that each successive variation was designed from the first to be selected. In that case, variation, struggle, and selection simply define the mechanism of "secondary causes" through which the "first cause" acts; and the doctrine of design is none the worse off because we know more of its *modus operandi*.

Darwin could not accept this mediating proposal. He admits or rather he asserts that it is "impossible to conceive this immense and wonderful universe including man with his capacity of looking far backwards and far into futurity as the result of blind chance or necessity." [1] But nevertheless he holds that since variations are in useless as well as useful directions, and since the latter are sifted out simply by the stress of the conditions of struggle for existence, the design argument as applied to living beings is unjustifiable; and its lack of support there deprives it of scientific value as applied to nature in general. If the variations of the pigeon, which under artificial selection give the pouter pigeon, are not preordained for the sake of the breeder, by what logic do we argue that variations resulting in natural species are pre-designed? [2]

IV

So much for some of the more obvious facts of the discussion of design *versus* chance, as causal principles of nature and of life as a

1. "Life and Letters," Vol. I., p. 282; cf. 285.
2. "Life and Letters," Vol. II, pp. 146, 170, 245; Vol. I., pp. 283–84. See also the closing portion of his "Variations of Animals and Plants under Domestication."

whole. We brought up this discussion, you recall, as a crucial instance. What does our touchstone indicate as to the bearing of Darwinian ideas upon philosophy? In the first place, the new logic outlaws, flanks, dismisses—what you will—one type of problems and substitutes for it another type. Philosophy forswears inquiry after absolute origins and absolute finalities in order to explore specific values and the specific conditions that generate them.

Darwin concluded that the impossibility of assigning the world to chance as a whole and to design in its parts indicated the insolubility of the question. Two radically different reasons, however, may be given as to why a problem is insoluble. One reason is that the problem is too high for intelligence; the other is that the question in its very asking makes assumptions that render the question meaningless. The latter alternative is unerringly pointed to in the celebrated case of design *versus* chance. Once admit that the sole verifiable or fruitful object of knowledge is the particular set of changes that generate the object of study together with the consequences that then flow from it, and no intelligible question can be asked about what, by assumption, lies outside. To assert—as is often asserted—that specific values of particular truth, social bonds and forms of beauty, if they can be shown to be generated by concretely knowable conditions, are meaningless and in vain; to assert that they are justified only when they and their particular causes and effects have all at once been gathered up into some inclusive first cause and some exhaustive final goal, is intellectual atavism. Such argumentation is reversion to the logic that explained the extinction of fire by water through the formal essence of aqueousness and the quenching of thirst by water through the final cause of aqueousness. Whether used in the case of the special event or that of life as a whole, such logic only abstracts some aspect of the existing course of events in order to reduplicate it as a petrified eternal principle by which to explain the very changes of which it is the formalization.

When Henry Sidgwick casually remarked in a letter that as he grew older his interest in what or who made the world was altered into interest in what kind of a world it is anyway, his voicing of a common experience of our own day illustrates also the nature of that intellectual transformation effected by the Darwinian logic. Interest shifts from the wholesale essence back of special changes to the question of how special changes serve and defeat concrete purposes; shifts from an intelligence that shaped things once for all to the particular intelligences which things are even now shaping; shifts from an ultimate goal of good to the direct increments of justice and happiness that intelligent administration of existent conditions may beget and that present carelessness or stupidity will destroy or forego.

In the second place, the classic type of logic inevitably set philosophy upon proving that life *must* have certain qualities and values—no matter how experience presents the matter—because of some remote cause and eventual goal. The duty of wholesale justification inevitably accompanies all thinking that makes the meaning of special occurrences depend upon something that once and for all lies behind them. The habit of derogating from present meanings and uses prevents our looking the facts of experience in the face; it prevents serious acknowledgment of the evils they present and serious concern with the goods they promise but do not as yet fulfil. It turns thought to the business of finding a wholesale transcendent remedy for the one and guarantee for the other. One is reminded of the way many moralists and theologians greeted Herbert Spencer's recognition of an unknowable energy from which welled up the phenomenal physical processes without and the conscious operations within. Merely because Spencer labeled his unknowable energy "God," this faded piece of metaphysical goods was greeted as an important and grateful concession to the reality of the spiritual realm. Were it not for the deep hold of the habit of seeking justification for ideal values in the remote and transcendent, surely this reference of them to an unknowable absolute would be despised in comparison with the demonstrations of experience that knowable energies are daily generating about us precious values.

The displacing of this wholesale type of philosophy will doubtless not arrive by sheer logical disproof, but rather by growing recognition of its futility. Were it a thousand times true that opium produces sleep because of its dormitive energy, yet the inducing of sleep in the tired, and the recovery to waking life of the poisoned, would not be thereby one least step forwarded. And were it a thousand times dialectically demonstrated that life as a whole is regulated by a transcendent principle to a final inclusive goal, none the less truth and error, health and disease, good and evil, hope and fear in the concrete, would remain just what and where they now are. To improve our education, to ameliorate our manners, to advance our politics, we must have recourse to specific conditions of generation.

Finally, the new logic introduces responsibility into the intellectual life. To idealize and rationalize the universe at large is after all a confession of inability to master the courses of things that specifically concern us. As long as mankind suffered from this impotency, it naturally shifted a burden of responsibility that it could not carry over to the more competent shoulders of the transcendent cause. But if insight into specific conditions of value and into specific consequences of ideas is possible, philosophy must in time become a method of locating and interpreting the more serious of the conflicts that occur in life, and a method of projecting ways for dealing with them: a method of moral and political diagnosis and prognosis.

The claim to formulate *a priori* the legislative constitution of the universe is by its nature a claim that may lead to elaborate dialectic developments. But it is also one that removes these very conclusions from subjection to experimental test, for, by definition, these results make no differences in the detailed course of events. But a philosophy that humbles its pretensions to the work of projecting hypotheses for the education and conduct of mind, individual and social, is thereby subjected to test by the way in which the ideas it propounds work out in practice. In having modesty forced upon it, philosophy also acquires responsibility.

Doubtless I seem to have violated the implied promise of my earlier remarks and to have turned both prophet and partisan. But in anticipating the direction of the transformations in philosophy to be wrought by the Darwinian genetic and experimental logic, I do not profess to speak for any save those who yield themselves consciously or unconsciously to this logic. No one can fairly deny that at present there are two effects of the Darwinian mode of thinking. On the one hand, there are making many sincere and vital efforts to revise our traditional philosophic conceptions in accordance with its demands. On the other hand, there is as definitely a recrudescence of absolutistic philosophies; an assertion of a type of philosophic knowing distinct from that of the sciences, one which opens to us another kind of reality from that to which the sciences give access; an appeal through experience to something that essentially goes beyond experience. This reaction affects popular creeds and religious movements as well as technical philosophies. The very conquest of the biological sciences by the new ideas has led many to proclaim an explicit and rigid separation of philosophy from science.

Old ideas give way slowly; for they are more than abstract logical forms and categories. They are habits, predispositions, deeply engrained attitudes of aversion and preference. Moreover, the conviction persists—though history shows it to be a hallucination—that all the questions that the human mind has asked are questions that can be answered in terms of the alternatives that the questions themselves present. But in fact intellectual progress usually occurs through sheer abandonment of questions together with both of the alternatives they assume—an abandonment that results from their decreasing vitality and a change of urgent interest. We do not solve them: we get over them. Old questions are solved by disappearing, evaporating, while new questions corresponding to the changed attitude of endeavor and preference take their place. Doubtless the greatest dissolvent in contemporary thought of old questions, the greatest precipitant of new methods, new intentions, new problems, is the one effected by the scientific revolution that found its climax in the "Origin of Species."

JOHN HERMAN RANDALL, JR.

The Changing Impact of Darwin on Philosophy (1961) †

In the Darwin Centennial Number of the *Rice Institute Pamphlet*, Professor James Street Fulton writes:

> An essay on the philosophy of evolution in the century since the publication of Darwin's *Origin of Species* can be written in two sentences. By the end of the first fifty years, everybody in the educated world took evolution for granted, but the idea was still intellectually exciting and its philosophical exploitation was entering upon its period of full maturity. By the end of the next fifty years, evolution belongs to "common sense" almost as thoroughly as the Copernican hypothesis and other early landmarks of the scientific revolution; but the idea is no longer exciting, and evolutionary philosophy is out of fashion.[1]

Professor Fulton's closing comment is not quite exact. "Evolutionary philosophy" may be out of fashion today, in the sense he intends of the philosophies of "cosmic evolution" of half a century ago. But, after all, the philosophies of Herbert Spencer or Henri Bergson represent only an early stage of the impact of Darwin on philosophizing; and, it has now become clear, the least important stage.

For Charles Darwin is one of those significant thinkers who is not technically a "philosopher." He is at once something less, and something more. He is one of those men, like Copernicus, Galileo, Newton, Freud, Planck, Einstein, and Franz Boas, who succeed in formulating ideas that make philosophers necessary, and to whom philosophers should therefore look with a mixture of extreme an-

† This article is based on two lectures on the theme, "Darwin and Philosophy," given on December 2 and 3, 1960, as part of the program of Darwin Centennial Lectures held at the University of California, Santa Barbara. It owes much to the suggestions offered in the panel discussion held on December 4 by the other participants, Mr. Aldous Huxley and Professors Harry Girvetz and Alexander Sesonske [Randall's note]. From the *Journal of the History of Ideas*, XXII (1961), 435–462. John Herman Randall, Jr. (b. 1899) is Woodbridge Professor Emeritus of Philosophy at Columbia University.
1. Fulton, "Philosophical Adventures of the Idea of Evolution, 1859–1959," *Rice Institute Pamphlet*, Darwin Centennial Number, v. 46 (1959), 1.

noyance and deep gratitude. It is safe to say, that had not Darwin
—or someone else—published the *Origin of Species* in 1859, there
is hardly a single subsequent thinker whose thought would not
have been different.

As a matter of fact, someone else *did*, Alfred Russel Wallace.
This makes clear, that in considering the idea of the evolution of
biological species, we are not dealing with the brilliant hypothesis
of a single man of genius, but rather with an idea for which men's
intellectual experience was ready and prepared. But this serves
only to make Darwin's own achievement the more significant. We
are considering a fundamental intellectual revolution, like those
associated with the other names mentioned, to which must be
added that of the great intellectual revolutionary of the XIIIth
century, a man who was a philosopher, Aristotle. For the coming
of Aristotelian science, at the end of the XIIth and the beginning
of the XIIIth centuries, set off the first of the great intellectual
revolutions through which our Western culture has passed.

Now, all these successive intellectual revolutions in our cultural
tradition illustrate a rather similar pattern of cultural change. The
impact of a revolutionary idea again and again provokes typical reactions. First, there appears a group of partisans of the new idea,
who see its promise, what illumination and suggestive further ideas
it can afford. In reaction against their one-sided enthusiasm for
the new idea, the partisans of the old, of tradition, consolidate
their forces. This usually is accomplished too late for them to fight
more than a rearguard action. By this time there has appeared a
third group, the adjusters—the compromisers and mediators—who
interpret the new idea in the light of the traditional notions with
which men are already familiar. They take it as really confirming in
a new way the older and familiar ideas.

These three stages of cultural adjustment to a novel conception
have normally in our tradition taken a generation or so to be
worked out. Only then do men begin to suspect, and far-seeing
thinkers to realize, that the new idea has been more disruptive and
subversive than it at first seemed. For when taken seriously it has
really been transforming the problems completely. And certain
pioneer thinkers begin to perceive implications of that novel conception which the vast majority even of intelligent men were at
first, and for about a generation, prevented from seeing by their
inability to loosen the hold of older preconceptions upon their
minds and imaginations. * * *

If "evolutionary philosophy" is now for us "out of fashion," the
reference is to the third group, the adjusters. In my own lifetime, I
have lived through the heyday of the evolutionary religious faiths,
of the philosophies of cosmic evolution. I have seen them come,

and I have seen them recede into the limbo of indifference. But we ourselves are in the midst of what I have distinguished as the work of the fourth stage, of the transformers. Even when, like so many philosophers today whose eyes are focused on new and quite different intellectual problems, we do not very clearly realize it, all our present-day philosophizing is still profoundly influenced by the intellectual consequences of accepting Darwinian evolution. * * *

In 1909, John Dewey gave a lecture in a course at Columbia University celebrating the fiftieth anniversary of the *Origin of Species*. He spoke on "The Influence of Darwinism on Philosophy." [2] * * *

* * * What Dewey pointed out was that while the "row" with the theologians had no philosophical significance, neither had the efforts at a "wholesale justification" of the meaning of life, of which he took Herbert Spencer's as the illustration. Evolution was not the answer to the old, traditional problems. Its significance for philosophy lay in its leading men to shift their attention to a wholly new set. For, said Dewey:

> In laying hands upon the sacred ark of absolute permanency, in treating the forms that had been treated as the types of fixity and perfection as originating and passing away, the "Origin of Species" introduced a *mode of thinking* that in the end was bound to transform the *logic of knowledge*, and hence the treatment of morals, politics, and religion. [3]

John Dewey has been proved right. The "new mode of thinking" is clearly the most important "influence" of Darwin on philosophy: the shifting of interest to a different set of problems. The realization of the further implications of the idea of evolution is not, of course, the only reason for this shift of interest. It has been helped also by the increasing impact of the experimental temper of mind: William James and John Dewey have been well called "the experimental method conscious of itself and its procedures." And it has been helped by the generalization of logical calculi into philosophies, in Bertrand Russell, the Logical Positivists, and the earlier Wittgenstein devoted to "logical atomism."

Having pointed out this major shift, we must at the same time recognize the persistence of the Hegelian evolution of human history. This remains not only in the Marxian world, where the Marxists still feel the need of a cosmic sanction for their social philosophy: Diamat in its orthodox form is the outstanding survivor today of the cosmically rooted "evolutionary faiths" of the end of

2. "The Influence of Darwinism on Philosophy," in *The Influence of Darwin on Philosophy and Other Essays in Contemporary Thought* (New York, 1910), 1–19.
3. John Dewey, *The Influence of Darwin on Philosophy*, 1.

the XIXth century. The Marxists now claim, and rightly, that theirs is the only philosophy today that really believes in the inevitability of "progress," in the good old-fashioned XIXth-century religious sense. The doubts the rest of us have come to share only reflect the contradictions of capitalist society. Marxism thus betrays in this as in so many other ways its origin in the complacent and uncritical atmosphere of XIXth-century "idealism."

Marxism is the last of the great Romantic faiths, lingering on in a scientific world. But there remain other XXth-century versions of Hegelianism, especially in cultural history, where Hegel's own thought originated: I have mentioned Cassirer and Brunschvicg. Having in our day lived through a fundamental revolution in physical theory, we have come to view science, even its best-founded branches, like physics, historically, as an institutionalized form of know-how by which a culture understands itself and directs its course. This is the deposit of Hegel modified by evolutionary anthropology, a combination, as it were, of Hegel, Darwin, and Franz Boas.

Dewey's lecture of 1909 emphasized certain specific points:

1) Change is no longer a sign of defect and unreality, but fundamental in all that exists. Knowledge and science can no longer aim at realities lying behind and beyond the processes of nature, but rather at mutual interactions of changing things; not at an Order of Nature, as XVIIth and XVIIIth-century science had aimed, but at events, situations, processes. This shift involved a fundamental temporalizing of all our thinking. For the first time since the abandonment of Aristotle in the XVIIth century for the mathematical order of nature, there was now a "taking time seriously," * * *

2) Thought is no longer concerned with the general and the wholesale, but with the specific and the particular, with the concrete problem. Thinking has become basically pluralistic. The Hegelian temporalism Darwin fundamentally pluralized, and shattered Hegel's own tight monism.

3) Closely allied to these two shifts, is the central emphasis on the experimental temper of mind * * *

4) Finally, there is involved a shift from a concern with the purposes of the Creator to ends and outcomes of natural processes, a shift from "design" to function, from antecedent "final causes," in the XVIIIth-century William Paley, Bernardin de Saint-Pierre sense, to specific means-ends relations.

These changes which Dewey signalized fifty years ago are all in what he called our "mode of thinking." But once the hold of the older problem of finding a new religious faith was broken, the employment of this new, genetic, pluralistic, experimental, and functional mode of thinking led to a great change in substantive views. Man's relation to nature was basically altered. He was no longer a fallen angel, but a great ape trying to make good, the last and best-born of nature's children. This alteration effected two great transformations: it transformed man, and it also transformed nature. It transformed nature, for a nature in which man and all his activities have suddenly become "natural" is very different from a nature sharply contrasted with the cardinal features of human life and experience. It also transformed man, altering the whole conception of the nature of human experience.

1. It was Darwin's ideas that generated the new "naturalism" of the XXth century. For among the characteristic features of nature are the various human activities she has uniformly provoked. In seeking to understand man and appraise the world in which we find ourselves, we can hardly afford to neglect the facts that it forces moral choice on men, inspires them to creative works of art, and leads or drives them to religious devotion, even as it stimulates some to scientific inquiry. Man's searching intelligence, his problems of moral choice and obligation, his ideal enterprises of art, science, and religion are all inescapable parts of nature; they are all ways in which man has learned to encounter and cooperate with his world. They all afford evidence of the character of the world in which they take place; their suggestions would have to be included in any transcription of nature that went beyond a diagram to a portrait. Nature must be understood as the kind of world in which they would all have an intelligible place. Inquiry can find out, and has, much about these natural human activities, about their conditions and consequences, about what they do and what they are good for; it has led us to criticise some of the beliefs commonly connected with them. But what inquiry thus finds is an addition to our knowledge, not the truly amazing discovery that they are not, or ought not to be.

The nature in which we live is a world with man in it. It cannot be taken as a world from which man and all his works have been carefully eliminated. Not only would a nature without man not be man's world: it would be a world in which there would be no knowledge, and nothing could be known. We can indeed conceive the world before man appeared in it, but we cannot conceive the world without the possibility that man would there appear, to find in it all he does find.[4] For strive as we may, we can never forget what was to come. All our theories of evolution are inescapably theories of how a world with man in it came to be.

4. See Dewey, "The Subject Matter of Metaphysical Inquiry," *Journal of Philosophy*, v. 12 (1915), 337–45. Re-printed in *John Dewey on Experience, Nature, and Freedom*, ed. Richard J. Bernstein (New York, 1960).

Nor is the nature we live in a world to be known and understood without reference to man. We cannot first work out a scheme for understanding the world to which everything human is irrelevant, and then claim to understand man in terms of that scheme—or man's world. For a world with man in it is a different world from a world defined regardless of man. It is a world in which things occur and are made and found that would not occur without man. And the world in which they occur cannot be understood as being what it is without their occurrence. Man's world cannot be reduced to a world without men—even if we then note man's presence, as something that introduces confusion and threatens to spoil it all, and so try to fit man and all his pursuits into the scheme in which we see the world. We shall not that way see the world. We shall see only those features which everything in the world possesses in common —stars and rocks and amoebae and men—atoms, perhaps, and what we used to call "laws." Man's finding of those common features, in himself as elsewhere, has been of momentous importance, and surely his making of such blueprints is one of his most significant arts. But that is to leave out all the features of the world that have been disclosed by man's presence in it—and all the possibilities revealed by his many other arts.

For all that man does, from birth to death, from walking to thinking, is a genuine co-working with the world. In realizing the world's possibilities, it is a revelation of what those possibilities are. Man's life in all its manifold productions makes clear what the intricate engines his blueprints describe can do, with man to direct them. The world is surely all that man can do in and with it and make out of it; it cannot be less. His doing and his making are a genuine discovery about the world. They are a finding of what the world contains.

A world with man in it contains the richness of human experience. It holds terror and love and thinking and imagination, good and evil and the wrestling with them, knowledge and ignorance and the search for truth, failure, frustration, defeat, beauty and vision and tragedy and comedy, the abyss of despair and the love of God. It has the reflective commentary of the spirit of man on all these wonders, the imaginative expression of what man has felt and suffered and thought and judged, the concentration of it all in words and paint and stone and sound. It has the pursuit of the ideal and the vision of the divine.

All these things are found in a nature with man in it. This is the nature that challenges us to tell how they are found and just how they are there. To be sure, it takes men to find them, even as it takes men to find the equations of physics. Without man's aid a star might well find other things and understand the world differently, or an angel. Stars, however, seem neither to find nor to understand anything. And angels, admirable creatures though they be, have left us no reports of their philosophic attainments. But surely there is no inference that because only men find anything, what they find is not found. The finding is a finding in nature, in cooperation with nature's possibilities.

This is a wisdom about nature that was known to the Greeks. It is the glory of Greek thought, of Plato and of Aristotle, that they took human life and experience as a revelation of what nature can accomplish on the human level. They understand the world as making possible the life of man. It was the theory of biological evolution that a century ago first put man fairly and squarely back into nature again. * * *

By common consent, it was the Greeks who looked most soberly and sanely on the natural setting of human life in the universe. They saw it steadily and whole. They managed to keep the best balance between the two contrasting relations in which man stands to the nature in whose midst he lives. On the one hand, man's life is part and parcel of the web of natural processes: he cannot live or act at all except by sharing in the great community of devices by which everything in nature takes place. He is one physical and chemical being among a host of others, inextricably involved in the interplay of nature's mechanisms. On the other hand, man acts in ways so distinct and unique that they are unparalleled by any other natural being. Both facts are important, man's unique ways of acting, and the continuity of the means by which he does so with the mechanisms of other natural processes. The Greeks, almost alone until our day, denied neither, and emphasized both. Again and again men have returned to the great Greek thinkers, to Plato and Aristotle, when they had forgotten one or the other of these essential facts of man's status in nature. * * *

Aristotle worked out the idea of "process," which has come to play so large a part in our new view of nature—of "process" in contrast to the motion from one place to another that mechanics treats of. Aristotle was at heart a biologist. To him the process by which an egg becomes a chicken was a fundamental kind of change. He was convinced that no science of nature's activities has done its job if it fails to explain the way an egg can grow into a chicken, or an acorn into an oak tree. He analysed living processes —what they do, how they function, the way the mechanisms involved in them work; for living processes, he held, reveal most clearly and fully what natural processes in general are like. Motion in place, though fundamental in all change, he took to be a limiting case of these more complex activities.

In contrast, the scientists of the early modern period took motion in place as typical. They won their triumphs in building up the science of dynamics by concentrating, not on the poultry-yard, but on the billiard table. Their blueprint, which read everything in the world as the motion of tiny billiard balls, had extraordinary fertility and power. But is is hardly surprising that it threw little light on the habits of eggs: it left out too much. It took no account of time—the time that is cumulative and progressive and irreversible, and so essential to the success of eggs. It paid no attention to the relations between means and ends, to outcomes and their necessary conditions, to what we call "functional" or "teleological" relations. Eggs have careers in time which demand the right conditions; billiard balls hardly can be said to enjoy careers.

When Darwin led men to take biology seriously once more, they had to reintroduce these functional concepts the physicists had forgotten—means and end, function, teleology, and time. Even when, with Darwin's generation, men interpreted living processes "mechanistically"—that is, when they tried to reduce them to *nothing but* chemical reactions—these reactions still remained the mechanisms by which living processes function. An egg is a chemical process, but it is not a mere chemical process. It is one that is going places—even when, in our world of chance and contingency, it ends up in an omelet and not in a chicken. Though it surely be a chemical process, we cannot understand it adequately without knowing the kind of chicken it has the power to become.

And then the physicists, seeking elements simpler than the "atom," found them cooperating from the start in a complex interrelated system, the "field." Physics has been forced by its new world of radiant energy to introduce very much the same functional relations, the same kind of temporal and systematic structures, the biologists had already been discovering. Gone are the tiny billiard balls; instead we find systematically organized electrical fields. Now the "field" of the physicists is not just like a chicken; but it is a lot more like one than is a billiard game.

As a result of this scientific advance, our present-day philosophies of nature no longer find living processes radically different from other natural processes. Both exhibit a similar type of relation and pattern, and require similar concepts for their understanding. Other natural processes are not so complex and intricate as those of living things; but they are much more so than the ways of billiard balls.

The consequences of this revolution in ideas precipitated by Darwin are far-reaching. First, we no longer ask whether "life" is to be understood in terms of its mechanisms or of its ends. The answer is, both. Means and ends are both seen to be inseparable aspects of natural processes. All processes involve and depend on some "mechanism," and the analysis and discovery of these mechanisms gives us a knowledge of *how* the processes take place. But all processes also involve the *functioning* of those mechanisms, the results they lead to, the outcomes they achieve, the way they cooperate with other natural processes. And only a study of those functionings can give us a knowledge of what these mechanisms *can do*—the results or ends they can effect. There will be no chicken unless the chemical processes of the egg interact with those of the environment. There is no thinking without a brain cooperating with nature. But what eggs—or brains—*can do*, is to be learned only from studying the way they operate. Chemistry will not tell us. Processes involve ends that are reached by means of some mechanism. The two are correlative. And only the Nothing-Butter emphasizes one exclusively, thus raising an issue and starting a fight.

The rediscovery of "process" and what it implies has reminded us of what the Greeks knew, that nature's processes are full of means and ends, of powers and their operations, that is, of functional and teleological relations and values. The very notion of "process" means the achievement of an end. There is, of course, no evidence that ends can ever bring themselves about, or serve as their own mechanisms. But nature is full of ends achieved through natural means and mechanisms.

A second consequence of our new view of nature is that the similarity between the mechanisms involved in all natural processes —including living and human processes—the fact that they are bound up in a community of interaction and can be stated in the same "laws"—is much less surprising. I do not mean that it is less surprising that an egg should become a chicken, or that a brain should think. Neither is what we should expect, before the event. But there is no evidence that nature was designed to meet human expectations. Until we have found how eggs and brains do act, what they manage to produce, we may well be surprised. But when we have found out, we should be surprised if they do not act that way, and we confidently expect them to do so.

What is less surprising, on our new view of nature, is that she should be so economical of means for her profusion of ends. If the simpler processes really follow a pattern very much like that of the most complex, it is not so hard to understand how a very similar type of mechanism can bring them all to pass. We can see how an egg, or a brain, which is itself an intricate and complex electrical system, can serve as the instrument of further complex processes like growing or thinking. But an egg or a brain that was really nothing but tiny billiard balls would offer little hope for our connecting its behavior with the obvious things that eggs and brains can do—little hope for the unification of our knowledge.

Thirdly, the fact that we can extend scientific method indefinitely to new fields becomes more plausible. A method developed to deal with billiard balls, and employing concepts quite adequate for that purpose, will not take you far in treating human life. Indeed, as Kant found, it stops short before the egg. But a method employing functional concepts: means and ends, mechanisms and their operations, systematic organization and vectors, can hope to get somewhere with living processes, and even with complex human activities. Just how it can be extended is no longer an issue to be fought over, but a problem to be worked out in detail.

Finally, nature is once more for us, as for the Greeks, full of implicit ends and ideals, full of "values," just because it is now an affair of processes, of means effecting ends, of things that are "necessary for," "better" and "worse for" other things. It contains so much "natural teleology," in terms of which its various factors can be "evaluated." It takes but a single flower to refute the contention that there are no "values" in nature, no achievement of ends through valuable means. We may even say it is obviously "good for" the planet to go round the sun. Of course, neither the flower nor the planet "finds" it good: only men "find" anything. But surely it does not follow that because only men find anything good or bad, better or worse, what they find is not found. The finding is a genuine cooperation with nature.

It is such a nature our best post-Darwinian knowledge and thought now reveals to us. Within it, there is no longer anything to prevent our working, desperately if we must, upon our pressing human problems. If we fall short, the responsibility is ours.

> The fault, dear Brutus, is not in our stars,
> But in ourselves, that we are underlings.

2. But Darwin's ideas not only transformed nature; they also transformed man. They led men to a new conception of the nature of human experience, and revolutionized that concept of "experience" that has been so fundamental in modern philosophy. With man now one animal, one biological organism among others, his experience became fundamentally that of any animal, an interaction between an organism and its environment. "Experience" ceased to be what it had been ever since Descartes and Newton, something exclusively mechanical, a being hit on the head—or the sense organs—by Cartesian particles or Newtonian tiny billiard balls, and seeing stars. For the phenomenalists, from David Hume to Ernst Mach, the billiard balls became dubious, and experience was just seeing stars in succession and coexistence. Such a conception of a purely mechanical experience is still to be found unquestioned in conservative empiricists like A. J. Ayer.

After Darwin, for those who listened—and this does not include the British empiricists—experience became fundamentally biological in character, an active process of adjusting to the environment, and in man, of reconstructing the environment of the organism.

Even Herbert Spencer had the sense to define experience as "the adjustment of internal to external relations." Such a biological conception was easily fused, with those who had read Hegel, with the Hegelian conception of experience as fundamentally social in character. Then men were back with Aristotle once more, for whom experience, though it always involves a physical mechanism, is primarily biological and social. * * *

Finally, Darwinian ideas led to an egalitarianism of differences and varieties of experience. All kinds and sorts are to be taken into account. All are, at the outset at least, on the same level. Thus of James's varieties of religious experience, none is "best." In ethics, for him, every claim is an obligation. In Dewey, every impulse, demand, and experienced good has a *prima facie* right to recognition in moral deliberation. The task of moral philosophy he sees suggesting such reconstruction of the pattern of living and social arrangements as will give them all the fullest possible fulfilment. Here is fused the Romantic openness to all varieties of experience, the experimental temper of mind, and evolutionary expansiveness—what Spencer called "heterogeneity," and Guyau, "fecundity."

3. The transformation of both nature and man effected by Darwinian ideas came to a head in a theme and an enterprise that has dominated philosophizing for a century: the appeal to experience as an instrument of criticism. This is the one theme that unites all present-day philosophical movements: they are all critical philosophies of experience. * * *

There was a fusion of the critical aims and methods of Romantic idealism and Darwinian thought in the appeals to immediate experience of most of the late XIXth-century and early XXth-century critical philosophies of experience. Nietzsche used his *Lebensphilosophie* to criticize the degenerate culture of the second *Reich*. Bergson used creative evolution to criticize mechanistic "finalism." James used his stream of consciousness to criticize association psychology, and to develop his radical empiricism in general. Dewey used experimental naturalism to criticize the classic tradition and the assumptions of modern philosophy. He appealed to direct experience to reconstruct such reflective experience, to art against theoretical vision, and to the social against the old individualism. Whitehead employed his philosophy of organism to criticize the abstractness and discreteness of Newton and Hume. Husserl resorted to the phenomenology of experience to criticize the psychologism and formalism of the Neo-Kantians, just as Bradley was doing in England. Heidegger and Jaspers have appealed to human *Existenz* to criticize the formalism and "essentialism" of Husserl's phenomenology. The Vienna Circle appealed to immediate observation formulated in protocol sentences to criticize German voluntarism and a-rationalism in general. Wittgenstein appealed to the linguistic usage of ordinary language, as the best clue to normal, undistorted experience, to criticize the logical atomism and reductive analysis he had originally shared with Bertrand Russell.

All these very diverse critical philosophies of experience have a common function. It is to criticize our theories about the world in the light of the world directly encountered: of the world "immediately experienced," say the Americans; of the experienced world "phenomenologically described," say the Continentals; of the world described in "protocol sentences," say the logical positivists; of the world implied in the many ways we use "ordinary language," say the elucidators of the "logical characteristics" of our uses of language.

But it is not merely the function of the appeal to direct experience that is common to all these critical philosophies. What is found through that appeal, as the setting for our reflective experience, for all our theories and systems, is likewise common. The world directly encountered is found, by all these varied methods, to be fundamentally temporal in character, to be specific and plural, a many rather than a neat one, to be capable of inquiry and manipulation in detail, to be subject to experimental reconstruction, and to be fundamentally functional in character, an affair of many specific means-end relations.

Now these are precisely the characters Dewey assigned in 1909 to the "new mode of thinking" initiated by Darwin. Though they speak in very different tongues, the startling agreement in conclusions among the different philosophical movements today seems to indicate that Darwin was right. The way he suggested we look at the world is still, to our best and most critical knowledge, pretty close to what the world is actually like. On the hundredth anniversary of the publication of his *magnum opus*, and hundred and fiftieth anniversary of his birth, could any featherless biped, or indeed any rational animal, claim a better record?

THOMAS HENRY HUXLEY

Evolution and Ethics (1893) †

* * *

The propounders of what are called the 'ethics of evolution', when the 'evolution of ethics' would usually better express the

---

† Thomas Henry Huxley's essay was the Romanes lecture for 1893; it is reprinted in Thomas Henry Huxley and Julian Huxley, *Touchstone for Ethics* (New York and London, 1947), pp. 67–112.

object of their speculations, adduce a number of more or less interesting facts and more or less sound arguments, in favour of the origin of the moral sentiments, in the same way as other natural phenomena, by a process of evolution. I have little doubt, for my own part, that they are on the right track; but as the immoral sentiments have no less been evolved, there is, so far, as much natural sanction for the one as the other. The thief and the murderer follow nature just as much as the philanthropist. Cosmic evolution may teach us how the good and the evil tendencies of man may have come about; but, in itself, it is incompetent to furnish any better reason why what we call good is preferable to what we call evil than we had before. Some day, I doubt not, we shall arrive at an understanding of the evolution of the æsthetic faculty; but all the understanding in the world will neither increase nor diminish the force of the intuition that this is beautiful and that is ugly.

There is another fallacy which appears to me to pervade the so-called 'ethics of evolution'. It is the notion that because, on the whole, animals and plants have advanced in perfection of organization by means of the struggle for existence and the consequent 'survival of the fittest'; therefore men in society, men as ethical beings, must look to the same process to help them towards perfection. I suspect that this fallacy has arisen out of the unfortunate ambiguity of the phrase 'survival of the fittest'. 'Fittest' has a connotation of 'best'; and about 'best' there hangs a moral flavour. In cosmic nature, however, what is 'fittest' depends upon the conditions. Long since,[1] I ventured to point out that if our hemisphere were to cool again, the survival of the fittest might bring about, in the vegetable kingdom, a population of more and more stunted and humbler and humbler organisms, until the 'fittest' that survived might be nothing but lichens, diatoms, and such microscopic organisms as those which give red snow its colour; while, if it became hotter, the pleasant valleys of the Thames and Isis might be uninhabitable by any animated beings save those that flourish in a tropical jungle. They, as the fittest, the best adapted to the changed conditions, would survive.

Men in society are undoubtedly subject to the cosmic process. As among other animals, multiplication goes on without cessation, and involves severe competition for the means of support. The struggle for existence tends to eliminate those less fitted to adapt themselves to the circumstances of their existence. The strongest, the most self-assertive, tend to tread down the weaker. But the influence of the cosmic process on the evolution of society is the

---

1. 'Criticisms on the Origin of Species,' 1864. *Collected Essays,* vol. ii, p. 91. [1894].

greater the more rudimentary its civilization. Social progress means a checking of the cosmic process at every step and the substitution for it of another, which may be called the ethical process; the end of which is not the survival of those who may happen to be the fittest, in respect of the whole of the conditions which obtain, but of those who are ethically the best.[2]

As I have already urged, the practice of that which is ethically best—what we call goodness or virtue—involves a course of conduct which, in all respects, is opposed to that which leads to success in the cosmic struggle for existence. In place of ruthless self-assertion it demands self-restraint; in place of thrusting aside, or treading down, all competitors, it requires that the individual shall not merely respect, but shall help his fellows; its influence is directed, not so much to the survival of the fittest, as to the fitting of as many as possible to survive. It repudiates the gladiatorial theory of existence. It demands that each man who enters into the enjoyment of the advantages of a polity shall be mindful of his debt to those who have laboriously constructed it; and shall take heed that no act of his weakens the fabric in which he has been permitted to live. Laws and moral precepts are directed to the end of curbing the cosmic process and reminding the individual of his duty to the community, to the protection and influence of which he owes, if not existence itself, at least the life of something better than a brutal savage.

It is from neglect of these plain considerations that the fanatical individualism [3] of our time attempts to apply the analogy of cosmic nature to society. Once more we have a misapplication of the stoical injunction to follow nature; the duties of the individual to the State are forgotten, and his tendencies to self-assertion are dignified by the name of rights. It is seriously debated whether the members of a community are justified in using their combined strength to constrain one of their number to contribute his share

2. Of course, strictly speaking, social life, and the ethical process in virtue of which it advances towards perfection, are part and parcel of the general process of evolution, just as the gregarious habit of innumerable plants and animals, which has been of immense advantage to them, is so. A hive of bees is an organic polity, a society in which the part played by each member is determined by organic necessities. Queens, workers, and drones are, so to speak, castes, divided from one another by marked physical barriers. Among birds and mammals, societies are formed, of which the bond in many cases seems to be purely psychological; that is to say, it appears to depend upon the liking of the individuals for one another's company. The tendency of individuals to over self-assertion is kept down by fighting. Even in these rudimentary forms of society, love and fear come into play, and enforce a greater or less renunciation of self-will. To this extent the general cosmic process begins to be checked by a rudimentary ethical process, which is, strictly speaking, part of the former, just as the 'governor' in a steam-engine is part of the mechanism of the engine. 3. See 'Government: Anarchy or Regimentation'. *Collected Essays*, vol. i. pp. 413–418. It is this form of political philosophy to which I conceive the epithet of 'reasoned savagery' to be strictly applicable. [1894.]

to the maintenance of it; or even to prevent him from doing his best to destroy it. The struggle for existence, which has done such admirable work in cosmic nature, must, it appears, be equally beneficent in the ethical sphere. Yet if that which I have insisted upon is true; if the cosmic process has no sort of relation to moral ends; if the imitation of it by man is inconsistent with the first principles of ethics; what becomes of this surprising theory?

Let us understand, once for all, that the ethical progress of society depends, not on imitating the cosmic process, still less in running away from it, but in combating it. It may seem an audacious proposal thus to pit the microcosm against the macrocosm and to set man to subdue nature to his higher ends; but I venture to think that the great intellectual difference between the ancient times with which we have been occupied and our day, lies in the solid foundation we have acquired for the hope that such an enterprise may meet with a certain measure of success. * * *

SIR JULIAN HUXLEY

Evolutionary Ethics (1943) †

* * *

I. T. H. Huxley's Antithesis Between Ethics and Evolution

* * * For T. H. Huxley, fifty years ago, there was a fundamental contradiction between the ethical process and the cosmic process. By the former, he meant the universalist ethics of the Victorian enlightenment, bred by nineteenth-century humanitarianism out of traditional Christian ethics, and in him personally tinged by a noble but stern puritanism and an almost fanatical devotion to scientific truth and its pursuit. And the cosmic process he restricted almost entirely to biological evolution and to the selective struggle for existence on which it depends. 'The ethical progress of society'—this was the main conclusion of his Romanes lecture—'consists, not in imitating the cosmic process, still less in running away from it, but in combating it'.

To-day, that contradiction can, I believe, be resolved—on the one hand by extending the concept of evolution both backward into the inorganic and forward into the human domain, and on the other by considering ethics not as a body of fixed principles, but as a product of evolution, and itself evolving. In both cases, the

† "Evolutionary Ethics" was the Romanes Lecture for 1943; it is reprinted   in *Touchstone for Ethics*, pp. 113–166.

intellectual tool which has given us new insight is that of developmental analysis—the scientific study of change, of becoming, of the production of novelty, whether of life from not-life, of a baby from an ovum and a man from a baby, of ants and swallows and tigers out of ancestral protozoa, of civilized societies out of barbarism and barbarism out of the dim beginnings of social life. * * *

V. *Evolutionary Levels and Directions*

During the thousand million years of organic evolution, the degree of organization attained by the highest forms of life increased enormously. And with this there increased also the possibilities of control, of independence, of inner harmony and self-regulation, of experience. Compared with what a protozoan or a polyp can show, the complexity of later forms of life, like bee or swallow or antelope, is stupendous, their capacity for self-regulation almost miraculous, their experience so much richer and more varied as to be different in kind.

And finally there is, in certain types of animals, an increase in consciousness or mind. Whether mind be a sudden emergent or, as biologists prefer to think, a gradual development of some universal property of the world-stuff, mind of the same general nature as ours is clearly present on the higher organizational levels of life, and at least in the birds and mammals we can trace its steady evolution towards greater capacities for feeling, knowing, willing, and understanding.

There is thus one direction within the multifariousness of evolution which we can legitimately call progress. It consists in the capacity to attain a higher degree of organization, but without closing the door to further advance. In the organic phase of evolution, this depends on all-round improvement as opposed to the limited improvement or one-sided specialiation which, it can be demonstrated, automatically leads sooner or later to a dead end, after which no true advance is possible, but only minor variations on an already existent theme. Insects appear to have reached an evolutionary dead end over 30 million years ago; birds a little later; and all the main lines of higher mammals except the primates—carnivores, ungulates, whales, bats, rodents, and so forth—at least no later than the early Pliocene. Most evolutionary lines or trends are specializations which either thus come to a stop or are extinguished; true progress or the unlimited capacity for advance is rare.

However, the details of biological evolution need not concern us overmuch, since during the last half-million years or so a new and more comprehensive type of order of organization has arisen; and on this new level, the world-stuff is once more introduced to altogether new possibilities, and has quite new methods of evolutionary operation at its disposal. Biological or organic evolution has at its upper end been merged into and largely succeeded by conscious or social evolution.

Just as biological evolution was rendered both possible and inevitable when material organization became self-reproducing, so conscious evolution was rendered both possible and inevitable when social organization became self-reproducing. This occurred when the evolving world-stuff, in the form of ancestral man, became capable of true speech and conceptual thought. For just as animal organization, however elaborate, had been transmissible across the generation by the vehicle of the chromosomes and genes, so from then on conscious experience could be transmitted down the stream of time on the vehicle of words and other symbols and representations. And somewhat as sexual fusion made possible the pooling of individual mutations, so reason made possible the pooling of individual experiences. For the first time in evolution, tradition and education became continuous and cumulative processes.

With this, a new type of organization came into being—that of self-reproducing society. So long as man survives as a species (and there is no reason for thinking he will not) there seems no possibility for any other form of life to push up to this new organizational level. Indeed there are grounds for suspecting that biological evolution has come to an end, so far as any sort of major advance is concerned. Thus further large-scale evolution has once again been immensely restricted in extent, being now it would seem confined to the single species man; but at the same time again immensely accelerated in its speed, through the operation of the new mechanisms now available.

In any case, it is only through social evolution that the world-stuff can now realize radically new possibilities. Mechanical interaction and natural selection still operate, but have become of secondary importance. For good or evil, the mechanism of evolution has in the main been transferred onto the social or conscious level. Part of the blind struggle for existence between separate individuals or groups is transposed into conflict in consciousness, either within the individual mind or within the tradition which is the vehicle of pooled social consciousness. The slow methods of variation and heredity are outstripped by the speedier processes of acquiring and transmitting experience. New tools of living originated *ex post facto* as biological adaptations or unconscious adjustments become increasingly unimportant compared with the tools deliberately produced by human design. Physical trial and error can be more and more transposed to the sphere of thought.

And in so far as the mechanism of evolution ceases to be blind and automatic and becomes conscious, ethics can be injected into the evolutionary process. Before man that process was merely amoral. After his emergence onto life's stage it became possible to introduce faith, courage, love of truth, goodness—in a word moral purpose—into evolution. It became possible, but the possibility has been and is too often unrealized. It is the business of an enlightened ethics to help in its realization.

The attainment of the social type of organization opens a new and apparently indefinite range of possibilities to the evolving world-stuff. It can now proceed to some understanding of the cosmos which gave it birth, and of the conflicts which it must endure; it can for the first time consciously both appreciate and create beauty, truth, and other values; it becomes aware of good and evil; it becomes capable of new emotional states like love, reverence, or mystical contemplation and peace; it can inject some of its own purpose into events; finally and most significantly, many of the new experiences that are being made available have inherent value.

Even in the brief space that man has been in existence, there has been considerable evolutionary advance in the degree of social organization, considerable realization of new possibilities previously unavailable to life. What is more, the general rate of advance, in spite of periodic setbacks, has been growing progressively quicker. There is every reason to believe that through the attainment of this new level of conscious and social organization, the evolutionary process has taken on a new and apparently indefinite lease of life.

VI. *Evolution and general ethical standards*

What guidance does all this give us in our search for independent ethical standards? There are, it seems to me, three rather separate areas in which such guidance may be found—that of nature as a whole, that of human society, and that of the human individual. All three must be considered from the dynamic angle of evolution or development; and when thus considered, all three are interlocked.

In the broadest possible terms evolutionary ethics must be based on a combination of a few main principles: that it is right to realize ever new possibilities in evolution, notably those which are valued for their own sake; that it is right both to respect human individuality and to encourage its fullest development; that it is right to construct a mechanism for further social evolution which shall satisfy these prior conditions as fully, efficiently, and as rapidly as possible.

To translate these arid-sounding generalities into concrete terms and satisfying forms is beyond the scope of a lecture; it is a task for an entire generation. But I must attempt a certain expansion, and some development of their implications.

When we look at evolution as a whole, we find, among the many directions which it has taken, one which is characterized by introducing the evolving world-stuff to progressively higher levels of organization and so to new possibilities of being, action, and experience. This direction has culminated in the attainment of a state where the world-stuff (now moulded into human shape) finds that it experiences some of the new possibilities as having value in or for themselves; and further that among these it assigns higher and lower degrees of value, the higher values being those which are more intrinsically or more pemanently satisfying, or involve a greater degree of perfection. * * *

If desirable direction of evolution provides the most comprehensive (though also the least specific) external standard for our ethics, then one very important corollary at once follows: namely that social organization should be planned, not to prevent change, nor merely to permit it, but to encourage it. Thus a static stability is undesirable, and a complete or static certitude of ethical belief itself becomes unethical. * * *

Furthermore, the rate as well as the direction of change is important. Theoretically, there must be an optimum rate of change, above which stability is endangered and the sacrifices of the present are excessive, below which advance is so slow that the welfare of future generations is needlessly impaired. Thus anything which retards advance below this optimum, even if it be moving in the same right direction, is wrong.

Next we have the guidance derived from an understanding of the workings of human societies. In the first place, it is clear on evolutionary grounds that the individual is in a real sense higher than the State or the social organism. The possibilities which are of value for their own sake, and whose realization must be one of our primary aims, are not experienced by society as a unit, but by some or all of the human beings which compose it.

All claims that the State has an intrinsically higher value than the individual are false. They turn out, on closer scrutiny, to be rationalizations or myths aimed at securing greater power or privilege for a limited group which controls the machinery of the State.

On the other hand the individual is meaningless in isolation, and the possibilities of development and self-realization open to him are conditioned and limited by the nature of the social organization. The individual thus has duties and responsibilities as well as rights and privileges, or if you prefer it, finds certain outlets and satisfactions (such as devotion to a cause, or participation in a joint enterprise) only in relation to the type of society in which he lives. * * *

With this we are brought into the area of the individual. The human individual is not merely inherently higher than the State, but the rightly-developed individual is, and will continue to be, the highest product of evolution, even though he needs the proper organization of society to achieve his welfare and realize his development.

The phrase *rightly-developed* begs a question. I would suggest that it includes not only the full, all-round development of potentialities, but also the one-sided development of particular possibilities or special talents, provided always that these restrict the development or interfere with the welfare of other individuals or groups as little as possible. * * *

If the right development of the individual is an evolutionary end in itself, then it is right that there should be universal equality of opportunity for development, and to the fullest degree. The reciprocal of this is the rightness of unselfishness and kindness, as the necessary means for realizing general well-being. Thus individual ethics will always in large measure be concerned with the conflict between the claims of self-expression and self-sacrifice, and their best reconciliation through love.

The Golden Rule, as various philosophers have pointed out, is an impossible ideal; it cannot ever be put into practice, not merely because of the imperfections of human nature, but also because it does not provide a real basis on which to make practical ethical decisions. However, it is the hyperbole beyond a perfectly practical ideal—the extension of more opportunity of fuller life to more human beings. Psychologically, this can be promoted by extending the child's love and sympathy to an ever-widening circle, and linking the idea of any and all avoidable suffering and stunting of development with his personal sense of wrong. And it can be promoted institutionally by the rational acceptance of certain moral principles, and then by laws and practical measures designed to give effect to those principles.

To accept this view is to give a new content to that sector of ethics concerned with justice. * * *

But in our grossly imperfect world the individual will continue to suffer painful conflict. He must reflect that this is one of the means by which we as a species have emerged into a new and more hopeful phase of evolution. It is part of the price we pay for being men.

And society will long be faced with the conflict between the general affirmation and the particular denial of principles that we know to be right. Our ethical principles assure us that war is a general wrong: yet to urge it may still be a particular right. Tolerance and kindness are general virtues: yet ruthless suppression of opponents may be a particular duty. It is the eternal conflict between means and ends. There is a slight comfort in the reflection that fuller understanding of general principles will give us more assurance of what ends are right.

Nor will clearer ethical vision prevent us from suffering what we feel as injustice at the hands of the cosmos—congenital deformity, unmerited suffering, physical disaster, the early death of loved ones. Such cosmic injustice represents the persistence of chance and its amorality into human life: we may gradually reduce its amount but we assuredly shall never abolish it. Man is the heir of evolution: but he is also its martyr. All living species provide their evolutionary sacrifice: only man knows that he is a victim.

But man is not only the heir of the past and the victim of the present: he is also the agent through whom evolution may unfold its further possibilities. Here, it seems, is the solution of our riddle of ethical relativity: the ultimate guarantees for the correctness of our labels of rightness and wrongness are to be sought for among the facts of evolutionary direction. Here, too, is to be found the reconciliation of T. H. Huxley's antithesis between the ethical and the cosmic process: for the cosmic process, we now perceive, is continued into human affairs. Thus man can impose moral principles upon ever-widening areas of the cosmic process, in whose further slow unfolding he is now the protagonist. He can inject his ethics into the heart of evolution.

PIERRE TEILHARD DE CHARDIN

The Phenomenon of Man (1955) †

Preface

If this book is to be properly understood, it must be read not as a work on metaphysics, still less as a sort of theological essay, but purely and simply as a scientific treatise. The title itself indicates

† Pierre Teilhard de Chardin (1881–1955), French priest and paleontologist, was banned from France for many years by his religious superiors because of the unorthodoxy of his thinking on human evolution. *The Phenomenon of Man*, representing the culmination of this thought, was written in 1938 but not permitted publication until 1955, after Teilhard's death. The present selections are from the Preface and from Book 4, Chapter 2, of the 1961 American edition.

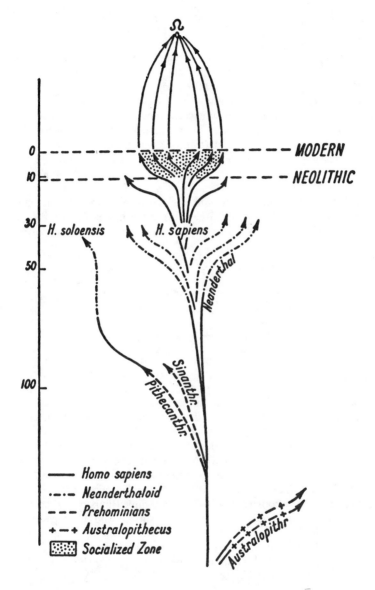

The development of the Human Layer. The figures on the left indicate thousands of years. They are a minimum estimate and should probably be at least doubled. The hypothetical zone of convergence on the point Omega is obviously not to scale. By analogy with other living layers, its duration should certainly run into millions of years.

that. This book deals with man *solely* as a phenomenon; but it also deals with the *whole* phenomenon of man.

In the first place, it deals with man *solely* as a phenomenon. The pages which follow do not attempt to give an explanation of the world, but only an introduction to such an explanation. Put quite simply, what I have tried to do is this; I have chosen man as the centre, and around him I have tried to establish a coherent order between antecedents and consequences. I have not tried to discover a system of ontological and casual relations between the elements of the universe, but only an experimental law of recurrence which would express their successive appearance in time. * * *

But this book also deals with the *whole* phenomenon of man. Without contradicting what I have just said (however much it may appear to do so) it is this aspect which might possibly make my suggestions *look* like a philosophy. * * *

1. *The Convergence of the Person and the Omega Point*

A. THE PERSONAL UNIVERSE

Unlike the primitives who gave a face to every moving thing, or the early Greeks who deified all the aspects and forces of nature, modern man is obsessed by the need to depersonalise (or impersonalise) all that he most admires. There are two reasons for this tendency. The first is *analysis*, that marvellous instrument of scientific research to which we owe all our advances but which, breaking down synthesis after synthesis, allows one soul after another to escape, leaving us confronted with a pile of dismantled machinery, and evanescent particles. The second reason lies in the discovery of the sidereal world, so vast that it seems to do away with all proportion between our own being and the dimensions of the cosmos around us. Only one reality seems to survive and be capable of succeeding and spanning the infinitesimal and the immense: energy—that floating, universal entity from which all emerges and into which all falls back as into an ocean; energy, the new spirit; the new god. So, at the world's Omega, as at its Alpha, lies the Impersonal.

Under the influence of such impressions as these, it looks as though we have lost both respect for the person and understanding of his true nature. We end up by admitting that to be pivoted on oneself, to be able to say 'I,' is the privilege (or rather the blemish) of the element in the measure to which the latter closes the door on all the rest and succeeds in setting himself up at the antipodes of the All. In the opposite direction we conceive the 'ego' to be diminishing and eliminating itself, with the trend to what is most real and most lasting in the world, namely the Collective and the Universal. Personality is seen as a specifically corpuscular and ephemeral property; a prison from which we must try to escape.

Intellectually, that is more or less where we stand today.

Yet if we try, as I have done in this essay, to pursue the logic and coherence of facts to the very end, we seem to be led to the precisely opposite view by the notions of space-time and evolution.

We have seen and admitted that evolution is an ascent towards consciousness. That is no longer contested even by the most materialistic, or at all events by the most agnostic of humanitarians. Therefore it should culminate forwards in some sort of supreme consciousness. But must not that consciousness, if it is to be supreme, contain in the highest degree what is the perfection of our consciousness—the illuminating involution of the being upon itself? * * *

All our difficulties and repulsions as regards the opposition between the All and the Person would be dissipated if only we understood that, by structure, the noosphere [1] (and more generally the world) represent a whole that is not only closed but also *centred*. Because it contains and engenders consciousness, space-time is necessarily *of a convergent nature*. Accordingly its enormous layers, followed in the right direction, must somewhere ahead become involuted to a point which we might call *Omega*, which fuses and consumes them integrally in itself. * * *

Seen from this point of view, the universe, without losing any of its immensity and thus without suffering any anthropomorphism, begins to take shape: henceforward to think it, undergo it and make it act, it is *beyond* our souls that we must look, *not the other way round*. In the perspective of a noogenesis, time and space become truly humanised—or rather super-humanised. Far from being mutually exclusive, the Universal and Personal (that is to say the 'centred') grow in the same direction and culminate simultaneously in each other.

It is therefore a mistake to look for the extension of our being or of the noosphere in the Impersonal. The Future-Universal could not be anything else but the Hyper-Personal—at the Omega Point.

B. THE PERSONALISING UNIVERSE

Personalisation. It is by this eternal deepening of consciousness upon itself that we have characterised the particular destiny of the

1. For an explanation of this and other words of Teilhard's coining, see the Huxley commentary which follows [Editor].

element that has become fully itself by crossing the threshold of reflection—and there, as regards the fate of individual human beings—we brought our inquiry to a provisional halt. *Personalisation:* the same type of progress reappears here, but this time it defines the collective future of totalised grains of thought. There is an identical function for the element as for the sum of the elements brought together in a synthesis. * * *

* * * It would be mistaken to represent Omega to ourselves simply as a centre born of the fusion of elements which it collects, or annihilating them in itself. By its structure Omega, in its ultimate principle, can only be a *distinct Centre radiating at the core of a system of centres;* a grouping in which personalisation of the All and personalisations of the elements reach their maximum, simultaneously and without merging, under the influence of a supremely autonomous focus of union.[2] That is the only picture which emerges when we try to apply the notion of collectivity with remorseless logic to a granular whole of thoughts.

And at this point we begin to see the motives for the fervour and the impotence which accompany every egoistic solution of life. Egoism, whether person or racial, is quite rightly excited by the idea of the element ascending through faithfulness to life, to the extremes of the incommunicable and the exclusive that it holds within it. It *feels* right. Its only mistake, but a fatal one, is *to confuse individuality with personality.* In trying to separate itself as much as possible from others, the element individualises itself; but in doing so it becomes retrograde and seeks to drag the world backwards towards plurality and into matter. In fact it diminishes itself and loses itself. To be fully ourselves it is in the opposite direction, in the direction of convergence with all the rest, that we must advance—towards the 'other.' * * *

* * * Thus, amongst the various forms of psychic inter-activity animating the noosphere, the energies we must identify, harness and develop before all others are those of an 'intercentric' nature, if we want to give effective help to the progress of evolution in ourselves.

Which brings us to the problem of love.

2. Love as Energy

We are accustomed to consider (and with what a refinement of analysis!) only the sentimental face of love, the joy and miseries it causes us. It is in its natural dynamism and its evolutionary significance that I shall be dealing with it here, with a view to determining the ultimate phases of the phenomenon of man.

2. It is for this central focus, necessarily autonomous, that we shall henceforward reserve the expression 'Omega Point.'

Considered in its full biological reality, love—that is to say the affinity of being with being—is not peculiar to man. It is a general property of all life and as such it embraces, in its varieties and degress, all the forms successively adopted by organised matter. * * * Driven by the forces of love, the fragments of the world seek each other so that the world may come to being. This is no metaphor; and it is much more than poetry. Whether as a force or a curvature, the universal gravity of bodies, so striking to us, is merely the reverse or shadow of that which really moves nature. To perceive cosmic energy 'at the fount' we must, if there is a *within* of things, go down into the internal or radial zone of spiritual attractions.

Love in all its subtleties is nothing more, and nothing less, than the more or less direct trace marked on the heart of the element by the psychical convergence of the universe upon itself.

This, if I am not mistaken, is the ray of light which will help us to see more clearly around us. * * *

We are often inclined to think that we have exhausted the various natural forms of love with a man's love for his wife, his children, his friends and to a certain extent for his country. Yet precisely the most fundamental form of passion is missing from this list, the one which, under the pressure of an involuting universe, precipitates the elements one upon the other in the Whole—cosmic affinity and hence cosmic direction. A universal love is not only psychologically possible; it is the only complete and final way in which we are able to love.

But, with this point made, how are we to explain the appearance all around of us of mounting repulsion and hatred? If such a strong potentiality is besieging us from within and urging us to union, what is it waiting for to pass from potentiality to action? Just this, no doubt that we should overcome the 'anti-personalist' complex which paralyses us, and make up our minds to accept the possibility, indeed the reality, of some *source* of love and *object* of love at the summit of the world above our heads. So long as it absorbs or appears to absorb the person, the collectivity kills the love that is trying to come to birth. As such the collectivity is essentially unlovable. That is where philanthropic systems break down. Common sense is right. It is impossible to give oneself to anonymous number. But if the universe ahead of us assumes a face and a heart, and so to speak personifies itself,[3] then in the atmosphere created by this focus the elemental attraction will immediately blossom. Then, no doubt, under the heightened pressure of an infolding world, the formidable energies of attraction, still dormant between human molecules, will burst forth. * * *

3. Not, of course, by becoming a person, but by charging itself at the very heart of its development with the dominating and unifying influence of a focus of personal energies and attractions.

3. The Attributes of the Omega Point

After allowing itself to be captivated in excess by the charms of analysis to the extent of falling into illusion, modern thought is at last getting acclimatised once more to the idea of the creative value of synthesis in the evolutionary sense. It is beginning to see that there is definitely *more* in the molecule than in the atom, *more* in the cell than in the molecule, *more* in society than in the individual, and *more* in mathematical construction than in calculations and theorems. We are now inclined to admit that at each further degree of combination *something* which is irreducible to isolated elements *emerges* in a new order. And with this admission, consciousness, life and thought are on the threshold of acquiring a right to existence in terms of science. But science is nevertheless still far from recognizing that this *something* has a particular value of independence and solidity. For, born of an incredible concourse of chances on a precariously assembled edifice, and failing to create any measurable increase of energy by their advent, are not these 'creatures of synthesis,' from the point of view of experiment, the most beautiful as well as the most fragile of things? How could they anticipate or survive the ephemeral union of particles on which their souls have alighted? So in the end, in spite of a half-hearted conversion to spiritual order, it is still on the *elementary* side—that is, towards matter infinitely diluted—that physics and biology look to find the eternal and the Great Stability.

In conformity with this state of mind the idea that some Soul of souls should be developing at the summit of the world is not as strange as might be thought from the present-day views of human reason. After all, is there any other way in which our thought can generalise the Principle of Emergence? At the same time, as this Soul coincides with a supremely improbable coincidence of the totality of elements and causes, it remains understood or implied that it could not form itself save at an extremely distant future and in a total dependence on the reversible laws of energy.

Yet it is precisely from these two restrictions (fragility and distance), both incompatible to my mind with the nature and function of Omega, that we want to rid ourselves—and this for two positive reasons, one of love, the other of survival.

First of all the *reason of Love.* Expressed in terms of internal energy, the cosmic function of Omega consists in initiating and maintaining within its radius the unanimity of the world's 'reflective' particles. But how could it exercise this action were it not in some sort loving and lovable *at this very moment?* Love, I said, dies in contact with the impersonal and the anonymous. With equal infallibility it becomes impoverished with remoteness in space—and still more, much more, with difference in time. For love to be possible there must be co-existence. Accordingly, however marvellous its foreseen figure, Omega could never even so much as equilibrate the play of human attractions and repulsions if it did not act with equal force, that is to say with the same stuff of proximity. With love, as with every other sort of energy, it is within the existing datum that the lines of force must at every instant be enclosed. Neither an ideal centre, nor a potential centre could possibly suffice. A present and real noosphere goes with a real and present centre. To be supremely attractive, Omega must be supremely present. * * *

In Omega we have in the first place the principle we needed to explain both the persistent march of things toward greater consciousness, and the paradoxical solidity of what is most fragile. Contrary to the appearances still admitted by physics, the Great Stability is not at the bottom in the infra-elementary sphere, but at the top in the ultra-synthetic sphere. It is thus entirely by its tangential envelope that the world goes on dissipating itself in a chance way into matter. By its radial nucleus it finds its shape and its natural consistency in gravitating against the tide of probability towards a divine focus of mind which draws it onward.

Thus something in the cosmos escapes from entropy, and does so more and more.

During immense periods in the course of evolution, the radial, obscurely stirred up by the action of the *Prime Mover ahead*, was only able to express itself, in diffuse aggregates, in animal consciousness. And at that stage, not being able, above them, to attach themselves to a support whose order of simplicity was greater than their own, the nuclei were hardly formed before they began to disaggregate. But as soon as, through reflection, a type of unity appeared no longer closed or even centred, but punctiform, the sublime physics of centres came into play. When they became centres, and therefore persons, the elements could at last begin to react, directly as such, to the personalising action of the centre of centres. When consciousness broke through the critical surface of hominisation, it really passed from divergence to convergence and changed, so to speak, both hemisphere and pole. Below that critical 'equator' lay the relapse into multiplicity; above it, the plunge into growing and irreversible unification. Once formed, a reflective centre can no longer change except by involution upon itself. To outward appearance, admittedly, man becomes corrupted just like any animal. But here and there we find an inverse function of the phenomenon. By death, in the animal, the radial is reabsorbed into the tangential, while in man it escapes and is liberated from it. So we come to escape from entropy by turning back to Omega: the *hominisation* of death itself.

Thus from the grains of thought forming the veritable and indestructible atoms of its stuff, the universe—a well-defined universe in the outcome—goes on building itself above our heads in the inverse direction of matter which vanishes. The universe is a collector and conservator, not of mechanical energy, as we supposed, but of persons. All round us, one by one, like a continual exhalation, 'souls' break away, carrying upwards their incommunicable load of consciousness. One by one, yet not in isolation. Since, for each of them, by the very nature of Omega, there can only be one possible point of definitive emersion—that point at which, under the synthesising action of personalising union, the noosphere (furling its elements upon themselves as it too furls upon itself) will reach collectively its point of convergence—at the 'end of the world.'

Three Scientists' Views of Teilhard

SIR JULIAN HUXLEY

Introduction to *The Phenomenon of Man* (1958) †

The Phenomenon of Man is a very remarkable work by a very remarkable human being. Père Teilhard de Chardin was at the same time a Jesuit Father and a distinguished palaeontologist. In *The Phenomenon of Man* he has effected a threefold synthesis—of the material and physical world with the world of mind and spirit; of the past with the future; and of variety with unity, the many with the one. He achieves this by examining every fact and every subject of his investigation *sub specie evolutionis*, with reference to its development in time and to its evolutionary position. Conversely, he is able to envisage the whole of knowable reality not as a static mechanism but as a process. In consequence, he is driven to search for human significance in relation to the trends of that enduring and comprehensive process; the measure of his stature is that he so largely succeeded in the search. * * *

† This selection is from Huxley's Introduction to the English translation of *The Phenomenon of Man.*

Père Teilhard starts from the position that mankind in its totality is a phenomenon to be described and analysed like any other phenomenon: it and all its manifestations, including human history and human values, are proper objects for scientific study.

His second and perhaps most fundamental point is the absolute necessity of adopting an evolutionary point of view. Though for certain limited purposes it may be useful to think of phenomena as isolated statically in time, they are in point of fact never static: they are always processes or parts of processes. The different branches of science combine to demonstrate that the universe in its entirety must be regarded as one gigantic process, a process of becoming, of attaining new levels of existence and organization, which can properly be called a genesis or an evolution. For this reason, he uses words like *noogenesis*, to mean the gradual evolution of mind or mental properties, and repeatedly stresses that we should no longer speak of a cosmology but of a *cosmogenesis*. Similarly, he likes to use a pregnant term like *hominisation* to denote the process by which the original proto-human stock became (and is still becoming) more truly human, the process by which potential man realized more and more of his possibilities. Indeed, he extends this evolutionary terminology by employing terms like *ultra-hominisation* to denote the deducible future stage of the process in which man will have so far transcended himself as to demand some new appellation.

With this approach he is rightly and indeed inevitably driven to the conclusion that, since evolutionary phenomena (of course including the phenomenon known as man) are processes, they can never be evaluated or even adequately described solely or mainly in terms of their origins: they must be defined by their direction, their inherent possibilities (including of course also their limitations), and their deducible future trends. He quotes with approval Nietzsche's view that man is unfinished and must be surpassed or completed; and proceeds to deduce the steps needed for his completion.

Père Teilhard was keenly aware of the importance of vivid and arresting terminology. Thus in 1925 he coined the term *noosphere* to denote the sphere of mind, as opposed to, or rather superposed on, the biosphere or sphere of life, and acting as a transforming agency promoting hominisation (or as I would put it, progressive psychosocial evolution). He may perhaps be criticized for not defining the term more explicitly. By *noosphere* did he intend simply the total pattern of thinking organisms (i.e. human beings) and their activity, including the patterns of their interrelations: or did he intend the special environment of man, the systems of organized

344 · Sir Julian Huxley

thought and its products in which men move and have their being, as fish swim and reproduce in rivers and the sea? [1] Perhaps it might have been better to restrict *noosphere* to the first-named sense, and to use something like *noosystem* for the second. But certainly *noosphere* is a valuable and thought-provoking word.

He usually uses *convergence* to denote the tendency of mankind, during its evolution, to superpose centripetal on centrifugal trends, so as to prevent centrifugal differentiation from leading to fragmentation, and eventually to incorporate the results of differentiation in an organized and unified pattern. Human convergence was first manifested on the genetic or biological level: after *Homo sapiens* began to differentiate into distinct races (or *subspecies*, in more scientific terminology) migration and intermarriage prevented the pioneers from going further, and led to increasing interbreeding between all human variants. As a result, man is the only successful type which has remained as a single interbreeding group of species, and has not radiated out into a number of biologically separated assemblages (like the birds, with about 8,500 species, or the insects with over half a million).

Cultural differentiation set in later, producing a number of psychosocial units with different cultures. However, these 'interthinking groups,' as one writer has called them, are never so sharply separated as are biological species; and with time, the process known to anthropologists as cultural diffusion, facilitated by migration and improved communications, led to an accelerating counter-process of cultural convergence, and so towards the union of the whole human species into a single interthinking group based on a single self-developing framework of thought (or noosystem).

In parenthesis, Père Teilhard showed himself aware of the danger that this tendency might destroy the valuable results of cultural diversification, and lead to drab uniformity instead of to a rich and potent pattern of variety-in-unity. However, perhaps because he was (rightly) so deeply concerned with establishing a global unification of human awareness as a necessary prerequisite for any real future progress of mankind, and perhaps also because he was by nature and inclination more interested in rational and scientific thought than in the arts, he did not discuss the evolutionary value of cultural variety in any detail, but contented himself by maintain-

---

1. In *Le Phénomène Humain* (p. 201) he refers to the *noosphere* as a new layer or membrane on the earth's surface, a 'thinking layer' superposed on the living layer of the *biosphere* and the lifeless layer of inorganic material, the *lithosphere*. But in his earlier formulation of 1925, in *La Vision du Passé* (p. 92), he calls it 'une sphère de la réflexion, de l'invention consciente, de l'union sentie des âmes.'

ing that East and West are culturally complementary, and that both are needed for the further synthesis and unification of world thought.

Before passing to the full implications of human convergence, I must deal with Père Teilhard's valuable but rather difficult concept of *complexification*. This concept includes, as I understand it, the genesis of increasingly elaborate organization during cosmogenesis, as manifested in the passage from subatomic units to atoms, from atoms to inorganic and later to organic molecules, thence to the first subcellular living units or self-replicating assemblages of molecules, and then to cells, to multicellular individuals, to cephalized metazoa with brains, to primitive man, and now to civilized societies.

But it involves something more. He speaks of complexification as an all-pervading tendency, involving the universe in all its parts in an *enroulement organique sur soi-même,* or by an alternative metaphor, as a *reploiement sur soi-même.* He thus envisages the world-stuff as being 'rolled up' or 'folded in' upon itself, both locally and in its entirety, and adds that the process is accompanied by an increase of energetic 'tension' in the resultant 'corpuscular' organizations, or individualized constructions of increased organizational complexity. For want of a better English phrase, I shall use *convergent integration* to define the operation of this process of self-complexification. * * *

Père Teilhard, extrapolating from the past into the future, envisaged the process of human convergence as tending to a final state,[2] which he called 'point *Omega,*' as opposed to the *Alpha* of elementary material particles and their energies. If I understand him aright, he considers that two factors are co-operating to promote this further complexification of the noosphere. One is the increase of knowledge about the universe at large, from the galaxies and stars to human societies and individuals. The other is the increase of psychosocial pressure on the surface of our planet. The result of the one is that the noosphere incorporates ever more facts of the cosmos, including the facts of its general direction and its trends in time, so as to become more truly a microcosm, which (like all incorporated knowledge) is both a mirror and a directive agency. The result of the other is the increased unification and the

2. Presumably, in designating this state as Omega, he believed that it was a truly final condition. It might have been better to think of it merely as a novel state or mode of organization, beyond which the human imagination cannot at present pierce, though perhaps the strange facts of extra-sensory perception unearthed by the infant science of parapsychology may give us a clue as to a possible more ultimate state.

increased intensity of the system of human thought. The combined result, according to Père Teilhard, will be the attainment of point Omega, where the noosphere will be intensely unified and will have achieved a 'hyperpersonal' organisation.

Here his thought is not fully clear to me. Sometimes he seems to equate this future hyperpersonal psychosocial organisation with an emergent Divinity: at one place, for instance, he speaks of the trend as a *Christogenesis*; and elsewhere he appears not to be guarding himself sufficiently against the dangers of personifying the nonpersonal elements of reality. Sometimes, too, he seems to envisage as desirable the merging of individual human variety in this new unity. Though many scientists may, as I do, find it impossible to follow him all the way in his gallant attempt to reconcile the supernatural elements in Christianity with the facts and implications of evolution, this in no way detracts from the positive value of his naturalistic general approach. * * *

Once he had grasped and faced the fact of man as an evolutionary phenomenon, the way was open towards a new and comprehensive system of thought. It remained to draw the fullest conclusions from this central concept of man as the spearhead of evolution on earth, and to follow out the implications of this approach in as many fields as possible. The biologist may perhaps consider that in *The Phenomenon of Man* he paid insufficient attention to genetics and the possibilities and limitations of natural selection,[3] the theologian that his treatment of the problems of sin and suffering was inadequate or at least unorthodox, the social scientist that he failed to take sufficient account of the facts of political and social history. But he saw that what was needed at the moment was a broad sweep and a comprehensive treatment. This was what he essayed in *The Phenomenon of Man*. In my view he achieved a remarkable success, and opened up vast territories of thought to further exploration and detailed mapping. * * *

GEORGE GAYLORD SIMPSON

Evolutionary Theology: The New Mysticism (1964) †

* * * The conflict between science and religion has a single and simple cause. It is the designation as religiously canonical of any con-

3. Though in his Institute for Human Studies he envisaged a section of Eugenics.
† This selection is from Chapter 11 of Simpson's *This View of Life* (New York, 1964). George Gaylord Simpson (b. 1902) is professor emeritus of Harvard University and professor of geosciences at the University of Arizona.

ception of the material world open to scientific investigation. That is a basis for conflict even when religion and science happen to agree as to the material facts. The religious canon (if normally designated as such) demands absolute acceptance not subject to test or revision. Science necessarily rejects certainty and predicates acceptance on objective testing and the possibility of continual revision. As a matter of fact, most of the dogmatic religions have exhibited a perverse talent for taking the wrong side on the most important concepts of the material universe, from the structure of the solar system to the origin of man. The result has been constant turmoil for many centuries, and the turmoil will continue as long as religious canons prejudge scientific questions. * * *

I am no theologian, natural or otherwise, and I am unwilling to pose as one. Here I am also not directly or primarily concerned with the conflict between science and religion, but with a peculiar, related interaction of the two. The path of religious intuition or of mystic communion need not have conscious connection with the material world, and indeed this is one of several ways in which the conflict with science can be successfully resolved. However, for some scientists there has seemed to be such a connection, and then some reconciliation or fusion of the two conceptual schemes has been sought. The relationships envisioned vary greatly. For Julian Huxley (*Religion Without Revelation*) theology itself becomes a subject for scientific investigation and religious emotion is a psychological fact centering on direct experience of sacredness in the universe. For Teilhard de Chardin the mystic conviction is overwhelming and primary; it is the premise for all interpretation and overrides any consideration of objective science. Huxley and Teilhard could hardly differ more as regards theories of evolution, attitudes toward science, and conclusions as to theology, but they both have proposed systems in which, in quite different ways and proportions, science and mysticism are involved.

It is that phenomenon that I shall discuss in the present chapter. This will be done mainly by reference to the works of three biologists whom I would call new mystics: Pierre Lecomte du Noüy, Edmund W. Sinnott, and P. Teilhard de Chardin. They are nearly alone, or at the least have been most eloquent, in expression of varieties of evolutionary theology or theological evolution. All three are both finalists and vitalists of sorts and so those minority schools, given short shrift elsewhere in this book, will have some notice. All agree with other finalists and vitalists that a naturalistic theory of evolution has not been and cannot be achieved. All make appeals to the supernatural, in these three cases to different forms of dogmatic Christianity, and all advocate concepts or theories of evolution in which the approaches of science and religion are confused. With varying degrees of overtness, all make some claims that their religious conclusions are derived from scientific premises and interpretations. That aspect has led in some instances to popularity among those piously concerned but not cognizant of the actual issues or capable of judging the theories. * * *

One of Teilhard's fundamental propositions is that all phenomena must be considered as developing dynamically, that is, in an evolutionary manner, in space-time. "It [i.e., evolution] is a general condition to which all theories, all hypotheses, all systems must bow and which they must satisfy henceforward if they are to be thinkable and true." On this basis, unimpeachable in itself, he reviews briefly the evolution of the cosmos and at greater length that of organisms and of man. He is not concerned with details but with the broadest features of the story as it moves onward. These are traced in a style often delightfully poetic but sometimes syntactically overcomplex and often obscurely metaphorical. The whole process, from dissociated atoms to man, is seen as a gradual progress with two revolutionary turning points among others of less importance: first, and early, the achievement of cellular organization; second, and late, the emergence of true man. Much of the intervening story is envisioned in terms of the succession and frequently the replacement of what Teilhard usually called "*nappes*," a term difficult to translate that is rendered as "layers" or "grades" in the English version. The *nappe* phenomenon involves the expansion or radiation of groups that had reached new structural and adaptive levels, and it has been extensively discussed by other evolutionists in those or similar terms.

Teilhard's book is not, however, strictly or even mainly concerned with describing the factual course of evolution. That is "the *without*" of things, and the author is concerned rather with "the *within*." The within is another term for consciousness (the French "*conscience*," another word without a really precise English equivalent), which in turn implies spontaneity and includes every kind of "psychism." Consciousness, in this sense, is stated to be a completely general characteristic of matter, whether in an individual atom or in man, although in the atom it is less organized and less evident. The origin of the cell was critical because it involved a "psychic mutation" introducing a change in the nature of the state of universal consciousness. The origin of man was again critical because at this stage consciousness became self-consciousness, reflection or thought. Now this as yet highest stage of consciousness begins a concentration or involution that will eventually bring it into complete unity, although without loss of personality in that collective hyper-personal. Then the consciousness of the universe, which will have evolved through man, will become eternally concentrated at the "Omega point," free from the perishable planets and material trammels. The whole process is intended; it is the *purpose* of evolution, planned by the God Who is also the Omega into which consciousness is finally to be concentrated. Mystical Christianity is to be the path or the vehicle to ecstatic union with Omega.

Teilhard's first sentence in *The Phenomenon of Man* is as follows:

> If this book is to be properly understood, it must be read not as a work on metaphysics, still less as a sort of theological essay, but purely and simply as a scientific treatise.

In the last chapter (before the epilogue, the postscript, and the appendix) he wrote:

> Man will only continue to work and to research so long as he is prompted by a passionate interest. Now this interest is entirely dependent on the conviction, strictly undemonstrable to science, that the universe has a direction and that it could—indeed, if we are faithful, it should—result in some sort of irreversible perfection. Hence comes belief in progress.

But the direction of evolution toward an irreversible perfection is the whole theme, and not merely a philosophical appendage, of the book. Hence we have a book submitted purely as a scientific treatise and yet devoted to a thesis admittedly undemonstrable scientifically. (The word here translated as "belief" is "*foi*," and the context makes it unmistakable that religious faith is meant.) The anomaly is partly explained by the fact that in this particular manuscript Teilhard did avoid explicit discussion of certain points in dogmatic theology. The origin and fate of the individual soul, Adam and Eve and original sin, and the divinity of Christ, for instance, are all alluded to or allowed for, but only briefly and in veiled terms. In addition the discussion begins as a sort of mystical science and only gradually, almost imperceptibly, becomes mystical religion. Identification of Omega with God is evident from the beginning to anyone already familiar with Teilhard's thought, but in this book it is not made explicit until the epilogue. In others of Teilhard's works, lacking the pretense of being scientific treatises, Omega is discussed in frankly theological-mystical terms.

The sense in which Teilhard's science, and not alone his theology, must be called mystical may be illustrated from an early passage in *The Phenomenon of Man* (Chapter II) that introduces concepts crucially used throughout all that follows. First he makes a distinction between material energy and spiritual energy, and points out that material energy, for instance that derived from bread, is not closely correlated either in intensity or in variety with spiritual energy, for instance that exhibited by human thought. But surely both of these can be described and at least conceivably may be explained in material terms. A reasonable mechanical analogy is provided by a television set, in which the activity and multiplicity of the pictures are not well correlated with the intensity and uniformity of the power in wires and tubes. One could speak of "picture energy" as distinct from "electron energy," but it would be evident that "energy" is not even roughly comparable in the two senses and that the metaphorical terminology obscures rather than promotes understanding of the phenomena. And surely it is further obfuscation when Teilhard goes on to explain:

> We shall assume that, essentially, all energy [i.e., both material and spiritual energy] is physical in nature; but add that in each particular element this fundamental energy is divided into two distinct components: A *tangential energy* which links the element with all others of the same order (that is to say of the same complexity and the same centricity) as itself in the universe; and a *radial energy* which draws it towards ever greater complexity and centricity—in other words forwards.

Alas! That is no better than double talk, from the statement that something *defined* as spiritual is nevertheless *assumed* to be physical onward through the whole discussion.

As to the mechanism of evolution, obviously a, or indeed *the*, crucial point of the scientific part of the inquiry, Teilhard accepted both Darwinism and Neo-Lamarckism as partial factors. He called Darwinism evolution by chance (although natural selection is the only objectively established antichance evolutionary factor) and therefore considered the nonchance Neo-Lamarckian factors more important (although, as he knew, most biologists consider them not merely unimportant but nonexistent). However, he maintained that these and all proposed material mechanisms of evolution are related only to various details of the process. The basic over-all pattern and also the essentially directional elements in its various lineages he ascribed to orthogenesis.

Orthogenesis was variously defined by Teilhard as the "law of controlled complication" which acts "in a predetermined direction," as "definite orientation regularizing the effects of chance in the play of heredity," as "the manifest property of living matter to form a system in which 'terms *succeed each other* experimentally, following the constantly increasing values of centro-complexity,'" or

as "*directed* transformation (to whatever degree and under what-ever influence 'the direction' may be manifested)." The last defi-nition, which is from a brief manuscript written just before Teilhard's death, is broad enough to include the effects of natural selection, but that was certainly not intended, because Teilhard repeatedly contrasted selection with orthogenesis and indeed usually treated them as complete opposites. Similar imprecision or contra-diction in definition is one of the constant problems in the study of the Teilhardian canon.

Indeed these and other usages of the term "orthogenesis" in Teilhard's work seem at first sight to have no explanatory meaning whatever but to be tautological or circular. History is inherently unrepeatable, so that any segment of a historical sequence (such as that of organic evolution) begins with one state and ends with another. It therefore necessarily has a direction of change, and if orthogenesis is merely that direction, it explains nothing and only applies a Greek term to what is obvious without the term. How-ever, when Teilhard says that the direction is "pre-determined" and that there is only one direction—toward greater "centro-com-plexity," toward Omega, ultimately toward God—then the state-ment is still not explanatory and is obviously not science, but it is no longer trivial.

Now it is easy enough to show that, although evolution is direc-tional as a historical process must always be, it is multidirectional; when all directions are taken into account, it is erratic and oppor-tunistic. Obviously, since man exists, from primordial cell to man was one of the directions, or rather a variety of them in succession, for there was no such sequence *in a straight line* and therefore literally orthogenetic. Teilhard was well aware of the consensus to that effect, but he brushed it aside and refused to grapple with it in terms of the detailed evidence.

Here we come to the real crux of the whole problem: Which are the premises and which the conclusions? One may start from ma-terial evidence and from interpretive probabilities established by tests of hypotheses, that is, from science. Despite the objections of some philosophers and theologians, it is then legitimate to proceed logically from these premises to conclusions regarding the nature of man, of life, or of the universe, even if these conclusions go beyond the realm of science in the strictest sense, and that is not only legit-imate but also necessary if science is to have value beyond serving as a base for technology. On the other hand, one may start from premises of pure faith, nonmaterial and nontestable, therefore non-scientific, and proceed to conclusions in the same field of the na-ture of the material cosmos. It cannot be argued that this approach

from metaphysical or religious premises is *ipso facto* illegitimate. It is, however, proper to insist that its conclusions should not be presented as scientific, and that when they are materially testable they should be submitted to that scientific discipline. Gradual recognition of that necessity has been evident in the historical change in the relationships between science and religion.

Teilhard's major premises are in fact religious and, except for the conclusion that evolution has indeed occurred, his conclusions about evolution derive from those premises and not from scientific premises. One cannot object to the piety or mysticism of *The Phenomenon of Man*, but one can object to its initial claim to be a scientific treatise and to the arrangement that puts its real premises briefly, in part obscurely, as a sort of appendage after the conclusions drawn from them. That this really is an inversion of the logic involved is evident from the whole body of Teilhard's philosophical writings and also from the statements, or admissions, made toward the end of this book. A passage indicating that the main thesis of the book is a matter of faith and not scientifically demonstrable has already been quoted. Elsewhere in Teilhard's work there is abundant testimony that his premises were always in Christian faith and especially in his own mystical vision.

That is evident, too, in the complex concept of Omega that is the key to Teilhard's personal religious system. He explained on various occasions that the concept is necessary in order to keep mankind on its job of self-improvement and in order to evade distasteful thoughts of aimlessness and eventual death—worthy but certainly not scientific premises. The following passage from another of his manuscripts may additionally represent this contribution of Teilhard's, also essential in *The Phenomenon of Man* but there even less clear:

> In order to resolve the internal conflict that opposes the innate evanescence of the planets against the necessary irreversibility developed on their surface by planetized life, it is not enough to draw a veil or to recoil. It is a case for radical exorcism of the specter of Death from our horizon.
>
> Very well, is it not that which permits us to form the idea (a corollary, as we have seen, of the mechanism of planetization) that there exists ahead of, or rather at the heart of, the universe, extrapolated along its axis of complexity, a divine center of convergence. Let us call it, to prejudge nothing and to emphasize its synthesizing and personalizing function, the *Omega point*. Let us suppose that from this universal center, this Omega point, there are continuously emitted rays perceptible only, up to now, by those whom we call "mystic souls." Let us further imagine that as mystical sensitivity or permeability increases with planeti-

zation, the perception of Omega comes to be more widespread, so that the earth is heated psychically while growing colder physically. Then does it not become conceivable that humanity at the end of its involution and totalization within itself may reach a critical point of maturation at the end of which, leaving behind earth and stars to return slowly to the vanishing mass of primordial energy, it will detach itself psychically from the planet in order to rejoin the Omega point, the only irreversible essence of things?

(Translated by me from an essay written in 1945, published in *L'Avenir de L'Homme*, Paris: Editions de Seuil, 1959, pp. 155–156.)

That is mysticism at its purest (if not exactly simplest), without vestige of either premise or conclusion in the realm of science. Teilhard's beliefs as to the course and the causes of evolution are not scientifically acceptable, because they are not in truth based on scientific premises and because to the moderate extent that they are subject to scientific tests they fail those tests. Teilhard's mystic vision is not thereby invalidated, because it does not in truth derive from his beliefs on evolution—quite the contrary. There is no possible way of validating or of testing Teilhard's mystic vision of Omega. Any assurance about it must itself be an unsupported act of mystic faith. * * *

P. B. MEDAWAR

Review of *The Phenomenon of Man* (1961) †

Everything does not happen continuously at any one moment in the universe. Neither does everything happen everywhere in it.
There are no summits without abysses.
When the end of the world is mentioned, the idea that leaps into our minds is always one of catastrophe.
Life was born and propagates itself on the earth as a solitary pulsation.
In the last analysis the best guarantee that a thing should happen is that it appears to us as vitally necessary.

This little bouquet of aphorisms, each one thought sufficiently important by its author to deserve a paragraph to itself, is taken

† *Mind*, LXX (1961), 99–106. P.B. Medawar (b. 1915), Nobel laureate in physiology and medicine, was director of the National Institute for Medical Research, London.

from Père Teilhard's *The Phenomenon of Man*. It is a book widely held to be of the utmost profundity and significance; it created something like a sensation upon its publication a few years ago in France, and some reviewers hereabouts have called it the Book of the Year—one, the Book of the Century. Yet the greater part of it, I shall show, is nonsense, tricked out by a variety of tedious metaphysical conceits, and its author can be excused of dishonesty only on the grounds that before deceiving others he has taken great pains to deceive himself. *The Phenomenon of Man* cannot be read without a feeling of suffocation, a gasping and flailing around for sense. There is an argument in it, to be sure—a feeble argument, abominably expressed—and this I shall expound in due course; but consider first the style, because it is the style that creates the illusion of content, and which is in some part the cause as well as merely the symptom of Teilhard's alarming apocalyptic seizures.

The Phenomenon of Man stands square in the tradition of *Naturphilosophie*, a philosophical indoor pastime of German origin which does not seem even by accident (though there is a great deal of it) to have contributed anything of permanent value to the storehouse of human thought. French is not a language that lends itself naturally to the opaque and ponderous idiom of nature-philosophy, and Teilhard has accordingly resorted to the use of that tipsy, euphoric prose-poetry which is one of the more tiresome manifestations of the French spirit. It is of the nature of reproduction that progeny should outnumber parents, and of Mendelian heredity that the inborn endowments of the parents should be variously recombined and reassorted among their offspring, so enlarging the population's candidature for evolutionary change. Teilhard puts the matter thus: it is one of his more lucid passages, and Mr. Wall's translation, here as almost everywhere else, captures the spirit and sense of the original.

> Reproduction doubles the mother cell. Thus, by a mechanism which is the inverse of chemical disintegration, *it multiplies without crumbling*. At the same time, however, it transforms what was only intended to be prolonged. Closed in on itself, the living element reaches more or less quickly a state of immobility. It becomes stuck and coagulated in its evolution. Then by the act of reproduction it regains the faculty for inner re-adjustment and consequently takes on a new appearance and direction. The process is one of pluralization in form as well as in number. The elemental ripple of life that emerges from each individual unit does not spread outwards in a monotonous circle formed of individual units exactly like itself. It is diffracted and becomes iridescent, with an indefinite scale of variegated tonalities. The

living unit is a centre of irresistible multiplication, and *ipso facto* an equally irresistible focus of diversification.

In no sense other than an utterly trivial one is reproduction the inverse of chemical disintegration. It is a misunderstanding of genetics to suppose that reproduction is only "intended" to make facsimiles, for parasexual processes of genetical exchange are to be found in the simplest living things. There seems to be some confusion between the versatility of a population and the adaptability of an individual. But errors of fact or judgement of this kind are to be found throughout, and are not my immediate concern; notice instead the use of adjectives of excess (misuse, rather, for genetic diversity is not indefinite nor multiplication irresistible). Teilhard is for ever shouting at us: things or affairs are, in alphabetical order, astounding, colossal, endless, enormous, fantastic, giddy, hyper-immense, implacable, indefinite, inexhaustible, inextricable, infinite, infinitesimal, innumerable, irresistible, measureless, mega-monstrous, mysterious, prodigious, relentless, super-, ultra-, unbelievable, unbridled, or unparalleled. When something is described as merely *huge* we feel let down. After this softening-up process we are ready to take delivery of the neologisms: biota, noosphere, hominization, complexification. There is much else in the literary idiom of nature-philosophy: *nothing-buttery*, for example, always part of the minor symptomatology of the bogus. "Love in all its subtleties is nothing more, and nothing less, than the more or less direct trace marked on the heart of the element by the psychical convergence of the universe upon itself." "Man discovers that he is *nothing else than evolution become conscious of itself*," and evolution is "nothing else than the continual growth of . . . 'psychic' or 'radial' energy". Again, "the Christogenesis of St. Paul and St. John is nothing else and nothing less than the extension . . . of that noogenesis in which cosmogenesis . . . culminates." It would have been a great disappointment to me if Vibration did not somewhere make itself felt, for all scientistic mystics either vibrate in person or find themselves resonant with cosmic vibrations; but I am happy to say that on page 266 Teilhard will be found to do so.

These are trivialities, revealing though they are, and perhaps I make too much of them. The evolutionary origins of consciousness are indeed distant and obscure, and perhaps so trite a thought does need this kind of dressing to make it palatable: "refracted rearwards along the course of evolution, consciousness displays itself qualitatively as a spectrum of shifting hints whose lower terms are lost in the night." (The roman type is mine.) What is much more serious is the fact that Teilhard habitually and systematically cheats with words. His work, he has assured us, is to be read, not as a metaphysical system, but "purely and simply as a scientific treatise" executed with "remorseless" or "inescapable" logic; yet he uses in metaphor words like energy, tension, force, impetus, and dimension *as if* they retained the weight and thrust of their special scientific usages. Consciousness, for example, is a matter upon which Teilhard has been said to have illuminating views. For the most part consciousness is treated as a manifestation of energy, though this does not help us very much because the word 'energy' is itself debauched; but elsewhere we learn that consciousness is a dimension, something with mass, something corpuscular and particulate which can exist in various degrees of concentration, being sometimes infinitely diffuse. In his lay capacity Teilhard, a naturalist, practised a comparatively humble and unexacting kind of science, but he must have known better than to play such tricks as these. On page 60 we read: "The simplest form of protoplasm is already a substance of unheard-of complexity. This complexity increases in geometrical progression as we pass from the protozoon higher and higher up the scale of the metazoa. And so it is for the whole of the remainder always and everywhere." Later we are told that the "*nascent* cellular world shows itself to be already infinitely complex". This seems to leave little room for improvement. In any event complexity (a subject on which Teilhard has a great deal to say) is not measureable in those scalar quantities to which the concept of a geometrical progression applies.

In spite of all the obstacles that Teilhard perhaps wisely puts in our way, it is possible to discern a train of thought in *The Phenomenon of Man*. It is founded upon the belief that the fundamental process or motion in the entire universe is *evolution*, and evolution is "a general condition to which all theories, all hypotheses, all systems must bow . . . a light illuminating all facts, a curve that all lines must follow". This being so, it follows that "nothing could ever burst forth as final across the different thresholds successively traversed by evolution . . . which has not already existed in an obscure and primordial way" (again my romans). Nothing is wholly new: there is always some primordium or anlage or rudiment or archetype of whatever exists or has existed. Love, for example— "that is to say, the affinity of being with being"—is to be found in some form throughout the organic world, and even at a "prodigiously rudimentary level", for if there were no such affinity between atoms when they unite into molecules it would be "physically impossible for love to appear higher up, with us, in 'hominized form". But above all consciousness is not new, for this would contradict the evolutionary axiom; on the contrary, we are "logically forced to assume the existence in rudimentary form . . . of some sort of psyche in every corpuscle", even in molecules; "by the very fact of the individualization of our planet, a certain mass of elementary consciousness was originally emprisoned in the matter of earth".

What form does this elementary consciousness take? Scientists have not been able to spot it, for they are shallow superficial fellows, unable to see into the inwardness of things—"up to now, has science ever troubled to look at the world other than from *without?*" Consciousness is an interiority of matter, an "inner fact that everywhere duplicates the 'material' external face, which alone is commonly considered by science". To grasp the nature of the within of things we must understand that energy is of two kinds: the 'tangential', which is energy as scientists use that word, and a radial energy (a term used interchangeably with spiritual or psychic energy) of which consciousness is treated sometimes as the equivalent, sometimes as the manifestation, and sometimes as the consequence (there is no knowing what Teilhard intends). Radial energy appears to be a measure of, or that which conduces towards, complexity or degree or arrangement; thus "spiritual energy, by its very nature, increases in 'radial' value . . . in step with the increasing chemical complexity of the elements of which it represents the inner lining". It confers *centricity*, and "the increase of the synthetic state of matter involves . . . an increase of consciousness".

We are now therefore in a position to understand what evolution is (is nothing but). Evolution is "the continual growth of . . . 'psychic' or 'radial' energy, in the course of duration, beneath and within the mechanical energy I called 'tangential' "; evolution, then, is "an ascent towards consciousness". It follows that evolution must have a "precise *orientation* and a privileged *axis*" at the topmost pole of which lies Man, born "a direct lineal descendant from a total effort of life".

Let us fill in the intermediate stages. Teilhard, with a penetrating insight that Sir Julian Huxley singles out for special praise, discerns that consciousness in the everyday sense is somehow associated with the possession of nervous systems and brains ("we have every reason to think that in animals too a certain inwardness exists, approximately proportional to the development of their brains"). The direction of evolution must therefore be towards cerebralization, *i.e.* towards becoming brainier. "Among the infinite modalities in which the complication of life is dispersed," he tells us, "the differentiation of nervous tissue stands out . . . as a significant transformation. *It provides a direction;* and by its consequences *it proves that evolution has a direction."* All else is equivocal and insignificant; in the process of becoming brainier we find "the very essence of complexity, of essential metamorphosis". And if we study the evolution of living things, organic evolution, we shall find that in every one of its lines, except only in those in which it does not occur, evolution is an evolution towards increasing complexity of the nervous system and cerebralization. Plants don't count, to be sure (because "in the vegetable kingdom we are unable to follow along a nervous system the evolution of a psychism obviously remaining diffuse") and the contemplation of insects provokes a certain shuffling of the feet (p. 153); but primates are "a phylum of *pure and direct cerebralization*" and among them "evolution went straight to work on the brain, neglecting everything else". Here is Teilhard's description of noogenesis, the birth of higher consciousness among the primates, and of the noosphere in which that higher consciousness is deployed:

> By the end of the Tertiary era, the psychical temperature in the cellular world had been rising for more than 500 million years. . . . When the anthropoid, so to speak, had been brought 'mentally' to boiling point some further calories were added. . . . No more was needed for the whole inner equilibrium to be upset. . . . By a tiny 'tangential' increase, the 'radial' was turned back on itself and so to speak took an infinite leap forward. Outwardly, almost nothing in the organs had changed. But in depth, a great revolution had taken place: consciousness was now leaping and boiling in a space of super-sensory relationships and representations. . . .

The analogy, it should be explained, is with the vaporization of water when it is brought to boiling point, and the image of hot vapour remains when all else is forgotten.

I do not propose to criticize the fatuous argument I have just outlined; here, to expound is to expose. What Teilhard seems to be trying to say is that evolution is often (he says always) accompanied by an increase of orderliness or internal coherence or degree of integration. In what sense is the fertilized egg that develops into an adult human being 'higher' than, say, a bacterial cell? In the sense that it contains richer and more complicated genetical instructions for the execution of those processes that together constitute development. Thus Teilhard's radial, spiritual or psychic energy may be equated to 'information' or 'information content' in the sense that has been made reasonably precise by modern communications engineers. To equate it to consciousness, or to regard degree of consciousness as a measure of information content, is one of the silly little metaphysical conceits I mentioned in an earlier paragraph. Teilhard's belief, enthusiastically shared by Sir Julian Huxley, that evolution flouts or foils the second law of thermodynamics is based on a confusion of thought; and the idea that evolution has a main track or privileged axis is unsupported by scientific evidence.

Teilhard is widely believed to have rejected the modern Mendelian-Darwinian theory of evolution or to have demonstrated its inadequacy. Certainly he imports a ghost, the entelechy of *élan vital* of an earlier terminology, into the Mendelian machine; but he seems to accept the idea that evolution is probationary and exploratory and mediated through a selective process, a "groping", a billionfold trial and error"; "far be it from me", he declares, "to deny its importance". Unhappily Teilhard has no grasp of the real weakness of modern evolutionary theory, namely its lack of a complete theory of variation, of the origin of *candidature* for evolution. It is not enough to say that 'mutation' is ultimately the source of all genetical diversity, for that is merely to give the phenomenon a name: mutation is so defined. What we want, and are very slowly beginning to get, is a comprehensive theory of the forms in which new genetical information comes into being. It may, as I have hinted elsewhere, turn out to be of the nature of nucleic acids and the chromosomal apparatus that they tend spontaneously to proffer genetical variants—genetical solutions of the problem of remaining alive—which are more complex and more elaborate than the immediate occasion calls for; but to construe this 'complexification' as a manifestation of consciousness is a wilful abuse of words.

Teilhard's metaphysical argument begins where the scientific argument leaves off, and the gist of it is extremely simple. Inasmuch as evolution is the fundamental motion of the entire universe, an ascent along a privileged and necessary pathway towards consciousness, so it follows that our present consciousness must "culminate forwards in some sort of supreme consciousness". In expounding this thesis, Teilhard becomes more and more confused and excited and finally almost hysterical. The Supreme Consciousness, which apparently assimilates to itself all our personal consciousness, is, or is embodied in, "Omega" or the Omega-point; in Omega "the movement of synthesis culminates". Now Omega is "already in existence and operative at the very core of the thinking mass", so if we have our wits about us we should at this moment be able to detect Omega as "some excess of personal, extra-human energy", the more detailed contemplation of which will disclose the Great Presence. Although already in existence, Omega is added to progressively: "All round us, one by one, like a continual exhalation, 'souls' break away, carrying upwards their incommunicable load of consciousness", and so we end up with "a harmonized collectivity of consciousnesses equivalent to a sort of super-consciousness".

Teilhard devotes some little thought to the apparently insuperable problem of how to reconcile the persistence of individual consciousnesses with their assimilation to Omega. But the problem yields to the application of "remorseless logic". The individual particles of consciousness do not join up any old how, but only centre to centre, thanks to the mediation of Love; Omega, then, "in its ultimate principle, can only be a distinct Centre radiating at the core of a system of centres", and the final state of the world is one in which "unity coincides with a paroxysm of harmonized complexity". And so our hero escapes from his appalling predicament: with one bound, Jack was free.

Although elsewhere Teilhard has dared to write an equation so explicit as "Evolution = Rise of Consciousness" he does not go so far as to write "Omega = God"; but in the course of some obscure pious rant he does tell us that God, like Omega, is a "Centre of centres", and in one place he refers to "God-Omega".

How have people come to be taken in by *The Phenomenon of Man?* We must not underestimate the size of the market for works of this kind, for philosophy-fiction. Just as compulsory primary education created a market catered for by cheap dailies and weeklies, so the spread of secondary and latterly of tertiary education has created a large population of people, often with well developed literary and scholarly tastes, who have been educated far beyond their capacity to undertake analytical thought. It is through their eyes that we must attempt to see the attractions of Teilhard, which I shall jot down in the order in which they come to mind.

1. *The Phenomenon of Man* is anti-scientific in temper (scientists are shown up as shallow folk skating about on the surface of things), and, as if that were not recommendation enough, it was written by a scientist, a fact which seems to give it particular authority and weight. Laymen firmly believe that scientists are one species of person. They are not to know that the different branches of science require very different aptitudes and degrees of skill for their prosecution. Teilhard practised an intellectually unexacting kind of science in which he achieved a moderate proficiency. He has no grasp of what makes a logical argument or of what makes for proof. He does not even preserve the common decencies of scientific writing, though his book is professedly a scientific treatise.

2. It is written in an all but totally unintelligible style, and this is construed as *prima facie* evidence of profundity. (At present this applies only to works of French authorship; in later Victorian and Edwardian times the same deference was thought due to Ger-

mans, with equally little reason.) It is because Teilhard has such wonderful *deep* thoughts that he's so difficult to follow—really it's beyond my poor brain but doesn't that just *show* how profound and important it must be?

3. It declares that Man is in a sorry state, the victim of a "fundamental anguish of being", "a malady of space-time", a sickness of "cosmic gravity". The Predicament of Man is all the rage now that people have sufficient leisure and are sufficiently well fed to contemplate it, and many a tidy little literary reputation has been built upon exploiting it; anybody nowadays who dared to suggest that the plight of man might not be wholly desperate would get a sharp rap over the knuckles in any literary weekly. Teilhard not only diagnoses in everyone the fashionable disease but propounds a remedy for it—yet a remedy so obscure and so remote from the possibility of application that it is not likely to deprive any practitioner of a living.

4. *The Phenomenon of Man* was introduced to the English-speaking world by Sir Julian Huxley, which seemed to give it a scientific benediction. Unlike myself, Sir Julian finds Teilhard in possession of a "rigorous sense of values", one who "always endeavoured to think concretely". He was speculative, to be sure, but his speculation was "always disciplined by logic". The only common ground between us is that Huxley, too, finds Teilhard somewhat difficult to follow ("If I understood him aright", p. 16 and again p. 18; "here his thought is not fully clear to me", p. 19, etc.). But then it does not seem to me that Huxley expounds Teilhard's argument; his Introduction does little more than to call attention to parallels between Teilhard's thinking and his own. Chief among these is the cosmic significance attached to a suitably generalized conception of evolution—a conception so diluted or attenuated in the course of being generalized as to cover all events or phenomena that are not immobile in time (pp. 12, 13). In particular, Huxley applauds the, in my opinion, superficial and ill thought out view that the so-called 'psycho-social evolution' of mankind and the genetical evolution of living organisms generally are two episodes of a continuous integral process (though separated by a "critical point", whatever that may mean). Yet for all this Huxley finds it impossible to follow Teilhard "all the way in his gallant attempt to reconcile the supernatural elements in Christianity with the facts and implications of evolution". But, bless my soul, this reconciliation is just what Teilhard's book is *about*! And so, it seems to me, Huxley contrives to enrage all parties—those who have some concern for rigorous analytical thought, and those who see in Teilhard's work the elements of a profound spiritual revelation.

I have read and studied *The Phenomenon of Man* with real distress, even with despair. Instead of wringing our hands over the Human Predicament, we should attend to those parts of it which are wholly remediable, above all to the gullibility which makes it possible for people to be taken in by such a bag of tricks as this. If it were an innocent, passive gullibility it would be excusable; but all too clearly, alas, it is an active willingness to be deceived.

ANDREW DICKSON WHITE

The Final Effort of Theology (1896) †

* * *

Darwin's *Origin of Species* had come into the theological world like a plough into an ant-hill. Everywhere those thus rudely awakened from their old comfort and repose had swarmed forth angry and confused. Reviews, sermons, books light and heavy, came flying at the new thinker from all sides.

The keynote was struck at once in the *Quarterly Review* by Wilberforce, Bishop of Oxford. He declared that Darwin was guilty of "a tendency to limit God's glory in creation"; that "the principle of natural selection is absolutely incompatible with the word of God"; that it "contradicts the revealed relations of creation to its Creator"; that it is "inconsistent with the fulness of his glory"; that it is "a dishonouring view of Nature"; and that there is "a simpler explanation of the presence of these strange forms among the works of God": that explanation being—"the fall of Adam." Nor did the bishop's efforts end here; at the meeting of the British Association for the Advancement of Science he again disported himself in the tide of popular applause. Referring to the ideas of Darwin, who was absent on account of illness, he congratulated himself in a public speech that he was not descended from a monkey. The reply came from Huxley, who said in substance: "If I had to choose I would prefer to be a descendant of a humble monkey rather than of a man who employs his knowledge and eloquence in misrepresenting those who are wearing out their lives in the search for truth."

This shot reverberated through England, and indeed through other countries.

The utterances of this the most brilliant prelate of the Anglican

† Andrew Dickson White (1832–1918), scholar-diplomat, was the first president of Cornell University. The text is from his *A History of the Warfare of Science with Theology in Christendom* (New York, 1896).

Church received a sort of antiphonal response from the leaders of the English Catholics. In an address before the "Academia," which had been organized to combat "science falsely so called," Cardinal Manning declared his abhorrence of the new view of Nature, and described it as "a brutal philosophy—to wit, there is no God, and the ape is our Adam."

These attacks from such eminent sources set the clerical fashion for several years. One distinguished clerical reviewer, in spite of Darwin's thirty years of quiet labour, and in spite of the powerful summing up of his book, prefaced a diatribe by saying that Darwin "might have been more modest had he given some slight reason for dissenting from the views generally entertained." Another distinguished clergyman, vice-president of a Protestant institute to combat "dangerous" science, declared Darwinism "an attempt to dethrone God." Another critic spoke of persons accepting the Darwinian views as "under the frenzied inspiration of the inhaler of mephitic gas," and of Darwin's argument as "a jungle of fanciful assumption." Another spoke of Darwin's views as suggesting that "God is dead," and declared that Darwin's work "does open violence to everything which the Creator himself has told us in the Scriptures of the methods and results of his work." Still another theological authority asserted: "If the Darwinian theory is true, Genesis is a lie, the whole framework of the book of life falls to pieces, and the revelation of God to man, as we Christians know it, is a delusion and a snare." Another, who had shown excellent qualities as an observing naturalist, declared the Darwinian view "a huge imposture from the beginning."

Echoes came from America. One review, the organ of the most widespread of American religious sects, declared that Darwin was "attempting to befog and to pettifog the whole question"; another denounced Darwin's views as "infidelity"; another, representing the American branch of the Anglican Church, poured contempt over Darwin as "sophistical and illogical," and then plunged into an exceedingly dangerous line of argument in the following words: "If this hypothesis be true, then is the Bible an unbearable fiction; . . . then have Christians for nearly two thousand years been duped by a monstrous lie. . . . Darwin requires us to disbelieve the authoritative word of the Creator." A leading journal representing the same church took pains to show the evolution theory to be as contrary to the explicit declarations of the New Testament as to those of the Old, and said: "If we have all, men and monkeys, oysters and eagles, developed from an original germ, then is St. Paul's grand deliverance—'All flesh is not the same flesh; there is one kind of flesh of men, another of beasts, another of fishes, and another of birds'—untrue."

Another echo came from Australia, where Dr. Perry, Lord Bishop of Melbourne, in a most bitter book on *Science and the Bible*, declared that the obvious object of Chambers, Darwin, and Huxley, is "to produce in their readers a disbelief of the Bible."

Nor was the older branch of the Church to be left behind in this chorus. Bayma, in the *Catholic World*, declared, "Mr. Darwin is, we have reason to believe, the mouthpiece or chief trumpeter of that infidel clique whose well-known object is to do away with all idea of a God."

Worthy of especial note as showing the determination of the theological side at that period was the foundation of sacro-scientific organizations to combat the new ideas. First to be noted is the "Academia," planned by Cardinal Wiseman. In a circular letter the cardinal, usually so moderate and just, sounded an alarm and summed up by saying, "Now it is for the Church, which alone possesses divine certainty and divine discernment, to place itself at once in the front of a movement which threatens even the fragmentary remains of Christian belief in England." The necessary permission was obtained from Rome, the Academia was founded, and the "divine discernment" of the Church was seen in the utterances which came from it, such as those of Cardinal Manning, which every thoughtful Catholic would now desire to recall, and in the diatribes of Dr. Laing, which only aroused laughter on all sides. A similar effort was seen in Protestant quarters; the "Victoria Institute" was created, and perhaps the most noted utterance which ever came from it was the declaration of its vice-president, the Rev. Walter Mitchell, that "Darwinism endeavours to dethrone God."[1]

In France the attack was even more violent. Fabre d'Envieu brought out the heavy artillery of theology, and in a long series of elaborate propositions demonstrated that any other doctrine than that of the fixity and persistence of species is absolutely contrary to

1. For Wilberforce's article, see *Quarterly Review*, July, 1860. For the reply of Huxley to the bishop's speech I have relied on the account given in *Quatrefages*, who had it from Carpenter; a somewhat different version is given in the *Life and Letters of Darwin*. For Cardinal Manning's attack, see *Essays on Religion and Literature*, London, 1865. For the review articles, see the *Quarterly* already cited, and that for July, 1874; also the *North British Review*, May, 1860; also F. O. Morris's letter in the *Record*, reprinted at Glasgow, 1870; also the *Addresses of Rev. Walter Mitchell* before the Victoria Institute, London, 1867; also Rev. B. G.

Johns, *Moses not Darwin, a Sermon*, March 31, 1871. For the earlier American attacks, see *Methodist Quarterly Review*, April, 1871; *The American Church Review*, July and October, 1865, and January, 1866. For the Australian attack, see *Science and the Bible*, by the Right Reverend Charles Perry, D. D., Bishop of Melbourne, London, 1869. For Bayma, see the *Catholic World*, vol. xxvi, p. 782. For the Academia, see *Essays* edited by Cardinal Manning, above cited; and for the Victoria Institute, see *Scientia Scientiarum*, by a member of the Victoria Institute, London, 1865.

Scripture. The Abbé Désorges, a former Professor of Theology, stigmatized Darwin as a "pedant," and evolution as "gloomy"; Monseigneur Ségur, referring to Darwin and his followers, went into hysterics and shrieked: "These infamous doctrines have for their only support the most abject passions. Their father is pride, their mother impurity, their offspring revolutions. They come from hell and return thither, taking with them the gross creatures who blush not to proclaim and accept them."

In Germany the attack, if less declamatory, was no less severe. Catholic theologians vied with Protestants in bitterness. Prof. Michelis declared Darwin's theory "a caricature of creation." Dr. Hagermann asserted that it "turned the Creator out of doors." Dr. Schund insisted that "every idea of the Holy Scriptures, from the first to the last page, stands in diametrical opposition to the Darwinian theory"; and, "if Darwin be right in his view of the development of man out of a brutal condition, then the Bible teaching in regard to man is utterly annihilated." Rougemont in Switzerland called for a crusade against the obnoxious doctrine. Luthardt, Professor of Theology at Leipsic, declared: "The idea of creation belongs to religion and not to natural science; the whole superstructure of personal religion is built upon the doctrine of creation"; and he showed the evolution theory to be in direct contradiction to Holy Writ.

But in 1863 came an event which brought serious confusion to the theological camp: Sir Charles Lyell, the most eminent of living geologists, a man of deeply Christian feeling and of exceedingly cautious temper, who had opposed the evolution theory of Lamarck and declared his adherence to the idea of successive creations, then published his work on the *Antiquity of Man*, and in this and other utterances showed himself a complete though unwilling convert to the fundamental ideas of Darwin. The blow was serious in many ways, and especially so in two—first, as withdrawing all foundation in fact from the scriptural chronology, and secondly, as discrediting the creation theory. The blow was not unexpected; in various review articles against the Darwinian theory there had been appeals to Lyell, at times almost piteous, "not to flinch from the truths he had formerly proclaimed." But Lyell, like the honest man he was, yielded unreservedly to the mass of new proofs arrayed on the side of evolution against that of creation.

At the same time came Huxley's *Man's Place in Nature*, giving new and most cogent arguments in favour of evolution by natural selection.

In 1871 was published Darwin's *Descent of Man*. Its doctrine had been anticipated by critics of his previous books, but it made, none the less, a great stir; again the opposing army trooped forth, though evidently with much less heart than before. A few were very violent. The *Dublin University Magazine*, after the traditional Hibernian fashion, charged Mr. Darwin with seeking "to displace God by the unerring action of vagary," and with being "resolved to hunt God out of the world." But most notable from the side of the older Church was the elaborate answer to Darwin's book by the eminent French Catholic physician, Dr. Constantin James. In his work, *On Darwinism, or the Man-Ape*, published at Paris in 1877, Dr. James not only refuted Darwin scientifically but poured contempt on his book, calling it "a fairy tale," and insisted that a work "so fantastic and so burlesque" was, doubtless, only a huge joke, like Erasmus's *Praise of Folly*, or Montesquieu's *Persian Letters*. The princes of the Church were delighted. The Cardinal Archbishop of Paris assured the author that the book had become his "spiritual reading," and begged him to send a copy to the Pope himself. His Holiness, Pope Pius IX, acknowledged the gift in a remarkable letter. He thanked his dear son, the writer, for the book in which he "refutes so well the aberrations of Darwinism." "A system," His Holiness adds, "which is repugnant at once to history, to the tradition of all peoples, to exact science, to observed facts, and even to Reason herself, would seem to need no refutation, did not alienation from God and the leaning toward materialism, due to depravity, eagerly seek to support in all this tissue of fables. . . ." * * * Wherefore the Pope thanked Dr. James for his book, "so opportune and so perfectly appropriate to the exigencies of our time," and bestowed on him the apostolic benediction. Nor was this brief all. With it there came a second, creating the author an officer of the Papal Order of St. Sylvester. The cardinal archbishop assured the delighted physician that such a double honour of brief and brevet was perhaps unprecedented, and suggested only that in a new edition of his book he should "insist a little more on the relation existing between the narratives of Genesis and the discoveries of modern science, in such fashion as to convince the most incredulous of their perfect agreement." The prelate urged also a more dignified title. The proofs of this new edition were accordingly all submitted to His Eminence, and in 1882 it appeared as *Moses and Darwin: the Man of Genesis compared with the Man-Ape, or Religious Education opposed to Atheistic*. No wonder the cardinal embraced the author, thanking him in the name of science and religion. "We have at last," he declared, "a handbook which we can safely put into the hands of youth."

Scarcely less vigorous were the champions of English Protestant orthodoxy. In an address at Liverpool, Mr. Gladstone remarked: "Upon the grounds of what is termed evolution God is relieved of the labour of creation; in the name of unchangeable laws he is discharged from governing the world"; and, when Herbert Spencer called his attention to the fact that Newton with the doctrine of gravitation and with the science of physical astronomy is open to the same charge, Mr. Gladstone retreated in the *Contemporary Review* under one of his characteristic clouds of words. The Rev. Dr. Coles, in the *British and Foreign Evangelical Review*, declared that the God of evolution is not the Christian's God. Burgon, Dean of Chichester, in a sermon preached before the University of Oxford, pathetically warned the students that "those who refuse to accept the history of the creation of our first parents according to its obvious literal intention, and are for substituting the modern dream of evolution in its place, cause the entire scheme of man's salvation to collapse." Dr. Pusey also came into the fray with most earnest appeals against the new doctrine, and the Rev. Gavin Carlyle was perfervid on the same side. The Society for Promoting Christian Knowledge published a book by the Rev. Mr. Birks, in which the evolution doctrine was declared to be "flatly opposed to the fundamental doctrine of creation." Even the *London Times* admitted a review stigmatizing Darwin's *Descent of Man* as an "utterly unsupported hypothesis," full of "unsubstantiated premises, cursory investigations, and disintegrating speculations," and Darwin himself as "reckless and unscientific." [2] * * *

2. For the French theological opposition to the Darwinian theory, see Pozzy, *La Terre et le Récit Biblique de la Création*, 1874, especially pp. 353, 363; also, Félix Ducane, *Études sur le Transformisme*, 1876, especially pp. 107 to 119. As to Fabre d'Envieu, see especially his Proposition xliii. For the Abbé Désorges, "former Professor of Philosophy and Theology," see his *Erreurs Modernes*, Paris, 1878, pp. 677 and 595 to 598. For Monseigneur Ségur, see his *La Foi devant la Science Moderne*, sixth ed., Paris, 1874, pp. 23, 34, etc. For Herbert Spencer's reply to Mr. Gladstone, see his *Study of Sociology;* for the passage in the *Dublin Review*, see the issue for July, 1871. For the review in the *London Times*, see *Nature* for April 20, 1871. For Gavin Carlyle, see *The Battle of Unbelief*, 1870, pp. 86 and 171. For the attacks by Michelis and Hagermann, see *Natur und Offenbarung*, Münster, 1861 to 1869. For Schund, see his *Darwin's Hypothese und ihr Verhältniss zu Religion und Moral*, Stuttgart, 1869. For Luthardt, see *Fundamental Truths of Christianity*, translated by Sophia Taylor, second ed., Edinburgh, 1869. For Rougemont, see his *L'Homme et le Singe*, Neuchâtel, 1863 (also in German trans.). For Constantin James, see his *Mes Entretiens avec l'Empereur Don Pédro sur le Darwinisme*, Paris, 1888, where the papal briefs are printed in full. For the English attacks on Darwin's *Descent of Man*, see the *Edinburgh Review*, July, 1871, and elsewhere; the *Dublin Review*, July, 1871; the *British and Foreign Evangelical Review*, April, 1886. See also *The Scripture Doctrine of Creation*, by the Rev. T. R. Birks, London, 1873, published by the S. P. C. K. For Dr. Pusey's attack, see his *Unscience, not Science, adverse to Faith*, 1878; also, *Darwin's Life and Letters*, vol. ii, pp. 411, 412.

PRESTON CLOUD

"Scientific Creationism"—A New Inquisition Brewing? (1977) †

The Creationist Movement

Religious bigotry is abroad again in the land. And, in addition to socialism, sex education, and birth control, it is tilting anew at an old *bête noire*—evolution. Within the larger fundamentalist movement, a small group of hard-core zealots, comprising the membership of the Creation Research Society (CRS), is riding a crest of supernaturalist fervor to battle against a basic liberating tenet of civilized peoples—the separation of church and state. The five hundred or so members and many supporters of this organization, who call themselves creationists, see the ancient Judeo-Christian creation myths of the first two chapters of Genesis as constituting a single, divinely revealed account of origins that must be restored to preeminence in public-school teaching. Toward this end, they insist, the biblical version(s) of creation must be given "equal time" with scientific accounts of the progressive development of life from simple to complex forms. It does not satisfy them that biblical creationism receives equal time with other religious accounts of origins in courses in comparative theology. They demand that creationism be presented as a "scientific" alternative to evolution in science textbooks that deal with the origin and subsequent development of life before such textbooks can be approved for use in the public schools. They have even prepared their own textbook to serve this end, *Biology: A Search for Order in Complexity* (J. N. Moore and H. S. Slusher, editors, 1974). The outlooks described are those encompassed under the terms *creationist* and *creationism* as used in the present paper.

The humanistic preference for rational thought, particularly as seen in the search for naturalistic explanations of natural phenomena, has, of course, always been unpopular among those who prefer the supernatural, whether it be benign, diabolical, or simply whimsical. But why this strong resurgence of the age-old struggle between naturalistic and mystic perceptions of the universe? How do the creationists arrive at and support their proposition?

† From "'Scientific Creationism'—A New Inquisition Brewing?" *The Humanist*, 37 (1977), 6–15. Preston Cloud (b. 1912) is a research biogeologist with the U.S. Geological Survey and professor emeritus of biogeology and environmental studies at the University of California, Santa Barbara.

A part of the credo to which all members of the CRS subscribe is that "all basic types of living things, including man, were made by direct creative acts of God during the creation week described in Genesis." Elaborating on this, their leading polemicist, H. M. Morris, emphasizes, on page 16 of his book *The Remarkable Birth of Planet Earth* (1972) that *"it is only in the Bible that we can possibly obtain any information about the methods of creation, the order of creation, the duration of creation, or any of the other details of creation."* The Bible, claimed to be not only inspired but factual, thus is seen as a scientific document, a document, moreover, that, coming from a supposedly infallible source, is not open to inquiry or interpretation. Scholarly documentation of pre-Hebraic antecedents, including the two different versions of creation given in the first two chapters of Genesis, is ignored or brushed aside, and the "days" and other terms of the King James version of the Bible are taken literally as written—*"If it really took five billion years for God to make all these things, why did He tell us it took six days?"* asks Morris (1972, p. 89).

Incredible as it may seem, such a rationale is held to comprise a "creation model," scientifically comparable to the greatly refined modern version of the theory of evolution by means of natural selection. This position is reinforced, in the creationist view, by adding that "evolutionism," like humanism, is itself a form of faith or religion anyhow. According to such an argument, it is then seen as only fair that the "creation model" be taught on an equal footing with the "evolution model." Apparently, the creationists either believe that rational judgment, in this instance, can and should be suspended, or it has not occurred to them that a balanced and critical consideration of the alternatives and their supporting sources is bound to bring out the "heathen" antecedents and internal inconsistencies of the Genesis account, its exclusive reliance on revelation for support, its predictive barrenness, and its total refutation by two centuries of geological and biological investigation and the refined measurements of modern geochronology.

Although the creationists may be irrational, they are not to be dismissed as a lunatic fringe that can best be treated by being ignored. In California, which accounts for about 10 percent of the public-school enrollment and thus exerts great leverage on textbook publishers, they have proven themselves to be skillful tacticians, good organizers, and uncompromising adversaries. As J. A. Moore has shown in his account of the California controversy (in *Daedalus*, v. 103, no. 3, pp. 173–89, 1974), creationists were able both to gain control of the State Board of Education from about 1963 to at least 1974, and, during the same time, to get an adherent to their views elected as Superintendent of Public Instruction until 1970.

This board then proceeded to revise the *Science Framework for California Public Schools*, prepared by the California State Advisory Committee on Science Education, in such a way as to distort the findings of the scientists on that committee and introduce a creationist bias: a situation that led to tough negotiation and uneasy compromise.

The position of scholarly theologians and a substantial majority of literate, practicing Christians regarding the creationism of CRS is well expressed by statements quoted by Moore of the Very Reverend C. Julian Bartlett, dean of Grace Cathedral in San Francisco, and Dr. Conrad Bonifazi, professor of philosophy and religion at the Pacific School of Religion in Berkeley. Bonifazi summarizes: "Broadly speaking, then, the situation is thus: an extremely conservative wing of Christian sectarianism, which has little or no repute in the world of theological scholarship, adheres to a literal interpretation of the Bible, and is therefore committed to saying that evolution contradicts the biblical account of creation. Its belief in the 'infallibility' of the Bible does not even permit it to recognize that in Genesis itself there are two accounts of creation, each differing from the other in background and in content. It is also true that the major *denominations* of Protestantism and the Roman Catholic Church in the United States recognize and condone the teaching of evolution in the disciplines of natural science. These denominations represent a large majority of Christians in this country," And Reverend Bartlett adds: "The Biblical myth-story was but one of many such which were developed by primitive religions . . . it is a religious and therefore theological document and not a scientific treatise."

If the creationists are deterred by such comments from these and other religious scholars and scholarly theologians, whose judgment one might think they would respect, there is no sign of it. As Moore has observed, and with good reason: "Scientists who have dealt with fundamentalists simply do not trust them; they rather imagine that, if the fundamentalists had the power, they would happily reinstitute an inquisition."

The Approach to Science and to Creationism

In trying to arrive at a balanced judgment of issues involved, the nature and methods of both science and creationism need to be understood. Science can be described as a special, *active* way of trying to understand the universe, solar system, and earth. It differs from subjects such as fundamentalist theology that seek their insights wholly from inspiration, meditation, intuition, or divine revelation, unhampered by experimental or naturalistic constraints. Inspiration, meditation, and intuition also play important parts in the mental processes of scientists, but ideas so arrived at do not become a part of science until checked against relevant evidence and found to be consistent with it.

Evidence relevant to science consists of measurements or observations that can be made or confirmed by human observers. If the evidence is experimental, the experiment must be repeatable by others, with the same results. Should the evidence be the results of natural processes, such as floods, earthquakes, climatic change, or exploding stars, the observations must be repeatable. Others observing the same results must be able to see and measure the same thing.

The rules under which science operates specify that scientists must strive for objectivity. That objectivity is difficult is a part of being human. Even the most self-disciplined are products of previous experience and social climate. Although *total* detachment is impossible, the work of the scientist is under constant scrutiny by other scientists and that promotes caution. Characteristically, the ability to do first-rate science is not fulfilled by a high level of intelligence alone. Intellectual as well as personal integrity, balanced and critical judgment, and independence from authority in affairs of the mind are also important. Unverifiable assumptions are not permitted. Assumptions made must be consistent with what is already known, and they must be clearly stated so that others can see, test, and challenge them.

The central assumptions of science are that there is order in the universe and that this order can be found and explained. Its twin goals are thus: (1) to search for order in the universe; and (2) where found, to attempt to explain it in terms of processes that can be detected and measured or in terms of processes whose results can be observed and shown to be consistent with causes that do not violate the facts or laws of nature. Science may not invoke supernatural causes—not even in support of divine revelation. There can be no intellectual conflict between science and theology because they are mutually exclusive realms of thought. That involves no value judgment at all. Supernaturalism is not science, and science is not supernaturalism. It is that simple.

The approach to theory in the *scientific* sense starts, not in books, but with *data* and the formulation of *hypotheses* (or a group of related hypotheses called a model). A hypothesis is an attempt to explain the observed data. Science requires that its hypotheses be consistent with known evidence from experimentation or nature and that they have *verifiable consequences*—that is, they must be capable of disproof. One way of increasing objectivity is to think of as many hypotheses as possible that are consistent with the evidence and have verifiable consequences. As competing hypotheses are tested, their believability grows or shrinks as they withstand or fail opportunities for disproof. From at first being simply permissible, they either are eliminated or grow in believability until the most successful hypothesis may become a *ruling hypothesis*. If such a ruling hypothesis continues to be successful in predicting previously unsuspected facts or relationships, and withstands all opportunities for disproof, and if it has broad application, it may finally be accepted as a *theory*, often modified from the original hypothesis. These distinctions are important. Although not always made, they should be. They express different levels of probability, which is what science is about.

It is essential in science to distinguish among observations and measurements, the hypotheses and theories that integrate and propose *mechanisms* to explain the facts observed, scientific principles that specify operating procedures, and the *laws* of science. The laws of science represent the highest level of supportable generalization. In order to be accepted as a law, the generalization must have proved invariable under all of many observed circumstances; or, if variations are observed, they must occur in systematic and predictable ways. The laws of science may not be broken. Angular momentum must be conserved. The entropy of a closed system may not be decreased. Water may not flow uphill without a pump. Hypotheses that run against established scientific law are not acceptable unless they can demonstrate that the law is wrong.

It is characteristic of science that it is controversial. Scientists love to explore new areas, methods, and ideas. Hypotheses, and even theories that once appeared well established, may be challenged, modified, and even overthrown as they are tested against new experimental or observational data or better measurements. As investigation continues, the explanations of science sort out at different levels of probability without ever being considered unchallengeable where new evidence suggests the possibility of other naturalistic causes. Science is thus dynamic, progressive, ever changing, never finished. It is like the expanding wave-front of a pebble flung into a sea of ignorance; its growth both widens the domain of scientific understanding and expands the surrounding circle of ignorance as new knowledge raises new questions. Moreover, previous knowledge, without necessarily being wrong, constantly needs reconsideration in the face of new knowledge or new scientific ways of looking at it. As science expands into space Euclidean geometry yields to hyperbolic geometry and Newtonian gravity is refined by relativistic gravity. Darwinian ideas of selection evolve into more complex theory as we probe the molecule, behavioral responses, and the rocks. The stable continents of a few decades ago become moving pieces in a great new game of geologic chess because of discoveries made on the ocean floor.

Creationism, on the contrary, is seen by its adherents as fixed, immutable, divinely revealed truth—unchanged and unchanging since the writing of the original Hebrew text, or perhaps the older but similar Babylonian and Sumerian accounts. No less an authority that H. M. Morris himself, the director of the Institute for Creation Research, assures us that "the Genesis record of creation was verified by God himself as He gave the ten commandments." Never mind the glaring discrepancies between Genesis and the evolutionary sequences of geology, of which Morris finds "at least twenty-five"—grass, herbs, and trees before the sun, for instance. To creationists, this simply demonstrates that such vegetation must have grown in the light of the divine presence itself.

In their many public debates, creationists employ a fivefold strategy: (1) Get out the vote by means of advance agents that arouse local fundamentalist groups in order to assure a strong claque of supporters in the audience. (2) Attack evolution on the grounds that, as is usual in science, some details of the sequence and mechanisms involved are not agreed upon. (3) Snow the unsophisticated with claims that evolution violates that most misunderstood of scientific generalizations, the second law of thermodynamics. (4) Deny the evidence for intermediate forms and their gradual appearance over geologically long spans of time, introducing whatever wild claims or denials appear best suited to that purpose. (5) Claim that a literal interpretation of the Bible provides the only foundation for morality in a wicked and changing age. Granted, then, that there is disagreement among evolutionists, however trivial that may be, and that the second law of thermodynamics and alleged lack of intermediate forms are seen by creationists as verifiable consequences of creationism, but contradictory to evolution, Genesis emerges in the eyes of the creationists as the only alternative, without need for documentation or discussion beyond the simple assertion that it is the word of God.

It is an appealing scenario to those enamored of simple, unwavering answers, but much too successful at winning over the uncritical popular mind to be brushed aside or underrated by scientists and other humanists who see reason as the quality that offers the best hope for mankind's eventual liberation from the tyranny of fear, superstition, suspicion, and hostility.

The Question of Origins

To turn now to the question of origins * * *

Evolution implies a systematic progression of related events—a continuous or stepwise process of change from one state to another. It is hard to think of systems that do not evolve—social, political, economic, or natural. Even though they may equilibrate temporarily, change sets in sooner or later. Historical geology attempts to trace the interrelated evolutions of life, air, water, and earth's rocky crust. Its results leave *no doubt that change from simple, slightly diversified to complex and greatly diversified forms of life has taken place over billions of years of geologic time*. In charging evolutionists with dogmatism, creationists both deny that fact and confuse it with the mechanism by which changes were achieved.

Although that mechanism is always open to debate, competing hypotheses have repeatedly failed to displace Charles Darwin's basic concept of progressive change brought about by selective processes acting on naturally varying systems over long periods of time in response to changing circumstances. Indeed, creationists are clever enough not to deny either natural variation or the effects of selective processes on local populations. What they do deny is time in excess of a few thousand years and the reality of the progressive changes observed. Instead, all the "basic kinds" of life are seen by them as having originated in a complete state of "perfection" during the third, fifth, and sixth days of creation, after which, giving vent to some unexplained whimsy, God decreed the second law of thermodynamics, whereby free energy decreases, order decreases, and the universe retrogresses from its initial state of perfection forever after. Things are getting worse all the time, 'tis said, and they will get still worse for those who fail to accept the gospel of H. M. Morris, D. T. Gish, (*Evolution: The Fossils Say No!*, 1973), H. S. Slusher, J. C. Whitcomb, Jr. (*The Early Earth*, 1972), and others.

In contrast to the creationist approach, the scientific way to assess evolutionary theory is to ask what it predicts, or "postdicts," about the past, about the geologic record of life. *Current* evolutionary theory, of course, is more complex than that visualized by Darwin, including a foundation of experimental evidence unknown to him, and it is still evolving. It does, however, predict the following: (1) Life either originated on earth under an essentially oxygen-free atmosphere not long after liquid water first began to accumulate, or it reached here from elsewhere in the universe. (2) The earliest forms of life were very simple cells without well-defined nuclei, which evolved in essentially oxygen-free environments until such time as their photosynthetic activities and tolerances to oxygen permitted that gas to accumulate in the atmosphere. (3) More complex, truly nucleated, and, eventually, fully sexual microorganisms evolved only after atmospheric oxygen increased to levels capable of supporting a fully oxidative metabolism. (4) Many-celled animals came later, the first of these being delicate, soft-bodied, thin-bodied forms because they depended on simple diffusion for their oxygen supply. (5) Multicellular animals acquired protective armor or external skeletons only later, as oxygen levels increased and internal oxygen-transport systems evolved. (6) There has been a general, although by no means regular, progression of increasing variety and complexity of life from that time until the present.

How do these predictions fit the geologic record? Not only have they been borne out by the steady growth of factual evidence, but nuclear age determinations confirm and amplify the observed sequences of geology. Such nuclear methods permit estimates in atomic years, equivalent to *present* sidereal or clock years, for about how long ago major changes occurred. Consider the predictions (postdictions) above in the order presented. (1) During the past 15 years we have learned that life and the beginnings of photosynthesis originated more than 2 billion years ago and probably more than 3.8 billion years ago. A substantial body of evidence has also accumulated in support of the chemical probability of steps leading toward the origin of life by chemical evolution from nonliving antecedents under oxygen-free conditions; that evidence, however, derives from chemically sophisticated laboratory experiments and cosmochemistry that will not be dealt with further here. (2) The oldest demonstrable organisms were very simple single-celled and filamentous forms, and the geochemical evidence indicates an absence or very low level of oxygen in the atmosphere at the time. Although some of these organisms probably were photosynthetic, oxygen did not accumulate because released oxygen was absorbed in vast sinks of reduced substances, including dissolved iron that formed our largest iron deposits during an episode of iron formation that has not been repeated on the scale earlier observed for the past 2 billion years. (3) Free oxygen first began to accumulate in the atmosphere about 2 billion years ago, as shown by the oldest records of oxidized sediments deposited on the continents of the time, while the oldest cells of a truly advanced nature so far known are younger—about 1.3 billion years old. (4) Many-celled animals are first known from rocks about 680 million years old; these delicate, soft-bodied, thin-bodied or thin-walled animals of primitive sorts are related to worms, jellyfish, and sea pens, but without shells or skeletons. (5) The first shell-bearing animals appeared about 600 million years ago; they were very simple types—trilobites and most of the main kinds of organisms did not appear until later. (6) Although early multicellular diversification was rapid, a natural consequence of the many then unoccupied ecologic niches and probably multiple origins, the progression was orderly. From then until now there has been an essentially continuous progression of increasing variety and complexity of multicellar animal life.

I have written above of my own field of specialization. The

results I have summarized so briefly come from forty years of independent study and research on life processes in earth history.

Let me now add some words about the discontinuities in the evolutionary record, of which creationists make so much. Populations of forms transitional from one successful form of life to another should be small, peripheral to larger populations of successful forms, and represent brief time spans. Only evolutionary successes become abundant enough to have a good statistical chance of leaving a fossil record, and those numerous forms that lack hard shells or skeletons are only rarely preserved. Because land deposits tend to be weathered and eroded, while marine ones tend to be preserved, marine fossils are more common than those of land animals; and on the continents, smart animals like man rarely become fossils by accident. Nevertheless, there *are* intermediate forms, as well as gaps; and although no person was there to witness the progress of evolution in prehuman times, its results are in the rocks for all to see. Just as we do not discard Newtonian or Einsteinian gravity because we do not have measurements of the mutual attractions between every particle in the universe, so the general evolutionary progression is clear, even though fossil remains are not found for every creature that ever lived—and even though more than a few new forms appear abruptly in the geologic record either because of its incompleteness or as a result of processes not yet well understood.

Evolution as a historical phenomenon rests on as sound and extensive a factual basis as any specific generalization we know.

The *mechanism* of evolution, as noted earlier, is a different matter. Although no one since 1859 has come up with a durable scientific alternative to the action of natural selection on varying populations or gene pools, the possibility of large jumps as a result of precocious sexual maturity or for other reasons is still debated, while the evolution of nonsexual organisms involves different patterns from that of sexual ones. The rules of science require that, if situations should be found in which natural selection is not consistent with the facts, it must be modified or abandoned. This doesn't mean, however, that it needs to be seriously reconsidered *without* the introduction of *new* evidence because a few people don't or won't understand it. Thus, among biological and biogeological scientists, natural selection in the modern sense, sometimes called "the synthetic theory of evolution," is the favored theory for the observation that organisms *have* evolved.

If evolution over a long time interval, as documented by the geologic record, is to be explained as the work of a deity, that also has some consequences, although not verifiable. The deity either set the rules by which evolution took place or personally created all of the millions of species that have ever lived, and in a generally systematic progression of increasing complexity and diversity.

Two last thoughts before turning to a consideration of particular creationist arguments against evolution. Creationists fear that without a literal acceptance of the Bible, there is no basis for morality. In contrast, it seems to me that the best testament to the basic goodness of mankind is that so many are honest and compassionate for reasons other than fear of punishment or religious conviction.

Then there is the matter of one's vision of divine cause. If one holds to the view of a supreme being, is it more elevating to think of that being as a grand architect who set the whole thing in motion with a divine plan of operation and then let it alone, or to think of her or him as the whimsical builder pictured by a literal interpretation of Genesis?

Some Observations on Particular Creationist Claims

Why, then, do creationists cling to an internally inconsistent six-day miracle where "creation science" is a contradiction in terms and even the word *creationism* has a different meaning to biblical scholars? On what grounds does the CRS attack evolution? Six of their central substantive arguments are briefly considered below.

1. *Creationists claim that intermediate or transitional forms predicted by evolution theory are not found in the fossil record.* I have already explained some of the reasons why deficiencies in the fossil record are to be expected and, in fact, are common. But real intermediate forms are *not* lacking. The creationists are aware of this but choose to deny the evidence. Consider four examples. (a) In the case of *Archaeopteryx*, intermediate between reptiles and birds, creationist D. T. Gish insists that, since it had wings, feathers, and flew, it was clearly a bird and nothing else. It is, of course, true that among living animals, feathers are found only among birds. Contemporary with *Archaeopteryx*, however, were good reptiles that also had wings and flew. *Archaeopteryx* also had teeth, which occur in no living birds. Indeed, Yale paleontologist J. H. Ostrom, who has restudied in detail all of the few known specimens of *Archaeopteryx*, reported in the British journal *Nature* in 1973 that, were it not for the associated impressions of feathers, he would have identified these specimens unequivocally as small theropod dinosaurs with birdlike pelvises. Because it had characteristics of both reptiles and birds, therefore, *Archaeopteryx* is intermediate by definition. But our ways of classifying animals do not provide for intermediate forms. We must choose between reptile and bird or invent a new class with some features of each. As a matter of simplicity and priority, *Archaeopteryx* is classified as a bird. (b) *Ichthyostega*, a

350-million-year-old creature, also denied as transitional by creationists, has the skeleton of and is regarded as a very fishlike amphibian, yet it might equally well be considered a very amphibianlike fish. (c) As for amphibians and reptiles, the differences are so gradational that one might say that the first amphibian to lay an egg that could survive desiccation and hatch out of water (an amniotic egg) was a reptile. (d) Intermediates between reptiles and mammals are so numerous that, although current opinion favors a single main line of evolution from reptile to mammal, there could have been several ancestral reptilian lines, all evolving mammalian characteristics at the same time. The classification of intermediate forms is, in fact, a major procedural problem in modern paleontology. I do not, of course, assert that there are no gaps. They appear to exist, and they are puzzling; but if evolutionary science is to progress toward a better understanding of them, this will not be achieved by using the creationist broom to sweep the problem under the rug.

2. In the creationist scientish-joke cartoon-strip "Have you been brainwashed?" D. T. *Gish states that "billions of highly complex animals—trilobites, brachiopods, corals, worms, jellyfish, etc.—just suddenly appear in the geological record at the base of the Cambrian."* He can be forgiven for this misstatement because part of it could be derived from careless reading of source materials, including my own writings. But it is *not* true. Since 1954, a variety of primitive microorganisms have been found to occur through a long sequence of rocks dating back to more than 2 billion years ago. We now also have evidence that a limited variety of multicellular animal life began about 680 million years ago, perhaps 80 million years before the shelly fossils of the Cambrian, and that higher forms appeared sequentially up to, through, and beyond the Cambrian. Also contrary to Gish, corals were never thought by people familiar with evidence to exist in earliest Cambrian time. Moreover, all of the forms mentioned are still simple forms of life compared with those that came in *successive* waves of greater complexity and diversity over the succeeding half-billion years of geologic time. The contrast with the creationist fantasy of a six-day creation week could not be greater.

3. *Creationists assert that time has been too short for evolution.* Geochronologists and cosmochronologists, they say, are mistaken about the great age of the universe, the solar system, and the earth. Slusher's "Critique of Radiometric Dating" attacks geochronologists for "apparent intellectual dishonesty." He states: *"Most creationists . . . have viewed the evidence regarding the age of the earth as pointing to a very young age of from about 7,000 years to 10,000 years."* All the elegant and internally consistent work of a host of geochronologists the world over, using a variety of sophisticated

instrumentation and self-checking systems for the last quarter-century, is rejected because it doesn't fit Genesis. One half-baked calculation by a creationist of the time required for decay of the earth's magnetic field (Slusher, 1973) gives an age that approaches the creationist preconception! *That* age is spurious because the assumptions are invalid. Earth's magnetic field, to be sure, does decay, and on a cycle of thousands of years; but it is constantly being renewed by motions in the earth's liquid core. I add only that the devoutly Christian E. A. Milne, in his 1952 deathbed treatise on "Modern Cosmology and the Christian Idea of God," found no problem with a great age for the earth or the universe. Indeed, he thought that classical clock time, based on inconstant relations, was slowing down relative to constant atomic time, so that the age of the earth in conventional clock years was probably vastly greater than its atomic age, now estimated at about 4.6 billion years.

4. *Creationists insist that all fossils were actually deposited at the time of the Great Noachian Flood* of about one year's duration. Apart from the problem this makes with the sequence of rocks and with geochronology is that of the volume of sediments needed to fall from suspension in a bit over a year. We know continuous sequences of stratified rock as much as 20 kilometers (12 miles) thick; and if all those known in time sequence were piled in the order of their deposition, they would be many hundreds of kilometers high. A modern reservoir, say 60 meters deep, made by damming a river in a rapidly eroding area, takes about 100 years to fill with sediment, even allowing for catastrophic floods. At that rate, it would take about 32,000 years for 20 kilometers of stratified sediment to accumulate, and remember that I speak of muddy river water, wet sediment (that would compact to much smaller thickness when dry), and a small reservoir. If one multiplies 32,000 by the hundreds, the years become millions, underscoring the difficulty of accounting for even a small fraction of the sedimentary rocks known by the deposits of one year's time. Indeed, the method of sedimentary rates used by early geologists to estimate the age of the earth gave numbers of around 100 to 400 million years. This, however, included little of pre-Cambrian history and left out erosion and nondeposition. We now find much longer ages, using precise, self-checking nuclear methods. I should add here, however, that the legend of a great lowland flood some thousands of years ago *is* widespread and that Cesare Emiliani, of the University of Miami, and others, in a paper in the American journal *Science*, in 1975, have suggested that such a flood may well have happened as a result of a rapid advance and melting of a very late Pleistocene ice sheet about 11,600 years ago—precisely as reported from early accounts by Pliny the Elder.

5. Similar to their claim that all fossils were formed at once during the biblical flood, *creationists assert that the use of fossils as age indicators is self-fulfilling* because when paleontologists find particular fossils they claim the assigned age. Here I would ask you to visualize the Grand Canyon, along whose walls is a succession of nearly horizontal, layered rocks that can be traced with the eye or on foot, always in the same succession with reference to one another. Geologists judge that the bottom ones were the older (deposited first) because there is no way of suspending the overlying ones above an open space while younger sediments were deposited over large areas beneath. That would indeed require a miracle! Successive layers, therefore, decrease in age before the present from the bottom upward, and everywhere the same distinctive kinds of fossils are found in the same layers, while different ones occur above and below. Similar relationships of varying time spans are found in many parts of the world. Such relationships, matched with one another like pieces of a jigsaw puzzle, allowed students of fossils over a century and a half ago to work out successions that gave *relative* ages in terms of older than, younger than, and contemporaneous with. Until measurements from nuclear-decay series became available, however, ages in years (before the present) could not be given. Now the consistency in sequence observed between atomic ages and fossil ages supports the evolutionary progression of life, the validity of nuclear geochronology, and the conclusion of both evolutionists and creationists that evolution needs lots of time—time measurable not in days but in hundreds or thousands of millions of years. The span of ages involved in the flat-lying rocks of the Grand Canyon alone is over 300 million years. The deformed rocks beneath them extend another 1,200 million years into the past.

6. Finally, I note the curious *creationist belief that evolution violates the second law of thermodynamics*. This law states that something called entropy always increases (in a closed system). In simplest terms this says, approximately, that free or available energy will be converted to bound, and thus unavailable, energy and that disorder will increase, to the extent order is not locally restored by investments of free energy. Creationists, most notably H. M. Morris, an engineer who ought to know better, insist that life and its diversity violate the second law of thermodynamics, presenting this as evidence of supernatural intervention. This is a misconception on several counts. One defect is that the earth is not closed with respect to energy. Instead, our planet receives new energy from the sun at the average rate of 178 trillion kilowatts daily. This energy, through photosynthesis, drives all life processes in the same way a pump drives water uphill. It is, incidentally, also the source of all of our fresh water, coal, oil, hydroelectric power, and much more. The second law applies only to the universe as a whole, or to

such parts of it as may exist separately as truly closed systems. Morris, in his "Entropy and Open Systems" (ICR *Impact Series*, No. 40, 1976), not unexpectedly, takes issue also with this position. He fails, however, to allow for exchange between energy and order. A simple illustration of this phenomenon is the following sequence: energy → bauxite → aluminum metal, in which energy is invested to transform disordered aluminum ore to the ordered elemental state of aluminum metal. When disorder sets in, as a result of the fabrication, use, and dispersal of beer cans from the aluminum metal, additional energy must be invested to restore order in the form of recycled aluminum ingots. Examples of this principle are seen throughout the universe. When an igneous rock crystallizes from a melt, order is created while free energy is consumed. The chemical elements themselves, the perception of whose ordered arrangement is one of the great artistic triumphs of science, are cooked in stars, novae, and supernovae as a product of the enormous temperatures found there. *Enegy from the sun,* through photosynthesis, *is the driving force of life and its evolution.* Indeed, one could argue that the ever growing diversity of life is itself a kind of entropic effect—where the maximal ordered condition might be visualized as the original population of simple unicellular organisms. In any case, through death, the molecules and elements of all living things are eventually restored to the physical system from which their substance was derived and in which they passed their lives. Entropy gets you in the end!

Summary

Fundamentalist creationism is not a science but a form of antiscience, whose more vocal practitioners, despite their advanced degrees in the sciences and their bland debating postures, play fast and loose with the facts of geology and biology. Creationism has been thoroughly and repeatedly considered over the generations and rejected as being outside the realm of science by the world scientific community. It is not a *scientific* alternative to any form of evolution theory; and unlike much of the Bible, it has no bearing on morals or ethics. Like flat-earthism, which branded photographs of the earth from space as frauds, it is of interest only for its historical aspects and as a sociological aberration.

Indeed, creation "research" is a contradiction in terms, for there is no research to be done if the task is complete, perfect, and fully described in the Bible. What the research of CRS consists of, in fact, is poring through the works of evolutionists in search of trivial inconsistencies, no matter how ancient or offbeat, that can be used to reinforce their admittedly preconceived ideas.

The real issue is not whether science or divine revelation offers better insights to the truth or even whose version of divine revelation is to be presented as an alternative to evolution. There are two more important and more manageable issues. One is whether the scientifically and theologically unsophisticated student is to be confused by treating these two very different modes of thought as if they were susceptible to similar treatment in the framework of science—a distortion of both science and religion. The other is whether an extremist group of religious bigots shall be permitted to abridge the constitutionally guaranteed separation of church and state— whether fundamentalist Old Testament orthodoxy is to be granted a privileged and improper place in the public educational system. If a person wants to believe that the earth is flat or that it and everything in it was created in six days, or to reject the proofs of its great age, he or she should have every right to do so. What he or she does not have a right to under the Constitution of the United States is to have such beliefs falsely presented as *science* in the classrooms of the public-school system.

The most serious threat of creationism is that, if successful, it would stifle inquiry. If everything were already completely set forth in biblical accounts, there would be nothing more to do, apart from suppressing heretical notions like natural selection while awaiting Judgment Day. We could close down the biological and medical research laboratories of the world and those branches of the school system that deal with subjects other than fundamentalist Judeo-Christian theology, industry, and driver training. The grand ideal of the Creation Research Society would have been achieved.

Two Letters on Evolution vs. Creationism (1972) †

Letter from 19 Nobel Laureate Scientists

To the California State Board of Education

We are appalled that you are considering a requirement that science textbooks include creation along with evolution as an explanation of the origin of life. Creation "theory" is *not* based on science and does *not* belong in a science textbook.

We urge you to support the recommendation of your own State Advisory Committee on Science Education in rejecting this unreasonable requirement for our science textbooks.

Respectfully yours,

† In 1972 a concentrated attempt was made to include the religious notion of the separate creation of species in biology textbooks in California. These documents were two of the protests made on that occasion by members of the scientific community. The first is a unanimous statement by all of the Nobel Prize scientists then living in California; the second is an elaboration of that statement by one of the nineteen signatories.

Luis W. Alvares
Nobel Laureate 1968, Physics
University of California

Carl David Anderson
Nobel Laureate 1936, Physics
California Institute of
  Technology

Felix Bloch
Nobel Laureate 1952, Physics
Stanford University

Melvin Calvin
Nobel Laureate 1961,
  Chemistry
University of California,
  Berkeley

Max Delbrück
Nobel Laureate 1969, Medicine
California Institute of
  Technology

Richard P. Feynman
Nobel Laureate 1965, Physics
California Institute of
  Technology

Murray Gell-Mann
Nobel Laureate 1969, Physics
California Institute of
  Technology

William F. Giauque
Nobel Laureate 1949,
  Chemistry
University of California,
  Berkeley

Donald A. Glaser
Nobel Laureate 1960, Physics
University of California,
  Berkeley

Robert Hofstadter
Nobel Laureate 1961, Physics
Stanford University

Robert W. Holley
Nobel Laureate 1968, Medicine
Salk Institute

Arthur Kornberg
Nobel Laureate 1959, Medicine
Stanford University

Joshua Lederberg
Nobel Laureate 1958, Medicine
Stanford University

Willard F. Libby
Nobel Laureate 1960,
  Chemistry
University of California at
  Los Angeles

Edwin M. McMillan
Nobel Laureate 1951,
  Chemistry
University of California,
  Berkeley

Linus Pauling
Nobel Laureate 1954,
  Chemistry; 1962, Peace
Stanford University

Glenn T. Seaborg
Nobel Laureate 1951,
  Chemistry
University of California,
  Berkeley

William Shockley
Nobel Laureate 1956, Physics
Stanford University

Harold C. Urey
Nobel Laureate 1934,
  Chemistry
University of California at
  San Diego

To the California State Board of Education:

Nineteen Nobel Laureate scientists who live in California have joined in deploring the attack on evolution and beclouding its significance in the science textbooks for our public schools.

The latest recommendation from the Curriculum Commission may seem innocuous in requiring "that dogmatism be changed to conditional statements where speculation is offered as explanation of origins." However, this is clearly tailored to make room for the "creation theory" as an alternative to evolution.

Conditional statements are appropriate when multiple theories have been proposed and none of these can be eliminated by the existing scientific evidence. However, this is not the case in the present argument. The "creation theory" of man does not stand as an alternative to the theory of evolution in this scientific sense. It is eliminated by existing data. Indeed, no alternative to the evolutionary theory of the origin of man exists today which gives an equally satisfactory explanation of the biological facts. Hence the incentive in applying this requirement selectively to the evolutionary theory, instead of, for example, the atomic theory, is clearly not scientific but religious.

None of these remarks is intended to foreclose further discussion of the theory of evolution posited as a scientific issue. Many of its details are a subject of continuing controversy. Students should by all means have the opportunity to be acquainted with the factual evidence on which scientists have based their conclusions, and, in the realm of scientific teaching, should not be biased by assertions based on arguments of faith rather than scientific evidence.

We urge you to reject modifications to the science framework which require the addition of non-scientific material to our science textbooks.

Sincerely yours,

Arthur Kornberg
Nobel Laureate 1959, Medicine
Professor of Biochemistry

A *Statement Affirming Evolution as a Principle of Science* (1977)†

For many years it has been well established scientifically that all known forms of life, including human beings, have developed by a lengthy process of evolution. It is also verifiable today that very primitive forms of life, ancestral to all living forms, came into being thousands of millions of years ago. They constituted the trunk of a "tree of life" that, in growing, branched more and more; that is, some of the later descendants of these earliest living things, in growing more complex, became ever more diverse and increasingly different from one another. Humans and the other highly organized types of today constitute the present twig-end of that tree. The human twig and that of the apes sprang from the same apelike progenitor branch.

Scientists consider that none of their principles, no matter how seemingly firmly established—and no ordinary "facts" of direct observation either—are absolute certainties. Some possibility of human error, even if very slight, always exists. Scientists welcome the challenge of further testing of any view whatever. They use such terms as *firmly established* only for conclusions founded on rigorous evidence that have continued to withstand searching criticism.

The principle of biological evolution, as just stated, meets these criteria exceptionally well. It rests upon a multitude of discoveries of very different kinds that concur and complement one another. It is therefore accepted into humanity's general body of knowledge by scientists and other reasonable persons who have familiarized themselves with the evidence.

In recent years, the evidence for the principle of evolution has continued to accumulate. This has resulted in a firm understanding of biological evolution, including the further confirmation of the principle of natural selection and adaptation that Darwin and Wal-

† Published in *The Humanist*, 37 (1977), 4–6. The Sponsoring Committee responsible for the statement comprised Bette Chambers, president, American Humanist Association; Isaac Asimov, associate professor of biochemistry, Boston University School of Medicine; Hudson Hoagland, president emeritus, the Worcester Foundation for Experimental Biology; Chauncey D. Leake, senior lecturer, University of California at San Francisco; Linus Pauling, research professor, Linus Pauling Institute of Science and Medicine; and George Gaylord Simpson, emeritus professor of vertebrate paleontology, Harvard University and professor of geosciences, University of Arizona at Tucson. The statement was adapted from an earlier paper by Hermann J. Muller, Distinguished Service Professor of Zoology at Indiana University and Nobel laureate in physiology and medicine. It was cosigned by 186 other professional people, most of them professors of biology in American universities.

lace over a century ago showed to be an essential part of the process of biological evolution.

There are no alternative theories to the principle of evolution, with its "tree of life" pattern, that any competent biologist of today takes seriously. Moreover, the principle is so important for an understanding of the world we live in and of ourselves that the public in general, including students taking biology in school, should be made aware of it, and of the fact that it is firmly established in the view of the modern scientific community.

Creationism is not scientific; it is a purely religious view held by some religious sects and persons and strongly opposed by other religious sects and persons. Evolution is the only presently known strictly scientific and nonreligious explanation for the existence and diversity of living organisms. It is therefore the only view that should be expounded in public-school courses on science, which are distinct from those on religion.

We, the undersigned, call upon all local school boards, manufacturers of textbooks and teaching materials, elementary and secondary teachers of biological science, concerned citizens, and educational agencies to do the following:

—Resist and oppose measures currently before several state legislatures that would require creationist views of origins be given equal treatment and emphasis in public-school biology classes and text materials.

—Reject the concept, currently being put forth by certain religious and creationist pressure-groups, that alleges that evolution is itself a tenet of a religion of "secular humanism," and as such is unsuitable for inclusion in the public-school science curriculum.

—Give vigorous support and aid to those classroom teachers who present the subject matter of evolution fairly and who often encounter community opposition.

PART V

Darwin and Society

A struggle is inevitable and it is a question of the survival of the fittest.

—Andrew Carnegie, 1900

The fortunes of railroad companies are determined by the law of the survival of the fittest.

—James J. Hill, 1910

The growth of a large business is merely the survival of the fittest.

—John D. Rockefeller, c. 1900

God gave me my money.

—John D. Rockefeller, 1915

History warns us * * * that it is the customary fate of new truths to begin as heresies and to end as superstitions. * * *

—Thomas Henry Huxley, 1880

Competition and Cooperation

RICHARD HOFSTADTER

The Vogue of Spencer (1955) †

As it seems to me, we have in Herbert Spencer not only the profoundest thinker of our time, but the most capacious and most powerful intellect of all time. Aristotle and his master were no more beyond the pygmies who preceded them than he is beyond Aristotle. Kant, Hegel, Fichte, and Schelling are gropers in the dark by the side of him. In all the history of science, there is but one name which can be compared to his, and that is Newton's * * *

—F. A. P. Barnard

I am an ultra and thoroughgoing American. I believe there is great work to be done here for civilization. What we want are ideas—large, organizing ideas—and I believe there is no other man whose thoughts are so valuable for our needs as yours are.

—Edward Livingston Youmans to Herbert Spencer

I

"The peculiar condition of American society," wrote Henry Ward Beecher to Herbert Spencer in 1866, "has made your writings far more fruitful and quickening here than in Europe." [1] Why Americans were disposed to open their minds to Spencer, Beecher did not say; but there is much to substantiate his words. Spencer's philosophy was admirably suited to the American scene. It was scientific in derivation and comprehensive in scope. It had a reassuring theory of progress based upon biology and physics. It was large enough to be all things to all men, broad enough to satisfy agnostics like Robert Ingersoll and theists like Fiske and Beecher. It offered a comprehensive world-view, uniting under one generalization everything in nature from protozoa to politics. Satisfying the desire of "advanced thinkers" for a world-system to replace the shattered Mosaic cosmogony, it soon gave Spencer a public influence that transcended Darwin's. Moreover it was not a technical creed for professionals. Presented in language that tyros in philosophy could understand, [2] it made Spencer the metaphysician

† From Chapter 2 of Hofstadter's *Social Darwinism in American Thought* (Boston, 1955). Richard Hofstadter (1916–1970) was professor of history at Columbia University.

1. David Duncan, *The Life and Letters of Herbert Spencer* (London, 1908), p. 128.

2. Spencer, wrote William James, "is the philosopher whom those who have no other philosopher can appreciate." *Memories and Studies*, p. 126.

of the homemade intellectual, and the prophet of the cracker-barrel agnostic. Although its influence far outstripped its merits, the Spencerian system serves students of the American mind as a fossil specimen from which the intellectual body of the period may be reconstructed. Oliver Wendell Holmes hardly exaggerated when he expressed his doubt that "any writer of English except Darwin has done so much to affect our whole way of thinking about the universe." [3] * * *

II

Herbert Spencer and his philosophy were products of English industrialism. It was appropriate that this spokesman of the new era should have trained to be a civil engineer, and that the scientific components of his thought—the conservation of energy and the idea of evolution—should have been indirectly derived from earlier observations in hydrotechnics and population theory. Spencer's was a system conceived in and dedicated to an age of steel and steam engines, competition, exploitation, and struggle. * * *

The aim of Spencer's synthesis was to join in one coherent structure the latest findings of physics and biology. While the idea of natural selection had been taking form in the mind of Darwin, the work of a series of investigators in thermodynamics had also yielded an illuminating generalization. Joule, Mayer, Helmholtz, Kelvin, and others had been exploring the relations between heat and energy, and had brought forth the principle of the conservation of energy which Helmholtz enunciated most clearly in his *Die Erhaltung der Kraft* (1847). The concept won general acceptance along with natural selection, and the convergence of the two discoveries upon the nineteenth-century mind was chiefly responsible for the enormous growth in the prestige of the natural sciences. Science, it was believed, had now drawn the last line in its picture of a self-contained universe, in which matter and energy were never destroyed but constantly changing form, whose varieties of organic life were integral, intelligible products of the universal economy. Previous philosophies paled into obsolescence much as pre-Newtonian philosophies had done in the eighteenth century. The transition to naturalism was marked by an efflorescence of mechanistic world-systems, whose trend is suggested by the names of Edward Büchner, Jacob Moleschott, Wilhelm Ostwald, Ernst Haeckel, and Herbert Spencer. Among these new thinkers, Spencer most resembled the eighteenth-century philosophers in his attempt to apply the implications of science to social thought and action.

3. M. De Wolfe Howe, ed., *Holmes-Pollock Letters* (Cambridge, 1941), I, 57–58. "Spencer," wrote Parrington, "laid out the broad highway over which American thought traveled in the later years of the century." *Main Currents in American Thought*, III, 198.

The conservation of energy—which Spencer preferred to call "the persistence of force"—was the starting point of his deductive system. The persistence of force, manifested in the forms of matter and motion, is the stuff of human inquiry, the material with which philosophy must build. Everywhere in the universe man observes the incessant redistribution of matter and motion, rhythmically apportioned between evolution and dissolution. Evolution is the progressive integration of matter, accompanied by dissipation of motion; dissolution is the disorganization of matter accompanied by the absorption of motion. The life process is essentially evolutionary, embodying a continuous change from incoherent homogeneity, illustrated by the lowly protozoa, to coherent heterogeneity, manifested in man and the higher animals.[4]

From the persistence of force, Spencer inferred that anything which is homogeneous is inherently unstable, since the different effects of persistent force upon its various parts must cause differences to arise in their future development.[5] Thus the homogeneous will inevitably develop into the heterogeneous. Here is the key to universal evolution. This progress from homogeneity to heterogeneity—in the formation of the earth from a nebular mass, in the evolution of higher, complex species from lower and simpler ones, in the embryological development of the individual from a uniform mass of cells, in the growth of the human mind, and in the progress of human societies—is the principle at work in everything man can know.[6]

The final result of this process, in an animal organism or society, is the achievement of a state of equilibrium—a process Spencer called "equilibration." The ultimate attainment of equilibration is inevitable, because the evolutionary process cannot go on forever in the direction of increasing heterogeneity. "Evolution has an impassable limit."[7] Here the pattern of universal rhythm comes into play: dissolution follows evolution, disintegration follows integration. In an organism this phase is represented by death and decay, built in society by the establishment of a stable, harmonious, completely adapted state, in which "evolution can end only in the establishment of the greatest perfection and the most complete happiness."[8]

This imposing positivistic edifice might have been totally unacceptable in America, had it not also been bound up with an important concession to religion in the form of Spencer's doctrine of

4. In the words of the original definition, "Evolution is an integration of matter and concomitant dissipation of motion; during which the matter passes from an indefinite, incoherent homogeneity to a definite, coherent heterogeneity; and during which the retained motion undergoes a parallel transformation." *First Principles* (4th Amer. ed., 1900), p. 407.
5. "The Instability of the Homogeneous," *ibid.*, Part II, chap. xix.
6. *Ibid.*, pp. 340–71.
7. *Ibid.*, p. 496.
8. *Ibid.*, p. 530.

the Unknowable. The great question of the day was whether religion and science could be reconciled. Spencer gave not only the desired affirmative answer, but also an assurance for all future ages that, whatever science might learn about the world, the true sphere of religion—worship of the Unknowable—is by its very nature inviolable.[9] * * *

III

Spencer's supposition that a general law of evolution could be formulated led him to apply the biologic scheme of evolution to society. The principles of social structure and change, if the generalizations of his system were valid, must be the same as those of the universe at large. In applying evolution to society, Spencer, and after him the social Darwinists, were doing poetic justice to its origins. The "survival of the fittest" was a biological generalization of the cruel processes which reflective observers saw at work in early nineteenth-century society, and Darwinism was a derivative of political economy. The miserable social conditions of the early industrial revolution had provided the data for Malthus' *Essay on The Principle of Population*, and Malthus' observations had been the matrix of natural-selection theory. The stamp of its social origin was evident in Darwinian theory. "Over the whole of English Darwinism," Nietzsche once observed, "there hovers something of the odor of humble people in need and in straits." [1]

Spencer's theory of social selection, also written under the stimulus of Malthus, arose out of his concern with population problems. In two famous articles that appeared in 1852, six years before Darwin and Wallace jointly published sketches of their theory, Spencer had set forth the view that the pressure of subsistence upon population must have a beneficient effect upon the human race. This pressure had been the immediate cause of progress from the earliest human times. By placing a premium upon skill, intelligence, self-control, and the power to adapt through technological innovation, it had stimulated human advancement and selected the best of each generation for survival.

Because he did not extend his generalization to the whole animal world, as Darwin did, Spencer failed to reap the full harvest of his insight, although he coined the expression "survival of the fittest." [2] He was more concerned with mental than physical evolution, and accepted Lamarck's theory that the inheritance of acquired characteristics is a means by which species can originate.

9. *Ibid.*, pp. 99, 103–4.
1. Quoted from *The Joyful Wisdom*, in Crane Brinton, *Nietzsche* (Cambridge, 1941), p. 147.
2. "A Theory of Population, Deduced from the General Law of Animal Fertility," *Westminster Review*, LVII (1852), 468–501, esp. 499–500; "The Development Hypothesis," reprinted in *Essays* (New York, 1907), I, 1–7; see *Autobiography*, 450–51.

This doctrine confirmed his evolutionary optimism. For if mental as well as physical characteristics could be inherited, the intellectual powers of the race would become cumulatively greater, and over several generations the ideal man would finally be developed. Spencer never discarded his Lamarckism, even when scientific opinion turned overwhelmingly against it.[3]

Spencer would have been the last to deny the primacy of ethical and political considerations in the formulation of his thought. "My ultimate purpose, lying behind all proximate purposes," he wrote in the preface to his *Data of Ethics*, "has been that of finding for the principles of right and wrong in conduct at large, a scientific basis." It is not surprising that he began his literary career with a book on ethics rather than metaphysics. His first work, *Social Statics* (1850), was an attempt to strengthen laissez faire with the imperatives of biology; it was intended as an attack upon Benthamism, especially the Benthamite stress upon the positive role of legislation in social reform. Although he consented to Jeremy Bentham's ultimate standard of value—the greatest happiness of the greatest number—Spencer discarded other phases of utilitarian ethics. He called for a return to natural rights, setting up as an ethical standard the right of every man to do as he pleases, subject only to the condition that he does not infringe upon the equal rights of others. In such a scheme, the sole function of the state is negative—to insure that such freedom is not curbed.

Fundamental to all ethical progress, Spencer believed, is the adaptation of human character to the conditions of life. The root of all evil is the "non-adaptation of constitution to conditions." Because the process of adaptation, founded in the very nature of the organism, is constantly at work, evil tends to disappear. While the moral constitution of the human race is still ridden with vestiges of man's original predatory life which demanded brutal self-assertion, adaptation assures that he will ultimately develop a new moral constitution fitted to the needs of civilized life. Human perfection is not only possible but inevitable:

> The ultimate development of the ideal man is logically certain —as certain as any conclusion in which we place the most implicit faith; for instance that all men will die. . . . Progress, therefore, is not an accident, but a necessity. Instead of civilization being artificial, it is a part of nature; all of a piece with the development of the embryo or the unfolding of a flower.[4]

Despite its radicalism on incidental themes—the injustice of private land ownership, the rights of women and children, and a peculiar Spencerian "right to ignore the state" which was dropped from his later writings—the main trend of Spencer's book was

3. See the controversy with Weismann in Duncan, *op. cit.*, pp. 342–52.　　4. *Social Statics*, pp. 79–80.

ultra-conservative. His categorical repudiation of state interference with the "natural," unimpeded growth of society led him to oppose all state aid to the poor. They were unfit, he said, and should be eliminated. "The whole effort of nature is to get rid of such, to clear the world of them, and make room for better." Nature is as insistent upon fitness of mental character as she is upon physical character, "and radical defects are as much causes of death in the one case as in the other." He who loses his life because of his stupidity, vice, or idleness is in the same class as the victims of weak viscera or malformed limbs. Under nature's laws all alike are put on trial. "If they are sufficiently complete to live, they *do* live, and it is well they should live. If they are not sufficiently complete to live, they die, and it is best they should die." [5]

Spencer deplored not only poor laws, but also state-supported education, sanitary supervision other than the suppression of nuisances, regulation of housing conditions, and even state protection of the ignorant from medical quacks.[6] He likewise opposed tariffs, state banking, and government postal systems. Here was a categorical answer to Bentham.

In Spencer's later writings social selection was less prominent, although it never disappeared. The precise degree to which Spencer based his sociology upon biology was never a matter of common agreement, and the inconsistencies and ambiguities of his system gave rise to a host of Spencer exegesists, among whom the most tireless and sympathetic was Spencer himself.[7] Accused of brutality in his application of biological concepts to social principles, Spencer was compelled to insist over and over again that he was not opposed to voluntary private charity to the unfit, since it had an elevating effect on the character of the donors and hastened the development of altruism; he opposed only compulsory poor laws and other state measures.[8]

Spencer's social theory was more fully developed in the *Synthetic Philosophy*. In *The Principles of Sociology* there is a long exposition of the organic interpretation of society, in which Spencer traces the parallels between the growth, differentiation, and integration of society and of animal bodies.[9] Although the purposes of a social organism are different from those of an animal organism,

5. *Ibid.*, pp. 414–15.
6. *Ibid.*, pp. 325–444.
7. In an article on "The Relations of Biology, Psychology, and Sociology," *Popular Science*, L (1896), 163–71, Spencer defended himself against the then-common charge that his sociology had been too dependent upon biology, and argued that he had always made ample use of psychology too. In a defense of his ethical writings he also

argued that he had not apotheosized the struggle for existence. "Evolutionary Ethics," *ibid.*, LII (1898), 497–502.
8. Duncan, *op. cit.*, p. 366.
9. "A Society Is an Organism," *The Principles of Sociology* (3rd ed., New York, 1925), Part II, chap. ii. For an excellent critique of Spencer's organismic theory see Judah Rumey, *Herbert Spencer's Sociology* (London, 1934), chap. 11.

he maintained that there is no difference in their laws of organization.[1] Among societies as among organisms, there is a struggle for existence. * * *

In *The Study of Sociology*, first published in the United States in 1872–73 in serial form by the *Popular Science Monthly* and incorporated in the International Scientific Series, Spencer outlined his conception of the practical value of social science. Written to show the desirability of a naturalistic social science and to defend sociology from the criticisms of theologians and indeterminists, the book had a notable influence on the rise of sociology in the United States.[2] Spencer was animated by the desire to foster a science of society that would puncture the illusions of legislative reformers who, he believed, generally operated on the assumption that social causes and effects are simple and easily calculable, and that projects to relieve distress and remedy ills will always have the anticipated effect. A science of sociology, by teaching men to think of social causation scientifically, would awaken them to the enormous complexity of the social organism, and put an end to hasty legislative panaceas.[3] Fortified by the Darwinian conception of gradual modification over long stretches of time, Spencer ridiculed schemes for quick social transformation.

The great task of sociology, as Spencer envisioned it, is to chart "the normal course of social evolution," to show how it will be affected by any given policy, and to condemn all types of behavior that interfere with it.[4] Social science is a practical instrument in a negative sense. Its purpose is not to guide the conscious control of societal evolution, but rather to show that such control is an absolute impossibility, and that the best that organized knowledge can do is to teach men to submit more readily to the dynamic factors in progress. Spencer referred to the function of a true theory of society as a lubricant but not a motive power in progress: it can grease the wheels and prevent friction but cannot keep the engine moving.[5] "There cannot be more good done," he said, "than that

---

1. Spencer was not consistent in carrying out his theory of the social organism. As Ernest Barker has pointed out, he was unable to overcome the antagonism between his individualistic ethics and his organic conception of society. Barker, *Political Thought in England*, pp. 85–132. From his individualistic bias Spencer seems to have derived the atomistic idea, most clearly expressed in *Social Statics* and *The Study of Sociology*, that a society is but the sum of its individual members and takes its character from the aggregate of their characters (*Social Statics*, pp. 28–29; *The Study of Sociology*, pp. 48–51). In *The Principles of Sociology*, however, Spencer says that there arises in the social organism "a life of the whole quite unlike the lives of the units, though it is a life produced by them" (3rd ed., I, 457). A similar dualism can be found in his ethical criteria, which are sometimes determined by the impersonal requirements of evolution and sometimes by personal hedonism. Cf. A. K. Rogers, *English and American Philosophy Since 1800*, pp. 154–57.

2. Charles H. Cooley, "Reflections on the Sociology of Herbert Spencer," *American Journal of Sociology*, XXVI (1920), pp. 129–45.

3. *The Study of Sociology*, chap. i.

4. *Ibid.*, pp. 70–71.

5. Duncan, *op. cit.*, p. 367.

of letting social progress go on unhindered; yet an immensity of mischief may be done in the way of disturbing, and distorting and repressing, by policies carried out in pursuit of erroneous conceptions." [6] Any adequate theory of society, Spencer concluded, will recognize the "general truths" of biology and will refrain from violating the selection principle by "the artificial preservation of those least able to take care of themselves." [7]

IV

With its rapid expansion, its exploitative methods, its desperate competition, and its peremptory rejection of failure, post-bellum America was like a vast human caricature of the Darwinian struggle for existence and survival of the fittest. Successful business entrepreneurs apparently accepted almost by instinct the Darwinian terminology which seemed to portray the conditions of their existence.[8] Businessmen are not commonly articulate social philosophers, but a rough reconstruction of their social outlook shows how congenial to their thinking were the plausible analogies of social selection, and how welcome was the expansive evolutionary optimism of the Spencerian system. In a nation permeated with the gospel of progress, the incentive of pecuniary success appealed even to many persons whose ethical horizons were considerably broader than those of business enterprise. "I perceive clearly," wrote Walt Whitman in *Democratic Vistas*, "that the extreme business energy, and this almost maniacal appetite for wealth prevalent in the United States, are parts of amelioration and progress, indispensably needed to prepare the very results I demand. My theory includes riches, and the getting of riches . . . " No doubt there were many to applaud the assertion of the railroad executive Chauncey Depew that the guests at the great dinners and public banquets of New York City represented the survival of the fittest of the thousands who came there in search of fame, fortune, or power, and that it was "superior ability, foresight, and adapta-

6. Spencer, *op. cit.*, pp. 401–2.
7. *Ibid.*, pp. 343–46.
8. "It would be strange," wrote a sociologist in 1896, "if the 'captain of the industry' did not sometimes manifest a militant spirit, for he has risen from the ranks largely because he was a better fighter than most of us. Competitive commercial life is not a flowery bed of ease, but a battle field where the 'struggle for existence' is defining the industrially 'fittest to survive.' In this country the great prizes are not found in Congress, in literature, in law, in medicine, but in industry. The successful man is praised and honored for his success. The social rewards of business prosperity, in power, in praise, and luxury, are so great as to entice men of the greatest intellectual faculties. Men of splendid abilities find in the career of a manufacturer or merchant an opportunity for the most intense energy. The very perils of the situation have a fascination for adventurous and inventive spirits. In this fierce, though voiceless contest, a peculiar type of manhood is developed, characterized by vitality, energy, concentration, skill in combining numerous forces for an end, and great foresight into the consequence of social events." C. R. Henderson, "Business Men and Social Theorists," *American Journal of Sociology*, I (1896), 385–86.

bility" that brought them successfully through the fierce competitions of the metropolis.[9] James J. Hill, another railroad magnate, in an essay defending business consolidation, argued that "the fortunes of railroad companies are determined by the law of the survival of the fittest," and implied that the absorption of smaller by larger roads represents the industrial analogy of the victory of the strong.[1] And John D. Rockefeller, speaking from an intimate acquaintance with the methods of competition, declared in a Sunday-school address:

> The growth of a large business is merely a survival of the fittest. . . . The American Beauty rose can be produced in the splendor and fragrance which bring cheer to its beholder only by sacrificing the early buds which grow up around it. This is not an evil tendency in business. It is merely the working-out of a law of nature and a law of God.[2]

The most prominent of the disciples of Spencer was Andrew Carnegie, who sought out the philosopher, became his intimate friend, and showered him with favors. In his autobiography, Carnegie told how troubled and perplexed he had been over the collapse of Christian theology, until he took the trouble to read Darwin and Spencer.

> I remember that light came as in a flood and all was clear. Not only had I got rid of theology and the supernatural, but I had found the truth of evolution. "All is well since all grows better," became my motto, my true source of comfort. Man was not created with an instinct for his own degradation, but from the lower he had risen to the higher forms. Nor is there any conceivable end to his march to perfection. His face is turned to the light; he stands in the sun and looks upward.[3]

* * *

Conservatism and Spencer's philosophy walked hand in hand. The doctrine of selection and the biological apology for laissez faire, preached in Spencer's formal sociological writings and in a series of shorter essays, satisfied the desire of the select for a scientific rationale. Spencer's plea for absolute freedom of individual enterprise was a large philosophical statement of the constitutional ban upon interference with liberty and property without due process of law. Spencer was advancing within a cosmic framework the same general political philosophy which under the Supreme Court's exegesis of the Fourteenth Amendment served so brilliantly to turn back the tide of state reform. It was this convergence of Spencer's philosophy with the Court's interpretation of due proc-

9. *My Memories of Eighty Years* (New York, 1922), pp. 383–84.
1. *Highways of Progress* (New York, 1910), p. 126; cf. also p. 137.
2. Quoted in William J. Ghent, *Our Benevolent Feudalism*, p. 29.
3. *Autobiography of Andrew Carnegie* (Boston, 1920), p. 327.

ess which finally inspired Mr. Justice Holmes (himself an admirer of Spencer) to protest that "the fourteenth Amendment does not enact Mr. Herbert Spencer's Social Statics." [4]

The social views of Spencer's popularizers were likewise conservative. Youmans took time from his promotion of science to attack the eight-hour strikers in 1872. Labor, he urged in characteristic Spencerian vein, must "accept the spirit of civilization, which is pacific, constructive, controlled by reason, and slowly ameliorating and progressive. Coercive and violent measures which aim at great and sudden advantages are sure to prove illusory." He suggested that, if people were taught the elements of political economy and social science in the course of their education, such mistakes might be avoided.[5] Youmans attacked the newly founded American Social Science Association for devoting itself to unscientific reform measures instead of a "strict and passionless study of society from a scientific point of view." Until the laws of social behavior are known, he declared, reform is blind; the Association might do better to recognize a sphere of natural, self-adjusting activity, with which government intervention usually wreaks havoc.[6] There was precious little scope for meliorist activities in the outlook of one who believed with Youmans that science shows "that we are born well, or born badly, and that whoever is ushered into existence at the bottom of the scale can never rise to the top because the weight of the universe is upon him." [7]

Acceptance of the Spencerian philosophy brought with it a paralysis of the will to reform. One day, some years after the publication of *Progress and Poverty*, Youmans in Henry George's presence denounced with great fervor the political corruption of New York and the selfishness of the rich in ignoring or promoting it when they found it profitable to do so. "What do you propose to do about it?" George asked. Youmans replied, "Nothing! You and I can do nothing at all. It's all a matter of evolution. We can only wait for evolution. Perhaps in four or five thousand years evolution may have carried men beyond this state of things." [8]

4. Lochner v. New York, 198 U.S. 45 (1905).
5. Youmans, "The Recent Strike," *Popular Science Monthly*, III (1872), 623–24. See also R. G. Eccles, "The Labor Question," *ibid.*, XI (1877), 606–11; *Appleton's Journal*, N. S., V (1878), 473–75.
6. "The Social Science Association," *Popular Science Monthly*, V (1874), 267–69. See also *ibid.*, VII (1875), 365–67.
7. "On the Scientific Study of Human Nature," reprinted in Fiske, *op. cit.*, p. 482. For other statements of the conservative Spencerian viewpoint, see Erastus B. Bigelow, "The Relations of Capital and Labor," *Atlantic Monthly*, XLII (1878), 475–87; G. F. Parsons, "The Labor Question," *ibid.*, LVIII (1886), 97–113. Also "Editor's Table," *Appleton's Journal*, N. S., V (1878), 473–75.
8. Henry George, *A Perplexed Philosopher*, pp. 163–64 n. Fiske shared Youman's conservatism, but was less alarmed at the menace of radicalism to the American future. See Fiske, *op. cit.*, pp. 381–82n. For the social outlook of an American thinker thoroughly influenced by Spencer, see Henry Holt, *The Civic Relations* (Boston, 1907), and *Garrulities of an Octogenarian Editor*, pp. 374–88.

Spencer's doctrines were imported into the Republic long after individualism had become a national tradition. Yet in the expansive age of our industrial culture he became the spokesman of that tradition, and his contribution materially swelled the stream of individualism if it did not change its course. If Spencer's abiding impact on American thought seems impalpable to later generations, it is perhaps only because it has been so thoroughly absorbed.[9] His language has become a standard feature of the folklore of individualism. "You can't make the world all planned and soft," says the businessman of Middletown. "The strongest and best survive—that's the law of nature after all—always has been and always will be."[1]

ANDREW CARNEGIE

The Gospel of Wealth (1900) †

* * * The price which society pays for the law of competition, like the price it pays for cheap comforts and luxuries, is also great; but the advantages of this law are also greater still than its cost—for it is to this law that we owe our wonderful material development, which brings improved conditions in its train. But, whether the law be benign or not, we must say of it, as we say of the change in the conditions of men to which we have referred: It is here, we cannot evade it; no substitutes for it have been found; and while the law may be sometimes hard for the individual, it is best for the race, because it insures the survival of the fittest in every department. We accept and welcome, therefore, as conditions to which we must accommodate ourselves, great inequality of environment; the concentration of business, industrial and commercial, in the hands of a few; and the law of competition between these, as being not only beneficial, but essential to the future progress of the race. * * *

Objections to the foundations upon which society is based are not in order, because the condition of the race is better with these than it has been with any other which has been tried. Of the effect of any new substitutes proposed we cannot be sure. The Socialist or Anarchist who seeks to overturn present conditions is to be regarded as attacking the foundation upon which civilization

9. See Thomas C. Cochran, "The Faith of Our Fathers," *Frontiers of Democracy*, VI (1939), 17–19.
1. Robert S. and Helen M. Lynd, *Middletown in Transition* (New York, 1937), p. 500.
† From Chapter 2 of Carnegie's *The*

Gospel of Wealth and Other Timely Essays (New York, 1900). Andrew Carnegie (1835–1919), American industrialist and philanthropist, wrote extensively on business and social problems.

itself rests, for civilization took its start from the day when the capable, industrious workman said to his incompetent and lazy fellow, "If thou dost not sow, thou shalt not reap," and thus ended primitive Communism by separating the drones from the bees. One who studies this subject will soon be brought face to face with the conclusion that upon the sacredness of property civilization itself depends—the right of the laborer to his hundred dollars in the savings-bank, and equally the legal right of the millionaire to his millions. Every man must be allowed "to sit under his own vine and fig-tree, with none to make afraid," if human society is to advance, or even to remain so far advanced as it is. To those who propose to substitute Communism for this intense Individualism, the answer therefore is: The race has tried that. All progress from that barbarous day to the present time has resulted from its displacement. Not evil, but good, has come to the race from the accumulation of wealth by those who have had the ability and energy to produce it. But even if we admit for a moment that it might be better for the race to discard its present foundation, Individualism,—that it is a nobler ideal that man should labor, not for himself alone, but in and for a brotherhood of his fellows, and share with them all in common, realizing Swedenborg's idea of heaven, where, as he says, the angels derive their happiness, not from laboring for self, but for each other,—even admit all this, and a sufficient answer is, This is not evolution, but revolution. It necessitates the changing of human nature itself—a work of eons, even if it were good to change it, which we cannot know.

It is not practicable in our day or in our age. Even if desirable theoretically, it belongs to another and long-succeeding sociological stratum. Our duty is with what is practicable now—with the next step possible in our day and generation. It is criminal to waste our energies in endeavoring to uproot, when all we can profitably accomplish is to bend the universal tree of humanity a little in the direction most favorable to the production of good fruit under existing circumstances. We might as well urge the destruction of the highest existing type of man because he failed to reach our ideal as to favor the destruction of Individualism, Private Property, the Law of Accumulation of Wealth, and the Law of Competition; for these are the highest result of human experience, the soil in which society, so far, has produced the best fruit. Unequally or unjustly, perhaps, as these laws sometimes operate, and imperfect as they appear to the Idealist, they are, nevertheless, like the highest type of man, the best and most valuable of all that humanity has yet accomplished.

We start, then, with a condition of affairs under which the best interests of the race are promoted, but which inevitably gives wealth to the few. Thus far, accepting conditions as they exist, the situation can be surveyed and pronounced good. The question then arises,—and if the foregoing be correct, it is the only question with which we have to deal,—What is the proper mode of administering wealth after the laws upon which civilization is founded have thrown it into the hands of the few? And it is of this great question that I believe I offer the true solution. It will be understood that fortunes are here spoken of, not moderate sums saved by many years of effort, the returns from which are required for the comfortable maintenance and education of families. This is not wealth, but only competence, which it should be the aim of all to acquire, and which it is for the best interests of society should be acquired.

There are but three modes in which surplus wealth can be disposed of. It can be left to the families of the decedents; or it can be bequeathed for public purposes; or, finally, it can be administered by its possessors during their lives. Under the first and second modes most of the wealth of the world that has reached the few has hitherto been applied. Let us in turn consider each of these modes. The first is the most injudicious. In monarchical countries, the estates and the greatest portion of the wealth are left to the first son, that the vanity of the parent may be gratified by the thought that his name and title are to descend unimpaired to succeeding generations. The condition of this class in Europe to-day teaches the failure of such hopes or ambitions. The successors have become impoverished through their follies, or from the fall in the value of land. Even in Great Britain the strict law of entail has been found inadequate to maintain an hereditary class. Its soil is rapidly passing into the hands of the stranger. Under republican institutions the division of property among the children is much fairer; but the question which forces itself upon thoughtful men in all lands is, Why should men leave great fortunes to their children? If this is done from affection, is it not misguided affection? Observation teaches that, generally speaking, it is not well for the children that they should be so burdened. Neither is it well for the State. Beyond providing for the wife and daughters moderate sources of income, and very moderate allowances indeed, if any, for the sons, men may well hesitate; for it is no longer questionable that great sums bequeathed often work more for the injury than for the good of the recipients. Wise men will soon conclude that, for the best interests of the members of their families, and of the State, such bequests are an improper use of their means.

It is not suggested that men who have failed to educate their sons to earn a livelihood shall cast them adrift in poverty. If any man has seen fit to rear his sons with a view to their living idle lives, or, what is highly commendable, has instilled in them the

402 · *Andrew Carnegie*

sentiment that they are in a position to labor for public ends without reference to pecuniary considerations, then, of course, the duty of the parent is to see that such are provided for in moderation. There are instances of millionaires' sons unspoiled by wealth, who, being rich, still perform great services to the community. Such are the very salt of the earth, as valuable as, unfortunately, they are rare. It is not the exception, however, but the rule, that men must regard; and, looking at the usual result of enormous sums conferred upon legatees, the thoughtful man must shortly say, "I would as soon leave to my son a curse as the almighty dollar," and admit to himself that it is not the welfare of the children, but family pride, which inspires these legacies.

As to the second mode, that of leaving wealth at death for public uses, it may be said that this is only a means for the disposal of wealth, provided a man is content to wait until he is dead before he becomes of much good in the world. Knowledge of the results of legacies bequeathed is not calculated to inspire the brightest hopes of much posthumous good being accomplished by them. The cases are not few in which the real object sought by the testator is not attained, nor are they few in which his real wishes are thwarted. In many cases the bequests are so used as to become only monuments of his folly. It is well to remember that it requires the exercise of not less ability than that which acquires it, to use wealth so as to be really beneficial to the community. Besides this, it may be said that no man is to be extolled for doing what he cannot help doing, nor is he to be thanked by the community to which he only leaves wealth at death. Men who leave vast sums in this way may fairly be thought men who would not have left it at all had they been able to take it with them. The memories of such cannot be held in grateful remembrance, for there is no grace in their gifts. It is not to be wondered at that such bequests seem so generally to lack the blessing.

The growing disposition to tax more and more heavily large estates left at death is a cheering indication of the growth of a salutary change in public opinion. The State of Pennsylvania now takes—subject to some exceptions—one tenth of the property left by its citizens. The budget presented in the British Parliament the other day proposes to increase the death duties; and, most significant of all, the new tax is to be a graduated one. Of all forms of taxation this seems the wisest. Men who continue hoarding great sums all their lives, the proper use of which for public ends would work good to the community from which it chiefly came, should be made to feel that the community, in the form of the State, cannot thus be deprived of its proper share. By taxing estates heavily at death the State marks its condemnation of the selfish millionaire's unworthy life.

It is desirable that nations should go much further in this direction. Indeed, it is difficult to set bounds to the share of a rich man's estate which should go at his death to the public through the agency of the State, and by all means such taxes should be graduated, beginning at nothing upon moderate sums to dependents, and increasing rapidly as the amounts swell, until of the millionaire's hoard, as of Shylock's, at least

> The other half
> Comes to the privy coffer of the State.

This policy would work powerfully to induce the rich man to attend to the administration of wealth during his life, which is the end that society should always have in view, as being by far the most fruitful for the people. Nor need it be feared that this policy would sap the root of enterprise and render men less anxious to accumulate, for, to the class whose ambition it is to leave great fortunes and to be talked about after their death, it will attract even more attention, and, indeed, be a somewhat nobler ambition, to have enormous sums paid over to the State from their fortunes.

There remains, then, only one mode of using great fortunes; but in this we have the true antidote for the temporary unequal distribution of wealth, the reconciliation of the rich and the poor—a reign of harmony, another ideal, differing, indeed, from that of the Communist in requiring only the further evolution of existing conditions, not the total overthrow of our civilization. It is founded upon the present most intense Individualism, and the race is prepared to put it in practice by degrees whenever it pleases. Under its sway we shall have an ideal State, in which the surplus wealth of the few will become, in the best sense, the property of the many, because administered for the common good; and this wealth, passing through the hands of the few, can be made a much more potent force for the elevation of our race than if distributed in small sums to the people themselves. Even the poorest can be made to see this, and to agree that great sums gathered by some of their fellow-citizens and spent for public purposes, from which the masses reap the principal benefit, are more valuable to them than if scattered among themselves in trifling amounts through the course of many years. * * *

This, then, is held to be the duty of the man of wealth: To set an example of modest, unostentatious living, shunning display or extravagance; to provide moderately for the legitimate wants of those dependent upon him; and, after doing so, to consider all surplus revenues which come to him simply as trust funds, which he is called upon to administer, and strictly bound as a matter of duty to administer in the manner which, in his judgment, is best calculated to produce the most beneficial results for the community—the man of wealth thus becoming the mere trustee and agent for his poorer brethren, bringing to their service his superior wisdom, experience, and ability to administer, doing for them better than they would or could do for themselves. * * *

* * * It were better for mankind that the millions of the rich were thrown into the sea than so spent as to encourage the slothful, the drunken, the unworthy. Of every thousand dollars spent in so-called charity to-day, it is probable that nine hundred and fifty dollars is unwisely spent—so spent, indeed, as to produce the very evils which it hopes to mitigate or cure. A well-known writer of philosophic books admitted the other day that he had given a quarter of a dollar to a man who approached him as he was coming to visit the house of his friend. He knew nothing of the habits of this beggar, knew not the use that would be made of this money, although he had every reason to suspect that it would be spent improperly. This man professed to be a disciple of Herbert Spencer; yet the quarter-dollar given that night will probably work more injury than all the money will do good which its thoughtless donor will ever be able to give in true charity. He only gratified his own feelings, saved himself from annoyance—and this was probably one of the most selfish and very worst actions of his life, for in all respects he is most worthy.

In bestowing charity, the main consideration should be to help those who will help themselves; to provide part of the means by which those who desire to improve may do so; to give those who desire to rise the aids by which they may rise; to assist, but rarely or never to do all. Neither the individual nor the race is improved by almsgiving. Those worthy of assistance, except in rare cases, seldom require assistance. * * *

Time was when the words concerning the rich man entering the kingdom of heaven were regarded as a hard saying. To-day, when all questions are probed to the bottom and the standards of faith receive the most liberal interpretations, the startling verse has been relegated to the rear, to await the next kindly revision as one of those things which cannot be quite understood, but which, meanwhile, it is carefully to be noted, are not to be understood literally. But is it so very improbable that the next stage of thought is to restore the doctrine in all its pristine purity and force, as being in perfect harmony with sound ideas upon the subject of wealth and poverty, the rich and the poor, and the contrasts everywhere seen and deplored? In Christ's day, it is evident, reformers were against the wealthy. It is none the less evident that we are fast recurring to that position to-day; and there will be nothing to surprise the student of sociological development if society should soon approve the text which has caused so much anxiety: "It is easier for a camel to enter the eye of a needle than for a rich man to enter the kingdom of heaven." Even if the needle were the small casement at the gates, the words betoken serious difficulty for the rich. It will be but a step for the theologian from the doctrine that he who dies rich dies disgraced, to that which brings upon the man punishment or deprivation hereafter.

The gospel of wealth but echoes Christ's words. It calls upon the millionaire to sell all that he hath and give it in the highest and best form to the poor by administering his estate himself for the good of his fellows, before he is called upon to lie down and rest upon the bosom of Mother Earth. So doing, he will approach his end no longer the ignoble hoarder of useless millions; poor, very poor indeed, in money, but rich, very rich, twenty times a millionaire still, in the affection, gratitude, and admiration of his fellow-men, and—sweeter far—soothed and sustained by the still, small voice within, which, whispering, tells him that, because he has lived, perhaps one small part of the great world has been bettered just a little. This much is sure: against such riches as these no bar will be found at the gates of Paradise.

PETER KROPOTKIN

Mutual Aid (1902) †

Introduction

Two aspects of animal life impressed me most during the journeys which I made in my youth in Eastern Siberia and Northern Manchuria. One of them was the extreme severity of the struggle for existence which most species of animals have to carry on against an inclement Nature; the enormous destruction of life which periodically results from natural agencies; and the consequent paucity of life over the vast territory which fell under my observation. And the other was, that even in those few spots where animal life teemed in abundance, I failed to find—although I was eagerly looking for it—that bitter struggle for the means of existence, *among animals belonging to the same species*, which was considered by most Darwinists (though not always by Darwin himself) as the dominant characteristic of struggle for life, and the main factor of evolution.

† Peter Kropotkin (1842–1921) was a Russian prince who spent much of his mature life in anarchist-nihilist activities. As a young man, however, he held a variety of military and diplomatic posts in Siberia and led geographical survey expeditions in Manchuria, where he observed some of the phenomena he described in *Mutual Aid*. The present selections are from the Introduction and the first two chapters.

The terrible snow-storms which sweep over the northern portion of Eurasia in the later part of the winter, and the glazed frost that often follows them; the frosts and the snow-storms which return every year in the second half of May, when the trees are already in full blossom and insect life swarms everywhere; the early frosts and, occasionally, the heavy snowfalls in July and August, which suddenly destroy myriads of insects, as well as the second broods of the birds in the prairies; the torrential rains, due to the monsoons, which fall in more temperate regions in August and September—resulting in inundations on a scale which is only known in America and in Eastern Asia, and swamping, on the plateaus, areas as wide as European States; and finally, the heavy snowfalls, early in October, which eventually render a territory as large as France and Germany, absolutely impracticable for ruminants, and destroy them by the thousand—these were the conditions under which I saw animal life struggling in Northern Asia. They made me realize at an early date the overwhelming importance in Nature of what Darwin described as "the natural checks to over-multiplication," in comparison to the struggle between individuals of the same species for the means of subsistence, which may go on here and there, to some limited extent, but never attains the importance of the former. Paucity of life, under-population—not over-population—being the distinctive feature of that immense part of the globe which we name Northern Asia, I conceived since then serious doubts—which subsequent study has only confirmed—as to the reality of that fearful competition for food and life within each species, which was an article of faith with most Darwinists, and, consequently, as to the dominant part which this sort of competition was supposed to play in the evolution of new species.

On the other hand, wherever I saw animal life in abundance, as, for instance, on the lakes where scores of species and millions of individuals came together to rear their progeny; in the colonies of rodents; in the migrations of birds which took place at that time on a truly American scale along the Usuri; and especially in a migration of fallow-deer which I witnessed on the Amur, and during which scores of thousands of these intelligent animals came together from an immense territory, flying before the coming deep snow, in order to cross the Amur where it is narrowest—in all these scenes of animal life which passed before my eyes, I saw Mutual Aid and Mutual Support carried on to an extent which made me suspect in it a feature of the greatest importance for the maintenance of life, the preservation of each species, and its further evolution.

And finally, I saw among the semi-wild cattle and horses in Transbaikalia, among the wild ruminants everywhere, the squirrels, and so on, that when animals have to struggle against scarcity of food, in consequence of one of the above-mentioned causes, the whole of that portion of the species which is affected by the calamity, comes out of the ordeal so much impoverished in vigour and health, that *no progressive evolution of the species can be based upon such periods of keen competition.*

Consequently, when my attention was drawn, later on, to the relations between Darwinism and Sociology, I could agree with none of the works and pamphlets that had been written upon this important subject. They all endeavoured to prove that Man, owing to his higher intelligence and knowledge, *may* mitigate the harshness of the struggle for life between men; but they all recognized at the same time that the struggle for the means of existence, of every animal against all its congeners, and of every man against all other men, was "a law of Nature." This view, however, I could not accept, because I was persuaded that to admit a pitiless inner war for life within each species, and to see in that war a condition of progress, was to admit something which not only had not yet been proved, but also lacked confirmation from direct observation.

On the contrary, a lecture "On the Law of Mutual Aid," which was delivered at a Russian Congress of Naturalists, in January 1880, by the well-known zoologist, Professor Kessler, the then Dean of the St. Petersburg University, struck me as throwing a new light on the whole subject. Kessler's idea was, that besides the *law of Mutual Struggle* there is in Nature *the law of Mutual Aid*, which, for the success of the struggle for life, and especially for the progressive evolution of the species, is far more important than the law of mutual contest. This suggestion—which was, in reality, nothing but a further development of the ideas expressed by Darwin himself in *The Descent of Man*—seemed to me so correct and of so great an importance, that since I became acquainted with it (in 1883) I began to collect materials for further developing the idea. * * *

* * * To reduce animal sociability to *love* and *sympathy* means to reduce its generality and its importance, just as human ethics based upon love and personal sympathy only have contributed to narrow the comprehension of the moral feeling as a whole. It is not love to my neighbour—whom I often do not know at all—which induces me to seize a pail of water and to rush towards his house when I see it on fire; it is a far wider, even though more vague feeling or instinct of human solidarity and sociability which moves me. So it is also with animals. It is not love, and not even sympathy (understood in its proper sense) which induces a herd of ruminants or of horses to form a ring in order to resist an attack of wolves; not love which induces wolves to form a pack for hunting; not love which induces kittens or lambs to play, or a dozen of species of young birds to spend their days together in the autumn; and it is neither love nor personal sympathy which induces many thousand fallow-deer scattered over a territory as large as France to

form into a score of separate herds, all marching towards a given spot, in order to cross there a river. It is a feeling infinitely wider than love or personal sympathy—an instinct that has been slowly developed among animals and men in the course of an extremely long evolution, and which has taught animals and men alike the force they can borrow from the practice of mutual aid and support, and the joys they can find in social life.

The importance of this distinction will be easily appreciated by the student of animal psychology, and the more so by the student of human ethics. Love, sympathy and self-sacrifice certainly play an immense part in the progressive development of our moral feelings. But it is not love and not even sympathy upon which Society is based in mankind. It is the conscience—be it only at the stage of an instinct—of human solidarity. It is the unconscious recognition of the force that is borrowed by each man from the practice of mutual aid; of the close dependency of every one's happiness upon the happiness of all; and of the sense of justice, or equity, which brings the individual to consider the rights of every other individual as equal to his own. Upon this broad and necessary foundation the still higher moral feelings are developed. * * *

After having discussed the importance of mutual aid in various classes of animals, I was evidently bound to discuss the importance of the same factor in the evolution of Man. This was the more necessary as there are a number of evolutionists who may not refuse to admit the importance of mutual aid among animals, but who, like Herbert Spencer, will refuse to admit it for Man. For primitive Man—they maintain—war of each against all was *the* law of life. * * *

Chapter I

MUTUAL AID AMONG ANIMALS

The conception of struggle for existence as a factor of evolution, introduced into science by Darwin and Wallace, has permitted us to embrace an immensely-wide range of phenomena in one single generalization, which soon became the very basis of our philosophical, biological, and sociological speculations. An immense variety of facts:—adaptations of function and structure of organic beings to their surroundings; physiological and anatomical evolution; intellectual progress, and moral development itself, which we formerly used to explain by so many different causes, were embodied by Darwin in one general conception. We understood them as continued endeavours—as a struggle against adverse circumstances—for such a development of individuals, races, species and societies, as would result in the greatest possible fulness, variety, and intensity of life. It may be that at the outset Darwin himself was not fully aware of the generality of the factor which he first invoked for explaining one series only of facts relative to the accumulation of individual variations in incipient species. But he foresaw that the term which he was introducing into science would lose its philosophical and its only true meaning if it were to be used in its narrow sense only—that of a struggle between separate individuals for the sheer means of existence. And at the very beginning of his memorable work he insisted upon the term being taken in its "large and metaphorical sense including dependence of one being on another, and including (which is more important) not only the life of the individual, but success in leaving progeny." [1]

While he himself was chiefly using the term in its narrow sense for his own special purpose, he warned his followers against committing the error (which he seems once to have committed himself) of overrating its narrow meaning. In *The Descent of Man* he gave some powerful pages to illustrate its proper, wide sense. He pointed out how, in numberless animal societies, the struggle between separate individuals for the means of existence disappears, how *struggle* is replaced by *co-operation*, and how that substitution results in the development of intellectual and moral faculties which secure to the species the best conditions for survival. He intimated that in such cases the fittest are not the physically strongest, nor the cunningest, but those who learn to combine so as mutually to support each other, strong and weak alike, for the welfare of the community. "Those communities," he wrote, "which included the greatest number of the most sympathetic members would flourish best, and rear the greatest number of offspring" (2nd edit., p. 163). The term, which originated from the narrow Malthusian conception of competition between each and all, thus lost its narrowness in the mind of one who knew Nature.

Unhappily, these remarks, which might have become the basis of most fruitful researches, were overshadowed by the masses of facts gathered for the purpose of illustrating the consequences of a real competition for life. Besides, Darwin never attempted to submit to a closer investigation the relative importance of the two aspects under which the struggle for existence appears in the animal world, and he never wrote the work he proposed to write upon the natural checks to over-multiplication, although that work would have been the crucial test for appreciating the real purport of individual struggle. Nay, on the very pages just mentioned, amidst data disproving the narrow Malthusian conception of struggle, the old Malthusian leaven reappeared—namely, in Dar-

---

1. *Origin of Species*, chap. iii.

win's remarks as to the alleged inconveniences of maintaining the "weak in mind and body" in our civilized societies (ch. v.). As if thousands of weak-bodied and infirm poets, scientists, inventors, and reformers, together with other thousands of so-called "fools" and "weak-minded enthusiasts," were not the most precious weapons used by humanity in its struggle for existence by intellectual and moral arms, which Darwin himself emphasized in those same chapters of *Descent of Man*.

It happened with Darwin's theory as it always happens with theories having any bearing upon human relations. Instead of widening it according to his own hints, his followers narrowed it still more. And while Herbert Spencer, starting on independent but closely-allied lines, attempted to widen the inquiry into that great question, "Who are the fittest?" especially in the appendix to the third edition of the *Data of Ethics*, the numberless followers of Darwin reduced the notion of struggle for existence to its narrowest limits. They came to conceive the animal world as a world of perpetual struggle among half-starved individuals, thirsting for one another's blood. They made modern literature resound with the war-cry of *woe to the vanquished*, as if it were the last word of modern biology. They raised the "pitiless" struggle for personal advantages to the height of a biological principle which man must submit to as well, under the menace of otherwise succumbing in a world based upon mutual extermination. Leaving aside the economists who know of natural science but a few words borrowed from second-hand vulgarizers, we must recognize that even the most authorized exponents of Darwin's views did their best to maintain those false ideas. In fact, if we take Huxley, who certainly is considered as one of the ablest exponents of the theory of evolution, were we not taught by him, in a paper on the 'Struggle for Existence and its Bearing upon Man,' that,

> "from the point of view of the moralist, the animal world is on about the same level as a gladiators' show. The creatures are fairly well treated, and set to fight; whereby the strongest, the swiftest, and the cunningest live to fight another day. The spectator has no need to turn his thumb down, as no quarter is given."

Or, further down in the same article, did he not tell us that, as among animals, so among primitive men,

> "the weakest and stupidest went to the wall, while the toughest and shrewdest, those who were best fitted to cope with their circumstances, but not the best in another way, survived. Life was a continuous free fight, and beyond the limited and temporary

relations of the family, the Hobbesian war of each against all was the normal state of existence." [2]

In how far this view of nature is supported by fact, will be seen from the evidence which will be here submitted to the reader as regards the animal world, and as regards primitive man. But it may be remarked at once that Huxley's view of nature had as little claim to be taken as a scientific deduction as the opposite view of Rousseau, who saw in nature but love, peace, and harmony destroyed by the accession of man. In fact, the first walk in the forest, the first observation upon any animal society, or even the perusal of any serious work dealing with animal life (D'Orbigny's, Audubon's, Le Vaillant's, no matter which), cannot but set the naturalist thinking about the part taken by social life in the life of animals, and prevent him from seeing in Nature nothing but a field of slaughter, just as this would prevent him from seeing in Nature nothing but harmony and peace. Rousseau had committed the error of excluding the beak-and-claw fight from his thoughts; and Huxley committed the opposite error; but neither Rousseau's optimism nor Huxley's pessimism can be accepted as an impartial interpretation of nature.

As soon as we study animals—not in laboratories and museums only, but in the forest and the prairie, in the steppe and the mountains—we at once perceive that though there is an immense amount of warfare and extermination going on amidst various species, and especially amidst various classes of animals, there is, at the same time, as much, or perhaps even more, of mutual support, mutual aid, and mutual defence amidst animals belonging to the same species or, at least, to the same society. Sociability is as much a law of nature as mutual struggle. Of course it would be extremely difficult to estimate, however roughly, the relative numerical importance of both these series of facts. But if we resort to an indirect test, and ask Nature: "Who are the fittest: those who are continually at war with each other, or those who support one another?" we at once see that those animals which acquire habits of mutual aid are undoubtedly the fittest. They have more chances to survive, and they attain, in their respective classes, the highest development of intelligence and bodily organization. If the numberless facts which can be brought forward to support this view are taken into account, we may safely say that mutual aid is as much a law of animal life as mutual struggle, but that, as a factor of evolution, it most probably has a far greater importance, inasmuch as it favours the development of such habits and characters as insure the maintenance and further development of the species, together with the greatest amount of welfare and enjoyment of life for the individual, with the least waste of energy. * * *

If we knew no other facts from animal life than what we know about the ants and the termites, we already might safely conclude that mutual aid (which leads to mutual confidence, the first condition for courage) and individual initiative (the first condition for intellectual progress) are two factors infinitely more important than mutual struggle in the evolution of the animal kingdom. In fact, the ant thrives without having any of the "protective" features which cannot be dispensed with by animals living an isolated life. Its colour renders it conspicuous to its enemies, and the lofty nests of many species are conspicuous in the meadows and forests. It is not protected by a hard carapace, and its stinging apparatus, how-ever dangerous when hundreds of stings are plunged into the flesh of an animal, is not of a great value for individual defence; while the eggs and larvæ of the ants are a dainty for a great number of the inhabitants of the forests. And yet the ants, in their thousands, are not much destroyed by the birds, not even by the ant-eaters, and they are dreaded by most stronger insects. When Forel emp-tied a bagful of ants in a meadow, he saw that "the crickets ran away, abandoning their holes to be sacked by the ants; the grass-hoppers and the crickets fled in all directions; the spiders and the beetles abandoned their prey in order not to become prey them-selves;" even the nests of the wasps were taken by the ants, after a battle during which many ants perished for the safety of the com-monwealth. Even the swiftest insects cannot escape, and Forel often saw butterflies, gnats, flies, and so on, surprised and killed by the ants. Their force is in mutual support and mutual confidence. And if the ant—apart from the still higher developed termites—stands at the very top of the whole class of insects for its intellectual capacities; if its courage is only equalled by the most courageous vertebrates; and if its brain—to use Darwin's words—"is one of the most marvellous atoms of matter in the world, perhaps more so than the brain of man," is it not due to the fact that mutual aid has entirely taken the place of mutual struggle in the communities of ants? * * *

Chapter II

MUTUAL AID AMONG ANIMALS (CONTINUED)

* * * I have to say yet a few words about the societies of mon-keys, which acquire an additional interest from their being the link which will bring us to the societies of primitive men.

It is hardly needful to say that those mammals, which stand at the very top of the animal world and most approach man by their structure and intelligence, are eminently sociable. Evidently we must be prepared to meet with all varieties of character and habits in so great a division of the animal kingdom which includes hundreds of species. But, all things considered, it must be said that sociability, action in common, mutual protection, and a high development of those feelings which are the necessary outcome of social life, are characteristic of most monkeys and apes. From the smallest species to the biggest ones, sociability is a rule to which we know but a few exceptions. The nocturnal apes prefer isolated life; the capuchins (*Cebus capucinus*), the monos, and the howling monkeys live but in small families; and the orang-outans have never been seen by A. R. Wallace otherwise than either solitary or in very small groups of three or four individuals, while the gorillas seem never to join in bands. But all the remainder of the monkey tribe—the chimpanzees, the sajous, the sakis, the mandrills, the baboons, and so on—are sociable in the highest degree. They live in great bands, and even join with other species than their own. Most of them become quite unhappy when solitary. The cries of distress of each one of the band immediately bring together the whole of the band, and they boldly repulse the attacks of most carnivores and birds of prey. Even eagles do not dare attack them. They plunder our fields always in bands—the old ones taking care for the safety of the commonwealth. The little tee-tees, whose childish sweet faces so much struck Humboldt, embrace and protect one another when it rains, rolling their tails over the necks of their shivering comrades. Several species display the greatest solicitude for their wounded, and do not abandon a wounded comrade during a retreat till they have ascertained that it is dead and that they are helpless to restore it to life. Thus James Forbes narrated in his *Oriental Memoirs* a fact of such resistance in reclaiming from his hunting party the dead body of a female monkey that one fully understands why "the witnesses of this extraordinary scene resolved never again to fire at one of the monkey race." [1] In some species several individuals will combine to overturn a stone in order to search for ants' eggs under it. The hamadryas not only post sentries, but have been seen making a chain for the transmission of the spoil to a safe place; and their courage is well known. Brehm's description of the regular fight which his caravan had to sustain before the hamadryas would let it resume its journey in the valley of the Mensa, in Abyssinia, has become classical. [2] The playfulness of the tailed apes and the mutual attachment which reigns in the families of chimpanzees also are familiar to the general reader. And if we find among the highest apes two species, the orang-outan and the

1. Romanes's *Animal Intelligence*, p. 472.
2. Brehm, i. 82; Darwin's *Descent of Man*, ch. iii. The Kozloff expedition of 1899–1901 have also had to sustain in Northern Thibet a similar fight.

gorilla, which are not sociable, we must remember that both—
limited as they are to very small areas, the one in the heart of
Africa, and the other in the two islands of Borneo and Sumatra—
have all the appearance of being the last remnants of formerly
much more numerous species. The gorilla at least seems to have
been sociable in olden times, if the apes mentioned in the *Periplus*
really were gorillas.

We thus see, even from the above brief review, that life in societies is no exception in the animal world; it is the rule, the law of
Nature, and it reaches its fullest development with the higher vertebrates. Those species which live solitary, or in small families only,
are relatively few, and their numbers are limited. Nay, it appears
very probable that, apart from a few exceptions, those birds and
mammals which are not gregarious now, were living in societies
before man multiplied on the earth and waged a permanent war
against them, or destroyed the sources from which they formerly
derived food. "On ne s'associe pas pour mourir," was the sound remark of Espinas; and Houzeau, who knew the animal world of
some parts of America when it was not yet affected by man, wrote
to the same effect.

Association is found in the animal world at all degrees of evolution; and, according to the grand idea of Herbert Spencer, so brilliantly developed in Perrier's *Colonies Animales*, colonies are at
the very origin of evolution in the animal kingdom. But, in proportion as we ascend the scale of evolution, we see association growing
more and more conscious. It loses its purely physical character, it
ceases to be simply instinctive, it becomes reasoned. With the
higher vertebrates it is periodical, or is resorted to for the satisfaction of a given want—propagation of the species, migration, hunting, or mutual defence. It even becomes occasional, when birds
associate against a robber, or mammals combine, under the pressure of exceptional circumstances, to emigrate. In this last case, it
becomes a voluntary deviation from habitual moods of life. The
combination sometimes appears in two or more degrees—the family
first, then the group, and finally the association of groups, habitually scattered, but uniting in case of need, as we saw it with the
bisons and other ruminants. It also takes higher forms, guaranteeing
more independence to the individual without depriving it of the
benefits of social life. With most rodents the individual has its own
dwelling, which it can retire to when it prefers being left alone;
but the dwellings are laid out in villages and cities, so as to guarantee to all inhabitants the benefits and joys of social life. And finally,
in several species, such as rats, marmots, hares, etc., sociable life is
maintained notwithstanding the quarrelsome or otherwise egotistic

inclinations of the isolated individual. Thus it is not imposed, as is the case with ants and bees, by the very physiological structure of the individuals; it is cultivated for the benefits of mutual aid, or for the sake of its pleasures. * * *

HERMANN J. MULLER

The Guidance of Human Evolution (1960) †

Even though natural selection has been the great guiding principle that has brought us and all other higher organisms to their present estate, every responsible student of evolution knows that natural selection is too opportunistic and shortsighted to be trusted to give an advantageous long-term result for any single group of organisms. Mankind constitutes one of those relatively rare, fabulously lucky lines whose ancestors did happen to win out—else we would not be here—while the incalculably vast majority of species sooner or later vanished—that is, there are no living descendants now. Of all the species existing at any one time, only a relatively few ever function as conveyors of germ plasm that is to continue indefinitely, but most of these few branch and rebranch to more than compensate for the far greater number that are lost. Do we have reasons for believing that our species belongs in that very limited category that is to continue into the geologically distant future? * * *

Results of the Continuation of Present Practices

On the average, the counterpressure of selection, consisting in the elimination of individuals with excess detrimental genes, almost exactly equals the pressure of mutation in producing these genes. There is evidence from more than one direction that, in man, at least one person in five, or 20 per cent, carries a detrimental gene which arose in the immediately preceding generation and that, therefore, this same proportion—one in five—is, typically, prevented by genetic defects from surviving to maturity or (if surviving) from reproducing. This equilibrium holds only when a population is living under conditions that have long prevailed. Modern techniques are so efficacious that, used to the full, they might today (as judged by recent statistics on deaths and births)

† From Sol Tax, ed., *Evolution after Darwin* (Chicago, 1960), II, pp. 423–461. Hermann J. Muller (1890–1967), geneticist and Nobel laureate in physiology and medicine, was Distinguished Service Professor of Zoology at Indiana University.

be able to save for life and for a virtually normal rate of reproduction some nine-tenths of the otherwise genetically doomed 20 per cent. Assuming this to be the case, there would in the next generation be 18 per cent who carried along those defects that would have failed to be transmitted in the primitive or equilibrium population, plus another 20 per cent (partly overlapping the 18 per cent) who had the most recently arisen defects. At this rate, if the effectiveness of the techniques did not diminish as their job grew, there would, after about eight generations, or 240 years, be an accumulation of about 100 "genetic deaths" (scattered over many future generations) per 100 persons then living, in addition to the regular "load of mutations" that any population would ordinarily carry. It can be estimated (on the supposition that human mutation rates are like those in mice) that this amount of increase in the load is about the same as would be brought about by an acute exposure of all the parents of one generation to 200 r of gamma radiation, a situation similar to that at Hiroshima, or by a chronic, low-dose-rate exposure of each of the eight generations to 100 r. * * *

Let us next suppose that this sparing of genetic deaths by the aid of technology were to continue indefinitely at the assumed rate, a rate at which a genetic defect, on the average, subjects a person to only a tenth as much risk as it would if he were living under primitive conditions. Eventually, after some tens of thousands of years, a new equilibrium would be reached at which the load of mutations would be about ten times as large as at present. Thus as many extinctions as mutations would again be occurring. If we are to keep to our previously chosen figure for mutations, there would be one extinction for every five individuals, or 20 per cent. The frequency of genetic deaths would therewith return to the level which it had in primitive times and would be far above that now prevailing, in spite of all technological efforts. At the same time, the average individual of that time, carrying ten times today's genetic load, would, if tested under primitive conditions, be found to be no longer subject to a risk of extinction of only 20 per cent, but to one of 200 per cent. This means that he would carry twice as much defect as would suffice to eliminate him. Man would thereby have become entirely dependent on the techniques of his higher civilization. Yet, even with these techniques, he would be subject to as high an incidence of genetic misfortunes as had afflicted him in primitive times. That is, his weaknesses would have caught up with him. * * *

Long before such an "advanced" stage of the genetic cul-de-sac was reached, however, this medical utopia would probably be subjected to such great strains as to throw men back toward more primitive ways of life. Many would find themselves incapable of such ways. To be sure, the difficulty then would in a sense be "self-rectifying." But so late and forced a rectification would be likely to cause the loss of much that had previously been gained. * * *

A favorite cliché with those who do not understand this situation is the statement that, by definition, natural selection must always be acting and must always be favoring the fitter. This statement overlooks the fact that the degree of genetically occasioned difference in reproductive rate—that is, the intensity of selection—can be far less in some situations than in others. But the major point disregarded here is that what is fitter in the immediate acts of life is not always fitter for a group or a species as a whole in the long run. In such a case the group is running a race toward debasement and sometimes toward extinction, in this respect following the great majority of species of the past. In the case of man, the trick factor in this connection is a very unusual one: culture. Although culture did serve to sharpen salutary types of human selection in the past, as we have seen, it has now reached a point at which its very efficiency, when not yet involving foresight in regard to genetics, has placed upon society the burden of supporting almost indiscriminately the ever increasing genetic failings of its members.

If, in accordance with the above cliché, we define fitness in the narrow (but erroneous) sense, by the criterion of leaving a larger number of immediate offspring, then, of course, later generations of man must, by definition, by increasingly fit. Yet this type of fitness is no longer the same as fitness in regard to the qualities conducive to the well-being and survival of mankind in general. In fact, it seems not unlikely that in regard to the human faculties of the highest group importance—such as those needed for integrated understanding, foresight, scrupulousness, humility, regard for others, and self-sacrifice—cultural conditions today may be conducive to an actually lower rate of reproduction on the part of their possessors than of those with the opposite attributes. * * *

The Protection of Our Genetic Heritage

The crux of the problem is the interference with salutary types of selection in man that has arisen incidentally as a by-product of the widespread and increased effectiveness of mutual aid when it utilizes the tools supplied by science. What means can be used to protect our genetic heritage from this paradoxical situation? Occasional reactionary voices are to be heard calling upon us to reduce our mutual aid in the name of "rugged individualism," "private enterprise," or the like, and others are asking for a moratorium on science and even for a return to a fancied golden age.

However, it has been exactly the combination of intelligence with co-operative behavior that has made culture possible and raised men above beasts, and these propensities brook no stopping point.

The enormous advances opening to men in consequence of the further extension of science (representing intelligence) and of a world-wide social organization (representing mutual aid) so utterly overshadow, in their potential effects within the next few hundred years, the damage that may be done in that period to men's genetic constitution that none but the unbalanced would consider now giving up, for genetic reasons, the march of civilization. * * *

What is most needed in this area of living is an extension of the feeling of social responsibility to the field of reproduction: an increasing recognition that the chief objective in bringing children into the world is not the glorification of the parents or ancestors by the mere act of having children but the well-being of the children themselves and, through them, of subsequent generations in general. When people come to realize that in some measure their gifts, as well as their failings and difficulties—physical, intellectual, and temperamental—have genetic bases and that social approval or disapproval will be accorded them if they take these matters into account in deciding how much of a family to beget, a big step forward will have been taken in the motivation of human reproduction.

It can become an accepted and valued practice to seek advice, though not dictation, in these matters, even as it is today in matters of individual health. Although no one enjoys admitting his faults, he can learn to take pride in exercising humility and ordering the most important of his biological functions—reproduction—in such ways as to win the approbation of himself and his fellows. This is, to be sure, a higher type of mutual aid, a superior moral code, than exists at present, but it can be just around the corner for people who from early youth have had the facts of genetics and evolution made vivid to them and who have been imbued with a strong sense of their participation in the attainment of human well-being. * * *

Two developments of our present period are powerful positive influences toward the needed change in motivation. One is the sudden realization of the damaging effects of radiation on heredity. This, by reason of having been made a political football, has done more to arouse the public and its leaders to the fact that our genetic constitution requires protection than all the propaganda that eugenicists have ever put forth. Characteristically, the danger has been greatly exaggerated in some quarters, for ulterior purposes quite unconnected rationally with the matter at issue, and has been just as unjustifiably dismissed or played down in other quarters, where there were other axes to grind. Nevertheless, the over-all effect of the controversy has been highly educational and has helped to make people far more genetics-conscious than they ever were before. It so happens that this same radiation problem is one of the *proper* faces of the ax which is here being ground. Thus it is fitting to take advantage of the receptivity created by political circumstances to awaken the public to the more general need for a reformation of attitudes toward reproduction.

The other relevant development of our time is the menace of overpopulation. Even publicists are at last becoming alarmed at the smothering of cultural advance and the disaster to democratic institutions that it can being about in a generation or two if unchecked. An absolute check will require not only that birth-control techniques be made available but also that large masses of people execute an about-face in their attitudes toward having children. They must recognize that to have or not to have children, and how many, should be determined primarily by the interests of the children themselves—that is, of the next and subsequent generations. If this change in outlook is effected—as it must be sooner or later—it is a relatively short step to the realization that the inborn equipment of the children also counts mightily in their well-being and opportunity for happiness. * * *

More Distant Prospects

Evolution in the past has been for the most part a matter of millions of years. In this larger view, what we have been discussing is but a matter of today—the step we are just about to take. So great are the present psychological impediments to this step, arising out of our traditions, that we have not had time to consider the enormous vistas beyond.

The rapid upgrading of our general intelligence must be accompanied and co-ordinated as closely as possible with a corresponding effort to infuse into the genetic basis of our moral natures the springs of stronger, more genuine fellow feeling. At the same time, especially interested groups will see to it that diverse abilities and proclivities of specific types will here and there be multiplied, both those of a more purely intellectual nature and those making possible more far-reaching and poignant appreciation of the varied kinds of experiences that life may offer. As all these genetic resources of mankind grow richer, they will increasingly be combined to give more of the population many of their benefits at once. Observation shows that these faculties are not antagonistic but rather mutually enhancing. Finally, increasing attention can be paid to what is called the physical side: bettering the genetic foundations of health, vigor, and longevity; reducing the need for sleep; bringing the induction of sedation and stimulation under better voluntary control; and increasing physical tolerances and aptitudes in general. * * *

There are sure to be powerful attempts to pull in diverse directions, in genetic just as in other matters, but we need not be afraid of this. The diversities will tend to enrich the genetic background, increasing the resources available for recombination. These partial attempts can then be judged by their fruits, and these fruits, where sound, will be added to our bounty.

It seems highly unlikely that, in a world-wide society at an advanced level of culture and technology, founded on the recognition of universal brotherhood, such diversities would proceed so far and for so long as again to split humanity on this shrunken planet into semi-isolated groups and that these groups would thenceforth undergo increasing divergence from one another. It is because man is potentially master of all trades that he has succeeded. And if his culture is to continue to evolve indefinitely, he must retain this essential plasticity and with it the feeling that all men are, at bottom, of his own kind.

Through billions of years of blind mutations, pressing against the shifting walls of their environment, microbes finally emerged as men. We are no longer blind; at least, we are *beginning* to be conscious of what has happened and of what may happen. From now on, evolution is what we make it, provided that we choose the true and the good. Otherwise, we shall sink back into oblivion. If we hold fast to our ideal, then evolution will become, for the first time, a conscious process. Increasingly conscious, it can proceed at a pace far outdistancing that achieved by trial and error—and in ever greater assurance, animation, and enthusiasm. That will be the highest form of freedom that man, or life, can have.

MARGARET MEAD

The Conditions of Conscious and Scientific Participation in the Evolutionary Process (1964) †

Increasingly in recent years thinkers concerned with contemporary problems have sought a place for man in the evolutionary process in which he is no longer the wholly unconscious or the half-conscious most recent development in a cosmic process but instead, having obtained some understanding of the nature of evolution, begins himself to direct its course.[1] Yet all too frequently discussion of the problem breaks down because of unexplored differences in the viewpoint of those who are temperamentally inclined to think

† From Chapters 10 and 11 of Margaret Mead, *Continuities in Cultural Evolution* (New Haven, 1964). Margaret Mead (1901–1978) was adjunct professor of anthropology at Columbia University and curator of the American Museum of Natural History.
1. Julian S. Huxley, "The Humanist Frame," in *The Humanist Frame*, 1962.

in terms of controlling the processes of nature and of those who are temperamentally inclined to envisage a role for man which is dependent on cooperative understanding of some cosmic design. At one extreme are those who, arguing for control, foresee that as man gains greater knowledge of genetics it will be possible by gene manipulation to control the kinds of individuals who will be born, or that, with a greater knowledge of drugs, it will be possible to control population size, or, in more elaborate fantasies, that it will be possible by the propagation of test-tube tissue to order a dozen "Churchills" to fill the needs of a dozen political positions.[2] The other extreme is best represented by the prophets of apocalyptic cults and by those who, accepting man's limitations, see history as a set of recurrent cycles, each as futile as the last, or see man's role as that of a gambler, taking a desperate chance on a seat in Heaven, or see man as a static figure, elegantly and pessimistically living out his existence.

We may examine these two versions of man's future possibilities in terms of their contemporary reference. Until the time when biological research has advanced far enough so that control can be assumed over plants, animals, and men, there are very few steps that can be recommended. One of these would be to make the modifications in the educational system that are necessary to produce more scientists to work on the problem. Meanwhile, the daydream of biological control has the reverse effect of a kind of nightmare, an alarming depiction of a world to come in which practically no one now alive would wish to live. The daydreamers themselves do not speak of genetic control as something by which they too would be controlled; instead, they picture men and women like themselves, in some future age, manipulating the germ plasm of others in ways guaranteed to improve the caliber of mankind to a point where problem solving on a huge scale would be very easy to accomplish.[3]

The suggestion that we replace man's long, slow, fumbling attempts to control the environment and to develop styles of life wherein he becomes increasingly more human, by automatic controls of various kinds—including not only those resulting from breeding or propagation but also those resulting from the application of somewhat crude and only partly known rules of behavior to a conditioning process—is an image that functions in the present as a deterrent to enthusiastic commitment to the future.[4] In addition, it is curiously out of step with the dominant feature of this age—that is, with the vast increase in man's freedom to travel, to know, to

2. William L. Laurence, "You May Live Forever," *Look*, 1953.
3. Hudson Hoagland and Ralph W. Burhoe, issue eds., "Evolution and Man's Progress," *Daedalus*, 1961; Sol Tax, ed., *Evolution after Darwin*, 1960.
4. Aldous Huxley, *Brave New World* and *Brave New World Revisited*, 1960.

understand. The transmutation of this great increase in freedom, this enlargement of the stage upon which every individual acts, into a picture of a future of rigid and predetermined controls involves a regressive flight from freedom of the kind that Fromm diagnosed for Nazi Germans,[5] or a continuation of reliance on strong but hated authority of the kind that characterized Old Russia and is still dominant in the Soviet Union,[6] or a conceptualization of human beings as machines, and human life as a machine-like process, a temptation to which Americans are very vulnerable.

Viewed as a new kind of mechanized power, man's greater control over biological evolution invokes a future in which more and more poultry will live out their lives crowded on beds of wood shavings. It invokes a future in which human mating will become a centrally controlled mechanism—whether this take the form of artificial insemination or selective birth control ensured by the use of drugs—for the production of the right kind of individual to develop and exercise more control. This mechanized image has great repellent power for most of the human race and has attraction only for those who, in such a situation, can comfortably see themselves in positions of power. Mechanization of this kind may be feasible. But viewed in the perspective of man's present situation, the image does not function to increase men's willingness to view their future state with enthusiasm and imagination or their readiness to undertake sacrifices for the future.

Perhaps not accidentally, those who are willing to hand over complete control of their destiny to some outside power emphasize divisiveness. Whether this abnegation of control is phrased in terms of predestination, or the attainment of Nirvana, or the dignified enactment of a role robbed even of tragedy by its meaningless culmination in a gratuitous act,[7] or the acquisition of the last few seats in Heaven reserved for Jehovah's Witnesses, an image of the future which is based on a conception of man's essential powerlessness has the effect of cutting off the individuals who pursue such a goal from all other men. The Christian born to be saved though other men are damned, the Existentialist turning the power of his imagination inward to feed on his own pride and despair, the Burmese Buddhist distributing alms for the sake of his own soul or entering a monastery to break his ties with everyday life—all roles of this kind are insufficiently inclusive. Acceptance of any of these positions tends to produce an elite group, the members of which pursue their way in disregard of the ways of lesser men as they seek a goal which is defined by its accessibility only to the insightful or the chosen.

5. Erich Fromm, *Escape from Freedom*, 1941.
6. Margaret Mead, *Soviet Attitudes toward Authority*, 1951.

7. Albert Camus, *The Stranger*, 1946; Nathan Leites, "Trends in Affectlessness," *American Imago*, 1947.

The inference is clear. Neither from those who dream of gaining power by genetic manipulation, by the manipulation of a behavioristic psychology, or by the use of a set of precisely operating drugs, nor from those who, individually and without regard for their fellow men, seek to ally themselves with or resign themselves to a power they are helpless to alter do we obtain an image of the future that is capable of inspiring the man of today to become an active and responsible participant in the world of tomorrow.

Yet at present an understanding of the evolutionary process can lead us at least to recognize that, over and over again, species have reached points of significant divergence—a possibility of evolution of too great specificity, for example, the outcome of which has determined whether a species has survived or has disappeared leaving open a zone into which species whose evolution has proceeded differently can expand. That these points of divergence have occurred in a context of mutation and cytoplasmic alternation and within the conditions set by the environment, while man's choices may be made in conferences held in the Kremlins and Pentagons of rival states, does not change the overall nature of the argument. Our knowledge of evolution suggests that any species may progressively become more, or less, able to survive.[8] And our knowledge of the process gives us an opportunity to exercise choice hitherto unknown on this planet, but it provides no guarantee that men will make the kinds of choices necessary for the survival of *Homo sapiens* and the intricately contrived cultures he has evolved as a result of his special methods of accumulating generational gains.

An examination of the history of past civilizations, the sure traces of many small and fragile human societies that have completely vanished, suggests that the "instinct of self-preservation," invoked so facilely by physical scientists in their moments of optimism,[9] has not yet been incorporated into human culture in any reliable way. That human societies rely on developing in crucial members a combination of self-oriented and other-oriented behaviors is fully documented, but up to the present the combination in each society has remained an unstable constellation, in which the cultural style has been inadequately directive of the diversity of individuals who have been called upon to discharge their culturally determined and evolutionarily significant roles as kings and chiefs, prime ministers, judges, prophets and preachers, artists, poets, philosophers and, in very recent days, scientists.

Stated simply and bluntly, there is no anthropological evidence of an adequately evolved and reliable *cultural* method of assuring the survival of a society or the survival of the human species. * * *

8. George G. Simpson, *The Major Features of Evolution*, 1953, pp. 206–12.
9. See "Symposium: The Physical Universe" (in which I. I. Rabi was a participant), in *Man's Contracting World in an Expanding Universe*, 1960.

We are therefore faced with a more urgent need so to involve ourselves consciously in evolution that we may be able to make the necessary inventions for the survival of mankind. In whatever field we would seek solutions initially, a first step is the straightforward admission that we do not have them. We do not know how to find the kinds of leaders we need; we do not know how to construct the kinds of social organization we need; we do not know how to persuade a large enough body of people to follow any course of action without simultaneously generating opposition to that very course of action. We do not know how to institutionalize a worldwide ideology so that the way in which it is structured does not defeat its stated goals. Most important, perhaps, we have not yet created, even on a pilot experimental basis, a type of social organization capable of finding, recruiting, educating, and providing for the innovative intelligence we need. Yet there is little doubt that among our living population as mankind is constituted—without resort to controlled eugenic manipulation—there is a sufficient number of highly gifted individuals who, given the proper cultural conditions in which to work, could go on to make the necessary innovations. * * *

In this discussion I have argued that the unit of cultural microevolution is a cluster of interacting individuals who within the special conditions provided by period and culture make choices which set a direction—a channel—in which events tend to flow until other points of divergence are reached. Further, I have considered the specific cultural conditions under which a given innovation is made possible, as well as the way in which period—the state of knowledge and the types of existing interaction among people—provides a context in which clusters of individuals act. For evolutionary activity, each of these conditions is essential. Cultural conditions and favorable period will not of themselves ensure that an outstanding man, the genius after whom a significant change is likely to be named, will actually make a contribution. Still less can they provide for the composition of the cluster of which he is a part.

The task of conscious participation, in which we put to use our existing knowledge of the nature of cultural evolution, necessarily includes an assay of each of these conditions and an estimate of the points at which intervention would be possible. Consequently we need accurate analyses of the particular cultural system in which we plan to work, analyses that focus on the particular cultural capacities for innovation and the particular cultural neutralities and actual blocks. * * *

At present our ability to characterize the period in which we live and to prefigure a coming period is also dependent on the geographical segmentation of areas of large-scale integrated research. Gunnar

Myrdal—outside of Sweden—worked on one set of problems in the United States, a second set for the Economic Commission for Europe (under the Economic and Social Council of the United Nations), and still another set in India. In Myrdal's case, these disparate researches have been united through the development of an encompassing theory.[1] But, more commonly, economists who are concerned, for example, with the consequences of automation in the United States are surprised by sudden political upheavals in Africa. Or the calculations of professional students of trade unionism in socialist countries are thrown off balance both by automation and by nationalist revolutions. Clearly, we have not yet developed a framework for looking at the entire world simultaneously or for developing solutions on a worldwide basis.

In order to identify choice points at which change is possible, it is not enough for us to develop methods of characterizing the period in which we are the living actors. We need also to develop methods by which we can simultaneously cross-check intraperiod sequences that arise from unique and only relatively predictable events. For example, a catastrophe like an earthquake, which causes thousands of deaths and great destruction of property, not only affects the society in which it occurs but also, given a worldwide system of communication, raises the level of awareness (or, if many earthquakes occur in rapid succession, may blunt interest) in other parts of the world.[2] Such changes in social perception may have far-reaching political consequences in influencing measures of soil conservation, flood control, dam construction, and technical assistance, as well as potential shifts in political orientation in countries desiring economic aid, differential allotments of public funds for education, defense, underground nuclear testing, and public works, the location of capital cities of new countries, and so on. However, we can arrive at an accurate understanding of the complex process by which a single event of this kind alters the state of the whole system only if the immediate effects are studied soon after the event and the later effects are also followed up. Furthermore, we shall need to assess rates of response to events of different magnitudes as these responses vary from one country to another, closer to and farther away from the place where a particular event has taken place.

Once we have developed methods of period analysis, based on very careful experimental retrospective studies and cross-checking simultaneous studies that measure the repercussions of single events throughout the system, we shall be able to work out prefigurative

1. Gunnar Myrdal, *The American Dilemma*, 1944; Myrdal, *The International Economy: Problems and Prospects*, 1956; Myrdal, *Rich Lands and Poor*, 1957; Myrdal, *Beyond the Welfare State*, 1960.

2. See, for example, Martha Wolfenstein, *Disaster*, 1957; also G. W. Baker and D. W. Chapman, eds., *Man and Society in Disaster*, 1962.

426 · *Margaret Mead*

indicators. These may or may not be single complexes, such as the uses of gold or uranium. Their purpose will be to indicate significant types of fluctuation in the whole system in which points of divergence may be developing.

It is my argument that the points of divergence, the points of greatest freedom in the system, may precede the peaks of significant change which later are defined as the turning points in history. The significance of a peak of this kind (for example, Darwin's presentation of the theory of evolution) is not that it determines a course of development, of which it is more likely to be the culmination than the origin, but rather that it gives direction to the *next* step in an evolutionary sequence. One purpose for which we need to develop methods of doing retrospective experimental analysis is to make possible a re-examination of the familiar arguments about the anticipation of particular famous men. So one might by experimental reconstruction work out the course of development without, specifically, Darwin or Freud or Marx. Actually, of course, such situations have occurred historically, as in the case of Mendel, whose work was virtually unknown and its significance overlooked when it was published,[3] and in the case of Stolypin.[4] Purposive, conscious, and responsible intervention in cultural evolution must be carried out in terms of a worldwide system, with awareness that events in any one part of the system will have repercussions on other parts of the system. This means that the prefigurative indicators must have reference to the whole and must give us information both about those developments which are already past the point at which intervention can be successful and those points at which intervention is possible.

As in modern society the sciences are taking over the ancient and respected role of the prophet, the vicissitudes of prophets in earlier ages become relevant. The prophet who led his people safely to the Promised Land; the prophet who, like Cassandra, could only discern a train of events long after the events were hopelessly in train, who could aggravate but not change the situation; the prophet who produced a self-fulfilling prophecy that became an active component of the system with which he was working—all these are analogues of what the application of scientific research to prediction may pro-

3. Thus, in the case of William Bateson, the incorporation of the rediscovered work of Mendel into his own work —at a time when he was just approaching the same discoveries in the orderly pursuit of his own scientific interests—resulted in a kind of overemphasis, overpartisanhip, and overacceptance of Mendel's work; the effect on his work might have been quite differ-ent if the discoveries had grown out of his own work or, on the contrary, if he could have built his thinking on the experimental work already done by Mendel. See Beatrice Bateson, *William Bateson, F. R. S., Naturalist*, 1928.
4. For a recent discussion of Stolypin, see Edmond Taylor, *The Fall of the Dynasties*, 1963, pp. 161–62, 172–73, 188, and 406.

duce. It is possible that by harnessing both description and prediction to a worldwide system, we may acquire some control over the competitive distortion that comes about when nations or industrial complexes are free to create their own "public" information.[5]

The state of a given culture, including the extent to which it is changing and is capable of change under new conditions, and the state of the world are both conditions in which cultural evolution takes place. An event that may become of evolutionary importance is not in and of itself something that can alter either the particular culture or the state of the world. However, if a particular event of potential evolutionary significance does set in motion a train of events, it will affect the later state of the culture and later periods in the world. It is more difficult for us to accept the culture, with its potentialities for certain types and rates of change, and the period, with its already inevitable contemporary characteristics, as *given*, than it is for us to deal with a desired change as if it had already occurred and at the same time to recognize that the small, potentially innovative detail is part both of a given culture and of the state of the world. We need a time-space model which makes simultaneous provision for various aspects of the future, including those aspects of the future which have already been determined by past events (for example, the upper limits of the world population between the ages of thirty and forty, twenty years from now), those aspects which allow for a limited number of alternatives (for example, the availability of different kinds of fuel), and those aspects which are completely unpredictable, at least in the present state of our knowledge (for example, the appearance of a new highly resistant virus, or an accidental major atomic explosion). And we need information about the ways in which the anticipation of future trains of events are, or may become, operative in the present.

Considerable work has been done on ways in which an individual's or a people's view of the past affects the present, but comparatively little work has been done on an individual's or a people's view of the future as a component in the present.[6] Yet any conscious attempt to bring about change becomes a component, however inconspicuous, of the present. Consequently, the likelihood that a next step in evolution will occur can be estimated not only from the state of the culture (particularly the accumulation of knowledge and skills and frames of reference) and the conditions of the period

5. For an outstanding example see George Creel, *Rebel at Large*, 1947; also James R. Mock and Cedric Larson, *Words That Won the War*, 1939, especially Chapter 2, on Creel. As one response to "image making," see Daniel J. Boorstin, *The Image or What Happened to the American Dream*, 1962.
6. Rhoda Metraux, "Immigrants and Natives in the Space Age," unpublished paper presented at the annual meeting of the American Orthopsychiatric Association, 1963.

(particularly the conditions of interrupted or uninterrupted communication, peaceful cooperation or active conflict, and so on), but also from existing germinal conscious attempts at innovation. ·

The population "explosion" provides us with one example. Even though no precise attempt is made to determine trends, statistical extrapolations of the present world population demonstrate very clearly that the changing ratio between men and natural resources will bring about other changes of a magnitude which may be expected to have evolutionary significance. This would be so even though actual demographic conditions went completely unrecognized by anyone. However, the population explosion has been recognized in many parts of the world, and this recognition has had significant effects at many levels on the relations between nation-states, as a factor in the preservation of peace, in orienting our thinking about food production, on the structure of the family, on the acceleration of space exploration, whether this is conceived of as a remedy for overpopulation or as a means of rescuing man from the disasters that will accompany overpopulation, and, finally, on our estimates of mankind and our estimates of the value of other men, our own family line, our own stock, our own nationality, the relative value of those already born and those not yet born, the near and the distant future, freedom of choice or central control.[7]

The issue of what shall be done to meet the problem is one that looms large and will loom larger, and we can be saved from facing this issue neither by natural catastrophe nor by the possibility of a man-made catastrophe of nuclear or biochemical war in which mankind may be wiped out. We can see shaping up around the world some of the main lines of response, already hardening, in part, to inevitability. The choice point in the position on traditional methods of contraception taken by the Roman Catholic Church has been passed. The selection of the issue of contraception by non-Catholics as a weapon against Catholicism has had the predictable effect of hardening the stand of the Roman Catholic Church. So, too, there is an apparent hardening of the general lines of strategy that will be pursued by those countries in the Free World which have a high standard of living—encouragement of the use of contraception by *other* peoples in poor and underdeveloped countries within their sphere of influence while, at the same time, they pride themselves on their own large families. The Communist countries may be expected to pursue a strategy of controlling the birthrate in their own countries by arbitrary measures for and against abortion or contraception while, at the same time, they make light of arguments advanced by the Free World about the impossibility of

7. Harrison Brown, James Bonner, and John Weir, *The Next Hundred Years*, 1957.

indefinitely expanding food production.[8] These three positions have given rise to various countersuggestions; for example, a suggestion that if it were not for the opposition of the Roman Catholic Church, the practice of contraception would rapidly spread around the world, and a suggestion that the number of children born can be limited by state-controlled sterilization, compulsory or voluntary, or by the deferment of marriage, and so on.[9]

Quite clearly, the principal positions and the countersuggestions are totally inadequate approaches to the overall problem of population limitation. Roman Catholics recommend deferred marriage and increased abstinence, but they have no means of commending their recommendations outside their own communion. New nations boast of their growing populations and are affronted by suggestions that they, but not Europeans or North Americans, should practice population control. The Communists at one time promote and at another discourage population increase as an adjunct of their world policy.[1] As things now stand, even if there are great improvements in existing agricultural practices, in the allocation of land, and in the types of crop grown, there will inevitably be an increase in malnutrition and its accompaniments—disease, differential death rates, impairment of functioning, and enlightened bitterness.

Population growth will provide a condition for evolutionary change. But the direction of change and the greater or lesser likelihood of mankind's survival may be determined by purposive intervention.

Within the whole complex it is possible to locate certain areas of activity. There are, for example, those who are experimenting with oral contraceptives with reversible effects; those who are experimenting with techniques which produce irreversible—and also reversible —sterility; those who are concerned with devising methods of international cooperation which override national boundaries in such ways that differences in population between nation-states lose some of their significance; those who are experimenting with ideas for limited warfare with "clean" bombs and various methods of biochemical warfare which have a high potential for wiping out part or all of the world's population; those who are developing a space technology adequate for the establishment of space colonies so that, independent of events on earth, a portion of the human species can

8. Harrison Brown and E. K. Federov, "Too Many People in the World?" *Saturday Review*, 1962; for a summary of recent shifts and changes in Chinese policy, see Robert Trumbull, "Peking Opens a New Drive to Limit Population," *The New York Times*, June 16, 1963.
9. Clyde V. Kiser, ed., *Research in*

Family Planning, 1962.
1. As for example, in the interventions by the Soviet Union at the United Nations Conference on the Application of Science and Technology for the Benefit of the Less Developed Areas, held in Geneva, February 1963; for China, see Trumbull, "Peking Opens a New Drive to Limit Population."

be preserved; those who are concerned with the simplification of the expensive, heavy, and bulky technology of the contemporary world in order to increase people's mobility and decrease their consumption of irretrievable resources and use of energy; those who are experimenting with new sources of food to short cut the present complicated food production cycle, eliminate expensive forms of transportation, and produce nutriments at enormously lowered cost and expenditure of natural resources. And, finally, there are those who are concerned with the overall ethical, philosophical, and religious implications of the choices that individuals must make in deciding whether or not to have children, whether to set a higher value on the welfare of their own unborn children than on the welfare of other children who are already born or, alternatively, to surrender—voluntarily or by coercion—some of their rights over their own individual reproductivity.

Interdisciplinary and worldwide exploration would greatly extend a list of this kind, and in extended form it could provide a basis for purposive innovation. Whether we then look at the population problem from the standpoint of the currents of world opinion that would be set in motion or from the standpoint of individual career choice, the relevance of what is done becomes salient. Individually, a biochemist may choose to work on the elaboration of biochemical warfare, the development of methods of oral contraception, or the production of new, less expensive, more compact foods, suitable for feeding enormous populations or for use in outer space. The sciences concerned with human behavior may direct their efforts toward the construction of new forms of international cooperation, such as world food banks, or they may undertake research on the consequences of the individual's reproductive status for his total health, or they may attempt to provide a scientific background for the kind of choice that must ultimately be made on the basis of a total world philosophy. Between precise knowledge of the possible consequences of a particular course of action for individual personality, on the one hand, and a world philosophy of human action, on the other, particular cultures, religious systems, and ideologies are the mediating variables of which account must be taken. Childlessness means one thing in a culture in which failure to reproduce means a loss of status in this world or the next. It means quite a different thing in a culture in which having children is regarded as a suitable reward for having worked to achieve a reasonable standard of living, and something different again in a culture in which a newly awakened sense of national identity requires each individual to make a personal contribution to his country's strength. It means still something else in a religion devoted to final annihilation of the personal self, and a different thing again in a religion in which individuality is a religious value and embodiment as a human being is a final actualization of a soul. And the fusing of children and cars and television sets in the secular rewards for economic conformity has still other consequences.

We already have the necessary methods for studying the overall problem at all these levels and for acquiring information on the individual psychological consequences of the kinds of choices that are made in different cultures and by those with different religious and ideological orientations. At every stage of any change in world orientation, the particular significance of change will be determined by the cultures and the religious and ideological groups which initiate, promote, and accept any particular type of solution. It would be possible for us to group areas of research so that they would have mutually reinforcing significance. For example, research on new foods could be grouped with research on oral contraceptives; or research on space colonization with research on the new uses of nuclear energy; or research on the individual with research on group correlates of different patterns of reproductivity. This kind of categorization would enable us to arrive at a division of labor whereby problems could be assigned to those parts of the world in which the culture, the religion, and the political ideology would foster a particular kind of research. For example, research on new, inexpensive foods to replace our present highly expensive methods of producing animal protein would encounter continuous obstruction in the Americas and Europe, but it might well be heavily supported in a country like China. Similarly, research on methods of sterilization might receive its greatest cultural support in Japan, the country which for many centuries has articulately faced population problems. And passionate agnosticism might be a suitable background for research on oral contraception, and so on.

A strategic assay of the world situation, a definition of the state of the period, and a systematic analysis of the potential for evolutionary change, or obstruction of change, in each part of the world's population, in national cultures, local scientific traditions, different religious and political orientations—these are the first steps we can take in planning for immediate and responsible participation in cultural evolution.

Aggression and Altruism

KONRAD LORENZ

On Aggression (1963) †

What is the value of all this fighting? In nature, fighting is such an ever-present process, its behavior mechanisms and weapons are so highly developed and have so obviously arisen under the selection pressure of a species-preserving function, that it is our duty to ask this Darwinian question. * * *

Darwin's expression, "the struggle for existence," is sometimes erroneously interpreted as the struggle between different species. In reality, the struggle Darwin was thinking of and which drives evolution forward is the competition between near relations. What causes a species to disappear or become transformed into a different species is the profitable "invention" that falls by chance to one or a few of its members in the everlasting gamble of hereditary change. The descendants of these lucky ones gradually outstrip all others until the particular species consists only of individuals who possess the new "invention."

There are, however, fightlike contests between members of different species: at night an owl kills and eats even well-armed birds of prey, in spite of their vigorous defense, and when these birds meet the owl by day they attack it ferociously. Almost every animal capable of self-defense, from the smallest rodent upward, fights furiously when it is cornered and has no means of escape. Besides these three particular types of inter-specific fighting, there are other, less typical cases; for instance, two cave-nesting birds of different species may fight for a nesting cavity. * * *

All the cases described above, in which animals of different species fight against each other, have one thing in common: every one of the fighters gains an obvious advantage by its behavior or, at least, in the interests of preserving the species it "ought to" gain one. But intra-specific aggression, aggression in the proper and narrower sense of the word, also fulfills a species-preserving function. * * *

† From Chapters 3 and 13 of Konrad Lorenz, *On Aggression* (first published in Austria, 1963; English translation, New York, 1966). Konrad Lorenz (b. 1903), the founder of ethology, shared the Nobel Prize in physiology and medicine in 1973.

Let us forget for a moment that the aggression drive has become derailed under conditions of civilization, and let us inquire impartially into its natural causes. For the reasons already given, as good Darwinians we must inquire into the species-preserving function which, under natural—or rather precultural—conditions, is fulfilled by fights within the species, and which by the process of selection has caused the advanced development of intra-specific fighting behavior in so many higher animals. It is not only fishes that fight their own species: the majority of vertebrates do so too, man included.

Darwin had already raised the question of the survival value of fighting, and he has given us an enlightening answer: It is always favorable to the future of a species if the stronger of two rivals takes possession either of the territory or of the desired female. As so often, this truth of yesterday is not the untruth of today but only a special case; ecologists have recently demonstrated a much more essential function of aggression. Ecology—derived from the Greek *oikos*, the house—is the branch of biology that deals with the manifold reciprocal relations of the organism to its natural surroundings—its "household"—which of course includes all other animals and plants native to the environment. Unless the special interests of a social organization demand close aggregation of its members, it is obviously most expedient to spread the individuals of an animal species as evenly as possible over the available habitat. To use a human analogy: if, in a certain area, a larger number of doctors, builders, and mechanics want to exist, the representatives of these professions will do well to settle as far away from each other as possible.

The danger of too dense a population of an animal species settling in one part of the available biotope and exhausting all its sources of nutrition and so starving can be obviated by a mutual repulsion acting on the animals of the same species, effecting their regular spacing out, in much the same manner as electrical charges are regularly distributed all over the surface of a spherical conductor. This, in plain terms, is the most important survival value of intra-specific aggression. * * *

Conceptual thought and speech changed all man's evolution by achieving something which is equivalent to the inheritance of acquired characters. We have forgotten that the verb "inherit" had a juridic connotation long before it acquired a biological one. When a man invents, let us say, bow and arrow, not only his progeny but his entire community will inherit the knowledge and the use of these tools and possess them just as surely as organs grown on the body. Nor is their loss any more likely than the rudimentation of an organ of equal survival value. Thus, within one or two generations a process of ecological adaptation can be achieved which, in normal phylogeny and without the interference of conceptual thought, would have taken a time of an altogether different, much greater order of magnitude. Small wonder, indeed, if the evolution of social instincts and, what is even more important, social inhibitions could not keep pace with the rapid development forced on human society by the growth of traditional culture, particularly material culture.

Obviously, instinctive behavior mechanisms failed to cope with the new circumstances which culture unavoidably produced even at its very dawn. There is evidence that the first inventors of pebble tools, the African Australopithecines, promptly used their new weapons to kill not only game, but fellow members of their species as well. Peking Man, the Prometheus who learned to preserve fire, used it to roast his brothers: beside the first traces of the regular use of fire lie the mutilated and roasted bones of Sinanthropus pekinensis himself. * * *

In human evolution, no inhibitory mechanisms preventing sudden manslaughter were necessary, because quick killing was impossible anyhow; the potential victim had plenty of opportunity to elicit the pity of the aggressor by submissive gestures and appeasing attitudes. No selection pressure arose in the prehistory of mankind to breed inhibitory mechanisms preventing the killing of conspecifics until, all of a sudden, the invention of artificial weapons upset the equilibrium of killing potential and social inhibitions. When it did, man's position was very nearly that of a dove which, by some unnatural trick of nature, has suddenly acquired the beak of a raven. One shudders at the thought of a creature as irascible as all prehuman primates are, swinging a well-sharpened hand-ax. Humanity would indeed have destroyed itself by its first inventions, were it not for the very wonderful fact that inventions and responsibility are both the achievements of the same specifically human faculty of asking questions.

Not that our prehuman ancestor, even at a stage as yet devoid of moral responsibility, was a fiend incarnate; he was by no means poorer in social instincts and inhibitions than a chimpanzee, which, after all, is—his irascibility notwithstanding—a social and friendly creature. But whatever his innate norms of social behavior may have been, they were bound to be thrown out of gear by the invention of weapons. If humanity survived, as, after all, it did, it never achieved security from the danger of self-destruction. If moral responsibility and unwillingness to kill have indubitably increased, the ease and emotional impunity of killing have increased at the same rate. The distance at which all shooting weapons take effect screens the killer against the stimulus situation which would otherwise activate his killing inhibitions. The deep, emotional layers of our personality simply do not register the fact that the crooking of the forefinger to release a shot tears the entrails of another man. No sane man would even go rabbit hunting for pleasure if the necessity of killing his prey with his natural weapons brought home to him the full, emotional realization of what he is actually doing.

The same principle applies, to an even greater degree, to the use of modern remote-control weapons. The man who presses the releasing button is so completely screened against seeing, hearing, or otherwise emotionally realizing the consequences of his action, that he can commit it with impunity—even if he is burdened with the power of imagination. Only thus can it be explained that perfectly good-natured men, who would not even smack a naughty child, proved to be perfectly able to release rockets or to lay carpets of incendiary bombs on sleeping cities, thereby committing hundreds and thousands of children to a horrible death in the flames. The fact that it is good, normal men who did this, is as eerie as any fiendish atrocity of war!

As an indirect consequence, the invention of artificial weapons has brought about a most undesirable predominance of intra-specific selection within mankind. * * *

Our Cro-Magnon warrior had plenty of hostile neighbors against whom to discharge his aggressive drive, and he had just the right number of reliable friends to love. His moral responsibility was not overtaxed by an exercise of function which prevented him from striking, in sudden anger, at his companions with his sharpened hand-ax. The increase in number of individuals belonging to the same community is in itself sufficient to upset the balance between the personal bonds and the aggressive drive. It is definitely detrimental to the bond of friendship if a person has too many friends. It is proverbial that one can have only a few really close friends. To have a large number of "acquaintances," many of whom may be faithful allies with a legitimate claim to be regarded as real friends, overtaxes a man's capacity for personal love and dilutes the intensity of his emotional attachment. The close crowding of many individuals in a small space brings about a fatigue of all social reactions. Every inhabitant of a modern city is familiar with the surfeit of social relationships and responsibilities and knows the disturbing feeling of not being as pleased as he ought to be at the visit of a friend, even if he is genuinely fond of him and has not seen him for a long time. A tendency to bad temper is experienced when the telephone rings after dinner. That crowding increases the propensity to aggressive behavior has long been known and demonstrated experimentally by sociological research.

On the other hand, there is, in the modern community, no legitimate outlet for aggressive behavior. To keep the peace is the first of civic duties, and the hostile neighboring tribe, once the target at which to discharge phylogenetically programmed aggression, has now withdrawn to an ideal distance, hidden behind a curtain, if possible of iron. Among the many phylogenetically adapted norms of human social behavior, there is hardly one that does not need to be controlled and kept on a leash by responsible morality. This indeed is the deep truth contained in all sermons preaching asceticism. Most of the vices and mortal sins condemned today correspond to inclinations that were purely adaptive or at least harmless in primitive man. Paleolithic people hardly ever had enough to eat and if, for once, they had trapped a mammoth, it was biologically correct and moral for every member of the horde to gorge to his utmost capacity; gluttony was not a vice. When, for once, they were fully fed, primitive human beings rested from their strenuous life and were as absolutely lazy as possible, but there was nothing reprehensible in their sloth. Their life was so hard that there was no danger of healthy sensuality degenerating into debauch. A man sorely needed to keep his few possessions, weapons and tools, and a few nuts for tomorrow's meal; there was no danger of his hoarding instinct turning into avarice. Alcohol was not invented, and there are no indications that man had discovered the reinforcing properties of alkaloids, the only real vices known of present-day primitive tribes. In short, man's endowment with phylogenetically adapted patterns of behavior met the requirements well enough to make the task of responsible morality very easy indeed. Its only commandment at the time was: Thou shalt not strike thy neighbor with a hand-ax even if he angers thee.

Clearly, the task of compensation devolving on responsible morality increases at the same rate as the ecological and sociological conditions created by culture deviate from those to which human instinctive behavior is phylogenetically adapted. Not only does this deviation continue to increase, but it does so with an acceleration that is truly frightening.

The fate of humanity hangs on the question whether or not responsible morality will be able to cope with its rapidly growing burden. We shall not lighten this burden by overestimating the strength of morality, still less by attributing omnipotence to it. We have better chances of supporting moral responsibility in its ever-increasing task if we humbly realize and acknowledge that it is "only" a compensatory mechanism of very limited strength and that, as I have already explained, it derives what power it has from the same kind of motivational sources as those which it has been created to control. * * *

The stress under which morally responsible behavior breaks down can be of varying kinds. It is not so much the sudden, one-time great temptation that makes human morality break down but the effect of any prolonged situation that exerts an increasing drain on the compensatory power of morality. Hunger, anxiety, the necessity to make difficult decisions, overwork, hopelessness and the like all have the effect of sapping moral energy and, in the long run, making it break down. Anyone who has had the opportunity to observe men under this kind of strain, for example in war or in prisoner-of-war camps, knows how unpredictably and suddenly moral decompensation sets in. Men in whose strength one trusted unconditionally suddenly break down, and others of whom one would never have expected it prove to be sources of inexhaustible energy, keeping up the morale of others by their example. Anyone who has experienced such things knows that the fervor of good intention and its power of endurance are two independent variables. Once you have realized this, you cease to feel superior to the man who breaks down a little sooner than you do yourself. Even the best and noblest reaches a point where his resistance is at an end: "*Eloi, Eloi, lama sabachthani?*" * * *

Militant enthusiasm is particularly suited for the paradigmatic illustration of the manner in which a phylogenetically evolved pattern of behavior interacts with culturally ritualized social norms and rites, and in which, though absolutely indispensable to the function of the compound system, it is prone to miscarry most tragically if not strictly controlled by rational responsibility based on causal insight. The Greek word *enthousiasmos* implies that a person is possessed by a god; the German *Begeisterung* means that he is controlled by a spirit, a *Geist*, more or less holy.

In reality, militant enthusiasm is a specialized form of communal aggression, clearly distinct from and yet functionally related to the more primitive forms of petty individual aggression. Every man of normally strong emotions knows, from his own experience, the subjective phenomena that go hand in hand with the response of militant enthusiasm. A shiver runs down the back and, as more exact observation shows, along the outside of both arms. One soars elated, above all the ties of everyday life, one is ready to abandon all for the call of what, in the moment of this specific emotion, seems to be a sacred duty. All obstacles in its path become unimportant; the instinctive inhibitions against hurting or killing one's fellows lose, unfortunately, much of their power. Rational considerations, criticisms, and all reasonable arguments against the behavior dictated by militant enthusiasm are silenced by an amazing reversal of all values, making them appear not only untenable but base and dishonorable. Men may enjoy the feeling of absolute righteousness even while they commit atrocities. Conceptual thought and moral responsibility are at their lowest ebb. As a Ukrainian proverb says: "When the banner is unfurled, all reason is in the trumpet."

The subjective experiences just described are correlated with the following, objectively demonstrable phenomena. The tone of the entire striated musculature is raised, the carriage is stiffened, the arms are raised from the sides and slightly rotated inward so that the elbows point outward. The head is proudly raised, the chin stuck out, and the facial muscles mime the "hero face," familiar from the films. On the back and along the outer surface of the arms the hair stands on end. This is the objectively observed aspect of the shiver!

Anybody who has ever seen the corresponding behavior of the male chimpanzee defending his band or family with self-sacrificing courage will doubt the purely spiritual character of human enthusiasm. The chimp, too, sticks out his chin, stiffens his body, and raises his elbows; his hair stands on end, producing a terrifying magnification of his body contours as seen from the front. The inward rotation of his arms obviously has the purpose of turning the longest-haired side outward to enhance the effect. The whole combination of body attitude and hair-raising constitutes a bluff. This is also seen when a cat humps its back, and is calculated to make the animal appear bigger and more dangerous than it really is. Our shiver, which in German poetry is called a *"heiliger Schauer,"* a "holy" shiver, turns out to be the vestige of a prehuman vegetative response of making a fur bristle which we no longer have. * * *

The first prerequisite for rational control of an instinctive behavior pattern is the knowledge of the stimulus situation which releases it. Militant enthusiasm can be elicited with the predictability of a reflex when the following environmental situations arise. First of all, a social unit with which the subject identifies himself must appear to be threatened by some danger from outside. * * *

A second key stimulus which contributes enormously to the releasing of intense militant enthusiasm is the presence of a hated enemy from whom the threat to the above "values" emanates. This enemy, too, can be of a concrete or of an abstract nature. It can be "the" Jews, Huns, Boches, tyrants, etc., or abstract concepts like world capitalism, Bolshevism, fascism, and any other kind of ism; it can be heresy, dogmatism, scientific fallacy, or what not. * * *

A third factor contributing to the environmental situation eliciting the response is an inspiring leader figure. Even the most emphatically antifascistic ideologies apparently cannot do without it, as the giant pictures of leaders displayed by all kinds of political parties prove clearly enough. Again the unselectivity of the phylogenetically programmed response allows for a wide variation in the conditioning to a leader figure. Napoleon, about whom so critical a man as Heinrich Heine became so enthusiastic, does not inspire me in the least; Charles Darwin does.

A fourth, and perhaps the most important, prerequisite for the full eliciting of militant enthusiasm is the presence of many other individuals, all agitated by the same emotion. Their absolute number has a certain influence on the quality of the response. Smaller numbers at issue with a large majority tend to obstinate defense with the emotional value of "making a last stand," while very large numbers inspired by the same enthusiasm feel the urge to conquer the whole world in the name of their sacred cause.

* * * The need to control, by wise rational responsibility, all our emotional allegiances to cultural values is as great as, if not greater than, the necessity to keep in check our other instincts. None of them can ever have such devastating effects as unbridled militant enthusiasm when it infects great masses and overrides all other considerations by its single-mindedness and its specious nobility. It is not enthusiasm in itself that is in any way noble, but humanity's great goals which it can be called upon to defend.

RICHARD E. LEAKEY and ROGER LEWIN

Aggression, Sex, and Human Nature (1977) †

Konrad Lorenz, one of the founders of modern ethology, wrote: 'There is evidence that the first inventors of pebble tools—the African australopithecines—promptly used their weapons not only to kill game, but fellow members of their species as well. Peking Man, the Prometheus who learned to preserve fire, used it to roast his brother: beside the first traces of the regular use of fire lie the mutilated and roasted bones of *Sinanthropus pekinensis* himself.'

Lorenz sounded these dramatic phrases a little more than ten years ago in his celebrated book *On Aggression*, the main burden of which is that the human species carries with it an inescapable legacy of territoriality and aggression, instincts which must be ventilated lest they spill over in ugly fashion. All these—the archeological evidence of cannibalism, the notions of territorial and aggressive instincts, and of an evolutionary career as killer apes—have been woven together to form one of the most dangerously persuasive myths of our time: that mankind is incorrigibly belligerent; that war and violence are in our genes.

The essentially pessimistic view of human nature was assimilated with unseemly haste into a popular conventional wisdom, an assimilation that was further enhanced by the elegant and catching prose

† From Chapter 9 of *Origins* (see above, p. 279).

of Desmond Morris (with *The Naked Ape*) and Robert Ardrey (with *African Genesis, The Territorial Imperative, Social Contract,* and more recently *The Hunting Hypothesis*). We emphatically reject this conventional wisdom for three reasons: first, on the very general premise that no theory of human nature can be so firmly proved as its proponents imply; second, that much of the evidence used to erect this aggression theory is simply not relevant to human behavior; and last, the clues that do impinge on the basic elements of human nature argue much more persuasively that we are a cooperative rather than an aggressive animal. If we seem to be faint-hearted by countering the proposition that 'humans are *definitely* aggressively disposed to one another' with 'no, we are *probably* a cooperative animal', then that is as it may be. There is simply no point in pretending that one has the absolute truth in the palm of one's hands, when really one is cradling a carefully-considered hypothesis. * * *

The rules for human behavior are simple, we believe, precisely because they offer such a wide scope for expression. By contrast, the proponents of innate aggression try to tie us down to narrow, well-defined paths of behavior: humans are aggressive, they propose, because there is a universal territorial instinct in biology; territories are established and maintained by displays of aggression; our ancestors acquired weapons, turning ritual displays into bloody combat, a development that was exacerbated through a lust for killing. And according to the Lorenzian school, aggression is such a crucial part of the territorial animal's survival kit that it is backed up by a steady rise in pressure for its expression. Aggression may be released by an appropriate cue, such as a threat by another animal, but in the protracted absence of such cues the pressure eventually reaches a critical point at which the behavior bursts out spontaneously. The difference between a piece of behavior that is elicited by a particular type of stimulus, and one that will be expressed whether or not cues occur is enormous and that difference is central to understanding aggression in the human context.

There is no doubt that aggression and territoriality are part of modern life: vandalism is a distressingly familiar mark of the urban scene; we lock the doors of our houses and apartments against strangers who might wander in; and there is war, an apparent display of territoriality and aggression on a grand scale. Are these unsavory aspects of modern living simply part of an inescapable legacy of our animal origins? Or are they phenomena with entirely different causes? These are the questions that must be answered since they are so clearly relevant to the future of our species.

To begin with, it is worth taking a broad view of territoriality and aggression in the animal world. Why are some animals territorial? Simply to protect resources, such as food, a nest, or a similar reproductive area. Many birds defend one piece of real estate in which a male may attract and court a female, and then move off to another one, also to be defended, in which they built a nest and rear young. The 'choking' by male kittiwakes, the lunging by stickle- backs, and the early morning chorus by gibbons are all displays announcing ownership of territory. Intruders who persist in violat- ing another's territory are soon met with such displays, the intention of which is quite clear. The clarity of the defender's response, and also of the intruder's prowess, is the secret of nature's success with these so-called aggressive encounters.

Such confrontations are strictly ritualized, so that on all but the rarest occasions the biologically fitter of the two wins without the infliction of physical damage on either one. This 'aggression' is in fact an exercise in competitive display rather than physical violence. The individuals engage in stereotyped lunges, thrusts, and postures which may or may not be similar to their responses when a real threat to their lives arises, as from a predator for instance. In either event, the outcome is a resolution of a territorial dispute with mini- mal injury to either party. The biological advantage of these mock battles is clear: a species that insists on settling disputes violently reduces its overall fitness to thrive in a world that offers enough environmental challenges anyway.

The biological common sense implicit in this simple behavioral device is reiterated again and again throughout the animal kingdom, and even as far down as some ants: disputes over territorial owner- ship, and over sexual rights too, are channeled into stereotyped, nonviolent competitions. This law is so deeply embedded in the nature of survival and success in the game of evolution that for a species to transgress, there must be extremely unusual circum- stances. We cannot deny that with the invention of tools, first made of wood and later of stone, an impulse to employ them occa- sionally as weapons might have caused serious injury, there being no stereotyped behavior patterns to deflect their risk. And it is possible that our increasingly intelligent ancestors may have understood the implications of power over others through the delivery of one swift blow with a sharpened pebble tool. But is it likely?

The answer must be no. An animal that develops a proclivity for killing its fellows thrusts itself into an evolutionarily disadvanta- geous position. Because our ancestors probably lived in small bands, in which individuals were closely related to one another, and had as neighbors similar bands which also contained blood relations, in most acts of murder the victim would more than likely have been kin to the murderer. As the evolutionary success is the production of as many descendants as possible, an innate drive for killing individuals of one's own species would soon have wiped that species out. Humans, as we know, did not blunder up an evolutionary blind alley, a fate that innate, unrestrained aggressiveness would undoubtedly have produced.

To argue, as we do, that humans are innately nonaggressive toward one another is not to imply that we are of necessity innately good-natured toward our fellows. In the lower echelons of the animal kingdom the management of conflict is largely through ritualized mock battles. But farther along the evolutionary path, carrying out the appropriate avoidance behavior comes to depend more and more on learning, and in social animals the channel of learning is social education. The capacity for that behavior is rooted in the animal's genes, but its elaboration depends also on learning. And, as we have stressed, humans are learning animals par excellence, so we must expect that techniques for coping with potential conflict are largely learned. * * *

A second crucial feature of animal conflict is its variability. It occurs, that is to say, both between animals of different species and between individuals of the same species, and under differing environmental conditions. Anyone who argues for inbuilt aggression in *Homo sapiens* must see aggression as a universal instinct in the animal kingdom. It is no such thing. * * * Simply because greylag geese and mockingbirds, for instance, enthusiastically defend their territory, we should not infer that all animals do so. And it is not surprising that hummingbirds show considerably more territorial aggression than lions, even though the king of beasts is a lethal hunter. Our closest animal relatives, the chimpanzees and gorillas, are notably nonterritorial. * * *

That territoriality is flexible should not be surprising. It is, after all, a biological adaption to environmental conditions so that the species may survive through sufficient access to food supplies and by unhampered reproduction. If food resources and space are scarce, then almost certainly there will be conspicuous territorial behavior. It is likewise inevitable that some individuals will fail to secure sufficient food or a place in which to rear a brood. These individuals are, of course, the weakest, and this is what survival of the fittest through natural selection really means. The pressure for selection applies with force only when resources are limited—in other words, when there is a good biological reason.

Territorial behavior is therefore triggered when it is required and remains dormant when it is not. The Lorenzians, however, take a different view: aggression, they say, builds up inexorably, to be released either by appropriate cues or spontaneously in the absence of any cues at all. A safety valve suggested by Lorenzians for human societies is competitive sport. But such a suggestion neglects the high correlation between highly competitive encounters and associated vandalism and physical violence—as players, referees, and crowds know to their cost through Europe and the Americas. More significantly, research now shows a close match between warlike behavior in countries and a devotion to sport. Far from defusing aggression, highly organized, emotionally-charged sporting events generate even more aggression and reflect the degree to which humans' deep propensity to group identity and cohesion can be manipulated.

We can say therefore that territoriality and aggression are not universal instincts as such. Rather they are pieces of behavior that are tuned to particular life styles and to changes in the availability of important resources in the environment. * * *

Altogether, then, the notion that humans are inherently aggressive is simply not tenable. We cannot deny that twentieth-century humans display a good deal of aggression, but we cannot point to our evolutionary past either to explain its origins, or to excuse it. For that is what the equating of territorial aggressiveness in the animal domain with waging war in the human one often amounts to—an excuse. The fallacy of thus adducing our animal origins should now be evident. Wars are planned and organized by leaders intent on increasing their power. And they are fought usually by people not driven by an innate aggression against an enemy they often do not see. In war men are more like sheep than wolves: they may be led to manufacture munitions at home, to release bombs, or to fire long-range guns and rockets—all as part of one great cooperative effort. It is not insignificant that those soldiers who engage in fierce and bloody hand-to-hand fighting are subjected to an intense process of desensitization before they can do it.

War is a battle for power over people and for resources such as land and minerals, neither of which are relevant in hunting and gathering societies. With the growth of agriculture and of materially-based societies, warfare has increased steadily in both ferocity and duration, culminating in our current capability to destroy even the planet: powerful leaders have found more and more to fight about, and increasingly effective ways of achieving their ends. We should not look to our genes for the seeds of war; those seeds were planted when, ten thousand years ago, our ancestors for the first time planted crops and began to be farmers. The transition from the nomadic hunting way of life to the sedentary one of farmers and industrialists made war possible and potentially profitable.

Possible, but not inevitable. For what has transformed the possible into reality is the same factor that has made human beings special in the biological kingdom: culture. Because of our seemingly limitless inventiveness and our vast capacity for learning, there is an

endless potential for difference among human cultures, as indeed
may be witnessed throughout the world. An essential element of
culture, however, consists in those central values that make up an
ideology. It is social and political ideologies, and the tolerance or
lack of it between them, that bring human nations to bloody conflict. Those who argue that war is in our genes not only are wrong,
but they also commit the crime of diverting attention from the real
cause of war.

This last criticism applies even more strongly to those who cite
innate aggression to explain violence within nations, particularly in
the overcrowded urban areas. There are many reasons why a youth
may spontaneously smash a window or attack an old lady, but an
inborn drive inherited from our animal origins is certainly not one
of them. Human behavior is extraordinarily sensitive to the nature
of the environment, and so it should not be particularly surprising
that a person reared in unpleasant surroundings, perhaps subjected
to material insecurity and emotional deprivation, should later
behave in a way that people blessed with a more fortunate life
might regard as unpleasant. Urban problems will not be solved by
pointing to supposed defects in our genes while ignoring real defects
in social justice.

EDWARD O. WILSON

Sociobiology: The New Synthesis (1975) †

The Morality of the Gene

Camus said that the only serious philosophical question is suicide. That is wrong even in the strict sense intended. The biologist,
who is concerned with questions of physiology and evolutionary history, realizes that self-knowledge is constrained and shaped by the
emotional control centers in the hypothalamus and limbic system of
the brain. These centers flood our consciousness with all the emotions—hate, love, guilt, fear, and others—that are consulted by ethical philosophers who wish to intuit the standards of good and evil.
What, we are then compelled to ask, made the hypothalamus and
limbic system? They evolved by natural selection. That simple biological statement must be pursued to explain ethics and ethical philosophers, if not epistemology and epistemologists, at all depths.

† From Chapters 1 and 27 of Edward
O. Wilson, *Sociobiology: The New Synthesis* (Cambridge, Mass., 1975). Edward O. Wilson (b. 1929) is Frank B.
Baird Jr. Professor of Science and curator of entomology at the Museum of
Comparative Zoology, Harvard University.

Self-existence, or the suicide that terminates it, is not the central question of philosophy. The hypothalamic-limbic complex automatically denies such logical reduction by countering it with feelings of guilt and altruism. In this one way the philosopher's own emotional control centers are wiser than his solipsist consciousness, "knowing" that in evolutionary time the individual organism counts for almost nothing. In a Darwinist sense the organism does not live for itself. Its primary function is not even to reproduce other organisms; it reproduces genes, and it serves as their temporary carrier. Each organism generated by sexual reproduction is a unique, accidental subset of all the genes constituting the species. Natural selection is the process whereby certain genes gain representation in the following generations superior to that of other genes located at the same chromosome positions. When new sex cells are manufactured in each generation, the winning genes are pulled apart and reassembled to manufacture new organisms that, on the average, contain a higher proportion of the same genes. But the individual organism is only their vehicle, part of an elaborate device to preserve and spread them with the least possible biochemical perturbation. Samuel Butler's famous aphorism, that the chicken is only an egg's way of making another egg, has been modernized: the organism is only DNA's way of making more DNA. More to the point, the hypothalamus and limbic system are engineered to perpetuate DNA.

In the process of natural selection, then, any device that can insert a higher proportion of certain genes into subsequent generations will come to characterize the species. One class of such devices promotes prolonged individual survival. Another promotes superior mating performance and care of the resulting offspring. As more complex social behavior by the organism is added to the genes' techniques for replicating themselves, altruism becomes increasingly prevalent and eventually appears in exaggerated forms. This brings us to the central theoretical problem of sociobiology: how can altruism, which by definition reduces personal fitness, possibly evolve by natural selection? The answer is kinship: if the genes causing the altruism are shared by two organisms because of common descent, and if the altruistic act by one organism increases the joint contribution of these genes to the next generation, the propensity to altruism will spread through the gene pool. This occurs even though the altruist makes less of a solitary contribution to the gene pool as the price of its altruistic act.

To his own question, "Does the Absurd dictate death?" Camus replied that the struggle toward the heights is itself enough to fill a man's heart. This arid judgment is probably correct, but it makes little sense except when closely examined in the light of evolutionary theory. The hypothalamic-limbic complex of a highly social

species, such as man, "knows," or more precisely it has been programmed to perform as if it knows, that its underlying genes will
be proliferated maximally only if it orchestrates behavioral responses
that bring into play an efficient mixture of personal survival, reproduction, and altruism. Consequently, the centers of the complex
tax the conscious mind with ambivalences whenever the organisms
encounter stressful situations. Love joins hate; aggression, fear;
expansiveness, withdrawal; and so on; in blends designed not to
promote the happiness and survival of the individual, but to favor
the maximum transmission of the controlling genes.

The ambivalences stem from counteracting pressures on the units
of natural selection. Their genetic consequences will be explored
formally later in this book. For the moment suffice it to note that
what is good for the individual can be destructive to the family;
what preserves the family can be harsh on both the individual and
the tribe to which its family belongs; what promotes the tribe can
weaken the family and destroy the individual; and so on upward
through the permutations of levels of organization. Counteracting
selection on these different units will result in certain genes being
multiplied and fixed, others lost, and combinations of still others
held in static proportions. According to the present theory, some
of the genes will produce emotional states that reflect the balance
of counteracting selection forces at the different levels.

I have raised a problem in ethical philosophy in order to characterize the essence of sociobiology. Sociobiology is defined as the systematic study of the biological basis of all social behavior. For the
present it focuses on animal societies, their population structure,
castes, and communication, together with all of the physiology
underlying the social adaptations. But the discipline is also concerned with the social behavior of early man and the adaptive features of organization in the more primitive contemporary human
societies. Sociology *sensu stricto*, the study of human societies at all
levels of complexity, still stands apart from sociobiology because of
its largely structuralist and nongenetic approach. It attempts to
explain human behavior primarily by empirical description of the
outermost phenotypes and by unaided intuition, without reference
to evolutionary explanations in the true genetic sense. It is most
successful, in the way descriptive taxonomy and ecology have been
most successful, when it provides a detailed description of particular
phenomena and demonstrates first-order correlations with features
of the environment. Taxonomy and ecology, however, have been
reshaped entirely during the past forty years by integration into neo-
Darwinist evolutionary theory—the "Modern Synthesis," as it is
often called—in which each phenomenon is weighed for its adaptive significance and then related to the basic principles of popu-

lation genetics. It may not be too much to say that sociology and the other social sciences, as well as the humanities, are the last branches of biology waiting to be included in the Modern Synthesis.
* * *

It is part of the conventional wisdom that virtually all cultural variation is phenotypic rather than genetic in origin. This view has gained support from the ease with which certain aspects of culture can be altered in the space of a single generation, too quickly to be evolutionary in nature. The drastic alteration in Irish society in the first two years of the potato blight (1846–1848) is a case in point. Another is the shift in the Japanese authority structure during the American occupation following World War II. Such examples can be multiplied endlessly—they are the substance of history. It is also true that human populations are not very different from one another genetically. When Lewontin[1] analyzed existing data on nine blood-type systems, he found that 85 percent of the variance was composed of diversity within populations and only 15 percent was due to diversity between populations. There is no a priori reason for supposing that this sample of genes possesses a distribution much different from those of other, less accessible systems affecting behavior.

The extreme orthodox view of environmentalism goes further, holding that in effect there is no genetic variance in the transmission of culture. In other words, the capacity for culture is transmitted by a single human genotype. Dobzhansky[2] stated this hypothesis as follows: "Culture is not inherited through genes, it is acquired by learning from other human beings . . . In a sense, human genes have surrendered their primacy in human evolution to an entirely new, nonbiological or superorganic agent, culture. However, it should not be forgotten that this agent is entirely dependent on the human genotype." Although the genes have given away most of their sovereignty, they maintain a certain amount of influence in at least the behavioral qualities that underlie variations between cultures. Moderately high heritability has been documented in introversion-extroversion measures, personal tempo, psychomotor and sports activities, neuroticism, dominance, depression, and the tendency toward certain forms of mental illness such as schizophrenia.[3] Even a small portion of this variance invested in population differences might predispose societies toward cultural differences. At

1. R. C. Lewontin, "The Apportionment of Human Diversity," *Evolutionary Biology*, 6 (1972), 381–398.
2. Theodosius Dobzhansky, "Anthopology and the Natural Sciences—the Problem of Human Evolution," *Current Anthropology*, 4 (1963), 138, 146–148.
3. P. A. Parsons, *The Genetic Analysis of Behaviour* (London, 1967); I. M. Lerner, *Heredity, Evolution, and Society* (San Francisco, 1968).

the very least, we should try to measure this amount. It is not valid to point to the absence of a behavioral trait in one or a few societies as conclusive evidence that the trait is environmentally induced and has no genetic disposition in man. The very opposite could be true.

In short, there is a need for a discipline of anthropological genetics. In the interval before we acquire it, it should be possible to characterize the human biogram by two indirect methods. First, models can be constructed from the most elementary rules of human behavior. Insofar as they can be tested, the rules will characterize the biogram in much the same way that ethograms drawn by zoologists identify the "typical" behavioral repertories of animal species. The rules can be legitimately compared with the ethograms of other primate species. Variation in the rules among human cultures, however slight, might provide clues to underlying genetic differences, particularly when it is correlated with variation in behavioral traits known to be heritable. * * *

The other indirect approach to anthropological genetics is through phylogenetic analysis. By comparing man with other primate species, it might be possible to identify basic primate traits that lie beneath the surface and help to determine the configuration of man's higher social behavior. This approach has been taken with great style and vigor in a series of popular books by Konrad Lorenz (*On Aggression*), Robert Ardrey (*The Social Contract*), Desmond Morris (*The Naked Ape*), and Lionel Tiger and Robin Fox (*The Imperial Animal*). Their efforts were salutary in calling attention to man's status as a biological species adapted to particular environments. The wide attention they received broke the stifling grip of the extreme behaviorists, whose view of the mind of man as a virtually equipotent response machine was neither correct nor heuristic. But their particular handling of the problem tended to be inefficient and misleading. They selected one plausible hypothesis or another based on a review of a small sample of animal species, then advocated the explanation to the limit. * * *

The correct approach using comparative ethology is to base a rigorous phylogeny of closely related species on many biological traits. Then social behavior is treated as the dependent variable and its evolution deduced from it. When this cannot be done with confidence (and it cannot in man) the next best procedure is the one outlined in Chapter 7: establish the lowest taxonomic level at which each character shows significant intertaxon variation. Characters that shift from species to species or genus to genus are the most labile. We cannot safely extrapolate them from the cercopithecoid monkeys and apes to man. In the primates these labile qualities include group size, group cohesiveness, openness of the group to others, involvement of the male in parental care, attention structure, and the intensity and form of territorial defense. Characters are considered conservative if they remain constant at the level of the taxonomic family or throughout the order Primates, and they are the ones most likely to have persisted in relatively unaltered form into the evolution of *Homo.* These conservative traits include aggressive dominance systems, with males generally dominant over females; scaling in the intensity of responses, especially during aggressive interactions; intensive and prolonged maternal care, with a pronounced degree of socialization in the young; and matrilineal social organization. This classification of behavioral traits offers an appropriate basis for hypothesis formation. It allows a qualitative assessment of the probabilities that various behavioral traits have persisted into modern *Homo sapiens.* * * *

Role Playing and Polyethism

Roles in human societies are fundamentally different from the castes of social insects. The members of human societies sometimes cooperate closely in insectan fashion, but more frequently they compete for the limited resources allocated to their role-sector. The best and most entrepreneurial of the role-actors usually gain a disproportionate share of the rewards, while the least successful are displaced to other, less desirable positions. In addition, individuals attempt to move to higher socioeconomic positions by changing roles. Competition between classes also occurs, and in great moments of history it has proved to be a determinant of societal change.

A key question of human biology is whether there exists a genetic predisposition to enter certain classes and to play certain roles. Circumstances can be easily conceived in which such genetic differentiation might occur. The heritability of at least some parameters of intelligence and emotive traits is sufficient to respond to a moderate amount of disruptive selection. Dahlberg[4] showed that if a single gene appears that is responsible for success and an upward shift in status, it can be rapidly concentrated in the uppermost socioeconomic classes. Suppose, for example, there are two classes, each beginning with only a 1 percent frequency of the homozygotes of the upward-mobile gene. Suppose further that 50 percent of the homozygotes in the lower class are transferred upward in each generation. Then in only ten generations, depending on the relative sizes of the groups, the upper class will be comprised of as many as 20 percent homozygotes or more and the lower class of as few as 0.5

4. G. Dahlberg, *Mathematical Methods for Population Genetics* (New York, 1947).

percent or less. Using a similar argument, Herrnstein[5] proposed that as environmental opportunities become more nearly equal within societies, socioeconomic groups will be defined increasingly by genetically based differences in intelligence.

A strong initial bias toward such stratification is created when one human population conquers and subjugates another, a common enough event in human history. Genetic differences in mental traits, however slight, tend to be preserved by the raising of class barriers, racial and cultural discrimination, and physical ghettos. The geneticist C. D. Darlington[6], among others, postulated this process to be a prime source of genetic diversity within human societies.

Yet despite the plausibility of the general argument, there is little evidence of any hereditary solidification of status. The castes of India have been in existence for 2000 years, more than enough time for evolutionary divergence, but they differ only slightly in blood type and other measurable anatomical and physiological traits. Powerful forces can be identified that work against the genetic fixation of caste differences. First, cultural evolution is too fluid. Over a period of decades or at most centuries ghettos are replaced, races and subject people are liberated, the conquerors are conquered. Even within relatively stable societies the pathways of upward mobility are numerous. The daughters of lower classes tend to marry upward. Success in commerce or political life can launch a family from virtually any socioeconomic group into the ruling class in a single generation. Furthermore, there are many Dahlberg genes, not just the one postulated for argument in the simplest model. The hereditary factors of human success are strongly polygenic and form a long list, only a few of which have been measured. IQ constitutes only one subset of the components of intelligence. Less tangible but equally important qualities are creativity, entrepreneurship, drive, and mental stamina. Let us assume that the genes contributing to these qualities are scattered over many chromosomes. Assume further that some of the traits are uncorrelated or even negatively correlated. Under these circumstances only the most intense forms of disruptive selection could result in the formation of stable ensembles of genes. A much more likely circumstance is the one that apparently prevails: the maintenance of a large amount of genetic diversity within societies and the loose correlation of some of the genetically determined traits with success. This scrambling process is accelerated by the continuous shift in the fortunes of individual families from one generation to the next. * * *

5. Richard Herrnstein, "I.Q.," *The Atlantic Monthly*, 228 (September 1971), 43–64. (See below, pp. 490–499.)

6. C. D. Darlington, *The Evolution of Man and Society* (New York, 1969).

Culture, Ritual, and Religion

Culture, including the more resplendent manifestations of ritual and religion, can be interpreted as a hierarchical system of environmental tracking devices. In Chapter 7 the totality of the biological responses, from millisecond-quick biochemical reactions to gene substitutions requiring generations, was described as such a system. At that time culture was placed within the scheme at the slow end of the time scale. Now this conception can be extended. To the extent that the specific details of culture are nongenetic, they can be decoupled from the biological system and arrayed beside it as an auxiliary system. The span of the purely cultural tracking system parallels much of the slower segment of the biological tracking system, ranging from days to generations. Among the fastest cultural responses in industrial civilizations are fashions in dress and speech. Somewhat slower are political ideology and social attitudes toward other nations, while the slowest of all include incest taboos and the belief or disbelief in particular high gods. It is useful to hypothesize that cultural details are for the most part adaptive in a Darwinian sense, even though some may operate indirectly through enhanced group survival.[7] A second proposition worth considering, to make the biological analogy complete, is that the rate of change in a particular set of cultural behaviors reflects the rate of change in the environmental features to which the behaviors are keyed. * * *

The sacred rituals are the most distinctively human. Their most elementary forms are concerned with magic, the active attempt to manipulate nature and the gods. Upper Paleolithic art from the caves of Western Europe shows a preoccupation with game animals. There are many scenes showing spears and arrows embedded in the bodies of the prey. Other drawings depict men dancing in animal disguises or standing with heads bowed in front of animals. Probably the function of the drawings was sympathetic magic, based on the quite logical notion that what is done with an image will come to pass with the real thing. The anticipatory action is comparable to the intention movements of animals, which in the course of evolution have often been ritualized into communicative signals. The waggle dance of the honeybee, it will be recalled, is a miniaturized rehearsal of the flight from the nest to the food. Primitive man might have understood the meaning of such complex animal behavior easily. Magic was, and still is in some societies, practiced by special people variously called shamans, sorcerers, or medicine

7. S. L. Washburn and F. C. Howell, "Human Evolution and Culture," in Sol Tax, ed., *Evolution After Darwin* (Chicago, 1960), II, 33–56; R. D. Masters, "Genes, Language, and Evolution," *Semiotica*, 2 (1970), 295–320.

men. They alone were believed to have the secret knowledge and power to deal effectively with the supernatural, and as such their influence sometimes exceeded that of the tribal headmen.

Formal religion *sensu stricto* has many elements of magic but is focused on deeper, more tribally oriented beliefs. Its rites celebrate the creation myths, propitiate the gods, and resanctify the tribal moral codes. Instead of a shaman controlling physical power, there is a priest who communes with the gods and curries their favor through obeisance, sacrifice, and the proffered evidences of tribal good behavior. In more complex societies, polity and religion have always blended naturally. Power belonged to kings by divine right, but high priests often ruled over kings by virtue of the higher rank of the gods. * * *

The enduring paradox of religion is that so much of its substance is demonstrably false, yet it remains a driving force in all societies. Men would rather believe than know, have the void as purpose, as Nietzsche said, than be void of purpose. At the turn of the century Durkheim rejected the notion that such force could really be extracted from "a tissue of illusions." And since that time social scientists have sought the psychological Rosetta stone that might clarify the deeper truths of religious reasoning. In a penetrating analysis of this subject, Rappaport[8] proposed that virtually all forms of sacred rites serve the purposes of communication. * * *

To sanctify a procedure or a statement is to certify it as beyond question and imply punishment for anyone who dares to contradict it. So removed is the sacred from the profane in everyday life that simply to repeat it in the wrong circumstance is a transgression. This extreme form of certification, the heart of all religions, is granted to the practices and dogmas that serve the most vital interests of the group. The individual is prepared by the sacred rituals for supreme effort and self-sacrifice. Overwhelmed by shibboleths, special costumes, and the sacred dancing and music so accurately keyed to his emotive centers he has a "religious experience." He is ready to reassert allegiance to his tribe and family, perform charities, consecrate his life, leave for the hunt, join the battle, die for God and country. *Deus vult* was the rallying cry of the First Crusade. God wills it, but the summed Darwinian fitness of the tribe was the ultimate if unrecognized beneficiary.

It was Henri Bergson who first identified a second force leading to the formalization of morality and religion. The extreme plasticity of human social behavior is both a great strength and a real danger. If each family worked out rules of behavior on its own, the result

8. R. A. Rappaport, "The Sacred in Human Evolution," *Annual Review of* *Ecology and Systematics*, 2 (1971), 23–44.

would be an intolerable amount of tradition drift and growing chaos. To counteract selfish behavior and the "dissolving power" of high intelligence, each society must codify itself. Within broad limits virtually any set of conventions works better than none at all. Because arbitrary codes work, organizations tend to be inefficient and marred by unnecessary inequities. As Rappaport succinctly expressed it, "Sanctification transforms the arbitrary into the necessary, and regulatory mechanisms which are arbitrary are likely to be sanctified." The process engenders criticism, and in the more literate and self-conscious societies visionaries and revolutionaries set out to change the system. Reform meets repression, because to the extent that the rules have been sanctified and mythologized, the majority of the people regard them as beyond question, and disagreement is defined as blasphemy.

This leads us to the essentially biological question of the evolution of indoctrinability.[9] Human beings are absurdly easy to indoctrinate—they *seek* it. If we assume for argument that indoctrinability evolves, at what level does natural selection take place? One extreme possibility is that the group is the unit of selection. When conformity becomes too weak, groups become extinct. In this version selfish, individualistic members gain the upper hand and multiply at the expense of others. But their rising prevalence accelerates the vulnerability of the society and hastens its extinction. Societies containing higher frequencies of conformer genes replace those that disappear, thus raising the overall frequency of the genes in the metapopulation of societies. The spread of the genes will occur more rapidly if the metapopulation (for example, a tribal complex) is simultaneously enlarging its range. Formal models of the process, presented in Chapter 5, show that if the rate of societal extinction is high enough relative to the intensity of the counteracting individual selection, the altruistic genes can rise to moderately high levels. The genes might be of the kind that favors indoctrinability even at the expense of the individuals who submit. For example, the willingness to risk death in battle can favor group survival at the expense of the genes that permitted the fatal military discipline. The group-selection hypothesis is sufficient to account for the evolution of indoctrinability.

The competing, individual-level hypothesis is equally sufficient. It states that the ability of individuals to conform permits them to enjoy the benefits of membership with a minimum of energy expenditure and risk. Although their selfish rivals may gain a momentary advantage, it is lost in the long run through ostracism

9. D. T. Campbell, "On the Genetics of Altruism and the Counterhedonic Components in Human Culture," *Journal of Social Issues*, 28 (1972), 21–37.

454 · *Edward O. Wilson*

and repression. The conformists perform altruistic acts, perhaps even to the extent of risking their lives, not because of self-denying genes selected at the group level but because the group is occasionally able to take advantage of the indoctrinability which on other occasions is favorable to the individual.

The two hypotheses are not mutually exclusive. Group and individual selection can be reinforcing. If war requires spartan virtues and eliminates some of the warriors, victory can more than adequately compensate the survivors in land, power, and the opportunity to reproduce. The average individual will win the inclusive fitness game, making the gamble profitable, because the summed efforts of the participants give the average member a more than compensatory edge.

Ethics

Scientists and humanists should consider together the possibility that the time has come for ethics to be removed temporarily from the hands of the philosophers and biologicized. The subject at present consists of several oddly disjunct conceptualizations. The first is *ethical intuitionism*, the belief that the mind has a direct awareness of true right and wrong that it can formalize by logic and translate into rules of social action. The purest guiding precept of secular Western thought has been the theory of the social contract as formulated by Locke, Rousseau, and Kant. In our time the precept has been rewoven into a solid philosophical system by John Rawls.[1] His imperative is that justice should be not merely integral to a system of government but rather the object of the original contract. The principles called by Rawls "justice as fairness" are those which free and rational persons would choose if they were beginning an association from a position of equal advantage and wished to define the fundamental rules of the association. In judging the appropriateness of subsequent laws and behavior, it would be necessary to test their conformity to the unchallengeable starting position.

The Achilles heel of the intuitionist position is that it relies on the emotive judgment of the brain as though that organ must be treated as a black box. While few will disagree that justice as fairness is an ideal state for disembodied spirits, the conception is in no way explanatory or predictive with reference to human beings. Consequently, it does not consider the ultimate ecological or genetic consequences of the rigorous prosecution of its conclusions. Perhaps explanation and prediction will not be needed for the millennium.

1. John Rawls, *A Theory of Justice* (Cambridge, Mass., 1971).

But this is unlikely—the human genotype and the ecosystem in which it evolved were fashioned out of extreme unfairness. In either case the full exploration of the neural machinery of ethical judgment is desirable and already in progress. One such effort, constituting the second mode of conceptualization, can be called *ethical behaviorism*. Its basic proposition, which has been expanded most fully by J. F. Scott,[2] holds that moral commitment is entirely learned, with operant conditioning being the dominant mechanism. In other words, children simply internalize the behavioral norms of the society. * * * The difference between ethical behaviorism and the current version of developmental-genetic analysis is that the former postulates a mechanism (operant conditioning) without evidence and the latter presents evidence without postulating a mechanism. No great conceptual difficulty underlies this disparity. The study of moral development is only a more complicated and less tractable version of the genetic variance problem (see Chapters 2 and 7). With the accretion of data the two approaches can be expected to merge to form a recognizable exercise in behavioral genetics.

Even if the problem were solved tomorrow, however, an important piece would still be missing. This is the *genetic evolution of ethics*. In the first chapter of this book I argued that ethical philosophers intuit the deontological canons of morality by consulting the emotive centers of their own hypothalamic-limbic system. This is also true of the developmentalists, even when they are being their most severely objective. Only by interpreting the activity of the emotive centers as a biological adaptation can the meaning of the canons be deciphered. Some of the activity is likely to be outdated, a relic of adjustment to the most primitive form of tribal organization. Some of it may prove to be *in statu nascendi*, constituting new and quickly changing adaptations to agrarian and urban life. The resulting confusion will be reinforced by other factors. To the extent that unilaterally altruistic genes have been established in the population by group selection, they will be opposed by allelomorphs favored by individual selection. The conflict of impulses under their various controls is likely to be widespread in the population, since current theory predicts that the genes will be at best maintained in a state of balanced polymorphism (Chapter 5). Moral ambivalency will be further intensified by the circumstance that a schedule of sex- and age-dependent ethics can impart higher genetic fitness than a single moral code which is applied uniformly to all sex-age groups. * * *

2. J. F. Scott, *Internalization of Norms: A Sociological Theory of Moral Commitment* (New York, 1971).

If there is any truth to this theory of innate moral pluralism, the requirement for an evolutionary approach to ethics is self-evident. It should also be clear that no single set of moral standards can be applied to all human populations, let alone all sex-age classes within each population. To impose a uniform code is therefore to create complex, intractable moral dilemmas—these, of course, are the current condition of mankind. * * *

Warfare

Throughout recorded history the conduct of war has been common among tribes and nearly universal among chiefdoms and states. When Sorokin[3] analyzed the histories of 11 European countries over periods of 275 to 1,025 years, he found that on the average they were engaged in some kind of military action 47 percent of the time, or about one year out of every two. The range was from 28 percent of the years in the case of Germany to 67 percent in the case of Spain. The early chiefdoms and states of Europe and the Middle East turned over with great rapidity, and much of the conquest was genocidal in nature. The spread of genes has always been of paramount importance. For example, after the conquest of the Midianites Moses gave instructions identical in result to the aggression and genetic usurpation by male langur monkeys:

> Now kill every male dependent, and kill every woman who has had intercourse with a man, but spare for yourselves every woman among them who has not had intercourse. (Numbers 31)

And centuries later, von Clausewitz conveyed to his pupil the Prussian crown prince a sense of the true, biological joy of warfare:

> Be audacious and cunning in your plans, firm and persevering in their execution, determined to find a glorious end, and fate will crown your youthful brow with a shining glory, which is the ornament of princes, and engrave your image in the hearts of your last descendants.

The possibility that endemic warfare and genetic usurpation could be an effective force in group selection was clearly recognized by Charles Darwin. In *The Descent of Man* he proposed a remarkable model that foreshadowed many of the elements of modern group-selection theory:

> Now, if some one man in a tribe, more sagacious than the others, invented a new snare or weapon, or other means of attack or defence, the plainest self-interest, without the assistance of much reasoning power, would prompt the other members to imitate

3. P. Sorokin, *Social and Cultural Dynamics* (Boston, 1957).

him, and all would thus profit. The habitual practice of each new art must likewise in some slight degree strengthen the intellect. If the invention were an important one, the tribe would increase in number, spread, and supplant other tribes. In a tribe thus rendered more numerous there would always be a rather greater chance of the birth of other superior and inventive members. If such men left children to inherit their mental superiority, the chance of the birth of still more ingenious members would be somewhat better, and in a very small tribe decidedly better. Even if they left no children, the tribe would still include their blood-relations, and it has been ascertained by agriculturists that by preserving and breeding from the family of an animal, which when slaughtered was found to be valuable, the desired character has been obtained.

Darwin saw that not only can group selection reinforce individual selection, but it can oppose it—and sometimes prevail, especially if the size of the breeding unit is small and average kinship correspondingly close. Essentially the same theme was later developed in increasing depth by Keith,[4] Bigelow,[5] and Alexander.[6] These authors envision some of the "noblest" traits of mankind, including team play, altruism, patriotism, bravery on the field of battle, and so forth, as the genetic product of warfare. * * *

The Future

When mankind has achieved an ecological steady state, probably by the end of the twenty-first century, the internalization of social evolution will be nearly complete. About this time biology should be at its peak, with the social sciences maturing rapidly. Some historians of science will take issue with this projection, arguing that the accelerating pace of discoveries in these fields implies a more rapid development. But historical precedents have misled us before: the subjects we are talking about are more difficult than physics or chemistry by at least two orders of magnitude.

Consider the prospects for sociology. This science is now in the natural history stage of its development. There have been attempts at system building but, just as in psychology, they were premature and came to little. Much of what passes for theory in sociology today is really labeling of phenomena and concepts, in the expected manner of natural history. Process is difficult to analyze because the fundamental units are elusive, perhaps nonexistent. Syntheses commonly consist of the tedious cross-referencing of differing sets of

4. A. Keith, *A New Theory of Human Evolution* (New York, 1949).
5. R. Bigelow, *The Dawn Warriors: Man's Evolution toward Peace* (Boston, 1969).
6. R. D. Alexander, "The Search for an Evolutionary Philosophy of Man," *Proceedings of the Royal Society of Victoria*, 84 (1971), 99–120.

definitions and metaphors erected by the more imaginative thinkers (see for example Inkeles[7] and Friedrichs.[8] That, too, is typical of the natural history phase.

With an increase in the richness of descriptions and experiments, sociology is drawing closer each day to cultural anthropology, social psychology, and economics, and will soon merge with them. These disciplines are fundamental to sociology *sensu lato* and are most likely to yield its first phenomenological laws. In fact, some viable qualitative laws probably already exist. They include tested statements about the following relationships: the effects of hostility and stress upon ethnocentrism and xenophobia (LeVine and Campbell[9]); the positive correlation between and within cultures of war and combative sports, resulting in the elimination of the hydraulic model of aggressive drive (Sipes[1]); precise but still specialized models of promotion and opportunity within professional guilds (White[2]); and, far from least, the most general models of economics.

The transition from purely phenomenological to fundamental theory in sociology must await a full, neuronal explanation of the human brain. Only when the machinery can be torn down on paper at the level of the cell and put together again will the properties of emotion and ethical judgment come clear. Simulations can then be employed to estimate the full range of behavioral responses and the precision of their homeostatic controls. Stress will be evaluated in terms of the neurophysiological perturbations and their relaxation times. Cognition will be translated into circuitry. Learning and creativeness will be defined as the alteration of specific portions of the cognitive machinery regulated by input from the emotive centers. Having cannibalized psychology, the new neurobiology will yield an enduring set of first principles for sociology.

The role of evolutionary sociobiology in this enterprise will be twofold. It will attempt to reconstruct the history of the machinery and to identify the adaptive significance of each of its functions. Some of the functions are almost certainly obsolete, being directed toward such Pleistocene exigencies as hunting and gathering and intertribal warfare. Others may prove currently adaptive at the level of the individual and family but maladaptive at the level of the group—or the reverse. If the decision is taken to mold cultures to fit the requirements of the ecological steady state, some behaviors

7. A. Inkeles, *What is Sociology? An Introduction to the Discipline and Profession* (Englewood Cliffs, N.J., 1964).
8. R. W. Friedrichs, *A Sociology of Sociology* (New York, 1970).
9. R. A. LeVine and D. T. Campbell, *Ethnocentrism: Theories of Conflict*

(New York, 1972).
1. R. G. Sipes, "War, Sports and Aggression: An Empirical Test of Two Rival Theories," *American Anthropologist,* 75 (1973), 64–86.
2. H. C. White, *Chains of Opportunity: System Models of Mobility in Organizations* (Cambridge, Mass., 1970).

can be altered experientially without emotional damage or loss in creativity. Others cannot. Uncertainy in this matter means that Skinner's dream of a culture predesigned for happiness will surely have to wait for the new neurobiology. A genetically accurate and hence completely fair code of ethics must also wait.

The second contribution of evolutionary sociobiology will be to monitor the genetic basis of social behavior. Optimum socioeconomic systems can never be perfect, because of Arrow's impossibility theorem and probably also because ethical standards are innately pluralistic. Moreover, the genetic foundation on which any such normative system is built can be expected to shift continuously. Mankind has never stopped evolving, but in a sense his populations are drifting. The effects over a period of a few generations could change the identity of the socioeconomic optima. In particular, the rate of gene flow around the world has risen to dramatic levels and is accelerating, and the mean coefficients of relationship within local communities are correspondingly diminishing. The result could be an eventual lessening of altruistic behavior through the maladaption and loss of group-selected genes (Haldane[3]; Eshel[4]). It was shown earlier that behavioral traits tend to be selected out by the principle of metabolic conservation when they are suppressed or when their original function becomes neutral in adaptive value. Such traits can largely disappear from populations in as few as ten generations, only two or three centuries in the case of human beings. With our present inadequate understanding of the human brain, we do not know how many of the most valued qualities are linked genetically to more obsolete, destructive ones. Cooperativeness toward groupmates might be coupled with aggressivity toward strangers, creativeness with a desire to own and dominate, athletic zeal with a tendency to violent response, and so on. In extreme cases such pairings could stem from pleiotropism, the control of more than one phenotypic character by the same set of genes. If the planned society—the creation of which seems inevitable in the coming century—were to deliberately steer its members past those stresses and conflicts that once gave the destructive phenotypes their Darwinian edge, the other phenotypes might dwindle with them. In this, the ultimate genetic sense, social control would rob man of his humanity.

3. J. B. S. Haldane, *The Causes of Evolution* (London, 1932).
4. I. Eshel, "On the Neighbor Effect and the Evolution of Altruistic Traits," *Theoretical Population Biology*, 3 (1972), 258–277.

STEPHEN JAY GOULD

Biological Potentiality vs. Biological Determinism
(1977) †

* * * The statement that humans are animals does not imply that our specific patterns of behavior and social arrangements are in any way directly determined by our genes. *Potentiality* and *determination* are different concepts.

The intense discussion aroused by E. O. Wilson's *Sociobiology* (Harvard University Press, 1975) has led me to take up this subject. Wilson's book has been greeted by a chorus of praise and publicity. I, however, find myself among the smaller group of its detractors. Most of *Sociobiology* wins from me the same high praise almost universally accorded it. For a lucid account of evolutionary principles and an indefatigably thorough discussion of social behavior among all groups of animals, *Sociobiology* will be the primary document for years to come. But Wilson's last chapter, "From Sociobiology to Sociology," leaves me very unhappy indeed. After twenty-six chapters of careful documentation for the nonhuman animals, Wilson concludes with an extended speculation on the genetic basis of supposedly universal patterns in human behavior. Unfortunately, since this chapter is his statement on the subject closest to all our hearts, it has also attracted more than 80 percent of all the commentary in the popular press.

We who have criticized this last chapter have been accused of denying altogether the relevance of biology to human behavior, of reviving an ancient superstition by placing ourselves outside the rest of "the creation." Are we pure "nurturists?" Do we permit a political vision of human perfectibility to blind us to evident constraints imposed by our biological nature? The answer to both statements is no. The issue is not universal biology vs. human uniqueness, but biological potentiality vs. biological determinism.

Replying to a critic of his article in the *New York Times Magazine* (October 12, 1975), Wilson wrote:

> There is no doubt that the patterns of human social behavior, including altruistic behavior, are under genetic control, in the sense that they represent a restricted subset of possible patterns that are very different from the patterns of termites, chimpanzees and other animal species.

† From Chapter 32 of Stephen Jay Gould, *Ever Since Darwin* (New York, 1977). Stephen Jay Gould (b. 1941) is professor of geology at Harvard University.

If this is all that Wilson means by genetic control, then we can scarcely disagree. Surely we do not do all the things that other animals do, and just as surely, the range of our potential behavior is circumscribed by our biology. We would lead very different social lives if we photosynthesized (no agriculture, gathering, or hunting —the major determinants of our social evolution) or had life cycles like those of the gall midges discussed in essay 10. (When feeding on an uncrowded mushroom, these insects reproduce in the larval or pupal stage. The young grow within the mother's body, devour her from inside, and emerge from her depleted external shell ready to feed, grow the next generation, and make the supreme sacrifice.)

But Wilson makes much stronger claims. Chapter 27 is not a statement about the range of potential human behaviors or even an argument for the restriction of that range from a much larger total domain among all animals. It is, primarily, an extended speculation on the existence of genes for specific and variable traits in human behavior—including spite, aggression, xenophobia, conformity, homosexuality, and the characteristic behavioral differences between men and women in Western society. Of course, Wilson does not deny the role of nongenetic learning in human behavior; he even states at one point that "genes have given away most of their sovereignty." But, he quickly adds, genes "maintain a certain amount of influence in at least the behavioral qualities that underlie variations between cultures." And the next paragraph calls for a "discipline of anthropological genetics."

Biological determinism is the primary theme in Wilson's discussion of human behavior; chapter 27 makes no sense in any other context. Wilson's primary aim, as I read him, is to suggest that Darwinian theory might reformulate the human sciences just as it previously transformed so many other biological disciplines. But Darwinian processes can not operate without genes to select. Unless the "interesting" properties of human behavior are under specific genetic control, sociology need fear no invasion of its turf. By interesting, I refer to the subjects sociologists and anthropologists fight about most often—aggression, social stratification, and differences in behavior between men and women. If genes only specify that we are large enough to live in a world of gravitational forces, need to rest our bodies by sleeping, and do not photosynthesize, then the realm of genetic determinism will be relatively uninspiring.

What is the direct evidence for genetic control of specific human social behavior? At the moment, the answer is none whatever. (It would not be impossible, in theory, to gain such evidence by standard, controlled experiments in breeding, but we do not raise people in *Drosophila* bottles, establish pure lines, or control environments for invariant nurturing.) Sociobiologists must therefore advance indirect arguments based on plausibility. Wilson uses three major strategies: universality, continuity, and adaptiveness.

1. Universality: If certain behaviors are invariably found in our closest primate relatives and among humans themselves, a circumstantial case for common, inherited genetic control may be advanced. Chapter 27 abounds with statements about supposed human universals. For example, "Human beings are absurdly easy to indoctrinate—they *seek* it." Or, "Men would rather believe than know." I can only say that my own experience does not correspond with Wilson's.

When Wilson must acknowledge diversity, he often dismisses the uncomfortable "exceptions" as temporary and unimportant aberrations. Since Wilson believes that repeated, often genocidal warfare has shaped our genetic destiny, the existence of nonaggressive peoples is embarrassing. But he writes: "It is to be expected that some isolated cultures will escape the process for generations at a time, in effect reverting temporarily to what ethnographers classify as a pacific state."

In any case, even if we can compile a list of behavioral traits shared by humans and our closest primate relatives, this does not make a good case for common genetic control. Similar results need not imply similar causes; in fact, evolutionists are so keenly aware of this problem that they have developed a terminology to express it. Similar features due to common genetic ancestry are "homologous"; similarities due to common function, but with different evolutionary histories, are "analogous" (the wings of birds and insects, for example—the common ancestor of both groups lacked wings). I will argue below that a basic feature of human biology supports the idea that many behavioral similarities between humans and other primates are analogous, and that they have no direct genetic specification in humans.

2. Continuity: Wilson claims, with ample justice in my opinion, that the Darwinian explanation of altruism in W. D. Hamilton's 1964 theory of "kin selection" forms the basis for an evolutionary theory of animal societies. Altruistic acts are the cement of stable societies, yet they seem to defy a Darwinian explanation. On Darwinian principles, all individuals are selected to maximize their own genetic contribution to future generations. How, then, can they willingly sacrifice or endanger themselves by performing altruistic acts to benefit others?

The resolution is charmingly simple in concept, although complex in technical detail. By benefiting relatives, altruistic acts preserve an altruist's genes even if the altruist himself will not be the one to perpetuate them. For example, in most sexually reproducing organisms, an individual shares (on average) one-half the genes of his sibs and one-eighth the genes of his first cousins. Hence, if faced with a choice of saving oneself alone or sacrificing oneself to save more than two sibs or more than eight first cousins, the Darwinian calculus favors altruistic sacrifice; for in so doing, an altruist actually increases his own genetic representation in future generations.

Natural selection will favor the preservation of such self-serving altruist genes. But what of altruistic acts toward nonrelatives? Here sociobiologists must invoke a related concept of "reciprocal altruism" to preserve a genetic explanation. The altruistic act entails some danger and no immediate benefit, but if it inspires a reciprocal act by the current beneficiary at some future time, it may pay off in the long run: a genetic incarnation of the age-old adage: you scratch my back and I'll scratch yours (even if we're not related).

The argument from continuity then proceeds. Altruistic acts in other animal societies can be plausibly explained as examples of Darwinian kin selection. Humans perform altruistic acts and these are likely to have a similarly direct genetic basis. But again, similarity of result does not imply identity of cause (see below for an alternate explanation based on biological potentiality rather than biological determinism).

3. Adaptiveness: Adaptation is the hallmark of Darwinian processes. Natural selection operates continuously and relentlessly to fit organisms to their environments. Disadvantageous social structures, like poorly designed morphological structures, will not survive for long.

Human social practices are clearly adaptive. Marvin Harris has delighted in demonstrating the logic and sensibility of those social practices in other cultures that seem most bizarre to smug Westerners (*Cows, Pigs, Wars, and Witches.* Random House, 1974). Human social behavior is riddled with altruism; it is also clearly adaptive. Is this not a prima facie argument for direct genetic control? My answer is definitely "no," and I can best illustrate my claim by reporting an argument I recently had with an eminent anthropologist.

My colleague insisted that the classic story of Eskimos on ice floes provides adequate proof for the existence of specific altruist genes maintained by kin selection. Apparently, among some Eskimo peoples, social units are arranged as family groups. If food resources dwindle and the family must move to survive, aged grandparents willingly remain behind (to die) rather than endanger the survival of their entire family by slowing an arduous and dangerous migration. Family groups with no altruist genes have succumbed to natural selection as migrations hindered by the old and sick lead to the death of entire families. Grandparents with altruist genes increase

464 · *Stephen Jay Gould*

their own fitness by their sacrifice, for they enhance the survival of close relatives sharing their genes.

The explanation by my colleague is plausible, to be sure, but scarcely conclusive since an eminently simple, nongenetic explanation also exists: there are no altruist genes at all, in fact, no important genetic differences among Eskimo families whatsoever. The sacrifice of grandparents is an adaptive, but nongenetic, cultural trait. Families with no tradition for sacrifice do not survive for many generations. In other families, sacrifice is celebrated in song and story; aged grandparents who stay behind become the greatest heroes of the clan. Children are socialized from their earliest memories to the glory and honor of such sacrifice.

I cannot prove my scenario, any more than my colleague can demonstrate his. But in the current context of no evidence, they are at least equally plausible. Likewise, reciprocal altruism undeniably exists in human societies, but this provides no evidence whatever for its genetic basis. As Benjamin Franklin said: "We must all hang together, or assuredly we shall all hang separately." Functioning societies may require reciprocal altruism. But these acts need not be coded into our consciousness by genes; they may be inculcated equally well by learning.

* * * We are both ordinary and special. The central feature of our biological uniqueness also provides the major reason for doubting that our behaviors are directly coded by specific genes. That feature is, of course, our large brain. * * *

Why imagine that specific genes for aggression, dominance, or spite have any importance when we know that the brain's enormous flexibility permits us to be aggressive or peaceful, dominant or submissive, spiteful or generous? Violence, sexism, and general nastiness *are* biological since they represent one subset of a possible range of behaviors. But peacefulness, equality, and kindness are just as biological—and we may see their influence increase if we can create social structures that permit them to flourish. Thus, my criticism of Wilson does not invoke a nonbiological "environmentalism"; it merely pits the concept of biological potentiality—a brain capable of the full range of human behaviors and rigidity predisposed toward none—against the idea of biological determinism—specific genes for specific behavioral traits.

But why is this academic issue so delicate and explosive? There is no hard evidence for either position, and what difference does it make, for example, whether we conform because conformer genes have been selected or because our general genetic makeup permits conformity as one strategy among many?

The protracted and intense debate surrounding biological determinism has arisen as a function of its social and political message.

As I argue in the preceding set of essays, biological determinism has always been used to defend existing social arrangements as biologically inevitable—from "for ye have the poor always with you" to nineteenth-century imperialism to modern sexism. Why else would a set of ideas so devoid of factual support gain such a consistently good press from established media throughout the centuries? This usage is quite out of the control of individual scientists who propose deterministic theories for a host of reasons, often benevolent.

I make no attribution of motive in Wilson's or anyone else's case. Neither do I reject determinism because I dislike its political usage. Scientific truth, as we understand it, must be our primary criterion. We live with several unpleasant biological truths, death being the most undeniable and ineluctable. If genetic determinism is true, we will learn to live with it as well. But I reiterate my statement that no evidence exists to support it, that the crude versions of past centuries have been conclusively disproved, and that its continued popularity is a function of social prejudice among those who benefit most from the status quo. * * *

We are both similar to and different from other animals. In different cultural contexts, emphasis upon one side or the other of this fundamental truth plays a useful social role. In Darwin's day, an assertion of our similarity broke through centuries of harmful superstition. Now we may need to emphasize our difference as flexible animals with a vast range of potential behavior. Our biological nature does not stand in the way of social reform. We are, as Simone de Beauvoir said, "l'être dont l'être est de n'être pas"—the being whose essence lies in having no essence.

ARTHUR CAPLAN

Ethics, Evolution, and the Milk of Human Kindness (1976) †

Sufficient time has elapsed since the publication of Edward O. Wilson's massive new book, *Sociobiology: The New Synthesis* (Cambridge: Harvard University Press, 1975) to permit a large body of critical review articles to accumulate. And accumulate they surely have. Nearly every journal concerned even peripherally with scientific issues has commissioned a review. While many reviewers have acclaimed Wilson's erudition and insight, others have criticized his efforts. This is not, of course, the first time that a new

† From the *Hastings Center Report*, 6 (April 1976), 20–25. Arthur Caplan (b. 1950) is associate for the humanities, The Hastings Center, and instructor, School of Public Health, Columbia University Medical School.

book has received a mixed set of notices. However, *Sociobiology* has been criticized and acclaimed on the basis of so many diverse arguments that it is natural to ask why the book provokes such divergent responses.

Many biologists have praised the book for its biological erudition and analytical insight into complex evolutionary phenomena. Much of the attention given the book has resulted, however, from claims that Wilson commits a series of damning mistakes in extending his evolutionary analysis to human social behavior. These ethical charges will bear the brunt of critical scrutiny in this essay. * * *

If Wilson's book had been confined solely to the compilation and explanation of social behaviors in animals by means of a new synthetic evolutionary approach, it is reasonable to assume that the book would have met with the acclaim and approval of most biologists. But the book contains two more interpretive and highly provocative chapters—the first chapter, entitled "The Morality of the Gene," and the last, called "Man: From Sociobiology to Sociology." If one had to pinpoint two book chapters written in the last year likely to create controversy in a scientific community already reeling from debates concerning the validity of IQ research, XYY screening programs, genetic transplantation, and the innately aggressive theory of human nature, these undoubtedly would be the chapters.

Sociobiology, as Wilson conceives of the field, draws under its mantle all aspects of social behavior in every species including man. In fact, because his social behavior is so rich and complex, man is perhaps the most interesting of all the species encompassed by sociobiological inquiry. Wilson shows no reluctance to pursue his inquiry into human social behavior. Ethics, aesthetics, politics, culture and religion, in his view, desperately need biologization. He cites such altruistic or seemingly altruistic human behaviors as homosexuality, philanthropy, celibacy, slavery, and martyrdom as all needing evolutionary explanations. Like every other structural and behavioral trait, such behaviors must have their origins in selection acting upon genes. A metaphysical commitment to environmentalism must not be permitted to blind scientific inquiry to the fact that much of what we are and how we got that way can be understood in terms of selection pressures on our ancestors' genetic components and organic traits.

Almost inevitably Wilson's willingness to ascribe a hereditary base and evolutionary origin to complex human behaviors, and his attempts to draw explanatory comparisons between animal and human behavior, have drawn a harsh critical response from those reviewers sensitive to the inherent ethical difficulties. In an impassioned letter to the editors in the *New York Review of Books*

(November 13, 1975), a Boston-based group of biologists and students warned of the ethical and political dangers lurking behind the "biological determinism" of Wilson's sociobiological approach to human behavior. Wilson's evolutionary explanations of human social behavior, they say, carry the seeds of a genetic justification of regressive sociopolitical policies. Similar speculations in earlier decades blossomed, they claim, into the horrors of eugenics movements, restrictive immigration policies, a rampant competitive ethos in business, and the construction of gas chambers in Nazi Germany. These "value critics" accuse Wilson of treating behavior and social structure simplistically, as the simple end-products of genetic synthesis. He is accused of ignoring the effects of cultural transmission, of facile comparative generalizations between humans and animals, of *ad hoc* arguments to explain complex human traits, and of a crude and outmoded hereditarianism in his scientific approach to human behavior.

In an equally impassioned response to this letter (December 11, 1975), Wilson decries what he sees as a distortion of the contents and intent of his arguments. Wilson reminds his critics that in *Sociobiology* and in a variety of concurrent articles in various scientific journals and the popular press he explicitly warned against the dangers of simple-minded hereditarianism, *ad hoc* advocacy arguments, facile comparative analogies, and simplistic valuational judgments. Moreover, he argues that sociobiology provides the best means of pursuing an investigation into human nature—a nature that, despite the wishes and desires of various liberal critics, is not infinitely malleable and plastic.

Unfortunately, the personal tone of the debate indicates that the controversy may degenerate into a murky morass of mud-slinging accusations and counter-accusations. This would be most unfortunate, for Wilson's book surely raises fundamental scientific and ethical issues that deserve serious discussion. Can human behavior or any behavioral trait be studied in the same way that structural or physiological organic properties have traditionally been approached by biologists? Is there any methodology for assessing similarities found to exist between animal and human behavior? And, more generally, of what significance are scientific findings and facts to valuational issues in ethics, religion, and politics? And what obligation, if any, should scientists feel about guarding against the possible abuse and misuse of their scientific speculations concerning human nature and human behavior?

It is somewhat puzzling that the "value critics" of Wilson's book fail to appreciate the theoretical significance of social behavior for evolutionary theorizing despite their admitted ethical distaste for extending evolutionary theorizing to human behavior. It is even more puzzling that, in their haste to formulate ethical criticisms of the book, these same critics seem to commit an important methodological mistake. For much of the hostility to Wilson's evolutionary examination of human social behavior appears to originate in a failure to distinguish clearly between his attempt to give an historical explanation or account of the origin of a trait or behavior, and his attempt to explain the maintenance or persistence of the same trait or behavior in a contemporary population of organisms.

There is a great difference between the explanations that can be invoked to explain the first or rudimentary appearance of a behavior and the explanations that can be used to explain why that same behavior can still be observed in living organisms today. What Wilson tries to do is not so much to explain the *present* manifestation of ethics, culture, and social behavior in contemporary human societies as to explain the *origins* of these behaviors in ancestral societies. It is the conflation of intended historical explanations with explanations of contemporary events that so strongly divides Wilson and his critics.

The error of blurring historical and contemporary accounts should not be a source of controversy once the aims and intentions of sociobiological inquiry are made evident. It is one thing to try and construct evolutionary explanations of rudimentary or primitive altruistic behaviors in ancestral man on the basis of selective environmental forces acting on a variable set of genes. It is quite a different matter to attempt to explain homosexual behavior in twentieth-century American males by means of these same explanatory premises and assumptions. Wilson can make certain assumptions about society, culture, and genetics in the former case that he surely cannot validly make to explain the latter phenomena. While Wilson certainly attempts to explain the origins of human sociality, this attempt can be made entirely independently of an explanation of contemporary human social behavior.

Not only do Wilson's "value-critics" fail to recognize this important distinction, but they also fail to distinguish adequately exactly what it is that they object to in the book on ethical grounds. Just as there are important differences in the assumptions and premises that can be used to explain the origin of a behavior in a population or society and the assumptions and premises used to explain the persistence and presence of the same behavior in a contemporary population or society, there is an important difference between studying the evolution of ethical or social behaviors, and arguing about the ethical validity or worth of behaviors that already exist. One cannot be sure exactly what error these "value-critics" think Wilson has made in engaging in an evolutionary study of human as well as animal sociality.

But perhaps one should not expect a great deal of clarity regarding such value questions. The nature of the relationship between empirical scientific knowledge and moral or value beliefs has long been a bone of contention among philosophers and scientists. It seems painfully obvious to a large number of philosophers and scientists that ethics and science exist in separate worlds, and that it is the most blatant of fallacies to attempt to formulate moral prescriptions on the basis of empirical scientific evidence. It seems equally obvious to an equally large number of philosophers and scientists that scientific findings directly influence the sorts of moral and ethical prescriptions held to be valid at any given moment. The notorious feuds, at the beginning of this century, between those who believed ethics to be reducible to the empirical properties discovered by science and those who denied that any such reduction was possible, have produced a schism between these two camps that few participants in either group seem willing to acknowledge, much less bridge. But if any answers are to emerge regarding issues such as the implications of empirical science for ethics, or the moral responsibilities of scientists, it is necessary at least to be clear about what the scientists, in this case Wilson, are up to.

There are at least three kinds of questions that can be distinguished concerning the relationship that obtains between ethics or values and science:

1. One question concerns the distinction alluded to previously between explaining the origins of a behavior or trait and the presence of the behavior in a living population. The scientific study of ethics is concerned with explaining the origins of primitive ethical behavior in human beings. The evolution of ethics may be a difficult area for scientific study due to a lack of fossil data concerning primitive behavior; nevertheless it seems to stand as a legitimate subject of scientific investigation and evolutionary analysis.

2. Entirely distinct from this scientific pursuit is the question of the ethics of evolution. Although similar-sounding, this question refers to the problem of determining whether trends or patterns can be seen in evolution that can be assessed in terms of their ethical worth or merit.

3. The final possible relationship between scientific evolutionary theorizing and ethics can be labeled evolutionary ethics. Scientists interested in evolutionary ethics are concerned with establishing an ethical or value system on the basis of a scientific understanding of empirical evolutionary events.

It is important to distinguish the problem of the evolution of ethics from the related but distinct questions of the ethics of evolution. The value assessments that can be offered of evolutionary events or the consequences of the evolutionary process raise issues that are quite distinct from attempts to understand the origins of ethical behavior. It may be that scientific speculations concerning human behavioral evolution influence the kinds of value assessments made concerning the evolutionary process. Nevertheless, disagreements concerning the future course of evolution should not be allowed to color the legitimacy of scientific inquiry into the evolution of ethics or any other human activity.

Another question that must be kept distinct is the topic of evolutionary ethics. This label refers to views which allege that evolution can supply a foundation or warrant for specific ethical prescriptions and value systems. Advocates of evolutionary ethics, from Herbert Spencer to Julian Huxley,[1] have claimed that evolution, and in particular, human evolution provides an external standard or foundation upon which it is possible to construct an ethical superstructure. Attempts have been made to justify competition and struggle as well as altruism and cooperation as the moral "goods" to be derived from evolutionary inquiry. It is with regard to this specific topic that the fact/value dichotomy and naturalism/non-naturalism debates loom largest. It is entirely possible for an individual to hold that certain conclusions may be drawn concerning the evolution of human ethics and the ethics of evolution without thereby being committed to a naturalistic belief in the legitimacy of evolutionary ethics.

If I am correct and it is possible to distinguish at least three issues arising concerning the relationship that exists between evolution and ethics, then what, if anything, can be said about Wilson's views on these topics and the views of his critics? Wilson certainly believes that the evolution of ethical and human social behavior constitutes a central problem for the nascent science of sociobiology. He seems to have little interest in discussing the issue of the ethics of evolution, either with regard to value assessment of historical events or prescriptive suggestions as to the future direction evolution should follow. Nor does Wilson appear to be committed to a belief in evolutionary ethics. Instead, contrary to the charges of his critics, Wilson seems merely to urge a new inquiry into the whole issue of ethical naturalism. Wilson seems to say that sociobiological inquiry might produce conclusions that could affect our beliefs about all aspects of human behavior. Surely this claim warrants the sort of serious critical assessment that has been sadly absent in the reviews. Moreover, in their haste to discredit the legitimacy of evolutionary ethics, Wilson's critics make the mistake of attempting to use the very same arguments to deprecate the legitimacy of the independent questions of the evolution of ethics and the ethics of

1. See above, pp. 328-334 and 389-399.

evolution. Little progress can be made toward resolving any of these questions until all parties manage to separate these issues and treat them independently. It is impossible to come to any conclusions concerning the moral responsibilities of scientists and the relationship that exists between their work and particular political beliefs and ideologies unless one understands the airs and intensions underlying the scientific investigation of any problem. Both Wilson and his critics can be faulted for failing to make clear exactly what specific value problems compel their interest in sociobiology.

Many of the objections raised by what I have termed the "value-critics" of Wilson's book are weakened by their inattention to theoretical difficulties that may exist for sociobiology and by the confusion that surrounds ethical issues arising in the context of evolutionary inquiry. There may, however, be a more important reason underlying the diverse nature of the responses that have been made to Wilson's book. For a number of years behavioral biologists have been feuding over the proper methodological approach to studying animal behavior. Europeans, under the influence of ethologists such as Konrad Lorenz and Niko Tinbergen, have tended to lean toward an evolutionary approach to the study of behavior. It is assumed that behavior, particularly innate, species-specific behavior, can be treated as any other organic feature in offering explanations for the presence or uniqueness of a particular behavior. Americans, on the other hand, under the influence of social scientists such as B. F. Skinner, Frank Beach, and T. C. Schneirla have leaned more toward a comparative psychological approach in the study of animal behavior. American researchers have been more concerned with studying the function of behavior than they have been with the origin or maintenance of the trait over long periods of evolutionary history. It may be that Wilson is unpalatable to an American audience because his approach follows in the spirit of the European ethological camp. Perhaps it is not the ethics or the analogies that Wilson's critics find offensive but, rather, the emphasis on heredity and evolution. This claim would ally the "value-critics" of Wilson's book with historical schools of behaviorism and operationalism that I imagine they would find quite distasteful. If I am correct, the sort of response one has to Wilson's book depends upon the sort of methodological approach one brings to bear on behavioral questions. But the subtle historical influences of ethology and comparative psychology in America and Europe on Wilson and his critics remain to be explored.

Evolution and Intelligence

JANE VAN LAWICK-GOODALL

In the Shadow of Man (1971) †

The amazing success of man as a species is the result of the evolutionary development of his brain which has led, among other things, to tool-using, toolmaking, the ability to solve problems by logical reasoning, thoughtful cooperation, and language. One of the most striking ways in which the chimpanzee biologically resembles man lies in the structure of his brain. The chimpanzee, with his capacity for primitive reasoning, exhibits a type of intelligence more like that of man than does any other mammal living today. The brain of the modern chimpanzee is probably not too dissimilar to the brain that so many millions of years ago directed the behavior of the first ape men.

Previous to that far off day when I first watched David Graybeard and Goliath[1] modifying grass stems in order to use them to fish for termites, the fact that prehistoric man made tools was considered to be one of the major criteria distinguishing him from other creatures. As I pointed out earlier, the chimpanzee does not fashion his probes to "a regular and set pattern"—but then, prehistoric man, before his development of stone tools, undoubtedly poked around with sticks and straws, at which stage it seems unlikely that he made tools to a set pattern, either.

It is because of the close association in most people's minds of tools with man that special attention has always been focused upon any animal able to use an object as a tool; but it is important to realize that this ability, on its own, does not necessarily indicate any special intelligence in the creature concerned. The fact that the Galápagos woodpecker finch uses a cactus spine or twig to probe insects from crevices in the bark is indeed a fascinating phenomenon, but it does not make the bird more intelligent than

† From Chapter 19 of Jane van Lawick-Goodall, *In the Shadow of Man* (Boston, 1971). Jane van Lawick-Goodall (b. 1934) is director of the Gombe Stream Research Centre and visiting professor in zoology, University of Dar es Salaam, Tanzania.

1. These are the names assigned to the chimps by the author. Others appear later in the text.—Ed.

a genuine woodpecker that uses its long beak and tongue for the same purpose.

The point at which tool-using and toolmaking, as such, acquire evolutionary significance is surely when an animal can adapt its ability to manipulate objects to a wide variety of purposes, and when it can use an object spontaneously to solve a brand-new problem that without the use of a tool would prove insoluble.

At the Gombe Stream alone we have seen chimpanzees use objects for many different purposes. They use stems and sticks to capture and eat insects and, if the material picked is not suitable, then it is modified. They use leaves to sop up water they cannot reach with their lips—and first they chew on the leaves and thus increase their absorbency. One individual used a similar sponge to clean out the last smears of brain from the inside of a baboon skull. We have seen them use handfuls of leaves to wipe dirt from their bodies or to dab at wounds. They sometimes use sticks as levers to enlarge underground bees' nests.

In captivity chimpanzees often use objects as tools quite spontaneously. One group that was studied intensively by Wolfgang Köhler used sticks to try to pry open box lids and to dig in the ground for roots. They wiped themselves with leaves or straw, scratched themselves with stones and poked straws into columns of ants in order to eat the insects rather as the Gombe Stream chimpanzees fish for termites. They often used sticks and stones as weapons during aggressive encounters. Sometimes they used bread to lure chickens close to their enclosure, whereupon they would suddenly prod the birds with sharp sticks, apparently for amusement. Extensive tests have been carried out in laboratory settings in order to find out more about the tool*making* ability of the chimpanzee. Results show that he can pile up to five boxes one on top of the other in order to climb to a hanging food lure, that he can fit up to three tubes together to reach food placed outside the bars of his cage, and that he can uncoil part of a length of wire for the same purpose. So far, however, no chimpanzee has succeeded in using one tool to make another. Even with tuition one chimpanzee, the subject of exhaustive tests, was not able to use a stone hand ax to break a piece of wood into splinters suitable for obtaining food from a narrow pipe. She could do this when the material was suitable for her to break off pieces with her teeth but, although she was shown how to use the hand ax on tougher wood many times, she never even attempted to make use of it when trying to solve the problem. However, many other chimpanzees must be tested before we say that the chimpanzee as a species is unable to perform this act. Some humans are mathematicians—others are not.

When the performance of the chimpanzee in the field is compared with his actual abilities in test situations, it would seem that, in time, he might develop a more sophisticated tool-culture. After all, primitive man continued to use his early stone tools for thousands of years, virtually without change. Then we find a more refined type of stone tool-culture suddenly appearing widespread across the continents. Possibly a stone-age genius invented the new culture and his fellows, who undoubtedly learned from and imitated each other, copied the new technique.

If the chimpanzee is allowed to continue living he, too, might suddenly produce a race of chimp superbrains and evolve an entirely new tool-culture. For it seems almost certain that, although the ability to manipulate objects is innate in a chimpanzee, the actual tool-using patterns practiced by the Gombe Stream chimpanzees are learned by the infants from their elders. We saw one very good example of this. It happened when a female had diarrhea: she picked a large handful of leaves and wiped her messy bottom. Her two-year-old infant watched her closely and then twice picked leaves and wiped his own clean bottom.

To Hugo and me, and assuredly to many scientists interested in human behavior and evolution, one significant aspect of chimpanzee behavior lies in the close similarity of many of their communicatory gestures and postures to those of man himself. Not only are the actual positions and movements similar to our own but also the contexts in which they often occur.

When a chimpanzee is suddenly frightened he frequently reaches to touch or embrace a chimpanzee nearby, rather as a girl watching a horror film may seize her companion's hand. Both chimpanzees and humans seem reassured in stressful situations by physical contact with another individual. Once David Graybeard caught sight of his reflection in a mirror. Terrified, he seized Fifi, then only three years old. Even such contact with a very small chimp appeared to reassure him; gradually he relaxed and the grin of fear left his face. Humans may sometimes feel reassured by holding or stroking a dog or some other pet in moments of emotional crisis.

This comfort, which chimpanzees and humans alike appear to derive from physical contact with another, probably originates during the years of infancy, when for so long the touch of the mother, or the contact with her body, serves to calm the frights and soothe the anxieties of both ape and human infants. So, when the child grows older and his mother is not always at hand, he seeks the next best thing—close physical contact with another individual. If his mother is around, however, he may deliberately pick her out as his comforter. Once when Figan was about eight years old he was threatened by Mike. He screamed loudly and hurried past six or seven other chimps nearby until he reached Flo; then he held his hand toward her and she held it with hers. Calmed, Figan stopped screaming almost at once. Young human beings, too, continue to unburden their hearts to their mothers long after the days of childhood have passed—provided, of course, that an affectionate relationship exists between them.

There are some chimps who, far more than others, constantly seem to try to ingratiate themselves with their superiors. Melissa, for one, particularly when she was young, used to hurry toward and lay her hand on the back or head of an adult male almost every time one passed anywhere near her. If he turned toward her, she often drew her lips back into a submissive grin as well. Presumably Melissa, like the other chimps who constantly attempt to ingratiate themselves in this way, is simply ill at ease in the presence of a social superior, so that she constantly seeks reasurance through physical contact. If the dominant individual touches her in return, so much the better.

There are many human Melissas: the sort of people who when trying to be extra friendly reach out to touch the person concerned and smile very frequently and attentively. Usually they are, for some reason or other, people who are unsure of themselves and slightly ill at ease in social contexts. And what about smiling? There is much controversy as to how the human smile has evolved. It seems fairly certain, though, that we have two rather different kinds of smile, even if a long time ago they derived from the same facial gesture. We smile when we are amused and we smile when we are slightly nervous, on edge, apprehensive. Some people, when they are nervous at an interview, smile in this way at almost everything that is said to them. And this is the sort of smile that can probably be closely correlated with the grin of the submissive or frightened chimpanzee.

When chimpanzees are overjoyed by the sight of a large pile of bananas they pat and kiss and embrace one another rather as two Frenchmen may embrace when they hear good news, or as a child may leap to hug his mother when told of a special treat. We all know those feelings of intense excitement or happiness which cause people to shout and leap around, or to burst into tears. It is not surprising that chimpanzees, if they feel anything akin to this, should seek to calm themselves by embracing their companions.

I have already described how a chimpanzee, after being threatened or attacked by a superior, may follow the aggressor, screaming and crouching to the ground or holding out his hand. He is, in fact, begging a reassuring touch from the other. Sometimes he will not relax until he has been touched or patted, kissed or embraced. Figan several times flew into a tantrum when such contact was withheld, hurling himself about on the ground, his screams cramping in his throat until the aggressor finally calmed him with a touch. I have seen a human child behaving in the same sort of way, following his mother around the house after she has told him off, crying, holding on to her skirt, until finally she picked him up and kissed and cuddled him in forgiveness. A kiss or embrace or some other gesture of endearment is an almost inevitable outcome once a matrimonial dispute has been resolved, and in many cultures the clasping of hands occurs to denote renewal of friendship and mutual forgiveness after a quarrel.

When one human begs forgiveness from or gives forgiveness to another there are, however, moral issues involved; it is when we consider these that we get into difficulties in trying to draw parallels between chimpanzee and human behavior. In chimpanzee society the principle involved when a subordinate seeks reassurance from a superior, or when a high-ranking individual calms another, is in no way concerned with the right or wrong of the aggressive act. A female who is attacked for no reason other than that she happens to be standing too close to a charging male is quite as likely to approach the male and beg a reassuring touch as is the female who is bowled over by a male while she attempts to take a fruit from his pile of bananas.

Again, while we may make a direct comparison between the effect on anxious chimpanzee or human of a touch or embrace of reassurance, the issue becomes complicated if we probe into the motivation that directs the gesture of the ape or the human who is doing the reassuring. Human beings are capable of acting from purely unselfish motives; we can be genuinely sorry for someone and try to share in his troubles in an endeavor to offer comfort and solace. It is unlikely that a chimpanzee acts from feelings quite like these; I doubt whether even members of one family, united as they are by strong mutual affections, are ever motivated by pure altruism in their dealings one with another.

On the other hand, there may be parallels in some instances. Most of us have experienced sensations of extreme discomfort and unease in the presence of an abject, weeping person. We may feel compelled to try to calm him, not because we are sorry for him in the altruistic sense, but because his behavior disturbs our own feeling of well-being. Perhaps the sight—and especially the sound—of a crouching, screaming subordinate similarly makes a chimpanzee uneasy; the most efficient way of changing the situation is for him to calm the other with a touch. * * *

When two chimpanzees greet each other after a separation, their behavior often looks amazingly like that shown by two humans in the same context. Chimpanzees may bow or crouch to the ground, hold hands, kiss, embrace, touch, or pat each other on almost any part of the body, especially the head and face and genitals. A male may chuck a female or an infant under the chin. Humans, in many cultures, show one or more of these gestures. Even the touching or holding of another's genitals is a greeting in some societies; in fact, it is described in the Bible, only it has been translated as the placing of the hand under the companion's thigh.

In human societies much greeting behavior has become ritualized. A man who smiles when greeting a friend, or who inclines his head when passing an acquaintance in the street, is not necessarily acknowledging that the other has a superior social status. Yet the nod undoubtedly derives from submissive bowing or prostration and the smile from a nervous grin. Often, though, human greetings still do serve to clarify the relative social status of the individuals concerned, particularly on formal occasions.

A greeting between two chimpanzees nearly always serves such a purpose—it reestablishes the dominance status of the one relative to the other. * * *

It is not only the submissive and reassuring gestures of the chimpanzee that so closely resemble our own. Many of his games are like those played by human children. The tickling movements of chimpanzee fingers during play are almost identical with our own. The chimpanzee's aggressive displays are not dissimilar to some of ours. Like a man, an angry chimpanzee may fixedly stare at his opponent. He may raise his forearm rapidly, jerk back his head a little, run toward his adversary upright and waving his arms, throw stones, wield sticks, hit, kick, bite, scratch, and pull the hair of a victim.

In fact, if we survey the whole range of the postural and gestural communication signals of chimpanzees on the one hand and humans on the other, we find striking similarities in many instances. It would appear, then, that man and chimp either have evolved gestures and postures along a most remarkable parallel or that we share with the chimpanzees an ancestor in the dim and very distant past; an ancestor, moreover, who communicated with his kind by means of kissing and embracing, touching and patting and holding hands.

One of the major differences between man and his closest living relative is, of course, that the chimpanzee has not developed the power of speech. Even the most intensive efforts to teach young chimps to talk have met with virtually no success. Verbal language represents a truly gigantic stride forward in man's evolution.

Chimpanzees do have a wide range of calls, and these certainly serve to convey some types of information. When a chimp finds good food he utters loud barks; other chimps in the vicinity instantly become aware of the good source and hurry to join in. An attacked chimpanzee screams and this may alert his mother or a friend, either of whom may hurry to his aid. * * *

While chimpanzee calls do serve to convey basic information about some situations and individuals, they cannot for the most part be compared to a spoken language. Man by means of words can communicate abstract ideas; he can benefit from the experiences of others without having to be present at the time; he can make intelligent and cooperative plans. All the same, when humans come to an exchange of emotional feelings, most people fall back on the old chimpanzee-type of gestural communication—the cheering pat, the embrace of exuberance, the clasp of hands. And when on these occasions we also use words, we often use them in rather the same way as a chimpanzee utters his calls—simply to convey the emotion we feel at that moment. "I love you. I love you," repeats the lover again and again as he strives to convey his overwhelming passion to his beloved—not by words but by his embraces and caresses. When we are surprised we utter inanities such as "Golly!" or "Gosh!" or "Gee whiz!" When we are angry we may express ourselves with swear words and other more or less meaningless phrases. This usage of words on the emotional level is as different from oratory, from literature, from intelligent conversation, as are the grunts and hoots of chimpanzees.

Recently it has been proved that the chimpanzee is capable of communicating with people in quite a sophisticated manner. There are two scientists in America, R. Allen and Beatrice Gardner, who have trained a young chimpanzee in the use of the approved sign language of the deaf. The Gardners felt that, since gesture and posture formed such a significant aspect of *chimpanzee* communication patterns, such a sign language might be more appropriate than trying to teach vocal words.

Washoe was brought up from infancy constantly surrounded by human companions. These people from the start communicated in sign language with Washoe and also with each other when in the chimp's presence. The only sounds they made were those approximating chimpanzee calls such as laughter, exclamations, and imitations of Washoe's own sounds.

Their experiment has been amazingly successful. At five years of age Washoe can understand some three hundred and fifty different symbols, many of which signify clusters of words rather than just a single word, and she can also use about one hundred and fifty of them correctly. * * *

I have not seen Washoe, but I have seen some film demonstrating her level of performance and, strangely enough, I was most impressed by an error she made. She was required to name, one after the other, a series of objects as they were withdrawn from a sack. She signed off the correct names very fast—but even so, it could be argued that an intelligent dog would ultimately learn to associate the sight of a bowl with a correct response of one scratch on the floor, a shoe with two scratches, and so on. And then a brush was shown to Washoe, and she made the sign for a comb. That to me was very significant. It is the sort of mistake a small child might make, calling a shoe a slipper or a plate a saucer—but never calling a shoe a plate.

Perhaps one of the Gardners' most fascinating observations concerns the occasion when for the first time Washoe was asked (in sign language) "Who is that?" as she was looking into a mirror. Washoe, who was very familiar with mirrors by that time, signaled back, "Me, Washoe."

This is, in a way, a scientific proof of a fact we have long known —that, in a somewhat hazy way, perhaps, the chimpanzee has a primitive awareness of Self. Undoubtedly there are people who would prefer not to believe this, since even more firmly rooted than the old idea that man is the only toolmaking being is the concept that man alone in the animal kingdom is Self-conscious. Yet, this should not be disturbing. It has come to me, quite recently, that it is only through a real understanding of the ways in which chimpanzees and men show similarities in behavior that we can reflect with meaning on the ways in which men and chimpanzees *differ*. And only then can we really begin to appreciate, in a biological and spiritual manner, the full extent of man's uniqueness. * * *

CARL SAGAN

The Dragons of Eden (1977) †

The great principle of biology—the one that, as far as we know, distinguishes the biological from the physical sciences—is evolution by natural selection, the brilliant discovery of Charles Darwin and Alfred Russel Wallace in the middle of the nineteenth century.[1] It

† From the Introduction and Chapters 5 and 9 of *The Dragons of Eden* (New York, 1977). Carl Sagan (b. 1934) is professor of astronomy and space sciences at Cornell University.
1. Since the time of the famous Victorian debate between Bishop Wilberforce and T. H. Huxley, there has been a steady and notably unproductive barrage fired against the Darwin/Wallace ideas, often by those with doctrinal axes to grind. Evolution is a fact amply demonstrated by the fossil record and by contemporary molecular biology. Natural selection is a successful theory devised to explain the fact of evolution. For a very polite response to recent criticisms of natural selection, including the quaint view that it is a tautology ("Those who survive survive"), see the article by Gould (1976) listed in the references at the back of this book. Darwin was, of course, a man of his times and occasionally given

is through natural selection, the preferential survival and replication of organisms that are by accident better adapted to their environments, that the elegance and beauty of contemporary life forms have emerged. The development of an organ system as complex as the brain must be inextricably tied to the earlier history of life, its fits and starts and dead ends, the tortuous adaptation of organisms to conditions that change once again, leaving the life form that once was supremely adapted again in danger of extinction. Evolution is adventitious and not foresighted. Only through the deaths of an immense number of slightly maladapted organisms are we, brains and all, here today.

Biology is more like history than it is like physics; the accidents and errors and lucky happenstances of the past powerfully prefigure the present. In approaching as difficult a biological problem as the nature and evolution of human intelligence, it seems to me at least prudent to give substantial weight to arguments derived from the evolution of the brain.

My fundamental premise about the brain is that its workings—what we sometimes call "mind"—are a consequence of its anatomy and physiology, and nothing more. "Mind" may be a consequence of the action of the components of the brain severally or collectively. Some processes may be a function of the brain as a whole. A few students of the subject seem to have concluded that, because they have been unable to isolate and localize all higher brain functions, no future generation of neuroanatomists will be able to achieve this objective. But absence of evidence is not evidence of absence. The entire recent history of biology shows that we are, to a remarkable degree, the results of the interactions of an extremely complex array of molecules; and the aspect of biology that was once considered its holy of holies, the nature of the genetic material, has now been fundamentally understood in terms of the chemistry of its constituent nucleic acids, DNA and RNA, and their operational agents, the proteins. * * *

There were, incidentally, manlike creatures who lived only a few tens of thousands of years ago—the Neanderthals and the Cro-Magnons—who had average brain volumes of about 1,500 cubic centimeters; that is, more than a hundred cubic centimeters larger than ours. Most anthropologists guess that we are not descended from

. . . to self-congratulatory comparisons of Europeans with other peoples. In fact, human society in pretechnological times was much more like that of the compassionate, communal and cultured Bushman hunter-gatherers of the Kalahari Desert than the Fuegians Darwin, with some justification, derided. But the Darwinian insights—on the existence of evolution, on natural selection as its prime cause, and on the relevance of these concepts to the nature of human beings—are landmarks in the history of human inquiry, the more so because of the dogged resistance which such ideas evoked in Victorian England, as, to a lesser extent, they still do today.

Neanderthals and may not be from Cro-Magnons either. But their existence raises the question: Who were those fellows? What were their accomplishments? Cro-Magnon was also very large: some specimens were well over six feet tall. We have seen that a difference in brain volume of 100 cubic centimeters does not seem to be significant, and perhaps they were no smarter than we or our immediate ancestors; or perhaps they had other, still unknown, physical impediments. Neanderthal was a lowbrow, but his head was long, front to back; in contrast, our heads are not so deep, but they are taller: we can certainly be described as highbrows. Might the brain growth exhibited by Neanderthal man have been in the parietal and occipital lobes, and the major brain growth of our ancestors in the frontal and temporal lobes? Is it possible that the Neanderthals developed quite a different mentality than ours, and that our superior linguistic and anticipatory skills enabled us to destroy utterly our husky and intelligent cousins?

So far as we know, nothing like human intelligence appeared on Earth before a few million, or at least a few tens of millions of years ago. But that is a few tenths of a percent of the age of Earth, very late in December in the Cosmic Calendar. Why did it appear so late? The answer clearly seems to be that some particular property of higher primate and cetacean brains did not evolve until recently. But what is that property? I can suggest at least four possibilities, all of which have already been mentioned, either explicitly or implicitly: (1) Never before was there a brain so massive; (2) Never before was there a brain with so large a ratio of brain to body mass; (3) Never before was there a brain with certain functional units (large frontal and temporal lobes, for example); (4) Never before was there a brain with so many neural connections or synapses. (There seems to be some evidence that along with the evolution of the human brain there may have been an increase in the number of connections of each neuron with its neighbor, and in the number of microcircuits.) Explanations 1, 2 and 4 argue that a quantitative change produced a qualitative change. It does not seem to me that a crisp choice among these four alternatives can be made at the present time, and I suspect that the truth will actually embrace most or all of these possibilities.

The British student of human evolution Sir Arthur Keith proposed what he called a "Rubicon" in the evolution of the human brain. He thought that at the brain volume of *Homo erectus*—about 750 cubic centimeters, roughly the engine displacement of a fast motorcyle—the uniquely human qualities begin to emerge. * * *

"Beasts abstract not," announced John Locke, expressing mankind's prevailing opinion throughout recorded history. Bishop Berkeley had, however, a sardonic rejoinder: "If the fact that brutes abstract not be made the distinguishing property of that sort of animal, I fear a great many of those that pass for men must be reckoned into their number." Abstract thought, at least in its more subtle varieties, is not an invariable accompaniment of everyday life for the average man. Could abstract thought be a matter not of kind but of degree? Could other animals be capable of abstract thought but more rarely or less deeply than humans? * * *

There is by now a vast library of described and filmed conversations, employing Ameslan and other gestural languages, with Washoe, Lucy, Lana and other chimpanzees studied by the Gardners and others. Not only are there chimpanzees with working vocabularies of 100 to 200 words; they are also able to distinguish among nontrivially different grammatical patterns and syntaxes. What is more, they have been remarkably inventive in the construction of new words and phrases.

On seeing for the first time a duck land quacking in a pond, Washoe gestured "water bird," which is the same phrase used in English and other languages, but which Washoe invented for the occasion. Having never seen a spherical fruit other than an apple, but knowing the signs for the principal colors, Lana, upon spying a technician eating an orange, signed "orange apple." After tasting a watermelon, Lucy described it as "candy drink" or "drink fruit," which is essentially the same word form as the English "water melon." But after she had burned her mouth on her first radish, Lucy forever after described them as "cry hurt food." A small doll placed unexpectedly in Washoe's cup elicited the response "Baby in my drink." When Washoe soiled, particularly clothing or furniture, she was taught the sign "dirty," which she then extrapolated as a general term of abuse. A rhesus monkey that evoked her displeasure was repeatedly signed at: "Dirty monkey, dirty monkey, dirty monkey." Occasionally Washoe would say things like "Dirty Jack, gimme drink." Lana, in a moment of creative annoyance, called her trainer "You green shit." Chimpanzees have invented swear words. Washoe also seems to have a sort of sense of humor; once, when riding on her trainer's shoulders and, perhaps inadvertently wetting him, she signed: "Funny, funny."

Lucy was eventually able to distinguish clearly the meanings of the phrases "Roger tickle Lucy" and "Lucy tickle Roger," both of which activities she enjoyed with gusto. Likewise, Lana extrapolated from "Tim groom Lana" to "Lana groom Tim." Washoe was observed "reading" a magazine—i.e., slowly turning the pages, peering intently at the pictures and making, to no one in particular, an appropriate sign, such as "cat" when viewing a photograph of a tiger, and "drink" when examining a Vermouth advertisement. Having learned the sign "open" with a door, Washoe extended the concept to a briefcase. She also attempted to converse in Ameslan with the laboratory cat, who turned out to be the only illiterate in the facility. Having acquired this marvelous method of communication, Washoe may have been surprised that the cat was not also competent in Ameslan. * * *

I would expect a significant development and elaboration of language in only a few generations if all the chimps unable to communicate were to die or fail to reproduce. Basic English corresponds to about 1,000 words. Chimpanzees are already accomplished in vocabularies exceeding 10 percent of that number. Although a few years ago it would have seemed the most implausible science fiction, it does not appear to me out of the question that, after a few generations in such a verbal chimpanzee community, there might emerge the memoirs of the natural history and mental life of a chimpanzee, published in English or Japanese (with perhaps an "as told to" after the by-line).

If chimpanzees have consciousness, if they are capable of abstractions, do they not have what until now has been described as "human rights"? How smart does a chimpanzee have to be before killing him constitutes murder? What further properties must he show before religious missionaries must consider him worthy of attempts at conversion? * * *

The long-term significance of teaching language to the other primates is difficult to overestimate. There is an arresting passage in Charles Darwin's *Descent of Man*: "The difference in mind between man and the higher animals, great as it is, certainly is one of degree and not of kind. . . . If it could be proved that certain high mental powers, such as the formation of general concepts, self-consciousness, et cetera, were absolutely peculiar to man, which seems extremely doubtful, it is not improbable that these qualities are merely the incidental results of other highly-advanced intellectual faculties; and these again mainly the results of the continued use of a perfect language." * * *

While more rather than less knowledge and intelligence seems so clearly the only way out of our present difficulties and the only aperture to a significant future for mankind (or indeed to any future at all), this is not a view always adopted in practice. Governments often lose sight of the difference between short-term and long-term benefits. The most important practical benefits have come about from the most unlikely and apparently impractical scientific advances. Radio is today not only the prime channel in the search for extraterrestrial intelligence, it is the means by which emergencies are responded to, news is transmitted, telephone calls relayed and global entertainment aired. Yet radio came about because a

Scottish physicist, James Clerk Maxwell, invented a term, which he called the displacement current, in a set of partial differential equations now known as Maxwell's equations. He proposed the displacement current essentially because the equations were aesthetically more appealing with it than without it.

The universe is intricate and elegant. We wrest secrets from nature by the most unlikely routes. Societies will, of course, wish to exercise prudence in deciding which technologies—that is, which applications of science—are to be pursued and which not. But without funding basic research, without supporting the acquisition of knowledge for its own sake, our options become dangerously limited. Only one physicist in a thousand need stumble upon something like the displacement current to make the support of all thousand a superb investment for society. Without vigorous, farsighted and continuing encouragement of fundamental scientific research, we are in the position of eating our seed corn: we may fend off starvation for one more winter, but we have removed the last hope of surviving the following winter. * * *

In the last chapter of *The Ascent of Man* [Jacob] Bronowski confessed himself saddened "to find myself suddenly surrounded in the West by a sense of terrible loss of nerve, a retreat from knowledge." He was talking, I think, partly about the very limited understanding and appreciation of science and technology—which have shaped our lives and civilizations—in public and political communities; but also about the increasing popularity of various forms of marginal, folk- or pseudo-science, mysticism and magic.

There is today in the West (but not in the East) a resurgent interest in vague, anecdotal and often demonstrably erroneous doctrines that, if true, would betoken at least a more interesting universe, but that, if false, imply an intellectual carelessness, an absence of toughmindedness, and a diversion of energies not very promising for our survival. Such doctrines include astrology (the view that which stars, one hundred trillion miles away, are rising at the moment of my birth in a closed building affect my destiny profoundly); the Bermuda Triangle "mystery" (which holds in many versions that an unidentified flying object lives in the ocean off Bermuda and eats ships and airplanes); flying saucer accounts in general; the belief in ancient astronauts; the photography of ghosts; pyramidology (including the view that my razor blade stays sharper within a cardboard pyramid than within a cardboard cube); Scientology; auras and Kirlian photography; the emotional lives and musical preferences of geraniums; psychic surgery; flat and hollow earths; modern prophecy; remote cutlery warping; astral projections; Velikovskian catastrophism; Atlantis and Mu; spiritualism; and the doctrine of the special creation, by God or gods, of mankind despite our deep relatedness, both in biochemistry and in brain physiology, with the other animals. It may be that there are kernels of truth in a few of these doctrines, but their widespread acceptance betokens a lack of intellectual rigor, an absence of skepticism, a need to replace experiments by desires. These are by and large, if I may use the phrase, limbic and right-hemisphere doctrines, dream protocols, natural—the word is certainly perfectly appropriate—and human responses to the complexity of the environment we inhabit. But they are also mystical and occult doctrines, devised in such a way that they are not subject to disproof and characteristically impervious to rational discussion. In contrast, the aperture to a bright future lies almost certainly through the full functioning of the neocortex—reason alloyed with intuition and with limbic and R-complex components, to be sure, but reason nonetheless: a courageous working through of the world as it really is.

JOHN C. LOEHLIN, GARDNER LINDZEY, AND J. N. SPUHLER

The Context of the Race-IQ Controversy (1975) †

The General Question

There is no issue in the history of the social sciences that has proved to be quite so persistently intrusive as the question of assessing *the relative importance of biological and environmental determinants of behavior.* Indeed, an interest in the contribution of what is given as opposed to what is learned far predates the emergence of the biological and social sciences. The modern versions of the question began to emerge following the formulations of Galton and Darwin in the nineteenth century and became more sophisticated early in the twentieth, after the development of the discipline of genetics from Mendel's discoveries and the appearance of a variety of techniques for measuring aspects of behavior quantitatively.

The initial presentations of the major ideas of Darwin, Galton, and Mendel occurred in the span of a few years even though it was to be many decades before all of these ideas were brought together and integrated. Darwin's *Origin of Species,* in which he developed his theory of evolution and particularly his view of the importance

† From Chapter 1 of John C. Loehlin, Gardner Lindzey, and J. N. Spuhler, *Race Differences in Intelligence* (San Francisco, 1975). John C. Loehlin (b. 1926) is professor of psychology and computer science at the University of Texas. Gardner Lindzey (b. 1920) is professor of psychology and dean of Graduate Studies at the University of Texas. J. N. Spuhler (b. 1917) is Leslie Spier Professor of Anthropology at the University of New Mexico.

of natural selection, was published in 1859. His emphasis upon the continuous and orderly development of new forms of life from other forms and the decisive role played by fitness, or reproductive advantage, was from the beginning linked to behavioral as well as physical attributes and thus directly relevant to social scientists. Galton's concern with the importance of inheritance in determining high levels of achievement was clearly influenced by the ideas of his cousin Darwin. Galton's studies, published under the title *Hereditary Genius* in 1869, can be seen as an application of Darwin's concepts to an area of human behavior of unusual interest. Galton was able to show that among persons judged to be outstanding in their achievements, the number that had biological relatives who were also judged to be outstanding vastly exceeded the number expected on the basis of chance. Galton also introduced the study of twins as a method of providing evidence concerning the relative contributions of heredity and environment. Altogether independent of the work of Darwin and Galton was the plant research of Mendel, first published in 1866, that provided the basis for the laws of segregation and independent assortment of inherited traits. But it was not until the turn of the century that the importance of Mendel's work was recognized and his two laws were suitably elaborated to serve as the foundation for the discipline of genetics. Shortly thereafter the term "gene" was applied to the basic unit that produced the regularities in inheritance that Mendel had noted. At almost the same time the label "genetics" was applied to this field of inquiry and the distinction was made between the *genotype*, the underlying biological makeup of an organism, and the *phenotype*, the external and observable aspect of the organism. What began as the study by a few persons of simple characters or attributes rapidly changed into an entire discipline that was concerned with simple and complex characters and their analysis at many different levels, ranging from molecular processes to the quantitative analysis of polygenic characters in large populations.

It was also around the turn of the century that psychologists began to show serious interest in individual differences and their measurement. The term "mental test," which was first suggested by J. McKeen Cattell,[1] provided a label for a set of diverse activities all of which were intended to identify and measure dimensions of variation among individuals that would be useful in predicting significant aspects of behavior. Initially most of these measures assessed simple sensory or sensory-motor components of behavior, but from almost the beginning of these developments there were psychologists who believed that complex and not simple processes

1. J. McK. Cattell, "Mental Tests and Measurements," *Mind*, 15 (1890), 373–380.

would prove to be the key to predicting "intelligent behavior." It was this perspective that eventually led Binet and Simon, in an attempt to predict the probability of educational success, to develop the Binet-Simon Scale (1908) that in the revision by Lewis Terman (1916) became the Stanford-Binet, the most famous of all tests of intelligence. This instrument, with its associated concept of the intelligence quotient or "IQ," pointed the way to the development of group testing of intelligence and other special abilities or aptitudes during World War I, and all of this signalled the onset of the Mental Testing Movement. The movement was marked by the vigorous development and application of a wide variety of tests in an extraordinarily diverse number of settings. Although psychological tests have not been without their detractors, even at the outset of the movement, there is little doubt that such tests represent one of the most significant technological accomplishments of the social sciences.

While mental tests were emerging and the discipline of genetics was developing, the social sciences were struggling also with the question of how to deal with the relation between genetic variation and behavior. Although social scientists had early contact with ideas of biological determination, particularly in the writings of Galton and Spencer, the social sciences as they developed in the United States demonstrated a very strong preference for formulations and findings that emphasized environmental control of behavior. A clear illustration of this is provided by the reactions to the writings of William McDougall and those of John B. Watson.

McDougall's instinct-based psychology emphasized the biological inheritance of mental characteristics:

> It will help to make clear the influence of innate qualities, if, by effort of imagination, we suppose every English child to have been exchanged at birth for an infant of some other nation (say the French) during some fifty years. At the end of that period the English nation would be composed of individuals of purely French origin or blood. . . . What would be the effect? . . . gradually, we must suppose, certain changes would appear; in the course of perhaps a century there would be an appreciable assimilation of English institutions to those of France at the present day, for example, the Roman Catholic religion would gain in strength at the cost of the Protestant.[2]

Watson, on the other hand, strongly influenced by Pavlov's findings and theories concerning the conditioned response, took a radically environmentalist position:

2. W. McDougall, *The Group Mind* (London, 1920), p. 165.

Give me a dozen healthy infants, well-formed, and my own specified world to bring them up in and I'll guarantee to take any one
at random and train him to become any type of specialist I might
select—a doctor, lawyer, artist, merchant-chief and, yes, even into
beggar-man and thief, regardless of his talents, penchants, tendencies, abilities, vocations and race of his ancestors.[3]

McDougall's views, after some modest contemporary popularity
in the United States, ebbed rapidly in influence. By contrast, Watson's Behaviorism captured the main body of American psychology
with a grip that has only begun to be loosened by the cognitive psychologies of the last decade or two and by the emergence of behavior genetics and psychobiology as interdisciplinary specialties.

Of course, most social scientists most of the time have taken positions somewhere between the hereditarian and environmentalist
extremes, accepting the reality that both the genotype and the environment contribute significantly to behavioral variation, but differing in the relative weights to be assigned to the two in accounting
for particular aspects of behavior. It was only in the heat of
polemic, or in the hands of enterprising journalists, that the joint
importance of these two factors was ever denied. Even McDougall
saw the changes in England as taking place "gradually," and
Watson, in the sentence immediately following the passage quoted
above, hedged: "I am going beyond my facts and I admit it . . ."
Nonetheless, the consensus position of American social science has
always been much closer to Watson than to McDougall. * * *

The Controversial Contemporary Question

It seems unlikely that there has ever been a controversy that has
involved a more complex tangle of ethical, public-policy, emotional,
measurement, design, and inference issues than the attempt to
determine the relative contribution of genetic and environmental
variation to group differences in intellectual performance. Since
publication of the controversial monograph by Arthur R. Jensen[4]
the debate has been carried on in speeches, interviews, and technical journals as well as in the mass media. Far from identifying areas
of clear agreement and resolvable differences, these discussions have
for the most part led to further polarization of positions and could
probably be assessed fairly as not having offered much enlightenment to the genuinely interested but uncommitted observer. Those
concerned with related public-policy issues have found little to

3. J. B. Watson, "What the Nursery Has to Say about Instincts," in C. Murchison, ed., *Psychologies of 1925* (Worcester, Mass., 1926), p. 10.

4. A. R. Jensen, "How Much Can We Boost IQ and Scholastic Achievement?" *Harvard Educational Review*, 39 (1969), 1–123.

guide or instruct them in making wise decisions. For every expert witness it seems possible to find another purporting to be equally expert who provides contrary advice.

Jensen's lengthy article was published by the *Harvard Educational Review* in 1969. The publication was titled "How much can we boost IQ and scholastic achievement?" and defended three major theses: (1) IQ tests measure a general-ability dimension of great social relevance; (2) individual differences on this dimension have a high degree of genetic determination (about 80 percent); and (3) educational programs have proved generally ineffective in changing the relative status of individuals and groups on this dimension. Jensen also took up Burt's[5] suggestion that because social mobility is linked to ability, social-class differences in IQ probably have an appreciable genetic component.

All of this would undoubtedly have produced some concern and response from environmentalists, particularly those actually involved in programs of compensatory education. This potential response, however, was enormously magnified by a very small portion of the article dealing with racial differences in intelligence and concluding with the statement:

> So all we are left with are various lines of evidence, no one of which is definitive alone, but which, viewed all together, make it a not unreasonable hypothesis that genetic factors are strongly implicated in the average Negro-white intelligence difference. The preponderance of the evidence is, in my opinion, less consistent with a strictly environmental hypothesis than with a genetic hypothesis, which, of course, does not exclude the influence of environment or its interaction with genetic factors (p. 82).

Although this statement is considerably more cautious and carefully qualified than many generalizations encountered in the social science literature, the sociopolitical climate of the times in the United States was such that the remark led to a storm of protest. The *Harvard Educational Review* alone published at least a dozen rejoinders, most of them highly critical, as well as a reply by Jensen. Critical commentaries have since appeared in dozens of other publications ranging from the technical journals to mass media; among the early sharp criticisms were articles by Hirsch[6] and Lewontin[7]. Many of Jensen's critics questioned or denied the validity of IQ tests; some of them disputed the evidence for the high heritability of intelligence; a number pointed out the logical hazards of arguing from individual to group differences on any trait; and almost all

5. C. Burt, "Intelligence and Social Mobility," *British Journal of Statistical Psychology*, 14 (1961), 3–24.
6. J. Hirsch, "Behavior-Genetic Analysis and Its Biosocial Consequences,"

Seminars in Psychiatry, 2 (1970), 89–105.
7. R. C. Lewontin, "Race and Intelligence," *Bulletin of the Atomic Scientists*, 26 (1970), 2–8.

found flaws in many of the studies cited by Jensen. In a recent book-length statement[8] Jensen has defended and extended his position on racial differences.

As the controversy widened, Jensen became the target of a variety of political and personal abuse, from both outside and within the academic community. A sobering account of this period is presented by Jensen in the preface to his collected writings on the topics of genetics and education.[9] An article by Herrnstein[1] dealing with genetic variation, social class, and intelligence also aroused a storm of controversy even though it said virtually nothing on the topic of racial-ethnic differences in intelligence. An expanded treatment of this topic[2] also includes a full discussion of the personal consequences of the controversy for the author. * * *

Predating the Jensen controversy, but to a considerable extent brought into public prominence by it, was a running argument in the United States between the Nobel laureate physicist William Shockley and his fellow members of the National Academy of Sciences. Shockley urged the Academy to take vigorous and positive action to investigate racial differences in IQ, and in particular, the possible dysgenic effect of the reproductive patterns of the black population of the United States. The Academy appointed several committees to consider Shockey's proposals and their work led to two reports[3] that, although acknowledging the legitimacy of research in this area, declined to consider it of special scientific urgency. A number of Shockley's attempts to present his views in public have also been associated with disruptions or threats of disruption leading to the cancellation or termination of the speeches.
* * *

RICHARD HERRNSTEIN

I.Q. (1971) †

Mental testing was one of many responses within psychology to Darwin's theory of evolution. In fact, the connection here is intimate and direct, for the idea of measuring mental ability objectively

8. A. R. Jensen, *Educability and Group Differences* (New York, 1973).
9. A. R. Jensen, *Genetics and Education* (New York, 1972).
1. R. Herrnstein, "I.Q.," *The Atlantic Monthly*, 228 (1971), 43–64. (See below, pp. 490–499.)
2. R. Herrnstein, *I.Q. in the Meritocracy* (Boston, 1973).
3. National Academy of Sciences, "A Statement by the Council of the Academy," *Proceedings of the National Academy of Sciences*, 59 (1968), 651–654; and "Recommendations with Respect to the Behavioral and Social Aspects of Human Genetics," *Proceedings of the National Academy of Sciences*, 69 (1972), 1–3.
† From Richard Herrnstein, "I.Q.," *The Atlantic Monthly*, 228 (1971), 43–64. Richard Herrnstein (b. 1930) is professor of psychology at Harvard University.

was first set forth by Francis Galton, the younger cousin of Charles Darwin. Far more versatile (perhaps smarter) than his great cousin, Galton was a geographer, explorer, journalist, mathematician, eugenicist (he coined the term), and articulate essayist. In 1869, just a decade after Darwin launched modern biology with the *Origin of Species*, Galton published *Hereditary Genius*, which applied evolutionary thinking to the question of intellect. Galton noted, first, that men varied greatly in their intellectual capacity and, second, that various kinds of excellence run in families, suggesting that the basis of intelligence may be inherited. Going back through British history, Galton found that judges, statesmen, prime ministers, scientists, poets, even outstanding wrestlers and oarsmen tended, for each kind of endeavor, to be related by blood. The eminent families of Great Britain were taken as evidence of superior human strains, comparable to the natural biological variations that figure so prominently in the doctrine of evolution. Today, our sensitivity to the role of the environment (not to mention such mundane complications as money and family connections) make us skeptical of his evidence. Nevertheless, in the first flush of Darwinian social theorizing, Galton called for constructive change. The inheritance of human capacity implied "the practicability of supplanting inefficient human stock by better strains," and led him "to consider whether it might not be our duty to do so by such efforts as may be reasonable, thus exerting ourselves to further the ends of evolution more rapidly and with less distress than if events were left to their own course."

Galton was not much more content with the genealogical approach to mental ability than are we today. Within a few years, he was trying to test mental ability directly, but the problem was how to do it. In 1882, Galton set up a small laboratory in a London museum where people could, for a fee, have their hearing, vision, and other senses tested. Galton knew that mental defectives—idiots and imbeciles—often lacked sensory acuity, and he guessed that there might be a reasonably consistent relation between intelligence and sensory keenness in general. As it turned out, his hunch was wrong, or at least not right enough to be useful as a way of testing on a large scale.

Galton was soon just one of many scientists searching for a practical intelligence test, with no one much worried at this point about the ultimate definition of intelligence. * * *

A person's I.Q. is a different sort of fact about him than his height or his weight or his speed in the hundred-yard dash, and not because of the difference between physical and mental attributes. Unlike inches, pounds, or seconds, the I.Q. is entirely a measure of relative standing in a given group. No such relativism is tolerated for the conventional measures. Gulliver may have looked like a giant in Lilliput and a mite in Brobdingnag, but he was just about 70 inches tall wherever he went. Relativism is tolerated for the I.Q. because, first of all, we have nothing better. If the testers came up with something like a platinum yardstick for mental capacity, it would quickly displace the I.Q. But more than this can be said for the I.Q. Because the group with which a child is implicitly compared is effectively the entire population of Western society, there is great stability to the comparison. The I.Q. gives one's standing among the people with whom one will live. And if it can be assumed that so large a sample of mankind is reasonably representative of the whole, then a relative measure is quite informative. An I.Q. of 100 would then indicate average intelligence, compared to people in general and not some small group; an I.Q. of 150 would denote high intelligence, and so on. * * *

It is one thing to note the correlation between social class and I.Q. but something else to explain, or even interpret it. It does not prove that the I.Q. is caused by social class, any more than it proves the reverse—that social class is caused by I.Q. More information is needed to sort out the possibilities. Since a family's social standing depends partly on the breadwinner's livelihood, there might be a further correlation between I.Q. and occupation. A large sample of enlisted men in the Air Force in World War II, drawn from seventy-four different civilian occupations, revealed in detail the expected I.Q. differences. Here are some of the findings, culled from a study by T. W. Harrell and M. S. Harrell published in 1945 in a periodical called *Educational and Psychological Measurement*:

Rank in list of 74 occupations	Civilian occupation	Average I.Q.
1	accountant	128.1
5	auditor	125.9
10	draftsman	122.0
15	sales manager	119.0
20	clerk-typist	116.8
25	radio repairman	115.3
30	laboratory assistant	113.4
35	musician	110.9
40	sales clerk	109.2
45	power lineman	107.1
50	riveter	104.1
55	bartender	102.2
60	molder	101.1
65	baker	97.2
70	lumberjack	94.7
74	teamster	87.7

Each occupation has a range of I.Q.'s: not-so-bright accountants and very bright bakers are far from unknown. But just as for good grades in school, a high I.Q. is necessary for some occupations, even if it is not sufficient. For example, among the seventy-four civilian occupations that turned up in the group, public relations proved to have the fourth highest average I.Q., with the top I.Q. an impressive 149. The top truck driver also registered 149, but truck drivers averaged sixty-seventh in the list of occupations, close to the bottom with lumberjacks and teamsters. The lowest PR man had an I.Q. of 100, while the dullest truck driver tested an unbelievable 16—essentially no tested intelligence at all. So it was in general. The more prestigious occupations—law, engineering, science, public relations, and so on—seem to require a certain minimum I.Q., well above the minimum for the less prestigious occupations—for the bakers, chauffeurs, barbers. As far as I.Q. alone is concerned, virtually anyone can be, for example, a welder, but half of mankind (the half below I.Q. 100) is not eligible for auditing, even if the brightest welder may equal the brightest auditor in I.Q. * * *

The top of the scale provided the subject of a massive longitudinal study by Lewis M. Terman and his associates at Stanford University. For almost forty years, they followed the lives of a large group of gifted people, publishing their results in five volumes between 1925 and 1959 under the general tile of *Genetic Studies of Genius.* * * *

Terman was unapologetic about where he thought I.Q. comes from. He believed in the inheritance of I.Q., at least to a considerable degree. Bluntly, but not dogmatically, he wrote in 1925:

> There are . . . many persons who believe that intelligence quotients can be manufactured to order by the application of suitable methods of training. There are even prominent educators and psychologists who are inclined to regard such a pedagogical feat as within the realm of possibility, and no one knows that it is not. If it is possible it is time we were finding out. Conclusive evidence as to the extent to which I.Q.'s can be artificially raised could be supplied in a few years by an experiment which would cost a few hundred thousand or at most a few million dollars. The knowledge would probably be worth to humanity a thousand times that amount.

The opening paragraphs of the disturbing and controversial article by Professor Arthur R. Jensen of the University of California, Berkeley, could be taken as the equally blunt answer to Terman's challenge, forty-four years later.

> Compensatory education has been tried and it apparently has failed.
> Compensatory education has been practiced on a massive scale

for several years in many cities across the nation. It began with auspicious enthusiasm and high hopes of educators. It had unprecedented support from Federal funds. It had theoretical sanction from social scientists espousing the major underpinning of its rationale: the "deprivation hypothesis," according to which academic lag is mainly the result of social, economic, and educational deprivation and discrimination—an hypothesis that has met with wide, uncritical acceptance in the atmosphere of society's growing concern about the plight of minority groups and the economically disadvantaged.

The chief goal of contemporary education—to remedy the educational lag of disadvantaged children and thereby narrow the achievement gap between "minority" and "majority" pupils—has been utterly unrealized in any of the large compensatory education programs that have been evaluated so far.

And the reason, Jensen goes on to say, why compensatory education has failed is that it has tried to raise I.Q.'s. which, he argues, are more a matter of inheritance than environment, and therefore not very amenable to corrective training. What evidence has he for this unexpected and unpopular conclusion?

The problem with nature and nurture is to decide which—inheritance or environment—is primary, for the I.Q. is exclusively the result of neither one alone. Advocates of environment—the clear majority of those who express themselves publicly on the subject—must explain why I.Q.'s usually stay about the same during most people's lives and also why high or low I.Q's tend to run in families. Those facts could easily be construed as signs of a genetic basis for the I.Q. The usual environmental answer argues that I.Q's remain the same to the extent that environments remain the same. If you are lucky enough to be wellborn, then your I.Q. will show the benefits of nurturing, which, in turn, gives you an advantage in the competition for success. If, on the other hand, you are blighted with poor surroundings, your mental growth will be stunted and you are likely to be stuck at the bottom of the social ladder. By this view, parents bequeath to their children not so much the genes for intelligence as the environment that will promote or retard it.

In one plausible stroke the environmentalist arguments seem to explain, therefore, not only the stability of the I.Q. but also the similarity between parents and children. The case is further strengthened by arguing that early training fixes the I.Q. more firmly than anything we know how to do later. And then to cap it off, the environmentalist may claim that the arbitrary social barriers in our society trap the underprivileged in their surroundings while guarding the overprivileged in theirs. Anyone who accepts this series of arguments is unshaken by Jensen's reminder that compensatory education has failed in the United States, for the answer seems to be ready and waiting. To someone who believes in the environmental theory, the failure of compensatory education is not disproof of his theory, but rather a sign that we need more and better special training earlier in a person's life.

To be sure, it seems obvious that poor and unattractive surroundings will stunt a child's mental growth. To question it seems callous. But even if it is plausible, how do we know it is true? By what evidence do we test the environmentalist doctrine? The simplest possible assessment of the inherited factor in I.Q. is with identical twins, for only environmental differences can turn up between people with identical genes. In an article recently published in the periodical *Behavior Genetics*, Professor Jensen surveys four major studies of identical twins who were reared in separate homes. Most of the twins had been separated by the age of six months, and almost all by the age of two years. The twins were Caucasians, living in England, Denmark, and the United States—all told, 122 pairs of them. The overall I.Q. of the 244 individuals was about 97, slightly lower than the standard 100. Identical twins tend to have slightly depressed I.Q.'s, perhaps owing to the prenatal hazards of twindom. The 244 individuals spanned the range of I.Q.'s from 63 to 132, a range that brackets most of humanity—or to be more precise, 97 percent of the general population on whom intelligence tests have been standardized.

Being identical twins, the pairs shared identical genetic endowments, but their environments could have been as different as those of random pairs of children in the society at large. Nevertheless, their I.Q.'s correlated by about 85 percent, which is more than usual between ordinary siblings or even fraternal twins growing up together with their own families. It is, in fact, almost as big as the correlations between the heights and weights of these twins, which were 94 percent and 88 percent respectively. Even environmentalists would expect separately raised twins to look alike, but these results show that the I.Q.'s match almost as well. Of course if the environment alone set the I.Q., the correlations should have been much smaller than 85 percent. It would, however, be rash to leap to the conclusion that the 85 percent correlation is purely genetic, for when twins are placed into separate homes, they might well be placed into similar environments. The children had been separated not for the edification of psychologists studying the I.Q., but for the weighty reasons that break families up—illness, poverty, death, parental incapacity, and so on—and the accidents of separation may not have yielded well-designed experiments. Some of the pairs were no doubt raised by different branches of the same family, perhaps assuring them considerable environmental similarity anyway. In such cases, the correlation of 85 percent would not be purely genetic, but at least partly environmental. Fortunately for our state of knowledge, one of the four studies examined by Jensen included ratings of the foster homes in terms of the breadwinner's occupation. Six categories sufficed: higher professional, lower professional, clerical, skilled, semiskilled, unskilled. Now, with this classification of homes, we know a little about whether the twins were raised in homes with a similar cultural ambience. To the extent that the environment in a home reflects the breadwinner's occupation, the answer is unequivocally negative, for there was literally no general correlation in the occupational levels of the homes into which the pairs were separated. At least for this one study—which happened to be the largest of the four—the high correlation in I.Q. resulted from something besides a social-class correlation in the foster homes, most likely the shared inheritance. * * *

Using the procedures of quantitative genetics, Jensen (and most other experts) estimates that I.Q. has a heritability between .80 and .85, but this is based almost entirely on data from whites. We may, therefore, say that 80 to 85 percent of the variation in I.Q. among whites is due to the genes. Because we do not know the heritability for I.Q. among blacks, we cannot make a comparable statement for them. But let us simply assume, for the sake of discussion, that .8 is the heritability for whites and blacks taken together. What could we say about the racial difference in I.Q. then? The answer is that we could still say nothing positive about it. Recall that the concept of heritability applies to a population as a whole. All we could say is that the differences between people, on the average and without regard to color, are 80 percent inherited. But within this broad generality, particular differences could and would be more or less inherited. Take, for example, the differences in I.Q. between identical twins. Even with the average heritability equal to .8, all twin differences have to be totally environmental, since their genes cannot differ. Or conversely, consider the differences between foster children in a given foster family. Because they are growing up in the same home, their I.Q. differences could easily be relatively more genetic than those of people taken at random. When this line of reasoning is applied to a racial (or ethnic) difference in I.Q., the only proper conclusion is that we do not know whether it is more genetic, less genetic, or precisely as genetic as implied by a heritability of .8.

Jensen notes that we lack a good estimate of the heritability of intelligence among blacks. Although there are scraps of evidence for a genetic component in the black-white difference, the overwhelming case is for believing that American blacks have been at an environmental disadvantage. To the extent that variations in the American social environment can promote or retard I.Q., blacks have probably been held back. But a neutral commentator (a rarity these days) would have to say that the case is simply not settled, given our present stage of knowledge. To advance this knowledge would not be easy, but it could certainly be done with sufficient ingenuity and hard work. To anyone who is curious about the question and who feels competent to try to answer it, it is at least irritating to be told that the answer is either unknowable or better not known, and both enjoinders are often heard. And there is, of course, a still more fundamental issue at stake, which should concern even those who are neither curious about nor competent to study racial differences in I.Q. It is whether inquiry shall (again) be shut off because someone thinks society is best left in ignorance.

Setting aside the racial issue, the conclusion about intelligence is that, like other important though not necessarily vital traits, it is highly heritable. It is not vital in the sense that it may vary broadly without markedly affecting survival, although it no doubt affects one's life-style. Does it do us any practical good to know how heritable intelligence is? We are not, for example, on the verge of Galton's vision of eugenics, even though we now have the mental test that he thought was the crucial prerequisite. For good or ill, and for some time to come, we are stuck with mating patterns as people determine them for themselves. No sensible person would want to entrust state-run human breeding to those who control today's states. There are, however, practical corollaries of this knowledge, more humble than eugenics, but ever more salient as the growing complexity of human society makes acute the shortage of high-grade intellect. * * *

Intelligence may be drifting up or down for environmental reasons from generation to generation, notwithstanding the high heritability. Height, for example, is said to be increasing—presumably because of diet and medicine—even with its .95 heritability. We can easily tell whether there has been a change in height, for the measures are absolute, and there is the tangible evidence of clothing, furniture, coffins, and the skeletons themselves. For intelligence, however, we have no absolute scales, only relative ones, and the tangible remains of intelligence defy interpretation. But if height has changed, why not intelligence? After all, one could argue, the I.Q. has a heritability of only .8, measurably lower than that of height, so it should be even more amenable to the influence of the environment. That, to be sure, is correct in principle, but the practical problem is to find the right things in the environment to change—the things that will nourish the intellect as well as diet does height. The usual assumption, that education and culture are crucial, is running into evidence that the physical environment—for example, early diet—might be more important. In fact, the twin studies that Jensen surveyed showed that the single most important environmental influence on I.Q was not education or social environment, but something prenatal, as shown by the fact that the twin heavier at birth usually grew up with the higher IQ.

Suppose we do find an environmental handle on I.Q.—something, let us say, in the gestating mother's diet. What then? Presumably society would try to give everyone access to the favorable factor, within the limits of its resources. Intelligence would increase accordingly. But that would not end our troubles with I.Q. Recall that heritability is a measure of relative variation. Right now, about 80 percent of the variation in I.Q. derives from the genes. If we make the relevant environment much more uniform (by making it as good as we can for everyone), then an even larger proportion of the variation in I.Q. will be attributable to the genes. The average person would be smarter, but intelligence would run in families even more obviously and with less regression toward the mean than we see today. It is likely that the mere fact of heritability in I.Q. is socially and politically important, and the more so the higher the heritability. * * *

The data on I.Q. and social-class differences show that we have been living with an inherited stratification of our society for some time. The signs point to more rather than less of it in the future, assuming that we are not plunged back into a state of primeval poverty by some cataclysm or do not turn back to rigidly and arbitrarily privileged classes. Recall that regression toward the mean depends upon the heritability and that improving the environment raises the heritability. The higher the heritability, the closer will human society approach a virtual caste system, with families sustaining their position on the social ladder from generation to generation as parents and children are more nearly alike in their essential features. The opportunity for social mobility across classes assures the biological distinctiveness of each class, for the unusual offspring—whether more or less able than his (or her) closest relatives—would quickly rise above his family or sink below it, and take his place, both biologically and socially, with his peers.

If this is a fair picture of the future, then we should be preparing ourselves for it instead of railing against its dawning signs. Greater wealth, health, freedom, fairness, and educational opportunity are *not* going to give us the egalitarian society of our philosophical heritage. It will instead give us a society sharply graduated, with ever greater innate separation between the top and the bottom, and ever more uniformity within families as far as inherited abilities are concerned. Naturally, we find this vista appalling, for we have been raised to think of social equality as our goal. The vista reminds us of the world we had hoped to leave behind—aristocracies, privileged classes, unfair advantages and disadvantages of birth. But it is different, for the privileged classes of the past were probably not much superior biologically to the downtrodden, which is why revolutions had a fair chance of success. By removing arbitrary barriers between classes, society has encouraged the creation of biological barriers. When people can freely take their natural level in society, the upper classes will, virtually by definition, have greater capacity than the lower.

The measurement of intelligence is one of the yardsticks by which we may assess the growing meritocracy, but other tests of human potential and performance should supplement the I.Q. in describing a person's talents, interests, skills, and shortcomings. The biological stratification of society would surely go on whether we had tests to gauge it or not, but with them a more humane and tolerant grasp of human differences is possible. And at the moment, that seems our best hope.

NOAM CHOMSKY

The Fallacy of Richard Herrnstein's IQ (1973) †

Harvard psychologist Richard Herrnstein's by now well-known *Atlantic* article, "IQ" (September 1971), has been the subject of considerable controversy. Unfortunately, this has tended to extend the currency of his ideas rather than to militate against them! Herrnstein purports to show that American society is drifting towards a stable hereditary meritocracy, with social stratification by inborn differences and a corresponding distribution of "rewards." The argument is based on the hypothesis that differences in mental abilities are inherited and that people close in mental ability are more likely to marry and reproduce,[1] so that there will be a tendency towards long-term stratification by mental ability, which Herrnstein takes to be measured by IQ. Second, Herrnstein argues that "success" requires mental ability and that social rewards "depend on success." This step in the argument embodies two assumptions: first, it is so in fact; and, second, it must be so for society to function effectively. The conclusion is that there is a tendency towards hereditary meritocracy, with "social standing" (which reflects earnings and prestige) concentrated in groups with higher IQs. The

† From Noam Chomsky, "The Fallacy of Richard Herrnstein's IQ," *Cognition*, I (1973), 285–298. Noam Chomsky (b. 1928) is Ferrari P. Ward Professor of Modern Languages and Linguistics at the Massachusetts Institute of Technology.
1. He does not specifically mention this assumption, but it is necessary to the argument.

tendency will be accelerated as society becomes more egalitarian, that is, as artificial social barriers are eliminated, defects in prenatal (e.g., nutritional) environment are overcome, and so on, so that natural ability can play a more direct role in attainment of social reward. Therefore, as society becomes more egalitarian, social rewards will be concentrated in a hereditary meritocratic elite.

Herrnstein has been widely denounced as a racist for this argument, a conclusion that seems to be unwarranted. There is, however, an ideological element in his argument that is absolutely critical to it. Consider the second step, that is, the claim that IQ is a factor in attaining reward and that this must be so for society to function effectively. Herrnstein recognizes that his argument will collapse if, indeed, society can be organized in accordance with the "socialist dictum, 'From each according to his ability, to each according to his needs.'" His argument would not apply in a society in which "income (economic, social, and political) is unaffected by success."

Actually Herrnstein fails to point out that his argument requires the assumption not only that success must be rewarded, but that it must be rewarded in quite specific ways. If individuals are rewarded for success only by prestige, then no conclusions of any importance follow. It will only follow (granting his other assumptions) that children of people who are respected for their own achievements will be more likely to be respected for their own achievements, an innocuous result even if true. It may be that the child of two Olympic swimmers has a greater than average chance of achieving the same success (and the acclaim for it), but no dire social consequences follow from this hypothesis. The conclusion that Herrnstein and others find disturbing is that wealth and power will tend to concentrate in a hereditary meritocracy. But this follows only on the assumption that wealth and power (not merely respect) must be the rewards of successful achievement and that these (or their effects) are transmitted from parents to children. The issue is confused by Herrnstein's failure to isolate the specific factors crucial to his argument, and his use of the phrase "income (economic, social, and political)" to cover "rewards" of all types, including respect as well as wealth. It is confused further by the fact that he continually slips into identifying "social standing" with wealth. Thus he writes that if the social ladder is tapered steeply, the obvious way to rescue the people at the bottom is "to increase the aggregate wealth of society so that there is more room at the top"—which is untrue if social standing is a matter of acclaim and respect. (We overlook the fact that even on his own tacit assumption redistribution of income would appear to be an equally obvious strategy.)

Consider then the narrower assumption that is crucial to his argument: Transmittable wealth and power accrue to mental ability and must do so for society to function effectively. If this assumption is false and society can be organized more or less in accordance with the socialist dictum, then nothing is left of Herrnstein's argument (except that it will apply to a competitive society in which his other factual assumptions hold). * * *

Lurking in the background of the debate over Herrnstein's syllogism is the matter of race, though he himself barely alludes to it. His critics are disturbed, and rightly so, by the fact that his argument will surely be exploited by racists to justify discrimination, much as Herrnstein may personally deplore this fact. More generally, Herrnstein's argument will be adopted by the privileged to justify their privilege on the grounds that they are being rewarded for their ability and that such reward is necessary if society is to function properly. The situation is reminiscent of nineteenth-century racist anthropology. Marvin Harris notes:

> Racism also had its uses as a justification for class and caste hierarchies; it was a splendid explanation of both national and class privilege. It helped to maintain slavery and serfdom; it smoothed the way for the rape of Africa and the slaughter of the American Indian; it steeled the nerves of the Manchester captains of industry as they lowered wages, lengthened the working day, and hired more women and children.[2]

We can expect Herrnstein's arguments to be used in a similar way and for similar reasons. When we discover that his argument is without force, unless we adopt unargued and implausible premises that happen to incorporate the dominant ideology, we quite naturally turn to the question of the social function of his conclusions and ask why the argument is taken seriously, exactly as in the case of nineteenth-century racist anthropology.

Since the issue is often obscured by polemic, it is perhaps worth stating again that the question of validity and scientific status of a particular point of view is, of course, logically independent from the question of its social function; each is a legitimate topic of inquiry, and the latter becomes of particular interest when the point of view in question is revealed to be seriously deficient on empirical or logical grounds.

The nineteenth-century racist anthropologists were no doubt quite often honest and sincere. They might have believed that they were simply dispassionate investigators, advancing science, following the facts where they led. Conceding this, we might, nevertheless, question their judgment, and not merely because the evidence was

2. M. Harris, *The Rise of Anthropological Theory* (New York: Thomas Y. Crowell, 1968), pp. 100–101. By the 1860s, he writes, "anthropology and racial determinism had become almost synonymous."

poor and the arguments fallacious. We might take note of the relative lack of concern over the ways in which these "scientific investigations" were likely to be used. It would be a poor excuse for the nineteenth-century racist anthropologist to plead, in Herrnstein's words, that "a neutral commentator . . . would have to say that the case is simply not settled" (with regard to racial inferiority) and that the "fundamental issue" is "whether inquiry shall (again) be shut off because someone thinks society is best left in ignorance." The nineteenth-century racist anthropologist, like any other person, is responsible for the effects of what he does, insofar as they can be clearly foreseen. If the likely consequences of his "scientific work" are those that Harris describes, he has the responsibility to take this likelihood into account. This would be true even if the work had real scientific merit—more so, in fact, in this case.

Similarly, imagine a psychologist in Hitler's Germany who thought he could show that Jews had a genetically determined tendency towards usury (like squirrels bred to collect too many nuts) or a drive towards antisocial conspiracy and domination, and soon. If he were criticized for even undertaking these studies, could he merely respond that "a neutral commentator . . . would have to say that the case is simply not settled" and that the "fundamental issue" is "whether inquiry shall (again) be shut off because someone thinks society is best left in ignorance"? I think not. Rather, I think that such a response would have been met with justifiable contempt. At best, he could claim that he is faced with a conflict of values. On the one hand, there is the alleged scientific importance of determining whether, in fact, Jews have a genetically determined tendency towards usury and domination (as might conceivably be the case). On the other, there is the likelihood that even opening this question and regarding it as a subject for scientific inquiry would provide ammunition for Goebbels and Rosenberg and their henchmen. Were this hypothetical psychologist to disregard the likely social consequences of his research (or even his undertaking of research under existing social conditions), he would fully deserve the contempt of decent people. Of course, scientific curiosity should be encouraged (though fallacious argument and investigation of silly questions should not), but it is not an absolute value.

The extravagant praise lavished on Herrnstein's flimsy argument and the widespread failure to note its implicit bias and unargued assumptions[3] suggest that we are not dealing simply with a question of scientific curiosity. Since it is impossible to explain this acclaim on the basis of the substance or force of the argument, it is natural to ask whether the conclusions are so welcome to many

3. See the correspondence in *Atlantic*, November 1971.

commentators that they lose their critical faculties and fail to perceive that certain crucial and quite unsupported assumptions happen to be nothing other than a variant of the prevailing ideology. This failure is disturbing, more so, perhaps, than the conclusions Herrnstein attempts to draw from his flawed syllogism.

Turning to the question of race and intelligence, we grant too much to the contemporary investigator of this question when we see him as faced with a conflict of values: scientific curiosity versus social consequences. Given the virtual certainty that even the undertaking of the inquiry will reinforce some of the most despicable features of our society, the intensity of the presumed moral dilemma depends critically on the scientific significance of the issue that he is choosing to investigate. Even if the scientific significance were immense, we should certainly question the seriousness of the dilemma, given the likely social consquences. But if the scientific interest of any possible finding is slight, then the dilemma vanishes.

In fact, it seems that the question of the relation, if any, between race and intelligence has little scientific importance (as it has no social importance, except under the assumptions of a racist society). A possible correlation between mean IQ and skin color is of no greater scientific interest than a correlation between any two other arbitrarily selected traits, say, mean height and color of eyes. The empirical results, whatever they may be, appear to have little bearing on any issue of scientific significance. In the present state of scientific understanding, there would appear to be little scientific interest in the discovery that one partly heritable trait correlates (or not) with another partly heritable trait. Such questions might be interesting if the results had some bearing, say, on hypotheses about the physiological mechanisms involved, but this is not the case. Therefore, the investigation seems of quite limited scientific interest, and the zeal and intensity with which some pursue or welcome it cannot reasonably be attributed to a dispassionate desire to advance science. It would, of course, be foolish to claim in response that "society should not be left in ignorance." Society is happily "in ignorance" of insignificant matters of all sorts. And with the best of will it is difficult to avoid questioning the good faith of those who deplore the alleged "anti-intellectualism" of the critics of scientifically trivial and socially malicious investigations. On the contrary, the investigator of race and intelligence might do well to explain the intellectual significance of the topic he is studying and thus enlighten us as to the normal dilemma he perceives. If he perceives none, the conclusion is obvious, with no further discussion.

As to social importance, a correlation between race and mean IQ (were this shown to exist) entails no social consequences except in a racist society in which each individual is assigned to a racial category and dealt with, not as an individual in his own right, but as a representative of this category. Herrnstein mentions a possible correlation between height and IQ. Of what social importance is that? None, of course, since our society does not suffer under discrimination by height. We do not insist on assigning each adult to the category "below six feet in height" or "above six feet in height" when we ask what sort of education he should receive or where he should live or what he should do. Rather, he is what he is, quite independent of the mean IQ of people of his height category. In a nonracist society, the category of race would be of no greater significance. The mean IQ of individuals of a certain racial background is irrelevant to the situation of a particular individual, who is what he is. Recognizing this perfectly obvious fact, we are left with little, if any, plausible justification for an interest in the relation between mean IQ and race, apart from the "justification" provided by the existence of racial discrimination.

The question of heritability of IQ might conceivably have some social importance, say, with regard to educational practice. However, even this seems dubious, and one would like to see an argument. It is, incidentally, surprising to me that so many commentators should find it disturbing that IQ might be heritable, perhaps largely so.[4] Would it also be disturbing to discover that relative height, or musical talent, or rank in running the 100-yard dash is in part genetically determined? Why should one have preconceptions one way or another about these questions, and how do the answers to them, whatever they may be, relate either to serious scientific issues (in the present state of our knowledge) or to social practice in a decent society?

JOHN C. LOEHLIN, GARDNER LINDZEY, and J. N. SPUHLER

Evolution, Intelligence, and Research (1975) [†]

Conclusions and Implications

We would urge that (1) scientists should consider research involving members of different U.S. racial-ethnic groups when (a)

4. An advertisement in the *Harvard Crimson* (November 29, 1971), signed by many faculty members, refers to the "disturbing conclusion that 'intelligence' is largely genetic, so that over many, many years society might evolve into classes marked by distinctly different levels of ability." Since the conclusion does not follow from the premise, as already noted, it may be that what disturbs the signers is the "conclusion that 'intelligence' is largely genetic." Why this should seem disturbing remains obscure.

† From Part III of *Race Differences in Intelligence* (see above, p. 485.)

1. E.g., C. J. MacLean and P. L. Workman, "Genetic Studies on Hybrid

this is the method of choice on scientific grounds, or when (b) practical questions related to the groups in question are at issue; that (2) when such research is done it be done honestly, with great care that the possible political implications of various answers not affect what answers are obtained; and that (3) considerable education be undertaken with minority-group members and the public in general concerning the social benefits of research of both kinds, along with continued scrutiny of the research undertaken to insure that it does indeed offer such benefits.

Some Promising Areas of Research

In indicating some of the kinds of research on racial-ethnic group ability differences that we feel to be interesting in themselves or to have special promise for illuminating socially important questions, we do not intend to be in any way prescriptive, but only to suggest some likely possibilities. We are sure that many other promising avenues of research are missing from this list, either because they didn't occur to us, or because we failed fully to appreciate their potential merits.

Studies causally linking abilities to specific genes or specific antecedent environmental conditions. This would permit much more powerful statements about racial-ethnic group differences in abilities than can be made at present, as both of these kinds of knowledge tend now either to be nonspecific or merely qualitative. A heritability coefficient says only that *some* unspecified genes and environmental factors contribute in such-and-such proportions to the variability of the trait in this population under these conditions. If one were able to identify *particular* genes and environmental factors and their respective contributions to the variation of the trait, one could ask directly whether those genes or environmental factors differed between the groups in question.

Studies that simutaneously compare several racial-ethnic groups on a number of ability measures. A comparison of two groups on a single ability measure, for example, blacks and whites on an IQ test, while it may sometimes provide data of practical interest, is virtually powerless to provide explanatory leads. Any of the multitude of differences between the two groups might conceivably be responsible.

Populations. I. Individual Estimates of Ancestry and Their Relation to Quantitative Traits," *Annals of Human Genetics*, 36 (1973), 341–351; W. Shockley, "Deviations from Hardy-Weinberg Frequencies Caused by Assortative Mating in Hybrid Populations," *Pro-ceedings of the National Academy of Sciences*, 70 (1973) 732–736; and T. E. Reed, "Number of Gene Loci Required for Accurate Estimation of Ancestral Population Proportions in Individual Human Hybrids," *Nature*, 244 (1973), 575–576.

In contrast, a varying pattern of ability differences between several racial-ethnic groups is much more constraining upon possible explanatory hypotheses, since very few environmental conditions, for example, are likely to vary in just the particular fashion among the groups that would fit the pattern of observed differences.

Developmental studies, especially on children in the first three years of life. As the evidence reviewed in Chapter 6 suggests that this is the period in which the primary racial-ethnic differentiation of abilities takes place, it would seem highly relevant to concentrate on environmental and biological factors known to be operating during this period. Furthermore, the pattern of changes of abilities over time, like the pattern of change across different groups, can place constraints on explanatory hypotheses that are much stronger, and hence more scientifically useful, than a difference noted at a single point in time.

Cross-racial adoptions. As increasing numbers of adoptions are made across racial lines in the U.S., a powerful means of partially disentangling genetic from family environmental factors becomes available. Such studies will be somewhat handicapped by the fact that families adopting children of a different race are a highly selected subset of U.S. families, as well as the fact that such adoptions are made almost entirely in one direction, i.e., minority-group children are adopted into majority-group homes. Clearly such studies must incorporate an assessment of selective factors in the adoption process. A particularly attractive type of family for research purposes is one in which several children of different racial origins are adopted into the same home.

Racial mixture studies in the United States. Such studies should ideally employ either good genealogical evaluation of racial mixture, or sophisticated empirical evaluation using blood-group and protein markers. The former method should work well where the racial mixture dates back only a few generations, as among some of the mixed racial-ethnic groups in Hawaii, for example. The latter approach has received recent theoretical development[1] but it is still not entirely clear how accurately such estimates can be made in practice. The pursuit of studies of this kind in extreme groups, such as U.S. blacks of very high IQ, should magnify their potential resolving power. A multivariate study, in which changes in the ability profile are examined across varying degrees of racial admixture, should also provide relatively powerful inferential possibilities.

Mixed-race offspring of U.S. soldiers overseas. The studies of the offspring of matings between German women and black and white

U.S. servicemen[2] are prototypic here. Studies of this kind should be possible in Japan, Korea, and Southeast Asia as well. If the studies could be expanded by military-test data from the fathers' service records, this would render them considerably more powerful, although the problem of accurately identifying parentage would doubtless be a formidable one. Presumably the mothers could be identified and tested, however. Again, a multiple-trait approach is clearly desirable.

Studies comparing genetic and social criteria of race. It would be useful to have studies in which blood groups or other genetic marker variables, physical cues to race such as skin color or facial features, and social and self-identification were studied concurrently in a mixed-racial population, in relation to abilities or other suitable dependent variables.

A large twin study of U.S. blacks and whites at different socioeconomic levels. It would be even better if this were expanded to include parent-offspring and ordinary sibling correlations in each group. Comparison of family correlations and heritabilities of different ability traits among the various groups should be most instructive; however, the study would need to be carried out on a considerably larger scale than existing investigations of this kind, if differences of a size likely to be found are to be statistically dependable. Extension to other racial ethnic groups would be attractive, but the required sample sizes might make this impractical.

Half-sibling studies. Comparison of the resemblance of maternally and paternally related half-siblings is a powerful test of maternal environmental effects. The fact that there are many half-siblings in some U.S. black groups should make such a study a promising way to evaluate the hypothesis that maternal influence plays a critical role in shaping observed ability patterns in blacks.

Educational, nutritional, and other environmental manipulations. There is a tremendous research potential inherent in the introduction of environmental changes that are undertaken primarily for reasons other than research.[3] With a little advance planning, the effects of a change in educational or nutritional practices, say, can be evaluated both within and across racial-ethnic groups. Such research may be highly instructive even though the change is made for reasons quite unrelated to racial-ethnic differences. If the change

2. K. Eyferth, "Leistungen verschiedener Gruppen von Besatzungskindern in Hamburg-Wechsler Intelligenztest für Kinder (HAWIK)," *Archiv für die gesamte Psychologie,* 113 (1961), 222–241.

3. D. T. Campbell, "Reforms as Experiments," *American Psychologist,* 24 (1969), 409–429.

508 · *Loehlin, Lindzey, and Spuhler*

is intended to affect such group differences, rational social policy would appear to dictate that an appropriate means of evaluating the effectiveness of the change be included as part of the process—and opportunities for informative and effective supplemental research become multiplied. Such an emphasis on the evaluation of social programs has been increasingly evident in recent U.S. government policy.

The kinds of research studies listed above seem to us particularly likely to shed light on the relative influence of genetic and environmental factors in producing differences between U.S. racial-ethnic groups in average levels and patterns of abilities. A host of other kinds of investigations—paleontological, anthropological, sociological, psychological, psychometric, linguistic, genetic, and many others—are essential to provide the matrix of knowledge within which studies like these may be most powerfully conceived, effectively implemented, and sensibly interpreted.

Above all, we would urge a diversity of research approaches. What falls through one net may be caught by another. A lingering doubt about a bias in one method may be dispelled when another approach, starting from different assumptions, yields confirming results. Investigators from different disciplines, through their differently distorting spectacles, can help keep one another honest. In the evolution of knowledge, as in the evolution of life, diversity plays a key and central role.

How Urgent Is Research on Racial-Ethnic Differences?

This is obviously a question to which no simple answer can be given. By almost any criterion, some kinds of such research are more urgent than others. If an educational or other ameliorative treatment is introduced with the avowed intention of decreasing average racial-ethnic differences in performance on IQ tests, it would appear to be fairly obvious and urgent that concomitant research should be carried out to determine whether in fact it does so, particularly if the treatment is costly, or may have unwanted side effects. By contrast, studying the genetics of intelligence by means of racial comparisons is likely to be grossly inefficient compared to studying it by twin and family studies within a race. One would seldom wish to incur considerable social cost in order to make the cross-racial study, if his main interest were in the development of intelligence in individuals.

For studies of human evolution, including the evolution of human behavior, the comparison of existing racial groups would seem to provide one of the more powerful methods available, and hence should deserve a reasonably high scientific priority. For studies of educational methods and policies, research into individual differences is almost certainly more critical than research into group differences, since more of the variation is associated with the former than with the latter. Still, group differences may be large enough to justify some degree of research attention. * * *

A Final Word

When we have mentioned our general conclusion to colleagues —that the solid evidence to date is compatible with a relatively broad range of intellectual positions on the "race-IQ" question—a typical response is "yes, but what do you *really* think?" Well, what we really think is just that. Based upon our reading of the available evidence, we would offer the following propositions for the consideration of fellow social scientists, public-policy makers, and concerned citizens in general.

1. Further evidence should be sought in order to narrow the range of positions that an intellectually honest person might take on this question—we have identified some reasonable research possibilities and we are confident that others exist.

2. Humane and enlightened public-policy measures need not be, and should not be, bound by either hereditarian or environmentalist dogmas. Improving the educational opportunities of U.S. blacks, for example, seems to us such a good idea that it should not be made to depend on the risky assumption that this will make the distribution of performance of U.S. blacks on IQ tests indistinguishable from that of U.S. whites (or American Indians, Asian Americans, or any other group). The same applies to improving the nutritional status of U.S. minorities.

3. Any public policy should be responsive to the fact that individual variation within U.S. racial-ethnic groups greatly exceeds average differences between groups. The empirical fact that many members of any U.S. racial-ethnic group exceed in intellectual performance the typical member of any other group is in itself a compelling case against racism. Ironically, some of the more intemperate critics of Jensen, Eysenck, and Herrnstein, by focusing attention on group averages as opposed to individual differences, have probably tended to detract from, rather than to strengthen, public understanding and acceptance of this truth.

4. Finally, although IQ is an empirically significant variable, it is not everything—not nearly everything. First, IQ-test performance is clearly not identical with intelligence as socially defined, although in an unselected sample of the U.S. population the correlation between these variables is likely to be quite high. Second, real-life

intellectual achievements are not solely a matter of ability, but reflect motivational, temperamental, and opportunity factors as well. And third, the correlation between intellectual achievement, however broadly defined, and the social rewards of money, leisure, power, affection, and esteem is surely only moderate at best.

While de-emphasizing IQ may have the soothing effect of somewhat down-playing the race-IQ controversy, it does raise a sobering possibility: Are we in for a re-enactment of the whole IQ affair in some other domain, such as personality traits? We sincerely hope not. There are, of course, some important differences. The personality domain is much more complex, contingent, and multidimensional in character, with no massive central axis like "general intelligence." Thus simple orders of merit between groups are much harder to come by, although not impossible to suggest. In addition, the technology of testing is much less advanced in the personality domain, and theory is very divergent, so that it would be much more difficult to claim scientific consensus in support of any particular public policy. Finally, we may at least hope that the lessons of the race-IQ controversy will not have been altogether lost on social scientists, policy makers, and the public. Thus the next time around, if there must be a next time, a higher proportion of the efforts and emotions of all concerned might be focused on decidable questions and the evidence that bears upon them, rather than on polemics and politics.

We do *not* believe that the lack of a definitive answer to the questions with which we began is either disastrous or disappointing. Moral and political questions never have had scientific answers. The factual questions involved, if phrased in limited and specific form, should indeed be answerable, and it is probably worth society's time and money to try to answer a good number of them. It is part of our own fundamental conviction as social scientists that on the whole better and wiser decisions are made with knowledge than without.

PART VI

Darwin and the Literary Mind

Evolution ever climbing after some ideal good,
And reversion ever dragging Evolution in the mud.
                                        —Alfred Tennyson, 1886

Vous savez * * * ce que c'est que le mot et que l'idée d'*Evolution* * * * que, depuis une vingtaine d'années, ils ont envahi, l'une après l'autre, pour les transformer ou les renouveler, toutes les provinces de l'érudition et de la science * * * puisque nous savons ce que l'histoire naturelle générale, ce que l'histoire, ce que le philosophie en ont déja tiré de profit, je voudrais examiner si l'histoire littéraire et la critique ne pourraient pas aussi l'utiliser à leur tour.
                                        —Ferdinand Brunetière, 1898

The theater is much older than the doctrine of evolution, but its one faith, asseverated again and again for every age and every year, is a faith in evolution, in the reaching and the climb of man toward distant goals, glimpsed but never seen, perhaps never achieved, or achieved only to be passed impatiently on the way to a more distant horizon.
                                        —Maxwell Anderson, 1947

LIONEL STEVENSON

Darwin among the Poets (1932) †

* * *

What the Poets Thought of Darwinism

In its simplest terms, the result of the evolutionary theory was the supplanting of the idea of permanence by the idea of relativity. Of course, the change had been imminent ever since science began to investigate the universe; but so long as the doctrines of orthodox religion were formally respected, most people rested secure. All the evil in the world was attributed to the original sin by which man had forfeited his primal perfection. One had only to live according to the precepts of religion and one could be confident of eternal happiness. Good or wicked deeds would be suitably rewarded or punished in the next world, and self-denial in earthly desires led to compensation by heavenly luxuries. On this solid basis of accepted fact, men established their view of life in which the human race was the pivot of the universe. When microscope and telescope began to reveal infinities surpassing the powers of imagination, man for a time tried to accept them as showing that God had been all the more generous in providing a wonderland for human occupancy; but more and more he became aware of his own insignificance, bounded by inefficient senses and "moving about in worlds not realized." And then the evolutionary theory completed the disruption of the old order. The definite act of creation was replaced by indeterminately long natural processes; the intelligent controlling deity succumbed to blind forces functioning mechanically. Since man was of one essence with the beasts, how could he have an immortal soul, destined for reward or punishment? Human life became a mysterious and melancholy thing, a brief struggle of consciousness against overwhelming and irrational external forces. Mankind appeared as an incidental and fortuitous episode in the age-long history of the stars.

This was the vast shift in human values which gradually revealed itself to the poets. Tennyson, a keen amateur of science, began to

† From Chapter 1 of Stevenson's *Darwin among the Poets* (New York, 1963; first published 1932). Lionel Stevenson (1902–1973) was James B. Duke Professor of English at Duke University.

perceive the problem about 1830; he recognized the immediate necessity of adapting the idea of God to keep pace with the new outlook. *In Memoriam*, written between 1833 and 1850, is a discussion of the doubts and difficulties involved, an exaltation of human intuition as transcending rational science, and—on that basis—a definition of God as a loving being who directs evolution toward beneficent ends. The other leading poet of the time, Browning, with less attention to scientific arguments, also preached a God of Love, and aligned himself with evolution by finding in human imperfection a promise of development still to come.

The appearance of the Darwinian theory made the problem acute. One of the most painful elements to the poetic mind was the revelation of cruelty in nature. The ruthless struggle for survival, the wasteful fecundity that entailed inevitable destruction, went counter to the belief in beneficence which had colored all previous poetry about nature. If any god existed, he could not be endowed with both omnipotence and benevolence—one or other attribute must be discarded. And if no god existed, nature was but a vast machine indifferent to the sufferings of living beings. Tennyson had to be content with the unsatisfactory conclusion that the world is as yet in the "red dawn" which will eventually develop into a golden noon. Browning dismissed the dilemma more summarily by declaring that suffering and dissatisfaction are necessary concomitants of progress: "Irks care the cropfull bird, frets doubt the maw-crammed beast?" Both Tennyson and Browning were convinced that progress was primarily a matter of the soul, in which earthly life was but an episode.

There were other poets who could not convince themselves of this encouraging possibility. In particular, Matthew Arnold and his friend Arthur Hugh Clough perceived the depressing aspect, and their work was colored with a melancholy fatalistic mood. In *Dover Beach* and *Stanzas in Memory of the Author of Obermann* Arnold spoke regretfully of the loss of faith which left the human spirit unsheltered and oppressed; he looked back to the period when Christianity was unquestioningly accepted, as to a golden age of security and happiness which was irrevocably fled. The fullest expression of his opinions is to be seen in *Empedocles on Etna* (1852) —it is significant that he took the first evolutionist as a mouthpiece to express the fatalism of the nineteenth-century rationalists. He preaches acquiescent endurance of fate and self-reliant defiance of weakness. After surveying the decay of orthodox belief in a benevolent deity who has prearranged man's happiness, he declares that man is conditioned by environment and heredity; his life is but a trivial repetition of an endless recurrent process; he deceives himself with illusions about life, while the world moves on indifferently. Nature has no special regard for humankind:

Nature, with equal mind,
Sees all her sons at play;
Sees man control the wind,
The wind sweep man away;
Allows the proudly riding and the founder'd bark.

Whether a man be good or evil, he is similarly the prey to fate; but instead of facing his lot fairly, "to fight as best he can," he has invented supernatural forces, finding it easier to suffer when he can rail at God and Fate for his ills. If any invisible power exists at all, it must be essentially identical with the phenomena and forces of nature, and therefore cannot be omnipotent:

All things the world which fill
Of but one stuff are spun,
That we who rail are still
With what we rail at, one;
One with the o'erlabour'd power that through the breadth and
    length

Of earth, and air, and sea,
In men, and plants, and stones,
Hath toil perpetually,
And travails, pants, and moans;
Fain would do all things well, but sometimes fails in strength.

This immanent life-force, creating and sustaining all nature with incomplete success, is the only God and Fate that can be rationally conceived, "this only *is*—is everywhere"; but man insisted on originating a more personal power to blame for his suffering. The next step of the anthropomorphic process comes when man believes that the gods, whom he first created to curse, are beneficent and will "perfect what man vainly tries." As man comes to realize his insignificance, he tends to impute to God the omniscience which he lacks in himself; but Empedocles scorns the argument as illogical. He sees the dream of immortality as a cowardly pretext by which men comfort themselves in the disappointments of life, and he declares that the only true and certain bliss is in making the most of what earthly life offers:

Is it so small a thing
To have enjoy'd the sun. . . .

That we must fain a bliss
Of doubtful future date,
And, while we dream on this,
Lose all our present state,
And relegate to worlds yet distant our repose?

In closing, Empedocles counsels a temperate happiness, neither despair because the orthodox faith is discountenanced by reason nor extravagant hope, but a determination to make the best of life.

This poem expresses all that was abhorrent to Tennyson and Browning. Its materialistic disbelief in a beneficent God and an immortal life, its fatalistic hedonism, are typical of what the new generation was deducing from the evolutionary theory. In Arnold an innate ethical tendency fostered the austere creed of defying fate's blows; but other poets were more blatantly materialistic. In the very year of *The Origin of Species,* Edward Fitzgerald published his version of the *Rubáiyát.* Although the poem did not refer directly to modern science, it won its popularity because it voiced exactly the pessimistic hedonism that so many people drew from evolution. Since an after-life was uncertain, and since man was powerless to overcome the blind fate in which he was enmeshed, life seemed to offer nothing better than self-indulgence.

Fitzgerald displayed this mood as world-weary and disillusioned; Swinburne, a few years later, endowed it with more virility. He combined it with praises of the Greek pantheon, and derived immense glee from his assaults upon the anthropocentric Christian god and the orthodox morality. However, he was not always the epicurean. His most significant evolutionary poems are the *Hymn of Man* and *Hertha,* in which a new creed is shaped—a pantheistic creed in which the human race is deified as the highest manifestation of nature. In the *Hymn of Man* he arraigns the orthodox creed for its selfishness:

> Therefore the God that ye made you is grievous, and gives not aid,
> Because it is but for your sake that the God of your making is made.
> Thou and I and he are not gods made man for a span,
> But God, if a God there be, is the substance of men, which is man.
> Our lives are as pulses or pores of his manifold body and breath;
> As waves of his sea on the shores where birth is the beacon of death.

He goes on to elaborate this concept of a god who is the sum total of mankind, "A God with the world inwound whose clay to his footsole clings." The evolutionary source of such an idea is obvious: man, as the final result of the creative process, is the most perfect embodiment of the life-force; the only spiritual element in the universe is that which has developed within the human species; and religion should be service to the cause of the race's further development rather than the selfish hope of individual salvation. It is true, Swinburne admits, that man is physically helpless and vulnerable, a servant of Change, but the spirit can overcome the cruel blind forces which hinder him. Man has made himself chains and blinded himself by creating an external god, thereby incurring the evils of dogma and priestcraft. As a result, man has suffered dread and doubt and contrition, has delayed his progress, and only now awakens to the tyranny he suffered. Man's mind has conquered space and comprehended the law of the universe; though the individual perish, the race is immortal:

> Men perish, but Man shall endure; lives die, but the life is not dead.
> He hath sight of the secrets of season, the roots of the years and the fruits,
> His soul is at one with the reason of things that is sap to the roots.
> He can hear in their changes a sound as the conscience of consonant spheres.
> He can see through the years flowing round him the law lying under the years.

Exulting that man is free from superstition, Swinburne proclaims that the anthropomorphic God is dead, and the poem closes with "the love-song of earth": "Glory to man in the highest! for Man is the master of things."

This is the positivist "religion of humanity" imbued with the fervor of a fanatic. Translated into analytic prose, it is unmistakably derived from scientific rationalism; but Swinburne's abundant emotion and imagery endow it with prophetic extravagance. *Hertha* is in the same mood, using the Teutonic earth-goddess as a symbol of the primordial force whence all life flows:

> I am that which began;
>   Out of me the years roll;
> Out of me God and man;
>   I am equal and whole;
> God changes, and man, and the form of them bodily; I am the
>   soul.
>
> First life on my sources
>   First drifted and swam;
> Out of me are the forces
>   That save it or damn;
> Out of me man and woman, and wild-beast and bird; before
>   God was, I am.

The poem goes on to illustrate the ubiquity of the force, after the usual mystical manner. Then we are told that men are reaching "the morning of manhood" and casting off "the Gods of their fashion"; being responsible for all things, it was this life-spirit that "set the shadow called God in your skies to give light," but now man is evolving beyond it. As component parts of the great life-tree, men are immortal; but the gods are worms in the bark, and perish. The great process of growth, going on eternally, is the sole "guerdon" of existence. Man's part is to further this growth by independence: "the lives of my children made perfect with freedom of soul were my fruits." Man need not pray to Hertha, he need only be free. The parasitic God that man made is stricken, and truth and love prevail. Man is at one with the universal spirit that brought him forth.

Inspired by precisely the same fact, Arnold and Swinburne reacted in diametrically opposite manners. In the discarding of orthodox faith, Arnold saw uncertainty, futility, and loss of confidence in supernatural protection; Swinburne saw progress, emancipation, and escape from fear of supernatural vengeance. Science had set the mind free in the vastitudes of space; Arnold felt that it revealed man's impotence, and Swinburne that it revealed his omnipotence. Both conclusions, being based on materialistic assumptions, were unsatisfactory to Tennyson and Browning, who clung to belief in God and immortality.

In the foregoing poems of Arnold and Swinburne may be found seminally most of the ideas which were expanded by the next important poets of the evolutionary theme, George Meredith and Thomas Hardy. As in the case of Arnold and Swinburne, the two poets, owing to temperamental differences, move from identical premises to incompatible conclusions. Both saw that the old supernaturalism was inadequate to explain evolution, and both saw that some metaphysical system of explanation was necessary. Meredith agreed with Arnold that the orthodox God was a product of man's selfish desire for an external power to blame or entreat; Hardy agreed with Swinburne that the orthodox God was defunct. To replace him, they both undertook to develop a system out of the evolutionary theory itself. Meredith accepted the idea of *Hertha*, that the cause of the human race is the highest thing in life, and that in the survival of the race the individual finds his immortality. Being essentially a nature poet, Meredith believed in an indwelling power in nature which made for progress, with man's assistance. Hardy accepted the idea of *Empedocles on Etna*, that if there is an invisible power it is a blind and limited one which cannot successfully carry out its designs. Being essentially a poet of fatalism, Hardy believed that progress was an illusion and that the primal force was merely a ceaseless craving for change in manifestation, unconscious of direction. Thus the two moods of Arnold and Swinburne, loosely labeled "pessimism" and "optimism," are reproduced in Hardy and Meredith.

By the nineties the period of evolutionary excitement in English poetry was at an end. Tennyson's late poems expressed a pantheistic creed in which the fact of evolution was accepted, with the corollary that its cruelties would be recompensed in a future spiritual development, and that progress was directed by God. Browning had died in his belief that the onward struggle was the greatest thing in this life and would continue in the next. Arnold had long abandoned poetry, and Swinburne had gradually modified the violence of his opinions until they practically vanished. Meredith and Hardy had given definite form to their systems in which the evolutionary theory was fundamental, and were merely elaborating them. The younger poets either adopted the Tennysonian pantheism or took the evolutionary principle for granted as an accepted phenomenon needing no discussion. The great shift in poetic outlook had been accomplished, and the poets were free to go back to some of the other topics of poetry which had been virtually neglected for a season. The mantle of prophecy and exegesis was laid aside, and the confraternity rather ostentatiously returned to the cultivation of its garden.

Thus the assimilating of the evolutionary idea appears as one of the chief currents of poetic thought during the Victorian era. Nowhere else, probably, can be found a more interesting illustration of the connection between poetic thought and contemporaneous developments in other spheres. * * *

JOSEPH WOOD KRUTCH

The Tragic Fallacy (1929) †

* * * Three centuries lay between the promulgation of the Copernican theory and the publication of the *Origin of Species*, but in sixty-odd years which have elapsed since that latter event the blows have fallen with a rapidity which left no interval for recovery. The structures which are variously known as mythology, religion, and philosophy, and which are alike in that each has as its function the interpretation of experience in terms which have human values, have collapsed under the force of successive attacks and shown themselves utterly incapable of assimilating the new stores of experience which have been dumped upon the world. With increasing completeness science maps out the pattern of nature, but the latter has no relation to the pattern of human needs and feelings.

Consider, for example, the plight of ethics. Historical criticism having destroyed what used to be called by people of learning and intelligence "Christian Evidences," and biology having shown how unlikely it is that man is the recipient of any transcendental knowledge, there remains no foundation in authority for ideas of right and wrong; and if, on the other hand, we turn to the traditions of the human race, anthropology is ready to prove that no consistent human tradition has ever existed. Custom has furnished the only

† From Chapters 1 and 5 of Krutch's *The Modern Temper* (New York, 1929). Joseph Wood Krutch (1893– 1970) was a naturalist and literary critic.

basis which ethics have ever had, and there is no conceivable human action which custom has not at one time justified and at another condemned. Standards are imaginary things, and yet it is extremely doubtful if man can live well, either spiritually or physically, without the belief that they are somehow real. Without them society lapses into anarchy and the individual becomes aware of an intolerable disharmony between himself and the universe. Instinctively and emotionally he is an ethical animal. No known race is so low in the scale of civilization that it has not attributed a moral order to the world, because no known race is so little human as not to suppose a moral order so innately desirable as to have an inevitable existence. It is man's most fundamental myth, and life seems meaningless to him without it. Yet, as that systematized and cumulative experience which is called science displaces one after another the myths which have been generated by need, it grows more and more likely that he must remain an ethical animal in a universe which contains no ethical element. * * *

And yet, nevertheless, the idea of nobility is inseparable from the idea of tragedy, which cannot exist without it. If tragedy is not the imitation or even the modified representation of noble actions it is certainly a representation of actions *considered* as noble, and herein lies its essential nature, since no man can conceive it unless he is capable of believing in the greatness and importance of man. Its action is usually, if not always, calamitous, because it is only in calamity that the human spirit has the opportunity to reveal itself triumphant over the outward universe which fails to conquer it; but this calamity in tragedy is only a means to an end and the essential thing which distinguishes real tragedy from those distressing modern works sometimes called by its name is the fact that it is in the former alone that the artist has found himself capable of considering and of making us consider that his people and his actions have that amplitude and importance which make them noble. Tragedy arises then when, as in Periclean Greece or Elizabethan England, a people fully aware of the calamities of life is nevertheless serenely confident of the greatness of man, whose mighty passions and supreme fortitude are revealed when one of these calamities overtakes him.

To those who mistakenly think of it as something gloomy or depressing, who are incapable of recognizing the elation which its celebration of human greatness inspires, and who, therefore, confuse it with things merely miserable or pathetic, it must be a paradox that the happiest, most vigorous, and most confident ages which the world has ever known—the Periclean and the Elizabethan—should be exactly those which created and which most relished the mightiest tragedies; but the paradox is, of course, resolved by the fact that tragedy is essentially an expression, not of despair, but of the triumph over despair and of confidence in the value of human life. If Shakespeare himself ever had that "dark period" which his critics and biographers have imagined for him, it was at least no darkness like that bleak and arid despair which sometimes settles over modern spirits. In the midst of it he created both the elemental grandeur of Othello and the pensive majesty of Hamlet and, holding them up to his contemporaries, he said in the words of his own Miranda, "Oh, rare new world that hath *such* creatures in it." * * *

It is, indeed, only at a certain stage in the development of the realistic intelligence of a people that the tragic faith can exist. A naïver people may have, as the ancient men of the north had, a body of legends which are essentially tragic, or it may have only (and need only) its happy and childlike mythology which arrives inevitably at its happy end, where the only ones who suffer "deserve" to do so and in which, therefore, life is represented as directly and easily acceptable. A too sophisticated society on the other hand—one which, like ours, has outgrown not merely the simple optimism of the child but also that vigorous, one might almost say adolescent, faith in the nobility of man which marks a Sophocles or a Shakespeare, has neither fairy tales to assure it that all is always right in the end nor tragedies to make it believe that it rises superior in soul to the outward calamities which befall it.

Distrusting its thought, despising its passions, realizing its impotent unimportance in the universe, it can tell itself no stories except those which make it still more acutely aware of its trivial miseries. When its heroes (sad misnomer for the pitiful creatures who people contemporary fiction) are struck down it is not, like Oedipus, by the gods that they are struck but only, like Oswald Alving, by syphilis, for they know that the gods, even if they existed, would not trouble with them, and they cannot attribute to themselves in art an importance in which they do not believe. Their so-called tragedies do not and cannot end with one of those splendid calamities which in Shakespeare seem to reverberate through the universe, because they cannot believe that the universe trembles when their love is, like Romeo's, cut off or when the place where they (small as they are) have gathered up their trivial treasure is, like Othello's sanctuary, defiled. Instead, mean misery piles on mean misery, petty misfortune follows petty misfortune, and despair becomes intolerable because it is no longer even significant or important. * * *

HERBERT J. MULLER

Modern Tragedy (1956) †

* * * In *The Experimental Novel* Zola argued that the novelist should give fiction the validity of a scientific experiment by operating objectively on his characters in a given situation, just as scientists operated in the laboratory. Although we need not take this theory seriously, the early naturalists did adopt the method of close, impersonal observation and analysis—"the modern method," as Zola proclaimed—and with it the mechanistic, deterministic doctrine of nineteenth-century science. Habitually they demonstrated that men were victims of their heredity and environment.

The theory of naturalism is plainly disastrous for tragedy. If man is merely a creature of brute compulsion, in no sense a free, responsible agent, his story can have no dignity or ideal significance of any sort. It is not clear why the naturalists should have had such a passion for telling this story. But as their passion suggests, their practice was often inconsistent and impure. The mixed consequences of naturalism may be illustrated by two playwrights—August Strindberg and Gerhardt Hauptmann. * * *

* * * Strindberg describes Miss Julia as a type of "man-hating half-woman" that may have existed in all ages, but has now come to the fore and begun to make a noise. In other plays, notably *The Father* and *The Dance of Death*, the battle of the sexes is still more desperate and elemental; man and wife fight to the death. Strindberg conceived this as Darwinian tragedy. To those who complained that it was too cruel and heartless he replied: "I find the joy of life in its violent and cruel struggles." A milder and perhaps fairer statement of his credo is this: "The true naturalism is that which seeks out those points in life where the great conflicts occur, which loves to see that which cannot be seen every day, rejoices in the battle of elemental powers, whether they be called love or hatred, revolt or sociability; which cares not whether a subject be beautiful or ugly, if only it is great." It was presumably the "greatness" of his conflicts that led Shaw to call Strindberg "the only genuinely Shakespearean modern dramatist."

For his distinctive purposes Strindberg originated a brilliant, if un-Shakespearean technique. Its essence is a fierce concentration. He reduced his cast to a minimum, usually three or four characters. He not only observed the unities but sought ideally a continuous

† From Chapter 6 of *The Spirit of Tragedy* (New York, 1956). Herbert J. Muller (b. 1905) is Distinguished Professor Emeritus of English at Indiana University.

action, without act intermissions. He confined himself to a single set on an almost bare stage, with the fewest possible props; in *The Father* he needed only a lamp and a strait jacket. Especially in this play he achieved a terrific intensity. In general, there is no denying the genius of Strindberg, and the unique power of his naturalistic drama. * * *

But we do not have a great tragic dramatist. Strindberg's naturalistic drama is the clearest illustration of Krutch's dismal thesis. The neurotic Miss Julia is much too mean to be a tragic figure; at most she stirs some pity—more than Strindberg intended, if we take him at his own word—in her utter bafflement. The heroes of his other tragedies are generally stronger, or at least fiercer, but no more admirable. They fight the battle of the sexes with an insane violence and mercilessness. Their madness is not, as with Hamlet and Lear, the result of their tragic experience—it is the mainspring of the tragedy. Though they illustrate the pathological extremes to which men are liable, the hell men can make of life, they are much too abnormal to represent the tragic fate of Man. * * *

At least the naturalists did not simply degrade man. Generally they tended to widen sympathies, create new values in literature. If the tragedy of low life has limited significance, high tragedy may also limit our awareness by accustoming us to an exalted realm where is enacted not the story of Man but of the heroic few. "As for our grand sorrows," remarked a simple woman in Santayana's *The Last Puritan,* "they are a parcel of our common humanity, like funerals; and the Lord designs them for our good to wean our hearts from this sad world. . . . And it's almost a pleasure to grieve, all hung in weeds, like a weeping willow. But the price of eggs, Mr. Oliver, the price of eggs!" Another reason why tragedy gives us pleasure is that it makes us forget the price of eggs, delivers us from all the petty, nagging, humiliating cares that we can never escape in life. No doubt this is all to the good, since we can count on having enough cares. But as Karl Jaspers observed in *Tragedy Is Not Enough*, the glamour of tragedy may obscure the appalling realities of human misery: the hopeless, helpless misery that the masses of men have always known; misery without greatness, without dignity, without any decent meaning whatever; misery that seems more intolerable because men have always tolerated it. We have no right to demand of artists that they treat such misery. As we value the tragic spirit and its essential humanity, we have no right either to condemn the naturalists who did treat it. * * *

Meanwhile most men in the West, including Christians, are still committed on principle as well as in practice to the humanistic belief in the value of life on earth, and of human enterprise to improve this life. They cannot accept the traditional Eastern wisdom of passivity, resignation, or renunciation, nor the traditional Christian view that the whole meaning and value of life derive from the life to come. They may agree with Reinhold Niebuhr that free reason, imagination, creativity—man's distinctive gifts and the source of his highest achievements—are also the source of all evil, which is therefore ineradicable; but like him they do not propose to cut the costs by discouraging the exercise of these gifts. In the democracies most are still committed, more specifically, to a belief in the values of freedom and individuality, the right of a man to a mind and a life of his own. And these distinctively Western beliefs, which gave rise to the tragic spirit, make it all the more relevant in a time of crisis.

To me, the tragic sense is the deepest sense of our humanity, and therefore spiritual enough. But all men may profit from it, whatever their faith. It is certainly valid as far as it goes, or this life goes. It sizes up the very reasons for religious faith, the awful realities that men must face up to if their faith is to be firm, mature, and responsible. It also makes for sensitiveness to the tragic excesses of all faiths, the inevitable corruptions of all ideals—in the West, more particularly, to the rugged, irresponsible individualism that has battened on the ideal of freedom, and the bigotry and self-righteousness that have flourished in the name of Jesus. It may deepen the sense of community that has been one end of religion. The tragic writer may most nearly realize the ideal mission of the artist stated by Joseph Conrad:

> He speaks to our capacity for delight and wonder, to the sense of mystery surrounding our lives; to our sense of pity, and beauty, and pain; to the latent feeling of fellowship with all creation—and to the subtle but invincible conviction of solidarity that knits together the loneliness of innumerable hearts, to the solidarity in dreams, in joy, in sorrow, in aspirations, in illusions, in hope, in fear, which binds men to each other, which binds together all humanity—the dead to the living and the living to the unborn.

For the many who are unable to believe that man was specially created in the image of God, and guaranteed that his earthly history will be consummated in eternity, herein may be the most available means—beyond animal faith—to spiritual acceptance and order, in a society that has lost its simple faith in progress but nevertheless remains committed to the belief that "something ought to be done" about all our problems, and can be. The tragic spirit can promote a saving irony, in the perception of the naïve or absurd aspects of this belief; a spirit of compassion, through the knowledge of irremediable evils and insoluble dilemmas; and a spirit of reverence, for the idealism that keeps seeking truth, goodness, and beauty even though human ideals are not everlasting. It is proof of the dignity of man, which remains a basic tenet of Western democracy. It is now perhaps the strongest proof because of the very realism, in modern thought and art, that has commonly led to a devaluation of man and nature.

At its best, the realistic spirit is itself a value, and a source of further values. It has meant tough-mindedness, the courage and honesty to admit that we really do not know all that we would like to know, and that most men have passionately claimed to know. In modern science it has meant the admission that our most positive, reliable knowledge of the physical universe is approximate, tentative, hypothetical, and that we cannot know the final, absolute truth about it: a respect for both fact and mystery that gives a pathetic air to the religious thinkers who have leaped to the odd conclusion that this admission of ultimate uncertainty proves the certainty of religious truth. In literature, realism as a technique has often meant superficiality, meagerness, fragmentariness, confusion; but as a controlling attitude it has also toughened the tragic faith. From Ibsen to Sartre, as from Hardy to Malraux, many writers have not only reasserted the dignity of the human spirit but proved its strength by holding fast in uncertainty, or even in the conviction that there is no power not ourselves making for righteousness. Although they cannot readily create heroes with the stature and symbolical significance of the ancient heroes, they may exhibit or exemplify a humbler, more difficult kind of heroism that may be more significant for our living purposes. They no longer leave the worst enemy in the rear.

All this necessarily falls far short of any promise of salvation, and so brings us back to "reality." The spirit of tragedy can never deliver us from tragedy. It cannot take the place of religion. Even in literature it cannot give us the kind of exaltation that some critics now soar to under the spell of Myth. In *The Timeless Theme*, for instance, Colin Still argues that the Living Art of all humanity, like all "authentic" myth and true religion, has "but one essential theme, namely: the Fall of the human Soul and the means of its Redemption." In irony one may remark that he proves his thesis by the easy expedient of dismissing art that lacks this theme as not authentic or living (even though it happens to have lived for a thousand years or so), and that he makes it still easier by asserting that this timeless truth can be grasped only by the Spirit, which most scholars and critics lack. In reverence one should acknowledge that this has in fact been a major theme in Western literature, and that it is the most inspiring theme to many men of good will. In truthfulness one must add that tragedy has had no such uniform, timeless theme, beyond the realities of suffering and death. Modern tragedy is particularly deficient in Spirit; it seldom exhibits or promises Redemption. At most it may help to redeem us from fear or despair, or from the vanity of cheap hopes.

I can conclude on no more exalted note than a verse of Thomas Hardy: "If way to the Better there be, it exacts a full look at the Worst." Come the worst, the survivors of atomic war—if any—will have little stomach for tragedy. Come the better, in something like One World, there will still be sufficient reason for pity and terror, and many more men to experience it with more intensity. The East is now stirring with the willful Western spirit, demanding more of the goods of this world. Tragedy might at last become a universal form, and redeem all the critics who have written so solemnly about its universal and eternal truths. But if so, it will be because the rest of the world has taken a fuller look at the worst, and is no longer resigned to the eternal verities, no longer content to surrender to the will of its gods.

PART VII

Epilogue and Postscript

PHILIP APPLEMAN

Darwin: On Changing the Mind (1969)

"Thought makes the whole
dignity of humankind."
—Pascal

I

Pascal's remark strikes us immediately as right; nevertheless, its very simplicity, out of context, tends to put us on our guard. Can "thought" be as unexceptionable as all that? Might thought also be our peculiar blemish? (We are, among many other things, "the mistaken animal, the foolish animal," writes evolutionist G. G. Simpson. "Other species doubtless have much more limited ideas about the world, but what ideas they do have are much less likely to be wrong. . . . White cats do not denigrate black, and dogs do not ask Baal, Jehovah, or other Semitic gods to perform miracles for them."[1]) To what extent is our "thinking" something we can properly call our own, and to what extent is it merely an unconscious reflection of various conditions in our environment? For we think —and we are aware that we think—within an intimidating maze of events and persuasions.

To be fair to Charles Darwin's originality of mind, we must see him boarding H.M.S. *Beagle* young, amateurish in science, a believer in Genesis. We should picture him carrying in his small library Lyell's new work, the *Principles of Geology*, but warned against its heresies by his respected master, Henslow. We must remember that he carried, too, the lessons of a close study of Paley's *Natural Theology*. ("I do not think I hardly ever admired a book more than Paley's," he was to write in his autobiography; "I could almost formerly have said it by heart.") And it was of course Paley more than anyone else who had already convinced a whole generation of readers that in the Deity's neatly constructed universe, "the marks of *design* are too strong to be gotten over."

Darwin also carried in his mental baggage the teachings of the distinguished Dr. William Whewell ("Next to Sir J. Mackintosh . . . the best converser on grave subjects to whom I ever listened"). And by an ironic trick of history, it was during the five years of the *Beagle*'s voyage that the British citadel of scientific respectability, the Royal Society, was administering the publication of the Bridgewater Treatises, a series of books by notable scientists and moralists commissioned specifically to illustrate "the power, wisdom, and goodness of God as manifested in the Creation"—so, while Darwin

1. George Gaylord Simpson, *This View of Life* (New York, 1964), p. viii.

was examining reptiles and fossils on the coast of Brazil, the grave Dr. Whewell, eminent mathematician and mineralogist, was writing for his Treatise: "If there be, in the administration of the universe, intelligence and benevolence, superintendence and foresight, grounds for love and hope, such qualities may be expected to appear in the constitution and combination of those fundamental regulations by which the course of nature is brought about, and made to be what it is." [2]

It is an awesome distance from that kind of reasoning to the conclusion of the *Origin of Species*: "Thus, from the war of nature, from famine and death, the most exalted object which we are capable of conceiving, namely, the production of the higher animals, directly follows"; and Darwin—cautious, skeptical, compulsively industrious, distrustful of his own talents and never daring to suspect himself of genius—Darwin did not make the voyage in a day.

It was not enough for Darwin that he was pre-eminently an empiricist: that for five years in exotic locales he had explored river beds and coral reefs; hiked pampas and climbed mountains; recorded stratifications of rocks and soil; examined the earth with lens, compass, clinometer, penknife, blowpipe, and acids; discovered fossils of conifers and shellfish, megatherium and mastodon; collected flowers, birds, insects, and reptiles. It was not enough that he was a subtle theorist, pondering the elevation and subsidence of volcanic strata, the causes of the earthquakes he experienced, the formation of coral reefs, and the relation of one species of ground sloth to another. Nor was it even enough that the maturing Darwin, widely respected as a naturalist after the *Beagle* voyage, should have come home to spend two decades in the dogged pursuit of a hypothesis: examining the many breeds of domestic pigeons, the skeletons of rabbits, the wings of ducks, the variations in ten thousand specimens of barnacles; keeping notebooks on "transmutation"; discussing the species problem with close scientific friends; and finally, twenty years after debarking for the last time from the *Beagle*, daring to begin to write his great book on "Natural Selection."

All this was not enough for Darwin, because he understood clearly the strength of conventional scientific opinion on the fixity of species. Lamarck's experience had been an object-lesson: he had challenged this conventional opinion, and his arguments had been systematically attacked by the French scientific establishment and discredited by Lyell. The author of *Vestiges of the Natural History of Creation*, that notorious evolutionary publication of 1844, had chosen discretion rather than valor, remaining anonymous. And

2. William Whewell, *Astronomy and General Physics Considered with Refer-* ence *to Natural Theology* (London, 1833), pp. 4–5.

other scientists, philosophers, and writers (including Darwin's own poetic grandfather) had speculated about the transmutation of species, but their work was never enough, either; it was always too hypothetical, too desultory, too superficial, too limited, too abstract, or too obscure to threaten in any serious way the established Truth of the fixity of species.

So, on June 18, 1858, after five years in the field, twenty years of patient observation and cautious speculation, and two years of busy writing on the manuscript of "Natural Selection," Darwin was still not ready to publish his challenge to prevailing opinion. On that day, however, he received the momentous letter from Alfred Russel Wallace describing Wallace's own recent discovery of the principle of natural selection. Darwin immediately wrote to Lyell: "Your words have come true with a vengeance—that I should be forestalled." But his dismay was temporary: his friends Lyell and Hooker arranged a joint presentation of short papers by both Wallace and Darwin at the Linnean Society in July, 1858, so the names of Darwin and Wallace are permanently linked as co-discoverers of the principle of natural selection. Wallace, however, was always modest about his contribution, since compared to Darwin's it was, as he said, as two weeks are to twenty years.

Darwin then went on, thanks to Wallace's unintentional prompting, and finished an "abstract" of his work: in March, 1859, he completed the *Origin*. It was published on November 24 of that year, and Darwin, tired and sickly, waited for the response.

II

The circumstances which have most influence on the happiness of mankind, the changes of manners and morals, the transition of communities from poverty to wealth, from knowledge to ignorance, from ferocity to humanity—these are, for the most part, noiseless revolutions. Their progress is rarely indicated by what historians are pleased to call important events. They are not achieved by armies, or enacted by senates. They are sanctified by no treaties, and recorded in no archives. They are carried on in every school, in every church, behind ten thousand counters, at ten thousand firesides.
—Thomas Babington Macaulay [3]

Macaulay died in 1859, but he had already written this appropriate epigraph for that eventful year back in 1828, when he was twenty-eight and at the beginning of a brilliant public career; when the aging Malthus, with six more years to live, had seen his portentous *Essay on Population* through the six editions of his lifetime; when Alfred Russel Wallace was a boy of five; and when Darwin was nineteen, "wasting" his time at Cambridge, collecting beetles and being "charmed" by Paley's logic. But it is not quite accurate to call the Darwinian revolution simply "noiseless." No cannon

3. Thomas Babington Macaulay, "History," *The Works of Lord Macaulay* (London, 1873), V, 156.

were fired, true (though Shaw later blamed World War I on "Neo-Darwinism in politics"), but there were enough broadsides of another sort to satisfy even the belligerent Thomas Henry Huxley, who wrote in 1873, "We are in the midst of a gigantic movement, greater than that which preceded and produced the Reformation."

Macaulay was full of admiration for the scientific revolution he was witnessing in the early nineteenth century, and in this, as in so many things, he typified his age. For him as for others, then and now, "science" meant only partly empiricism, a method of looking at data. More immediately, more tangibly, "science" meant the secondary results of that method: the products of technology. During the long reign of Queen Victoria, "science" transformed many of the conditions of people's lives. The first railroad was built in England in 1825, when Victoria was a little girl; before that, the maximum speed of land travel was—for up-to-date Englishmen as it had been for Caesars and Pharaohs—the speed of the horse. But before the Queen and Empress died, almost all of Britain's now existing railroads had been built: "science" had begun that liberation of man from animal muscle, that acceleration toward inconceivable velocities which is so characteristic of our own age and is still as impressive to us as it was to the Victorians.

Impressive: "science" was *doing* things, making things *work*. The practical, empirical, positivistic British temperament was fascinated. While Victoria occupied the throne, transatlantic steamship service was begun; power-driven machines revolutionized industry; the telegraph became a practical instrument and the telephone was developed; the electric lamp and the automobile were produced. Eight years before the *Origin*, the Victorians celebrated Progress at the first world's fair, in the fabulous Crystal Palace, where Macaulay felt as reverent as at St. Peter's. "Science" was making things happen; it could predict their occurrence; its success precluded doubt. It seemed to many, at the time, final and unambiguous. One could depend on it. That was the context of attitudes which curiously eluded the perceptive Matthew Arnold: "I cannot understand why all you scientific people make such a fuss about Darwin. Why it's all in Lucretius." Of course it was. It was "in" Hegel, too, and "in" Erasmus Darwin. But, as a biographer of Darwin's has pointed out, "No divination of poetry or philosophy can anticipate the knowledge that comes from dissecting barnacles and observing fossil armadillos and studying the methods of pigeon-breeders. . . . A conjecture—even a fortunate one by a Lucretius about evolution—is quite idle until some Darwin breathes life into it." [4]

"Theology," wrote Dr. Pusey, "precipitates nothing." Apropos

4. Henshaw Ward, *Charles Darwin: The Man and His Warfare* (Indianapolis, 1927), pp. 25, 27.

of Erasmus Darwin's evolutionism, compare Auden: "Poetry makes nothing happen." One may object that both theology and poetry do indeed "make things happen" in terms of human values and behavior; but science compels rational assent. And since Copernicus shunted people off from the center of the universe to a minor planet of a fifth-rate star, no scientific discovery had been so staggering to the popular mind as Darwin's. One could not simultaneously accept his evidence and the plain words of Genesis; no reconcilement was possible, T. H. Huxley insisted, "between free thought and traditional authority. One or the other will have to succumb."

What was at stake was nothing less than a world-view. In the seventeenth century, Bishop Ussher had calculated that man was created at 9:00 A.M. on October 23 in the year 4004 B.C.; and Paley had "proved" that the whole creation was wonderfully and intricately designed by a rational Creator. But natural selection was a prodigiously time-consuming process, in which six thousand years are as a single sunset; and it was the reverse of rational: it was fortuitous. Darwin's universe ended up looking much the same as Paley's (as of course it had to); but both its past and its process were new, revolutionary, heretical—and persuasive.

Persuasive because "science" was persuasive, evolution became a watchword to the late Victorians. By the end of the century, hardly a field of thought remained unfertilized by the "new" concept. Historians had begun looking at the past as "a living organism"; legal theorists studied the law as a developing social institution; critics examined the evolution of literary types; anthropologists and sociologists invoked "natural selection" in their studies of social forms; apologists for the wealthy showed how the poor are the "unfit" and how Progress, under the leadership of the "fit," was inevitable; novelists "observed" their creatures as they evolved in an "empirical" way; and poets hymned a creative life-force. Half a century after the publication of the *Origin*, evolution, which in 1800 had been a word used mostly in rather narrow and technical scientific senses, seemed capable of explaining anything. The titles of grave volumes of the period are symptomatic: *The Evolution of Morality* (1878), *The Evolution of Religion* (1894), *The Evolution of Modern Money* (1901), *The Evolution of Immortality* (1901), *The Evolution of the Soul* (1904).

In 1857, the naturalist Philip Gosse could still write:

I assume that each organism which the Creator educed was stamped with an indelible specific character, which made it what it was, and distinguished it from everything else, however near or like. I assume that such character has been, and is, indelible and immutable; that the characters which distinguish species now, were as definite at the first instant of their creation as now, and are as distinct now as they were then. If any choose to maintain . . . that species were gradually brought to their present maturity from humbler forms, he is welcome to his hypothesis, but I have nothing to do with it. . . . I believe . . . there is a large preponderance of the men of science . . . who will be at one with me here.[5]

And Gosse was right about that last point; respectable scientists who believed in the transmutation of species in 1857 were almost as rare as believers in the transmutation of lead into gold. After all, Gosse's world of 1857 was the only world a sane person, scientist or otherwise, could desire. As far as the biologists were concerned, it was a dependable world—the classical world, still, of fixed definitions. "To Aristotle," Herbert J. Muller writes, "definition was not merely a verbal process or a useful tool of thought; it was the essence of knowledge. It was the cognitive grasp of the eternal essences of Nature, a fixed, necessary form of knowing because an expression of the fixed, necessary forms of Being."[6]

Into that satisfied and satisfying universe, the quiet, kindly, unassuming Charles Darwin had dropped a bomb.

III

There is a well-known nineteenth-century epigram which proposes that it is the fate of all great scientific discoveries to pass through three stages: in the first stage, people say, "It's absurd"; in the second, "It's contrary to the Bible"; and in the third, "Oh, we've known *that* all along." Evolution passed through all three stages during Darwin's own lifetime, so that in his last revision of the *Origin* he could write:

As a record of a former state of things, I have retained in the foregoing paragraphs, and elsewhere, several sentences which imply that naturalists believe in the separate creation of species; and I have been much censured for having thus expressed myself. But undoubtedly this was the general belief when the first edition of the present work appeared. I formerly spoke to very many naturalists on the subject of evolution, and never once met with any sympathetic agreement. It is probable that some did then believe in evolution, but they were either silent, or expressed themselves so ambiguously that it was not easy to understand their meaning. Now things are wholly changed, and almost every naturalist admits the great principle of evolution.[7]

Scientific revolutions depend upon (among other things) the perceptiveness and the industriousness—and sometimes the aggressive-

5. Philip Gosse, *Omphalos* (London, 1857), pp. 111–112. It should perhaps be added that although Gosse was a respectable naturalist, he was a laughing-stock as a self-appointed reconciler of Genesis and geology.

6. Herbert J. Muller, *Science and Criticism* (New Haven, 1943), p. 21.

7. See above, p. 126.

ness—of their protagonists. Darwin had had the perception to discover natural selection and the industriousness to fill hundreds of pages with minutely observed facts and close reasoning; friends, when necessary, supplied the aggressiveness; and the world was changed: converted, in a very few years, from an almost total belief in the permanence of species to an almost total belief (among the educated) in the transmutation of species. This in itself was a monumental conversion, but the "Darwinian revolution" implies much more.

It implies, for instance, a transformation of attitudes, of outlook, on the part of other scientists. Since 1859 it has been necessary to think in post-Darwinian terms in order to understand the drift of modern paleontology, comparative anatomy, genetics, ecology, embryology, taxonomy—and in fact virtually all branches of botany and zoology. The "Darwinian revolution" goes well beyond science and scientists, however. It implies a basic change in ways of looking at all ideas, all phenomena. Relativity and flux were not nineteenth-century inventions, of course, but there was an imperiousness about nineteenth-century relativism that was new—new precisely because of the impressiveness of nineteenth-century "science" in general. To the conservative-minded, the terrifying thing about the implications of Darwinism was that nothing was sacrosanct: evolution became not only the science of sciences—worse still, it became the philosophy of philosophies. For those least prepared for change, the impact of all this was shattering. Seventy years after the publication of the *Origin*, Joseph Wood Krutch surveyed the wreckage in his book *The Modern Temper:*

> Three centuries lay between the promulgation of the Copernican theory and the publication of the *Origin of Species,* but in sixty-odd years which have elapsed since that latter event the blows have fallen with a rapidity which left no interval for recovery. The structures which are variously known as mythology, religion, and philosophy, and which are alike in that each has as its function the interpretation of experience in terms which have human values, have collapsed under the force of successive attacks and shown themselves utterly incapable of assimilating the new stores of experience which have been dumped upon the world. With increasing completeness science maps out the pattern of nature, but the latter has no relation to the pattern of human needs and feelings.[8]

"Mythology, religion, and philosophy" did not succumb without a struggle; counterattacks from the faithful were swift and fierce. Priests, parsons, and bishops defended not only their own faith but also "true Baconian induction" in the pages of the quarterly and theological reviews, where scientific "experts" could flourish

8. *Temper.* See above, pp. 519–521.

536 · Philip Appleman

in protective anonymity. "The theory of evolution," wrote a truculent contributor to the *Catholic World*, "has no scientific character, is irreconcilable with the conclusions of natural history, and has no ground to stand upon except the worn-out fallacies of a perverted logic. To call it 'hypothesis' is therefore to do it an honor which it does not deserve. A pile of rubbish is not a palace, and a heap of blunders is not a hypothesis." [9] The aging Anglican sage, Dr. Pusey, sternly repudiated Darwin: "Never probably was any system built upon so many 'perhaps,' 'probably,' 'possibly,' 'it may be,' 'it seems to be,' 'most likely,' 'it must be,' 'it requires but a slight stretch of imagination to conceive,' as that mythological account of the origin of all which has life, and, at last of ourselves, which is now being every where or widely acknowledged by unscientific minds as if it were axiomatic truth; some of whose adherents claim that it will revolutionise every other science." [1] And Pope Pius IX, writing to a French anti-Darwinian author, was thoroughly contemptuous:

> We have received with pleasure, dear son, the work in which you refute so well the aberrations of Darwinism. A system which is repudiated by history, by the traditions of all peoples, by exact science, by the observation of facts, and even by reason itself, would seem to have no need at all of refutation, if alienation from God and the penchant for materialism, both stemming from corruption, were not avidly searching for support in this fabric of fables. . . . But the corruption of this century, the guile of the depraved, the danger of oversimplification demand that such dreamings, absurd as they are, since they wear the mask of science, be refuted by true science. [2]

It need hardly be said that this rather novel concern of theologians for "true science" was not wholly disinterested. Theologians worried because they saw, perhaps more clearly than others, the philosophical implications of post-Darwinian thought. It was not just that Darwin had complicated the reading of Genesis; or even that he had furnished impressive scientific authority for the nineteenth-century habit of thinking in terms of wholes and continuities rather than in discrete parts and rigidities; or that the evolutionary orientation stressed context and complexity—though all of these influences could be bothersome when used by "materialists." The worst threat of all was that Darwin's universe operated not by Design but by natural selection, a self-regulating mechanism. ("Paley's divine watchmaker was unemployed," Gavin de Beer

9. "Dr. Draper and Evolution," *Catholic World*, XXVI (1878), 775.
1. Edward Bouverie Pusey, *Un-Science, Not Science, Adverse to Faith* (London, 1879), p. 32.

2. Quoted in Constantin James, *L'Hypnotisme expliqué et Mes Entretiens avec S. M. l'Empereur Don Pédro sur le Darwinisme* (Paris, 1888), pp. 84–85; translation by the editor.

writes, "because the wonderful property of organisms is that they make and mar themselves.") Natural selection pictured the world in a constant process of change, but without any apparent prior intention of going anywhere in particular or of becoming anything in particular.

That was a devastating proposition to the conventional theologian—more so, perhaps, than the Copernican theory had been, because it struck so close to home. Natural selection therefore seemed, to many, hopelessly negative, fraught with blasphemy and conducive of despair. Science, with all of its impressiveness of fact and achievement, was moving in on theologians and philosophers, *taking over*: constantly enlarging the domain of fact and consequently reducing the domain of speculation. Given objective knowledge, people tend (it was already clear) to give up the guessing-games of ignorance—conjecture about which of the "humors" is overbalanced in a person whose blood pressure is abnormal; or whether or not Adam and Eve had navels; or what influence the planets have on our destinies. So it *made a difference* to philosophers and theologians that man not only evolved, but evolved by natural selection rather than by a vital force or cosmic urge of some sort. Darwinism seemed uncompromisingly non-teleological, non-vitalist, and non-finalist, and that basic fact could not help but affect the work of philosophers. "Once man was swept into the evolutionary orbit," Bert James Loewenberg has written, "a revolution in Western thought was initiated. Man was seen to be a part of nature, and nature was seen to be a part of man. The Darwinian revolution was not a revolution in science alone; it was a revolution in man's conception of himself and in man's conception of all his works." [3]

Of course, philosophers and theologians had always seen human beings as a "part of nature," but as a much grander part: as the crowning achievement of God's universe, a little below the angels. It was the Darwinian demotion of humans from that lofty station that not only caused tremors among the professional thinkers but also rattled quite ordinary people. Krutch describes the debilitating effects of this: "When [one's] instinctive faith in that correspondence between the outer and the inner world fades, his grasp upon the faith that sustained him fades also, and Love or Tragedy or what not ceases to be the reality which it was because he is never strong enough in his own insignificant self to stand alone in a universe which snubs him with its indifference." [4] Those charged with protecting people from their own weakness repeatedly denounced the new heresy. Pope Pius IX wrote, apropos of Darwinism: "Pride, having rejected the Creator of all things and proclaimed man inde-

3. Bert James Loewenberg, ed., *Charles Darwin: Evolution and Natural Selec-* tion (Boston, 1959), p. 21.
4. Krutch, p. 136.

pendent, wishing him to be his own king, his own priest, and his own God, pride having come this far by all these madnesses of its own contriving, then reduces this same man to the level of the dumb animals, perhaps even to raw matter, thus unintentionally confirming the divine word: *When pride cometh, then cometh shame.*"[5]

A century ago the faithful still trusted this kind of righteous indignation; but it gradually became apparent that wishful thinking would no longer serve. With the passing of decades, the tone of the theologians had to be modified and the strategies of philosophers altered: direct opposition to Darwin (in all but the intellectual backwaters) gradually made way for accommodation. The first edition of the *Catholic Encyclopedia* (1909), for instance, still clung to the older attitude, saying of natural selection that "As a theory, it is scientifically inadequate," and adding, "The third significance of the term *Darwinism* arose from the application of the theory of selection to man, which is likewise impossible of acceptance." [6] By 1967, however, the *New Catholic Encyclopedia* was looking at these things differently: "Today, with a much better understanding of both the theological sources of the Judeo-Christian revelation and of evolutionary theory, the compatibility of God's creative and directive action is more easily comprehended . . . the solution of the basic difficulties [with Darwinism] was soon found to lie in Biblical research and scholarship and not in the rejection of the new theory. . . . In his encyclical *Humani generis* [1950], Pope Pius XII [asserted] that general evolution, even of the body of man (and woman), should be professionally studied by both anthropologist and theologian." [7]

"Present-day theologians," says a recent Catholic commentator, "are far more moderate in their claims than were their predecessors." [8]

The activities of science, relentlessly pushing back the margins of the unknown, have in effect been forcing the concept of "God" into a perpetual retreat into the still-unknown, and it is in this condition that "God" has frequently come to have meaning for people. The final retreat is of course into the strongholds of the Infinite and the Eternal, and with the scientists' continuing success in exploring the littleness and vastness of the finite, one may assume that, for any practical purpose, that final retreat has long since occurred. The implications of all this have led some people to a renewed humanism: to the proposition that humans, cut off from

5. James, p. 84; translation by the editor.
6. *Catholic Encyclopedia* (New York, 1909), V, 655.
7. *New Catholic Encyclopedia* (New York, 1967), V, 693.

8. Robert W. Gleason, "A Note on Theology and Evolution," in Walter J. Ong, S.J., ed., *Darwin's Vision and Christian Perspectives* (New York, 1960), p. 104.

theological presumption, might still have sufficient reason to exist
—even to respect themselves—simply as human beings. At the
beginning of this century, Bertrand Russell wrote:

> That Man is the product of causes which had no prevision of the
> end they were achieving; that his origin, his growth, his hopes and
> fears, his loves and his beliefs, are but the outcome of accidental
> collocations of atoms; that no fire, no heroism, no intensity of
> thought and feeling, can preserve an individual life beyond the
> grave; that all the labours of the ages, all the devotion, all the
> inspiration, all the noonday brightness of human genius, are des-
> tined to extinction in the vast death of the solar system, and that
> the whole temple of Man's achievement must inevitably be bur-
> ied beneath the debris of a universe in ruins—all these things, if
> not quite beyond dispute, are yet so nearly certain, that no phi-
> losophy which rejects them can hope to stand. Only within the
> scaffolding of these truths, only on the firm foundation of un-
> yielding despair, can the soul's habitation henceforth be safely
> built.[9]

It is possible to argue that there has been, in consequence of the
retreat of "God," a genuine spiritual gain. To discuss "God" in
terms of the Unknown seems to some contemporary thinkers (as
indeed it did to Herbert Spencer) a more dignified and tenable
procedure than to carry on that discussion in terms of oak trees or
thunderbolts. The possible attitudes toward this "Unknown" are
various: they can be put in terms of release and new potentiality,
as in Bertrand Russell's further comment, "It is well to exalt the
dignity of Man, by freeing him as far as possible from the tyranny
of non-human Power"; or of guarded optimism, like Julian Huxley's, seeing humanity as the Vicar of Evolution on Earth, a conscious directing factor in our progress toward an unknown destiny;
or of a kind of ecstasy, like Albert Einstein's, in "rapturous amaze-
ment" at the harmony of nature. But in any case, people now seem
able to view the human condition not in terms of a fall from grace
to degradation but rather as the reverse—as a long struggle to
escape from mere animalism, red in tooth and claw, and to establish
upon ourselves—upon our own best knowledge of ourselves—a tenable ethical ground.

Scientists have rarely been simple materialists, after all. It is important to scientists, as scientists, to restrict their investigations to
the knowable; but they have not often contended that the results
of their researches were the summation of all Truth, or that one
should act as though the world were purely deterministic. Moreover, some scientists, like T. H. Huxley and his grandson, Julian
Huxley, have been consistently interested in the relationship be-

9. Bertrand Russell, *Mysticism and Logic* (New York, 1957), pp. 45–46.

tween science (particularly evolution) and ethics. Their conclusions have been hopeful, not pessimistic, and one may cite, as illustrative examples, both T. H. Huxley's belief that "there lies within [humanity] a fund of energy, operating intelligently and so far akin to that which pervades the universe, that it is competent to influence and modify the cosmic process" and Julian Huxley's insistence that "in so far as the mechanism of evolution ceases to be blind and automatic and becomes conscious, ethics can be injected into the evolutionary process. Before man that process was merely amoral. After his emergence onto life's stage it became possible to introduce faith, courage, love of truth, goodness—in a word moral purpose—into evolution."[1] So it is not after all strange, or even unusual, to hear the very scientists who remind us of our cosmic littleness at the same time assuring us of our individual dignity in terms which, if not so dogmatic as those of the theologians, are nevertheless heartening.

The point is worth stressing partly because non-scientists have at times in the past tended to disparage science as an amoral or even an immoral study. Erasmus Darwin, Charles's grandfather, once declined to discuss one of his botanical books because, he said, "some Ladies have intimated to me, that the Loves of the Plants are described in too glowing colours." If science had any relation to ethics at all, it was often held to be that of a lowly subordinate. Zoology, for instance, as a recent commentator has noted, was taken to be a mere handmaiden of ethics:

> Animals were studied not to observe their actual characteristics but to find moral examples in their nature or behavior. Topsell's *Historie of Foure-footed Beastes*, a popular book on animals published in 1607, avowed its purpose to be the leading of men to "heavenly meditations upon earthly creatures" and was particularly recommended for Sunday reading.
>
> In such works morality naturally took precedence over accuracy. Many "impossible falsities," said Sir Thomas Browne, "do notwithstanding include wholesome moralities, and such as expiate the trespass of their absurdities."[2]

Today the shoe is pretty snugly on the other foot; few moralists would now be willing to propagate error on the ground that it taught a "wholesome morality." They would tend, in fact, to doubt that a really wholesome morality could be the product of palpable falsehoods. Some scientists have gone further than this and argued that a scientifically accurate view of the world is the best basis for ethics. "Duty arises from our potential control over the course of events," Whitehead proposed; "where attainable knowledge could

1. Julian Huxley and T. H. Huxley, *Touchstone for Ethics* (New York and London, 1947). See above, pp. 325–334.

2. Bergen Evans, *The Natural History of Nonsense* (New York, 1958), p. 29.

have changed the issue, ignorance has the guilt of vice." This is a momentous principle, and one to which scientists are, I believe, more generally alert than are other people. C. H. Waddington, the English zoologist, has shown how scientific awareness can broaden our sense of moral responsibility. "Our ethical notions," he writes,

> are fundamentally based on a system of individual responsibility for individual acts. The principle of statistical correlation between two sets of events, although accepted in scientific practice, is not usually felt to be ethically completely valid. If a man hits a baby on the head with a hammer, we prosecute him for cruelty or murder; but if he sells dirty milk and the infant sickness or death rate goes up, we merely fine him for contravening the health laws. And the ethical point is taken even less seriously when the responsibility, as well as the results of the crime, falls on a statistical assemblage. The whole community of England and Wales kills 8,000 babies a year by failing to bring its infant mortality rate down to the level reached by Oslo as early as 1931, which would be perfectly feasible; but few people seem to think this is a crime.[3]

Those who persist in seeing scientists as "materialists" and non-scientists as "humanists" will no doubt have difficulty accepting all this, but one must hope that such naïveté must now be getting rare. There is grandeur, Darwin insisted, in his scientific view of the world, for, he said, it ennobled humanity. Man has risen, he added later, "to the very summit of the organic scale; and the fact of his having thus risen, instead of having been aboriginally placed there, may give him hope for a still higher destiny in the distant future."[4]

IV

As some of the foregoing suggests, the moment one transplants the discussion of evolution from the field of science to the fields of philosophy or ethics or theology, one has to recognize that the discussion has probably become analogical rather than straightforwardly analytical, "Darwinistic" rather than Darwinian. ("Darwinism," writes Morse Peckham, "is a scientific theory about the origin of biological species from pre-existent species. . . . Darwinisticism can be an evolutionary metaphysic about the nature of reality and the universe. It can be an economic theory, or a moral theory, or an aesthetic theory, or a psychological theory."[5]) Darwin's propositions, like many other bright and fashionable ideas before and since, caught people's imaginations; and many thinkers picked up the new concepts and exploited them as analogies (or apologies) in their

3. C.H. Waddington, *The Scientific Attitude* (London, 1948), p. 31.
4. See the concluding paragraphs of the *Origin of Species* and *The Descent of Man.*
5. Morse Peckham, "Darwinism and Darwinisticism." See above, p. 304.

own fields of work, often less in the hope of being led to new perceptions by the analogies than with the intention of reinforcing
old positions or of scoring debater's points with them. Whitehead
reflected on the dangers of this indiscriminate and tendentious use
of Darwinistic ideas. "The last words of science," he wrote, "appeared to be Struggle for Existence and Natural Selection. Darwin's
own writings are for all time a model of refusal to go beyond the
direct evidence, and of careful retention of every hypothesis. But
those virtues were not so conspicuous in his followers, and still
less in his camp-followers." [6]

We see this tendency perhaps most clearly in the application
of a Darwinistic pattern to society itself. The publication of the
Origin and the American Civil War were almost coincident, and in
the years following those two traumatic events, the United States
was industrializing very rapidly. The late nineteenth century became
the pre-eminent period in our history of the Rugged Individualist,
the Robber Baron, the Captain of Industry, the accumulators of
great wealth. It was also a period of sweatshops, of union-busting, of
goon squads and strike-breaking massacres, of a dollar a day for
working people, of tenements without sanitation, of widespread
malnutrition.

It was not simple, in a "Christian society," to reconcile such
contradictions. The economic establishment had, since the beginnings of the industrial revolution, been casting about for sanctions,
for justifications. Manchester political economy had been a powerful sanction for the establishment, emphasizing as it did the
necessity for untrammelled individual enterprise, the automatic enlightenment of self-interest, and the "iron" laws of economics.
("There is no more possibility of defeating the operation of these
laws," Carnegie once said, "than there is of thwarting the laws of
nature which determine the humidity of the atmosphere or the revolution of the earth upon its axis." [7]) Curiously enough, there were
religious sanctions, too, for had not material things always been corrupting to people, and was it not therefore self-evident that the
lower classes had to be kept poor to be kept virtuous—and, para-
doxically, could not the virtuous and industrious among the poor
expect to be rewarded, even in this world? ("He that gets all he
can honestly," Ben Franklin had declared, "and saves all he gets
will certainly become rich, if that Being who governs the world, to
whom all should look for a blessing on their endeavors, doth not,
in His wise providence, otherwise determine." To which a railroad
president added, a century later: "The rights and interests of the

6. Alfred North Whitehead, *Science and the Modern World* (New York, 1925), p. 158.

7. Andrew Carnegie, *The Empire of Business* (London, 1902), p. 67.

laboring man will be protected and cared for by the Christian men to whom God has given control of the property rights of the country." [8]

And always, in the nineteenth century, there was that court of last resort, the sanction of Progress, in whose name all contradictions were resolved—or ignored.

But in natural selection the economic establishment found a massive sanction which gathered into one grand synthesis all of the previous ones and added to them its own profound, "scientific" prestige. Natural selection and the struggle for existence lent authority to laissez-faire economics (the state, said Herbert Spencer, should refrain from action calculated to interfere with the struggle for existence in the industrial field [9]); absorbed the older religious sanctions (the "laws" of natural selection, said one economist, were "merely God's regular methods of expressing his choice and approval" [1]); and seemed to make Progress inevitable (evolution, said Spencer, "can end only in the establishment of the greatest perfection and the most complete happiness"; "Progress," he said, "is not an accident, but a necessity" [2]).

Among American economists, the most thoroughgoing advocate of these views was William Graham Sumner, whose reading of Spencer in the early 1870s convinced him that Spencer was right in seeing the world as "a harsh, exacting nature, enforcing a bitter struggle for the meager goods available to humankind. To him the laws of individual and social existence were simple and rigorous. Rewards and punishments are meted out with impartial justice. Property, the enjoyment of family life, health, social preference go to the fit, while poverty, disease, and starvation are the lot of the unfit." And thus "the millionaires are a product of natural selection, acting on the whole body of men to pick out those who can meet the requirement of certain work to be done." [3] This is conservative "social Darwinism" in a nutshell. (I put the phrase in quotation marks to indicate its spuriousness: Darwin should not, of course, be held responsible for this—or any other—brand of Darwinisticism.)

The Captains of Industry were quick to pick up this Darwinistic vocabulary. "The growth of a large business," said John D. Rockefeller (speaking to a Sunday-school class), "is merely a survival of the fittest. . . . The American Beauty rose can be produced in the

8. Quoted in Matthew Josephson, *The Robber Barons* (New York, 1934), p. 299.
9. Edward S. Corwin, "The Impact of the Idea of Evolution on the American Political and Constitutional Tradition," in Stow Persons, ed., *Evolutionary Thought in America* (New Haven, 1950), p. 186.

1. Thomas Nixon Carver, quoted in Richard Hofstadter, *Social Darwinism in American Thought* (Boston, 1955), p. 40.
2. Hofstadter, p. 40.
3. See Maurice R. Davis, ed., *Sumner Today* (New Haven, 1940), p. 92, and Hofstadter, p. 58.

splendor and fragrance which bring cheer to the beholder only by sacrificing the early buds which grow up around it. This is not an evil tendency in business. It is merely the working-out of a law of nature and of God." [4] Similarly, James J. Hill held that "the fortunes of railroad companies are determined by the law of the survival of the fittest." [5] And Carnegie once warned his lieutenants, upon his break with the Steel Pool, that "a struggle is inevitable and it is a question of the survival of the fittest." [6]

Carnegie was the most introspective and easily the most articulate of the Rugged Individualists. He was strongly attracted to Spencer's theories, and his own speech and writings became full of Spencer's phraseology. He quickly adopted Spencer's easy optimism about progress; he believed firmly that the "fit" who survived in the struggle were the "best," and that these people would lead the rest to certain progress. "The exceptional man in every department," he said, "must be permitted and encouraged to develop his unusual powers, tastes, and ambitions in accordance with the laws which prevail in everything that lives or grows. The 'survival of the fittest' means that the exceptional plants, animals, and men which have the needed 'variations' from the common standard, are the fructifying forces which leaven the whole." [7]

But there were all sorts of anomalies in this use of the evolutionary sanctions: anomalies of language, for instance. To scientists, the word "natural" meant simply "the way things occur in nature"; but used by the apologists for "social Darwinism," it always implied "the way things ought to be." "Survival" was similarly converted into a term of generalized approbation—so persistently that William James was prompted to object: "The entire modern deification of survival *per se*, survival returning to itself, survival naked and abstract, with the denial of any substantive excellence in *what* survives, except the capacity for more survival still, is surely the strangest intellectual stopping-place ever proposed by one man to another." [8] The most abused of all of the evolutionary terms, however, was the word "fit." Spencer and Sumner insisted that the wealthy must be the "fit," for obvious reasons, and conversely, that the poor must be the "unfit," since the latter were, as Spencer held, the "stupid, vicious, or idle," or, to use Sumner's words, the "negligent, shiftless, inefficient, silly, and imprudent." The fallacies of this terminology are obvious and have often been objected to. T. H. Huxley insisted that the biologically "fittest" were by no means always the "highest" order of creatures, and G. G. Simpson

4. Quoted in Robert E. L. Faris, "Evolution and American Sociology," in Persons, p. 163.
5. James J. Hill, quoted in Hofstadter, p. 45.
6. Josephson, p. 420.
7. Andrew Carnegie, *Problems of Today* (New York, 1933), p. 125.
8. Quoted in Hofstadter, p. 201.

has pointed out that, inchoately in Darwin and definitely for neo-Darwinians, "fittest" means simply: leaving the most descendants over a number of generations. Lester Ward, from a less biological, more moralistic point of view, observed that Sumner's definition of the "fit" was based on the "fundamental error that the favors of this world are distributed entirely according to merit." [9]

Another anomaly in the way the conservative "social Darwinists" used Darwinistic analogies was in their tendency to apply them selectively. Capitalistic theory required a "struggle for existence" among competing economic organizations; in practice, however, those very Rugged Individualists who appealed to the competitive Darwinistic analogy against social reforms often tried to thwart its effects upon themselves. They secured the passage of tariffs to protect their individualism from foreign competition, for instance, and tried hard to eliminate all domestic production struggles. Rockefeller, for one, seemed "convinced that the competitive system . . . was a mistake," that "it was a crime against order, efficiency, economy"; and he came to the characteristic conclusion that "it could be eliminated only by abolishing all rivals." [1] Even Carnegie, "individualist" that he proclaimed himself, nevertheless operated a working monopoly in steel. Walter Lippmann has commented wryly that "most men have shown in their behavior that they wished to impose free capitalism on others and to escape it themselves." [2]

It stands as at least a qualified tribute to the humanity of human beings that many people simply would not accept the callousness of conservative "social Darwinism," however much it attempted to justify itself by the appeal to "scientific" prestige. Richard Tawney once argued that one sees the true character of a social philosophy most clearly in "the way it regards the misfortunes of those of its members who fall by the way." [3] Those who fell by the way in late nineteenth-century America were assured by the conservative apologists that this was their "natural" lot, that "science" proved that they were the unavoidable by-products of a beneficent Struggle for Existence, without which there could be no Progress; but meanwhile, people with less emotional investment in maintaining the economic status quo were questioning whether the implications of evolution were really as somberly deterministic as the conservatives made out. As early as the 1870s some zoologists had been investigating the implications of cooperation, as well as competition, in the natural world, and in 1902 Peter Kropotkin was to publish his *Mutual Aid*, revealing that he had

9. Quoted in Hofstadter, p. 79.
1. John T. Flynn, *God's Gold* (New York, 1932), p. 221.
2. Walter Lippmann, *The Method of* *Freedom* (New York, 1934), p. 25.
3. Richard Tawney, *Religion and the Rise of Capitalism* (New York, 1926), p. 247.

failed to find—although I was eagerly looking for it—that bitter struggle for the means of existence, *among animals belonging to the same species*, which was considered by most Darwinists (though not always by Darwin himself) as the dominant characteristic of struggle for life, and the main factor of evolution. . . . On the other hand, wherever I saw animal life in abundance . . . I saw Mutual Aid and Mutual Support carried on to an extent which made me suspect in it a feature of the greatest importance for the maintenance of life, the preservation of each species, and its further evolution.[4]

And he generalized, from this pattern, that

it is not love and not even sympathy upon which Society is based in mankind. It is the conscience—be it only at the stage of an instinct—of human solidarity. It is the unconscious recognition of the force that is borrowed by each man from the practice of mutual aid; of the close dependency of every one's happiness upon the happiness of all; and of the sense of justice, or equity, which brings the individual to consider the rights of every other individual as equal to his own. Upon this broad and necessary foundation the still higher moral feelings are developed.[5]

Thomas Henry Huxley had already made the famous distinction, in his Romanes lecture of 1893, that "the ethical progress of society depends, not on imitating the cosmic process, still less in running away from it, but in combating it." [6] "Social progress," he said, "means a checking of the cosmic process at every step and the substitution for it of another, which may be called the ethical process; the end of which is not the survival of those who may happen to be the fittest, in respect of the whole of the conditions which obtain, but of those who are ethically the best." [7]

By the end of the century, then, there were developing some serious demurrers to narrowly conservative Darwinistic social thought. Some naturalists were broadening the evolutionary view of life to show that nature was not always and simply competitive. And some social and ethical thinkers were attempting to demonstrate that even though ruthless competition does exist in nature, it is not therefore necessarily a proper pattern for human behavior.

V

Discussions of Darwinism and Darwinisticism inevitably return to the *impressiveness* of science, its ineluctable ability to demonstrate, to convince, its power to change the conditions and directions of our lives. Literary people, heirs to thousands of years of

---

4. Peter Kropotkin, *Mutual Aid* (London, 1902), pp. vii–ix.
5. Kropotkin, pp. xiii–xiv.
6. See above, p. 328.
7. See above, p. 327.

a general cultural hegemony, have not always welcomed the intrusion of this new power into their lives. The Victorian author George Gissing once wrote:

> I hate and fear "science" because of my conviction that for long to come if not forever, it will be the remorseless enemy of mankind. I see it destroying all simplicity and gentleness of life, all beauty of the world; I see it restoring barbarism under the mask of civilization; I see it darkening men's minds and hardening their hearts; I see it bringing a time of vast conflicts, which will pale into insignificance "the thousand wars of old," and, as likely as not, will whelm all the laborious advances of mankind in blood-drenched chaos.[8]

Writers' responses to Darwin in particular were often hostile. In novel, story, and poem, frontal attacks and attacks by innuendo and ridicule appeared regularly throughout the last decades of the nineteenth century. But thoughtful writers were at the same time busy assimilating the evolutionary doctrine into their work. Some had been using evolution before 1859: Tennyson was proud of having discussed evolution in his verse not only before the *Origin of Species* but even before the *Vestiges of Creation*. Browning, too, had mentioned evolutionary ideas prior to 1859, and both poets continued to write about the subject, off and on, for the rest of their lives. After 1859, however, evolution cropped up everywhere: in the novels of Bulwer-Lytton, Charles Reade, Mrs. Humphry Ward, Gissing, and Charles Kingsley and in scores of satires and romances, evolution was cited, discussed, and absorbed.

The most distinguished propagators of evolution to the late-Victorian reading public were George Meredith, Thomas Hardy, and A. C. Swinburne, and (in a rather different way and somewhat later) Samuel Butler, H. G. Wells, and George Bernard Shaw. The first three (despite Hardy's gloom) tended to see the outcome of human tribulations, in a world that is red in tooth and claw, as true progress. Meredith built a "philosophy of earth" around this belief, even though at times he, like Tennyson, only faintly trusted the larger hope that somehow, eventually, good would be the final goal of ill. Equally familiar is the story of how Butler, Wells, and Shaw all turned consciously away from Darwin and toward a Neo-Lamarckian version of evolution. The Lamarckian thesis was more attractive to them than Darwin's natural selection because it seemed more "optimistic"—it allowed more easily a teleological interpretation, a hope that somehow a Purpose did guide our steps aright.

Some writers needed this kind of reassurance; others did not. The influence of Darwinistic thinking upon late-nineteenth-century naturalism is too well known to need recounting here, but it

8. George Gissing, *The Private Papers of Henry Ryecroft*, Chapter 18.

might be recorded that the naturalists saw themselves as tough-minded students of the nature of evolving humanity, observers of environmental influences, of the objective facts of life. Darwin had revealed our true corporeal history, and the naturalistic writers pursued this record of the flesh with the intensity of devoted researchers. "Given a strong man and an unsatisfied woman," Zola proposed to "seek in them the beast, to see nothing but the beast . . ."

Less familiar is the story of those professional students of the arts in England, France, Germany, and America who saw and explained the arts in terms of Darwinian analogies. John Addington Symonds, like Walter Bagehot, Sir Leslie Stephen, and others, analyzed what he considered to be the inevitable aesthetic consequences of Darwinian thought. First of all, he said, evolution means that "all things in the universe exist in process." One must not attempt, then, to discuss a work of art without reference to its antecedents. This, Symonds believed, would revitalize aesthetic history and criticism. Second, evolution involves the principle of uniformity: "It implies the rejection of miraculous interferences, abrupt leaps and bounds in Nature." Finally, evolution implies the principle of increasing complexity, or "the passage of all things, inorganic and organic, by the action of inevitable law, from simplicity to complexity." [9]

Symonds became so engrossed with the concept of evolution that he could hardly write on any subject without pointing out that it had gone through a process of development. He was particularly impressed with the image of the growth cycle and the similarity of the growth of an art to the growth of an organism; he saw all arts as developing through three stages, corresponding to physical youth, maturity, and decline. This sort of "evolutionary" perspective, he said,

> lent the charm of biography or narrative to what had previously seemed so dull and lifeless—the history of art or letters. Illuminated by this idea, every stage in the progress of culture acquired significance. The origins and incunabula of art, viewed in their relation to its further growth, ceased to have a merely antiquarian interest. Periods of decadence were explicable and intelligible on the principle that every organism, expanding from the germ, passing through adolescence to maturity, is bound at last to exhaust its motive force and perish by exaggerating qualities implicit in the mature type.[1]

Explicit adaptations of evolutionary notions into the practice and study of the arts were characteristic of the late nineteenth century, but have been far less so of the twentieth. In part at least this

9. John Addington Symonds, *Essays Speculative and Suggestive* (London, 1890), I, 8, 42–43.

1. *Essays Speculative and Suggestive*, I, 11.

is because the nineteenth century had to go through the difficult process of changing its mind, of adapting itself to evolution; the twentieth century simply accepts it. Evolution has become one of those topics so well founded as not really to be exciting to educated people any more, and consequently direct references to evolution in literature are almost as rare as direct references to the laws of gravity. The indirect influence of evolution on our literature has, on the other hand, been tremendous. Whitehead once proposed, in a much-repeated statement, that students of the history of ideas should not look for those ideas which are under constant discussion in any age, but instead should look for those basic assumptions which are so fundamental to our way of thinking that we do not even realize we are assuming them. Evolution has by now become such an unconscious assumption in our society.

One of the supposed literary effects of Darwinian assumptions has already been mentioned: Joseph Wood Krutch (among others) has maintained that Darwin's ideas have eroded human values and therefore destroyed high tragedy in our century. "With increasing completeness," Krutch wrote in *The Modern Temper*, "science maps out the pattern of nature, but the latter has no relation to the pattern of human needs and feelings." This fact, Krutch said, precludes tragedy because "the Tragic Fallacy depends ultimately upon the assumption which man so readily makes that something outside his own being . . . confirms him in his feeling that his passions and his opinions are important. . . . We can no longer tell tales of noble men because we do not believe that noble men exist." [2]

Looking about us from the perspective of the last decades of the twentieth century, we can recognize the symptoms of Krutch's diagnosis. Nevertheless, the case as he states it can hardly be the whole story. For one thing, we ought to consider the negative instances. If Darwin destroyed twentieth-century tragedy, who then was responsible for the palpable failure of early nineteenth-century tragedy, or for the failure of eighteenth-century tragedy? In fact, the occurrence of high tragedy has always been far rarer than its non-occurrence; to expect every age to produce a Sophocles or a Shakespeare is overoptimistic.

For another thing: it is not simply axiomatic that a physically mechanistic world is necessarily a morally valueless one. Those who propose that it is seem to regret that natural selection is an automatic process, that it acts independently of teleological considerations, and that it, together with Mendelian genetics, makes such a satisfactory explanation of organic evolution; and they sometimes attempt to ignore all this and postulate instead some sort of "will"

2. See above, pp. 519–521.

or "preference" or "emergent evolution." Since Darwin, however, reasonable people have simply had to abandon naturalistic teleology—one cannot, any more, look to nature for revealing patterns of goal-directed process. Or, to put it another way, goal-direction in nature must now be divorced from final causes or preternatural factors. However, as John Herman Randall, Jr., has pointed out,

> nature is once more for us, as for the Greeks, full of *implicit* ends and ideals, full of "values," just because it is now an affair of processes, of means effecting ends, of things that are "necessary for," "better" and "worse for" other things. It contains so much "natural teleology," in terms of which its various factors can be "evaluated." It takes but a single flower to refute the contention that there are no "values" in nature, no achievement of ends through valuable means. We may even say it is obviously "good for" the planet to go round the sun. Of course, neither the flower nor the planet "finds" it good: only men "find" anything. But surely it does not follow that because only men find anything good or bad, better or worse, what they find is not found. The finding is a genuine cooperation with nature.
>
> It is such a nature our best post-Darwinian knowledge and thought now reveal to us.[3]

I would propose not that Darwinism has killed human values and therefore great and tragic art in our time, but something nearer the reverse: that since Darwin, we have been forced, in art as in life, to mature to finiteness. I mean maturing as human beings not simply by realizing that there are no usable absolutes for us—for that mere realization is still a kind of adolescence—but by accepting our finiteness and learning to live with it with some degree of sanity and integrity.

Oedipus, Antigone, and Lear are not great tragic figures simply because they stand in relation to the gods as flies to wanton boys, after all, but because of their own impressive human characters. And we have not stopped defending our uniqueness. If we are unique because of a certain type of brain rather than some supernatural prerogative, and if we have chosen a perhaps disagreeable scientific fact in preference to a pretty illusion, the case is nevertheless the same: our uniqueness, our dignity, remain important to us. Twentieth-century literature taken as a whole—despite absurdity, disillusion, black humor, anti-heroism, existential angst, and cosmic nausea—remains a human-centered, human-valued literature. We need not look for the tragic spirit only in drama. The greatest of the modern writers in all genres—Dickinson, Lawrence, Joyce, Faulkner, Camus, Woolf, Yeats, Frost, Brecht, Beckett—have kept

3. John Herman Randall, Jr., "The Changing Impact of Darwin on Philosophy," *Journal of the History of Ideas*, XXII (1961), 458–459.

aspiring humanity as at least the implied focus of their work, so that even when we read as a gray failure, we are still the ghostly negative of an implicitly positive picture.

Looking back at a million years of our struggle to be human, at our errant and painful attempts to be a special kind of animal—the animal who thinks, the animal who creates—it seems to me that despite our shortcomings, we have some cause for satisfaction. "Thought makes the whole dignity of humankind." Yes. Despite its simplicity, despite our sad reflections on the inadequacy of our thinking, on its stunted and twisted travesties in history and our daily lives, we must end by agreeing with Pascal. *Homo* is unique and valuable precisely because he is *sapiens*. We are worth keeping because, given our remarkable past, we may continue to hope that we have, as Darwin surmised, "a still higher destiny in the future."

PHILIP APPLEMAN

Postscript: Darwin among the Moralists (1979)

I

In the last decade, the biological sciences have been astir with original, important, and often highly controversial research, and much of this work has consciously Darwinian origins, as the following examples indicate.

1. The continuing discoveries of hominid fossils in East Africa have pushed back proto-human evolutionary history millions of years farther into the past. Discussing these new additions to the fossil record, Richard Leakey writes in *Origins* (1977):

> Perhaps more prophetic than anything else in *The Descent of Man* was its suggestion that the African continent was the cradle of mankind. Darwin reasoned that "in each great region of the world the living mammals are closely related to the extinct species of the same region. It is, therefore, probable that Africa was formerly inhabited by extinct apes closely allied to the gorilla and chimpanzee; and as these two species are now man's nearest allies, it is somewhat more than probable that our early progenitors lived on the African continent than elsewhere." The current accumulation of fossil evidence strongly supports Darwin's hunch. . . .

(See above, pp. 279–284.)

· *Philip Appleman*

2. Recombinant DNA research, or "gene splicing" as it is more conveniently called, is a technique first successfully used in 1973. It is "in essence a method of chemically cutting and splicing DNA, the molecular material which the genes of living organisms are made of. It enables biologists to transfer genes from one species to another, and in doing so to create new forms of life." (See above, pp. 285–293.) Thus a revolutionary development in biological science has opened the door to unprecedented evolutionary manipulation and also to unpredictable evolutionary risks. In *The Ultimate Experiment* (1977), a book about gene splicing, Nicholas Wade writes, "The fusion of Darwin's theory with Watson and Crick's discovery [of the structure of DNA] has provided a remarkable insight into the evolutionary history of life. . . . Living species . . . are all the product of some three billion years of evolution. . . . [But] man can now create a new species . . . and dump it into the system without notice."[1]

3. Ethology is the study of animal behavior; it emphasizes the interplay of genetic and environmental influences, and thus, as one recent commentator says, "Its point of departure and of rest is in the theory of evolution."[2] Konrad Lorenz and two other founders of ethology were awarded a Nobel Prize in 1973, bringing to a new level of public consciousness provocative ideas about our evolutionary inheritance from allegedly aggressive forebears. These ideas have been popularized by books with titles like *The Naked Ape, The Territorial Imperative,* and *The Imperial Animal*—"pop ethology," as Stephen Jay Gould calls them. Actually, Lorenz's Nobel Prize was awarded not for his speculations on human aggression but for solid ethological work on other species; nevertheless, in his best-known book the central question is, "What is the value of . . . fighting?" And he comments: "It is our duty to ask this Darwinian question." (See above, p. 432.)

4. The comparatively new discipline of sociobiology is, according to its chief spokesman, Edward O. Wilson,

> defined as the systematic study of the biological basis of social behavior in every kind of organism, including man, and is being pieced together with contributions from biology, psychology, and anthropology. There is of course nothing new about analyzing social behavior, and even the word "sociobiology" has been around for some years. What is new is the way facts and ideas are being extracted from their traditional matrix of psychology and ethology . . . and reassembled in compliance with the principles of genetics and ecology.

1. Nicholas Wade, *The Ultimate Experiment: Man-Made Evolution* (New York, 1977), pp. 15, 108–109.

2. George Stade, "K. Lorenz and the Dog Beneath the Skin," *The Hudson Review*, 26 (1973), 60.

In sociobiology, there is a heavy emphasis on the comparison of societies of different kinds of animals and of man, not so much to draw analogies . . . but to devise and to test theories about the underlying hereditary basis of social behavior.[3]

Sociobiology is now becoming an established academic discipline, buttressed by Wilson's landmark compilation of research, *Sociobiology* (1975), and it has been both highly praised and sharply criticized by other biologists. In the first chapter of his massive book, Wilson refers to "the neo-Darwinist evolutionary theory—the 'Modern Synthesis' as it is often called," and he observes: "It may not be too much to say that sociology and the other social sciences, as well as the humanities, are the last branches of biology waiting to be included in the Modern Synthesis." (See above, pp. 444–459.) Later he adds, "Sociobiology will perhaps be regarded by history as the last of the disciplines to have remained in the 'unknown land' beyond the route charted by Darwin's *Origin of Species.* . . . Now let us proceed to a deeper level of analysis based at last on the principle of natural selection."[4]

5. Students of human intelligence have for a decade been caught up in a continuing controversy over possible race- and class-related genetic factors in intelligence. John C. Loehlin, Gardner Lindzey, and J. N. Spuhler, writing in 1975 about the origins of this subject, noted that "Darwin's . . . emphasis upon the continuous and orderly development of new forms of life from other forms and the decisive role played by fitness, or reproductive advantage, was from the beginning linked to behavioral as well as physical attributes and thus directly relevant to social scientists." (See above, pp. 504–510.)

6. Recent work with primates has established that chimpanzees and gorillas are sufficiently intelligent to learn at least the symbolic rudiments of human languages, thus raising far-reaching ethical questions about the "human" treatment of "nonhuman" beings. In *The Dragons of Eden*, Carl Sagan, discussing the evolution of intelligence, wrote in 1977:

There is an arresting passage in Charles Darwin's *Descent of Man*: "The difference in mind between man and the higher animals, great as it is, certainly is one of degree and not of kind. . . . If it could be proved that certain high mental powers, such as the formation of general concepts, self-consciousness, et cetera, were absolutely peculiar to man, which seems extremely doubtful, it is not improbable that these qualities are merely the incidental

3. Edward O. Wilson, "Human Decency Is Animal," *New York Times Magazine*, October 12, 1975, p. 39.

4. Edward O. Wilson, *Sociobiology* (Cambridge, Mass., 1975), p. 63.

results of other highly-advanced intellectual faculties; and these again mainly the results of the continued use of a perfect language."

(See above, pp. 479-485.)

7. Alarmed by the successful efforts of religionists to have the doctrine of separate creation included in science textbooks, American biological scientists have increasingly felt obliged to issue public statements in support of the principle of evolution by natural selection and in opposition to the insertion of religious ideas in science texts. In 1977, two hundred professional scholars, most of them professors of biology in American universities, signed a position paper affirming that "the evidence for the principle of evolution has continued to accumulate . . . including the further confirmation of the principle of natural selection and adaptation that Darwin and Wallace over a century ago showed to be an essential part of the process of biological evolution." (See above, pp. 382-386.)

II

What this persistent contemporary invocation of Darwin's work and words makes clear is that Darwin is not one of those pioneers of science who are no longer studied—at any rate, not among professional biologists. On the contrary, Darwin remains among them today almost like a living presence, his great organizing idea still functional and indeed ineluctable, his testimony on countless subjects still respected, his originality of mind still admired. Darwin, in short, is indispensable; that is one thing recent biological developments have in common.

Another thing they have in common is their ability to provoke emotional responses and to cause noisy and sometimes violent controversies. In West Virginia, night riders bomb schoolhouses where evolution is taught. In Washington, shouting demonstrators interrupt Edward O. Wilson as he is about to address the American Association for the Advancement of Science, and douse him with water. Everywhere, scientists and social scientists dispute fervently with each other: Wilson's critics attack his ideas as akin to the social Darwinism which, they say, "provided an important basis for the enactment of sterilization laws and restrictive immigration laws by the United States . . . and also for the eugenics policies which led to the establishment of gas chambers in Nazi Germany."[5] And Wilson answers hotly, "I resent this ugly, irresponsible, and totally false accusation."[6] Ethological theories of aggression are sharply rejected by many anthropologists, paleontologists, and others who hold that human beings have as much cooperation as competition in their evolutionary inheritance. The notion of genetically determined and race-linked intelligence levels is indignantly repudiated by those who maintain that there is neither evidence for such ideas nor, given their potential for social damage, sufficient reason even to pursue them.

Darwin's theory began in controversy, and its various offspring survive in controversy because the issues involved go to our deepest conceptions of ourselves, to our pride in our origins, to our sense of our present dignity, to our hopes for the future. Many people find it difficult to accept facts which do not patently flatter their self-esteem or theories which strike them as socially retrograde. Violence aside, all of that is understandable, and perhaps, in the long run, healthy, the ferment of ideas out of which better ideas may arise. In the short run, too, the persistent controversy suggests not only hot tempers or bad manners but also welcome evidence of moral commitment and intellectual freedom.

And yet, despite the rising level of discord, despite the remarkable discoveries, the laboratory breakthroughs, and the daring speculations, one recognizes in many of the new bottles some very old wine. Criticizing Wilson's theories, Stephen Jay Gould asserts: "The issue is not universal biology vs. human uniqueness, but biological potentiality vs. biological determinism." (See above, p. 460.) It is, in other words, the issue that has for decades been debated as heredity versus environment, or nature versus nurture (and, for that matter, much the same issue that was once argued as free will versus determinism). The stakes are the same as they have always been: on the one hand, the hope for a better understanding of human nature; on the other hand, the risk of blaming what are really social shortcomings on imagined innate human defects. That the argument is an old one, however, neither diminishes its relevance nor blunts its emotive force.

Each of the biological controversies of the 1970s has a long history. The quarrel between ethologists and anthropologists over the competitive or cooperative nature of human behavior has its logical and biological roots in the Victorian era, in the divergent views of Herbert Spencer and Peter Kropotkin, among others. (See above, pp. 389–399 and 405–415.) The current hostility between "creation research" religionists and biological scientists goes back in a virtually unbroken line to the first outraged reviews of the *Origin of Species*, written by clergymen. The more these things change, the more their emotional potential remains the same.

But disputes between moralists on the one hand and scientists on the other are rather less interesting than the fact that scientists are so often conscious moralists themselves. Perhaps the experience of the atomic physicists in World War II deters other scientists from viewing their own work as existing in a social vacuum. Whatever the cause, biological scientists do have explicit ethical concerns, and they frequently discuss these concerns in the course of their scientific work. Robert Sinsheimer, a biologist who is now chancellor of the University of California, Santa Cruz, has cautioned his colleagues about the potential hazards of gene splicing, for instance. He warns that, although truth is the goal of science,

> truth is necessary but not sufficient, that scientific inquiry, the revealer of truth, needs to be coupled with wisdom if our object is to advance the human condition. . . . Our thrusts of inquiry should not too far exceed our perception of their consequence.
>
> (See above, p. 291.)

"Truth . . . coupled with wisdom," Sinsheimer says: without wisdom, our knowledge could be dangerous. But there are no college courses in wisdom, not even in graduate school, no seminars in good judgment, not even a freshman course in introductory common sense. These qualities are taken, negatively, to be unteachable, or sometimes positively, as obliging corollaries of advanced training. So ethical problems surface in all directions, of sufficient urgency to raise tempers, and hands, not only among the bombers of schoolhouses but even in the august assemblage of the American Association for the Advancement of Science; and everywhere it is assumed that ethical decisions are required and that wise choices are available —and yet there is no agreement at all on how such choices are to be made.

But if wisdom itself is elusive, it may be useful to identify three categories of contemporary dispute, and for each of them to try to distinguish the stronger arguments from the weaker. By making such distinctions, it may be possible to sketch out patterns of attitudes appropriate to each of the three categories.

III

In one category of biological controversy is a debate currently carried on between virtually the entire biological community on the one hand, and religious organizations calling themselves "creation research societies" on the other. These societies are engaged in a sustained effort to have the biblical notion of separate creation taught in American high school biology courses as a valid "scientific" interpretation of biological data. This attempt has its roots in the broader and older issues that have often pitted modern science against ancient religion, and is a linear descendant of that famous twentieth-century confrontation, the Scopes trial. A brief review of that event will shed light on the present controversy.

In 1925 the Tennessee legislature forbade the teaching of evolution in the public schools. In May of that year John Thomas Scopes, a science teacher at Dayton High School, consented to be the defendant in a court test of the law. He was arrested and indicted by a grand jury and stood trial in July. Defended by the American Civil Liberties Union, Scopes was represented by, among others, the noted trial lawyer Clarence Darrow; the prosecution was assisted by William Jennings Bryan, thrice-defeated presidential candidate. These men broadened the case from a simple issue of law to a forum for the debate over the merits of the Darwinian explanation of biological facts as opposed to the fundamentalists' literal interpretation of Genesis.

In the end Scopes was convicted, and although Bryan and the fundamentalists' cause were made to look foolish to the educated public, there was a flurry of antievolutionary activity in the "Bible Belt" states, led by fundamentalist religious groups. In 1926 and 1927, similar laws were passed in Mississippi and Arkansas, and these, together with the Tennessee law, survived, though almost wholly unenforced, until very recently. Tennessee repealed its law in 1967, and in 1968 the United States Supreme Court declared the Arkansas law unconstitutional—thus also nullifying the last remaining antievolutionary law, which is still on the books in Mississippi.

One would have to be naive, however, to suppose that legalities tell the whole story. Even in states where sectarian beliefs are not enacted into law, they may flourish through "gentleman's agreement"; and that is in fact what happened in the case of American high school biology teaching. For four decades after the Scopes trial, many wary authors and publishers simply omitted the word "evolution" and the name of Darwin from public school biology textbooks.[7] By 1959, the centenary of the publication of *The Origin of Species*, the Nobel laureate geneticist Hermann J. Muller felt called upon to protest, in an article called "One Hundred Years Without Darwinism Are Enough." "It ill befits the American people," Muller wrote,

> four generations after Darwin published his epochal discovery, to turn their backs on it, to pretend that it is unimportant or uncertain, to adopt euphemistic expressions to hide and soften its impact, to teach it only as one alternative theory, to leave it for advanced courses in universities, where the multitudes cannot encounter it, or, if it is dealt with at all in a school biology course, to present it as unobtrusively and near the end of the course as possible, so that the student will fail to appreciate how

7. Dorothy Nelkin, "The Science-Textbook Controversies," *Scientific American*, 234 (April 1976), 33.

every other feature and principle found in living things is in reality an outgrowth of its universal operation.[8]

Finally the National Science Foundation, attempting to repair the long neglect, sponsored the development of biology textbooks for the public schools which would deal with biology as what, in fact, it is: a science founded upon and depending upon evolutionary premises. The new books were introduced in 1964. Within five years, a revived fundamentalist opposition succeeded in having inserted into the California Board of Education's official guidelines a statement that the creation story from Genesis should be taught in biology courses as an acceptable "scientific" alternative to evolution.

The fundamentalists have been fortified in these latter-day crusades not so much by old-fashioned Bible-thumping publicists like William Jennings Bryan as by some technically trained persons who refer to themselves as scientists, although most of them are engineers or technicians, having neither a scientific temper of mind or method of working nor credentials in any field of biology. They have set up "creation research societies," which purport to supply new and scientific support for fundamentalist beliefs. However, their "research" has yielded nothing that is new to anyone familiar with the 120 years of post-Darwinian controversy. They cling to obsolete ideas, such as the biblical age of the earth (that is, about 6,000 years), closing their eyes to the abundant evidence of its billions of years of existence, and urging people to believe that the creation really did require only six days, as Genesis says. They point to discontinuities in the paleontological record, as if those were their own discovery; whereas in fact Darwin recognized them and discussed the problems they raised, in chapter ten of *The Origin of Species*. (see above, pp. 103–108.) They distort the significance of geological and biological phenomena, such as the Cambrian "explosion" of biological forms. And they promote odd notions, such as that evolution "violates" the second law of thermodynamics, proving in the process only that they misunderstand the second law of thermodynamics as thoroughly as they misunderstand biology. (See above, pp. 368–382.)

As a social phenomenon the creation research societies are a curiosity, and one that would, like the flat earth society, make for comic relief in a tense age, except that they have been disturbingly successful at political lobbying. It should perhaps not be surprising that they are so successful, since they bring a passionate commitment to what is almost an intellectual vacuum. Preaching pseudoscience to a

8. Hermann J. Muller, "One Hundred Years Without Darwinism Are Enough," *The Humanist*, 19 (1959), 139.

public whom they and their predecessors have managed largely to deprive of a sound scientific education, they are working under conditions ideal for their cause. An ill-educated populace which can so easily be taken in, in large numbers, by astrologers, self-proclaimed prophets, Bermuda Triangle mystics, U.F.O. visionaries, Velikovskian enthusiasts, and pyramidologists is fertile ground for the planting and growing of antiscience.

That is not to say that genuine scientists necessarily have the final word on these or any other subjects. On the contrary, the work of genuine scientists constantly reminds us that in science there are no final answers, that there are strong limits on the certainty of all knowledge, including scientific knowledge. Science in fact depends upon this principle in order to progress; it builds and grows by constant testing and revision of existing ideas. In this respect, too, the creationists reveal their antiscientific temper, since they are characteristically absolutist: they begin with fixed ideologically based conclusions and select only such data as support those conclusions, rather than working with tentative hypotheses, continually but cautiously modified to encompass more data.

In spite of their glaring inadequacies as scientists, the creationists are all too effective at political lobbying, and they need to be confronted at that level. Despite open letters, public testimony, and position papers submitted by large numbers of genuine scientists, the interests of science are not now being supported in public forums in a really effective or organized way. That remains a largely unanswered challenge to the scientific and educational community.

IV

In a second category of contemporary dispute, the venturesome but disturbing speculations of some scientists are pitted against the strongly held scientific and ideological convictions of other scientists. Two such cases have troubled biologists and social scientists for the last ten years: the controversy about sociobiologists' claims of genetically influenced human behavior, and the controversy about possible race-and-class related genetic factors in human intelligence.

The sociobiologists are more consciously and explicitly ethical theorists than are most other scientists. Edward O. Wilson begins his book on sociobiology with an essay called "The Morality of the Gene," and in the first paragraph he leads us through the following close argument:

Camus said that the only serious philosophical question is suicide. That is wrong even in the strict sense intended. The biologist, who is concerned with questions of physiology and evolutionary history, realizes that self-knowledge is constrained and shaped by the emotional control centers in the hypothalamus and limbic system of the brain. These centers flood our consciousness with all the emotions—hate, love, guilt, fear, and others—that are consulted by ethical philosophers who wish to intuit the standards of good and evil. What, we are then compelled to ask, made the hypothalamus and limbic system? They evolved by natural selection. That simple biological statement must be pursued to explain ethics and ethical philosophers, if not epistemology and epistemologists, at all depths.

(See above, pp. 444.)

Teasing out the strands of that compact statement, one recognizes that Wilson is using the words "philosophical," "consciousness," and "knowledge" so as to emphasize their rational or objective implications. These, he says, are complemented and complicated by signals in the form of emotions, which must be taken seriously as information about, and modifiers of, the total human experience. However, these signals are not rational or objective; they are consulted, Wilson says, in order to "intuit" the "standards of good and evil." Furthermore, the signals themselves have been bred into specific locations in the human brain in much the same way the nesting or honeycomb-building instincts are bred into birds and bees: by the incessant Darwinian process of natural selection.

If we have followed this reasoning, we have been led a long way from what we normally consider rationality; which is exactly where Wilson wants us. He is now ready to propose how, according to his theory, our genetically programmed emotions "tax the conscious mind with ambivalences" in order to stimulate activities that will promote not personal satisfaction or social well-being, but rather, long-term genetic success.

That, again, is a new way of putting an old theory of ethics; Darwin himself anticipated it in *The Descent of Man*, where he proposed that "the moral nature of man has reached its present standard, partly through the advancement of his reasoning powers and consequently of a just public opinion, but especially from his sympathies having been rendered more tender and widely diffused through the effects of habit, example, instruction, and reflection. It is not improbable that after long practice virtuous tendencies may be inherited." (See above, pp. 132–208.) But Wilson's formulation is not "merely" a new way of putting an old hypothesis; it is also the beginning of a serious attempt to establish a systematic investigation of genetic factors in ethical behavior. Dissenting biologists assert that in this, as in most other matters relating to human beings, the sociobiologists have yet to establish their hypotheses on a basis of convincing empirical data. Furthermore, critics like Stephen Jay Gould believe that to argue for a genetic role in human behavior could have the unfortunate side effect of reinforcing existing social arrangements, thus undermining efforts at social reform. Morally significant human activities are not genetically or otherwise predetermined in any specific way, Gould maintains, since our range of potential behavior, whatever our genetic endowment, is still vast. Richard Leakey agrees: "Very few behavioral patterns are built into the human brain," he writes; "it is built in such a way as to maximize *behavioral* adaptability. Within reasonable biological limits, humans, it is fair to say, could adapt to living in almost limitless numbers of ways. Indeed, this flexibility is manifest in the rich pattern of cultures expressed throughout the world."[9]

Sociobiologists willingly agree that people are capable of diverse behavior; but their new explorations of the sources of that behavior are fortified by the fact that for at least a generation now, geneticists have recognized that traits are usually not determined exclusively by the genes or by the environment. Rather, one must ask of the variance in any trait, in a given population and environment, what proportion is due to genetic differences, what proportion is due to environmental differences, and what proportion is due to covariance and interaction. Wilson argues that the behavioral evidence he has compiled, together with the general presence of genetically based variation in human and other animal traits of all kinds, make it unlikely that there is no genetically based variance in general human traits such as aggression or intelligence. Of course it is also unlikely that there would be no environmental influences on these traits. The existence of strong environmental effects on a trait is, after all, compatible with strong genetic differentiation among individuals in a particular environment.

Sociobiologists are working on the assumption that the prolongation of this controversy is due to a deficiency of reliable data. As their research goes on, it will be seen whether they will be able satisfactorily to distinguish and quantify the various factors in trait variation and thus, presumably, to resolve the issue.[1] Critics of sociobiology, however, do not believe that nature-nurture problems can ever be resolved as they are now formulated, partly because the very terms of the argument are defective. What exactly is a trait, they ask. Is aggression, territoriality, or dominance a "thing" upon which selection can act? If genes act differently in different environments, where is the pure "thing" that expresses the amount of a behavioral character that is due to genes? Such fundamental doubts

9. Richard E. Leakey and Roger Lewin, *Origins* (New York, 1977), p. 245.
1. Here and elsewhere in this Postscript

I am indebted to Professor Craig E. Nelson for helpful suggestions. He is not, of course, responsible for the personal opinions expressed in the essay.

about the sociobiologists' whole enterprise make any early resolution of this controversy seem unlikely.

In the other related controversy, some students of human intelligence have consciously grounded their work in evolutionary principles. Richard Herrnstein, in a well-known article on IQ, writes:

> Mental testing was one of many responses within psychology to Darwin's theory of evolution. In fact, the connection here is intimate and direct, for the idea of measuring mental ability objectively was first set forth by Francis Galton, the younger cousin of Charles Darwin. . . . In 1869, just a decade after Darwin launched modern biology with the *Origin of Species*, Galton published *Hereditary Genius*, which applied evolutionary thinking to the question of intellect.
>
> (See above, pp. 490–499.)

Herrnstein, Arthur Jensen, and others have published what they consider valid evidence and reasoning to support the contention that intelligence is not only largely genetically determined, but also racially and socially linked.

Opposition to this particular allegation of genetic influence on human behavior has been even more intense than in the case of sociobiology. The tactics of the opposition have been of two types, of very different degrees of legitimacy: rebuttals by reason and rebuttals by fiat. Stephen Jay Gould, whose disagreement with Edward O. Wilson is cogently expressed (see above, pp. 460–465), equally well represents the rebuttal by reason of Arthur Jensen's widely discussed article linking race to IQ.[2] Gould argues first that to equate IQ with intelligence is questionable; second, that the evidence for high heritability of IQ is shaky and partially fraudulent; and third, that Jensen confuses within-group and between-group variations in intelligence, thus invalidating his conclusions. That kind of argument, regardless of who happens to be right, is at least in the acceptable tradition of scholarly debate.

The second kind of rebuttal, the rebuttal by fiat, reflects less credit on the disputants. In its extreme form, this kind of tactic is analogous to schoolhouse bombing: it includes physical assault, shouting down teachers and public speakers, and barricading lecture halls. But even its characteristic nonviolent expression is disturbing: what this kind of critic wants is to prevent the controversial research from proceeding at all. That may be a tempting course, since studies like Arthur Jensen's could conceivably have unfortunate side effects; indeed, his opponents argue that it is already

2. A. R. Jensen, "How Much Can We Boost IQ and Scholastic Achievement?" *Harvard Educational Review*, 39 (1969), 1–123; cf. Stephen Jay Gould, *Ever Since Darwin* (New York, 1977), chapter 31, and D. D. Dorfman, "The Cyril Burt Question," *Science*, 201 (29 September, 1978), 1177–1186.

having such effects, denying people opportunities as a result of racial stereotyping. Preventing the research, then, might be thought a socially progressive act, simply as a way of stifling a troublesome social doctrine. But then again, perhaps things will turn out to be more complicated than that: perhaps that research, however pernicious its current implications may seem, could lead to genuinely useful results. There are such possibilities, as John Loehlin and others have pointed out: studies linking abilities to specific genes or specific environmental conditions; studies comparing several racial-ethnic groups on a number of ability measures; developmental studies of children; educational, nutritional, and other environmental manipulations; and others. "For studies of human evolution," Loehlin writes, "including the evolution of human behavior, the comparison of existing racial groups would seem to provide one of the more powerful methods available, and hence should deserve a reasonably high scientific priority."[3]

Clearly this controversy, like the sociobiology argument, is a specialized replay of the heredity-environment debate. No doubt both sides are partially right; but there seems to be no way to resolve such issues in the present frame of debate. One way resolution might come is from a reductionist approach, wherein the action of a particular defined gene—whether for some component of "intelligence" or "altruism" or some other characteristic—can be described in biological and biochemical terms through the various steps by which it produces the observed characteristic—as can now be done, for instance, for the gene whose defect results in sickle-cell anemia. Lacking such clarification, or other substantial evidence, the debate is ideological.

But quite apart from the merits of the case, it is hardly fitting for American academics, schooled in the First Amendment and the guiding principle of academic freedom, to attempt to deny or limit that freedom for others, even in an apparently good cause. Noam Chomsky, debating Richard Herrnstein, argues, "Of course, scientific curiosity should be encouraged . . . but it is not an absolute value."[4] Many people would agree that there are no absolute values, or absolute anything else; but if there are any things in human experience having genuine and demonstrated value, surely scientific curiosity is one of them. If in protecting that value we must also protect the expression of ideas we consider repugnant, that is certainly nothing new, and it should not alter our commitment to free speech and academic freedom. That is not to argue that our commitment to social justice be any less firm, but rather that our

3. John C. Loehlin, Gardner Lindzey, and J. N. Spuhler, *Race Differences in Intelligence* (San Francisco, 1975), p. 250.

4. Noam Chomsky, "Comments on Herrnstein's Response," *Cognition*, 1 (1973), 321.

values are interrelated, and that any erosion of our commitment to freedom will almost certainly, at least in the long run, subvert our commitment to justice.

V

In the third category of evolutionary dispute, the freedom of scientific investigation itself is being directly called into question because of its potential hazards. The unknown risks involved in recombinant DNA research, or gene splicing, have caused politicians, public-interest groups, and scientists themselves to urge caution in proceeding with the research. In 1978 a government high-containment laboratory was opened, in which the potential dangers of gene splicing were to be assessed. There were pickets on hand at the opening of the laboratory, denouncing the planned research on the grounds that it was the first step toward genetic manipulation of humans. The pickets were invoking the specter of genetic conditioning, as in the test-tube propagation of Aldous Huxley's *Brave New World*. That is a long-range social threat that people have a right to be uneasy about. Margaret Mead once observed:

> The suggestion that we replace man's long, slow, fumbling attempts to control the environment and to develop styles of life wherein he becomes increasingly more human, by automatic controls of various kinds—including not only those resulting from breeding or propagation but also those resulting from the application of somewhat crude and only partly known rules of behavior to a conditioning process—is an image that functions in the present as a deterrent to enthusiastic commitment to the future.
>
> (See above, pp. 420–431.)

Ominous as that image is, however, there are two other kinds of problems associated with genetic engineering which are more immediately threatening: the medical problem and the evolutionary problem. The medical problem arises from the possibility that gene splicing may produce new types of organisms that are dangerous to current forms of life (including humans) and are not containable in laboratories. That would be a considerable worry in any case, but it is intensified by the fact that the organism of choice for gene splicing is *Escherichia coli*, a bacterium which inhabits the intestinal tracts of humans and other vertebrates. That we ourselves are the hosts of this organism would make it seem a poor choice for genetic manipulation; nevertheless, it remains the organism of choice because it is comparatively well studied. To wait until some other organism were as well understood as *E. coli* would require some years; and biological researchers are understandably impatient at any such delay.

Some scientists have been reassured by reports at a 1977 conference in Falmouth, Massachusetts, that a genetically enfeebled strain of *E. coli*, called K12, is a safer host than had been thought: that even deliberate attempts to convert it into an epidemic pathogen have not worked, and that therefore an accidental conversion would be unlikely. Other scientists find this position unconvincing, pointing out that there was no consensus on this subject at the Falmouth conference. Even the enfeebled organisms, they argue, may be able to transmit their reconstructed plasmids to viable ones. Despite reassurances, then, the potential for danger remains a real risk, in the opinion of some scientists.

In addition to the social and medical risks of gene splicing, there is what must be called an evolutionary risk. Robert Sinsheimer insists that it is "extraordinarily anthropocentric" to emphasize the threats to human health in gene splicing, rather than the evolutionary threat to our environment. For one cannot responsibly undertake a basic restructuring of the materials of life without considering this question: can abrupt, irreversible, and self-replicating biological inventions fail to disturb our environmental balance? It may seem advantageous in the abstract to create new varieties or species which would produce insulin (as is already being done), or manufacture growth hormones, or fix nitrogen. But can such processes be entrusted to novel, self-propagating species whose biological interest would be to increase and multiply? Any answer to that question must begin with, and return to, a consideration of Darwin's fundamental changing of our way of understanding nature and our place in it. In the Epilogue, above, are cited two world views—a pre-Darwinian one, and Darwin's own—in assessing this fundamental change. The pre-Darwinian view was put forth by William Whewell, a clergyman and one of the most eminent scientific methodologists of his day, writing in 1833:

> If there be, in the administration of the universe, intelligence and benevolence, superintendence and foresight, grounds for love and hope, such qualities may be expected to appear in the constitution and combination of those fundamental regulations by which the course of nature is brought about, and made to be what it is.
>
> (See above, p. 530.)

That is to say, the characteristics of the Godhead (intelligence, benevolence, and so on) are known by divine revelation; in a world directly created and superintended by an immanent deity, then, these same qualities must be built into the natural laws which govern us. Whatever is, is right because divine omnipotence has so willed it.

Now consider the philosophical difference in Darwin's total reversal of these assumptions. Having looked at nature closely, ignoring theological postulates, he concluded the *Origin of Species* with this penultimate sentence:

> Thus, from the war of nature, from famine and death, the most exalted object which we are capable of conceiving, namely, the production of the higher animals, directly follows.

(See above, p. 131.)

In turning the book of Genesis topsy-turvy, this new understanding committed us to a world in which there is no biological superintendence or special creation, only adaption for survival. In the long run, then, in Darwinian terms, whatever is, is "right" not because of divine intervention, not because animals and plants are "beautifully designed" for their environments; but because, without successful adaptation to the demands of a given environment, a biological species simply could not be there at all.

So it is that any move, intentional or unintentional, which alters our environment in a significant way, may be a threat to the adaptations that have evolved in humans and other species over vast reaches of time. We are only beginning to realize to what extent even seemingly minor human interventions in our biosphere have already complicated our chances for survival: chlorofluorocarbons in the atmosphere; oil and pesticides in the sea; tobacco smoke in the human lung; vinyl chloride in the liver; saccharine in our coffee, nitrites in our meat; and Mirex, Kepone, dieldrin, DES, PCB, PBB, DDT, and so on. There are some sixty thousand chemicals now in active industrial use, and we optimistically assume that most of them are not dangerous to human life or to the environment. However, the constantly growing list of pathogenic ones must make us a little skeptical of those who reassure us of the safety of new technologies.

If even relatively crude and external environmental changes have a substantial impact on our lives, can we suppose that the abrupt introduction of new forms of life will always be harmless? Gene splicing, Robert Sinsheimer says, would "introduce quantum jumps into the evolutionary process," with unpredictable results. Those who defend recombinant DNA research argue that existing organisms are so well adapted to their evolutionary niches that novel organisms will almost certainly be less well adapted and hence will not survive. Most mutations have always been harmful, because they disturb an organism's finely tuned development orchestration. Furthermore, they point out, gene-splicing "experiments" have been proceeding in nature for billions of years; the vast majority of new combinations have no doubt been tried, and the useful mutations have been found and adapted. Consequently, essentially all mutations are now selected against, and this would apply as much to laboratory changes as to random ones.

This argument, in the judgment of Sinsheimer and others, takes a very static view of evolution, one which assumes that nature has already tried virtually all of the possibilities; and they see no compelling reason to make such an assumption. Erwin Chargaff, professor emeritus of biochemistry at Columbia University, adds this strong cautionary note: "We are dealing here much more with an ethical problem than with one in public health. . . . Have we the right to counteract, irreversibly, the evolutionary wisdom of millions of years . . .?" If we proceed with this "irreversible attack on the biosphere," he adds, "the future will curse us for it." (See above, p. 290.) That, as Chargaff sees it, is the disturbing conclusion from the basic Darwinian principle that we are what our environment has made of us over a very long period of time.

Why, then, is DNA research proceeding? That seems a fair question, and a fair answer must include the fact that most of the scientists directly involved are convinced that the dangers are negligible. Searching everywhere for the truth about nature, they are of course eager to seek in this very promising direction. Besides that purely scientific reason for doing DNA research, many biologists also foresee practical applications of great value for humanity. David Baltimore, a Nobel laureate from the Massachusetts Institute of Technology, has testified that "DNA research is our best hope for understanding diseases like cancer, heart disease, and malfunctions of the immune system."[5] And gene splicing might be used to develop bacteria which could produce hormones, antibiotics, and other valuable proteins for medicine and industry. Such hopes constitute respectable motives for proceeding with DNA research, and, the researchers believe, justify what they take to be the very slight risks involved.

The problems raised by Sinsheimer, Chargaff, and other scientists have not disappeared, however, despite the optimism and good intentions of the DNA researchers; and it has long since become apparent that the terms of this category of dispute are different from the two preceding categories. In those, the issues are serious but comparatively abstract; their social implications may seem ominous, but they are presumably open to resolution by further data and by informed public debate; and the debates themselves are protected both by explicit constitutional guarantees and by the principle of academic freedom.

In the gene-splicing dispute, however, we are on different ground, neither abstract nor perhaps even subject to correction. What is at risk is the possibility of a dangerous and irreversible evolutionary shift. People everywhere (as well as other animals, and even plants) have a life-or-death stake in it. Threatened with potential danger,

5. Wade, *The Ultimate Experiment*, p. 115.

ordinary citizens have a right to expect that scientists would pursue this research in accordance with the scruples of their more cautious colleagues. Chargaff has proposed that there be congressional action to take the following steps:

> (i) a complete prohibition of the use of bacterial hosts that are indigenous to man; (ii) the creation of an authority, truly representative of the population of this country, that would support and license research on less objectionable hosts and procedures; (iii) all forms of "genetic engineering" remaining a federal monopoly; (iv) all research eventually being carried out in one place, such as Fort Detrick.[6]

Scientists, however, are not being as cautious as that. Research is now going ahead in scores of laboratories, and already there have been violations of the National Institutes of Health safety guidelines, at Harvard and at the University of California, San Francisco, as well as reports of ignoring the guidelines in industrial laboratories. Industry is not at present required by law to adhere to the NIH guidelines, and potential hazards are multiplied by their current and prospective volume-oriented production of self-replicating organisms.

If there is a serious accident as a result of using *E. coli* in all this research, how, Nicholas Wade asks, will historians explain to future generations the continued use of this laboratory organism? The answer, Wade writes, would have to be:

> Prohibition of *E. coli* . . . would have delayed gene-splicing research for . . . several years . . . Researchers were unwilling to accept a major delay for what seemed to most to be a purely speculative risk . . . Research and the pursuit of knowledge being fundamental values of industrialized societies, the majority of the public was favorably disposed to accept the scientists' arguments.[7]

VI

We are always moralists, Dr. Johnson said, but only occasionally mathematicians. It is sometimes assumed that science strictly speaking has no ethics, that the gap between what is and what ought to be is broad and unbridgeable. But our ethics, whatever its source, can hardly emerge from a vacuum of knowledge; in fact our knowledge often tempers our ethical inclinations. Scientific knowledge has at the bare minimum a selective ethical function, identifying false issues which we can reasonably ignore: imagined astrological influ-

6. Erwin Chargaff, "On the Dangers of Genetic Meddling," *Science*, 192 (1976), 938.

7. Wade, *The Ultimate Experiment*, p. 84.

ences on our ethical decisions, for instance. Science offers us the opportunity of basing our ethical choices on factual data and true relationships, rather than on misconceptions or superstitions; that must be considered a valuable service.

Beyond that selective function, biological information has often been directly used (and misused) to support various types of ethical thinking. Unscrupulous people have sometimes appealed to spurious readings of scientific data in order to bulwark their arguments; this happened to Darwinism when Nazis perverted it in an attempt to legitimize their racist ideology. (It is an understandable wariness of this kind of perversion which heats up the dispute about race and intelligence today.) More characteristically, though, the growth of scientific knowledge has tended to have socially progressive implications. Factual knowledge of the physical world has on the whole been a better basis for human understanding, human solidarity, and human sympathy than were folklore or superstition. The old myth-supported notions of tribal and racial supremacy have been at least partly superseded, among educated persons, by the biological knowledge that we are one people, one species, in one world.

Finally, the scientific temper of mind is itself of service to moralists, showing itself as sometimes supplementary to, and sometimes superior to, those more primitive feelings that Edward O. Wilson says have typically been consulted to "intuit" ethical standards. Konrad Lorenz, working with assumptions similar to Wilson's, writes:

> The scientist who considers himself absolutely "objective" and believes that he can free himself from the compulsion of the "merely" subjective should try—only in imagination, of course—to kill in succession a lettuce, a fly, a frog, a guinea pig, a cat, a dog, and finally a chimpanzee. He will then be aware how increasingly difficult murder becomes as the victim's level of organization rises. The degree of inhibition against killing each one of these beings is a very precise measure for the considerably different values that we cannot help attributing to lower and higher forms of life.[8]

We "cannot help" this feeling, Lorenz believes. He obviously is not thinking about the American Rifle Association, or the whaling fleets, or the G.I.'s at My Lai, Vietnam. The fact is that the toleration, even the enjoyment, of killing "higher forms of life" must of necessity emerge from those same "emotional control centers" in the brain that Wilson appeals to as sources of ethical standards. One problem with this sociobiological and ethological theory of ethics is that it seems to operate on the assumption that if you have

8. Konrad Lorenz, *On Aggression* (New York, 1966), p. 218.

an "emotional" or "intuitive" sense of right and wrong, you will choose what is right. Ethical philosophers, however, have almost always thought otherwise. We cannot in fact trust emotion as an unassisted ethical guide; Hitler was as passionate as Jesus.

So the objectivity that Lorenz finds morally inconsequential (and, in his brief critique of Kant, a bit ludicrous) may have something to offer to ethics, after all. It is the "objective" scientists, these days, who are in the vanguard of ethical thought: who are, for instance, enlarging our understanding of the capacities of the higher mammals and of our moral responsibilities with respect to them. The fascinating work of Jane van Lawick-Goodall with chimpanzee societies in Africa has broadened our knowledge of primate behavior and, in the process, has illuminated the kinship of humans and the higher animals. Human beings, proud of the role of *Homo faber*, the creative animal, the toolmaker, now have to share this role with the clever chimps, who, Jane Goodall tells us, can "manipulate objects to a wide variety of purpose," and "can use an object spontaneously to solve a brand-new problem that without the use of a tool would prove insoluble." (See above, pp. 472–479.) The revolutionary laboratory work begun by Beatrice and Allen Gardner[9] has indicated that chimpanzees even have a distinct sense of self, thus belying the old and rather arrogant belief that human beings are unique among animals in their awareness of selfhood. No wonder, then, that scientists are now beginning to ask, quite seriously, as Carl Sagan does, questions like this: "If chimpanzees have consciousness, if they are capable of abstractions, do they not have what until now has been described as 'human rights'? How smart does a chimpanzee have to be before killing him [or her] constitutes murder?" (See above, pp. 479–485.)

There are no more absolute values in ethics than in anything else, but there are relative values in the various existing ethical systems; and one could make a persuasive case that those systems that are not only the most altruistic but also sensitive to the broadest constituencies are, by virtue of those qualities, superior to the others. Richard Dawkins writes, "If I say that I am more interested in preventing the slaughter of large whales than I am in improving housing conditions for people, I am likely to shock some of my friends." And he adds, "Whether the ethic of 'speciesism,' to use Richard Ryder's term, can be put on a logical footing any more sound than that of 'racism,' I do not know. What I do know is that it has no proper basis in evolutionary biology."[1] With a growing recognition among biologists of the ugly and self-defeating aspects of "speciesism," we may have reason to foresee a future consensus that a

9. For a useful survey of the language-learning abilities of chimpanzees, see Carl Sagan, *The Dragons of Eden* (New York, 1977).

1. Richard Dawkins, *The Selfish Gene* (New York, 1977), pp. 10–11.

narrowly species-centered ethics is inadequate, not so much to our emotions (which have almost always failed us in this matter) as to our reason, now under instruction by new biological perceptions.

In the truly well-balanced human being (that will o' the wisp of utopian thought) reason and emotion would be always in harmony, indeed in symbiotic function. In the meantime, it is reassuring to discover that biologists, engaged in "objective" research, so often become passionate about their work, and about the world it affects. Our perception of truth, it appears, sometimes causes, and sometimes is served by, moral fervor.

None of this would be so evident or so pertinent to our lives if biology were not a science so thoroughly unified by the principle of evolution as to afford philosophical perspectives of its own; and that unification, of course, we owe to Charles Darwin. In 1834, a year after William Whewell wrote the words quoted above, about the divine "administration of the universe," the polymath Samuel Taylor Coleridge died, believing, despite Whewell's comforting words, that the science of zoology was in danger of falling apart because of its huge mass of uncoordinated factual information. That was just four years before Darwin picked up Malthus's *Essay on the Principle of Population* and was inspired with the great organizing principle that would for the first time make a mature and coherent science of biology. Evolution by natural selection continues to serve biologists in their professional work and to inspire them to earnest pondering about our place in the universe: some of the wisest thinkers writing about the human condition today are biologists. That their ethical conclusions are diverse should not trouble us; the opposite would in fact be disturbing. It goes almost without saying that, while the physical world may be better understood by virtue of a unifying principle, the moral complexities of life will never be accounted for by simplistic propositions. "The moral faculties," Darwin wrote in *The Descent of Man*, "are generally and justly esteemed as of higher value than the intellectual powers. But we should bear in mind that the activity of the mind in vividly recalling past impressions is one of the fundamental though secondary bases of conscience. This affords the strongest argument for educating and stimulating in all possible ways the intellectual faculties of every human being." (See above, p. 201.)

Selected Readings

The number of books and articles written about Darwin's work is (to use one of Darwin's favorite words) staggering. This brief listing is meant merely to be suggestive. For more comprehensive guidance, one may examine the various bibliographies cited below. Titles available in paperback editions are starred.

I. BIBLIOGRAPHICAL MATERIALS

Freeman, R. B., *The Works of Charles Darwin: An Annotated Bibliographical Handlist*. London, 1965.

See also the annual bibliographies in *Isis* and *Victorian Studies* and extensive listings of scientific contributions in Julian Huxley, ★ *Evolution: The Modern Synthesis* (London, 1963) and of sociological contributions in Ashley Montagu, *Darwin: Competition & Cooperation* (New York, 1952). For an extensive discussion of studies in various fields, see Bert James Loewenberg, "Darwin and Darwin Studies, 1959–63," *History of Science*, IV (1965), 15–54.

II. BIOGRAPHY

Barlow, Nora, ed., ★ *The Autobiography of Charles Darwin, 1809–1882, with Original Omissions Restored*. New York, 1969.
————, *Darwin and Henslow: The Growth of an Idea; Letters 1831–1860*. London, 1967.
Darwin, Francis, ed., *The Life and Letters of Charles Darwin*. New York, 1959.
Darwin, Francis and A. C. Seward, eds., *More Letters*. London, 1903.
De Beer, Gavin, ★ *Charles Darwin: A Scientific Biography*. New York, 1964.

III. DARWIN'S WORK

★ *The Structure and Distribution of Coral Reefs* . . . London, 1842.
Journal of Researches into the Natural History and Geology of the Countries Visited during the Voyage of H. M. S. 'Beagle' . . . London, 1845.
★ *On the Origin of Species by Means of Natural Selection* . . . London, 1859.
The Variation of Animals and Plants under Domestication. London, 1868.
The Descent of Man . . . London, 1871.
★ *The Expression of the Emotions in Man and Animals*. London, 1872.
The Formation of Vegetable Mould . . . London, 1881.

IV. GENERAL OR MISCELLANEOUS STUDIES

Barnett, S. A., ed., *A Century of Darwin*. London, 1958.
Eiseley, Loren C., ★ *Darwin's Century*. New York, 1959.
Ghiselin, Michael T., ★ *The Triumph of the Darwinian Method*. Berkeley and Los Angeles, 1969.
Gruber, Howard and Paul Barrett, *Darwin on Man: A Psychological Study of Scientific Creativity*. New York, 1974.
Huxley, Julian, ★ *Evolution in Action*. New York, 1953.
Huxley, Thomas Henry, *Darwiniana*. New York, 1893.
Persons, Stow, ed., *Evolutionary Thought in America*. New Haven, 1950.
Simpson, George Gaylord, ★ *The Meaning of Evolution*. New Haven, 1949.
Tax, Sol, ed., *Evolution after Darwin*. Chicago, 1960.
Vorzimmer, Peter, *Charles Darwin: The Years of Controversy: The Origin of Species and Its Critics 1859–1882*. Philadelphia, 1970.

V. DARWIN AND SCIENCE

Bateson, W., *Problems of Genetics*. Oxford, 1913.
Bell, P. R., ed., ★ *Darwin's Biological Work*. Cambridge, England, 1959.
Dawkins, Richard, *The Selfish Gene*. New York, 1977.
De Beer, Gavin R., *Embryos and Ancestors*. Oxford, 1940.
DeVries, Hugo, *Species and Varieties*. Chicago and London, 1905.
Dobzhansky, Theodosius, ★ *Genetics and the Origin of Species*. New York, 1937.
————, ★ *Heredity and the Nature of Man*. New York, 1964.

573

574 · Selected Readings

Fisher, Ronald A., *The Genetical Theory of Natural Selection*. Oxford, 1930.
Gould, Stephen Jay, *Ever Since Darwin*. New York, 1977.
Gray, Asa, ★ *Darwiniana*. New York, 1876.
Hull, David L., *Darwin and His Critics: The Reception of Darwin's Theory of Evolution by the Scientific Community*. Cambridge, Mass., 1973.
Huxley, Julian, ★ *Evolution: The Modern Synthesis*. New York, 1942; revised, 1963.
Leakey, Richard E., and Roger Lewin, *Origins*. New York, 1977.
———, *People of the Lake*. New York, 1978.
Mayr, Ernst, *Animal Species and Evolution*. Cambridge, Mass., 1963.
Medawar, P. B. and J. S , *The Life Science*. New York, 1977.
Morgan, T. H., *Evolution and Genetics*. Princeton, 1925.
———, *The Scientific Basis of Evolution*. London, 1932.
Sagan, Carl, ★ *The Dragons of Eden*. New York, 1977.
Simpson, George Gaylord, *Horses*. New York, 1961.
van Lawick-Goodall, Jane, *In the Shadow of Man*. Boston, 1971.
Wade, Nicholas, *The Ultimate Experiment: Man-Made Evolution*. New York, 1977.
Wallace, Alfred Russell, *Darwinism*. London and New York, 1889.
Wilson, Edward O., *Sociobiology*. Cambridge, Mass. and London, 1975.
———, *On Human Nature*. Cambridge, Mass. and London, 1978.

VI. DARWIN AND PHILOSOPHICAL AND THEOLOGICAL THOUGHT
Bergson, Henri, *Creative Evolution*. London, 1911.
Dewey, John, ★ *The Influence of Darwin on Philosophy and Other Essays in Contemporary Thought*. New York, 1910.
Fiske, John C., *Darwinism*. London and New York, 1879.
★ Greene, John C., *Darwin and the Modern World View*. Baton Rouge, 1961.
★ Hardin, Garrett James, *Nature and Man's Fate*. New York, 1959.
Huxley, Thomas Henry and Julian Huxley, *Touchstone for Ethics*. New York and London, 1947.
★ Medawar, P. B., *The Future of Man*. London, 1960.
Passmore, John, "Darwin's Impact on British Metaphysics," *Victorian Studies*, III (1959), 41–54.
Peckham, Morse, "Darwinism and Darwinisticism," *Victorian Studies*, III (1959), 3–40.
Popper, Karl, *Objective Knowledge: An Evolutionary Approach*. Oxford, 1972.
Randall, John Herman, Jr., "The Changing Impact of Darwin on Philosophy," *Journal of the History of Ideas*, XXII (1961), 435–462.
Raphael, D. D., "Darwinism and Ethics," in Barnett, *A Century of Darwin* (q.v.).
Simpson, George G., ★ *This View of Life*. New York, 1964.
★ Waddington, C. H., *The Ethical Animal*. London, 1960.
White, Andrew Dickson, ★ *A History of the Warfare of Science with Theology in Christendom*. New York, 1896.

VII. DARWIN AND SOCIETY
Banton, Michael, ed., *Darwinism and the Study of Society*. London and Chicago, 1961.
Burrow, J. W., *Evolution and Society*. Cambridge, England, 1966.
Burton, D. H., "Theodore Roosevelt's Social Darwinism and Views on Imperialism," *Journal of the History of Ideas*, XXVI (1965), 103–118.
Carnegie, Andrew, ★ *The Gospel of Wealth and Other Timely Essays*. New York, 1900.
Goldman, Irving, "Evolution and Anthropology," *Victorian Studies*, III (1959), 55–75.
Gordon, Scott, "Darwinism and Social Thought," in H. H. J. Nesbitt, ed., *Darwin in Retrospect*. Toronto, 1960.
Graham, Loren, *Science and Philosophy in the Soviet Union*. New York, 1972.
Hofstadter, Richard, ★ *Social Darwinism in American Thought*. Boston, 1955.
Huxley, Julian, *Soviet Genetics and World Science*. London, 1949.
Kropotkin, Peter, ★ *Mutual Aid*. London, 1902.
Loehlin, John C., Gardner Lindzey, and J. N. Spuhler, ★ *Race Differences in Intelligence*. San Francisco, 1975.
Lorenz, Konrad, ★ *On Aggression*. New York, 1966.
MacRae, Donald G., "Darwin and Social Sciences," in Barnett, *A Century of Darwin* (q.v.).
Mead, Margaret, *Continuities in Cultural Evolution*. New Haven, 1964.
Montagu, Ashley, *Darwin: Competition & Cooperation*. New York, 1952.
Zirkle, Conway, *Evolution, Marxian Biology, and the Social Scene*. Philadelphia, 1959.

Selected Readings · 575

VIII. DARWIN AND THE LITERARY MIND

★ Barzun, Jacques, *Darwin, Marx, Wagner: Critique of a Heritage.* New York, 1941.

Beach, Joseph Warren, *The Concept of Nature in Nineteenth-Century English Poetry.* New York, 1936.

★ Bush, Douglas, *Science and English Poetry* (New York, 1950).

★ Ellegard, Alvar, *Darwin and the General Reader.* Göteborg, 1958.

Fleming, Donald, "Charles Darwin, the Anaesthetic Man," *Victorian Studies,* IV (1961), 219–236.

Henkin, Leo J., *Darwinism in the English Novel, 1860–1910.* New York, 1940.

★ Hyman, Stanley Edgar, *The Tangled Bank. Darwin, Marx, Frazer and Freud as Imaginative Writers.* New York, 1962.

Irvine, William, "The Influence of Darwin on Literature," *Proceedings of the American Philosophical Society,* CIII (1959), 616–628.

Krutch, Joseph Wood, ★ *The Modern Temper.* New York, 1929.

★ Muller, Herbert J., *Science and Criticism.* New York, 1956.

★ Shaw, George Bernard, *Back to Methuselah. London,* 1921.

Stevenson, Lionel, *Darwin among the Poets.* Chicago, 1932.

Willey, Basil, *Darwin and Butler: Two Versions of Evolution.* London, 1960.

Index

Norton Critical Editions in the History of Ideas